Old Master Drawings at Bowdoin College

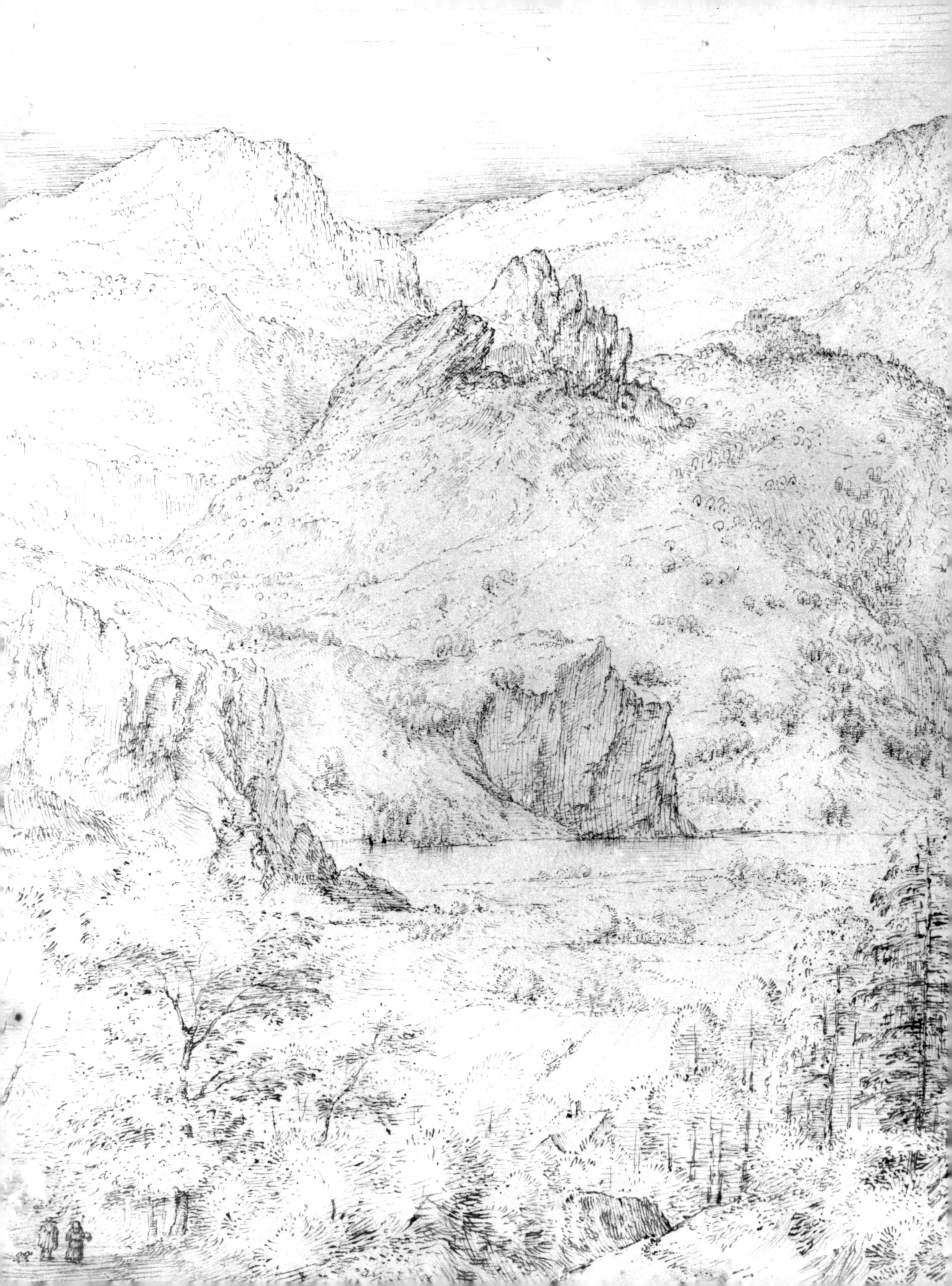

Old Master Drawings at Bowdoin College

DAVID P. BECKER

Bowdoin College Museum of Art

BRUNSWICK · MAINE · 1985

Bowdoin College Museum of Art
BRUNSWICK, MAINE

MAY 17 – JULY 7, 1985

Sterling and Francine Clark Art Institute
WILLIAMSTOWN, MASSACHUSETTS

SEPTEMBER 14 – OCTOBER 27, 1985

Helen Foresman Spencer Museum of Art
University of Kansas
LAWRENCE, KANSAS

JANUARY 19 – MARCH 2, 1986

Art Gallery of Ontario
TORONTO, CANADA

MAY 17 – JUNE 29, 1986

Published with the assistance of
the National Endowment for the Arts, a federal agency;
the Samuel H. Kress Foundation;
and the J. Paul Getty Trust.

COVER: Jan Baptist Weenix,
Landscape with Stream and Ruins.
Bequest of James Bowdoin III. 1811.140 (detail).

FRONTISPIECE: Pieter Bruegel the Elder,
Alpine Landscape (View of Waltensburg).
Bequest of James Bowdoin III. 1811.142 (detail).

ISBN 0–916606–08–2
Library of Congress Catalog Card Number: 84–072390

This catalogue has been composed, printed, and bound by
Meriden-Stinehour Press. The design is by Stephen Harvard.

TO THE MEMORY OF

James Bowdoin III

Henry Johnson

AND

Susan Dwight Bliss

WHO BUILT THE COLLECTION

OF OLD MASTER DRAWINGS

AT BOWDOIN COLLEGE

Contents

Foreword

> The place of the Museum on the College grounds forbids us to suppose that it was put here only that its contents might amuse the leisure of the visitor. It stands here to affirm, conspicuously and deliberately, that Art is a great instrument in man's education, that it rounds and completes a training which would be imperfect without it.
>
> MARTIN BRIMMER, founder and first president,
> Museum of Fine Arts, Boston
> *Walker Art Building Inaugural Speech, June 1894*
> *Adopted as part of Statement of Purpose,*
> *Bowdoin College Museum of Art, May 1984*

OF ALL ART FORMS, there is no greater teaching tool than drawing—both in the study of the finished work and in its execution. In no other medium are the artist's thoughts and style so purely stated; in no other medium is there closer affinity between the idea and its physical expression. Certainly it is the belief expressed by Martin Brimmer that "Art is a great instrument in man's education," as well as the beauty of the individual sheets, that have led collectors of drawings to make gifts to the Bowdoin College Museum of Art. And it is especially appropriate that this catalogue be dedicated to the principal donors to the collection: James Bowdoin III (1752–1811) and Susan Dwight Bliss (d. 1966).

Also honored in the dedication is Henry Johnson (1855–1918), professor of modern languages at the College and a scholar-collector, for his long study of the drawings, his early recognition of their importance, and his additions to the collection. The issuing of *Old Master Drawings at Bowdoin College* celebrates, too, the one-hundredth anniversary of the publication of the first listing of the drawings, which was compiled in 1885 by Dr. Johnson.

Many individuals have contributed to the catalogue's completion. A large measure of gratitude is owed to David P. Becker, a member of Bowdoin's class of 1970, who first came to know the drawings as an undergraduate. In the years immediately following his graduation, he worked as curatorial assistant and registrar for the art museum, which allowed him to learn the collection thoroughly. Following his departure from Maine, Mr. Becker worked at the Houghton Library at Harvard University as assistant curator of printing and graphic arts and earned his Master's degree from the Institute of Fine Arts, New York University. He is currently an assistant curator in the Department of Prints, Drawings, and Photographs at the Museum of Fine Arts, Boston. In January of 1981, Mr. Becker accepted the responsibility of authorship. I am deeply indebted to him for his devotion to the project and for the courageous spirit with which he undertook the challenge. His task was formidable. Of the approximately 300 sheets which constitute the collection, only a handful had been published previously by other scholars. His major achievement has been the establishment for the first time of the identity of the collection.

An especially happy development is that the exhibition will be shared with three other institutions: the Sterling and Francine Clark Art Institute in Williamstown, Massachusetts; the Helen Foresman Spencer Museum of Art at the University of Kansas, Lawrence, Kansas; and the Art Gallery of Ontario, Toronto, Canada. I wish to express my appreciation to David S. Brooke, director, and Rafael A. Fernandez, curator of prints and drawings, at the Clark Art Institute; Jay Gates, director, and Laura Giles, curator of painting and sculpture, at the Spencer Museum of Art; and William J. Withrow, director, and Katharine A. Lochnan, curator of prints and drawings, at the Art Gallery of Ontario.

The catalogue was funded from a number of sources. The National Endowment for the Arts offered essential support, not only for the research and writing of the text, but also for the publication of the catalogue and the conservation of the drawings. The Samuel H. Kress Foundation has funded the photographing of all the drawings. The J. Paul Getty Trust has provided, as part of its publication program, the funding necessary for duotone illustrations of the major works and small-scale reproduction of the drawings which accompany the checklist. A portion of the annual contributions to the Associates Program of the Museum of Art has been used to complete the funding of the publication, and as a result, every member has become a participant in the catalogue production. May I extend my thanks to you all.

A final word of gratitude is due the administration and Governing Boards of Bowdoin College, whose support of the Museum of Art and understanding of its purpose on the campus is fundamental to the achievement of every major project. In particular, I wish to thank A. LeRoy Greason, president of the College, and Alfred H. Fuchs, dean of the faculty, whose interest and encouragement have been important to the completion of the catalogue and the organization of the exhibition.

KATHARINE J. WATSON
Director
Bowdoin College Museum of Art

Acknowledgments

ONE OF MY FIRST TASKS as a student assistant at the Bowdoin College Museum of Art in the fall of 1967 was to remat some of the old master drawings in the collection. From that point, I was fascinated with their history, purposes, and beauty, and I determined to learn more about them. The publication of the present catalogue is the culmination of a personal dream to see the riches of the collection made known to a wider audience. That I—with the immeasurable help of the colleagues and friends mentioned below—should be the author is at once an honor, a great pleasure, and a greater labor than I foresaw those years ago.

One of my final tasks upon finishing my researches is to thank the many individuals who have encouraged and aided me. Any catalogue of a wide-ranging collection of old master drawings which attempts completeness is dependent on a host of drawings connoisseurs and scholars, and this work is no exception. From the first, scholars and curators in this country and abroad have without exception responded enthusiastically to news of this cataloguing project and have helped me at every stage.

Within the drawings field, my principal mentor has been Konrad Oberhuber of the Fogg Art Museum; he was the first to instill in me the courage to undertake this project, and he has been unstinting with help and advice. I am most grateful to him for visiting Bowdoin in 1977, for reviewing the entire collection, and for helping considerably to sort out schools and degrees of quality.

Several other individuals have aided me particularly in reviewing large groups of drawings. Lawrence Turčić and Jacob Bean of the Metropolitan Museum of Art have been very generous with their help and have granted me access to photographic and archival files in the Department of Drawings. Professor Egbert Haverkamp Begemann of the Institute of Fine Arts, New York University, reviewed the northern drawings with me and made a second trip to Bowdoin in 1982 to go over them in person; many pleasurable conversations about drawings have ensued. On my visits to England, Nicholas Turner of the British Museum has been of very great help in attributing and researching several of the more difficult Italian sheets; his indefatigable hospitality and correspondence are also greatly appreciated. Also in London, Philip Pouncey has generously spent much time discussing difficult attributions. At Bowdoin College, particular thanks go to Susan Wegner of the Department of Art, whose enthusiasm, personal encouragement, and prodigious help with knotty iconographical questions have been essential to my progress. Chiara d'Afflitto, in several conversations with Katharine Watson in 1982, offered many useful comments on the Italian drawings.

As noted above, other scholars have responded in correspondence and in person to my inquiries. In this country and Canada, the following were particularly helpful: Barbara

Weiden Boyd, Miles Chappell, Roger Clisby, Elizabeth Cropper, Bruce Davis, Elaine Evans Dee, Cara Denison, Diane De Grazia, Ann Sutherland Harris, John Herrmann, Catherine Johnston, Thomas da Costa Kaufmann, George Keyes, David Kiehl, Louise Lippincott, Anne-Marie Logan, Agnes Mongan, Helen Mules, Mary Myers, Ann Percy, Bobby Rainwater, Andrew Robison, Jane Shoaf, Felice Stampfle, Miriam Stewart, and Eunice Williams. European scholars who answered my inquiries include the following: Keith Andrews, David Brown, James Byam Shaw, Jan Piet Filedt Kok, Heinrich Geissler, John Gere, Dieter Graf, Richard Harprath, Henrietta McBurney, Manuela Mena Marqués, Catherine Monbeig Goguel, M. S. Robinson, Peter Schatborn, David Scrase, Simonetta Prosperi Valenti Rodinò, Carl van de Velde, and Hilary Wayment.

The photographic resources of the Frick Art Reference and Witt Libraries have been invaluable; Rupert Hodge of the latter extended his help to me on numerous occasions. The staffs of the libraries of the Metropolitan Museum of Art; the Institute of Fine Arts, New York University; the Fogg Art Museum, Harvard University; and the Museum of Fine Arts, Boston, have been consistently efficient and helpful. Dianne Gutscher of Special Collections in the Bowdoin College Library aided me considerably in archival research on the history of the collection.

My warmest and inadequate thanks go to my friends at the Bowdoin College Museum of Art, who have extended themselves extraordinarily to help my efforts and state of mind at every stage. They have made writing a catalogue primarily at long distance as easy as possible. Lynn Yanok, administrative assistant to the director, has handled administrative burdens and supplied prodigious amounts of personal support to the author for over fifteen years, for which I am very grateful. Brenda Pelletier, former registrar, and Henrietta Tye, present registrar, have been enormously helpful, as have John Coffey, curator, José Ribas '76, preparator, and Paula Volent, former curatorial assistant. Suzanne Bergeron, secretary to the director, deserves special recognition as coordinator of manuscripts for the catalogue and helper in innumerable ways. Maria Parker has diligently and efficiently typed the final manuscript. Helen Semerdjian, clerk-typist, has done last-minute typing, and both she and Alison Murray, coordinator of educational programs, have cheerfully pitched in to proofread. Student assistants Shelley Langdale '85 and Maria Teresa Arteiro '86 compiled the concordances and assisted with checking the photographs.

Judy Walsh, formerly of the Williamstown Regional Conservation Laboratory, has discussed examination and conservation problems with me on several occasions, and I am grateful for her careful work and personal help.

The final publication process has been efficiently and enthusiastically coordinated by Lucie Teegarden, Bowdoin's associate director of public relations and publications, and Rachel Dutch, assistant director of public relations and publications. My debt to my editor, Susan Ransom, is enormous and a great pleasure to acknowledge here. She has worked long and hard on my various drafts. Our discussions have been most beneficial in addition to being very enjoyable. Rosa Pellegrini, lecturer in Italian at Bowdoin, checked the Italian usage and spelling. This catalogue is the third on which I have had the pleasure of working with Stephen Harvard, and I am gratified to have the benefit of his advice and design, in addition to the superlative abilities of The Stinehour Press and Meriden Gravure Company. The photographs of the drawings are the work of Allan Ludwig, who has accomplished a difficult task with grace and professionalism.

Personal debts extend to all my friends, who are probably very tired of hearing about the mythical "Bowdoin catalogue" for all these months. Particular thanks go to Marjorie Cohn, Pearl Freiberg, Philip Hofer, Judith Lyczko, John McKee, Betty Smith, and Roger Wieck. My colleagues in the Department of Prints, Drawings, and Photographs at the Museum of Fine Arts, Boston, have been greatly supportive, particularly in the hectic last stages of this project.

Richard West, former director of the Museum of Art, discussed some of the drawings with me when I was a student, trained me in sensitive curatorial practices, and has consistently encouraged my research. His eye and explorations among the Bowdoin drawings have also been helpful. Marvin Sadik, also former director, is my first mentor in the curatorial field, and his standards of catalogue research, writing, and presentation have always been my models. My greatest debt, however, is to Katharine Watson, present director. Her support from the very inception of this project, even from her arrival at the museum, has been an honor for me. At every stage our dialogue has been helpful to me and to the project. She has contributed a large amount of work in reading the catalogue entries and questioning many of my art historical flights of fancy. Truly, without her the present publication would not be. Though I have happily dedicated my work to the three individuals who built the drawing collection at Bowdoin, it is to Katharine that I wish to present the very next copy.

Introduction

History of the Collection

THE COLLECTION OF DRAWINGS in the Bowdoin College Museum of Art contains the first old master drawings to arrive in this country, at some time during the second quarter of the eighteenth century. It is certainly the oldest public collection of drawings, having been established in 1811 by the bequest of James Bowdoin III (1752–1811) to the College. A major portion, perhaps the entirety, of that group of 141 sheets was almost certainly owned by the colonial portrait painter John Smibert (1688–1751), who was born in Edinburgh, trained principally in London, and settled in Boston by 1729.

Smibert's recently discovered autograph account book in the Public Records Office in London reveals that he purchased at least 251 drawings in Florence during a two-year stay in Italy.[1] Indeed, the very first purchase recorded during his sojourn was of 250 drawings on 1 February 1720 from "Sigre. Scatchati floure painter."[2] Miles Chappell has determined that this flower painter was probably a member of the Florentine family of artists which included the flower specialist Andrea Scacciati (1642–1704/10) and the engraver also named Andrea Scacciati (1725–1771).[3] Nine days later, Smibert additionally bought a cartoon by "Sallviator," whom Chappell identifies as Salvator Rosa.[4] Smibert almost certainly was acting as an agent for one or more patrons during his stay in Italy, as he made some considerable purchases of paintings and art objects there.[5] However, balancing the cost of the drawings he acquired with the other works of art purchased in the period 1 February to 28 October 1720, as recorded in his notebook (ca. 18 *scudi* against ca. 1,500 *scudi*), it is reasonable to suppose that he kept these drawings for himself, as artistic sources for study.[6]

He is known to have executed several portrait commissions during his sojourn, in addition to his regular course of copying paintings by Renaissance and Baroque masters.[7] It is fairly well established that several of Smibert's painted copies of old masters are now at Bowdoin College, having also been acquired and subsequently bequeathed by James Bowdoin III.[8] Smibert had an active studio in Boston from his arrival there in 1729 until his death in 1751, and the contents of his studio remained intact under the care of his nephew John Moffatt (d. 1777) and afterward until the turn of the century. Most important for the argument presented here, the presence of drawings in the studio was recorded in both Smibert's and his nephew's estates and in the possession of his son Williams.[9] Indeed, such native-born artists as Copley, Trumbull, Vanderlyn, and Allston visited Smibert's studio and received inspiration from the European works of art (and copies from them) to be seen there.[10]

Concrete evidence for a Smibert provenance for the drawings in the Bowdoin bequest lies in the inscriptions including Smibert's name on three of the sheets or their mounts (Cat. 10, 202, and 209). At one time, all three of the drawings were ascribed to Smibert himself,[11] but two of them are clearly sixteenth-century (Cat. 10, 202) and the third is most probably seventeenth-century (Cat. 209). Therefore, the inscriptions probably refer to ownership by John Smibert at one time.

The conclusion that the major portion, perhaps all, of the group of master drawings in the Bowdoin bequest came from John Smibert's purchases is further supported by the physical evidence of the drawings themselves. Every drawing which has been securely attributed to a known artist can be dated before 1728, when Smibert left England for this country.[12] The presence within this group of drawings of some eighteen sheets attributable to Carlo Maratti and his followers accords well with Smibert's arrival in Rome in 1720, as Maratti himself had died there in 1713, and Pietro de' Pietri (ca. ten sheets can be given to him alone) had died in 1716 in the same city. In addition, the drawing by Tommaso Redi (Cat. 81) may have been purchased by Smibert directly from Redi himself, as he is recorded as having bought a "pictor" from the artist on 25 May 1720.[13]

Only three collectors' marks appear on five of the drawings. They are the marks of the artist Sir Peter Lely, who died in 1680 (Lugt 2092, on Cat. 41); Lely's own assistant, P. H. Lankrink, who died in 1692 (Lugt 2090, on Cat. 19); and the Amsterdam art dealer, auctioneer, and collector Jan Pietersz. Zomer, who died in 1724 (Lugt 1511, on Cat. 34, 37, and 103). Though the sale of Zomer's personal collection did not take place until the 1720s, Lugt notes that he applied his mark on drawings passing through his trade, which had begun at least by 1690.

In quite a few cases, the original drawing mounts have been saved, many of which bear eighteenth-century English or Dutch watermarks; the style of the mount decoration and inscriptions reveal English origins.[14] Of significance is the fact that all of the traditional attributions or inscriptions on the drawings or mounts are to artists active before 1728. It is also quite possible though improbable that Smibert acquired these or other sheets in England after his return from Italy in 1721. It is further possible that once in America, Smibert purchased drawings from his London agent, Arthur Pond (ca. 1705–1758), as it is known that he ordered artists' supplies and prints from him; however, none of the drawings bear Pond's characteristic annotations.[15]

It seems increasingly unlikely that the collection was purchased by James Bowdoin III during his tour as minister to France and Spain from 1805 to 1808, as had previously been thought, for it would seem that at least some of the drawings would date from the later eighteenth century. No purchases of drawings are recorded by him during that tour of duty or on two earlier trips to Europe in 1771/72 and 1775/76.[16] Unfortunately, there is also no record of any purchase of drawings from Smibert's studio by Bowdoin or any other member of his family, though one is assumed. Katharine Watson has speculated that Bowdoin may have purchased paintings and drawings from Smibert's studio specifically as teaching materials for the college he was endowing in his father's memory in Maine.[17]

In any case, two "Folios" of drawings, valued originally at $7.75, were included in the collections of art, books, and scientific materials bequeathed by James Bowdoin III to Bowdoin College in 1811.[18] Considered part of the library, the drawings remained virtually undisturbed until their discovery some seventy years later. That bequest of 141 sheets[19] constitutes just under half the present old master drawing collection at the museum. Contained in that original foundation of the collection are the supreme Bruegel landscape (Cat. 8), the Vellert stained glass study (Cat. 2), the two Koninck landscapes (Cat. 24 and 25), the Beccafumi fresco study (Cat. 32), and the studies by Taddeo Zuccaro and Carlo Maratti (Cat. 40 and 65), among many other notable sheets.

The next major group of old master drawings came to the collections through the offices of Professor Henry Johnson (1855–1918), a remarkable teacher and scholar and the first director of the Museum of Art. Born in Gardiner, Maine, the son of a hardware store proprietor, Johnson graduated from Bowdoin in 1874, a member of Phi Beta Kappa. Almost immediately he went to Europe, studying literature at the Universities of Göttingen and Paris.[20] He was appointed instructor in modern languages at Bowdoin in 1877 and also in that year was awarded an A.M. degree by the College. He became professor of modern languages in 1881; the following year he returned to Germany for two years at the Universities of Leipzig and Berlin, achieving his doctorate at the latter in 1884. While teaching at the College, Professor Johnson was librarian from 1880 to 1885 and the curator of the art collections from 1881 to 1887 and 1892 to 1914, in which year he was appointed the first director of the museum. Johnson was a noted author and translator, publishing editions of Shakespeare, Schiller, and Heredia and a complete translation of Dante's *Divine Comedy*, which appeared in 1915. He also published a book of his own poems. Johnson was awarded an honorary doctorate of literature by the College in 1914.

Professor Johnson was deeply committed to caring for and building up the art collections at Bowdoin, particularly the growing classical group being assembled by Edward Perry Warren and the drawings in the Bowdoin bequest. The latter had been rediscovered near the time he had been appointed curator, and he was responsible for publishing the only complete listing of the drawing bequest, in 1885. It is clear that he wished to add to that collection by small purchases of his own. In the 1930 *Catalogue of the Art Collections*, a group of over thirty drawings is listed in the "Johnson Collection" as a supplement to the original collection. In 1932, this group was acquired from the family as a memorial to Johnson through funds donated by James Phinney Baxter. Baxter, who had received from Bowdoin both an A.M. in 1881 and a Litt. D. in 1904, was an Overseer of the College and a former mayor of Portland. Four other drawings from Johnson's collection were bequeathed to the museum in 1958 by his daughter, Helen Johnson (Mrs. Stanley P.) Chase. Further, this writer believes that the group of 105 drawings which entered the collections in 1930 under somewhat unclear circumstances were purchased by Professor Johnson for the museum. The group of drawings collected by Johnson includes such notable sheets as the Rubens (Cat. 13), the Cambiaso (Cat. 35), the Balducci (Cat. 46), the Guercino (Cat. 55), and the Stella (Cat. 86).

The methods by which Johnson assembled this collection are not entirely known, but, extraordinarily, most seem to have been ordered by him sight unseen from Europe through book dealers' catalogues. A scant three records survive of his purchases: an invoice dated 20 February 1886 from Charles T. Jefferies & Sons, Bristol, England, for "Drawings by Old Masters, at £30" from their catalogue 112; a letter dated 31 May 1892 from Henry Sotheran & Co., London, referring to Johnson's purchase of an "Atlas folio of scrapbook studies from the old masters"; and a letter of 31 May 1893 from Karl W. Hiersemann, a book and art dealer in Leipzig, referring to an order for an unspecified number of drawings (but see Cat. 144).[21] It is possible that he had seen some of these or other drawings on one of his several trips to Europe in the 1880s and 1890s, but the above orders were apparently all made from catalogue listings. The largest single group (some twenty-nine sheets) within the Johnson drawings is from the collection of William Bates (1824–1884), a professor at Queen's University, Birmingham, England, most noted for his collection of drawings by Thomas Rowlandson.[22] The sale of his drawings took place at Sotheby's London on 19 January 1887.

Finally, a small but distinguished group of drawings was presented to the museum by Miss Susan Dwight Bliss, a New York collector who was most generous in her benefactions to the Metropolitan and Newark Museums; Harvard, Yale, and Princeton Universities; and Bowdoin College. She collected drawings, prints, and other works of art in Europe and New York City from the early years of this century until her death in 1966. Unfortunately, few records survive of her purchases, but it would appear that many of her drawings were acquired at the American Art Association and other galleries in New York during the 1920s and 1930s. Her gifts to Bowdoin include the Stradanus and Berchem print studies (Cat. 6 and 26), the two Castiglione sheets (Cat. 56 and 57), and the major Maratti study (Cat. 64).

Of the ninety-four drawings selected to be featured in this catalogue and the accompanying exhibition, over half (fifty-two) are from the original Bowdoin bequest; of the remainder, Henry Johnson bought twenty-four, and Susan Dwight Bliss gave fourteen sheets. The four other drawings in this selection were purchased with the modest acquisition funds available to the museum. Of interest is the purchase in 1918 of the Flaxman (Cat. 94) through a fund devoted to classical art.

Previous Scholarship

THE HISTORY OF SCHOLARLY RESEARCH into the old master drawing collection began with the rediscovery of the drawings in the Bowdoin bequest in an "old box" in the college library by two students, Frederick W. Hall (A.B. 1880, A.M. 1883) and Horace Henderson (A.B. 1879).[23] Hall undertook a manuscript listing of them, which he finished in 1881 and gave to Henry Johnson, the newly-appointed curator of the art collections.[24] Utilizing

Hall's manuscript, Professor Johnson then prepared a careful description of the 142 sheets in the group, as the first part in a proposed catalogue of the art collections.[25] This volume was published in November of 1885 and previous to the present catalogue was the sole publication of the entire Bowdoin bequest of drawings. Though fairly inaccurate (of seventy-six attributions in the 1885 *Catalogue*, only eighteen can be accepted today, ten of which are to a single artist), Johnson's descriptive listing is a scrupulous record of the physical appearance of the sheets. In addition, he recorded the inscriptions on many of the drawings and their mounts; quite a few of the latter were removed in the early part of this century and lost. The 1885 *Catalogue* is also notable for Johnson's decision to publish fifty large-paper copies which included original photographs of twelve of the sheets. Many of these copies were sent by him to museums and university libraries. Charles Eliot Norton, the influential professor of art history at Harvard, received a copy and sent back several comments and corrections in a warm letter to Johnson.[26]

The very next year saw the publication of sixteen of the drawings in a portfolio of photogravure reproductions (twenty in all) of art works at Bowdoin, published by the college library and with commentaries by the Reverend Fred H. Allen of Lewiston, Maine.[27] The author of several general guides to art appreciation, Allen supplied glowing notices for each work in this publication, which was a relatively early instance of facsimile reproduction in this country. Upon the opening of the Walker Art Building in 1894, the entire Bowdoin drawing collection was placed on permanent display on racks in the Bowdoin Gallery (fig. 1), remaining there for over thirty years. As a result of such

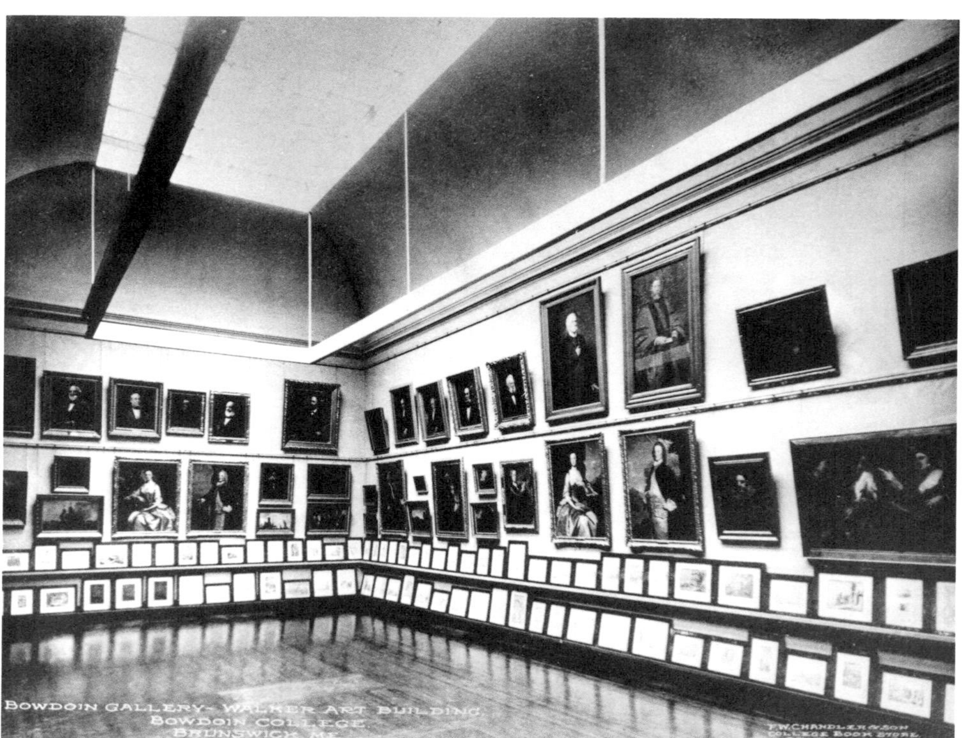

FIG. I

extended exposure in a gallery lit by natural light, many of the drawings show considerable fading of certain media, particularly ink and wash pigments (see Cat. 108–9). Fortunately, most of the sheets retain much of their original character, especially those executed in chalk.

Johnson's catalogue was responsible for the first publication of several drawings in the wider scholarly literature. In the first volume of the *Art Bulletin* of 1913, Frank Jewett Mather, Jr., a professor of art history and director of the museum at Princeton, illustrated nine of the Italian sheets, offering a few new attributions and considerable discussion and indicating that his first knowledge of the collection came from the 1885 *Catalogue*.[28] The next year Mather published a group of the northern drawings and had the honor of being the first to recognize the masterpiece and best-known drawing of the entire collection, the Bruegel landscape (Cat. 8), previously classed as unknown by Johnson and Allen.[29]

During his curatorship, Johnson had seen to the photographing of all the drawings in the Bowdoin bequest, and in 1913 sent photographs of them to Filippo di Pietro of the Uffizi, who returned them with notations as to his agreement with the attributions or alternative suggestions.[30] His general classification of many of the sheets was a beginning in sorting out national schools within the collection. Over twenty years of apparent inactivity followed, until the appointment of Philip C. Beam as curator of the museum. Largely through his efforts, photographs of the collection at that time (including the Johnson drawings purchased in 1932) were sent to Sir Robert Witt, the London drawings collector who was setting up a photographic library for the study of art history, which remains today as the Witt Library of the Courtauld Institute. Upon receipt of the photographs, Sir Robert sent many of his own comments on the attributions to the museum in 1936.[31] The photographs have remained in London, a few of them gathering inscriptions and attributions which were recorded by this writer in 1983.[32]

Since that time, and with the increasing knowledge in art historical circles of the drawing collection (spurred by the fame of the Bruegel), a limited yet growing number of scholars and connoisseurs have visited the collection and at times have left their comments in the museum files. These have included, during the late 1930s and 1940s, Agnes Mongan and Jakob Rosenberg of the Fogg Art Museum, Felice Stampfle of the Pierpont Morgan Library, and Frits Lugt, the Dutch scholar and collector, who made many helpful attributions of the northern drawings during his 1945 visit. More recently, the drawings have been examined by Jacob Bean, Egbert Haverkamp Begemann, Horst Gerson, Julius Held, Michael Jaffé, Catherine Johnston, J. Richard Judson, Jennifer Montagu, Konrad Oberhuber, Erwin Panofsky, Stephen Pepper, William Robinson, Pierre Rosenberg, Richard Spear, Mary Cazort Taylor, Hans Tietze, Erika Tietze-Conrat, and Walter Vitzthum. The present writer's efforts have been aided immeasurably by these scholars' comments, many of which are reflected in the individual catalogue entries which follow.

During the 1960s and 1970s, a few individual sheets from the collection have been published in the scholarly literature. However, it should be stated that of the ninety-four drawings which are extensively described in the first part of the present catalogue, only just over one-third have been reproduced or discussed in previous literature. The collection of old master drawings at Bowdoin College has until the present remained essentially unpublished. With the exceptions of the Bruegel and the Rubens, very few of the drawings have traveled to exhibitions outside the state of Maine,[33] and the occasion of the present traveling exhibition is in its own way an inauguration of the collection.

The Present Catalogue

ONCE THE DECISION WAS MADE several years ago to publish a proper catalogue of the old master drawings at Bowdoin, it was hoped that the publication could be as complete a document as possible. It was felt that, in addition to featuring the finer sheets in the collection, a full historical record of the original Bowdoin bequest should be presented, as probably the oldest collection of European drawings in this country. From that point, it was determined to make this publication a complete catalogue of the entire collection.

This catalogue is divided into two parts. The first, which also serves as the catalogue for a traveling exhibition of ninety-four drawings, contains in most cases rather full discussions of the purpose and context of each sheet, with some biographical information about the artist, if known. It is hoped that these longer entries may be of interest to students, teachers, and visitors to the museum, without being tiresome for drawings scholars. The drawings in this section are reproduced in large format and are set in chronological order within broad schools in order of the artists' birth dates. Anonymous drawings in the catalogue are placed roughly in chronological order.

The second part of the publication is an illustrated checklist of the remainder of the collection of old master drawings at Bowdoin. A very small number of nineteenth-century copies of older sheets and truly disreputable examples of drawing have been eliminated entirely.[34] However, every sheet in the Bowdoin bequest has been included. Full technical and bibliographic information has been attached, with occasional comments referring to attributions or subject matter. It is hoped that this fully illustrated section may yet reveal discoveries to other connoisseurs. Concordances to both the 1885 and 1930 editions of Professor Johnson's catalogue of the Bowdoin bequest have been appended to aid those who have annotated copies of those publications. Another concordance with the museum accession/inventory numbers has been included.

The drawing collection is made up primarily of the Italian and Netherlandish (Dutch and Flemish) schools, with a lesser proportion of French sheets (almost all of these coming from the Bliss gift). There are a minimum of German drawings, and virtually no English or Spanish. The collection of old master drawings at Bowdoin College contains one supreme drawing, several striking rarities, and a considerable number of sheets of both aesthetic beauty and art historical interest. The drawings are done in many different media and are the result of many different artistic motivations. As such, the collection is an excellent resource for both learning and enjoyment.

NOTES

1. The entire notebook has been reproduced and transcribed in *Smibert Notebook* 1969. 2. Ibid., p. 99. 3. Chappell 1982, p. 137; the latter artist engraved facsimile reproductions of drawings in the Uffizi later in the century. 4. Ibid. 5. *Smibert Notebook* 1969, p. 100. 6. Ibid., pp. 99–102; during the same period, he is recorded to have received "on account" some 1,665 *scudi* from a Mr. William Aikman for an unknown patron. Saunders (1984, p. 315) feels that that patron may have been Sir Francis Grant (1658–1726) of Monymusk, a patron of Smibert's in England whose portrait he painted (repr. Saunders 1984, p. 316, fig. 6). 7. Smibert's entire stay in Italy has been discussed at length in recent literature in Chappell 1982 and Saunders 1984. 8. See Sadik 1966, pp. 211–18, for the fullest discussion of the provenance of these works; see also Chappell 1982 and Saunders 1984 for their attributions. The possibility that the Bowdoin bequest of drawings had once been owned by Smibert had been tentatively ventured by several scholars in previous literature, including Sadik (1966, pp. 211–18) and James Thomas Flexner, in a lecture delivered at Wildenstein and Company, New York, on 13 September 1966 (published by the Museum of Art in 1967, pp. 11–13). 9. Sadik 1966, p. 217. 10. See, for instance, Flexner, op. cit., and D. A. Brown, *Raphael and America* (exh. cat.) (Washington: National Gallery of Art, 1983), p. 23. 11. *Catalogue* 1885, nos. 70–72; *Catalogue* 1930, nos. 73–75. 12. Some sixty-three sheets; in addition, the greater portion of the remaining drawings is datable to the sixteenth or seventeenth centuries. 13. *Smibert Notebook* 1969, p. 100. 14. Most of the identifiable watermarks on the mounts are of continental manufacture (Garden of Holland, Strasbourg bend, arms of Amsterdam, etc.) used in the seventeenth and eighteenth centuries. As Miss Agnes Mongan first pointed out to me in conversation in 1983, the style of mounts with heavy gold bands surrounding and extending to the edge of the original drawing itself is an English trait. 15. See Lugt 2038, 157, 158, and 2873. 16. Sadik 1966, pp. 137–39, and pp. 208–22 ("James Bowdoin III as Art Collector"). During a brief period in 1771, Bowdoin was a student at Christ Church College, Oxford, and it is tempting to speculate that he may have seen the large collection of drawings there, which were bequeathed by General John Guise in 1765 (see Byam Shaw 1976, p. 1 and n. 1). However, there is no mention of such a viewing. 17. Manuscript notes for a public lecture given on 19 September 1983. 18. *Catalogue* 1930, p. 9. 19. For many years, a chiaroscuro woodcut by Ugo da Carpi after Raphael's *Death of Ananias* tapestry cartoon (Bartsch 27) was considered part of the drawing collection, thus actually making 142 sheets in the original bequest as listed in the early catalogues. (The woodcut is Inv. no. 1811.72—*Catalogue* 1885, no. 6 [as Polidoro da Caravaggio]; *Catalogue* 1930, no. 6 [the same].) 20. Johnson's autograph journal from his European stay at this time is in Special Collections, Bowdoin College Library. It is a very personal record of his disciplined studies, his work as a tutor to support himself, and his growing passion for studying works of art. 21. Information from files in the museum. 22. See biography under Lugt 2604. The ex-Bates drawings at Bowdoin (see Index of Previous Owners) are of frankly uneven quality; perhaps the highlight of his entire collection is the drawing of a nude youth by Rubens now in the Pierpont Morgan Library, New York (repr. in New York 1979, cat. no. 12). 23. Letter in museum files dated 4 February 1936 from Philip C. Wilder (A.B. 1923), recording a conversation with Henderson. 24. Letters of 9 and 21 March 1881 from Hall to Henry Johnson in museum files; in the second letter, Hall stated his belief that all the drawings were indeed "originals." 25. Only 141 are drawings; see note 19 above. 26. Letter dated 23 November 1885 to Johnson in museum files; Norton commented in it, "the collection is a very interesting one, and I desire much to see it." 27. See Allen 1886. 28. Mather 1913, p. 244. 29. Mather 1914, p. 108. 30. In most cases, these photographs are still in the museum files, with a pencilled "X" affirming the attribution or suggesting other names or schools if he was not in agreement. 31. Correspondence in museum files; individual comments are recorded on the record cards for relevant drawings. 32. Unfortunately, many of the photos were placed in anonymous files or so far out of their fields that they eluded any comments. 33. The major scholarly exceptions are those included in the Italian and French exhibitions organized by Vitzthum and Rosenberg respectively (see Regina and Montreal 1970 and Toronto 1972). A small group was included in an American Federation of Arts traveling exhibition during 1962 and 1963, and another small group was shown at Wildenstein and Company, New York, concurrently with the *Colonial and Federal Portraits* exhibition in 1966. The AFA exhibition included only a checklist, and the latter had no publication. 34. These almost entirely come from a small number bequeathed in 1935 to the College by Charles Potter Kling.

NOTES TO THE CATALOGUE

Measurements of the drawings are of the sheet, height before width, unless specified otherwise.

The support of each drawing is white or off-white antique laid paper, unless specified otherwise.

As used in this catalogue, the *mount* of a drawing refers to the heavier card or board to which drawings are often adhered (implied by the term "laid down"); a *mat* is the overlaid board with a window used in frames to separate the drawing surface from the glass.

Inscriptions are not assumed to be in the artist's hand unless specified otherwise.

Full references to works cited in abbreviated form may be found in the list of Frequently Cited References.

In the bibliographic notes, earlier attributions are not included if the attribution has not changed or if the drawing was formerly listed as Unknown and now is classified by country or city.

Most of the sheets bear one of two stamps used in the past by the museum, in addition to the written accession number:

WALKER ART BUILDING　　　BCMA

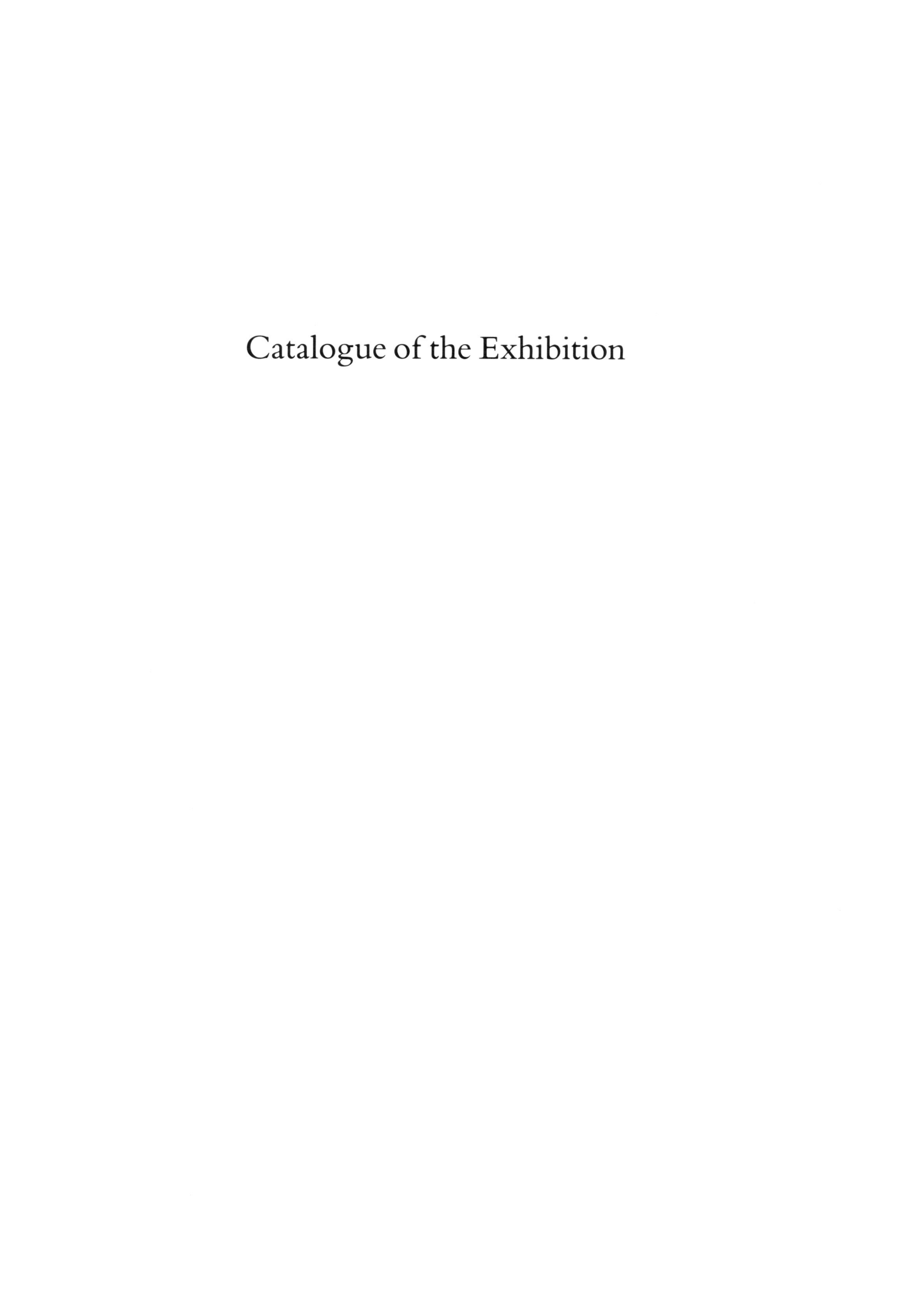

Catalogue of the Exhibition

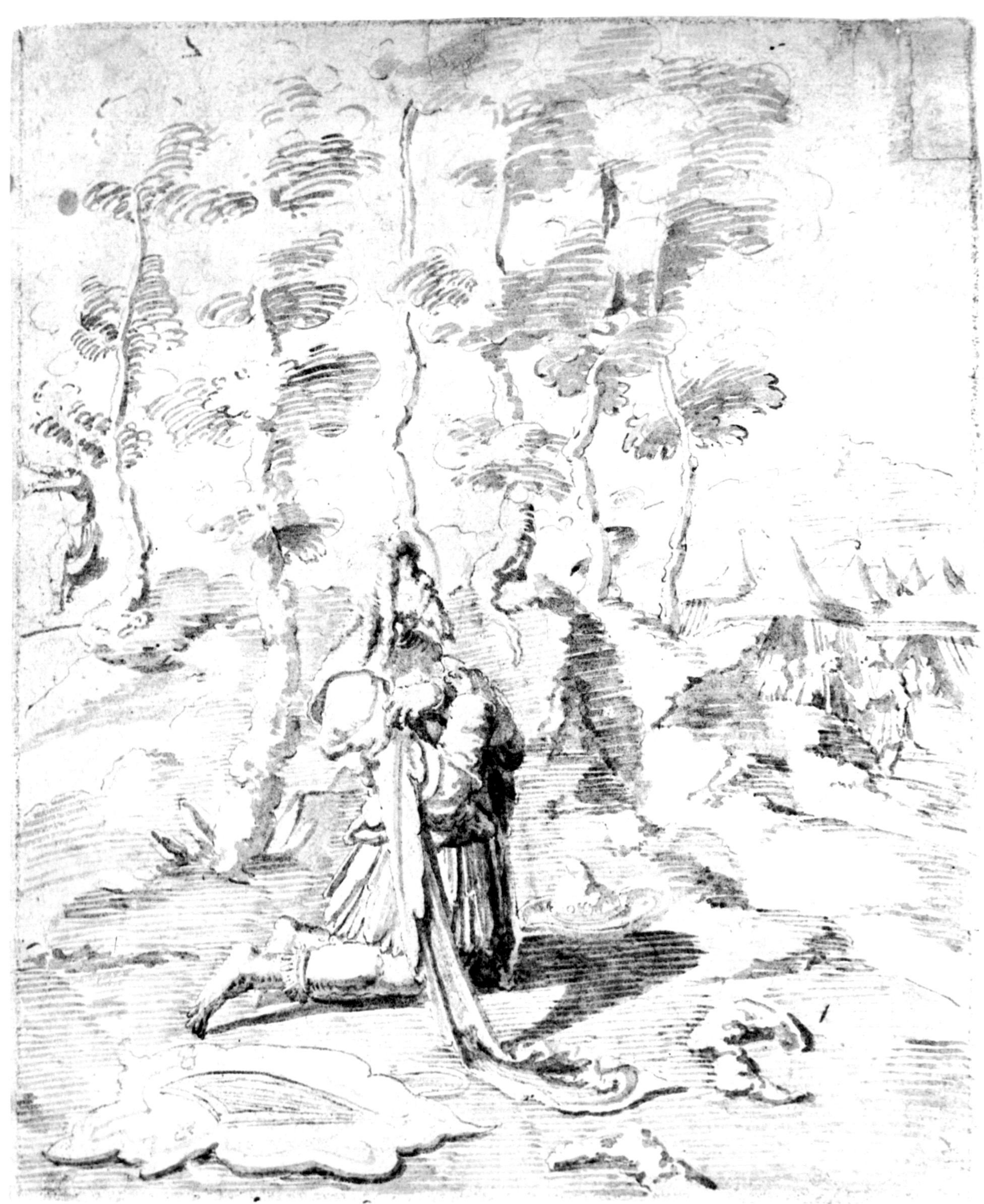

Dutch, Flemish, and German

MASTER OF 1527

LEIDEN, active during first half of the sixteenth century

1 *King David Praying*

Museum Purchase (1930.155) Pen and brown ink, grey wash, traces of black chalk, losses upper center and right. 231 x 191 mm. (9 1/8 x 7 1/2 in.) Watermark: Crowned shield with three fleur-de-lis, F below (Briquet 1817: Bruges 1524–25). Illegible initials in pen and ink on verso. PROVENANCE: Professor Henry Johnson. BIBLIOGRAPHY: Bruyn 1960, p. 112, no. 3* (as Aertgen van Leyden, subject identified as Joshua); Haverkamp Begemann and Logan 1970, vol. 1, p. 181, fig. 28 (as Master of 1527).

THE IDENTITY of the artist of this drawing has been the subject of much discussion. The sheet belongs to a group first isolated in 1928 by Wescher.[1] He placed the artist in the time of Lucas van Leyden (1489/1494–1533) and named him from a drawing dated 1527 in the Louvre.[2] Van Regteren Altena[3] and Bruyn[4] then ascribed this group and other sheets to Aertgen van Leyden (Leiden 1498–1564 Leiden), who had studied in the studio of Cornelis Engelbrechtsz. with Lucas. The Bowdoin sheet was first attributed to Aertgen by Gerson.[5] Bruyn then published it as such, while Haverkamp Begemann and Logan preferred to leave it with the more clearly defined Master of 1527 group. A sizable number of drawings of confusing variety has been placed under Aertgen's name. Indeed, Boon has recently stated that any attribution of the entire group to a single artist can be at best a hazardous venture.[6]

The media, technique, and style of the figures place the Bowdoin sheet clearly with the Master of 1527 drawings. In addition to the Paris sheet cited above, there are other drawings by this hand in Berlin, Yale, and Stockholm, and formerly in the Kneppelhout, Koenigs, and Lord Milford collections.[7] Another group of scenes from the Life of Christ is quite close to these.[8] A further group of three related allegories is close in technique but more mannered than the above.[9]

The figure in the Bowdoin drawing was identified by Bruyn as Joshua but certainly is David, because of his shield depicting a harp and the presence in the left background of his son Absalom hanging by his hair from a tree. This drawing probably comes from a series devoted to the story of Absalom's death, as told in 2 Samuel 18:9–15, for the sheet by this master in Berlin depicts the actual murder in the background. The technique and size of the Berlin sheet (229 x 187 mm.) are virtually identical with those of the Bowdoin drawing.

1. Wescher 1928, pp. 251–54. 2. Ibid., p. 253, fig. 7; Lugt 1968, pp. 33–34, no. 99, pl. 51. 3. Van Regteren Altena 1939, pp. 231–34. 4. Bruyn 1960, pp. 112–14. 5. Letter to Carl N. Schmalz, museum files, 8 October 1957. 6. Florence-Paris 1980–1981, pp. 145–46. 7. Respectively, Staatliche Museen Preussischer Kulturbesitz, *Vom späten Mittelalter bis zu Jacques Louis David* (exh. cat.) (Berlin, 1973), cat. no. 24, repr.; Haverkamp Begemann and Logan 1970, vol. 1, pp. 180–81, no. 330, and vol. 2, pl. 176; Bruyn 1960, p. 112, no. 4; Van Regteren Altena 1939, p. 75, fig. 2; Bruyn 1960, p. 92, fig. 31, and p. 111, fig. 44. 8. Düsseldorf (repr. Van Regteren Altena 1939, p. 130, fig. 2) and Berlin (repr. Wescher 1928, p. 252, fig. 6. This sheet was owned and retouched by Rubens, see Staatliche Museen Preussischer Kulturbesitz, *Peter Paul Rubens: Kritischer Katalog der Zeichnungen* [exh. cat. by H. Mielke and M. Winner] [Berlin, 1977], cat. no. 16, repr.). 9. Lugt Collection, Fondation Custodia, Institut Néerlandais, Paris (Florence-Paris 1980–1981, pp. 144–47, cat. no. 102, pl. 14, with references to the other two sheets).

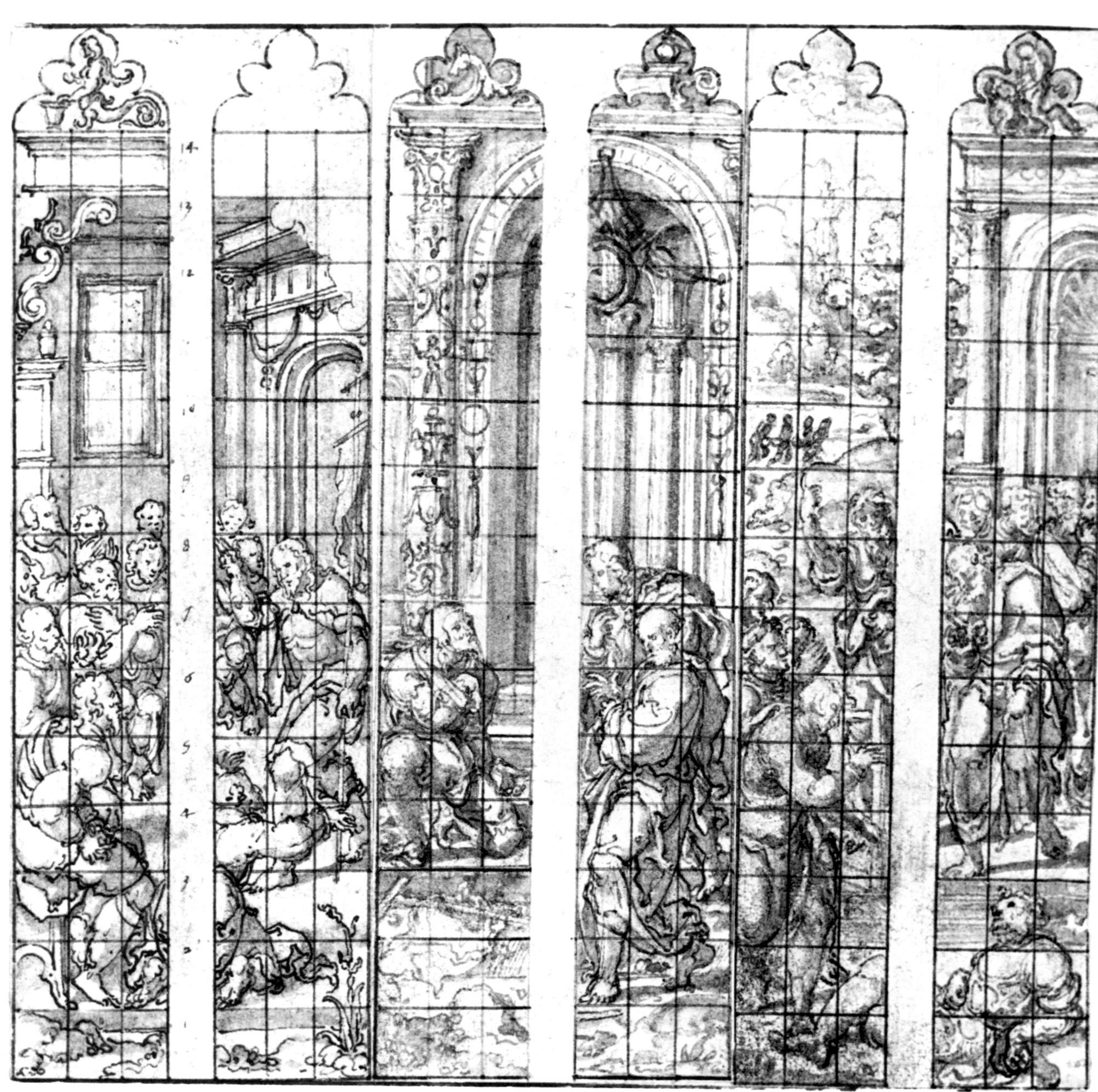

DIERICK VELLERT and Workshop
AMSTERDAM ca. 1480–after 1547 ANTWERP

2 *Three Designs for Stained Glass Windows*

Bequest of James Bowdoin III (1811.109) Pen and brown ink, grey wash over black chalk (traces of red chalk). Five sheets of paper, laid down (three sheets laid down, with two additional figural groups cut out from another sheet and laid down on center design). Compass used to emboss arch in center design, pin pricks on cinquefoils and ends of cross lines. 168 x 175 mm. (6 5/8 x 6 7/8 in.) No watermark visible. Inscribed with numbers of ferramenta in pen and ink, left design; traces of numbering on other designs. PROVENANCE: James Bowdoin III. BIBLIOGRAPHY: *Catalogue* 1885, no. 122 (as Unknown); *Catalogue* 1930, no. 122 (as Unknown); Boon 1964, pp. 153–56, pl. 20; Wayment 1972, pp. 20, 96, 101, and pl. 8, fig. 2; M. J. Friedländer, *Jan van Scorel and Pieter Coeck van Aelst*, vol. 12 of *Early Netherlandish Painting* (Leyden and Brussels, 1975), p. 135, n. 169; *Handbook* 1981, p. 164; H. G. Wayment, *King's College Chapel Cambridge—The Great Windows: Introduction and Guide* (Cambridge, 1982), p. 11, a detail repr. p. 4; H. G. Wayment, "Three *Vidimuses* for the Windows in King's College Chapel, Cambridge," *Master Drawings*, vol. 22, no. 1 (Spring 1984), pp. 43–46, repr. pl. 34. EXHIBITIONS: American Federation of Arts 1962–1963, no. 41 (as van Orley, attributed to); Waterville 1978, cat. no. 5, repr., exhibited in Brunswick.

THIS DRAWING is the only known surviving design for the stained glass of King's College Chapel, Cambridge, England. The twenty-five "great" windows of the chapel were glazed between 1515 and ca. 1547 and constitute a significant monument of northern Renaissance stained glass. Painters and glaziers from England, Germany, and the Netherlands took part in the commission. Dierick Vellert, perhaps the most renowned glass designer and painter in Antwerp of the 1520s and 1530s, contributed a major portion of the designs for King's College. He may even have traveled to England himself to work on the glass.[1]

Vellert came to Antwerp in the first decade of the century, joining the Guild of St. Luke there in 1511. His early artistic training is obscure. In addition to producing many designs for glass, Vellert was an inspired printmaker and maintained a studio of assistants. Albrecht Dürer paid him several visits during Dürer's stay in Antwerp in 1520/21. Vellert was still alive in 1547.

Formerly attributed to Barent van Orley, the Bowdoin drawing was first given to Vellert by Boon, who further recognized it as a design for the King's College windows (Judson had brought the drawing to his attention). Wayment then discussed it in detail in his 1972 monograph devoted to the windows. At that time, he accepted the attribution of the sheet to Vellert and convincingly demonstrated that it was an original working design for the windows and not copied after them. Upon a recent examination of the drawing itself, however, Wayment has modified his views somewhat, while still maintaining its important position within the design process.[2] The Bowdoin drawing is a "vidimus"—an exact study on a smaller scale for the glaziers to follow while preparing full-scale cartoons for the manufacture of the windows. According to Wayment, a vidimus must "correspond exactly . . . to the proportions of the opening, . . . and must repeat exactly the pattern of the *ferramenta*, the horizontal and vertical iron bars to which the completed panels are to be attached on the outside."[3] The original design would have been kept by the patron or his agent as part of the contract, thus necessitating an accurate duplicate working model—the vidimus—which could be done by the master-glazier (i.e., Vellert), but need not be.[4]

Wayment feels that the Bowdoin designs were indeed executed in the Vellert workshop, and he has attributed different sections of the sheet to different hands. That the designs are prior to the windows is proven primarily by 1) the major change of position of the lame man's left leg, which in the window is extended downward, and 2) the precise correspondence of the grids of the drawing and the actual windows and the numbering of the ferramenta in the drawing (the latter feature necessary for a vidimus but not for a copy).

In an analysis of the draughtsmanship, Wayment feels that Vellert himself was not responsible for the majority of the drawing, which was first laid down in washes and then reinforced with pen and ink contours. He attributes the left design of Christ appearing to the Apostles to the so-called Lazarus Master, who painted the scene of the Raising of Lazarus in Window 8.2.[5] He does attribute to Vellert much of the center drawing, particularly the figures of Peter and John. The right-hand design remains an anonymous product of the workshop.

The Bowdoin study is composed of designs for three scenes in two of the great windows on the south side of the chapel.[6] Each of the six sections in the drawing was then enlarged to a "light" measuring approximately seventeen and a half feet high and two and a half feet wide. The individual scenes portrayed from left to right in the drawing are Christ's appearance to the Apostles (John 20:12–23), Peter and John healing the Lame Man (Acts 3:1–10), and the Death of Ananias (Acts 5:1–6). The total iconographic program of the chapel windows derives principally from the Life of the Virgin, including the Life, Passion, and Resurrection of Christ, with prefigurations of each event from the Old Testament, and in addition three windows showing various acts of the Apostles. Much of the imagery ultimately derives from fifteenth-century blockbooks, particularly the *Speculum Humanae Salvationis* and the *Biblia Pauperum*.[7]

Wayment has discussed in detail specific features revealed in the Bowdoin designs, relating to original placement of the windows, smaller changes in decoration between design and glass, and visual sources for Vellert's representations. The pose of Peter in the right design, for instance, derives from Raphael's tapestry cartoon of the same subject, which was reproduced in a woodcut by Ugo da Carpi in 1518.[8] Wayment dates the windows related to the Bowdoin designs ca. 1538, during Vellert's later period of work on the King's College commission.

1. Wayment 1972, pp. 20–22. 2. Visit to the museum, 1982; I am most grateful to Dr. Wayment for sharing his observations with me. 3. Wayment 1972, p. 30. 4. Letter from H. G. Wayment to author, 8 July 1982. 5. The Lazarus window is repr. in Wayment 1972, pl. 79. 6. Repr. in Boon 1964, pp. 153–55, figs. 1–3 and in Wayment 1972, pls. 129, 135, and 137. 7. Wayment 1972, pp. 5–8. 8. Ibid., p. 102.

PIETER COECKE VAN AELST, Workshop of

AELST 1502–1550 BRUSSELS

3 *The Triumph of Sloth*

James Phinney Baxter Fund in Memory of Professor Henry Johnson (1932.37) Pen and brown ink, brush and grey wash, old vertical fold center. 222 x 398 mm. ($8^{3}/_{4}$ x $15^{11}/_{16}$ in.) Watermark: cross and orb with one cross bar (as in Briquet 3067). Inscribed pen and grey ink bottom center "1537"; graphite, verso "D. Barents." PROVENANCE: William Bates (1824–1884) (Lugt 2604); Professor Henry Johnson. BIBLIOGRAPHY: *Catalogue* 1930, p. 95, no. 645 (as Anonymous); Marlier 1966, p. 338; Haverkamp Begemann and Logan 1970, p. 261, fig. 48; Bauer 1981, p. 57.

COECKE PURSUED his apprenticeship in Antwerp, where he then spent the major part of his career. He was a prolific painter and designer for tapestries and stained glass. In 1533 he traveled to Constantinople, making a series of drawings of its topography and people which were later published as woodcuts. In 1539 he published and illustrated the first volume of an influential Flemish translation of Sebastiano Serlio's treatise on architecture, first published in Venice two years before. Pieter Coecke's earlier style reflects the influences of Dierick Vellert and Barent van Orley. He was in Brussels after 1546.

The Bowdoin sheet had formerly been attributed to Dirck Barendsz. and Lambert Lombard. However, as first pointed out by Jakob Rosenberg and Agnes Mongan, it is a close copy of a Coecke drawing in the Ecole des Beaux-Arts, Paris.[1] The Paris drawing seems to be the earliest study for the Triumph of Sloth, one of the tapestries in a series of the Seven Capital Sins.[2] The drawing at Bowdoin more closely resembles the finished tapestry. The most notable difference between the two is the elaboration of the wheels of the chariot on the Bowdoin sheet. Both drawings are in reverse to the tapestry. Marlier suggests that the Bowdoin design is a close workshop copy of the Paris sketch and that it established the definitive design which then would be enlarged for the cartoon preparatory to the tapestry manufacture.[3] Recently, Wayment has tentatively suggested that the Bowdoin sheet could have been a close copy by Coecke himself, but agrees that the less lively and strong draughtsmanship of some features argues against that hypothesis. Haverkamp Begemann and Logan state simply that Bowdoin's sheet is a copy. Other workshop copies for these tapestry designs probably by the same hand as Bowdoin's are at Frankfurt and Yale.[4] The Frankfurt drawing is similarly inscribed with the date 1537, which serves as a possible *terminus ante quem* for these designs.

The iconography for this series is described at some length in a near-contemporary document now in the Biblioteca Nacional in Madrid.[5] However, the document is incomplete, and much of the discussion of the representation of Sloth is missing. The Paris sketch does have inscriptions identifying two of the subjects: Sleep (the figure riding the ass at the left) and Sardanapalus (within the palace in the right distance).

Using these guides and other representations of Sloth, Bauer has reconstructed a plausible iconography for this particular subject.[6] Upon the chariot slumps the winged and horned Sloth, supported by a pillow (recalling a Netherlandish proverb that "Sloth is the devil's pillow"). The chariot is pulled slowly by two asses, also symbols of sloth. The standard-bearer at the left (Sleep) wearily rides an ass, barely holding his banner. An empty snail shell lies in the left foreground.

The figures of a young man and an elder are surmised by Bauer to represent Alexander the Great and Aristotle, as the latter is reputed to have exhorted the young prince against laziness. The representation here of the two figures walking purposefully away from the procession is taken as an

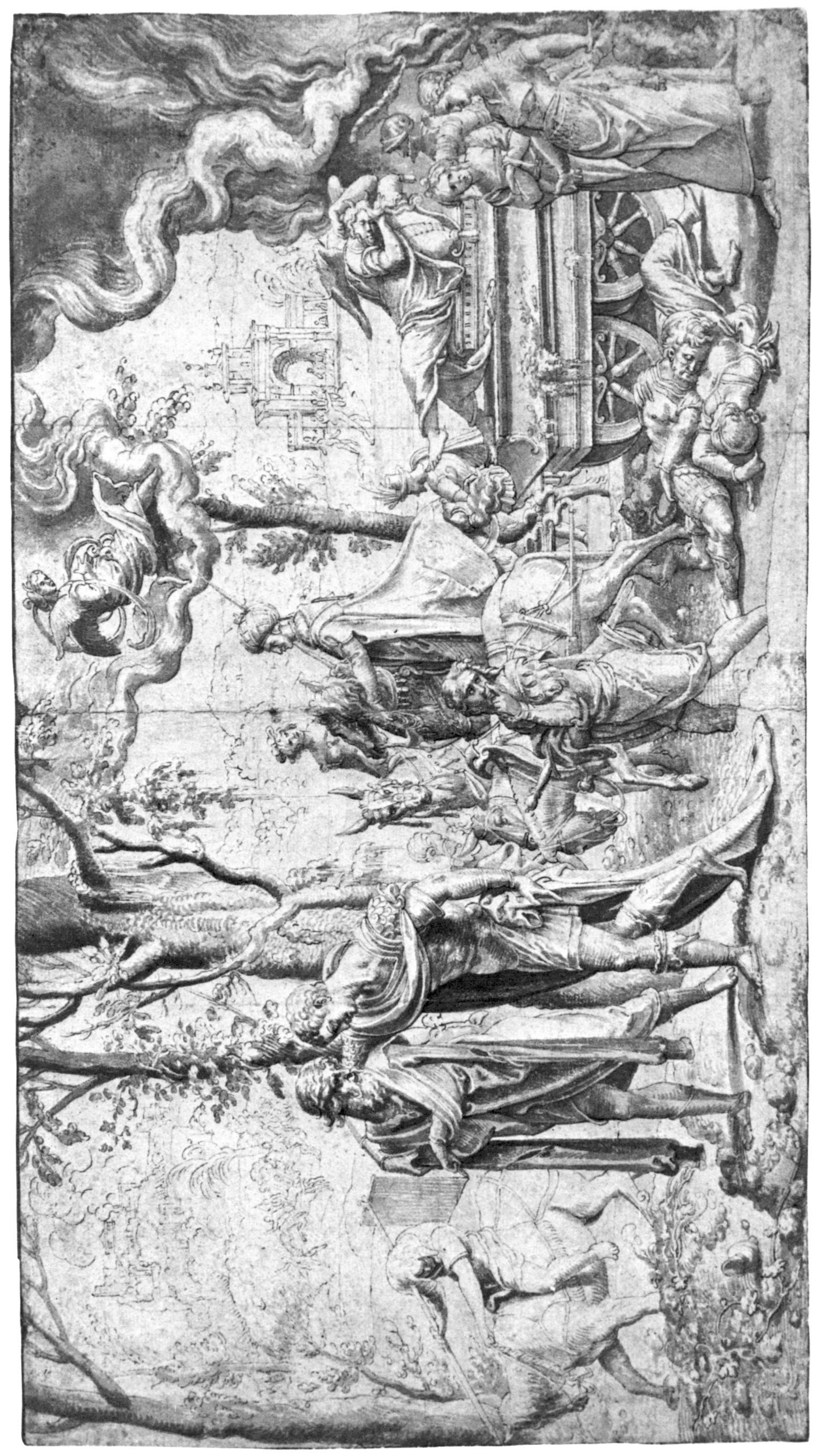

example of virtue, contrary to the vice of sloth. The figures of the young man in the center, the two riders in splendid robes on the other side of the chariot, and the three people lying beneath it remain unidentified.

As mentioned above, the grand palace in the right distance is taken to be that of Sardanapalus, the Assyrian king noted for his pampered and lustful ways, who allowed his kingdom to dissipate while he spent his days in his harem. In the left distance is a burning castle surrounded by a besieging army, presumed to represent Sardanapalus's legendary end. Bauer ventures the guess that the richly dressed and turbaned horseman next to Sloth's chariot is Sardanapalus himself.

Finally, the figures walking behind the chariot are a warrior who has drawn his sword but hides it (Cowardice) and two women (Timidity and Despair). The dark flames behind them are those of hell, populated in the tapestry by Death, monsters, and ghosts. The watchful female figure at the top of the composition is probably a symbol of Vigilance or Fortitude.

1. Repr. Marlier 1966, p. 336, fig. 277; Bauer 1981, p. 69, fig. 25. 2. Repr. Marlier 1966, p. 337, fig. 278; Bauer 1981, pl. 30. 3. Marlier 1966, p. 338. 4. Frankfurt: ibid., p. 334, fig. 273; Inv. no. 15320; Yale: Haverkamp Begemann and Logan 1970, no. 491, repr. vol. 2, pl. 255; Inv. no. 1961.64.7. 5. Bauer 1981, pp. 56–57, 90–99. 6. Ibid., pp. 68–70.

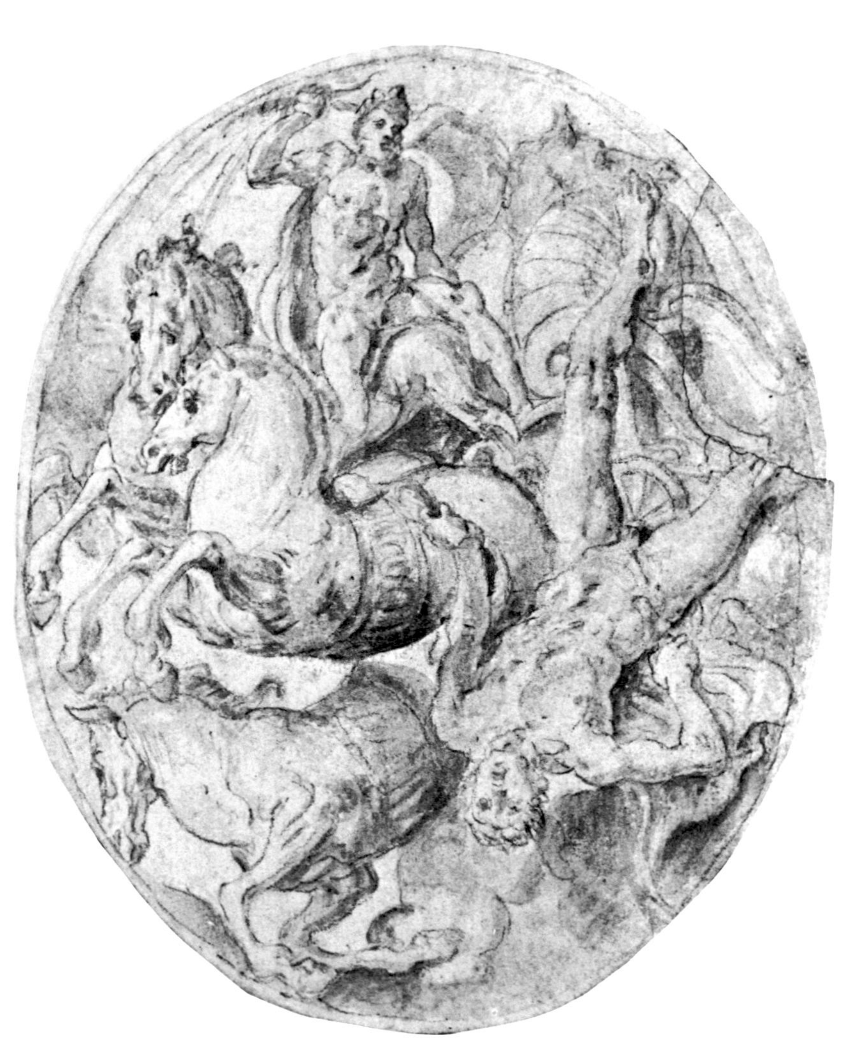

FRANS FLORIS

ANTWERP ca. 1519/20–1570 ANTWERP

4 *The Fall of Phaeton*

Bequest of James Bowdoin III (1811.108) Brush and light brown ink over black chalk (repaired tear upper right). 130 x 109 mm. ($5^1/_8$ x $4^1/_4$ in.) No watermark. PROVENANCE: James Bowdoin III. BIBLIOGRAPHY: *Catalogue* 1885, no. 123 (as Unknown); *Catalogue* 1930, no. 123 (as Unknown).

FLORIS BECAME A MEMBER of the Guild of St. Luke in Antwerp in 1540, having been a student of Lambert Lombard. After 1542, he went to Italy, where he studied ancient art and the works of contemporary masters, particularly Michelangelo. By 1547, Floris was back in Antwerp, where he established a large studio and became one of the most celebrated painters of his time. He decorated and built an elaborate house, which served as an inspiration for Rubens's own house fifty years later. Many of Floris's designs were circulated in some 150 engravings, and his influence was carried on in the work of his many students (numbering close to 120, according to Van Mander).

Originally classed as anonymous, this sheet was first ascribed by Lugt to a Flemish artist of about 1580.[1] Oberhuber then suggested an attribution to Floris, which was affirmed by Van de Velde on the basis of a photograph.[2] The drawing is closely related to three other sheets of the same subject by Floris in Paris, Brussels, and Dresden.[3] The Louvre drawing is particularly close to the Bowdoin sheet, though somewhat larger. It also includes the figures of the river god Eridanus and Phaeton's sisters. Floris has compressed the figures on the Bowdoin sheet into a tight oval, with Jupiter's eagle practically riding the horses. The horses and Phaeton have been placed very close to the picture plane, and the perspective has been tilted. It is conceivable that this design is a study for a ceiling painting or for a panel high on a wall (as also suggested by Van de Velde in correspondence). Van de Velde dates the Bowdoin drawing ca. 1555 or a little later.

The story of Phaeton is told by Ovid in the *Metamorphoses*, book 2, verses 1–400. Floris's depiction owes an obvious debt to Michelangelo's celebrated drawings of the theme. The most finished of these is at Windsor Castle, presented to Tommaso de' Cavalieri in 1533.[4] The dramatically upended figure of Phaeton rendered by Floris in the Bowdoin sheet is quite similar to one in a print engraved by Cornelis Cort after his design of *Hercules and the Pygmies*.[5] It further recalls the contorted figures in a painting of the *Last Judgment* in Brussels.[6] Crispijn van den Broecke, one of Floris's students, also portrayed the fall of Phaeton in a drawing, now in Munich.[7]

1. Visit to the museum, 1945. 2. Letter to the author, 6 July 1982. 3. Van de Velde 1975, cat. nos. T39, T37, and T38, figs. 136–38. 4. British Museum, *Drawings by Michelangelo* (exh. cat.) (London, 1975), cat. no. 126, repr. 5. Van de Velde 1970, fig. 209. 6. Ibid., fig. 91. 7. Wegner 1973, no. 20, pl. 30.

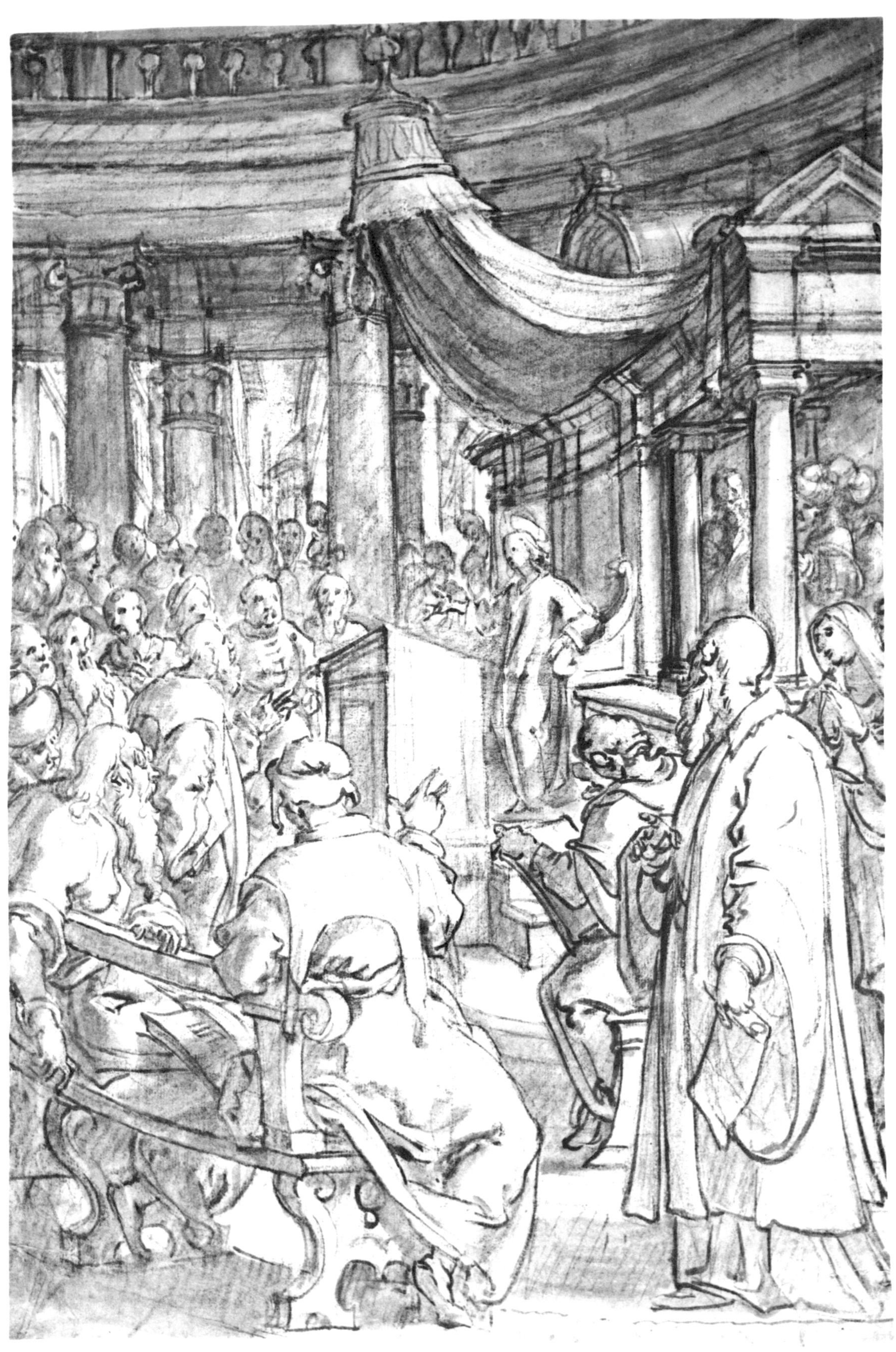

JAN VAN DER STRAET, called Stradanus

BRUGES 1523–1605 FLORENCE

5 *Christ among the Doctors*

Bequest of James Bowdoin III (1811.129) Brush and brown ink and brown wash over black chalk. 409 x 278 mm. (16 1/8 x 10 15/16 in.) Watermark: sun (similar to Briquet 13953-Pisa 1576). PROVENANCE: James Bowdoin III. BIBLIOGRAPHY: *Catalogue* 1885, no. 108 (as Unknown); *Catalogue* 1930, no. 108 (as Unknown); *Handbook* 1981, p. 165 (as Stradanus).

STRADANUS WAS ADMITTED to the Guild of St. Luke in Antwerp in 1545 and left for Italy two years later. He stayed first in Venice, then in Florence. During 1550, he worked in Rome with Daniele da Volterra and Francesco Salviati. Returning to Florence in 1551, Stradanus began a lengthy period of study and collaboration with Giorgio Vasari and then worked independently as a painter and designer, primarily of tapestries and prints. Although he took journeys to Naples and Flanders, he remained in Florence for the rest of his life.

Previously listed as anonymous Italian, this large drawing was first recognized by Oberhuber as a work of Stradanus. It is a preliminary study for a more finished drawing of only slightly larger dimensions in the Uffizi, Florence.[1] The compositions of the two drawings are virtually identical, the only significant change being an adjustment of the top angle of Christ's lectern to render a more accurate perspective in the Uffizi drawing. The architectural setting has been slightly changed, particularly in the background colonnade. The higher degree of finish in that drawing has solidified the space and figures. The Bowdoin sheet apparently was once a bit larger at both sides and top, for additional details are revealed at the edges of the Uffizi sheet. Thiem has ventured, from the elaborate technique and similarity to known painting designs, that the latter drawing is a study for a lost painting.[2]

The Bowdoin and Uffizi sheets are closely related to at least two others. In a private collection in Fort Worth, there is a sheet of the Adoration of the Shepherds of virtually identical dimensions and technique to the Bowdoin sketch.[3] And there is another highly finished drawing of the Visitation of the same format in the Uffizi.[4] Perhaps all these drawings were part of a projected larger series on the Life of the Virgin. Another series of drawings on the Life of the Virgin in smaller format is at Windsor Castle[5] (a series later engraved by Adriaen Collaert in Antwerp[6]), which includes *Christ among the Doctors*. There is a very small sketch related to the Windsor drawing in the Cooper-Hewitt Museum, New York.[7]

1. Inv. no. 5154S (Gernsheim Corpus no. 23920). 2. Thiem 1958, p. 102. 3. Reproduced in E. Pillsbury and J. Caldwell, *Sixteenth-Century Italian Drawings—Form and Function* (exh. cat.) (New Haven: Yale University Art Gallery, 1974), cat. no. 22. 4. Repr. Thiem 1958, p. 98, fig. 9. 5. J. van Puyvelde, *The Flemish Drawings in the Collection of His Majesty the King at Windsor Castle* (London, 1942), p. 23, no. 147, repr. 6. Hollstein *Dutch and Flemish*, vol. 4, p. 202. 7. Inv. no. 1901-39-116v.

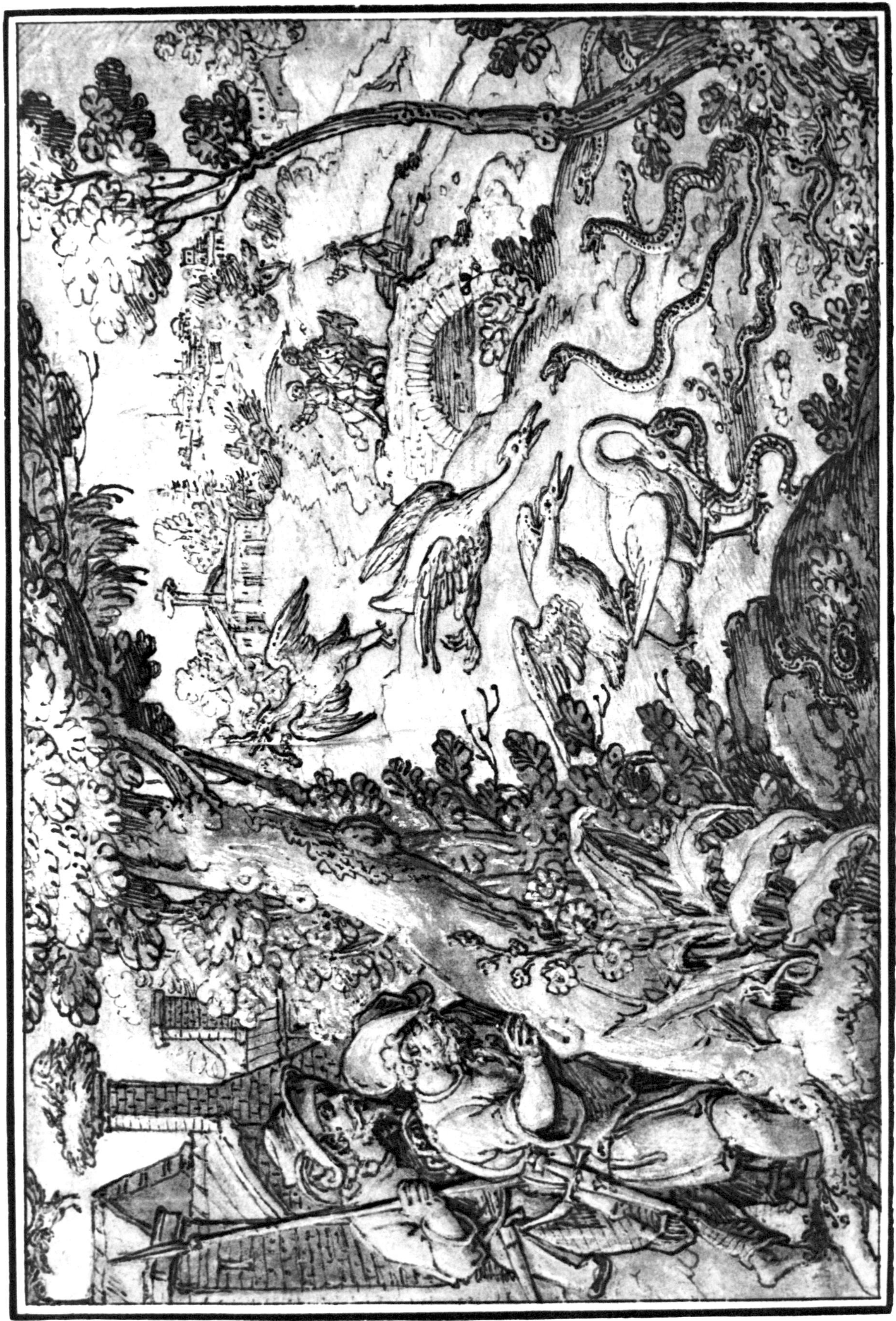

JAN VAN DER STRAET, called Stradanus

6 *Storks Fighting Snakes*

Gift of Miss Susan Dwight Bliss (1956.24.266) Pen and dark brown ink, brown wash, heightened with white (oxidized in places), on brown laid paper, traced with a stylus for transfer, laid down. 181 x 268 mm. (7 1/8 x 10 9/16 in.) No watermark visible. Inscribed in graphite on mount, verso: "3089 242/Stradanus." PROVENANCE: John or Thomas Thane (Lugt 1544 or 2461); Sir Thomas Lawrence (Lugt 2445); Susan Dwight Bliss. BIBLIOGRAPHY: *Handbook* 1981, p. 165.

STRADANUS WAS COMMISSIONED around 1566 by the Grand Duke Cosimo I de' Medici to prepare designs for a series of twenty-eight tapestries depicting hunting scenes. They were to decorate his villa at Poggio a Caiano near Florence and were woven at the court tapestry works, the Arazzeria Medicea. In 1570, the Antwerp publisher Hieronymus Cock published six engravings after Stradanus's designs. They proved so popular that another series of twelve prints was issued several years later. Stradanus then began producing independent designs for hunting prints; Bok-van Kammen has estimated that he designed more than 150 hunting subjects over a period of almost forty years.[1]

Another publisher in Antwerp, Philip Galle, soon issued two further series of engravings after these designs, totaling 104 subjects. The translated title of Galle's series is "The hunts of quadrupeds, birds and fishes, the fights with animals and of animals against each other." The Bowdoin drawing is a final study for an engraving in the second series, which comprised sixty-one scenes and was probably published between 1596 and 1602.[2] This particular group depicted exotic animals and hunting practices from distant lands, whereas Stradanus's earlier subjects had been more common to Europe.[3] The Bowdoin sheet shows storks attacking snakes, derived from a description by Pliny in his *Natural History*, book 10. He specifies that in Thessaly storks were protected by law for their helpful control of the snake population.[4]

The engraving after the Bowdoin drawing has a four-line Latin verse below the image composed by Cornelis Kiel, a philologist and poet who worked for the Antwerp printer-publisher Christoph Plantin.[5] Kiel's verse adds cranes to Pliny's description (to which Stradanus seems faithful) and changes the locale: "Vast Appulia nourishes the scaly snakes. The crane and the stork attack their offspring. Here they wage a bitter war with beak and bite. This sportive event is watched by many farmers." Kiel wrote the verses while working in Antwerp from the finished drawings which the artist had sent from Florence. Bok-van Kammen has determined that Stradanus relied on personal observation, pictorial sources, and literary descriptions for depictions of individual animals in his designs.

Approximately half of Stradanus's finished drawings for these engravings have been located in various collections, among them Amsterdam (Rijksmuseum), Paris (Louvre and Institut Néerlandais), Florence (Uffizi), Stockholm (Nationalmuseum), and Providence (Rhode Island School of Design).[6] In addition, the Cooper-Hewitt Museum in New York possesses numerous small sketches for the hunting prints, though none for the Bowdoin sheet. This drawing has been traced with a thin point, or stylus, to transfer the design directly to the printing plate; hence the design appears reversed in the final engraving. Stradanus used white highlighting fairly extensively to indicate to the engraver the areas to remain light in the print. The latter is quite faithful to the design of the drawing, but becomes drier in the transformation. It is unsigned, and the engraver is unknown.

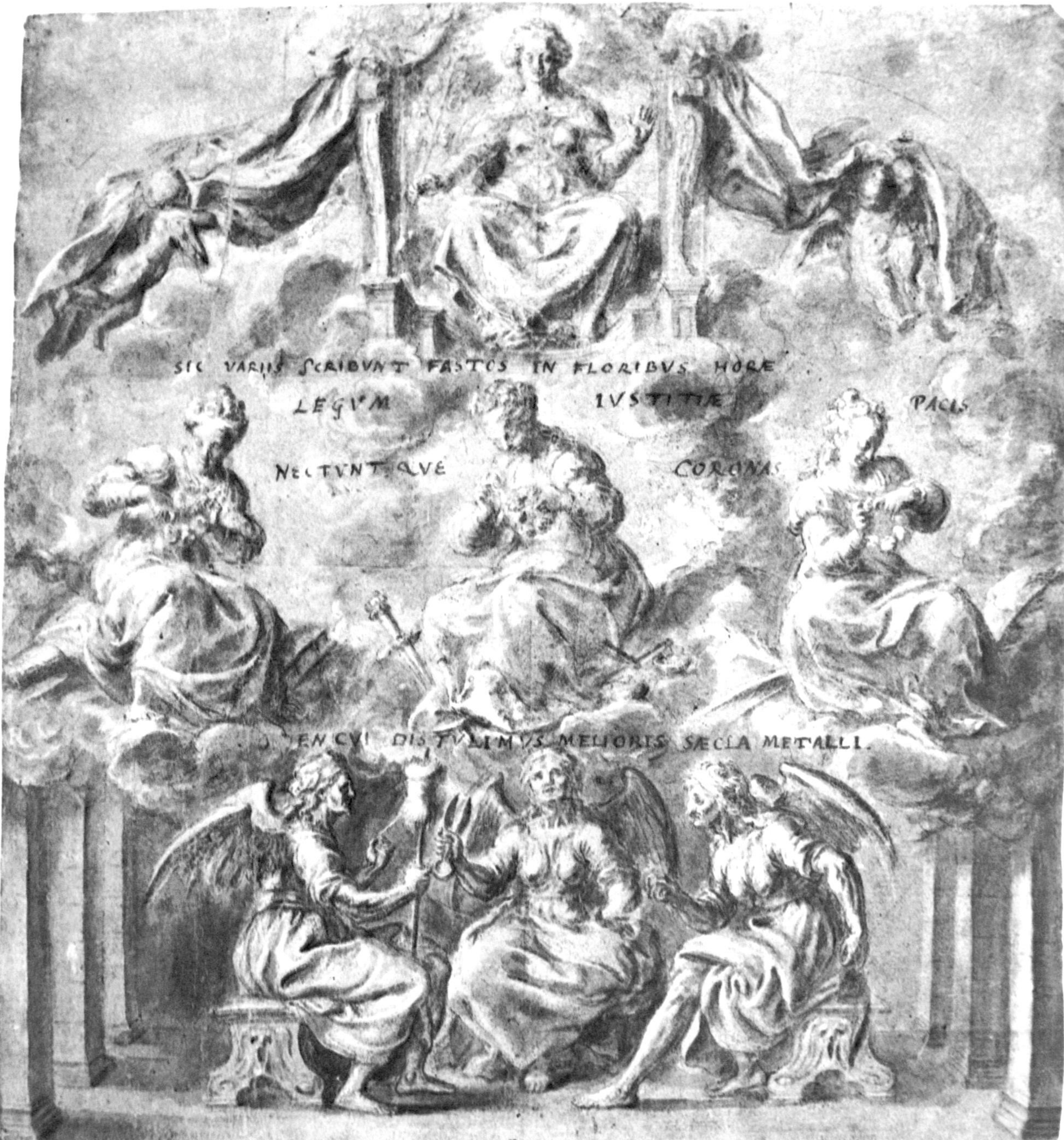
SIC VARIIS SCRIBUNT FASTOS IN FLORIBUS HORE
LEGUM
IUSTITIE
PACIS
NECTUNTQUE
CORONAS
EN CUI DISTULIMUS MELIORIS SECLA METALLI

1. Bok-van Kammen 1980, p. 6. 2. Ibid., p. 36. 3. Ibid., p. 35. 4. Ibid., p. 424. 5. The museum owns an impression of the print, Inv. no. 1976.39; ibid., p. 41. 6. Bok-van Kammen has the most complete list, with references to publications of the individual drawings, although she did not know of the Bowdoin drawing. The Institut Néerlandais drawings are published in Florence-Paris 1980–1981, cat. nos. 136–37.

CRISPIJN VAN DEN BROECK

MALINES ca. 1524–before 1591 ANTWERP

7 *Allegory with the Hours and Fates*

Museum Purchase (1930.223) Pen and brush and black ink, black chalk, heightened with white (oxidized), on blue-grey laid paper (old horizontal and vertical folds, some losses at edges). 432 x 401 mm. (17 x 15$^3/_4$ in.) No watermark visible. Inscribed recto pen and brown ink "SIC VARIIS SCRIBVNT FASTOS IN FLORIBVS HORÆ / LEGVM IVSTITIÆ PACIS / NECTVNTQVE CORONAS / EN CVI DISTVLIMVS MELIORIS SÆCLA METALLI"; inscribed verso, graphite "WS." PROVENANCE: Charles Rogers (1711–1784) (Lugt 624); Professor Henry Johnson [Note: the initials on the verso do not resemble those of William Sharp—cf. Lugt 2650].

VAN DEN BROECK entered the studio of Frans Floris (see Cat. 4) around 1550 and joined the Guild of St. Luke in Antwerp in 1555/56. He spent most of his career in the latter city, with a stay in Middelburg in 1584. There is some evidence for a trip to Italy before 1559. Van den Broeck's work shows a considerable stylistic debt to his master, Floris, and also to Marten de Vos. Many of his compositions were engraved, and he designed numerous book illustrations for the Antwerp publisher Christoph Plantin.

Entering the collections with an anonymous Flemish attribution, this large sheet has been given to various artists of the later sixteenth century, including de Vos, Jacob de Wit, and van den Broeck. The latter attribution, suggested by Haverkamp Begemann and Oberhuber, seems to be the most convincing, especially considering the facial and figural style of the three lowest figures, so reminiscent of his master, Floris. The loose draughtsmanship is also reflected in van den Broeck's known drawings, such as those in the Albertina; the Institut Néerlandais, Paris; and the Louvre, to name only a few.[1] There are a number of his drawings in various collections, many of which have previously carried Floris attributions.

The allegorical intent of the Bowdoin drawing is not completely clear; however, most of the elements composing it can be identified. The enthroned woman at the top probably represents the goddess Themis, who in Greek mythology was the incarnation of law. She was the second wife of Zeus and by his authority presided over assemblies of men and gods. She was the mother by Zeus of the three Hours and the three Fates, who are depicted here.

According to Hesiod, the Hours were named Eunomia (Order), Dice (Justice), and Eirene (Peace). Their identifications and attributes are confirmed by the inscriptions on the drawing. The Hours were also associated with the seasons and the stages of vegetation (thus the wreath of flowers each weaves). Each sits on her attributes, most clearly seen in Justice (sword and scales) and Peace (palm branch). Homer also indicates that the Horae had the duty of guarding the gates of heaven, which here are probably symbolized by the columns at the bottom and the obscuring clouds (which are controlled by the Hours).

The three Fates at the lower center sit spinning the thread of life. They are Clotho, at the left, who spins the thread; Lachesis, at the right, who winds it (determining the length of each mortal's life); and Atropos, in the center, who cuts each thread with her shears.[2] This composition might be an allegory either for a wise ruler or the proper moral conduct of human lives, perhaps drawing a connection between longevity and a person's propriety during life. The translated inscription reads:

> Thus do the Hours inscribe the annals on the various flowers
> of the laws, of justice, of peace, and they weave wreaths;
> behold, here is the one for whom we have delayed the generations of a nobler metal.

The first and third lines are paraphrased from the poet Claudius Claudianus (ca. 370–ca. 404 A.D.), whose works were particularly favored among Renaissance humanists.[3]

The ultimate purpose of this drawing is also unclear, but it is tempting to associate it with a print commission, perhaps for a thesis. There is another drawing of the three Fates by van den Broeck in the Ashmolean Museum, Oxford.[4] There they are depicted in an interior with other figures and Death, who often is included in such scenes.

1. Benesch 1928, nos. 119–26, repr.; Florence-Paris 1980–1981, nos. 36–40, pls. 70–74; Lugt 1968, nos. 384–95, pls. 141–43. 2. Much of the above is derived from the *Oxford Classical Dictionary*, 2nd ed.; and P. Grimal, ed., *Larousse World Mythology* (New York, 1965), p. 110. 3. The first line is taken from his *Panegyricus dictus Probino et Olybrio consulibus* (Claudian 1.278). The entire inscription was translated and the sources researched by Barbara Weiden Boyd, assistant professor of classics, Bowdoin College. I am very grateful to her for her aid. 4. Parker 1938, vol. 1, no. 29: pen and ink with bistre wash, 190 x 279 mm.

PIETER BRUEGEL the Elder

BREDA ca. 1525/30–1569 BRUSSELS

8 *Alpine Landscape (View of Waltensburg)*

Bequest of James Bowdoin III (1811.142) Pen and brown ink, laid down, darkened by exposure to light. 320 x 274 mm. (12 5/8 x 10 13/16 in.) No watermark visible. Inscribed in pen and brown ink at top center: "156 Waltersspurg"; in graphite, verso: "den ouden breugol [?] No. 56." PROVENANCE: James Bowdoin III. BIBLIOGRAPHY: *Catalogue* 1885, no. 98 (as Unknown); Allen 1886, pt. 4, no. 15, repr. (as Unknown); Mather 1914, p. 108, fig. 1 (as Bruegel); *Catalogue* 1930, no. 98 (as Unknown); C. de Tolnay, *Pierre Bruegel l'Ancien* (Brussels, 1935), p. 102, supp. no. 5, repr. pl. 116, fig. 198 (as Bruegel, as are all following); C. de Tolnay, *History and Technique of Old Master Drawings* (New York, 1943), p. 134, no. 172, repr.; [Siber] 1947, p. 118 and fig. 2; A. Mongan, *One Hundred Master Drawings* (Cambridge, 1949), p. 62, repr.; *Handbook* 1950, p. 21, fig. 15; de Tolnay 1952, pp. 58–59, no. 16, repr. pl. 9; Benesch 1953, p. 79; Grossmann 1954, pp. 54, 76, 84; Auner 1956, p. 75; Münz 1961, pp. 14, 210, no. 19, pl. 19; S. E. Lee, *Chinese Landscape Painting*, 2nd ed. (Cleveland, 1962), p. 79, fig. E; F. Grossmann, *Bruegel—The Paintings* (London, 1966), p. 15; I. Moskowitz, ed., *Great Drawings of All Time* (New York, 1962), vol. 2, no. 497, repr.; G. Arpino and P. Bianconi, *L'Opere completa di Bruegel* (Milan, 1967), p. 85, repr.; C. D. Cuttler, *Northern Painting from Pucelle to Bruegel* (New York [1968]), p. 470, fig. 654; B. Claessens and J. Rousseau, *Our Bruegel* (Antwerp, 1969), p. 60, fig. 5, and p. 151; W. Stechow, *Pieter Bruegel the Elder* (New York, 1969), pp. 18, 37, fig. 23; C. Eisler, *The Seeing Hand—A Treasury of Great Master Drawings* (New York, 1975) [p. 73], no. F.8, repr.; H. Spencer, *The Image Maker—Man and His Art* (New York, 1975), pp. 189–91, fig. 133; W. S. Gibson, *Bruegel* (London, 1977), pp. 34–35, fig. 12; P. Bianconi, *Bruegel* (Bologna and New York, 1979), p. 20, repr.; Müller Hofstede 1979, pp. 106–7 (n. 120–21), 111, 125; Palais des Beaux-Arts, *Bruegel, Une Dynastie des Peintres* (exh. cat.) (Brussels, 1980), pp. 32, repr., 64; Oberhuber 1981, p. 151; C. D. Denison and H. B. Mules, *European Drawings, 1375–1825* (New York, 1981), p. 56; *Handbook* 1981, pp. 152–53, repr. EXHIBITIONS: New London, Lyman Allen Museum, *Drawings*, 1936, cat. no. 46; Boston, Museum of Fine Arts, *A Thousand Years of Landscape East and West*, 1945, cat. no. 6; Cambridge, Fogg Art Museum, *Seventy Master Drawings*, 1948–1949, cat. no. 27; Philadelphia, Philadelphia Museum of Art, *Masterpieces of Drawing—Diamond Jubilee Exhibition*, 1950–1951, cat. no. 48, repr.; New York, Pierpont Morgan Library, *Landscape Drawings and Watercolors: Bruegel to Cézanne*, 1953, cat. no. 49; Montreal, Montreal Museum of Fine Arts, *Five Centuries of Drawings*, 1953, cat. no. 8, repr.; Cleveland, Cleveland Museum of Art, *Chinese Landscape Painting*, 1954–1955, cat. no. 119, repr. p. 86; Waterville, Colby College Art Museum, *An Exhibition of Drawings*, 1956, cat. no. 5; Lawrence, University of Kansas Museum of Art, *Thirtieth Anniversary Exhibition: Masterworks from University and College Collections*, 1958, cat. no. 38, repr.; Newark, The Newark Museum, *Old Master Drawings*, 1960, cat. no. 20, repr.; Durham, University of New Hampshire, *Art Collections of New England Colleges*, 1960; Los Angeles, Los Angeles County Museum of Art, *Prints and Drawings of Pieter Bruegel the Elder*, 1961, cat. no. 103, repr. p. 11; Utica, Munson-Williams-Proctor Institute, and Rochester, Rochester Memorial Art Gallery, *Masters of Landscape: East and West*, 1963, cat. no. 21, repr.; Santa Barbara, Santa Barbara Museum of Art, *European Drawings*, 1964, cat. no. 7, repr.; Cambridge, Busch-Reisinger Museum, *Northern Renaissance*, 1967; Albuquerque, University of New Mexico Art Museum, *Prints and Drawings by Pieter Bruegel the Elder*, 1968; Cambridge, Busch-Reisinger Museum, *Dürer and Bruegel: A Century of Humanism*, 1970; Berlin 1975, cat. no. 57a, repr. fig. 88a; Waterville 1978, cat. no. 6, repr., exhibited in Brunswick.

BRUEGEL DREW his celebrated mountain landscapes presumably from direct experience on a journey through the Alps, at the time of a stay in Italy from 1552 to 1553. In his biography of the artist in the *Schilderboek* of 1604, Karel van Mander stated that Bruegel swallowed up the mountains and then spat them out onto his canvases upon his return. Direct evidence for his Alpine journey

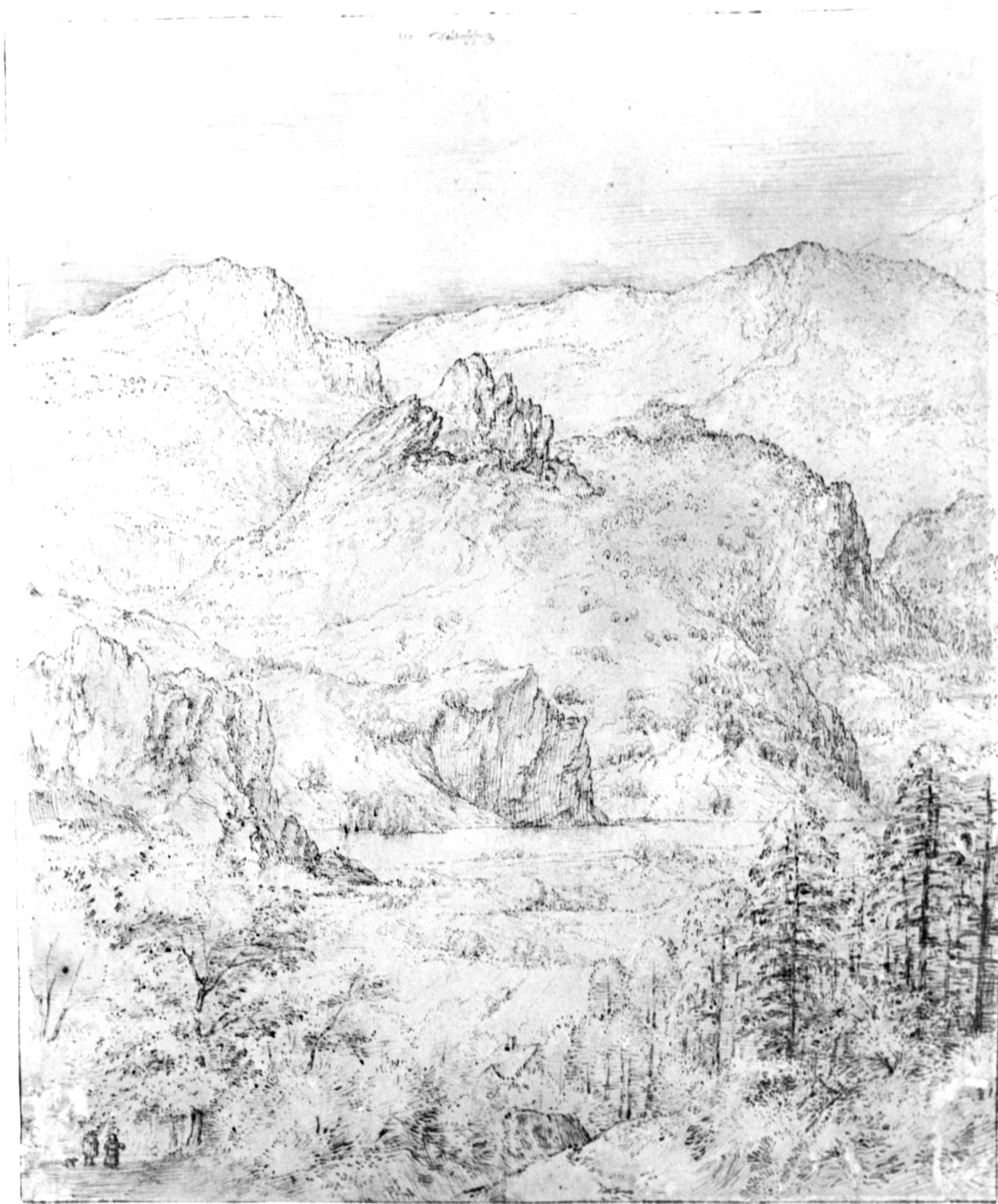

depends on a very few existing drawings of identifiable sites and on references to lost works depicting known sites. One of these is the Bowdoin landscape, unquestionably the masterpiece of the drawing collection.

The sheet remained completely unidentified (despite the inscription on the verso) until Mather published it as Bruegel's work in 1914, although its exceptional quality had been acknowledged by its inclusion in the 1886 facsimile publication of sixteen of the Bowdoin drawings. Otto Benesch was the first to propose that the landscape could be identified with the upper Rhine valley in the Grabünden (Grisons) district of Switzerland, near the small town of Waltensburg. He based his identification on the inscription at the top of the sheet, saying it could be in Bruegel's hand. The site is just north of the St. Gotthard Pass, also the subject of a Bruegel painting listed in Rubens's studio.[1] Auner attempted to disprove a lengthy Alpine journey, saying it was an itinerary too difficult and irrational for an artist of the time.[2] However, all other scholars have agreed that the evidence of the drawings themselves is too strong to deny the trip. Auner did establish that the inscription on the Bowdoin sheet could not be autograph, an opinion affirmed by Mielke, though the latter stated that it probably dates from the sixteenth century. Mielke still feels that the inscription refers to Waltensburg.[3] Other scholars, however, have felt that a firm identification would depend upon direct examination on the spot, as first suggested by Grossmann. There is a photograph in the museum files of the valley at Waltensburg; the visual evidence it offers is inconclusive.

There are two other Bruegel drawings which bear a remarkable affinity in technique and subject matter to the Bowdoin sheet. One is the *Mountain Landscape with River and a Cross* in the Museum Boymans-van Beuningen, Rotterdam,[4] and the other is perhaps Bruegel's most impressive work in this genre, the *Landscape in the Upper Rhine Valley* in the Pierpont Morgan Library, New York.[5] Benesch has proposed that the Morgan drawing depicts the castle Jörgensberg and village of Ruiz, between Truns and Ilanz, slightly east of Waltensburg.[6] The landscape in the Rotterdam drawing is tantalizingly similar—seemingly portraying the same site from a different viewpoint—without being precisely identical. Grossmann's study of the landscape drawings notes these resemblances but stresses that while Bruegel may have been inspired by the same view, these compositions are probably not direct studies from nature.[7]

All three drawings are highly finished (the Rotterdam sheet has been overlaid with pen and brush, probably by the artist Roelant Savery), both in their carefully composed formats and in the detailed and varied pen strokes delineating trees and rocks. The atmosphere of great height and distance is evoked by subtle gradations of penwork. Most authorities agree that the three drawings are compositions worked up from preliminary rough sketches (though not evident in the Bowdoin sheet, some pen drawings have slight black chalk sketches underneath). The three sheets are similarly anchored at the right side by tall stands of fir trees. Close examination of the Bowdoin drawing reveals that the two prominent outcroppings of rock in the central portion have been worked over previously drawn and gentler slopes. These changes are skillfully camouflaged by the artist in order to make the new formations appear entirely "natural." The additions considerably strengthen the drawn composition and reinforce the argument that these landscape drawings are "assembled" from different elements.

Müller Hofstede has suggested that the Morgan sheet and others like it were prepared by Bruegel as elaborate presentation drawings for friends and collectors in the Netherlands, as souvenirs of his Alpine trip.[8] Its consummate technique and considered composition would suggest a similar function for the Bowdoin drawing. It has also been suggested that the vertical format of the Bowdoin sheet resulted from its being cut down at some point from a larger, horizontal composition.[9] That seems unlikely, for the walking couple at the left and the large group of trees at the right adequately frame the sheet and present a balanced composition. The format is, however, relatively rare in Bruegel's Alpine landscape drawings, although he used it often in his forest scenes.[10]

The remaining scholarly question about these landscape drawings is their dating. Most scholars have placed the highly finished views such as the Bowdoin sheet during or soon after Bruegel's return journey from Italy to Antwerp—i.e., ca. 1553/54, postulating an Alpine journey on his way home. Recently, Konrad Oberhuber has proposed a redating of some of these landscapes to 1551/52, during Bruegel's outward journey to Italy, basing much of his argument on the large drawing in the Fogg Art Museum, Cambridge.[11] He has characterized the major mountain group of that sheet (it was done in three distinct stages, the left foreground being the last) as an essentially "optical" view, without a highly developed landscape aesthetic, which he states Bruegel learned only in Italy. Thus he places the Morgan and Bowdoin sheets and the major portion of the Fogg drawing before Bruegel's arrival in Italy, in contrast to such progressively "organized" views as that dated 1553 in the Louvre[12] or one formerly in the Seilern collection,[13] also datable to 1553. As there is no documentary proof for either a journey through the Alps in 1551/52 or for the early dating of the Bowdoin drawing, any conclusion as to its dating remains tentative.

1. Benesch 1953, p. 79. 2. Auner 1956, pp. 64–75. 3. Ibid., p. 75; Berlin 1975, p. 53. 4. Münz 1961, no. 20. 5. Ibid., no. 21. 6. Benesch 1953, p. 79. 7. Grossmann 1954, pp. 54, 84. 8. Müller Hofstede 1979, p. 98. 9. De Tolnay 1952, cat. nos. 41–49. 10. Cf. Berlin 1975, cat. nos. 41–49. 11. Oberhuber 1981, *passim*; the Fogg drawing is repr. in Münz 1961, no. 18. 12. Münz 1961, no. 5. 13. Ibid., no. 15.

SOUTH NETHERLANDISH OR GERMAN, second half of the sixteenth century

9 *The Passage of the Ark through the Jordan River*

Museum Purchase (1930.135) Pen and brown ink, black wash, heightened with white, on paper prepared with brown wash, losses upper left. 202 x 287 mm. (7 15/16 x 11 5/16 in.) No watermark. Inscribed verso, pen and brown ink: "Italiaens van/La Tombe/Suardian." PROVENANCE: Pieter (?) de La Tombe; Professor Henry Johnson.

THE PUZZLING ICONOGRAPHY of this drawing presented a riddle for many years. Described when it entered the collections as depicting a funeral procession, the sheet was first identified by Panofsky in 1954 as representing the Return of the Ark of the Covenant to Jerusalem (2 Samuel 6). However, this author has concluded that it refers to an earlier episode in the Old Testament, the entry of the Israelites into the Promised Land, after their flight from Egypt. Under the leadership of Joshua, who had been designated as Moses' successor, they came to the Jordan River, with Jericho lying opposite. As the priests carrying the ark entered the river, the flow of water miraculously ceased, allowing thousands of people to cross on the dry riverbed. Joshua is seen watching at the center right, while the priests and ark have stopped in the middle until all have passed.

The identification of this episode is rendered certain by the men in the foreground picking up large stones. As related in Joshua 4, one man from each of Israel's twelve tribes was chosen to take a stone from the riverbed and place it on the opposite riverbank as a permanent memorial to the Lord's miracle performed that day.

Although not a common subject, the Crossing of the Jordan is depicted at least twice in Netherlandish art from this period. Pieter Coecke van Aelst included it in his series of large tapestries of the History of Joshua (Vienna, Kunsthistorisches Museum), dating from the 1530s.[1] The twelve chosen men picking up the stones are featured prominently in the foreground in both the tapestry and a preliminary sketch.[2] The episode is likewise shown in a large engraving by Cornelis Bos and copied from an unknown model, dated 1547.[3] Traditionally thought to be after Giovanni da Udine, the print could possibly be after a lost painting by Jan van Scorel, mentioned by Karel van Mander.[4] The passage through the Jordan without the gathering of stones was illustrated in several German sixteenth-century Bibles, probably beginning with the Bible produced by the Cranach workshop in 1524.[5] The subject appeared also in Italian art, one instance being Ghiberti's bronze doors of the Baptistry in Florence (even to the stone-gathering).

The eccentric draughtsmanship of this sheet has so far eluded any firm attribution to a particular artist or school. Lugt first suggested that it was the work of a follower of Jan van Scorel. Haverkamp Begemann and Wayment independently have recently suggested looking in the circle of Pieter Coecke van Aelst. In 1977, Oberhuber associated the style of the Bowdoin drawing with that of the so-called Master of the Liechtenstein Adoration, who has been extremely difficult to identify.[6] This drawing almost certainly was not done by that master, but it does exhibit similar characteristics: exaggerated postures, fluttering draperies, dramatic composition, and a prepared background. Indeed, many of the names which have been suggested for the Liechtenstein master have likewise been brought up in connection with this sheet. In 1982, Oberhuber suggested an influence from Melchior Lorch.[7] At the risk of injecting further confusion into the ever-growing list of names, there are striking compositional and iconographic parallels between this drawing and sheets in Christ Church, Oxford, and in a private collection in London.[8] Byam Shaw attributes them to an Italian artist, perhaps Bolognese, of the mid-sixteenth century. They depict the Worship of the Golden Calf and Pharoah's Army Submerged in the Red Sea, two Old Testament episodes

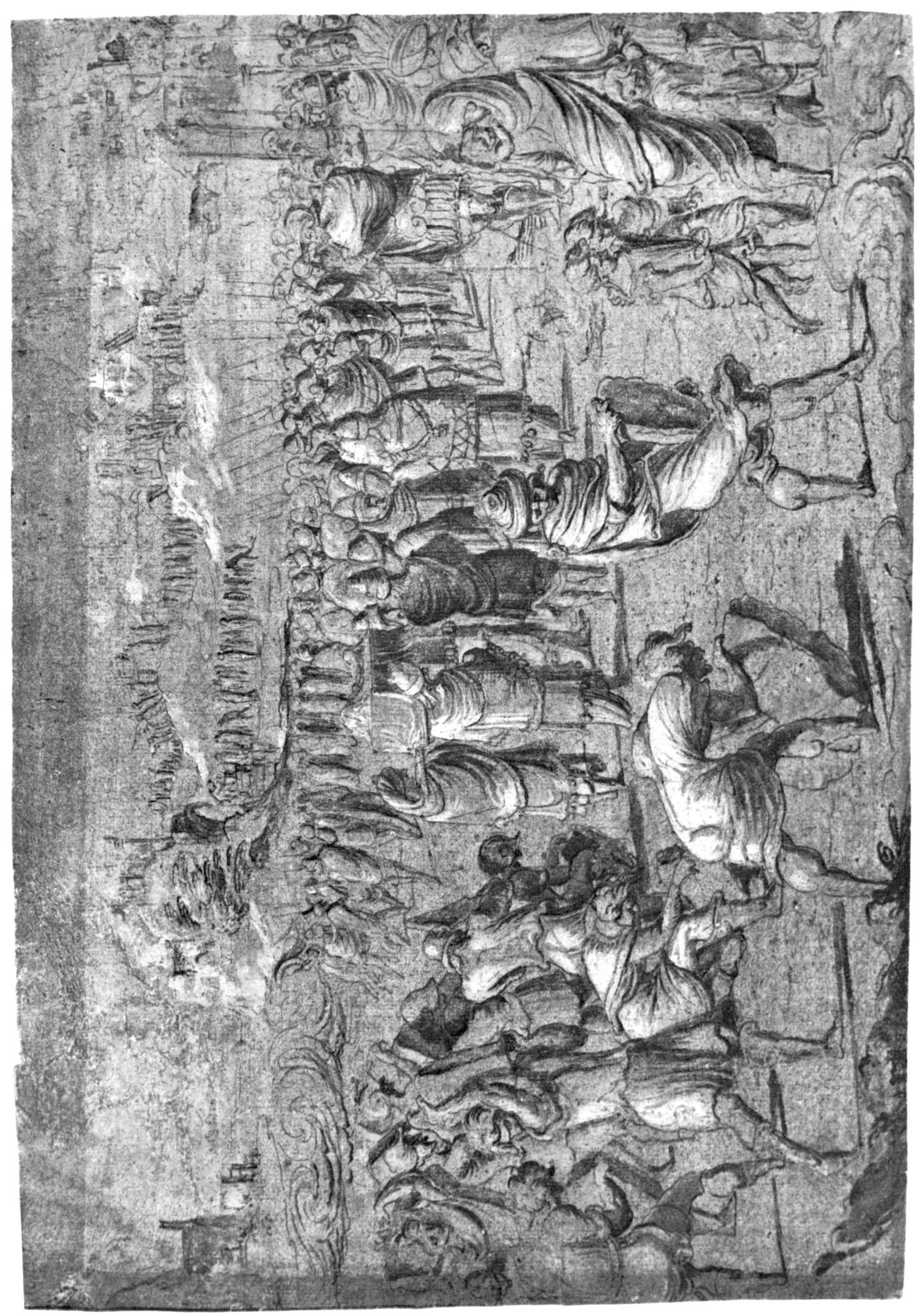

not far from that of the Bowdoin sheet. During the seventeenth century, this drawing had in fact an Italian attribution. The inscription on the verso led an earlier cataloguer to attribute the drawing to Nicolas de La Tombe (1616–1676), a Dutch artist. Rather, as Haverkamp Begemann kindly pointed out in 1982, the inscription probably refers to Pieter de La Tombe, an Amsterdam art dealer active from the 1630s who must have once owned this drawing: translated, the inscription reads "Italian, from La Tombe."[9]

1. Marlier 1966, p. 329, fig. 266. 2. For the latter, see Bauer 1981, p. 23, fig. 3. 3. S. Schéle, *Cornelis Bos* (Stockholm, 1965), no. 19, pls. 6–7; Hollstein *Dutch and Flemish*, vol. 3, p. 121, no. 22. 4. A. de Hevesy, "Quelques tableaux inconnus de Jean Scorel," *Oud Holland*, vol. 49 (1932), p. 138. 5. Cf. reproduction in *Lucas Cranach d. A 1472–1553*, J. Jahn, ed. (Munich, 197?), p. 754. 6. Cf. discussion in Princeton-Washington 1982–1983, cat. no. 7, with references to previous literature. 7. Cf. a drawing in the Achenbach Foundation, San Francisco (Inv. no. 1965.53, Princeton-Washington 1982–1983, cat. no. 13, repr.). 8. Byam Shaw 1976, cat. no. 878, repr. vol. 2, pl. 535; also see vol. 1, fig. 62. 9. See Hind 1926, pp. 134–35, for a discussion of the de La Tombes.

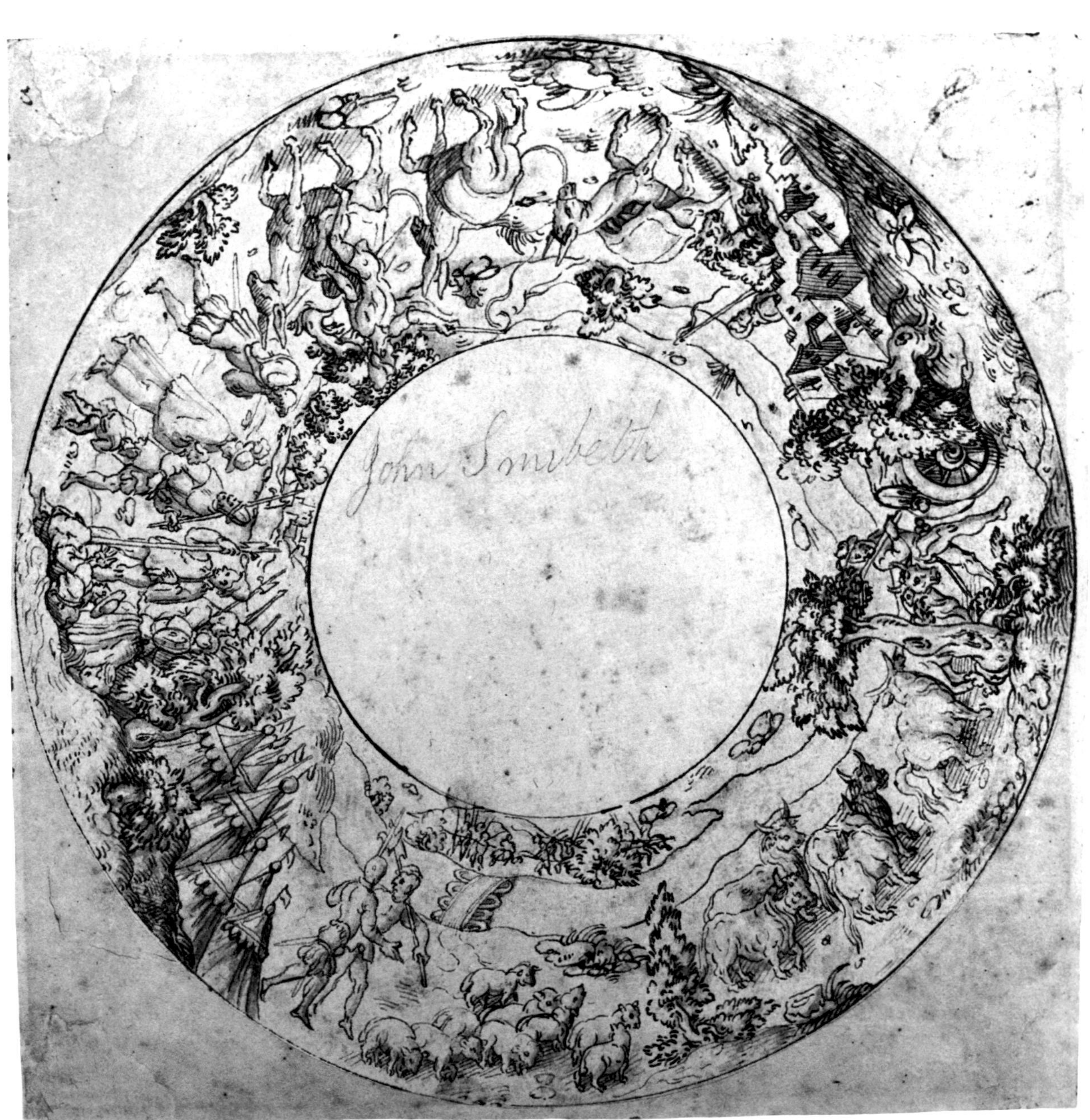
John Smibeth

GERMAN (NUREMBERG), mid-sixteenth century

10 *Design for a Circular Dish*

Bequest of James Bowdoin III (1811.56) Pen and brown ink and brown wash. Diameter 159 mm. (6 1/4 in.) Inscribed graphite center "John Smibeth"; pen and brown ink verso "No. 457/illn. [monogram]." Watermark: crowned L between two fleur-de-lis on crowned shield (similar to Briquet 8287, probably Lorraine manufacture, sixteenth century). PROVENANCE: John Smibert (?); James Bowdoin III. BIBLIOGRAPHY: *Catalogue* 1885, no. 72 (as Smibert); *Catalogue* 1930, no. 75 (as Smibert); Foote 1950, p. 232 (as sixteenth-century); Sadik 1966, pp. 216–17 (as not by Smibert); Chappell 1982, p. 137 (as not Smibert). EXHIBITION: Waterville 1978, cat. no. 2, repr. (as German, sixteenth century), exhibited in Brunswick.

THIS SHEET is significant for being one of three in the original Bowdoin bequest to be inscribed with the name of John Smibert (see Cat. 202 and 209), thus constituting the primary concrete evidence for the Smibert provenance for the collection (see Introduction). None of the three drawings has anything to do with Smibert's own art, and this particular design was quickly established by several scholars as dating from the sixteenth century.[1] Though Frits Lugt thought it was of Flemish origin, more recently most authorities have placed it in Germany, probably in the area of Nuremberg.[2]

The design has been thought to be a model for a silver dish. It could also conceivably have been a model for a ceramic piece, a box lid, or even an engraving in a model book. The scene is of a caravan of animals and armed soldiers traversing countryside which includes a camp among hills, towns, and a river with a pontoon bridge across it. The sketchiness and small size of the figures hamper an accurate attribution, but parallels with the draughtsmanship of Nuremberg artists of the time can be found. A larger sheet attributed to Erhard Schön (ca. 1491–1542) in the Germanischen Nationalmuseum, Nuremberg, depicting a similar subject, has similarities in figure type and landscape style.[3] The cruder pen work in the Bowdoin drawing could be attributable to its being a contemporary copy of another, more sophisticated study. Designs for works of art in other media were often copied and circulated within (and outside of) workshops.

1. Comments in museum files: Sir Robert Witt "German, ca. 1550"; Hans Tietze "at least 200 years earlier than Smibert"; Frits Lugt "Flemish 16th cen. style of Hans Bol." 2. Ingrid Weber and Konrad Oberhuber independently suggested such an origin. 3. Inv. no. Hz 194, repr. in F. Zink, *Die Handzeichnungen bis zur Mitte des 16. Jahrhunderts*, vol. 1, *Die deutschen Handzeichnungen* (Nuremberg, 1968), p. 139, cat. no. 109.

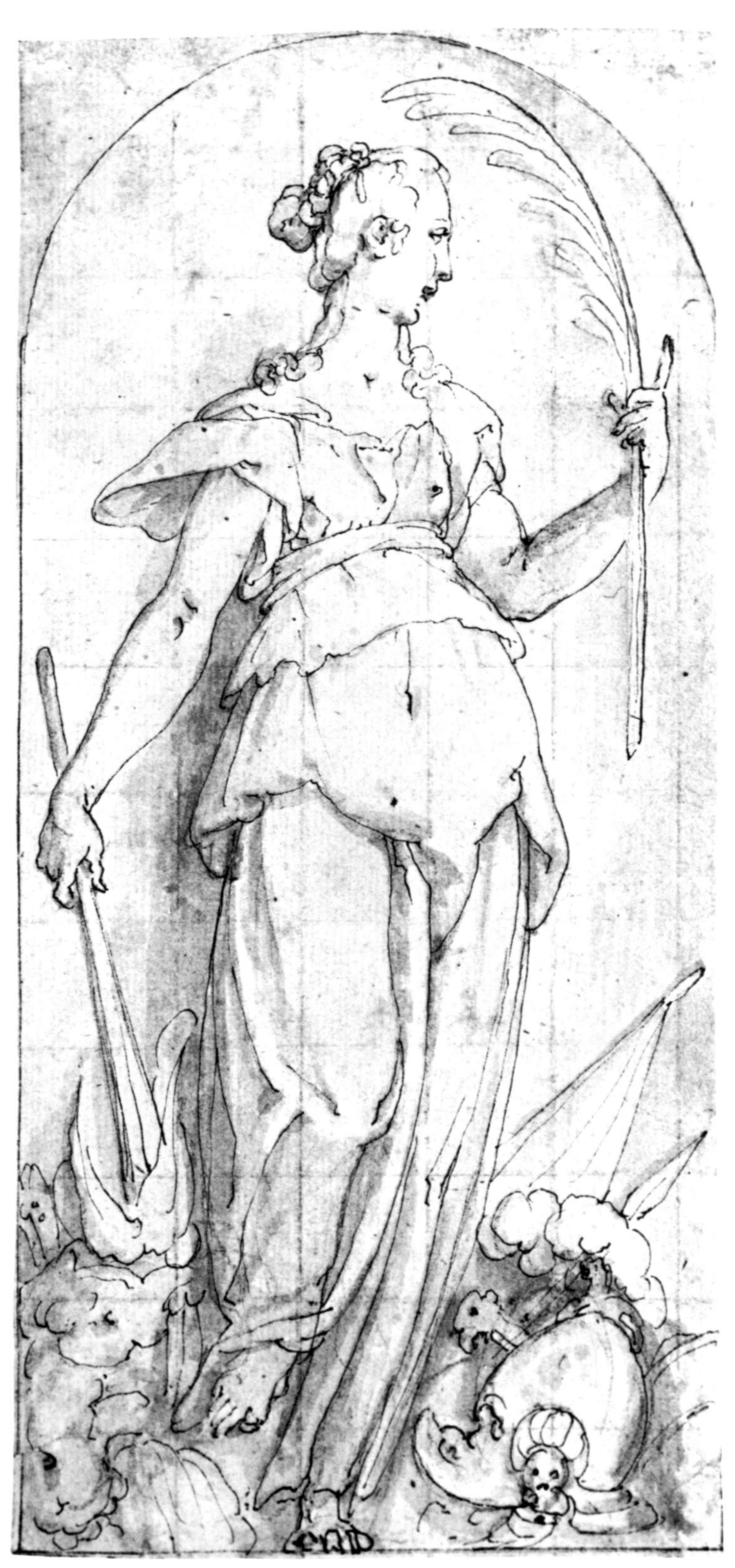

FRIEDRICH SUSTRIS
VENICE(?) ca. 1540–1599 MUNICH

11 *Allegory of Peace*

Bequest of James Bowdoin III (1811.15) Pen and black ink, grey wash over black chalk, squared for transfer in black chalk. 197 x 94 mm. (7⅞ x 3¾ in.) No watermark. Inscribed verso pen and brown ink "icus Sustris" (beginning of inscription cut by edge of sheet). Inscribed pen and ink on former mount "Perino del Vago." PROVENANCE: James Bowdoin III. BIBLIOGRAPHY: *Catalogue* 1885, no. 8 (as Perino del Vaga); Allen 1886, pt. 5, no. 19, repr. (as Perino); *Catalogue* 1930, no. 8 (as Perino); *Handbook* 1981, p. 165 (as Sustris). EXHIBITION: Princeton-Washington 1982–1983, cat. no. 40, repr.

SUSTRIS WAS THE SON of the Dutch artist Lambert Sustris, who emigrated to Italy from Amsterdam and worked in Venice and Padua. Friedrich was probably trained by his father and then worked from 1563 to 1567 in Florence, primarily with Giorgio Vasari. He participated in the decoration of the Palazzo Vecchio and the design of Michelangelo's tomb, among other projects. In 1568 he was commissioned by Hans Fugger to execute designs for the interior and exterior of his house in Augsburg. From 1573, Sustris worked for Crown Prince Wilhelm of Bavaria (the future Duke Wilhelm V), at first in Landshut, and then after 1580 in Munich. There he became virtually the court artist, being entrusted with the design and supervision of all important artistic activities.

This sheet entered the collections with a traditional attribution to Perino del Vaga, which was rejected by Davidson and Jaffé, both of whom ascribed it instead to a northern artist. Oberhuber first recognized it in 1977 as an autograph drawing by Sustris and suggested it was a design for the allegorical paintings in the Knight's Hall in Trausnitz Castle in Landshut. This attribution was affirmed by Heinrich Geissler, who also tentatively associated it with the Trausnitz designs.[1] In 1981, the sheet was removed from the original mount, revealing the inscription on the verso and reinforcing the Sustris ascription.

The style of the Bowdoin sheet is closely related to two similar designs by Sustris for female personifications in the Graphische Sammlung Staatsgalerie, Stuttgart.[2] They are figures of Concordia and Potestá and are of very similar dimensions to the Bowdoin design. One known study of Mars for the Trausnitz Knight's Hall is in the Staatliche Graphische Sammlung, Munich.[3]

The figure of Peace in the Bowdoin drawing is shown as a woman holding a palm branch in her left hand and a torch in her right, with which she is setting fire to a pile of weapons. Kaufmann points out that this same iconography was used in a painting by Francesco Salviati in the Palazzo Vecchio, Florence, which Sustris would of course have seen during his work there. Kaufmann was not able to find a painting specifically related to the Bowdoin design at Trausnitz. The iconography of Peace which does appear in a painting there shows a female figure holding a palm branch and a laurel, seemingly alighting from above. Hence he suggests that the Bowdoin sheet could be a preliminary study by Sustris for the painting, and therefore datable to the period of his work at the castle in the 1570s.[4]

1. Letter, 8 April 1981, to the author. 2. Inv. no. C70/2023, 201 x 196 mm. (repr. in H. Geissler, "Neues zu Friedrich Sustris," *Münchner Jahrbuch der bildenden Kunst*, 3rd ser., vol. 29 [1978], p. 74, fig. 11). 3. Repr. in K. Steinbart, "Die niederländischen Hofmaler der bairischen Herzöge," *Marburger Jahrbuch für Kunstwissenschaft*, vol. 4 (1928), p. 103, fig. 17. 4. Princeton-Washington 1982–1983, under cat. no. 40.

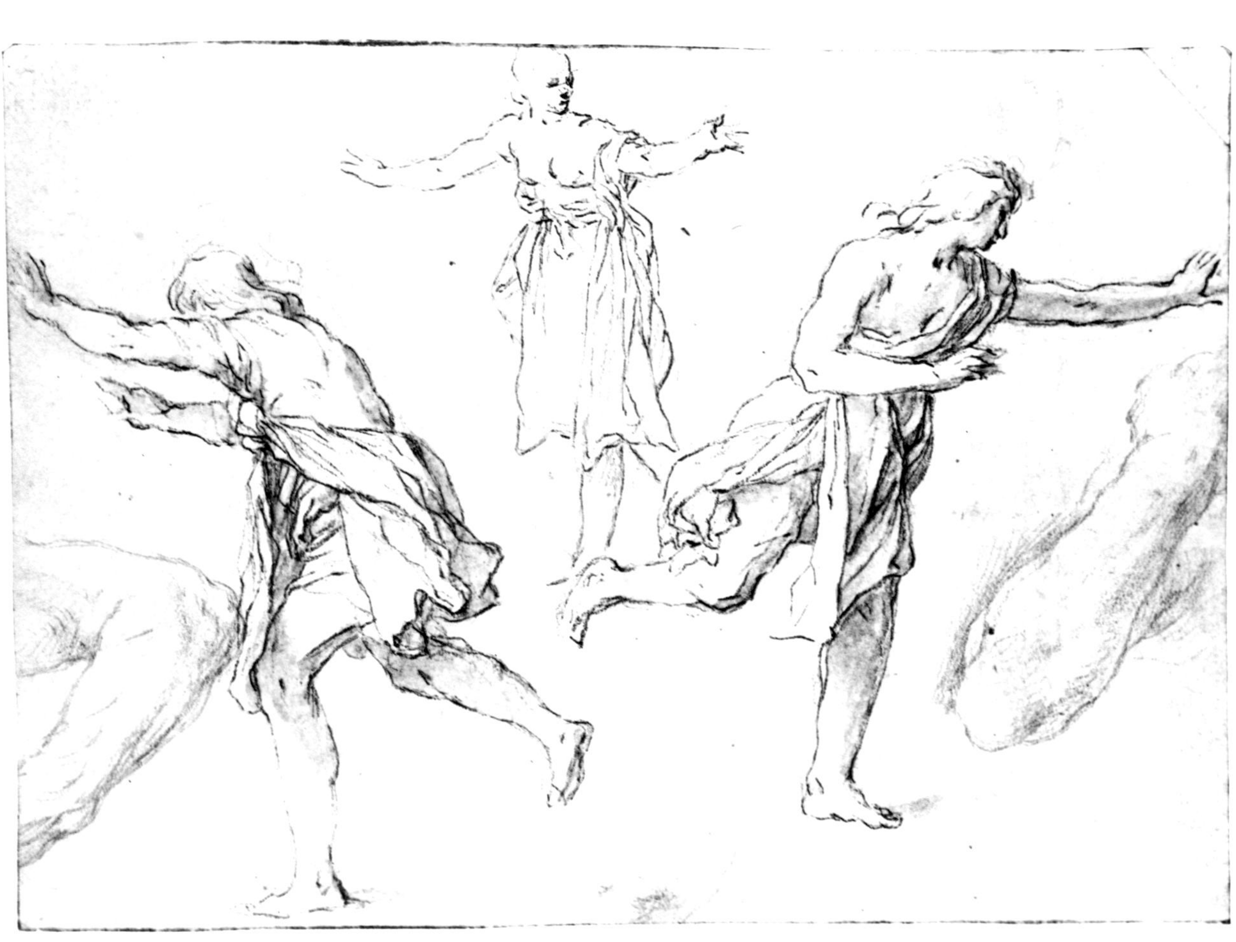

ABRAHAM BLOEMAERT

DORDRECHT 1564–1651 UTRECHT

12 *Studies of Running Figures*

Bequest of James Bowdoin III (1811.81) Pen and brown ink and brown wash over black chalk, heightened with white (arm fragments at left and right edge in red chalk) on brown laid paper, clipped upper right corner. 117 x 163 mm. (4⅝ x 6⅜ in.) No watermark. PROVENANCE: James Bowdoin III. BIBLIOGRAPHY: *Catalogue* 1885, no. 48; *Catalogue* 1930, no. 62. EXHIBITION: Poughkeepsie, Vassar College Art Gallery, *Dutch Mannerism—Apogee and Epilogue* [cat. ed. by W. Stechow], 1970, cat. no. 22, repr.

ONE OF THE most important exponents of the northern mannerist style, Bloemaert worked primarily in Utrecht, where he had first been a pupil of Joos de Beer. Bloemaert was one of the few major painters of his time not to travel to Italy; his sole foreign study was in Paris from 1580 to 1583. While in Amsterdam for two years after 1591, he was strongly influenced by the nearby Haarlem school of mannerism exemplified by artists such as Hendrik Goltzius, Karel van Mander, and Cornelis Cornelisz. Returning to Utrecht, Bloemaert was a co-founder of the Guild of St. Luke there in 1611 and became its dean in 1618.

This sheet of sketches entered the collections with a traditional attribution to Bloemaert written on the old mount. It contains three related sketches of running figures (two seem to be the same model viewed from different angles), with two fragments of bent arms in red chalk drawn on a larger scale. The sheet was removed from the old mount in 1981 and revealed no sketches on the verso. The technique of nervous pen work over black chalk is also seen in very comparable sketch sheets in Darmstadt, Munich, and Berlin.[1]

The Bowdoin sketches are not related to those figure and gesture sketches which were utilized for the plates of the drawing manual (*Tekenboek*) engraved by Bloemaert's son Frederick. The authors of the Vassar exhibition catalogue related the running figures to those in the background of the painting *The Crowning of Theagenes* of 1626 in the Utrecht Museum. However, as first suggested by Ronni Baer in conversation, the male figures in the Bowdoin sheet appear more suitably to be studies for similar figures in compositions of the Annunciation to the Shepherds. Bloemaert treated this subject in several drawn compositions, notably in two sheets in the Albertina, one in the British Museum, and one in a private collection in New York.[2] The Darmstadt sheet noted above certainly also relates to this subject, depicting various studies for shepherds "sore afraid," shielding themselves from the angels' brilliance. The story of the angels' appearance to the shepherds announcing Christ's birth is told in Luke 2:8–14.

The dating of Bloemaert's drawings from his long career is rendered difficult by both the lack of dated drawings and the continuity of style and subjects within his work. The Bowdoin sheet is no exception, and several comparable drawings have been dated from the 1590s to 1650. It clearly does not belong to Bloemaert's earliest and most mannerist style of the 1590s, but a more accurate placement within his mature work is uncertain without a clear framework. No painting definitively related to the Bowdoin studies is known.

1. Inv. no. AE 626, Gernsheim 24329; Inv. no. 9994, Wegner 1973, no. 243; Inv. no. 279, Gernsheim 47149.
2. Benesch 1928, nos. 446–47; Popham 1932, p. 91, no. 4, pl. 38; Cornell University, Herbert Johnson Museum, *Dutch Drawings of the Seventeenth Century* (exh. cat.) (Ithaca, 1979), cat. no. 1, repr.

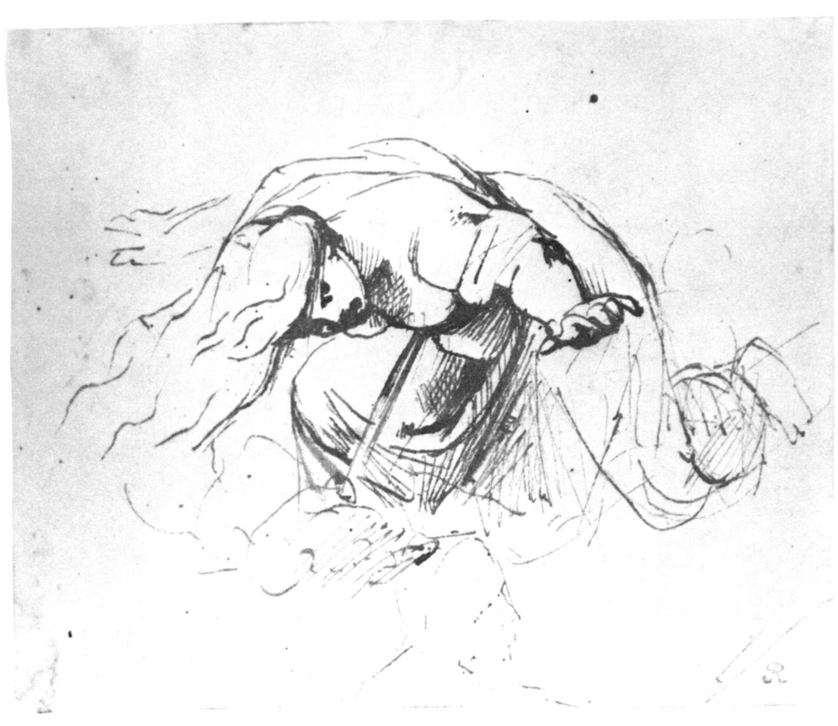

PETER PAUL RUBENS

SIEGEN 1577–1640 ANTWERP

13 *The Death of Dido*

Bequest of Helen Johnson Chase (1958.67) Pen and brown ink. 95 x 115 mm. (3 3/4 x 4 1/2 in.) No watermark. Verso: slight pen and brown ink sketch of figure head and top of a staff. PROVENANCE: Jonathan Richardson, Sr. (1655–1745) (Lugt 2184); Professor Henry Johnson; Helen Johnson (Mrs. Stanley P.) Chase. BIBLIOGRAPHY: Mather 1914, p. 115, repr. fig. 8 (as not by Rubens, perhaps Van Dyck); *Catalogue* 1930, p. 95, no. 635 (as Rubens); Lugt 1949, vol. 1, pp. 53–54, under no. 591 (as Van Dyck); M. Jaffé, "Rubens and Giulio Romano at Mantua," *Art Bulletin*, vol. 40, no. 4 (December 1958), p. 326 (as Rubens, as are all following); Held 1959 vol. 1, pp. 23, 97, no. 9, vol. 2, pl. 10, note: wrong measurements; L. Burchard and R.-A. d'Hulst, *Rubens Drawings* (Brussels, 1963), p. 129, under no. 77; J. Müller Hofstede, review of L. Burchard and R.-A. d'Hulst, *Rubens Drawings*, in *Master Drawings*, vol. 4, no. 4 (Winter 1966), p. 448, under no. 77; M. Jaffé, "A Sheet of Studies from Rubens's Italian Period," *Master Drawings*, vol. 8, no. 1 (Spring 1970), p. 47; Victoria and Albert Museum, and elsewhere, *Flemish Drawings of the Seventeenth Century from the Collection of Frits Lugt Institut Néerlandais Paris* (exh. cat.) (London, 1972), p. 95, under no. 73; Jaffé 1977, pp. 29, 64, fig. 219; E. Waterhouse, review of M. Jaffé, *Rubens and Italy*, in *Art Bulletin*, vol. 60, no. 3 (September 1978), p. 556; British Museum, *Rubens Drawings and Sketches* (exh. cat. by J. Rowlands) (London, 1977), p. 27, under no. 11; E. McGrath, "Rubens, the Gonzaga, and the *Adoration of the Trinity*," in Victoria and Albert Museum, *Splendours of the Gonzaga* (exh. cat.) (London, 1981–1982), p. 214; *Handbook* 1981, pp. 154–55, repr., note: wrong measurements. EXHIBITIONS: Cambridge, Fogg Art Museum, and New York, Pierpont Morgan Library, *Drawings and Oil Sketches by P. P. Rubens from American Collections*, 1956, cat. no. 2, note: wrong measurements; Cologne 1977, cat. no. 29, repr., note: wrong measurements; Waterville 1978, cat. no. 9, repr., exhibited in Brunswick.

THIS BRAVURA SKETCH was traditionally thought to represent the death of Thisbe, from Ovid's *Metamorphoses*. Recently, however, Elizabeth McGrath has suggested that it shows the suicide of

Dido, queen of Carthage, as related in the *Aeneid*.[1] After failing to dissuade Aeneas from continuing his journey, Dido has a mock funeral pyre built for his hastily abandoned possessions (including their shared bed). She pronounces terrible curses upon Aeneas and his descendants, mounts the pyre, and hurls herself upon a sword which had been her gift to him. McGrath convincingly argues that the Bowdoin sheet and a closely related one in the Louvre represent Dido, for the figure in several of the sketches wears a crown and, in one instance, bends over a pyre.[2]

Although the Bowdoin drawing entered the collections with a traditional attribution to Rubens, Mather placed it rather with the young Van Dyck, or even an Italian artist, declaring it "far too good for Rubens." Lugt affirmed the Van Dyck attribution. However, Held, Jaffé, and all other scholars have firmly given this and related sketches to Rubens at the time of his Italian sojourn. Indeed, in a letter to the museum, Held decisively stated that in his opinion, "nothing is too good for Rubens."[3]

The Bowdoin sketch has been cut from a larger sheet, now in the Louvre, which includes five further studies of Dido.[4] By the eighteenth century, the two sheets were in separate collections (the Louvre sheet was in the collection of P. J. Mariette, 1694–1774).[5] Four of the studies on the Louvre sheet similarly show Dido actually upon her sword; the largest study at the lower left shows her bent over in an attitude of lament, but before the act of suicide. All six extant studies are fascinating variations of pose, angle, and expression.

Much scholarship has been devoted to Rubens's eight years of prodigious work and study in Italy, primarily by Jaffé and Müller Hofstede. Both scholars have discussed the Bowdoin-Louvre sheets within the context of works by earlier masters whom Rubens was studying and of his own thematic and artistic endeavors. He had left Antwerp in 1600 and traveled widely in Italy, studying ancient and contemporary masters (he even went to Spain on a mission for the Gonzaga family of Mantua). Held dated the Dido sketches during this period, ca. 1602–5; Jaffé generally dated them between 1600 and 1606; and Müller Hofstede has placed them probably toward the end of 1601, or before the artist's departure for Spain in 1603. McGrath includes the Bowdoin and Louvre studies in an entire Aeneas cycle which Rubens evidently had designed just before his Spanish trip. She also includes the painting at Fontainebleau of the Departure from Troy of around 1602 in the same cycle.[6]

Other drawings, closely related in technique to these sketches, are in the Herzog Anton Ulrich Museum, Brunswick, Germany, and the Institut Néerlandais, Paris, Lugt Collection.[7] The verso of the Louvre Dido sheet has a sketch of a seated figure for a Judgment of Paris similar to sketches on the versos of sheets in the Metropolitan Museum and the Devonshire Collection at Chatsworth.[8] That figure was used in two paintings of the subject dated ca. 1601.[9] Jaffé has associated the very dramatic expression in all the Dido sketches with Rubens's reaction to seeing Leonardo's Last Supper fresco in Milan, and also has described the Bowdoin and Louvre sheets in particular as "brilliantly Raphaelite."[10] In the Bowdoin sketch, the dramatic, compressed treatment of the foreshortened hand and downward thrusting body of the queen of Carthage, her hair tossed by her movement, is extraordinarily evocative. No painted version of Dido's death is known from the same period, though Rubens did execute one in the 1630s which is now in the Louvre.[11]

1. Book 4, pp. 642–705. 2. McGrath 1981–1982. I am grateful to Anne-Marie Logan for bringing this reference to my attention. 3. 15 December 1952. 4. Lugt 1949, vol. 1, pp. 53–54, no. 591, pl. 54, as Van Dyck; Held 1959, no. 8. 5. Lugt 1852. 6. McGrath 1981–1982, p. 214. 7. Cologne 1977, no. 21 and Jaffé 1977, fig. 181; Jaffé 1977, fig. 205. 8. Held 1959, no. 6 and Jaffé 1977, fig. 205; Held 1959, no. 7. 9. Jaffé 1977, figs. 207–8. 10. Ibid., pp. 29 and 64. 11. Inv. no. RF1942–33. Repr. in A. Roy, ed., *Le XVIIe Siècle flamand au Louvre, Histoire des Collections* (Paris, 1977), pp. 48–49, no. 187.

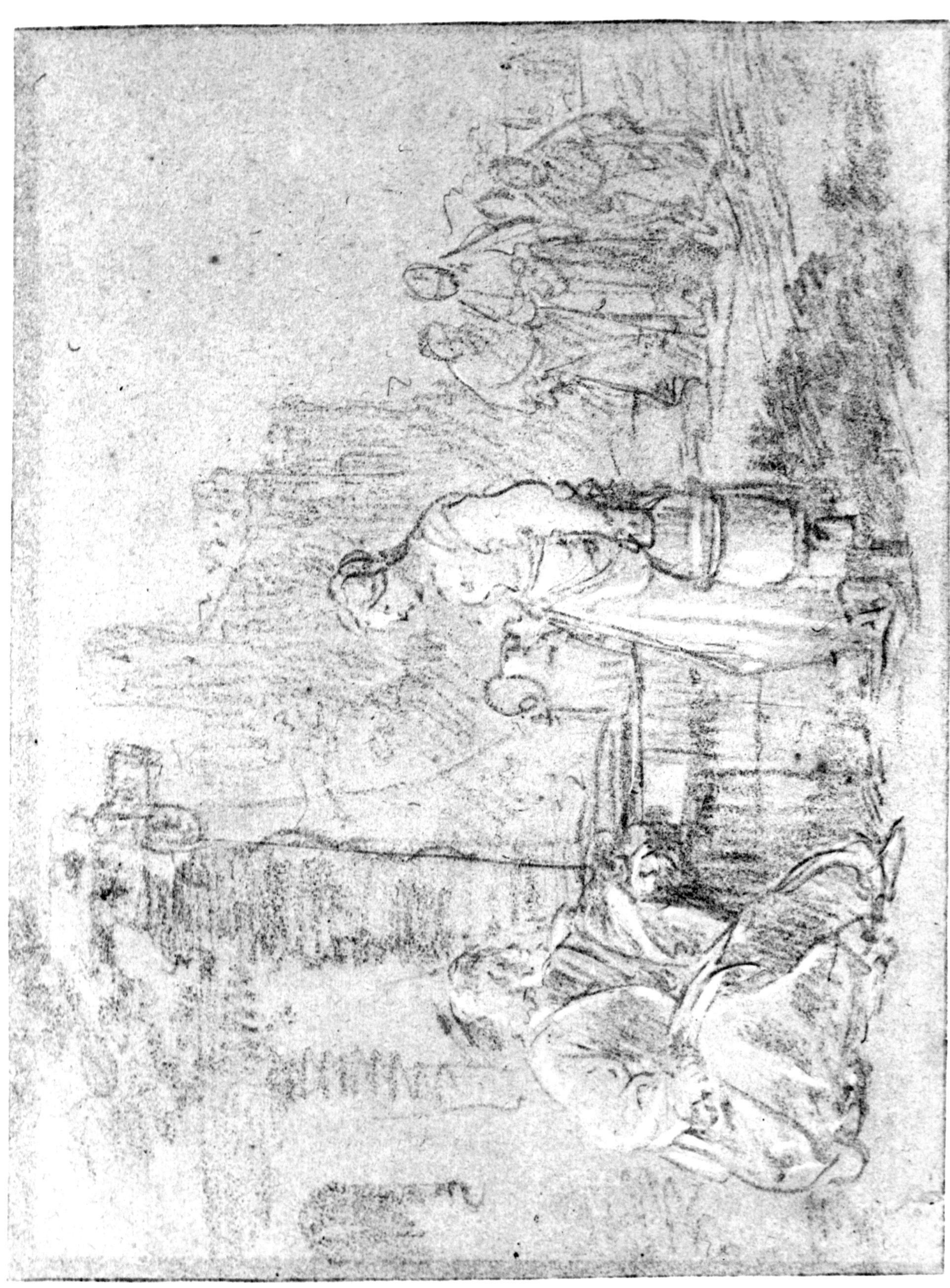

CLAES CORNELISZ. MOEYAERT
1590/91–1655 AMSTERDAM

14 *Christ and the Samaritan Woman*

Bequest of James Bowdoin III (1811.94) Black and white chalk on blue laid paper (faded by exposure to light). 195 x 258 mm. ($7^{11}/_{16}$ x $10^{1}/_{8}$ in.) No watermark. PROVENANCE: James Bowdoin III. BIBLIOGRAPHY: *Catalogue* 1885, no. 94 (as Unknown); *Catalogue* 1930, no. 94 (as Unknown); *Handbook* 1981, p. 166 (as Moeyaert). EXHIBITION: Sacramento 1974, cat. no. 27, repr.

MOEYAERT'S BIRTHPLACE is uncertain, but he was in Amsterdam from about 1605 and spent virtually his entire career there. The course of his artistic studies is unknown. He received many portrait commissions (especially from the Catholic Church) and was associated with the Amsterdam Theater. In 1638 he participated in the designs for the entry into Amsterdam of Marie de' Medici (some of which were used to illustrate the commemorative volume by C. van Baerle, *Medicae Hospes*, 1638). He also executed a number of etchings. Some of Moeyaert's notable pupils include Salomon Koninck, Nicolaes Berchem (cf. Cat. 26), Jacob van der Does, and Jan Baptist Weenix (cf. Cat. 27). Moeyaert is most often included among the group of early seventeenth-century artists called the Pre-Rembrandtists, which include Jan and Jacob Pynas, Pieter Lastman, and Moses van Uyttenbroeck. In his later years, however, Moeyaert was often influenced by the younger Rembrandt. Like other artists of his circle, Moeyaert specialized in historical and biblical scenes of often obscure iconography.

This drawing remained unidentified until Lugt attributed it to Moeyaert in 1945. The story of the interview between Christ and the Samaritan Woman is related in John 4:7–29. As Tümpel points out, the moment shown here is just after Christ reveals himself as the Messiah, while his disciples are seen approaching in the right background. Tümpel dates this sheet to the period of Moeyaert's work after 1639, when his figures become less stiff and their contours dissolve. She points out that the silhouette presentation of the disciples in the background is typical of his style from this point. She characterizes the Bowdoin drawing as a less finished, rather "cursory" work.[1]

There are no other known drawings by Moeyaert of this subject, and no painting was listed by Tümpel in her 1974 catalogue of his work. However, this subject was treated several times by Rembrandt, in two etchings from 1634 and ca. 1657/58,[2] two paintings of 1655,[3] and at least two drawings.[4] Other members of Rembrandt's circle treated this subject, among them Ferdinand Bol and Philips Koninck.[5]

Moeyaert was a fairly prolific draughtsman, and there are quite a few drawings by him in American collections.[6] There are two other drawings by him in the original Bowdoin collection, an early sheet of *Tobias Frightened by the Fish*[7] and the following number in this catalogue. Bowdoin also owns an early copy after Moeyaert, *Joseph Sold by His Brothers*,[8] and in 1970 the museum purchased a large Moeyaert painting of ca. 1636, *The Meeting of Jacob and Joseph in Egypt*.[9]

1. Sacramento 1974, p. 39. 2. Bartsch 71 and 70. 3. A. Bredius, *The Complete Edition of the Paintings—Rembrandt*, 3rd. ed. rev. by H. Gerson (London, 1969), nos. 588 (Berlin) and 589 (Metropolitan Museum). 4. Benesch 611 and 978. Three more drawings which may be by students are listed by Benesch, nos. A80, A100, and A118. 5. For Bol: Sumowski 1979ff., vol. 1, 221x, 222x (1640s); for Koninck: vol. 6, 1352 (1671), 1381x, 1383x (1655/8), and 1445x (1671). 6. Cf. Sacramento 1974. 7. Inv. no. 1811.63 (Cat. 111). Sacramento 1974, cat. no. 18, repr. 8. Inv. no. 1811.101 (Cat. 112). 9. Inv. no. 1970.41. Sacramento 1974, cat. no. 16, repr.

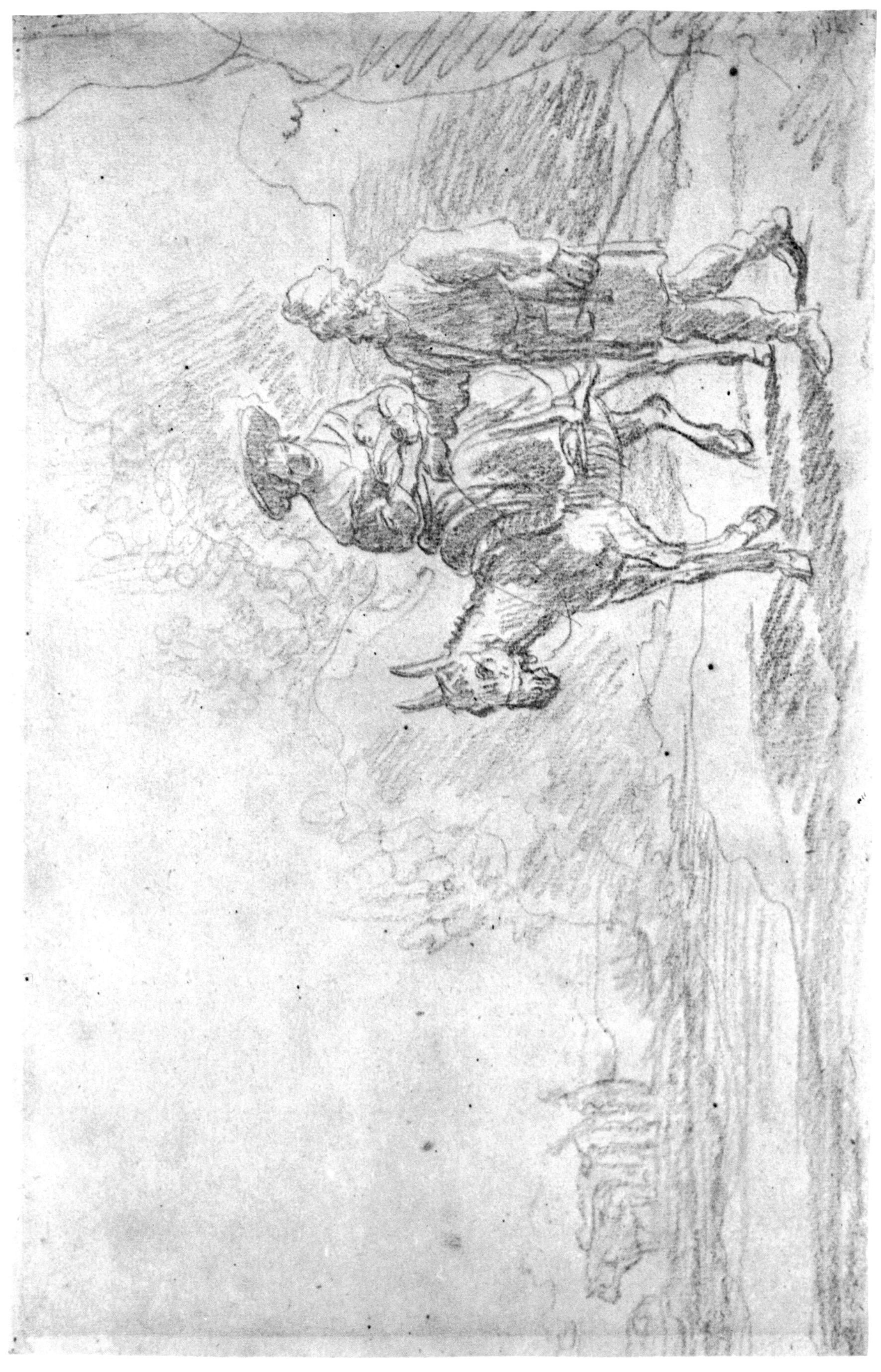

CLAES CORNELISZ. MOEYAERT

15 *The Flight into Egypt*

Bequest of James Bowdoin III (1811.52) Red chalk (counterproof). 170 x 270 mm. (6 7/8 x 10 5/8 in.) No watermark. Inscribed on old mount (lost): "Claudio Gille detto Loranese." PROVENANCE: James Bowdoin III. BIBLIOGRAPHY: *Catalogue* 1885, no. 68 (as Claude Lorraine); Allen 1886, pt. 3, no. 12, repr. (as Claude); Mather 1914, p. 112, fig. 5 ("ascribed" to Claude); *Catalogue* 1930, no. 71 (as Claude); [Siber] 1947, p. 119, no. 7, repr. (with Claude ascription, awaiting "further study"); Tümpel 1974, p. 259, under no. 107, fig. 241 (as Moeyaert); *Handbook* 1981, p. 166 (as Moeyaert). EXHIBITION: Sacramento 1974, cat. no. 26, repr.

THIS SHEET was published several times with its traditional attribution to Claude, though both Allen and Mather noted the obvious Dutch characteristics of the figures and their costume. Sir Robert Witt dismissed the Claude attribution and also recognized that this is a counterproof of another drawing. The correct attribution to Moeyaert was made by Lugt in 1945 and later affirmed by Judson and Tümpel. A counterproof was made by placing a blank sheet of paper over a drawing (usually chalk) and rubbing it with great pressure, thus transferring an impression of the earlier sheet in reverse. The process was often employed to copy a design or to experiment with such compositional reversals. A counterproof also enabled an artist to develop a subject further while retaining an earlier stage of the design.

The clearest indication that this sheet is a counterproof lies in the fact that most of the shading lines go from upper left to lower right, which is opposite from Moeyaert's normal stroke (as can be seen in Cat. 14). His usual technique indicates that he was right-handed; the direction of the shading here would be difficult to execute with the right hand.[1] A chalk counterproof usually exhibits a characteristic smooth surface, and red chalk examples often have an orange coloration.

Tümpel does not ascribe a date to this drawing, though it can be tentatively associated with others from the 1630s, such as two sheets also in chalk in Amsterdam.[2] There are three references to paintings by Moeyaert of this subject in Tümpel's catalogue: one in a north German private collection, one listed on the art market in 1950, and one cited in a 1653 estate inventory.[3] The original drawing from which this counterproof was taken is not known.

1. I am grateful to Miss Agnes Mongan for these observations concerning the general appearance of counterproofs. 2. Sacramento 1974, p. 37, figs. 57–58. 3. Ibid., p. 104, and Tümpel 1974, p. 259, nos. 107–109.

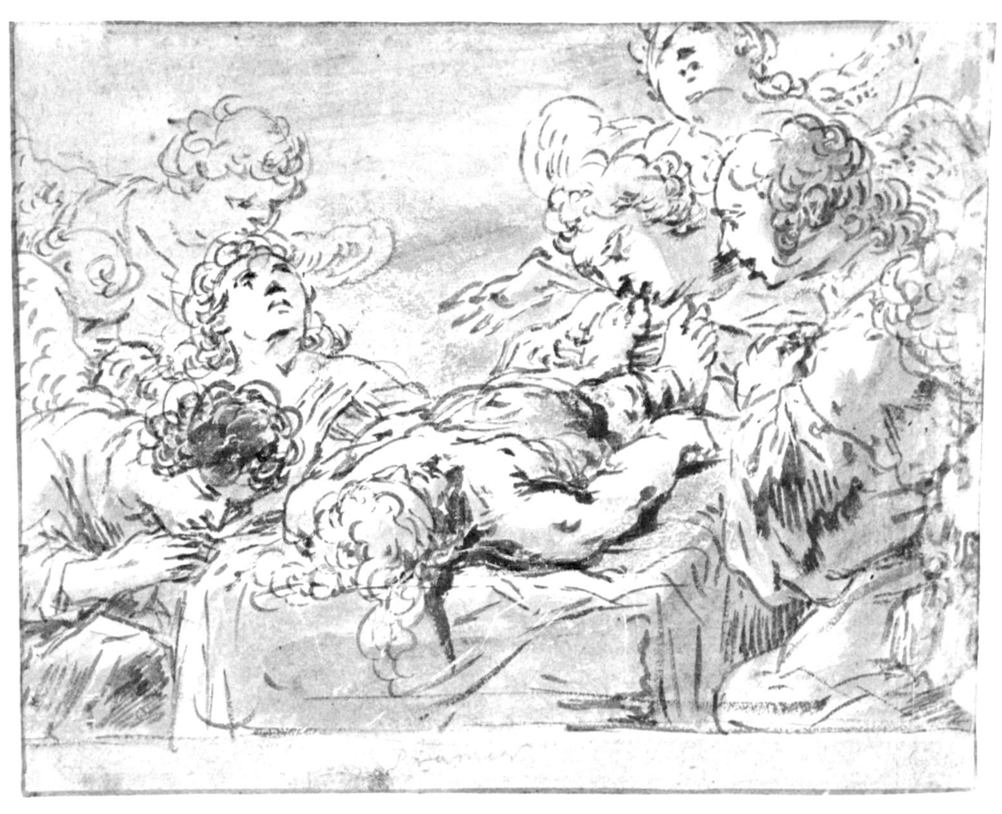

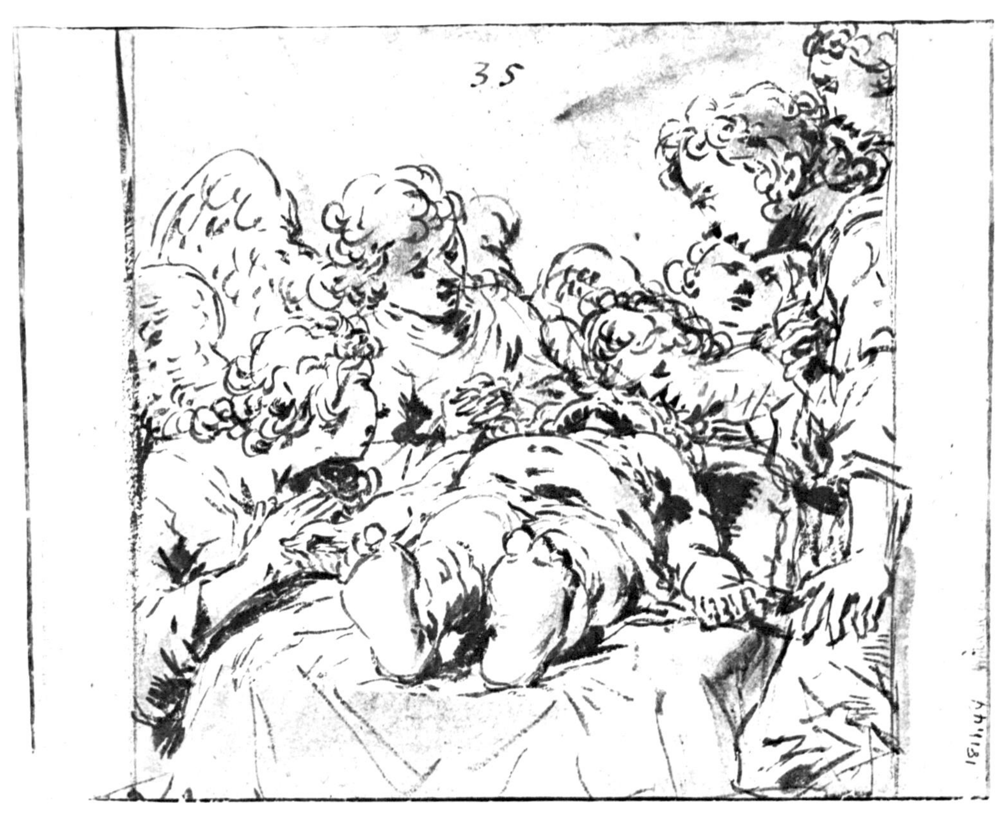

LEONARD BRAMER

DELFT 1596–1674 DELFT

16 *Dead Christ with Angels* (recto and verso)

Bequest of James Bowdoin III (1811.44) Brush and black ink and grey wash, heightened with white, on brown laid paper (perhaps faded from blue). 165 x 209 mm. (6½ x 8¼ in.) No watermark. Inscribed recto in graphite bottom "Bramer"; verso, pen and brown ink upper center "35." PROVENANCE: James Bowdoin III. BIBLIOGRAPHY: *Catalogue* 1885, no. 73; Mather 1914, p. 116; *Catalogue* 1930, no. 63.

BRAMER TRAVELED EXTENSIVELY in France and Italy from 1614 until 1627. He spent six years in Rome, where he was particularly influenced by Adam Elsheimer and Gerrit van Honthorst, a Dutch Caravaggist. He entered the Guild of St. Luke in Delft in 1629 and served as its governor several times. He painted many wall and ceiling decorations and even executed frescoes. Dramatically lit nocturnal scenes are characteristic of his painted work. Bramer was a most prolific draughtsman, often executing large series of biblical and literary subjects. The most important collections of his drawings are in Munich,[1] Bremen,[2] Paris,[3] Amsterdam, Berlin, and Vienna. The 1923 monograph by Wichmann contains an extensive catalogue of his paintings and drawings.

This drawing presumably comes from a series of New Testament or Passion scenes, indicated by the number 35 on the verso. A sheet of similar dimensions and style showing the Deposition is in Darmstadt[4] and is numbered 22. Bramer very often (as he does here) experimented with close variations of the same subject. The composition seems to be influenced by Mantegna's famous painting of the Dead Christ now in the Brera, Milan. Bramer's drawing style is quite recognizable in its rough sketchiness and lack of detailed finish. No painting of this subject was noted by Wichmann, and the Bowdoin sheet was unknown to him. Bauch has cited these two designs as "typical examples of Bramer's earlier Italianizing style."[5]

1. Wegner 1973, cat. nos. 327–475, pls. 199–230. 2. Inv. nos. 374–448, 457–501 (Wichmann 1923, p. 170, nos. 29–30); also many illustrated in Gernsheim Corpus. 3. Lugt 1929, cat. nos. 137–52, pl. 21. 4. Inv. no. AE 848, Gernsheim 24319. 5. Letter in museum files, 25 January 1956.

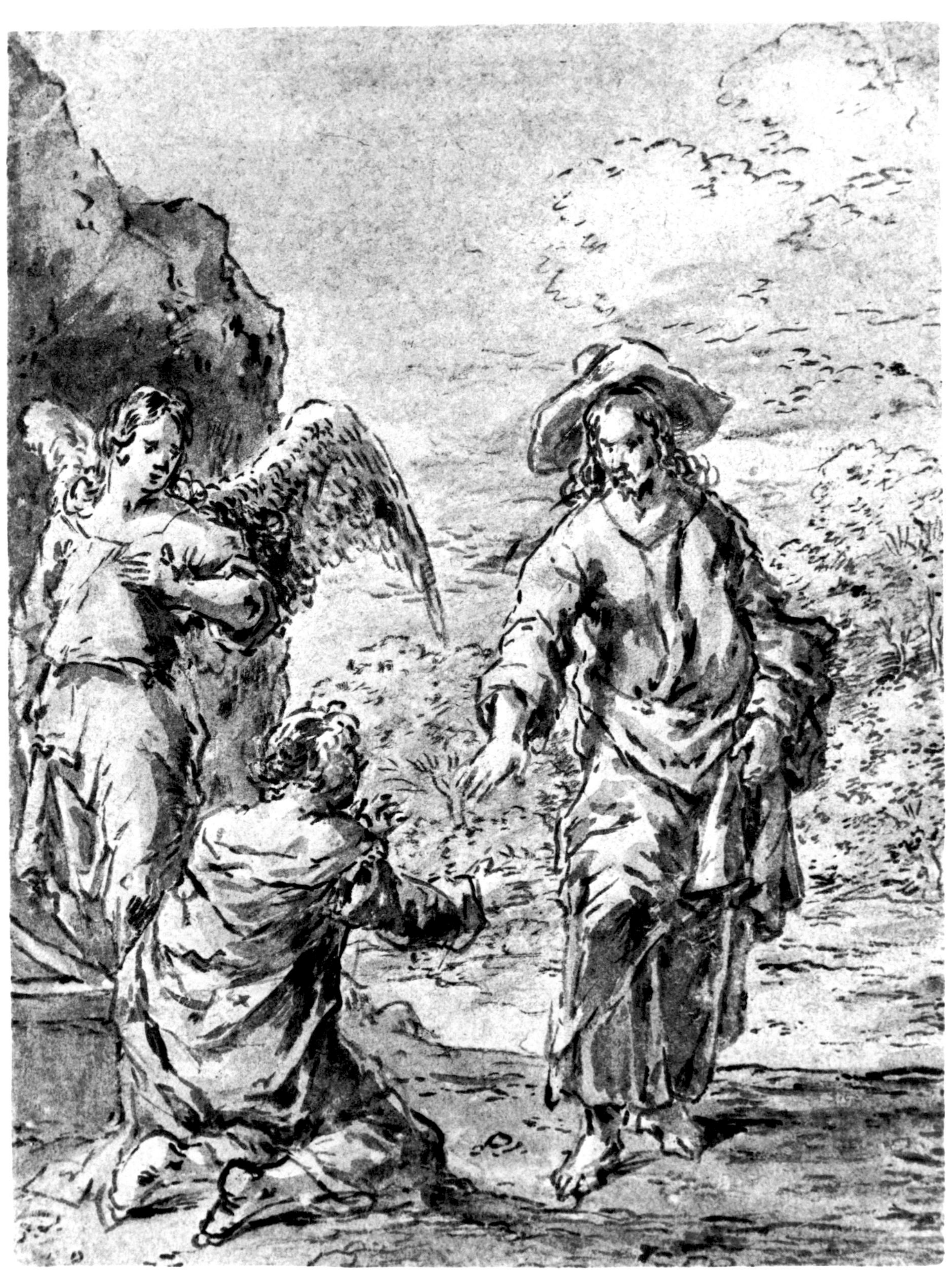

LEONARD BRAMER

17 *Noli Me Tangere*

James Phinney Baxter Fund in Memory of Professor Henry Johnson (1932.34) Pen and black ink, grey wash, heightened with white, on blue laid paper (faded by exposure to light), laid down at upper corners. 195 x 148 mm. ($7^{11}/16$ x $5^{13}/16$ in.) No watermark. Inscribed verso graphite: "412 No. 26 Bloemart No. 29"; on old mount, recto, pen and ink "141"; graphite "Bleomart"; verso, graphite "3851.69." PROVENANCE: Professor Henry Johnson. BIBLIOGRAPHY: *Catalogue* 1930, p. 95, no. 639 (as Bloemaert).

THIS DRAWING depicts the moment after the Resurrection when Mary Magdalene has come to the tomb and found it empty. As she looks for his body, Christ appears to her and reveals himself, saying "Do not hold me, for I am not yet ascended into Heaven." The encounter is fully described in John 20: 14–18. Christ is usually portrayed with a warning gesture of his hand; the tomb is shown at the left. He is often shown as a gardener, as he is here, holding a spade or shovel.

Formerly attributed to Bloemaert, this sheet was first correctly credited to Bramer by Lugt in 1945. Wichmann's monograph lists no paintings of this subject or individual drawings, though Bramer executed several extensive series of drawings of New Testament subjects. There is a sheet in Leiden of Christ on the Mount of Olives which is stylistically very close to the Bowdoin drawing and has almost identical dimensions, which may indicate that the two come from the same New Testament series.[1] The pose and gesture of Christ in both sheets are quite comparable. A sheet in the Yale University Art Gallery of Christ Presented to the People (Ecce Homo) is also quite close in technique.[2]

1. University Prentenkabinet, Inv. no. 116, 200 x 152 mm., Gernsheim 34951. 2. Inv. no. 1972.47.

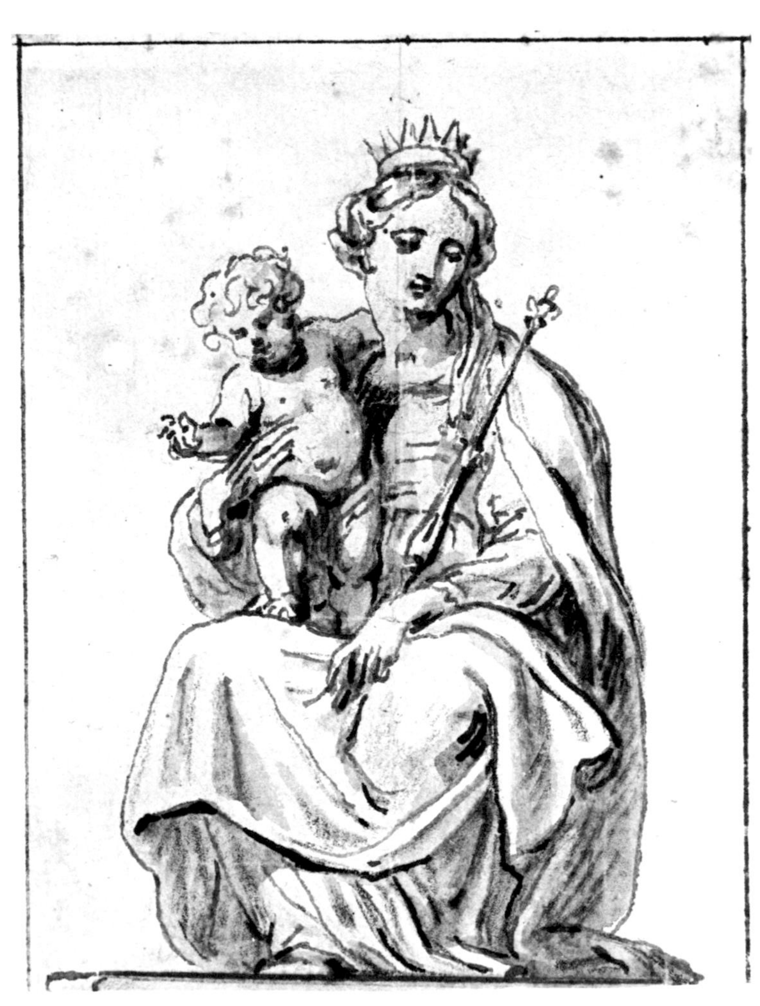

ABRAHAM VAN DIEPENBEECK
'S-HERTOGENBOSCH 1596–1675 ANTWERP

18 *Madonna and Child Enthroned*

Bequest of James Bowdoin III (1811.45) Pen and brown ink, brown wash, over traces of graphite and black chalk. 129 x 100 mm. (5 1/16 x 3 15/16 in.) Watermark: letters IHS with cross over small fleur-de-lis. Inscribed pen and brown ink verso: "P. de Jode/Nº 238"; pen and black ink (over earlier graphite inscription) on old mount "P. de Jode." PROVENANCE: James Bowdoin III. BIBLIOGRAPHY: *Catalogue* 1885, no. 62 (as Pieter de Jode [?]); *Catalogue* 1930, no. 65 (as Pieter de Jode [?].

VAN DIEPENBEECK'S FATHER, a glass painter, was probably his first teacher. Van Diepenbeeck moved to Antwerp in 1621 and began receiving commissions for both stained glass and paintings. In 1638 he became a member of the Guild of St. Luke. He evidently had a fiery temperament, for he became involved in several lawsuits and was expelled from the painter's guild in 1642. (After another suit, he was eventually readmitted in 1672.) He probably made at least two trips to France, one in the early 1630s and the second in 1650. Van Diepenbeeck painted several large windows early in his career but increasingly turned to painting and designing book illustrations. The most famous of the latter were those for Michel de Marolles, *Tableaux du Temple des Muses* (Paris, 1655). He also designed several series of large wall tapestries. Steadman has estimated that van Diepenbeeck produced well over 750 drawings.[1] Although never a student of Rubens, he was strongly influenced by the older artist. The Bowdoin bequest contains four drawings by van Diepenbeeck—the three discussed here and a Madonna and Child Appearing to St. Ignatius.[2]

This sheet had been traditionally attributed to Pieter de Jode II (1606–after 1674), an Antwerp painter and engraver, who was also much influenced by Rubens. The correct attribution was made verbally by Steadman in 1972 and later affirmed by Held and Haverkamp Begemann. There is another version of this subject in the Pushkin Museum, Moscow, which is more finished and slightly different stylistically.[3] The linearity of the Bowdoin drawing probably indicates that it is an early work. It also supports Steadman's observation that van Diepenbeeck never learned to draw hands very skillfully.

1. Steadman 1973, vol. 1, p. 72. Much of the biographical information comes from Steadman's thesis. 2. Cat. 103, Inv. no. 1811.42. 3. Steadman 1973, vol. 2, pl. 95.

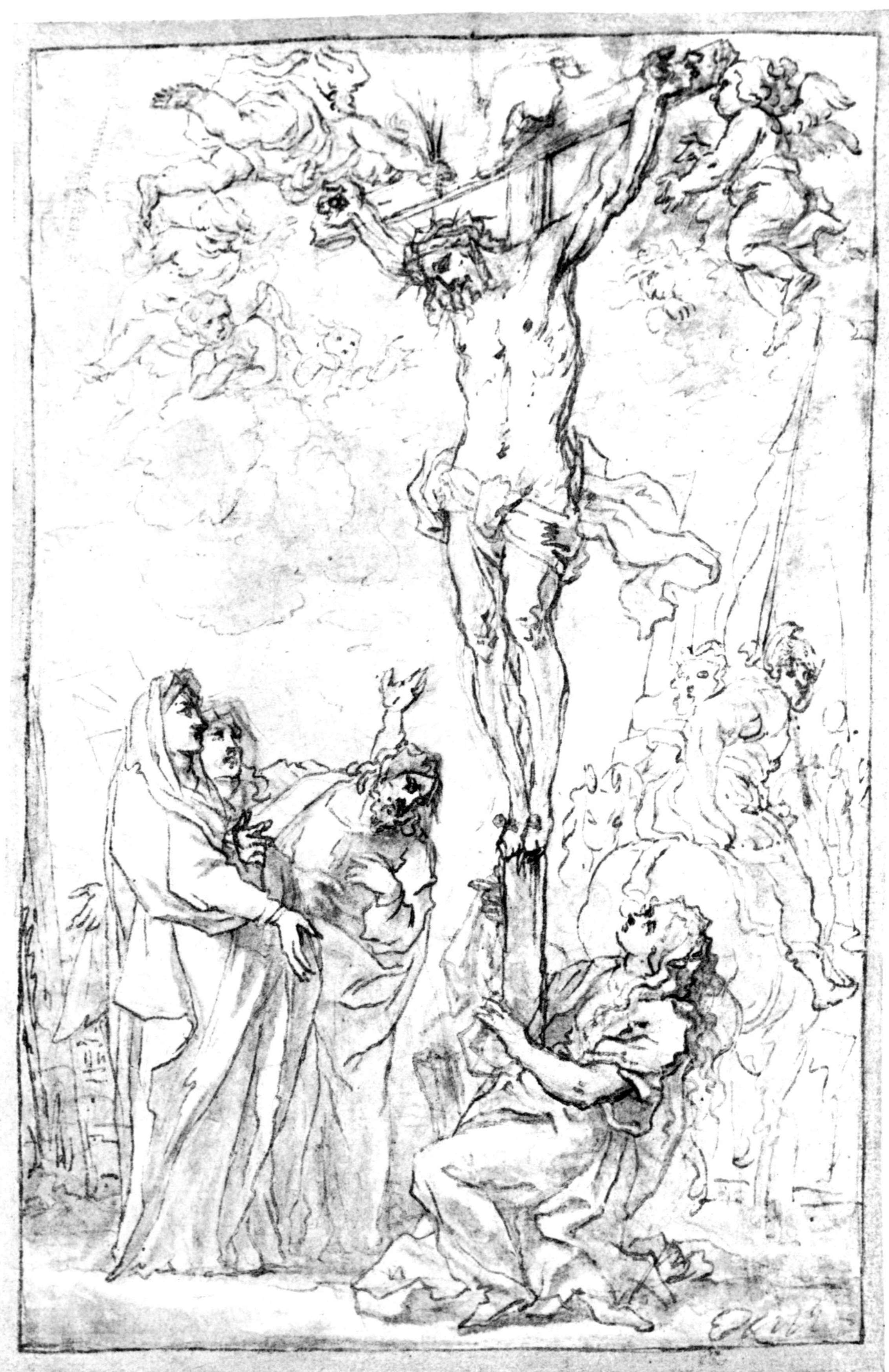

ABRAHAM VAN DIEPENBEECK

19 *Crucifixion*

Bequest of James Bowdoin III (1811.83) Pen and brown ink, brown and grey wash, over graphite; verso, black chalk, sketch of Crucifixion. 241 x 159 mm. (9½ x 6¼ in.) Inscribed pen and brown ink on old mount (removed): "Diepimbec"; verso of old mount, pen and ink "P.56, LL.6, No. 43." PROVENANCE: P. H. Lankrink (1628–1692) (Lugt 2090); James Bowdoin III. BIBLIOGRAPHY: *Catalogue* 1885, no. 52; *Catalogue* 1930, no. 52.

THE SUBJECT of the Crucifixion was depicted often by Flemish artists of the early seventeenth century. Rubens and Van Dyck had both executed altarpieces of the subject by the 1630s. Van Dyck in particular influenced van Diepenbeeck's representations. The latter completed at least two oils: a sketch dating from the 1640s now in the Fitzwilliam Museum, Cambridge,[1] and an altarpiece in the Church of St. Amelberga at Zanthoven, finished in 1652.[2] The Fitzwilliam sketch is thought by Steadman to have been specifically designed to be engraved; there are prints after that depiction by Paulus Pontius and Cornelis Visscher.[3] In addition to the Bowdoin sheet, there is another van Diepenbeeck drawing of the Crucifixion in the Uffizi.[4]

The format and figural composition of the Bowdoin and Fitzwilliam *Crucifixions* are similar, but with certain differences. They are in reverse to each other; the Fitzwilliam sketch includes the Good and Bad Thieves and eliminates the profusion of hovering putti seen here. The disposition of Christ and his attendant figures, including the departing soldiers, is much the same. The Bowdoin drawing could have been a preliminary idea for the more fully developed composition in the engravings after the Fitzwilliam model.

1. Inv. no. PD 77–1972, 450 x 328 mm.; discussed in Steadman 1973, pp. 66–68, 162–163, cat. no. 46, repr. pl. 141. 2. Repr. Steadman 1973, vol. 2, pl. 99. 3. The Metropolitan Museum owns two impressions of prints after the Fitzwilliam oil, both in reverse: a larger engraving, expanded horizontally, with three figures added, published by Visscher (Inv. no. 51.501.1641); and a reduced copy by Abraham Cuenradus (Inv. no. 51.501.1616). 4. Inv. no. 14228F (Kloek 1975, no. 399; photo in Witt Library).

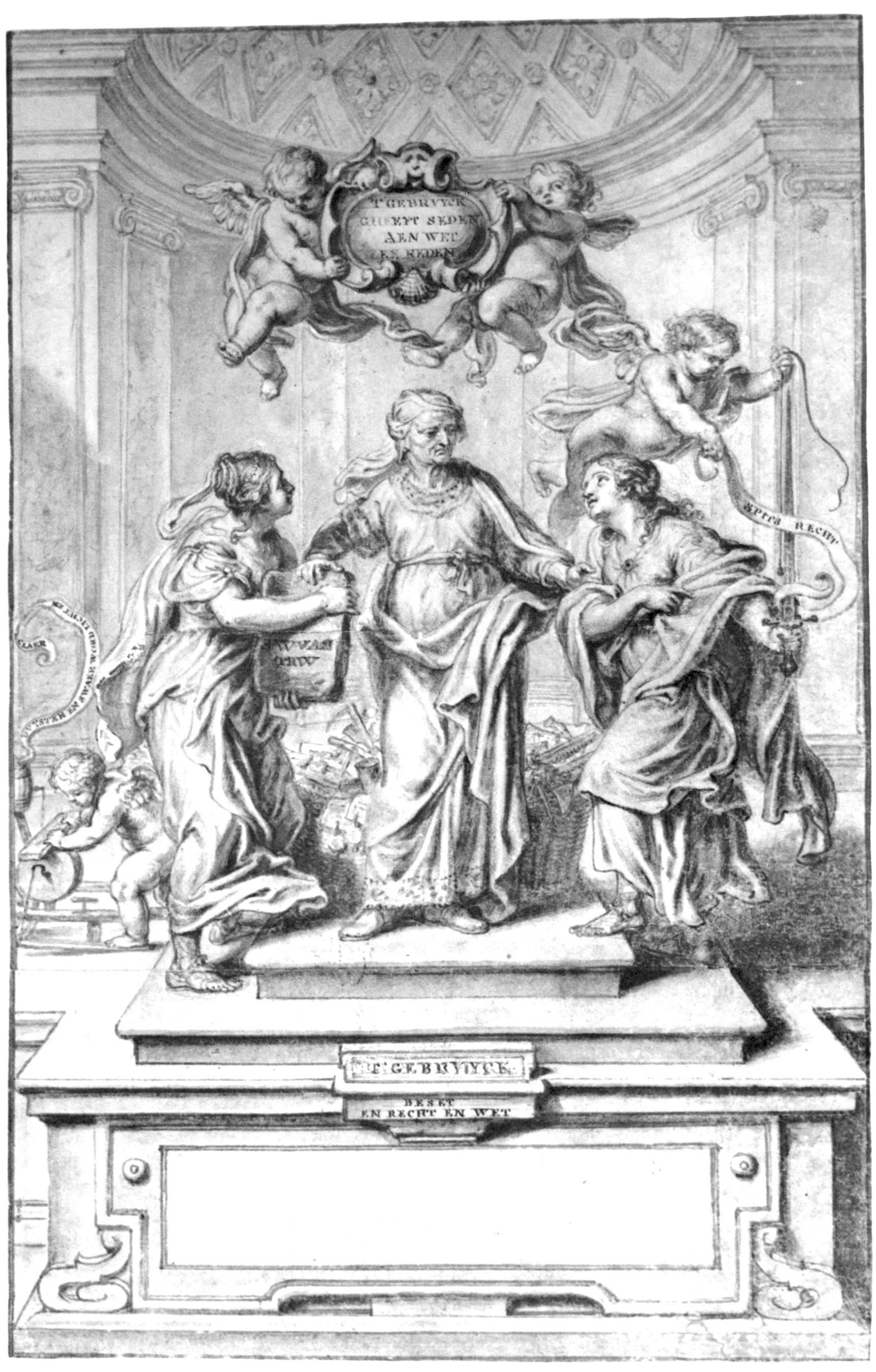

'T GEBRVYCK
GHEEFT SEDEN
AEN WET
EN REDEN
SPITS RECHT
'T GEBRVYCK
BESET
EN RECHT EN WET

ABRAHAM VAN DIEPENBEECK

20 *Design for a Title Page*

Bequest of James Bowdoin III (1811.135) Pen and brown ink, black chalk, heightened with white, traced with a stylus for transfer, on two sheets of paper. 343 x 224 mm. (13 1/2 x 8 13/16 in.) No watermark. Inscribed pen and brown ink on plaque held by putti top center: "T GEBRVYCK / GHEEFT SEDEN / AEN WET / EN REDEN"; on the ribbon center left "DVYSTER EN SWAER WORD LICHT EN CLAER"; on the tablet held by the figure at left (letters backward) "RAVWE / WET"; on the ribbon at center right "SPITS RECHT"; on pedestal bottom "T'GE-BRVYCK / BESET / EN RECHT EN WET"; verso, pen and brown ink "C Nº 22/Diepenbeeck/ 2." PROVENANCE: James Bowdoin III. BIBLIOGRAPHY: *Catalogue* 1885, no. 95 (as Unknown); *Catalogue* 1930, no. 95 (as Unknown); Steadman 1973, vol. 1, p. 78, vol. 2, pl. 173 (as van Diepenbeeck); *Handbook* 1981, p. 166 (as van Diepenbeeck).

THIS DESIGN remained among the anonymous drawings until Haverkamp Begemann recognized it as the work of van Diepenbeeck in 1966. The attribution was affirmed by Jaffé and Steadman, who identified it as the design for the engraved title of *Costumen van het Graefschap van Vlaenderen* by Laurens van den Hane, published in Antwerp and Ghent in 1674, a lengthy (over 1,000 pages) compendium of the laws and regulations of the County of Flanders. Van Diepenbeeck's drawing was engraved in reverse by Cornelis van Caukercken (1626–1680).[1]

Van Diepenbeeck designed at least thirty-six title pages between the late 1630s and his death in 1675.[2] Steadman points out that the artist's major period of activity designing book illustrations began after he had been expelled from the painter's guild and after the death of Rubens in 1640.[3] Rubens had himself designed quite a few engraved book title pages, achieving a new standard in the art. He had transformed the primarily decorative title into a compact and rich visual synopsis of the contents of a book.[4] Antwerp at this time was one of the most active publishing centers in Europe, and van Diepenbeeck had a ready market for his designs, which were perhaps inevitably strongly influenced by Rubens's designs.

The iconography of this drawing relates to the history and laws of Flanders, which appears personified as the central figure, unifying earlier common law on the left and the figure of Justice with her sword on the right (assisted by a flying putto holding a plumb bob, a further symbol of justice). The putto at the left is shown applying himself diligently to a grindstone, with a banner reading "Dark and murky becomes light and clear." The large basket behind the main figures contains numerous tools and symbols of craftsmen's trades.

The Bowdoin title design contains several elements used in previous titles by Rubens and others of his school: the platform upon which the figures stand, which serves as the tablet for the title; the unifying element of the sculptural niche behind the figures; the complex iconography; and the central group of three figures joined together. The latter group is reminiscent of Rubens's design for S. Pietrasanta, *De Symbolis Heroicis*, Antwerp, 1634.[5]

At least seven other drawings by van Diepenbeeck for book titles have been located by Steadman in Moscow, Frankfurt, Vienna, Berlin, Darmstadt, Leningrad, and London (Courtauld Institute).[6] In addition, the Metropolitan Museum of Art recently acquired a title design (formerly in the Mariette Collection) showing St. Paul dictating. The Metropolitan drawing was evidently never engraved.[7] These title designs serve as datable guides to the evolution of his draughtsmanship. The Bowdoin drawing was done at the very end of his career and is more sculpturally finished than earlier designs, but his strong outlines and characteristic putti are evident. In an unpublished

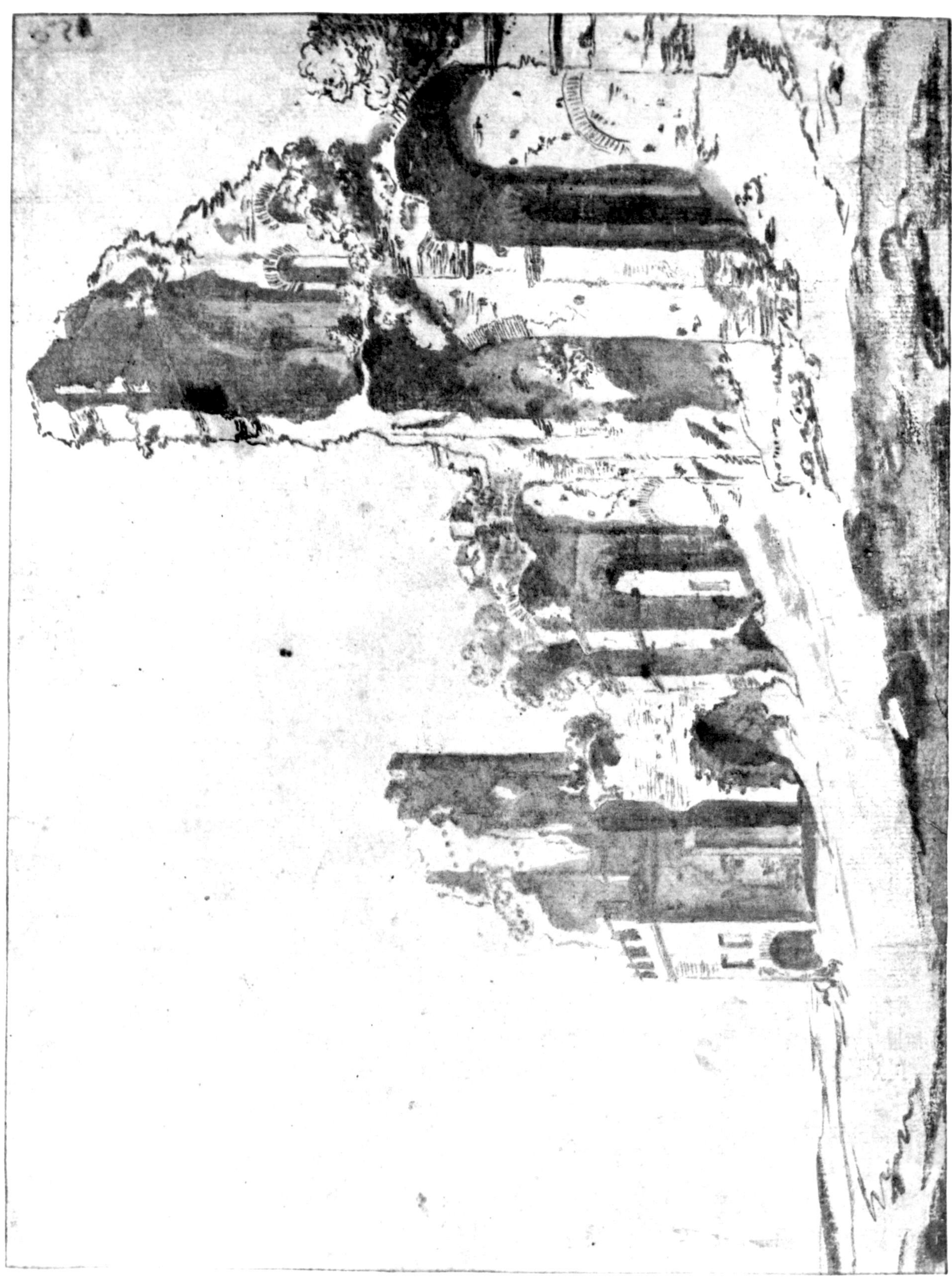

article written about 1956, Ludwig Burchard praised van Diepenbeeck's book designs for their spirit and variety, worthy of the best Italian illustrators.[8]

1. An impression of the engraved title only is in the Department of Prints and Photographs, Metropolitan Museum of Art (inv. no. 56.515.55). According to the *National Union Catalogue*, there is no copy of the whole book in this country. A later edition of the book published in Ghent in 1676 contains a copy of van Diepenbeeck's title design engraved by Henrik (Hans?) Janssen, of which there is a copy in the Harvard University Law Library, International Division. 2. Steadman 1973, vol. 1, p. 72. 3. Ibid., p. 70. 4. See especially J. R. Judson and C. van de Velde, *Book Illustrations and Title Pages* [*Corpus Rubenianum Ludwig Burchard*, vol. 21], 1978; and J. S. Held, ed., *Rubens and the Book* (exh. cat.) (Williamstown, 1977). 5. Judson and van de Velde above, no. 69, fig. 234. 6. Steadman 1973, vol. 2, pls. 154, 155, 160, 163, 167, 169, and 171, respectively. 7. Inv. no. 1981.289. 8. Cited by Steadman 1973, p. 7.

BARTHOLOMEUS BREENBERGH
DEVENTER 1598–1657 AMSTERDAM

21 *View of the Aurelian Walls of Rome*

Bequest of James Bowdoin III (1811.132) Brush and brown ink and brown wash over black chalk. 261 x 344 mm. (10¼ x 13 9/16 in.) No watermark visible. Inscribed pen and ink verso of old mount "No. 14 Bishop." PROVENANCE: James Bowdoin III. BIBLIOGRAPHY: *Catalogue* 1885, no. 57 (as Corneille Bishop [sic]); *Catalogue* 1930, no. 57 (as Corneille Bishop); *Handbook* 1981, p. 166 (as Breenbergh).

PERHAPS RECEIVING his early training in Amsterdam, Breenbergh went to Rome in 1619 and stayed at first with Paul Bril. He was one of the founders in 1623 of the *Schilderbent*, a group of Dutch painters working in Rome, which included Cornelis van Poelenburgh. Breenburgh left Italy by 1629 and settled in Amsterdam. His innovative use of brush and ink wash to define form and shadow was perhaps an influence on Claude Lorrain's draughtsmanship. The two artists probably knew each other during the later 1620s.[1] Breenbergh's oeuvre includes about 200 drawings, the majority of which are studies of landscapes and classical ruins.

Based on the verso inscription on the old mount, this sheet was first attributed to Cornelis Bisschop, although the reference was probably to Jan de Bisschop (see Cat. 29), some of whose Italian landscapes resemble Breenbergh's. It was given to Breenbergh by Sir Robert Witt, and this attribution has been generally accepted by scholars, including Roethlisberger.[2] Occasionally the name of van Poelenburgh has been suggested, because of the similarity of these two artists' drawing styles when they were working in Rome, often depicting the same monuments. The Bowdoin drawing, however, exhibits the stronger contrasts of light and shade and slightly greater freedom of brushwork characteristic of Breenbergh. Comparable sheets are those in the Uffizi, the Louvre, and the van Leeuwen Collection.[3] The ruins have been identified by John Herrmann as a portion of the Aurelian city walls of Rome, built between 270 and 310 A.D.[4] The place is more specifically localized to a spot inside the walls near the Porta Metronia by another drawing in the Albertina attributed to Breenbergh of exactly the same site, which additionally shows the church of Santo Stefano in Monte Celio (Santo Stefano Rotondo) in the far left distance.[5] No paintings for which the Bowdoin and Albertina drawings are specific models can be determined. As Roethlisberger

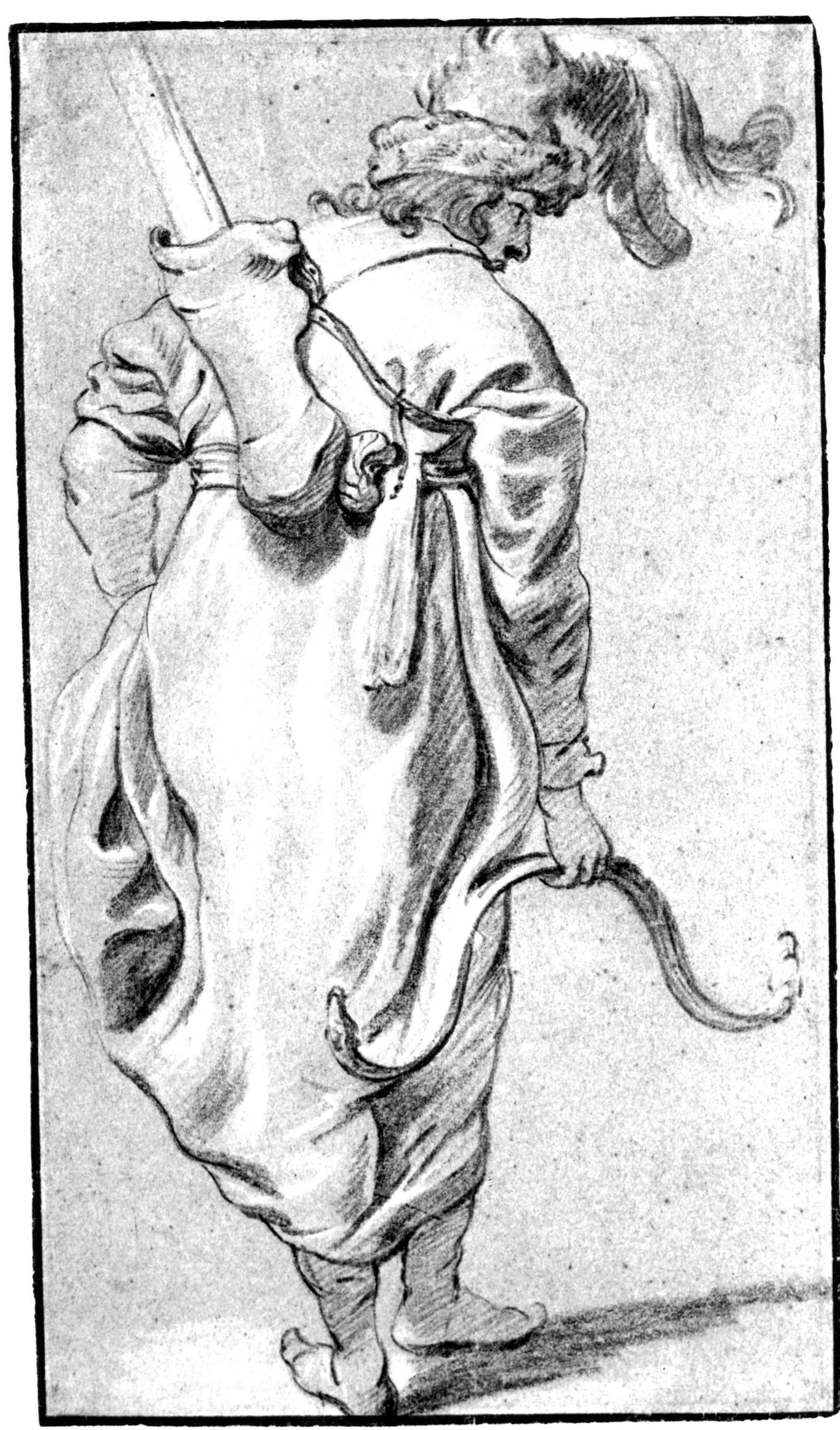

points out, Breenbergh freely used certain features from his drawn studies while completely eliminating or changing others. He is convinced, however, that Breenbergh's drawings are topographically accurate views.[6]

1. H. D. Russell, *Claude Lorrain, 1600–1682* (exh. cat.) (Washington, 1982), p. 53. 2. Letter to the museum, 9 January 1966. 3. M. Roethlisberger, *Bartholomäus Breenbergh Handzeichnungen* (Berlin, 1969), nos. 9, 108, and 139, repr. 4. In conversation with the author, 1984; I am grateful to Dr. Herrmann for his aid in identifying the location. 5. Inv. no. 9368, repr. in Bernt 1957–1958, no. 125. 6. M. Roethlisberger, *Bartholomeus Breenbergh—The Paintings* (Berlin and New York, 1981), p. 48.

JACOB ADRIAENSZ. BACKER
HARLINGEN 1608–1651 AMSTERDAM

22 *Study of an Archer*

Museum Purchase (1930.231) 357 x 208 mm. (14 1/8 x 8 3/16 in.) Black and white chalk on blue laid paper (faded by exposure to light), old vertical fold through center. No watermark. PROVENANCE: William Bates (1824–1884) (Lugt 2604); Professor Henry Johnson. BIBLIOGRAPHY: Sumowski 1979ff, vol. 1, pp. 44–45, no. 15x, repr.; *Handbook* 1981, p. 167. EXHIBITION: Waterville 1978, cat. no. 15, repr.

APPARENTLY entering the collections without an attribution, this sheet was first recognized as Backer's work by Lugt on his visit to the museum in 1945. This attribution was subsequently affirmed by Gerson[1] and published by Sumowski in his 1979 catalogue of Backer's drawings. Backer studied with the painter Lambert Jacobsz. in Leeuwarden from about 1630, as did Govaert Flinck, with whose drawings Backer's are often confused. In 1633, Backer moved to Amsterdam, becoming strongly influenced by Rembrandt's work, though he most probably never studied with him.[2] His work consists of portraits, mythological and biblical scenes, and allegories.

Sumowski has pointed out the difficulty of arranging Backer's drawings in any chronological order: there are few dated works or clear stylistic distinctions.[3] However, he relates the Bowdoin sheet clearly to a group of single figure studies, particularly two drawings in Vienna and one in the Lugt Collection, Institut Néerlandais, Paris.[4] All these drawings exhibit similar technique and three-dimensionality, which Sumowski attributes to the influence of Lambert Jacobsz. rather than to that of Rembrandt. Therefore he feels these studies may be dated to the early 1630s and perhaps may be for a painting entitled *Calling Back of Joseph's Brothers*.[5] Sumowski observes that the great part of Backer's drawings probably come from the collection of his brother, Tjerk Adriaensz., whose 1659 estate inventory lists two portfolios with eighty-four sheets by Jacob.[6]

1. Letter to Carl Schmalz, 8 October 1957. 2. Schatborn 1981, p. 129. 3. Sumowski 1979ff, vol. 1, p. 15. 4. Ibid., nos. 1, 13x, and 14x respectively. 5. Ibid., p. 16. 6. Ibid., p. 15.

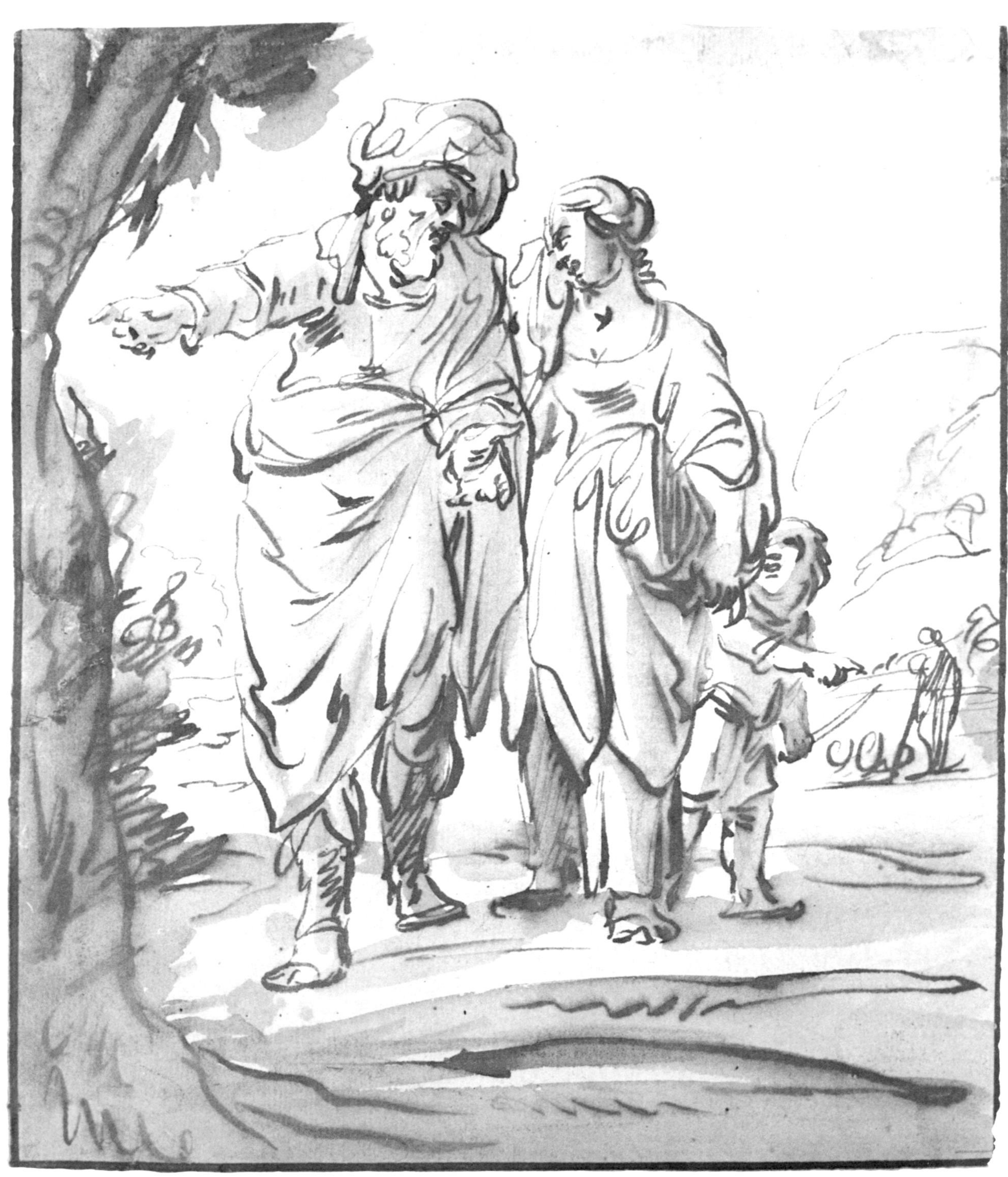

PIETER JANSZ.

AMSTERDAM 1612–1672 AMSTERDAM

23 *The Expulsion of Hagar*

James Phinney Baxter Fund in Memory of Professor Henry Johnson (1932.35) Pen and brown ink and brown and grey washes over traces of graphite. 190 x 165 mm. (7 1/2 x 6 1/2 in.) According to an old photograph in the museum files, this sheet has been trimmed at the top by ca. 20 mm. Inscribed graphite verso "Klaes Jansse Moiyaart." Watermark: foolscap (fragment). PROVENANCE: Professor Henry Johnson. BIBLIOGRAPHY: *Catalogue* 1930, p. 95, no. 640 (as Moeyaert); S. D. Kuretsky, review of Sacramento 1974 in *Art Bulletin*, vol. 58 (1976), p. 624. EXHIBITION: Sacramento 1974, cat. no. 7, repr. (as copy after Lastman).

BEARING A TRADITIONAL ATTRIBUTION to Moeyaert (see Cat. 14), this sheet was subsequently given to another of the so-called Pre-Rembrandtists, Pieter Lastman (ca. 1583–1633), by Kurt Bauch.[1] Bauch related the Bowdoin sheet to several others in the same technique, two of which are of the identical composition—one in Bremen and one formerly in the Houthakker Collection, Amsterdam.[2] Lastman executed this subject in 1612 in a painting which is in the Kunsthalle, Hamburg.[3] Astrid Tümpel, however, recognized that these stylistically similar drawings did not greatly resemble Lastman's proven draughtsmanship and instead called them copies after him.[4]

Recently, Marijn Schapelhouman has proposed the attribution of this group to Pieter Jansz., an Amsterdam glass and landscape painter who was trained by Jan van Bouckhorst (ca. 1588–1631) in Haarlem.[5] The draughtsmanship of the Bowdoin and related sheets is certainly reminiscent of van Bouckhorst's strong and fluid pen work.[6] Jansz. is also known for being the drawing teacher of the noted Amsterdam art dealer, collector, and amateur Jan Pietersz. Zomer.[7] The story of Abraham's expulsion of Hagar and their son Ishmael is related in Genesis 21:9–14.

1. Letter in museum files, 25 January 1956. 2. The Bremen drawing is repr. in K. Bauch, "Entwurf und Komposition bei Pieter Lastman," *Münchner Jahrbuch der bildenden Kunst*, ser. 3, vol. 6 (1955), p. 217, fig. 8, along with other sheets; the Houthakker sheet is repr. in the sale catalogue of that collection, Amsterdam, Sotheby Mak van Waay, 17–18 November 1975, lot no. 183. 3. Sacramento 1974, p. 60. 4. Ibid. 5. I am very grateful to Peter Schatborn for telling me of this discovery; Mr. Schapelhouman is currently preparing an article on the Jansz. attribution. 6. Schatborn 1981, p. 42, fig. 1. 7. Thieme-Becker, vol. 18, p. 418.

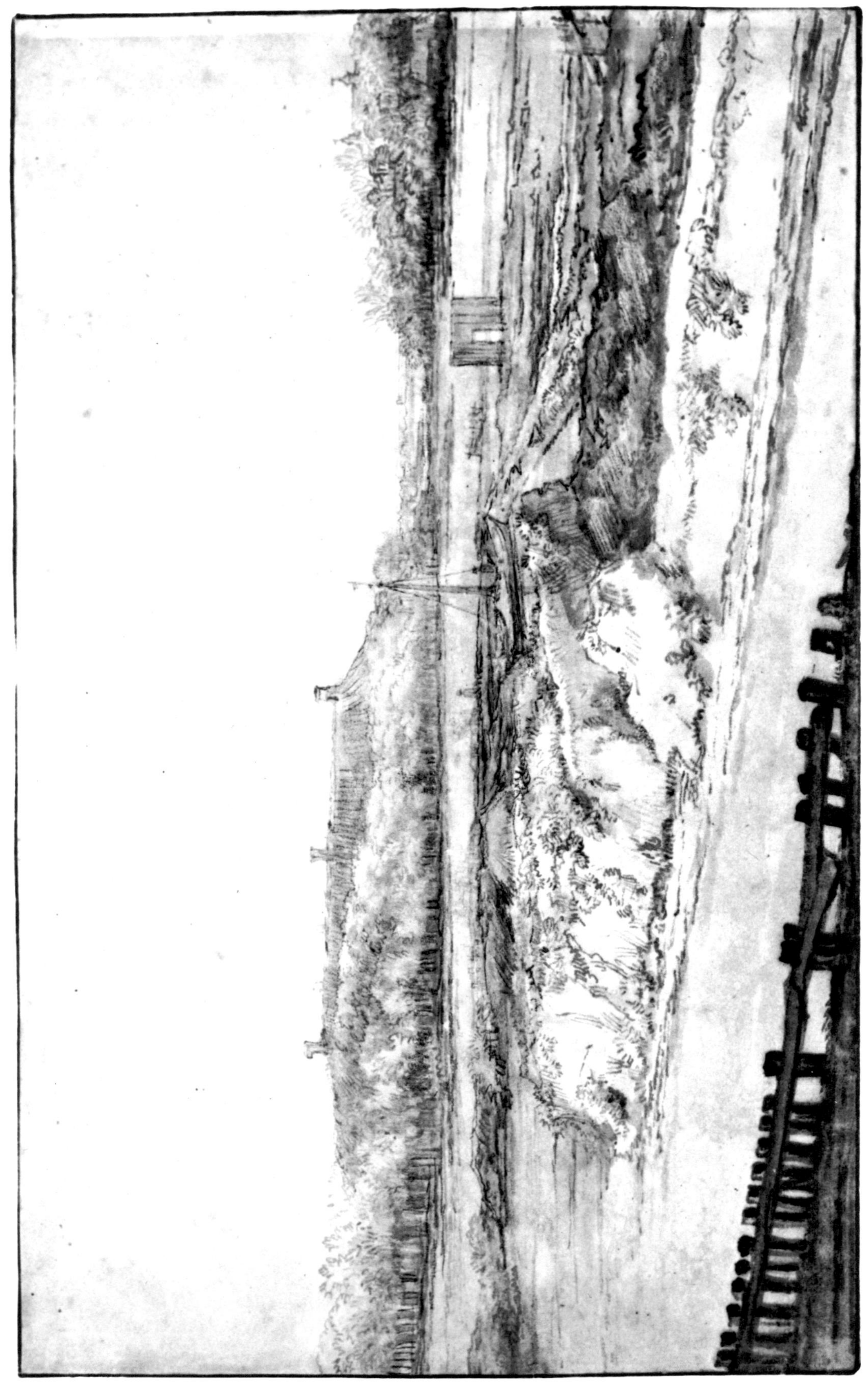

PHILIPS KONINCK
AMSTERDAM 1619–1688 AMSTERDAM

24 *River Landscape*

Bequest of James Bowdoin III (1811.82) Pen and brown ink, brown wash, black chalk, heightened with white. 199 x 317 mm. (7 13/16 x 12 1/2 in.) Watermark: arms of Amsterdam. Inscribed in graphite on old mount "Rembrant"; verso, red chalk "p ko" (cf. Broos 1981, p. 161, fig. 8); graphite "p - koning" (cf. Broos 1981, p. 161, fig. 1–2); "philip konink"; pen and brown ink "LT" (see Broos 1981, cat. no. 43). PROVENANCE: James Bowdoin III. BIBLIOGRAPHY: *Catalogue* 1885, no. 49 (as Rembrandt); Allen 1886, pt. 1, no. 1, repr. (as Rembrandt); Mather 1914, pp. 111–12, fig. 4 (as Rembrandt imitator, suggests Koninck, per Valentiner); *Catalogue* 1930, no. 49 (as Rembrandt); Gerson 1936, pp. 65, 140, no. Z20, repr. pl. 38 (as Koninck, as are all following); Broos 1981, p. 157; Sumowski 1979ff, vol. 6, no. 1501x, repr.; *Handbook* 1981, p. 167. EXHIBITIONS: Chicago 1969–1970, cat. no. 189, repr.; Poughkeepsie 1976, cat. no. 31, repr.

KONINCK RECEIVED his first artistic training from his brother Jacob in Rotterdam before returning permanently to Amsterdam by 1641. He was part of Rembrandt's circle there, and the latter's influence can be seen in both his figure studies and his landscapes. Abraham Furnerius, his brother-in-law (ca. 1620/28-ca. 1654), studied with Rembrandt in the 1640s. Koninck's landscapes are influenced by Rembrandt's etchings and drawings of the 1640s, and also by the panoramas of Hercules Segers (ca. 1589/90-ca. 1638). But Koninck created his own characteristic views of the Dutch landscape, often incorporating a high viewpoint. He also pursued a second career as a merchant, running a shipping line to Rotterdam.

Although bearing traditional attributions to Rembrandt, this and the following drawing were recognized fairly soon after their publication in 1885. Indeed, Valentiner suggested Koninck's name by 1914.[1] This ascription was confirmed by Gerson in his 1936 monograph and is accepted by all other scholars. The inscriptions on this and on the verso of the following drawing appear on many Koninck drawings.[2] As yet this scene has not been specifically identified, although many of his views can be localized.

The two Bowdoin drawings are closely related to each other in technique and dating. Gerson, Haverkamp Begemann, and Logan have related them to a 1663 drawing of farm buildings which is in Berlin.[3] Sumowski, however, draws a close parallel to another scene of a similar subject formerly in the Koenigs Collection, Haarlem, which is dated 1660.[4] The Bowdoin sheets are particularly closely related in technique and dimensions to a view in the Gemeentemuseum, Amsterdam, of windmills near Amsterdam.[5] Based on these comparisons, Sumowski dates both Bowdoin sheets to the early 1660s. Baer has dated them earlier, to the 1650s.[6] As Haverkamp Begemann and Logan have noted, these carefully observed views reflect Rembrandt's treatment of similar scenes, especially in etchings and drawings, of the 1640s and early 1650s.[7] In conversation, Professor Haverkamp Begemann revised his earlier opinion that the fence in the foreground was reinforced by another hand. He now believes that Koninck himself dulled the fence with white chalk (which has since darkened), a technique also characteristic of Rembrandt.

1. Mather 1914, pp. 111–12. 2. See Broos 1981, p. 161; comment by Haverkamp Begemann, 1982. 3. Sumowski 1979ff, vol. 6, no. 1360. 4. Ibid., no. 1358. 5. Ibid., no. 1359; Broos 1981, cat. no. 43. 6. Poughkeepsie 1976, cat. nos. 31–32. 7. Chicago 1969–1970, under cat. no. 189, referring particularly to drawings Benesch 1227 and 1234, both datable ca. 1650.

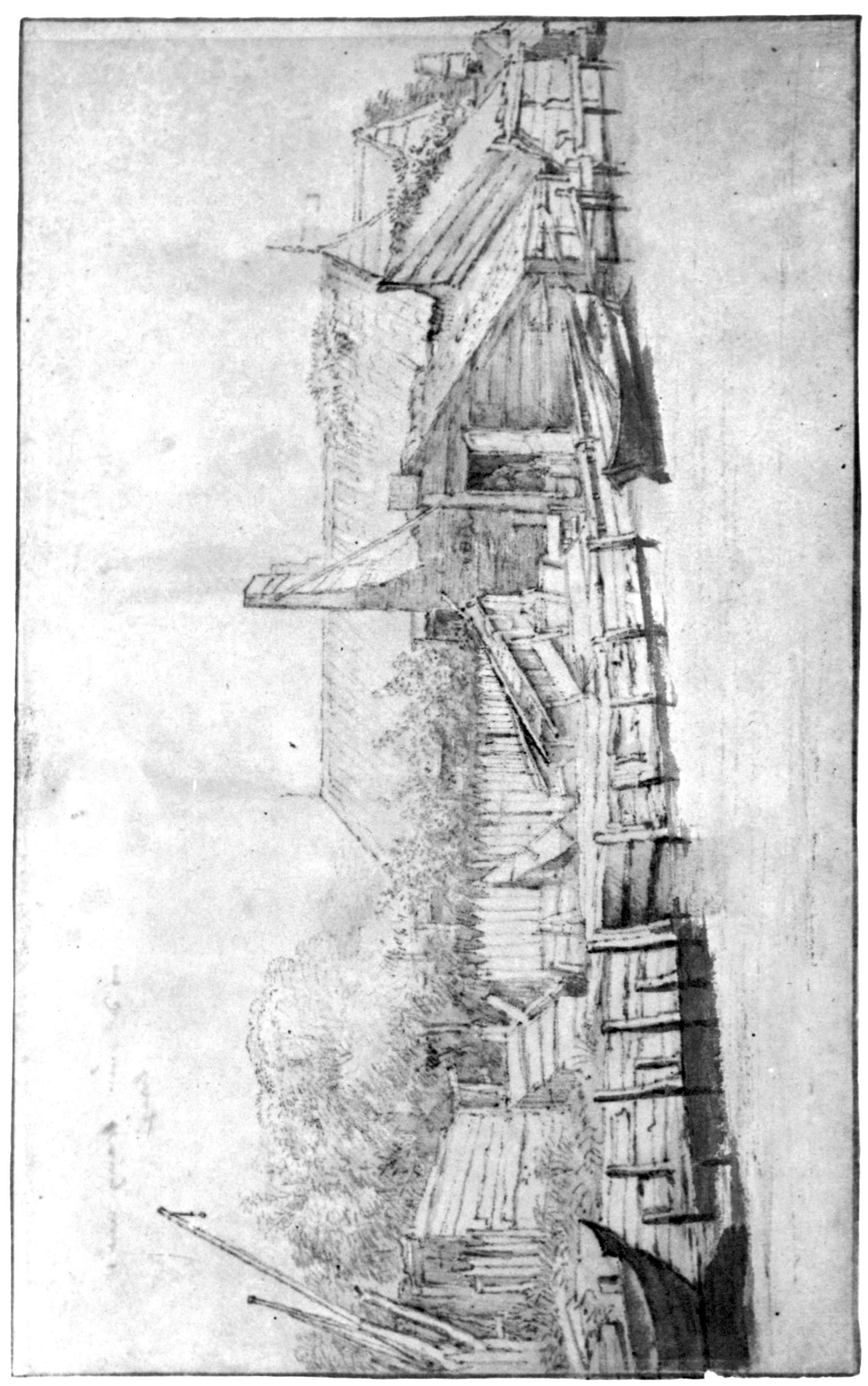

PHILIPS KONINCK

25 *Sheds by the Water*

Bequest of James Bowdoin III (1811.79) Pen and brown ink, brown wash, traces of black chalk, paper darkened by exposure to light. 199 x 318 mm. ($7^{13}/16$ x $12^{1}/2$ in.) Watermark: (four letters difficult to decipher, probably a countermark). Inscribed verso, red chalk "p ko" (cf. Broos 1981, p. 161, fig. 8); graphite "p - koning" (cf. Broos 1981, p. 161, figs. 1–2); "philip konink"; pen and brown ink "LT" (cf. Broos 1981, cat. no. 43); pen and brown ink, several indecipherable words [in artist's hand, according to Gerson in conversation]. On old mount (lost) "No 52 Rembrant." PROVENANCE: James Bowdoin III. BIBLIOGRAPHY: *Catalogue* 1885, no. 50 (as Rembrandt); Allen 1886, pt. 3, no. 2, repr. (as Rembrandt); Mather 1914, pp. 111–12, fig. 3 (as Rembrandt imitator, suggests Koninck, per Valentiner); *Catalogue* 1930, no. 50 (as Rembrandt); Gerson 1936, pp. 65, 140, no. Z20, repr. pl. 38 (as Koninck, as are all following); Broos 1981, p. 157; Sumowski 1979ff, vol. 6, no. 1503x; *Handbook* 1981, p. 167. EXHIBITION: Poughkeepsie 1976, cat. no. 32, repr.

THIS DRAWING is closely related stylistically to the other Bowdoin sheet (Cat. 24), as pointed out by Sumowski. He also dates this view to the early 1660s. He dismisses Baer's suggestion that this composition is based upon Rembrandt's etching *Hut behind the Picket Fence* of 1648 (Bartsch 232), for this motif is a common one in landscapes of the period. As it is in the Bowdoin *River Landscape*, Koninck's treatment of the foliage and individual features of the fence and buildings is particularly subtle. In conversation, Haverkamp Begemann has suggested that the dark washes at the water's edge may have been added later.

NICOLAES BERCHEM
HAARLEM 1620–1683 AMSTERDAM

26 *Laundresses and Cowherds*

Gift of Miss Susan Dwight Bliss (1956.24.187) Pen and brown ink, brown wash, traces of white heightening, traced with a stylus, and verso prepared with red chalk for transfer. 260 x 365 mm. (10 1/4 x 14 3/8 in., includes drawn border of sheet) Watermark: fleur-de-lis over shield (Strasbourg bend). Signed lower left, pen and brown ink "Berchem Fe." PROVENANCE: Duke of Rutland (according to Bliss inventory); Susan Dwight Bliss. BIBLIOGRAPHY: *Handbook* 1981, p. 167. EXHIBITION: Waterville 1978, cat. no. 19, repr.

BERCHEM FIRST STUDIED with his father, the still-life painter Pieter Claesz., and then with Jan van Goyen, Claes Moeyaert (Cat. 14), and Jan Wils. He most probably visited Italy during the period from 1650 to 1653 and lived in Haarlem and Amsterdam after 1677. He was one of the most noted of the Italianate school of Dutch painters, who were inspired by the southern landscape and light and utilized many classical motifs. Other artists of this group include Jan Both, Jan Baptist Weenix (Cat. 27), Jan Asselijn, Adam Pynacker, and Pieter van Laer. Berchem produced an extensive body of work, including paintings, drawings, and etchings. His works have always been popular and were often reproduced in prints, particularly during the eighteenth century.

The Bowdoin sheet is very characteristic of Berchem, with its delicate draughtsmanship, soft light, pastoral theme, and classical ruins above the scene. David Levine first identified this drawing in 1973 as preparatory to an etching by Jan de Visscher (ca. 1634–after 1692).[1] The print is a faithful reproduction in reverse of the Bowdoin sheet in every detail and in the same dimensions but does lose some of the fluidity and tone of the original. It is one of a series of four etchings after similar subjects by Berchem.[2] One other drawing from the series is known; it is in the Fitzwilliam Museum, Cambridge.[3] A drawing of similar technique, also preparatory to a print by de Visscher, is in the Pierpont Morgan Library, New York, and is dated 1657.[4] Hollstein lists almost 400 prints by various artists after Berchem designs, of which 82 are by Jan de Visscher.[5] Over 500 drawings and 850 paintings by Berchem are known.[6]

1. Hollstein *Dutch and Flemish*, vol. 1, p. 279, no. 370. An impression is in the Department of Prints and Photographs, Metropolitan Museum of Art (Inv. no. 53.600.1700[1]). There is also a reverse copy of this print in the same collection (Inv. no. 53.600.1700[2]). 2. Ibid., nos. 367–70. 3. Inv. no. P. D. 142–1963, preparatory to Hollstein 367. 4. New York 1979, cat. no. 101, repr. 5. Hollstein, vol. 1, pp. 278–279. 6. New York 1979, p. 126, under no. 99.

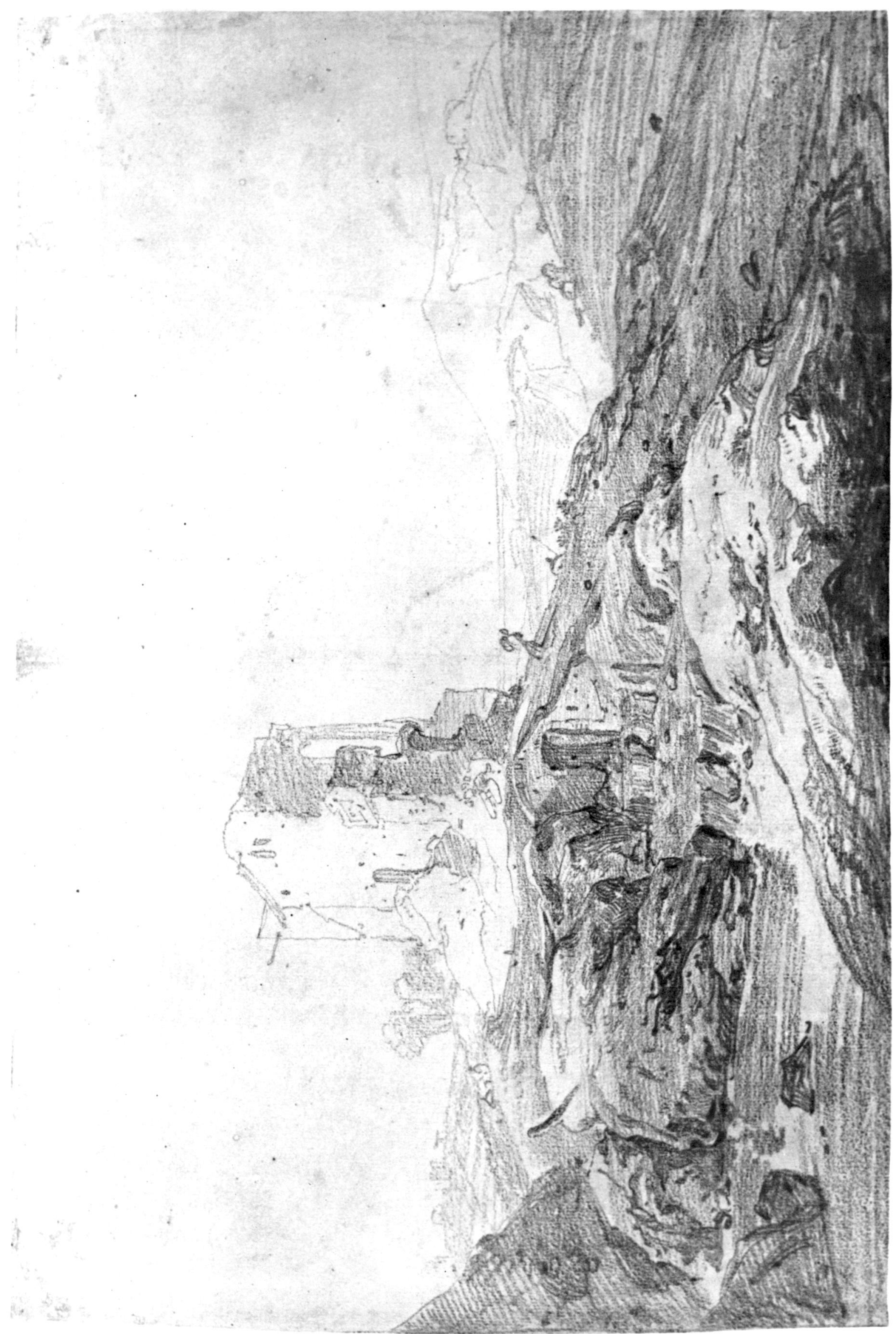

JAN BAPTIST WEENIX

AMSTERDAM 1621–ca. 1660 HUIS TER MEY, near Utrecht

27 *Landscape with Stream and Ruins*

Bequest of James Bowdoin III (1811.140) Red chalk, three vertical folds, rubbed on verso. 276 x 412 mm. ($10^{7}/_{8}$ x $16^{1}/_{4}$ in.) Watermark: HR. Inscribed graphite upper right with figures [101?]. PROVENANCE: James Bowdoin III. BIBLIOGRAPHY: *Catalogue* 1885, no. 102 (as Unknown); *Catalogue* 1930, no. 102 (as Unknown); *Handbook* 1981, p. 167 (as Weenix). EXHIBITION: Waterville 1978, cat. no. 21, repr., exhibited in Brunswick.

WEENIX STUDIED with Jan Micker, Claes Moeyaert and Abraham Bloemaert (Cat. 12) in Amsterdam. Going to Rome about 1643, he joined the group of Dutch artists known as the *Bentveughels*, which at that time included Jan Asselijn, Karel Dujardin, and Nicolaes Berchem (Cat. 26). Weenix received several painting commissions; among them was at least one from Cardinal Pamphili, later Pope Innocent X. He specialized in classicizing landscapes, at times in collaboration with other painters such as Asselijn and Berchem. He returned to Holland about 1647 and eventually settled in Utrecht.

Frits Lugt ascribed this large sheet to Moeyaert; Judson and van Regteren Altena were the first to attribute it to Weenix. His early landscape style does show affinities with that of the Pre-Rembrandt school typified by his teacher, Moeyaert. However, the Bowdoin sheet is much closer to Weenix's mature landscape drawings, many of which are executed in red chalk. Van Regteren Altena pointed out similarities to sheets in the Kestner-Museum, Hanover,[1] and William Robinson has drawn attention to a drawing in the Van Leeuwen Collection, Utrecht.[2] These drawings show particular parallels in technique with Bowdoin's sheet in architectural elements, foliage, and the broad treatment of the distant landscape. The Bowdoin drawing is one of the largest known by Weenix. Other comparable red chalk drawings are in Munich[3] and Hamburg.[4]

Upon removing the sheet from its old mount in 1978, Judy Walsh observed that the verso had been rubbed, undoubtedly in the process of transferring a counterproof of the design onto another sheet (see Cat. 15). The location of that work, if extant, is not known. The scene depicted could be an actual site in the Roman Campagna but more likely is a later composition done after the artist's return to Holland.

1. Letter to the museum, 20 December 1960; the Hanover sheets are published in Kestner-Museum, *Handzeichnung I (Die Niederländer des 16. bis 18. Jahrhunderts)* (cat. by C. von Heusinger) (Hanover, 1960), nos. 132–34, repr. pl. 42. 2. Repr. in Centraal Museum, *Nederlandse Tekeningen uit drie Eeuwen* (exh. cat.) (Utrecht, 1978), cat. no. 114. 3. Wegner 1973, nos. 1062, 1064–65, repr. pl. 233. 4. Inv. no. 22711, Gernsheim 17780.

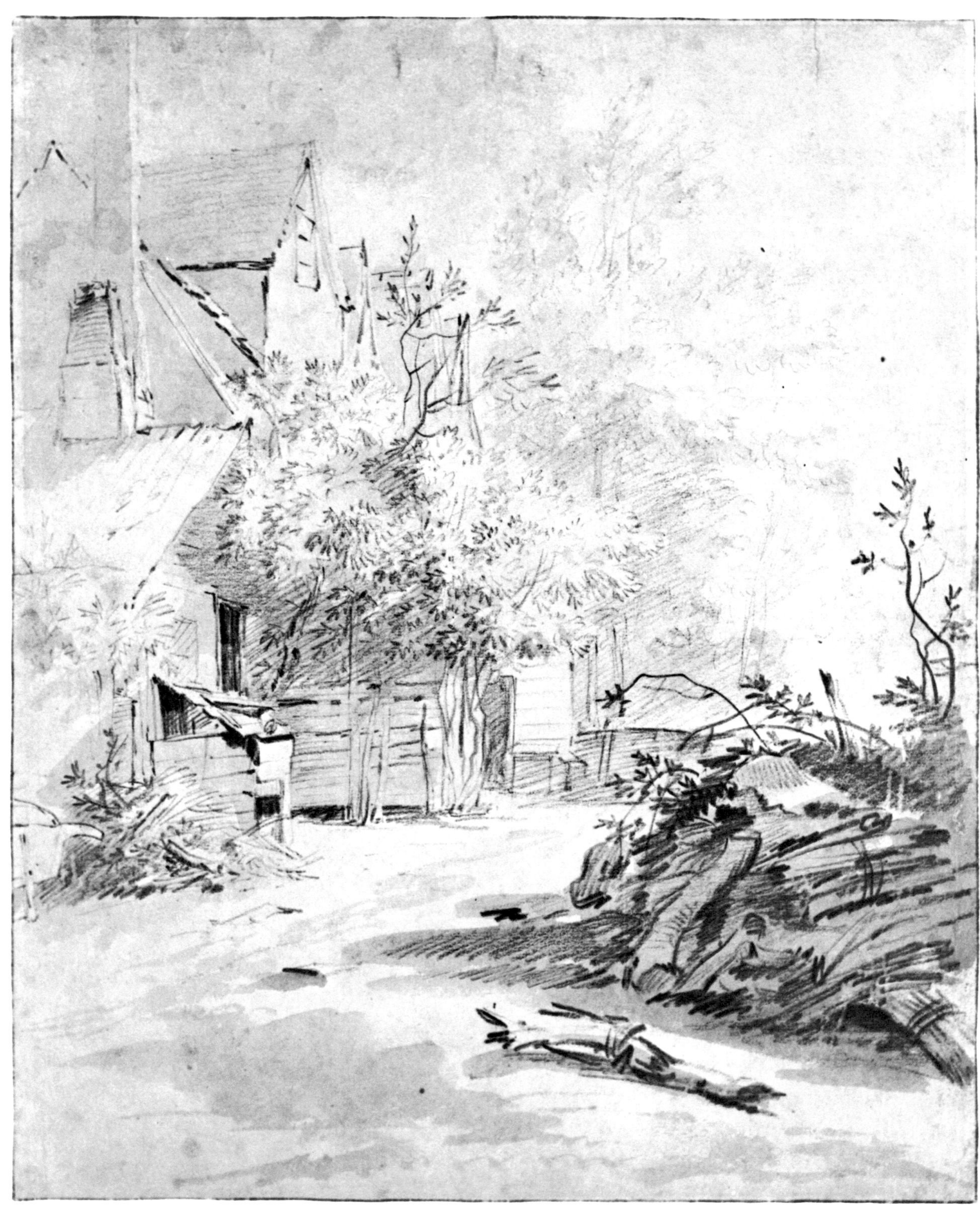

DUTCH, late seventeenth century

28 *Farm Buildings*

Bequest of James Bowdoin III (1811.137) Black crayon, black chalk, and grey wash. 333 x 275 mm. (13 1/8 x 10 13/16 in.) Watermark: Strasbourg bend, fleur-de-lis above. PROVENANCE: James Bowdoin III. BIBLIOGRAPHY: *Catalogue* 1885, no. 99 (as Unknown); *Catalogue* 1930, no. 99 (as Unknown).

THE FORMER ATTRIBUTION to Nicolaes Berchem (see Cat. 26) for this sheet has not been accepted, but the notation in the museum files as "Style of" Berchem is closer to the truth.[1] Other suggestions have been made: a member of the van der Does family, by William Robinson; or an artist in the circle of Adam Pynacker, by Egbert Haverkamp Begemann. George Abrams has suggested the Haarlem painter Vincent Laurentsz. van der Vinne (1629–1702). Several drawings which have been attributed both to him and to his son, Laurens Vincentsz. van der Vinne (1658–1729), are very much in the manner of Berchem. Laurens, in fact, studied with Berchem.

Landscapes attributed to the van der Vinnes which depict the ruins at Brederode, near Haarlem, are in the Ecole des Beaux-Arts, Paris;[2] the Rijksuniversiteit, Leiden;[3] and the Pierpont Morgan Library, New York.[4] All three are datable to 1676 and have similarities, particularly in the depiction of trees and leaves, with the Bowdoin sheet. There seems to be no consensus as to which member of the van der Vinne family may have executed these studies.[5]

1. Horst Gerson, for instance, in 1969, noted "later than Berchem." 2. F. Lugt, Ecole Nationale Supérieure des Beaux-Arts, *Inventaire général des dessins des écoles du nord*, vol. 1, *Ecole hollandaise* (Paris, 1950), p. 87, no. 710, pl. 91. 3. Bernt 1957–1958, vol. 2, no. 641, repr. 4. New York 1979, cat. no. 103, repr. 5. See discussion in New York 1979, p. 129, under cat. no. 103.

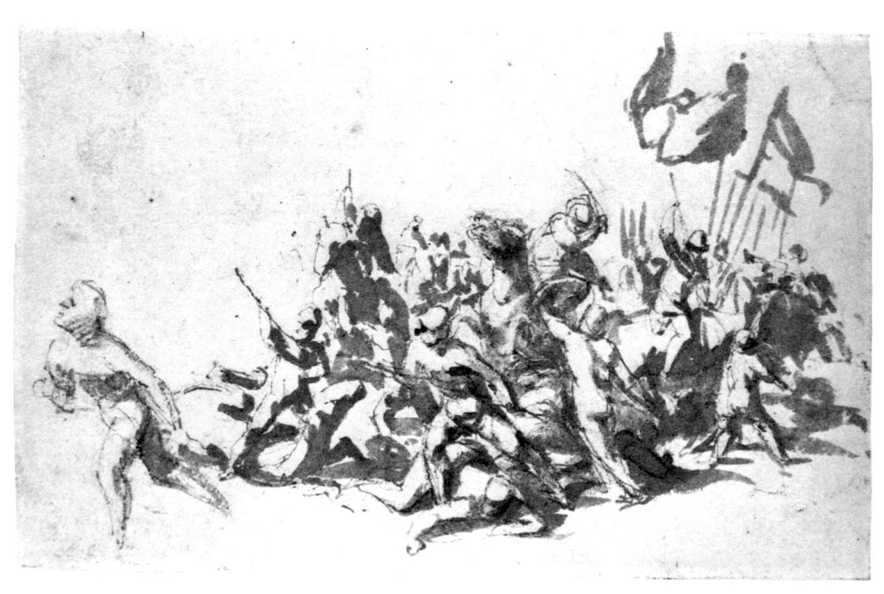

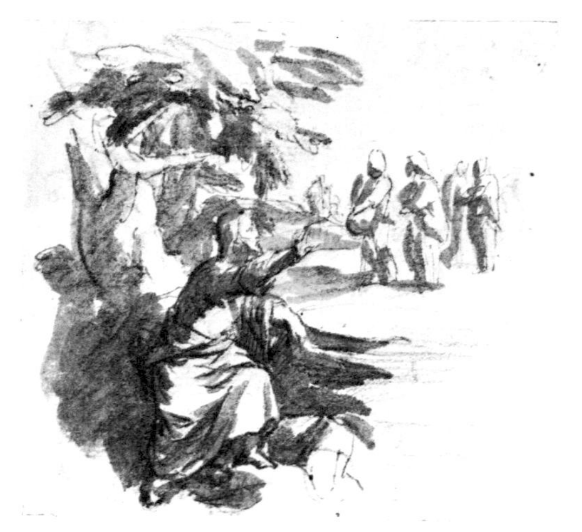

JAN DE BISSCHOP

AMSTERDAM 1628–1671 THE HAGUE

29 Two Sketches: *A Battle Scene / Christ Preaching*

Bequest of James Bowdoin III (1811.111–.112) Pen and brown ink, brush and brown wash over red chalk. 72 x 115 mm. / 63 x 69 mm. ($2^{13}/16$ x $4^{1}/2$ in. / $2^{1}/2$ x $2^{11}/16$ in.) No watermark. Inscribed pen and ink verso of old mount (now lost): "Bishop." PROVENANCE: James Bowdoin III. BIBLIOGRAPHY: *Catalogue* 1885, nos. 58–59 (as Corneille Bishop [sic]); *Catalogue* 1930, nos. 58–59 (as Corneille Bishop).

JAN DE BISSCHOP was a most accomplished amateur artist and theorist who was a member of the highest intellectual and cultural circles in seventeenth-century Holland. He studied law at the University of Leiden from 1648 to 1652, and as an advocate he practiced primarily in The Hague. Accomplished drawings by him are known from 1648, and Van Gelder has suggested that his drawing teacher could have been Bartholomeus Breenbergh (Cat. 21), based on stylistic resemblance and two etched copies de Bisschop made after the other artist's paintings.[1] In 1655 or 1657 he went on a study tour in Italy. In pursuing his professional legal career and his artistic hobby of drawing and etching, de Bisschop was part of a long tradition of dilettanti, as was his lifelong friend Constantin Huygens the Younger, also a talented landscape artist.[2] De Bisschop drew throughout his life and published two series of etchings after antique sculpture (*Signorum veterum Icones*, 1669) and drawings by earlier masters (*Paradigmata Graphices*, 1671). He is also known for over two hundred sunlit landscape drawings done in Holland and Italy, one of the largest being a view of Rome in the Pierpont Morgan Library.[3] His drawings are often characterized by a rusty-brown ink, which was his own recipe and was called "Bisschops inkt."[4] With several others he founded a small drawing academy in The Hague which met in the evenings, and he promoted the practice of drawing both from models and from antique sculpture.[5] Intending his two publications to serve as model-books for artists and amateurs, de Bisschop wrote in his introduction to the *Signorum veterum Icones* that he tried to "select the beautiful from the works of the ancients and thereby to enhance life as a whole which otherwise tends to be oppressive and uncertain . . ."[6] De Bisschop was often known by the Latin form of his name, Episcopius.

The old inscriptions on the verso of the original mounts for these two small sheets undoubtedly refer to traditional attributions to Jan de Bisschop, but the drawings were first catalogued under Cornelis Bisschop. However, they are clear examples of Jan's copies of compositions by earlier masters, even to the use of his characteristic ink. The attribution is further confirmed by Van Gelder's annotation "Jan" on the photographs of these drawings in the Witt Library (filed under Cornelis). In this case, the two original compositions are probably Italian, but remain so far unidentified. Other, larger examples of de Bisschop's copies after old masters are illustrated in articles by Van Gelder and Golahny.[7] Van Gelder dates these late in the artist's career, ca. 1660–1671. The small size of the sketches, however, could indicate their composition as "on the spot" records and so suggest that they were made during his 1655/57 trip to Italy.

1. Van Gelder 1971, pp. 205–6. 2. Ibid., pp. 206–7. 3. New York 1979, cat. no. 118, repr. 4. Van Gelder 1971, p. 217. 5. Ibid., pp. 211, 217. 6. Ibid., p. 219. 7. Ibid., figs. 5, 44–53, 68, 76, and 84; J. G. Van Gelder, "Rubens Marginalia," *Burlington Magazine*, vol. 120, pp. 455–57, 842–44 (July and December 1978); A. Golahny, "Jan de Bisschop's 'St. Helena' after Veronese," *Master Drawings*, vol. 19, no. 1 (Spring 1981), pp. 25–27, pl. 22.

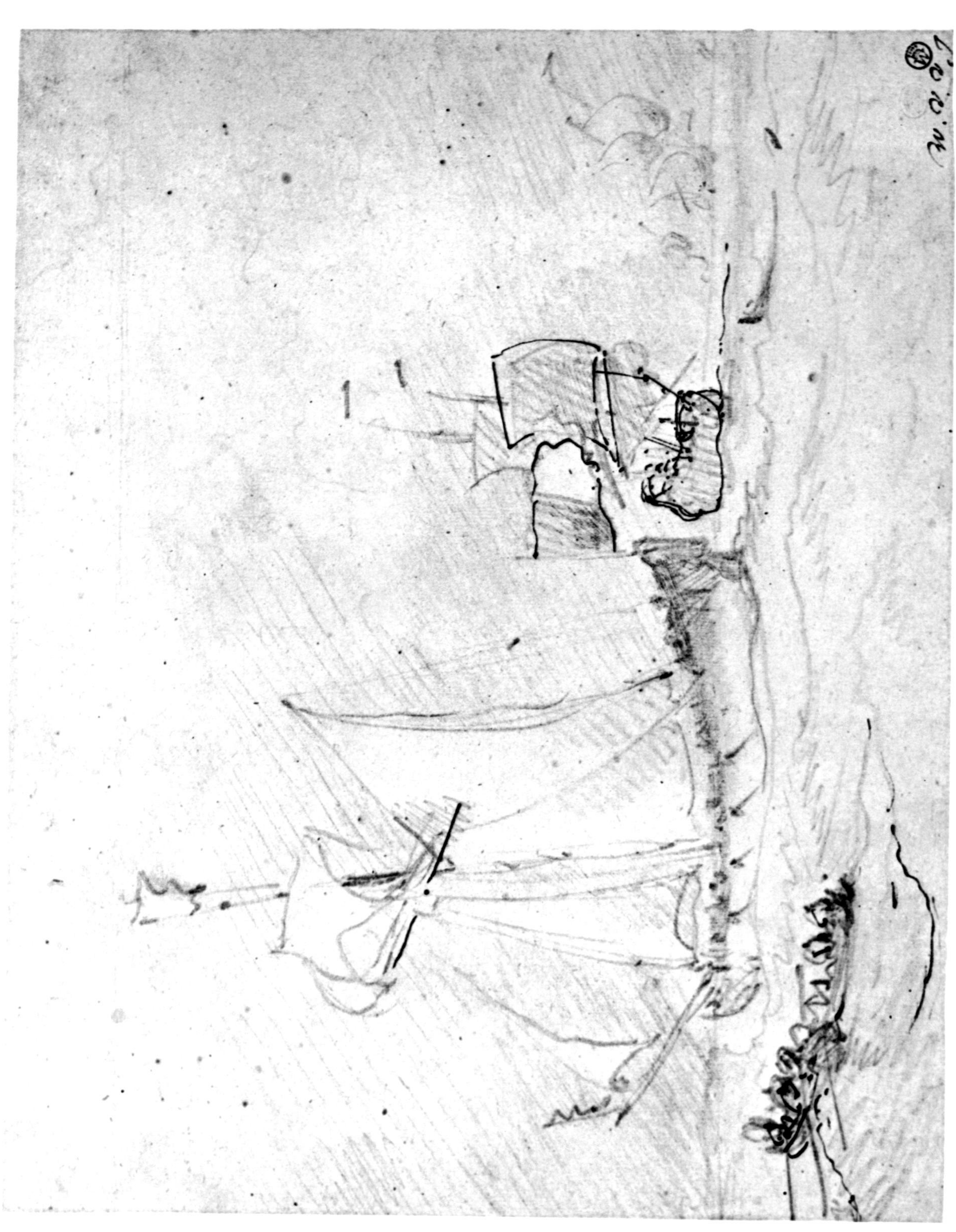

WILLEM VAN DE VELDE the Younger
LEIDEN 1633–1707 LONDON

30 *The Royal Yacht Cleveland in a Breeze*

Gift of Miss Susan Dwight Bliss (1956.24.268) Black chalk and pen and brown ink on beige laid paper, laid down (old horizontal fold at top of yacht's mast). 233 x 292 mm. (9³/16 x 11½ in.) Initialled lower right, pen and brown ink "W.V. V J"; inscribed graphite verso "a 60811/18." PROVENANCE: Earl of Warwick (1818–1893) (Lugt 2600) perhaps Christie's London, 20–21 May 1896, total of 140 van de Velde drawings in 13 lots; Victor W. Newman (b. 1860) (Lugt 2540); Susan Dwight Bliss (acquired from American Art Association).

VAN DE VELDE was the son of the marine painter Willem van de Velde the Elder (1611–1693) and brother of the landscapist Adriaen. He studied with his father and Simon de Vlieger. Both Willem the Younger and his father were employed to record naval ships and battles, first for the Dutch and then for the English (the latter after 1672). Thousands of drawings are known, the largest groups being preserved in the National Maritime Museum at Greenwich, the British Museum, and the Museum Boymans-van Beuningen, Rotterdam. The van de Veldes' depictions of battles were carefully studied at the time and served as official documentation. Willem the Younger is regarded as the most important marine painter and draughtsman in seventeenth-century Holland. Many of his works are true "portraits" of individual vessels and are accurate sources for their appearance and construction.

The principal craft portrayed in this sheet was identified by M. S. Robinson as the English royal yacht *Cleveland*, built at Portsmouth in 1671 and sold about 1716.[1] For the first few years of her service, the *Cleveland* was the yacht used most often by Charles II. There are closely related drawings in the British Museum,[2] the National Maritime Museum,[3] and the Fitzwilliam Museum, Cambridge.[4] All are probably preliminary studies for a painting dated 1678, bequeathed in 1963 to M. S. Robinson by Sir Bruce Ingram.[5] In all the studies, the *Cleveland* itself is portrayed similarly on the left of the composition in a stiff breeze, with the accessory vessels being varied in number and placement. The artist often made counterproofs of his compositional sketches; the faintness of the chalk lines in the Bowdoin drawing may indicate that such a counterproof was taken from this sheet.

1. E. Croft-Murray and P. Hulton, *Catalogue of British Drawings [in the British Museum]*, vol. 1, *XVI and XVII Centuries* (London, 1960), p. 516, under no. 63. 2. Ibid., no. 63, repr. pl. 269. 3. Robinson 1958–1974, p. 84, no. 438, pl. 99. 4. Inv. no. PD 804–1963. 5. Robinson 1958–1974, vol. 2, p. 34, under no. 1089–90. These latter two drawings are considered by Robinson perhaps to be copies after the painting. I am most grateful to Mr. Robinson for sending me a draft entry on this painting, which will be included in his forthcoming catalogue raisonné.

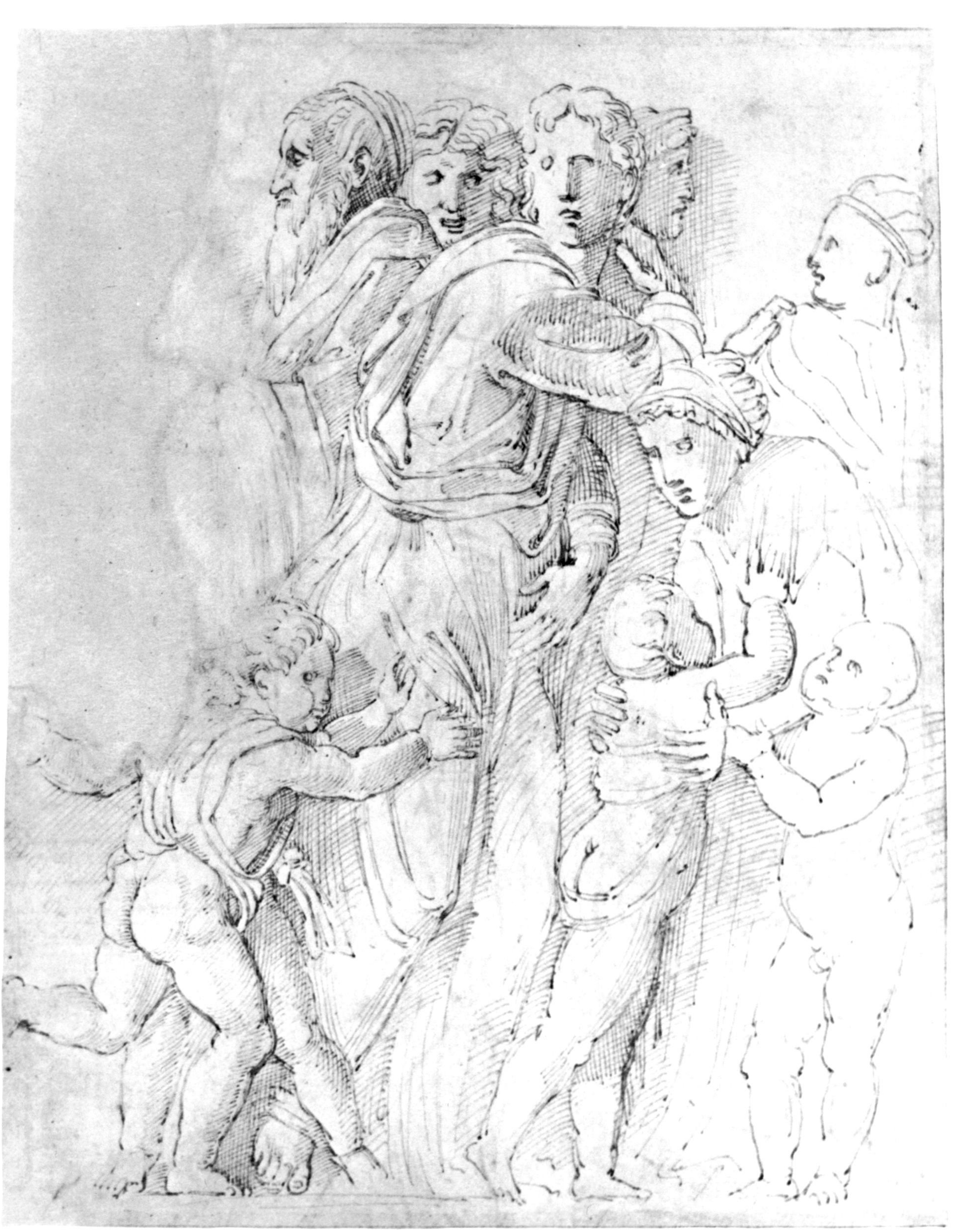

Italian

RAPHAEL (Raffaello Santi), School of
URBINO 1483–1520 ROME

31 *Copy from Donatello's "Miracle of the Miser's Heart"* (recto and verso)

Bequest of James Bowdoin III (1811.6 r and v) Pen and brown ink, loss at upper left corner of recto. 251 x 204 mm. (10 1/16 x 8 in.) Watermark: anchor in circle, six-pointed star above. Inscribed graphite, recto bottom: "Polidor Caravaggio" (now removed). PROVENANCE: James Bowdoin III. BIBLIOGRAPHY: *Catalogue* 1885, no. 7 (as Polidore [sic] da Caravaggio after Donatello); *Catalogue* 1930, no. 7 (as Polidore [sic] da Caravaggio after Donatello); *Handbook* 1981, p. 164 (as Giulio Romano).

THIS DRAWING is intriguing for the study of Raphael's artistic sources. It bears an old ascription to Polidoro da Caravaggio (1490/1500–1543?) and was recognized when first catalogued as a copy from Donatello, although the subject was misidentified as the Fall of Troy.[1] Both sides of this sheet are actually taken from the right portion of Donatello's bronze relief of the Miracle of the Miser's Heart on the high altar of Sant' Antonio, Padua. It is one of a group of four depicting miracles performed by St. Anthony; all four are dated ca. 1446–50.[2]

In 1969, Michael Jaffé suggested that this sheet is closer to the manner of Pirro Ligorio (1513/14–1583) than to that of Polidoro.[3] Oberhuber recognized it in 1977 as a copy from the Donatello reliefs and associated it within the immediate circle of Raphael, as a copy perhaps of a lost drawing by the master rather than of the reliefs themselves. At that time, he attributed the Bowdoin drawing to Giulio Romano (1499–1546). More recently he has suggested that Giovanni Francesco Penni (d. ca. 1528), another of Raphael's assistants, is a more likely possibility. The precise attribution of drawings from Raphael's studio, particularly just before and after his death, is the subject of much scholarly debate.[4]

There are no autograph Raphael drawings known which are direct copies of Donatello sculptures;[5] the nearest parallel from his hand is in Munich. It depicts the entombment of a bishop and is very close to the relief which is copied in the Bowdoin sheet.[6] Yet in several instances Raphael unquestionably incorporated elements from Donatello in his own compositions. Among these, the central three figures on the recto of the Bowdoin drawing appear virtually unchanged on the very right edge of Raphael's *School of Athens* fresco of 1509/10 in the Stanza della Segnatura in the Vatican, and the figure of the fleeing woman appears in the *Massacre of the Innocents*, later engraved by Marcantonio Raimondi.[7]

At least three other drawn copies of this particular relief exist, in the Uffizi, the Albertina, and the Biblioteca Reale in Turin; the same figures portrayed in the Bowdoin sheet appear in all.[8] The Uffizi and Turin studies—both of which had traditionally been given to Raphael himself—are quite rapid, loosely delineated sketches. One side of the Albertina sheet, which Stix and Frölich-Bum attributed perhaps to Penni (the sheet has an old inscription to him), has been very fully developed into solid relief and considerable chiaroscuro. The reverse of that sheet is loosely sketched after the original relief.

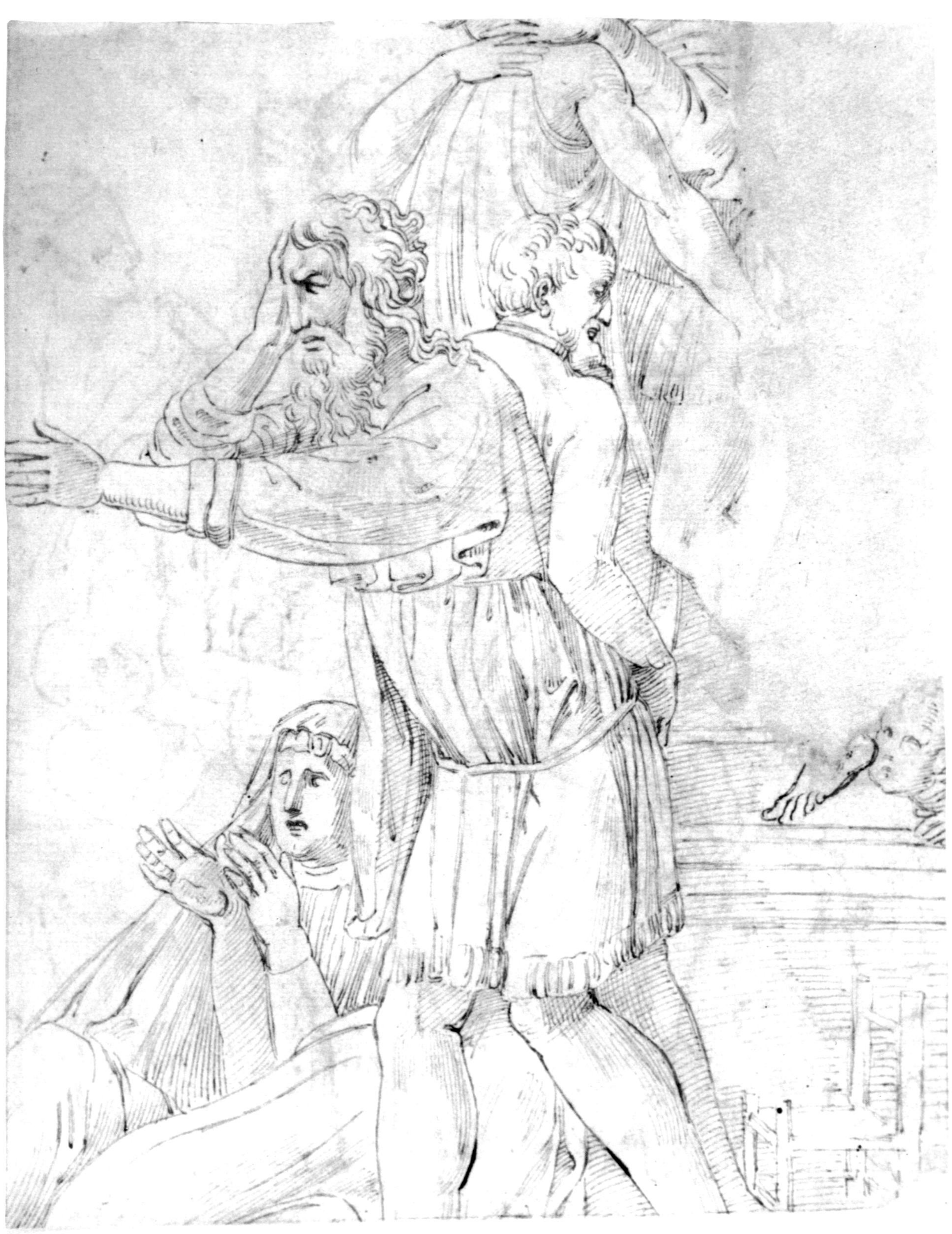

In the Bowdoin study, the plasticity of the relief is carefully developed, particularly for the central figures of the recto, and the penwork seems more deliberate. This quality leads to the tentative conclusion that the Bowdoin drawing may be placed within Raphael's studio. Comparison of the several drawn studies with the relief reveals small variations in the attitudes of the figures, with the Bowdoin version seeming the more restrained, in keeping with the original relief and with Raphael's final use of the group in the *School of Athens*. (Mitsch points out that in the Albertina copy, the kneeling woman with the two children is twisted into greater sculptural depth than in the relief.[9]) An original study after Donatello by Raphael would be datable before 1509. If the Bowdoin rendition was taken by either Giulio or Penni from such a drawing, this copy would be dated after their arrival in Raphael's studio around 1515.

1. *Catalogue* 1885, no. 7, and subsequent publications cited above. 2. H. W. Janson, *The Sculpture of Donatello* (Princeton, 1957), vol. 2, p. 162ff. The Miracle of the Miser's Heart relief is repr. in vol. 1, pls. 309, 312. 3. Comment in museum files. For another drawing attributed to Pirro Ligorio after another of the Miracle reliefs, see Jaffé 1977, pl. 134. 4. See J. Gere and N. Turner, *Drawings by Raphael* (exh. cat.) (London: British Museum, 1983), p. 230. 5. Oberhuber, in conversation with the author, 1983. 6. Inv. no. 2457, repr. in Fischel 1913, vol. 4, cat. no. 213; Joannides 1983, no. 192. Pouncey and Gere (*Italian Drawings in the Department of Prints and Drawings in the British Museum—Raphael and His Circle* [London, 1962], p. 45, under no. 57) relate the Munich sheet to another derived from Donatello in the British Museum and suggest both are early copies; Joannides accepts the Raphael attribution. 7. See Vöge 1896, p. 11, fig. 6. For the *School of Athens*, see Düssler 1971, pp. 73–74, pl. 124. 8. Uffizi: Inv. no. 1484, 218 x 280 mm., repr. Vöge 1896, pls. 1A and B; Albertina: 199 x 150 mm., repr. Stix and Fröhlich-Bum 1932, cat. no. 124, pl. 40; Turin, Biblioteca Reale: Inv. no. 15750, 185 x 244 mm., repr. Bertini 1958, cat. no. 518. 9. *Raphael in der Albertina* (exh. cat. by E. Mitsch) (Vienna: Graphische Sammlung Albertina, 1983), under cat. no. 77, repr. in color.

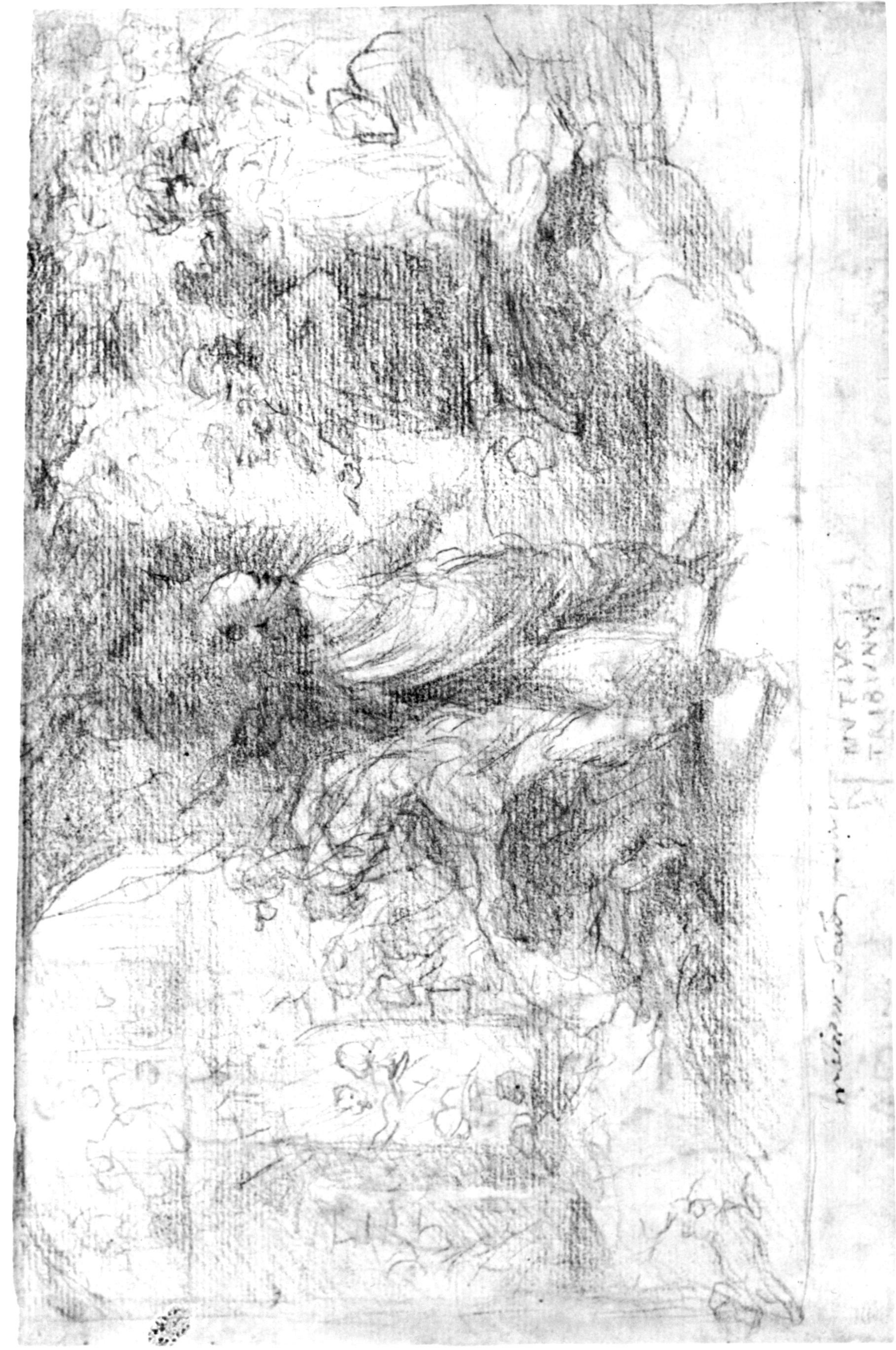

DOMENICO BECCAFUMI

VALDIBIENA near Siena ca. 1486–1551 SIENA

32 *Publius Mutius Condemning His Colleagues to Be Burnt*

Bequest of James Bowdoin III (1811.85) Red chalk (verso: pen and brown ink). 189 x 285 mm. (7 7/16 x 11 3/16 in.) No watermark. Inscribed in red chalk below center "MVTIVS / TRIBVNVS"; pen and brown ink bottom left "matrem Szad [fiduca?]." PROVENANCE: James Bowdoin III. BIBLIOGRAPHY: *Catalogue* 1885, no. 117 (as Unknown); *Catalogue* 1930, no. 117 (as Unknown); C. Monbeig Goguel, *Il manierismo fiorentino* (Milan, 1971), pl. 7, pp. 81–82 (as Beccafumi, as are all following); J. Bean, review of "Selection of Italian Drawings from North American Collections," in *Master Drawings*, vol. 9, no. 1 (Spring 1971), p. 69; *Handbook* 1981, p. 164. EXHIBITIONS: American Federation of Arts 1962–1963, no. 5; Regina and Montreal 1970, cat. no. 2, repr.; Providence 1973, cat. no. 15, repr., cat. entry by C. F. Tyler.

SPENDING MOST of his career in Siena, Beccafumi traveled several times to Rome and Florence, probably around 1511, 1519, and 1541. He also undertook individual commissions in Genoa and Pisa during the 1530s. Although it is apparent that he was impressed by the major works of Michelangelo and Raphael, Beccafumi developed during the early 1530s and always retained a highly personal, exaggerated style which Freedberg credits as anticipating the high Maniera of the 1540s.[1] In Siena he completed frescoes for palaces, churches, and public buildings. For the cathedral, he designed the mosaic pavements and monumental bronze candelabra. He also was an accomplished printmaker.

This sheet remained unattributed in both authorship and subject matter until Vitzthum recognized it in 1962 as an early compositional sketch for a Beccafumi painting from the ceiling of the Sala del Concistoro in the Palazzo Pubblico in Siena, executed between 1529 and 1535. The iconographic program of the ceiling consists of an elaborate series of allegories of civic justice, with references to contemporary events in Siena.[2] This particular drawing depicts an episode from Roman history described by Valerius Maximus, that of the Tribune Publius Mutius condemning nine colleagues to be burnt for their part in a plot to overthrow the government. This gruesome example of strict justice is portrayed at the left of the sketch; in the center, Publius Mutius gestures for support to the group of spectators on the right, while pointing to the furnace that awaits enemies of the state. The individual figures are considerably clearer in the final ceiling fresco, which was singled out by Vasari for its vivid depiction of the fire.[3]

There are several differences in composition between the Bowdoin sketch and the final painting: the addition of figures at the left edge, the deletion of the group to the left of the Tribune, the change in the attitude of the Tribune's head, and the arrangement of the spectators at the right.

The pen and ink sketches of a nude male on the verso are unsophisticated but not entirely incompatible with Beccafumi's rapid sketches.[4] The strong and rough chalk draughtsmanship of the recto finds a parallel in the drawing for an etching of two male nudes at Chatsworth.[5] A more highly finished red chalk drawing of another Roman hero is in the Pierpont Morgan Library.[6]

1. Freedberg 1979, p. 244. 2. The program is summarized in Providence 1973, pp. 18–19, with reference to earlier literature. 3. The fresco is repr. in D. Sanminiatelli, *Domenico Beccafumi* (Milan, 1967), pl. 47i; Vasari's comment is cited in Providence 1973, p. 18. 4. Cf. R. Liphart Ratshoff, "Un libro di schizzi di Domenico Beccafumi," *Rivista d'arte*, vol. 17 (1935), pp. 33–70, 162–200. 5. *Old Master Drawings from Chatsworth* (exh. cat.) (Washington: National Gallery of Art, et al., 1962–1963), cat. no. 7, repr. 6. Bean and Stampfle 1965, cat. no. 64, repr.

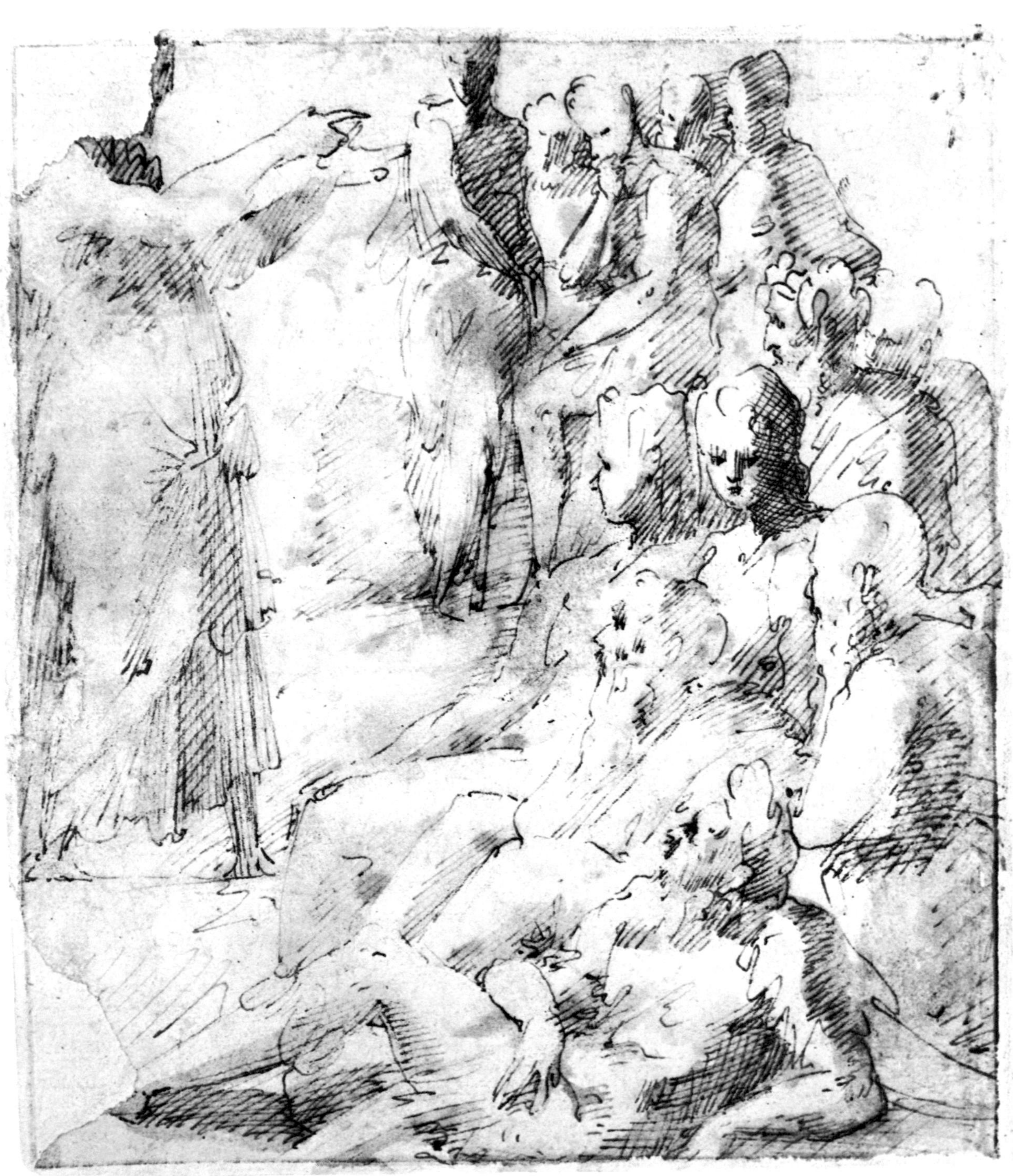

DOMENICO BECCAFUMI

33 *Christ Preaching*

Museum Purchase (1930.153) Pen and brown ink, brown wash over black chalk (verso: red chalk), losses upper and lower left corners (Christ's head partially filled in). 213 x 189 mm. (8 3/8 x 7 7/16 in.) Indecipherable pen and brown ink inscription (French?) verso. No watermark. PROVENANCE: Professor Henry Johnson.

THE TENTATIVE ATTRIBUTION to Beccafumi in the museum's files was recently affirmed by Turner, Pouncey, and Gere.[1] This drawing serves as a good example of Beccafumi's pen style, which can be compared to the style in the red chalk drawing of Publius Mutius condemning his colleagues (Cat. 32). Other sheets which exhibit the same rapid outlines and cursory cross-hatching are in the Louvre and the Uffizi.[2] This drawing is not related to any known project by Beccafumi. The subject could conceivably be St. John the Baptist preaching, but he is normally depicted holding his tall, thin cross. The cramped composition of this sheet indicates either that it was trimmed or that it was intended for a very small space.

1. From a photograph, June 1983, in conversation with the author.

2. Sanminiatelli 1967, cat. disegni, nos. 43, 50, 84, repr.

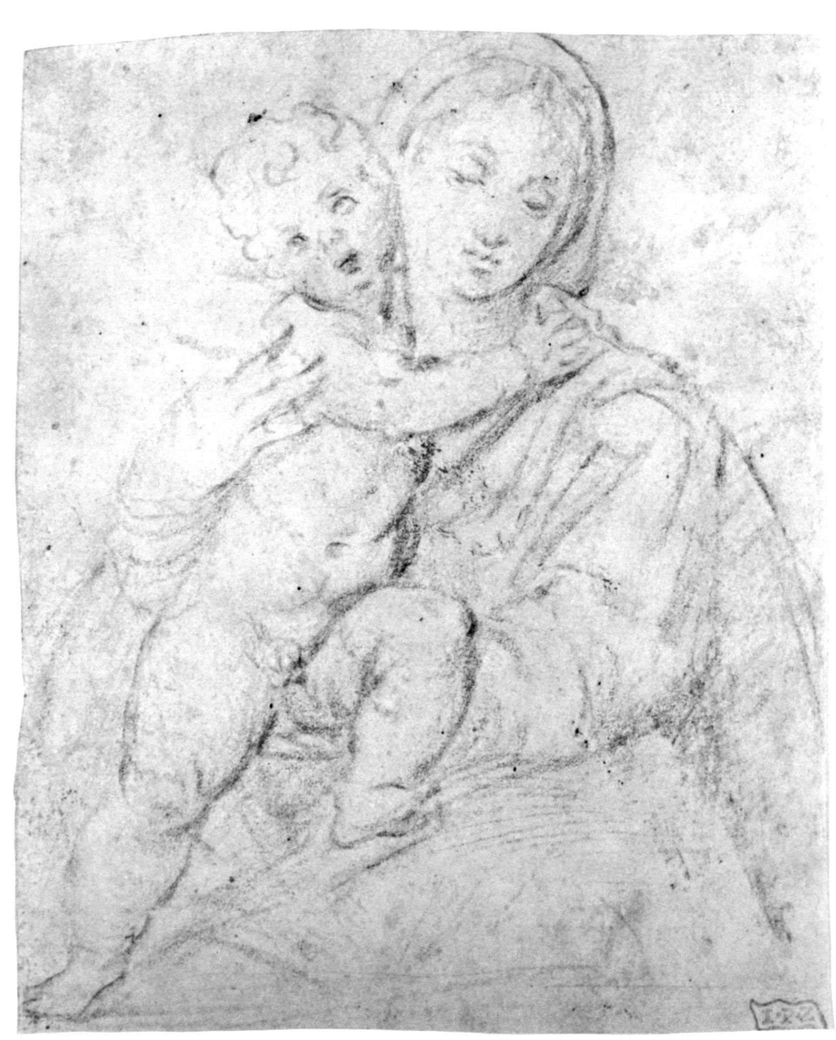

POMPONIO AMALTEO

MOTTA DI LIVENZA 1505–1588 PORDENONE

34 *Madonna and Child*

Bequest of James Bowdoin III (1811.33) Red chalk (verso: red chalk offset of large baby's head from another drawing). 132 x 108 mm. (5 3/16 x 4 1/4 in.) No watermark. Inscribed verso, pen and brown ink, "Purdeno"; pen and ink, verso of former mount (lost) "Titian." PROVENANCE: Jan Pietersz. Zomer (1641–1724) (Lugt 1511); James Bowdoin III. BIBLIOGRAPHY: *Catalogue* 1885, no. 1 (as Titian); Allen 1886, pt. 4, repr. (as Titian); Mather 1913, p. 248 (as style of Sassoferrato); *Catalogue* 1930, no. 1 (as Titian); Uffizi, *Tiziano e il disegno veneziano del suo tempo* (exh. cat. by W. R. Rearick) (Florence, 1976), p. 143, under cat. no. 101 (as Amalteo); C. E. Cohen, "Considerazioni e proposte sui disegni di Pomponio Amalteo," in Pordenone 1980, p. 76, fig. 5 (as Amalteo); *Handbook* 1981, p. 164 (as attributed to Caroto).

AMALTEO WAS THE PRINCIPAL STUDENT and closest follower of Giovanni Antonio da Pordenone (1484–1539). He may have inherited a number of commissions from Pordenone after the elder artist began working primarily in Venice in the 1530s. Amalteo had a very long career, which he spent entirely in the provincial area north of Venice known as the Friuli.[1] His work consists largely of altarpieces for the parish churches and cathedrals of the region. As his style often followed that of his master, Amalteo's drawings have frequently been confused with those of Pordenone, and the Bowdoin sheet is no exception.

The verso inscription on the drawing reflects an early attribution to Pordenone, but the work came to the collections mounted with an optimistic upgrading to Titian. Mather placed it in the seventeenth century, but it was subsequently ascribed to Giovanni Francesco Caroto (1480–1555/8), a Veronese painter. It was first recognized by Rearick as a study by Amalteo, and this attribution has been accepted by Cohen. The latter cites a comparable red chalk sketch of the Holy Family by Amalteo in the Uffizi; he places that sheet earlier than Bowdoin's because of its less skillful rendering of anatomy.[2] Cohen dates the Uffizi sketch to the early 1530s. He points out the facial and figural style of the Bowdoin drawing as being typical of Amalteo's style, to which can be added the characteristic "chunkiness" of the figures, particularly the Christ Child. The Madonna and Child in similar poses and with similar expressions are included in several altarpieces by Amalteo, such as those in the Church of Santo Stefano at Cesclans (1537), the Cathedral of Tolmezzo (1537), and the cathedral in Motta di Livenza (1556); even the Flight into Egypt in Pordenone Cathedral (1565) depicts a comparable pair.[3]

1. C. E. Cohen, "Drawings by Pomponio Amalteo," *Master Drawings*, vol. 11, no. 3 (Autumn 1973), pp. 239–40. 2. Pordenone 1980, pp. 75–76, fig. 4. 3. Ibid., cat. nos. 6, 7, 12, and 16, all repr.

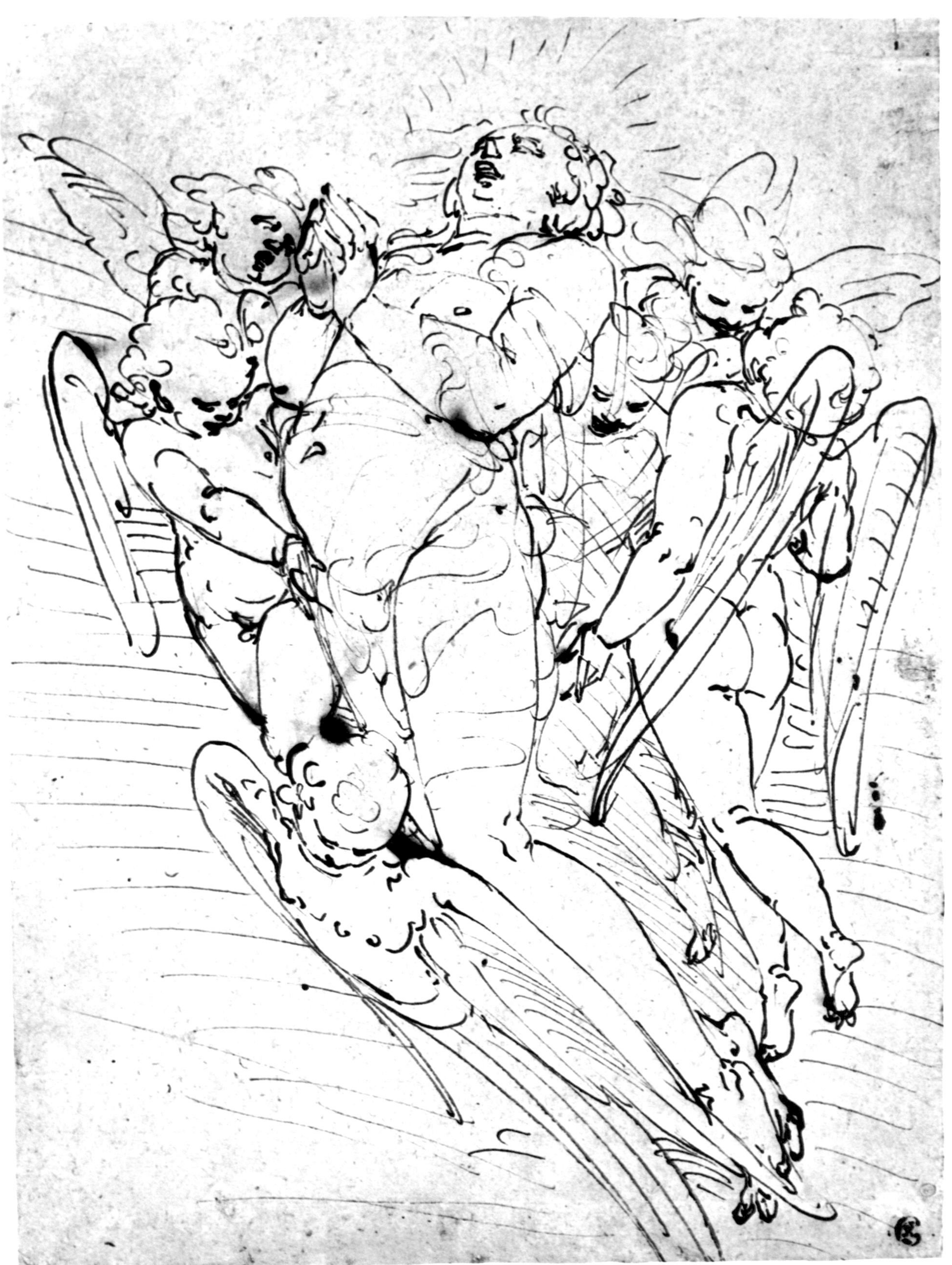

LUCA CAMBIASO

MONEGLIA 1527–1585 MADRID

35 *The Assumption of the Magdalene*

James Phinney Baxter Fund in Memory of Professor Henry Johnson (1932.8) Pen and brown ink on brown laid paper, laid down at edges. 360 x 273 mm. (14 3/16 x 10 3/4 in.) No watermark. Inscribed verso, pen and brown ink "Luca Cangiazo." PROVENANCE: Richard Cosway (1740–1821) (Lugt 629); William Bates (1824–1884) (Lugt 2604); Professor Henry Johnson. BIBLIOGRAPHY: *Catalogue* 1930, p. 94, no. 620.

CAMBIASO RECEIVED his early artistic training from his father, Giovanni, and also studied frescoes by Perino del Vaga, Beccafumi, and Pordenone, which were close at hand in Genoa. After a sojourn in Lombardy and Rome during the early 1540s, Cambiaso returned to Genoa, where he held a leading position as a fresco painter until he was called to Spain in 1583 by Philip II. His painting style was inventive and influential; Georges de la Tour's nocturnal paintings are probably derived from Cambiaso's earlier works in that mode. He also developed a unique drawing style during the later 1560s, exaggerating a strict geometrical vision of human anatomy. His so-called cubistic works are quite common and exist in many versions. Students were often assigned to copy them as an exercise. This factor renders connoisseurship of Cambiaso's drawings difficult.

This large sheet was first identified as an apotheosis when it entered the Bowdoin collections. However, the group of six angels and the indications of a halo are more typical of the assumption of a religious figure. That the central figure is Mary Magdalene and not the Virgin Mary is shown by her near-nakedness and uncovered head.

The style of this drawing does not have the fully developed block construction of Cambiaso's most familiar works, but indications of it appear in the hands of the figures and the Magdalene's nose. The boldness and grace of this sheet still point to an attribution to Cambiaso himself, although recently Giovanni Battista Castello (1509–1569), who collaborated with Cambiaso during the 1550s and 1560s, has been suggested as the artist.[1] Byam Shaw has raised an interesting point by observing that almost no genuine Cambiaso drawing known to him contains chalk underdrawing. He suggests that Cambiaso sketched directly in pen and ink, while his students and copyists first roughed out their compositions in chalk, thus reinforcing the attribution to Cambiaso of this sheet.[2]

There are quite a number of versions of this composition in Cambiaso's oeuvre, none quite like the Bowdoin drawing. Two drawings, in Stockholm and in the Victoria and Albert Museum, are probably studies for a print after Cambiaso by Raffaello Schiaminossi (1570–after 1619).[3] Other versions are in the Uffizi, the Louvre, Stuttgart, Munich, and formerly in Paris at the Sambon Gallery.[4] Several of these are related compositionally to his depictions of the Assumption of the Virgin.[5]

1. Note on the mount signed CJO. 2. Byam Shaw 1976, p. 306, under no. 1226; Popham felt similarly (cf. Popham and Wilde 1949, p. 201, under no. 148). Yet, Ward-Jackson in one instance felt differently (Ward-Jackson 1979, p. 49, under no. 87). 3. Bjurström 1979, no. 312, repr., and Suida-Manning and Suida 1958, fig. 360, respectively. 4. Suida-Manning and Suida 1958, figs. 362 and 358; Ragghianti Collobi 1959, p. 169, fig. 95; Thiem, Stuttgart, 1977, cat. no. 23, repr.; and Galerie Sambon, *Les dessins de Luca Cambiaso et de Gian Francesco Barbieri* (exh. cat.) (Paris, 1929), cat. no. 21, repr. pl. 4, respectively. 5. Cf. Ragghianti Collobi 1959, p. 169, figs. 96–97.

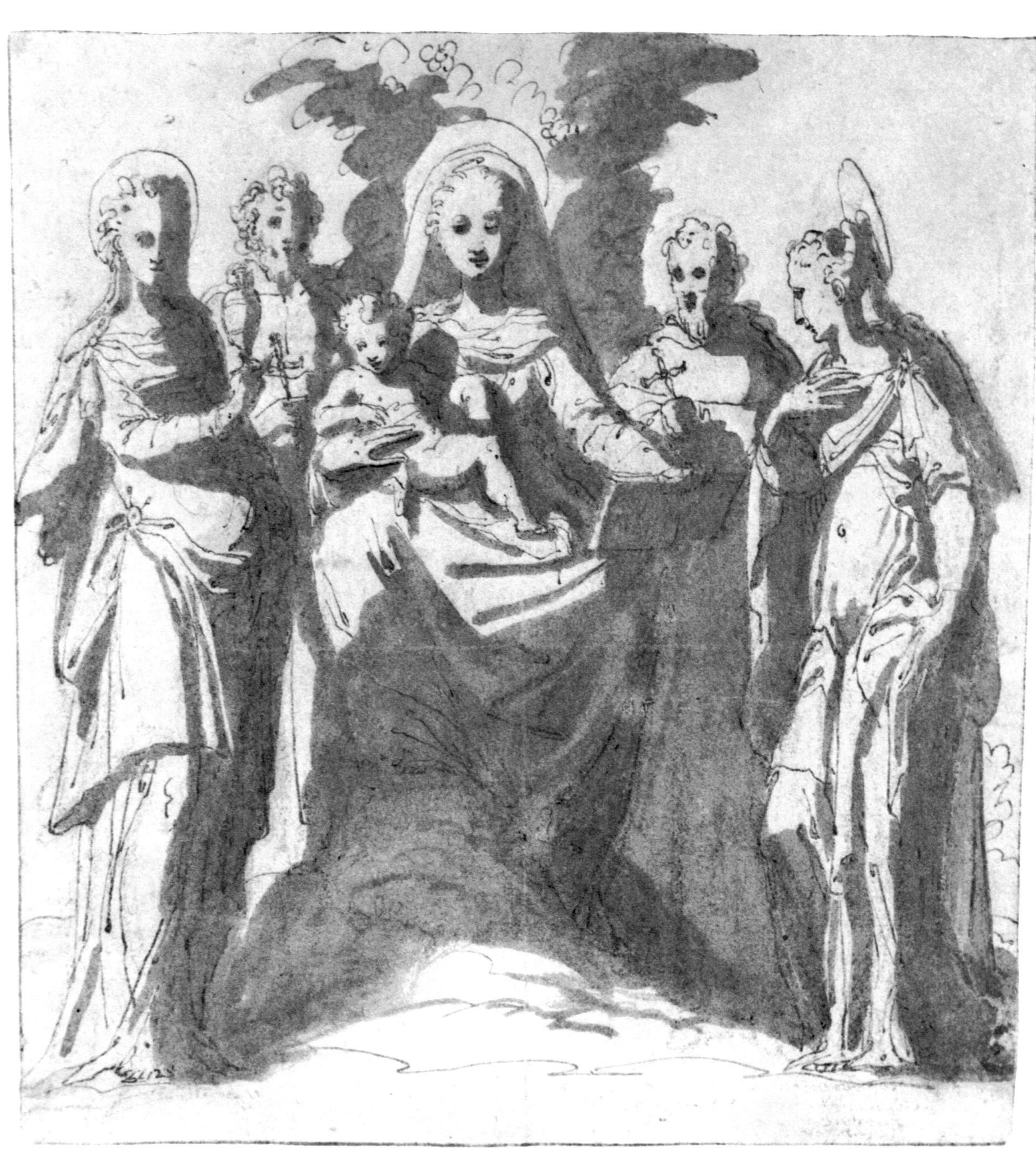

BERNARDINO INDIA
VERONA 1528–1590 VERONA(?)

36 *Madonna and Child with Two Saints and Two Monks*

Bequest of James Bowdoin III (1811.5) Pen and brown ink, brush and brown wash, over black chalk. 171 x 156 mm. (6¾ x 6⅛ in.) Indecipherable watermark of initials. Indistinct inscriptions verso, pen and brown ink [one perhaps "P. India"]; graphite inscription on old mount (lost) "Correggio." PROVENANCE: James Bowdoin III. BIBLIOGRAPHY: *Catalogue* 1885, no. 5 (as Correggio); *Catalogue* 1930, no. 5 (as Correggio); *Handbook* 1981, p. 165 (as India).

INDIA SPENT VIRTUALLY his entire career in and around Verona, executing altarpieces and decorations for local churches and villas. He collaborated with the architect Andrea Palladio on the decoration of at least two of the latter's commissions.[1] His style, particularly for his drawings, has only recently been defined, and few works are known.[2]

The Bowdoin sheet was traditionally attributed to Correggio and then, more reasonably, to the school of Parmigianino. The attribution to India was made independently in 1975 by the author and Mario di Giampaolo.[3] Typical features of India's style are the prominent "dot" eyes, the delicate curly hair, and the thin, attenuated draughtsmanship of the figures and drapery. The strong shading of the washes is also characteristic. Particularly close is a sheet in the National Gallery of Art, Washington, also of a Madonna and Child enthroned.[4]

More drawings by India have been found among the anonymous mannerist sheets in various collections. Studies have been identified for known paintings, such as both a preliminary study and a finished design for an altarpiece in the Pellegrini Chapel of San Bernardino in Verona.[5] A drawing in the Janos Scholz collection of a group of music-making figures in clouds is a study for a painting on an organ loft in the church of San Giorgio in Braida, also in Verona.[6] Further characteristic sheets are in the British Museum; Christ Church, Oxford; the Metropolitan Museum; and the Bick Collection.[7] Considering the decorative work India did for Palladio and others, more drawings by him should exist among collections specializing in architectural ornamentation.

Although there are records of India having painted altarpieces of the Madonna enthroned with saints, none can be related to the Bowdoin drawing. The Virgin in the Bowdoin design holds a book, traditionally the book of Wisdom, symbolizing the Virgin Mary as the Mother of Wisdom. The figure at the far left is Mary Magdalene, denoted by the vial of ointment she holds. The two male figures appear to be wearing the cowls and robes of a monastic order. The figure at the far right is difficult to identify, as she has no visible attributes.

1. A. Palladio, *I quattro libri dell'architettura* (Venice, 1570), bk. 2, pp. 12, 58. 2. Recently, groups of his drawings have been published by T. Mulally (*Disegni veronesi* [exh. cat.] [1971], cat. nos. 74–75, repr.) and L. Magagnato (Verona 1974). 3. The latter attribution was noted on the mount of the Witt Library photo. 4. National Gallery of Art, *Recent Acquisitions* (Washington, 1974), p. 200, Inv. no. B-26,202, repr. 5. Respectively, British Museum and Accademia, Venice (repr. Verona 1974, figs. 71, 70). 6. Repr. Verona 1974, figs. 74, 73. 7. Respectively, repr. Byam Shaw 1976, fig. 53; Byam Shaw 1976, cat. nos. 807–810, figs. 488–92; and Bean and Turčić 1982, cat. no. 105; E. J. Mundy, *Master Drawings Rediscovered* (exh. cat.) (South Hadley, Mass., and elsewhere, 1981–1982), cat. no. 13.

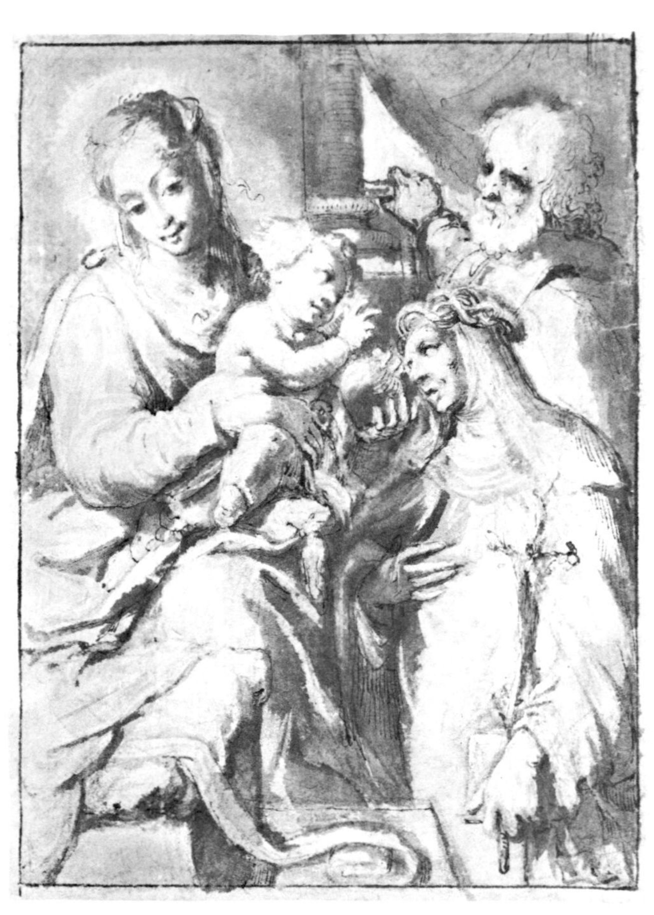

CENTRAL ITALIAN, mid-sixteenth century

37 *Holy Family with Saint Catherine*

Bequest of James Bowdoin III (1811.46) Pen and brown ink, brown wash, red chalk, heightened with white. 115 x 86 mm. ($4^{1}/_{2}$ x $3^{3}/_{8}$ in.) Inscribed pen and brown ink verso "N° 238 V. Salembeni"; on former mount below (removed) "V. Salembert"; also on former mount "65/93/ No. 305–6." Indistinguishable watermark, possibly a jug. PROVENANCE: Jan Pietersz. Zomer (1641–1724) (Lugt 1511); James Bowdoin III. BIBLIOGRAPHY: *Catalogue* 1885, no. 61 (as "Salembert"); *Catalogue* 1930, no. 66 (as Salembeni).

SCHOLARS HAVE RECENTLY DISMISSED the traditional attribution of this sheet to the Sienese painter Ventura Salimbeni (1568–1613) but have not been able to assign another name to it.[1] Suggestions by Nicholas Turner and Philip Pouncey have placed it in the Emilian region.[2] The elaborate technique of overlays of white wash and pen accents was used in drawings by such artists as Bernardino Gatti and Giorgio Gandini, and the facial expressions have reminded Mr. Pouncey of the work of Michelangelo Anselmi.[3] This work is not a traditional sketch or a preliminary study but could be either a very careful record of a larger work or perhaps a small presentation drawing. The attributes of a cross with a lily and a crown of thorns identify the female saint as St. Catherine of Siena, reinforcing (but not necessitating) a Sienese origin for this sheet. The saint is seen receiving the flaming heart from Christ to be placed within her own breast.[4]

1. Susan Wegner first denied the Salimbeni attribution in 1980. 2. Turner tentatively suggested Gatti, and Pouncey thought possibly near either Perino del Vaga or Anselmi. 3. For characteristic drawings by these artists and the most recent literature, see De Grazia 1984. 4. The iconography was pointed out to the author by Susan Wegner in conversation, 1984.

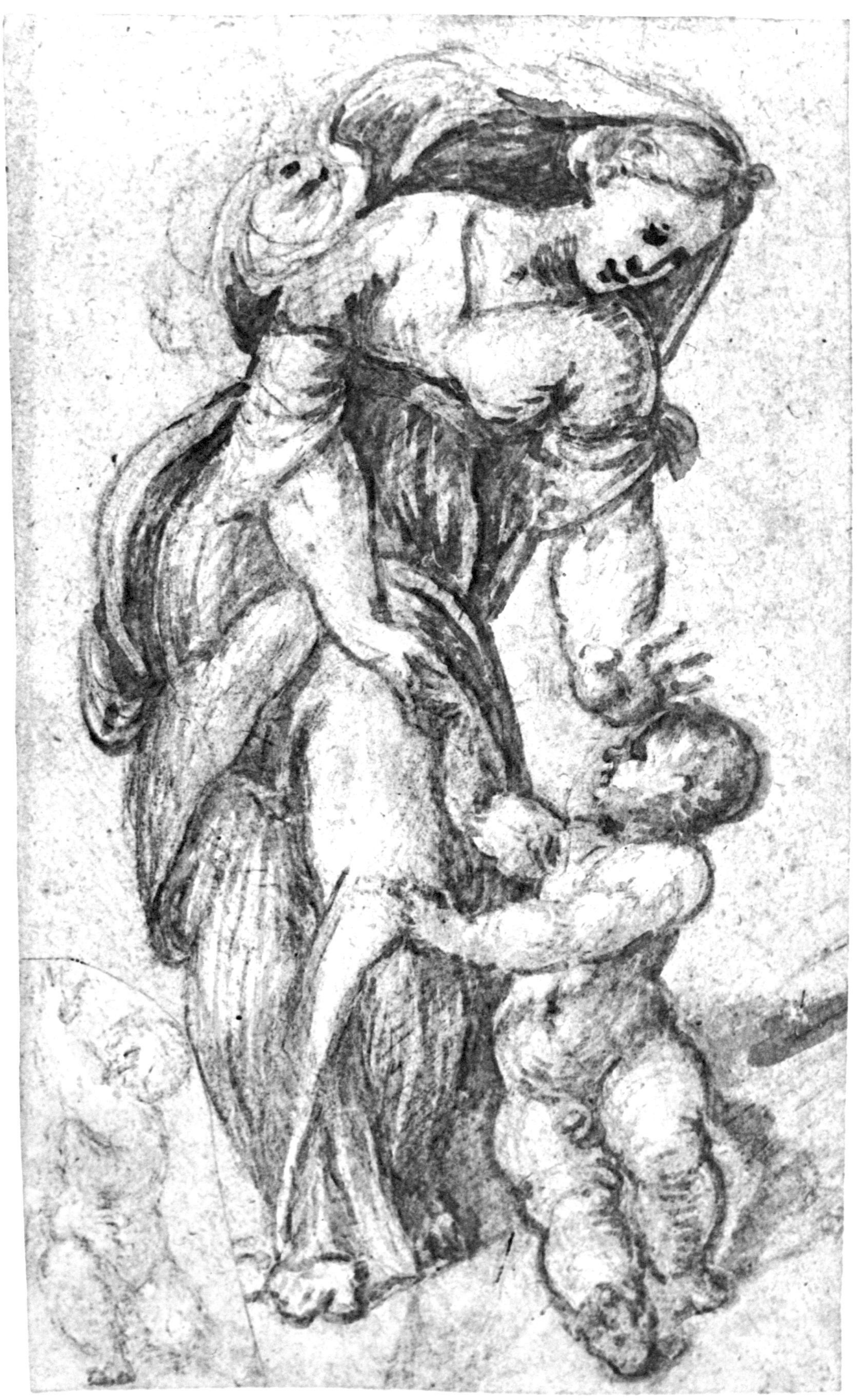

LATTANZIO GAMBARA
BRESCIA ca. 1530–1573/74 BRESCIA

38 *Woman and Child*

Bequest of James Bowdoin III (1811.35) Brush and brown ink, highlighted in white, over black chalk, on blue paper (faded to brown); additional figure lower left on attached sheet (that sheet has been affixed with a page from a fifteenth- or early sixteenth-century Dutch book). 224 x 140 mm. ($8^{13}/16$ x $5^{1}/2$ in.) No watermark. Inscribed pen and ink on old mount, "Paulo Farinate"; red chalk initials on verso of attached book page. PROVENANCE: James Bowdoin III. BIBLIOGRAPHY: *Catalogue* 1885, no. 11 (as Farinati, as are all following); Allen 1886, pt. 5, repr.; Mather 1913, pp. 247–48, repr. fig. 15; *Catalogue* 1930, no. 11; *Handbook* 1981, p. 165.

GAMBARA STUDIED WITH Antonio Campi in Brescia and went with him to Cremona for a period. Returning to Brescia around 1552, he studied with Girolamo Romanino. He worked primarily in that city but executed projects in Mantua, Cremona, and Parma. From 1567 until 1571 Gambara decorated the nave of Parma Cathedral with a cycle of frescoes from the Life of Christ.

Traditionally associated with Paolo Farinati (1524–1606), the Bowdoin drawing is not consistent with his style, and Oberhuber was the first to suggest Gambara as its author. This attribution was affirmed by De Grazia on the basis of a photograph.[1] She tentatively associated it with the fresco of the Massacre of the Innocents in the cathedral at Parma, as perhaps a rejected study, for there are no precisely corresponding figures in the painting.[2] A compositional study for the entire fresco is in the Pierpont Morgan Library (formerly Scholz Collection).[3] There are similarities of draughtsmanship with the Bowdoin sheet in the prominent outlining of facial features and the very regular, stylized definition of drapery. The Bowdoin study cannot be associated firmly with any other painting by Gambara, although a very similar figural group of a mother restraining a small child can be seen in another fresco in Parma of Christ Healing the Sick.[4]

The prominent outlining in the Bowdoin sheet is also clear in a drawing of a seated woman in the Ashmolean Museum, Oxford, and in an earlier sketch for a decorative frieze in the Palazzo Averoldi in Brescia, now in a private Italian collection.[5] These same features are even more evident in Gambara's painted frescoes, such as those for his own house in Brescia or those for the monastery at Rodengo (in which a putto has a very similar pose to that in the Bowdoin drawing).[6] The figures and drapery in an impressive study in the British Museum depicting Jael and Sisera are also similar in style.[7] Here the artist experiments with two different versions of the child's pose. Gambara seems most often to have drawn on colored papers, judging from known works, evidently preferring to draw in a chiaroscuro-like manner.

1. Letter to the author, 8 February 1983. 2. The fresco is repr. in P. V. Begni Redona and G. Vezzoli, *Lattanzio Gambara, Pittore* (Brescia, 1978, p. 185. 3. Ibid., p. 249, no. 26, repr. 4. Ibid., p. 187, repr. 5. Respectively, repr. in ibid., p. 249, no. 28; and p. 243, no. 5. 6. Ibid., pp. 125 and 208, repr. 7. Ibid., p. 246, no. 16.

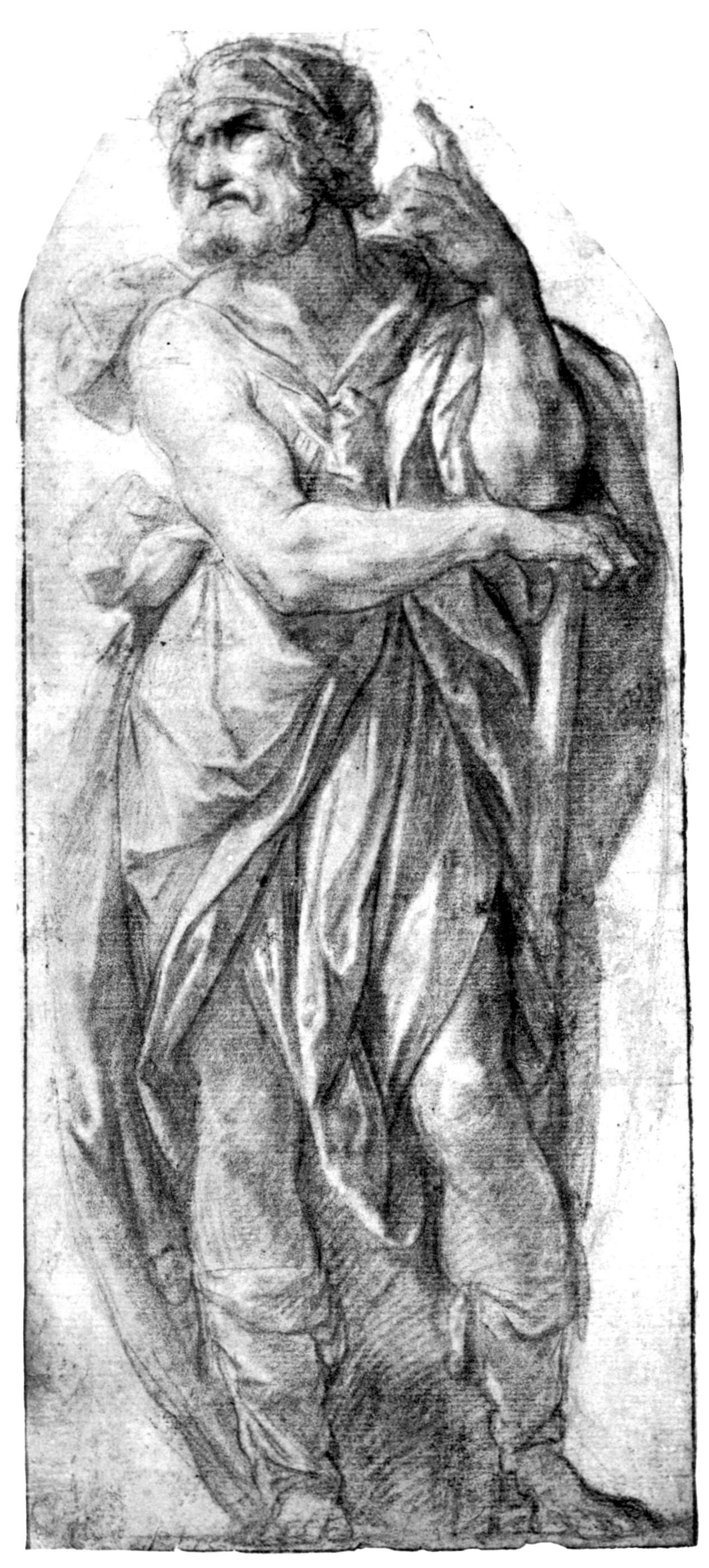

BOLOGNESE, late sixteenth century

39 *Standing Man*

Bequest of James Bowdoin III (1811.36) Red chalk. 275 x 123 mm. (10 13/16 x 4 7/8 in.) Inscribed pen and brown ink on former mount (removed) "Dominiken." Watermark: fleur-de-lis within circle (cf. Briquet 1706—Ferrara 1583). PROVENANCE: James Bowdoin III. BIBLIOGRAPHY: *Catalogue* 1885, no. 18, repr. in large paper edition (as Domenichino, as are all following); Allen 1886, pt. 1, no. 2, repr.; *Catalogue* 1930, no. 18.

THIS SHEET came to the collection with a traditional attribution to Domenichino. Richard Spear, however, suggested looking near Giuseppe Cesari (d'Arpino), and Konrad Oberhuber felt that it is the work of an earlier Bolognese artist working in the 1580s or 1590s. He noted that the strong draughtsmanship resembles the style of Bartolomeo Passarotti, but Passarotti's most characteristic drawings are executed in pen and ink, and red chalk studies by him are not familiar.

Oberhuber has tentatively suggested an artist such as Giovanni Francesco Bezzi, called Nosadella; Lorenzo Sabatini; or Orazio Samacchini. The latter's forceful draughtsmanship can be seen in a study for a seated prophet in the Scholz Collection in the Pierpont Morgan Library.[1] The Bowdoin study would also seem to be for a prophet or hero figure in a decorative project, obviously influenced by Florentine draughtsmanship deriving from Michelangelo.

1. Inv. no. 1981.20, repr. Ottawa 1982, cat. no. 15. Drawings by Sabatini and Samacchini are often confused; the most recent discussion of draughtsmanship of this school is in De Grazia 1984, pp. 330–340.

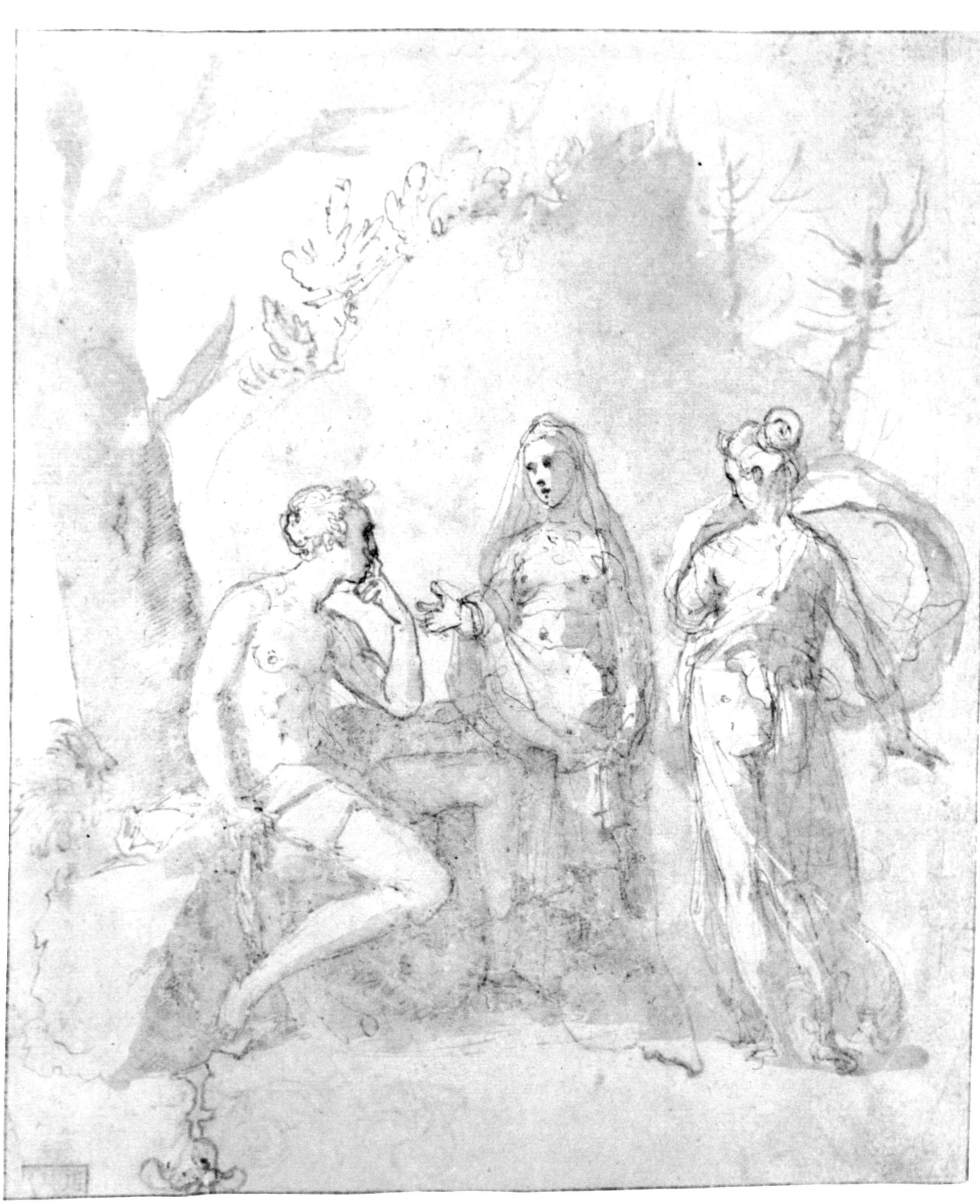

TADDEO ZUCCARO
SANT'ANGELO IN VADO (Marches) 1529–1566 ROME

40 *The Choice of Hercules (?)*

Bequest of James Bowdoin III (1811.62) Pen and brown ink, brown wash, and black chalk (considerable deterioration in areas of young man's legs from iron gall ink; sheet backed with Japanese tissue). 229 x 192 mm. (9 x 7⁹/₁₆ in.) Watermark: fleur-de-lis within double circle with pommel. Verso: sketches of foliate designs in pen and brown ink. PROVENANCE: James Bowdoin III. BIBLIOGRAPHY: *Catalogue* 1885, no. 86 (as Unknown); *Catalogue* 1930, no. 86 (as Unknown); *Handbook* 1981, p. 165 (as Federico Zuccaro). EXHIBITION: Regina and Montreal 1970, cat. no. 15, repr. (as Federico Zuccaro).

TADDEO ZUCCARO came to Rome in 1543 or 1544 and studied the many monuments and paintings there, as recorded in a series of drawings depicting events in his life by his younger brother Federico (1540/41–1609).[1] He began receiving commissions, including one from Pope Julius III, and was called to Urbino in 1551 to help decorate the cathedral there. He made a journey north to Verona in 1552 and was back in Rome the next year. Taddeo spent the rest of his brief career in or near Rome and executed decorations in the Vatican and Farnese Palaces in Rome and Caprarola.

Attributions of drawings by the Zuccaro brothers have frequently been interchanged; this sheet was first attributed to Federico by Vitzthum. Recently, however, both Turner and Pouncey felt it to be Taddeo's. Gere affirmed this attribution, without being able to connect it with a specific project.[2]

The identification of the subject presents some difficulty. The poses and number of the figures certainly resemble Hercules choosing between Virtue and Vice, but the male figure has neither club nor lion skin, the traditional attributes of Hercules. His depiction as a slight youth without attributes is comparatively rare, though certainly not unprecedented.[3] The veiled woman presumably represents Virtue, while Vice has thrown off her veil to tempt the young man. The Choice of Hercules was an extremely popular theme during the Renaissance and occasionally was used as an allegory for the choice open to a young prince contemplating marriage or the inheritance of the realm. Federico Zuccaro used it as an allegory of the artist's struggle to achieve glory.[4]

The technique of the Bowdoin drawing is typical of Taddeo, with the pen outlines, accents, and delicate wash. There are considerable chalk pentimenti under the pen lines, most apparent in the area of the young man's left arm. Unfortunately, the sheet has suffered fading and deterioration of the paper by the ink, but it can be compared with similar studies in the Rosenbach Foundation, Philadelphia; the British Museum; and the Louvre.[5]

1. Gere 1969, pp. 28–29. 2. In conversation with the author, June 1983, from a photograph. 3. See E. Panofsky, *Herkules am Scheidewege* (Berlin, 1930), pls. 53, 61, for instance. 4. See K. Herrmann-Fiore, "Die Fresken Federico Zuccaris in seinem römischen Kunstlerhaus," *Römisches Jahrbuch für Kunstgeschichte*, vol. 18 (1979), esp. pp. 47–54. 5. Gere 1969, pls. 44, 105, 134–36.

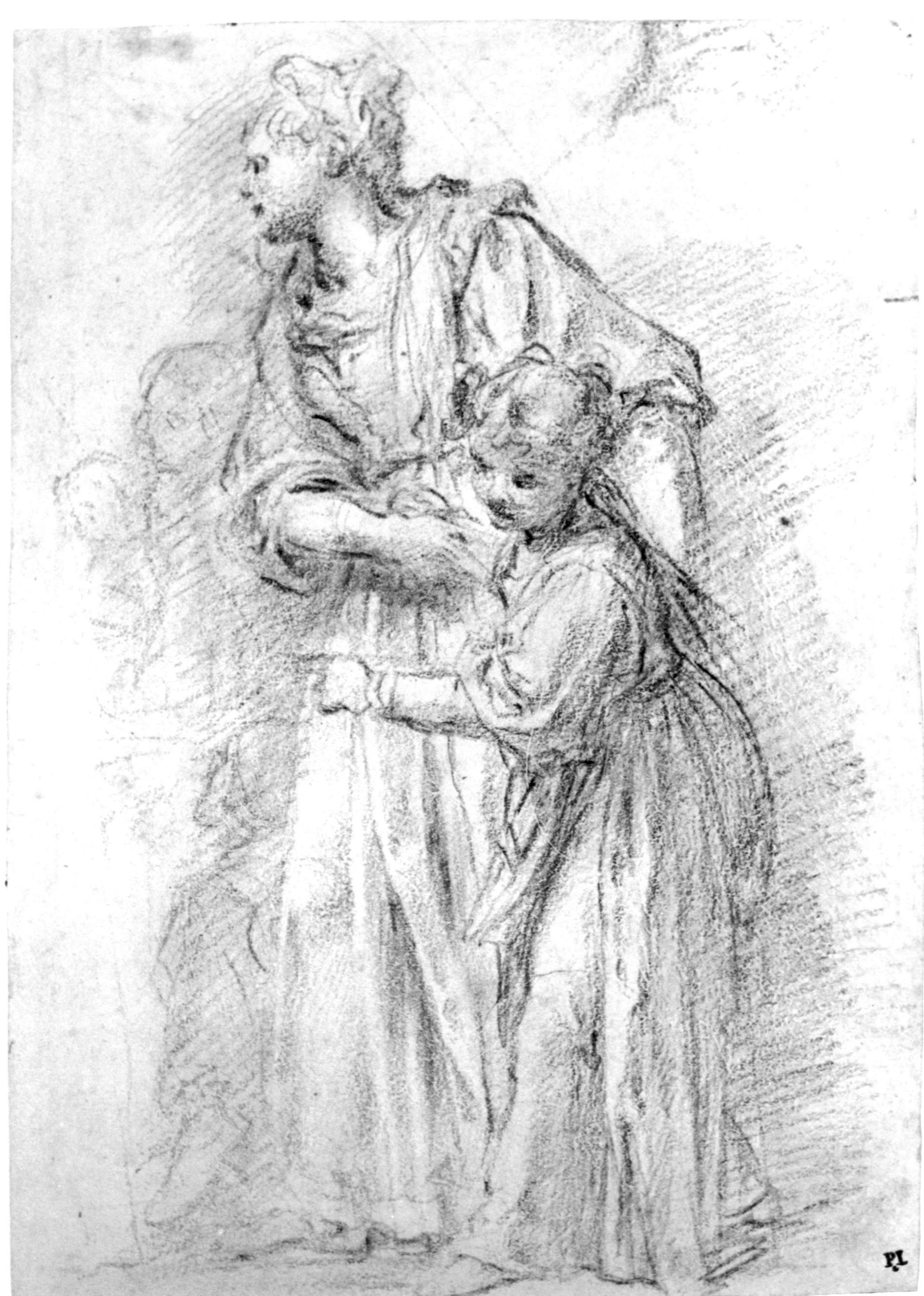

BERNARDINO POCCETTI (Barbatelli)
FLORENCE 1548–1612 FLORENCE

41 *Woman and Child*

Bequest of James Bowdoin III (1811.10) Black and red chalk. 225 x 162 mm. (8⁷/₈ x 6³/₈ in.) Verso black chalk sketch of a leg; inscribed pen and brown ink verso "F. Zuccaro 3.2. / F. Zuc$^{ro.}$" No watermark. PROVENANCE: Sir Peter Lely (1618–1680) (Lugt 2092); James Bowdoin III. BIBLIOGRAPHY: *Catalogue* 1885, no. 14 (as Federico Zuccaro); Mather 1913, p. 248, fig. 14 (as possibly Poccetti); *Catalogue* 1930, no. 14 (as Zuccaro); W. Vitzthum, *Die Handzeichnungen des Bernardino Poccetti* (Ph.D. diss., 1955) (Berlin, 1972), pp. 73–74 (as Poccetti, as are all following); Frerichs 1973, p. 35, under no. 105; Gibbons 1977, vol. 1, p. 161, under no. 500; Florence 1980, p. 80, under no. 62; *Handbook* 1981, p. 165. EXHIBITIONS: Regina and Montreal 1970, cat. no. 27, repr.; Cleveland 1979, cat. no. 21, recto and verso repr.

POCCETTI ENTERED the Guild of St. Luke in Florence in 1570 and the drawing academy there three years later. Trained first as a decorator and painter of facades, he made a trip to Rome ca. 1579/80 and studied architecture with Bernardo Buontalenti. He became a prolific fresco painter in the churches and palaces in and near Florence. Many of his drawings are preserved, primarily in the Uffizi, the Biblioteca Marucelliana, and the Berlin Collections.[1] A group of eight are in the Metropolitan Museum.[2]

Tentatively associated with Poccetti by Mather, this drawing was firmly identified by Vitzthum as a study for one of Poccetti's later commissions. From 1604 to 1612, he painted fourteen lunettes in the Chiostri dei Morti of SS. Annunziata, Florence, depicting incidents from the history of the resident Servite Order. This sketch is a detail study for the figures at the far right of the lunette showing the founding of the order.[3] The curved edge of the lunette format may be seen to the right of the woman's head and behind the child. Vitzthum dated the related fresco ca. 1604–6.[4] Hamilton has compiled the most complete list of the preparatory drawings for this cycle.[5]

Frerichs published an early study by Poccetti for the woman in the Bowdoin drawing in the Rijksprentenkabinet, Amsterdam.[6] It is a large figure study, possibly from life, with the woman's pose not yet completely resolved. Recently, a pen and ink compositional sketch for the entire lunette has been acquired by the Fitzwilliam Museum.[7] The Bowdoin sketch is probably a final preparatory study, as the attitudes of the woman and child are just as in the fresco, having been changed from the earlier Fitzwilliam sketch. The lightly indicated figures to the left of the woman in the Bowdoin drawing are not present in the fresco, and the head of the man also visible here at the left is turned out toward the viewer.

1. Thiem 1977, p. 265. 2. Bean and Turčić 1982, nos. 180–87, repr. 3. Repr. in Venturi, vol. 9, pt. 7, p. 607, fig. 329. 4. Regina and Montreal 1970, p. 38. 5. Florence 1980, pp. 78–82, cat. nos. 66–80. 6. Frerichs 1973, cat. no. 105, repr. 7. Inv. no. PD 15–1980; I am grateful to Lawrence Turčić for bringing this sheet to my attention.

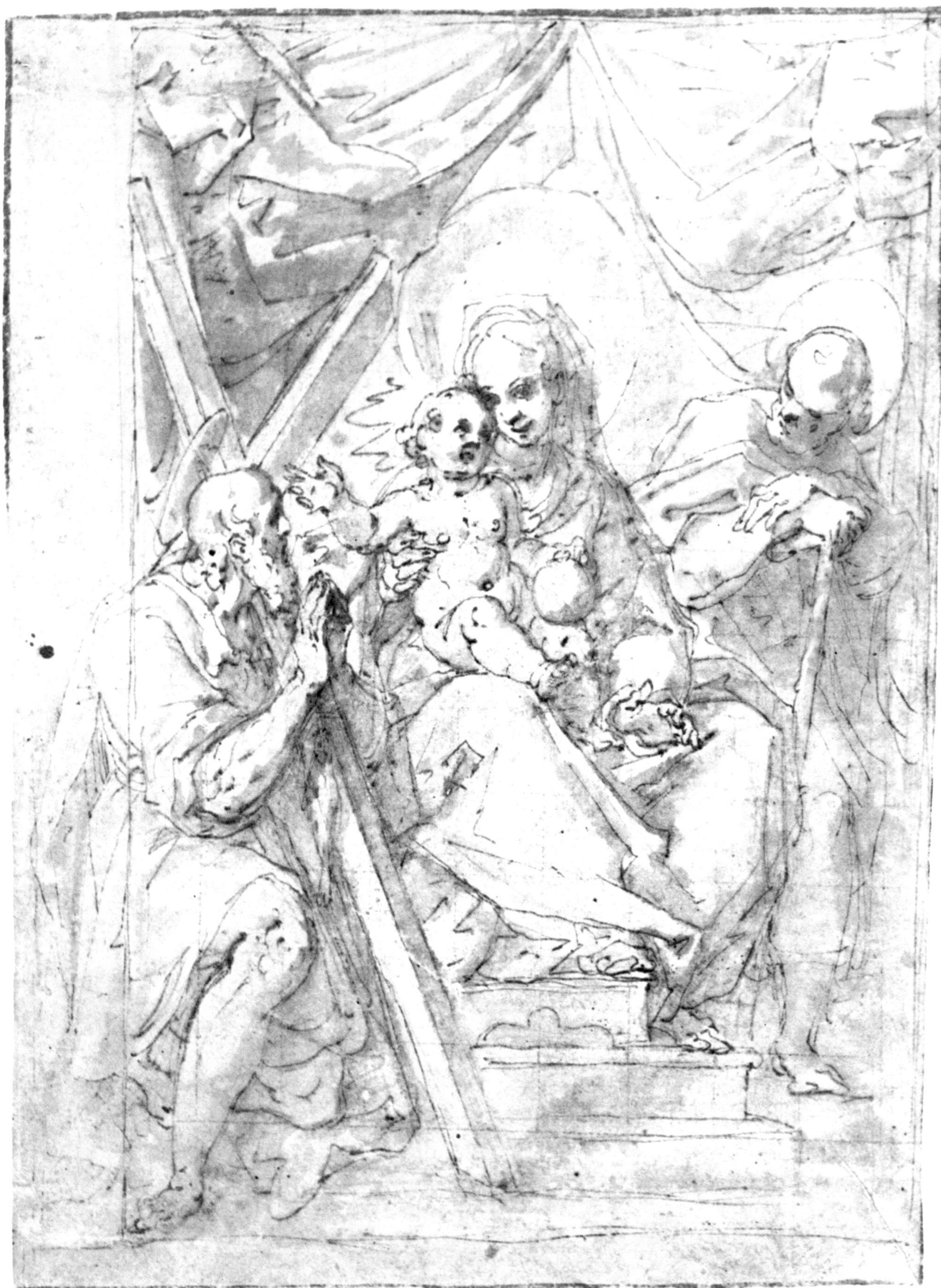

FILIPPO BELLINI

URBINO 1550/55–1604 MACERATA

42 *Holy Family with Saint Andrew*

Bequest of James Bowdoin III (1811.4) Pen and brown ink, brown wash over black chalk, squared in black chalk. 275 x 202 mm. (10 13/16 x 8 in.) Watermark: pilgrim with staff within circle (similar to Briquet 7567). Inscribed on verso of old mount (removed) "No. 8 Coregio." PROVENANCE: James Bowdoin III. BIBLIOGRAPHY: *Catalogue* 1885, no. 4 (as Correggio); Allen 1886, pt. 1, repr. (as Correggio); *Catalogue* 1930, no. 4 (as Correggio); [Siber] 1947, p. 119, repr. fig. 9 (as sixteenth-century Italian influenced by Correggio).

PRESUMABLY ON THE BASIS of the old inscription, this sheet was traditionally given to Correggio, until Witt and Tietze disposed of that attribution.[1] Oberhuber tentatively suggested a Genoese origin close to Paggi, but in 1980 Lawrence Turčić attributed it to Bellini, whose draughtsmanship has only recently been clarified by Monbeig Goguel.[1] She has accepted the Bellini attribution for the Bowdoin drawing.[3]

Although often cited as a student of Federico Barocci, Bellini cannot be shown to have had actual contact with him. He presumably received his early training in Urbino, living there until about 1580. He seems to have worked entirely in the province of Ancona and at Macerata. He worked primarily for the clergy, painting altarpieces and decorations for parish churches and oratories.[4]

The strongly emphasized hand gestures and the fluid pen and wash technique of the Bowdoin drawing are characteristic of Bellini's style. Comparable sheets are in the Hermitage,[5] the Louvre,[6] and the Metropolitan Museum.[7] The saint at the lower left can be identified as St. Andrew by his attributes, a large cross and a fish. No painting for which this sheet is a study has been identified.

1. Notations in museum files from visits. 2. Turčić attributed it from a photograph. 3. Letter to the author, 6 April 1981. 4. Cf. Monbeig Goguel 1975, p. 348ff. 5. Ibid., p. 364, no. 30, repr. M. B. Dobroklonsky, *Hermitage Museum—Drawings of the Italian School of XVII–XVIII Centuries* (Leningrad, 1961), no. 955, pl. 70 (as L. Carracci). 6. Monbeig Goguel 1975, p. 366, no. 59, repr. pl. 11. 7. Ibid., p. 365, no. 47, repr. pl. 9 (also Bean and Turčić 1982, cat. no. 31, repr.).

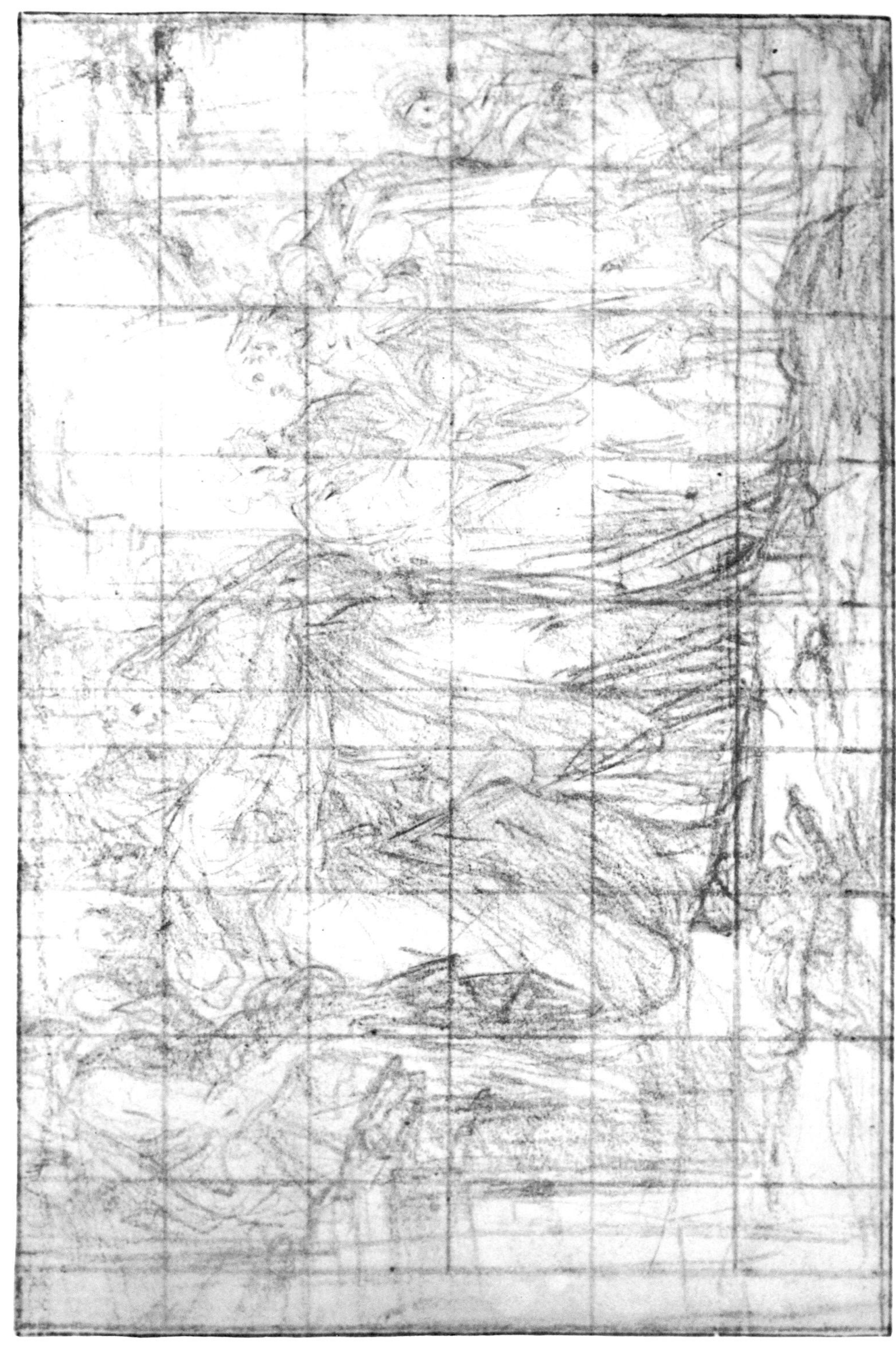

CAMILLO PROCACCINI

BOLOGNA ca. 1555–1629 MILAN

43 *The Visitation*

Bequest of James Bowdoin III (1811.104) Red chalk with touches of black chalk, squared in red chalk, pin holes at ends of squaring lines. 128 x 191 mm. (5 1/16 x 7 1/2 in.) No watermark. Inscribed pen and ink verso of former mount (removed): "G-6./G-22." PROVENANCE: James Bowdoin III. BIBLIOGRAPHY: *Catalogue* 1885, no. 135 (as Unknown); *Catalogue* 1930, no. 135 (as Unknown).

AFTER REMAINING stubbornly among the anonymous Italian drawings for years, this sheet was recently recognized independently by Nicholas Turner and Philip Pouncey as a characteristic work of Procaccini. A member of a dynasty of painters, Camillo was trained in Bologna by his father, Ercole (1520–1595), and moved in 1587 to Milan, where he remained for the rest of his career. He traveled to Rome ca. 1580.

Procaccini executed at least four paintings of the Visitation, and the Bowdoin study is preparatory to his fresco of the subject finished by 1609 for the nave of Piacenza Cathedral.[1] He had been called for the commission in 1605 by Duke Ranuccio Farnese and shared the task with Lodovico Carracci. Procaccini also painted a Death of the Virgin, two Sibyls, and a Pentecost for the cathedral.[2] The Bowdoin study corresponds closely with the finished painting, though the former has apparently been cropped at the top edge. Nancy Neilson knows of no other studies for this painting.[3] Other Procaccini drawings very close to this one in their energized red chalk technique are *David Playing Before Saul* in the Fogg Art Museum[4] and *Flaying of Marsyas* in the British Museum.[5]

1. Neilson 1979, p. 55, no. 77, repr. fig. 146. 2. Ibid., p. 57, under no. 80. 3. Letter to the author, 29 August 1984. 4. Inv. no. 1932.292 (repr. Neilson 1979, fig. 86). 5. Inv. no. 1939-3-11-24 (repr. Neilson 1979, fig. 316).

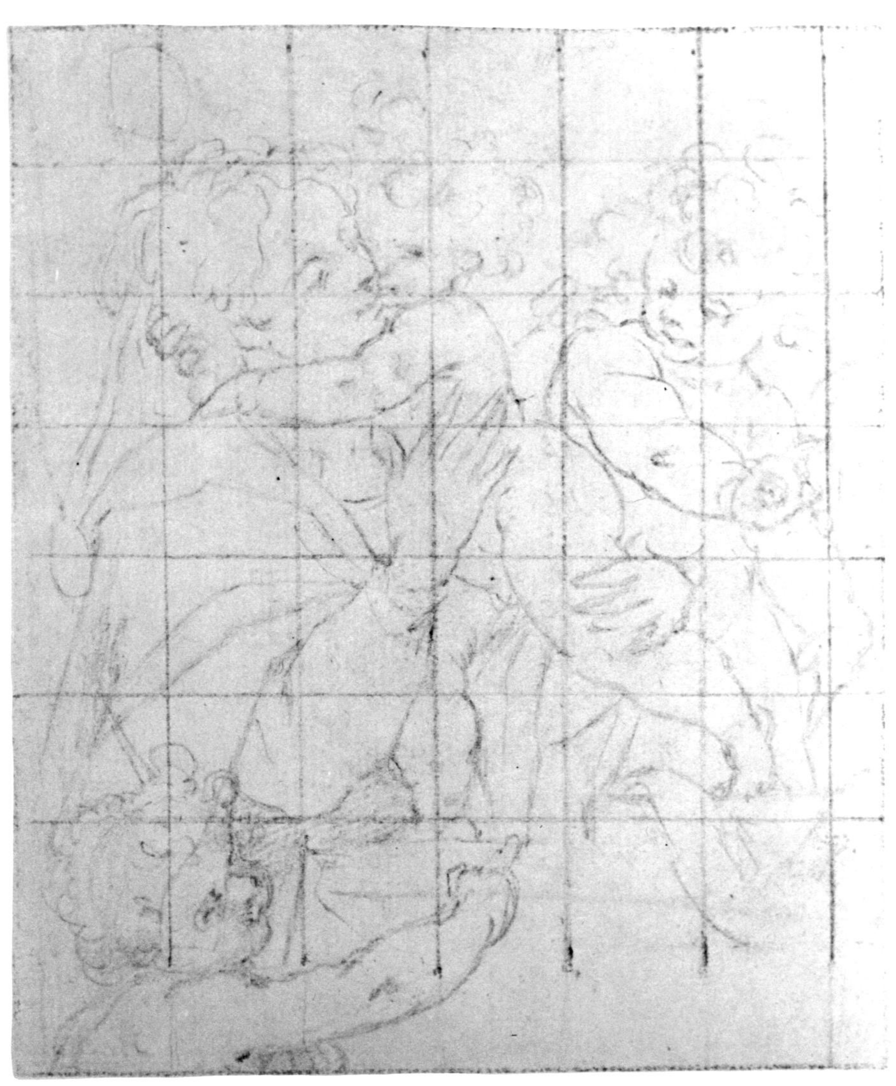

CRISTOFANO RONCALLI

POMERANCE 1551/53–1626 ROME

44 *Madonna and Child with St. John*

Bequest of James Bowdoin III (1811.99) Red chalk, squared in red chalk. 141 x 118 mm. (5 9/16 x 4 5/8 in.) No watermark. Verso sketches and offset black chalk inscriptions. PROVENANCE: James Bowdoin III. BIBLIOGRAPHY: *Catalogue* 1885, no. 82 (as Unknown); *Catalogue* 1930, no. 82 (as Unknown).

RONCALLI'S EARLY ARTISTIC TRAINING is obscure; he moved to Siena in the mid-1570s and to Rome by 1578. There he received many commissions for palace decorations and altarpieces. Pope Clement VIII chose Roncalli to supervise the decoration of his chapel in St. Peter's from 1599 to 1604. He worked often for the Oratory of Filippo Neri. In 1606 he traveled through Europe as far as London, and from 1605 to 1615 he was engaged in Loreto painting frescoes for the Santa Casa there. A member of the Accademia di San Luca in Rome from 1588, Roncalli was a leading exponent of the Counter-Maniera of the 1580s and 1590s.

After tentative attributions had been made to Vanni and Salimbeni, Susan Wegner recognized this sheet as Roncalli's work, citing the more finished version of the same composition in the Uffizi.[1] In that drawing, the forms are fully developed, and the figure of the young St. John at the lower left is not present. Otherwise, the two drawings are identical. Kirwin dates the Uffizi sheet stylistically to 1578–81, soon after Roncalli moved to Rome, when he was feeling the particular influence of his contemporary, Raffaellino da Reggio.[2] Kirwin was not able to connect the Uffizi study to a specific painting but did note two panel paintings, one in the Borghese Gallery, Rome, and the other in a private collection.[3] In both these works, the child to the right of the Madonna and Child in the drawing has been replaced with Joseph. Further, the panel in the private collection also includes the young St. John at the lower left pointing toward the Holy Family—as in the Bowdoin study. Therefore, the latter drawing seems to be a transitional study that Roncalli made while deciding where to place St. John. Indeed, two St. Johns are included: the fact that both the attendant children can be identified with St. John is confirmed by the attributes, the cross held by the left child and the staff with serpent held by the right child. The Uffizi drawing was probably traced to transfer the outlines for the Bowdoin version; the Bowdoin St. John is obviously drawn over the previously traced lower portion of the Uffizi composition. Another instance of Roncalli's use of this outline method of transfer can be seen in a drawing of Charity in the Uffizi.[4]

1. Inv. no. 10081 F, repr. in Uffizi, Gabinetto Disegni e Stampi, *Disegni dei Toscani a Roma (1580–1620)* (exh. cat.) (Florence, 1979), cat. no. 3, fig. 6. 2. Ibid. A lengthy study of Roncalli's drawings was published by Kirwin in "The Life and Drawing Style of Cristofano Roncalli," *Paragone*, no. 335 (1978), pp. 18–62, figs. 28–60. 3. Ibid.; the two paintings are repr. in C. Volpe, "Una precisazione sul Roncalli," *Paragone*, no. 335 (1978), pp. 87–89, figs. 88, 89a. 4. Inv. no. 10015 (Gernsheim 19615).

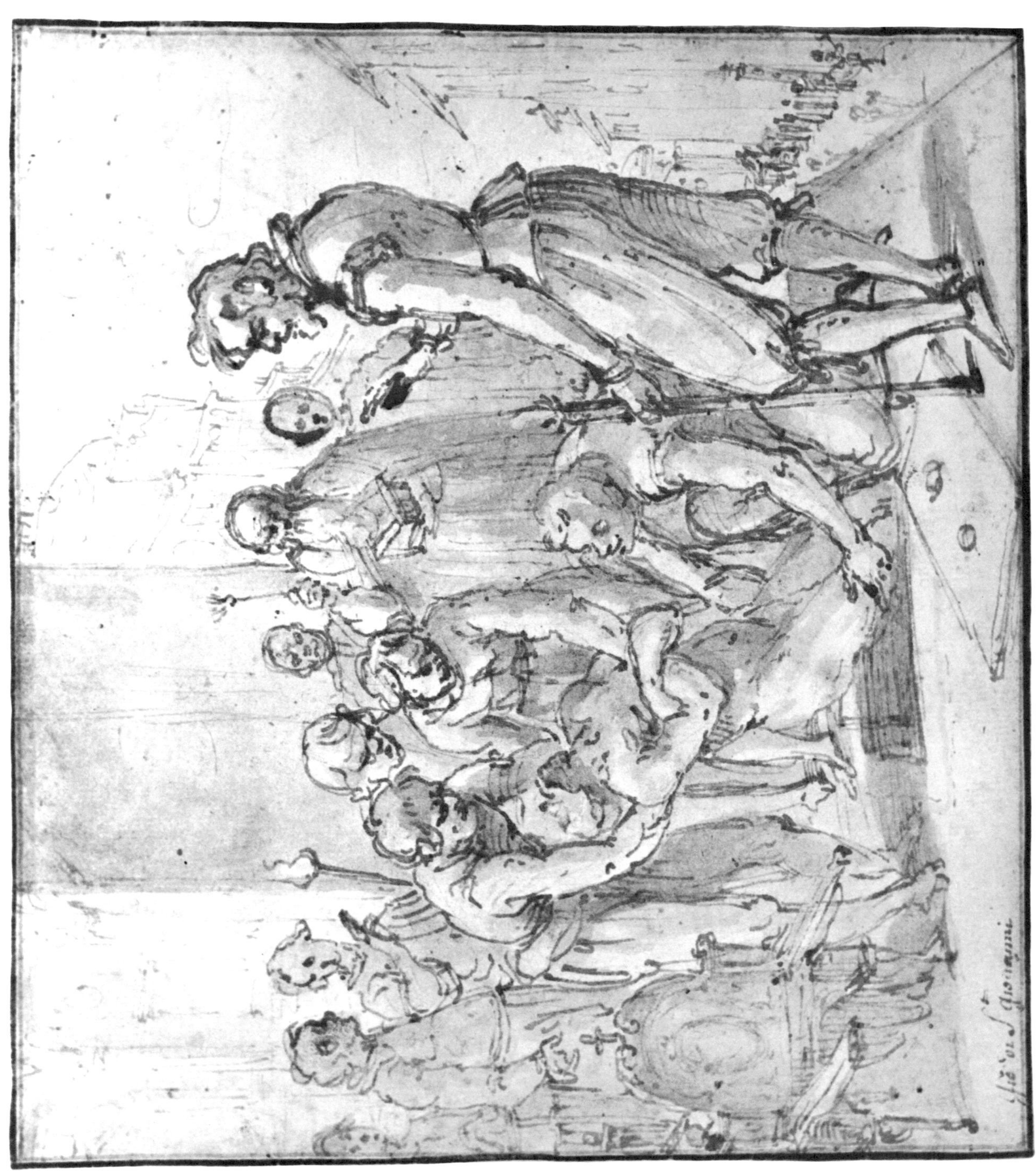

JACOPO CHIMENTI, called da Empoli

FLORENCE 1551–1640 FLORENCE

45 *An Entombment*

Bequest of James Bowdoin III (1811.8) Pen and brown ink with brown wash over graphite and black chalk. 184 x 203 mm. (7¼ x 8 in.) Inscribed pen and brown ink lower left "Gio' di S Giovanni"; graphite verso "C. 7." No watermark. PROVENANCE: James Bowdoin III. BIBLIOGRAPHY: *Catalogue* 1885, no. 19 (as Giovanni da San Giovanni, as are all following); *Catalogue* 1930, no. 19; *Handbook* 1981, p. 166.

THE TRADITIONAL ATTRIBUTION of this sheet to Giovanni Manozzi, called da San Giovanni (1592–1636), has not been accepted by scholars.[1] Though firmly rooted in Florentine baroque draughtsmanship, the drawing's authorship remains less than certain. Philip Pouncey has most firmly proposed Jacopo da Empoli, but other suggestions have been made, including such close contemporaries as Cosimo Gamberucci (ca. 1560–1621) and Lodovico Buti (ca. 1550–1611).[2]

Jacopo da Empoli studied with Maso da San Friano in Florence and entered the Accademia del Disegno in 1576. He is known to have copied the works of Renaissance masters such as Fra Bartolommeo and Pontormo. During the first decades of the seventeenth century, he worked almost exclusively in Tuscany but participated in decorations for Medici festivities and the paintings for the Casa Buonarroti in Florence.

The view in the right distance of the Bowdoin drawing may be a scene in Florence, but the subject, an interment, remains unrecognized. The figure carries no attributes such as religious vestments to aid an identification. The draughtsmanship may be compared with similar composition studies by Jacopo da Empoli in the Ecole des Beaux-Arts, Paris, and the Uffizi.[3] The largest group of his drawings, over four hundred sheets, is in the Uffizi.[4]

1. A Manozzi sheet of a very similar subject in a quite different style is at Oxford (Parker 1956, no. 897, vol. 2, repr. pl. 194). 2. Pouncey first stated his attribution in correspondence with Walter Vitzthum in 1962 and verbally reaffirmed his opinion to the author. The latter two suggestions are from David Scrase and Nicholas Turner, respectively. 3. Thiem 1977, cat. nos. 15, 17; Gabinetto Disegni e Stampe degli Uffizi, *Jacopo da Empoli* (exh. cat. by Anna Forlani) (Florence, 1962), fig. 1. 4. Thiem 1977, p. 272.

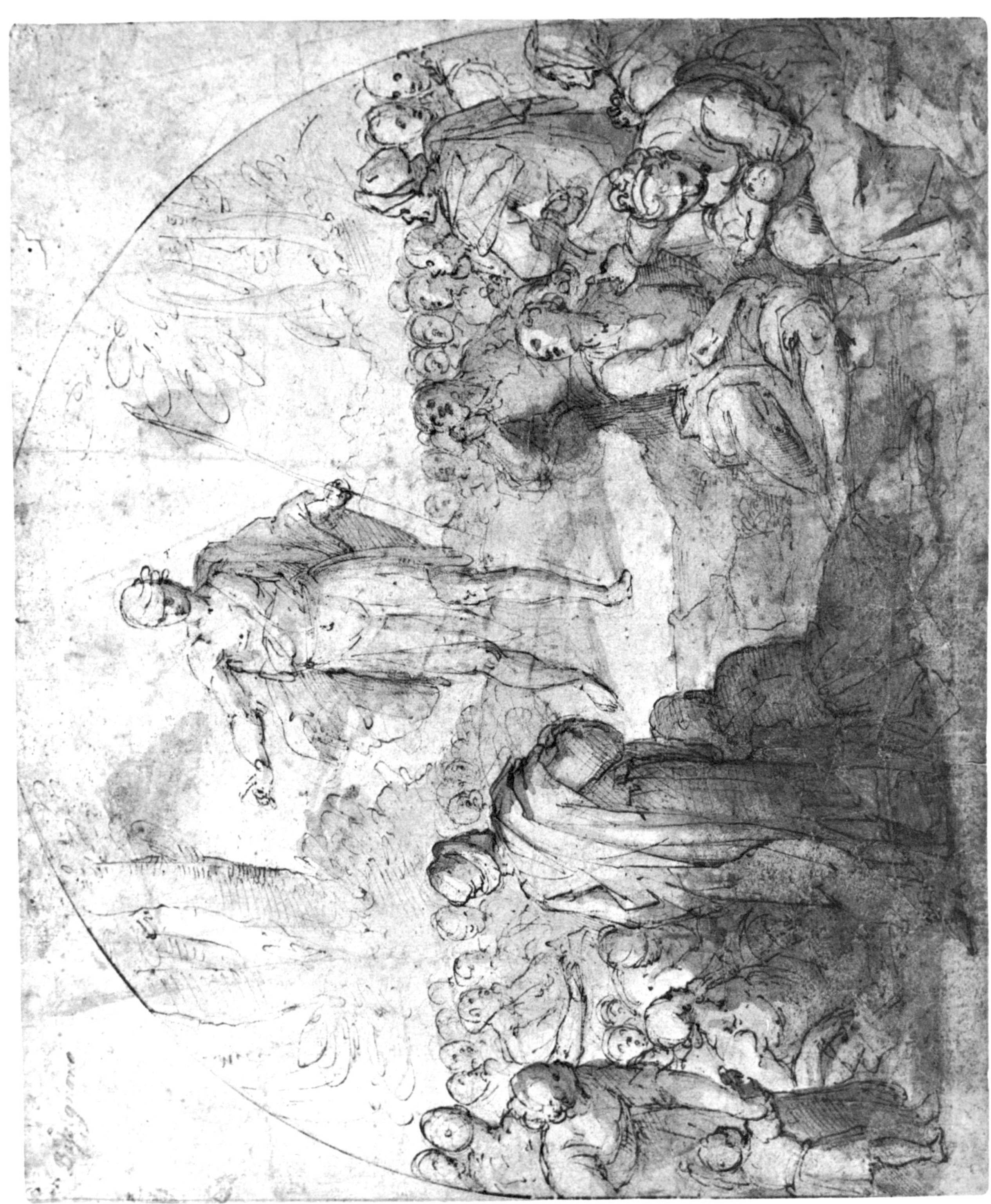

GIOVANNI BALDUCCI (Cosci)
FLORENCE ca. 1560–after 1631 NAPLES

46 *St. John the Baptist Preaching*

James Phinney Baxter Fund in Memory of Professor Henry Johnson (1932.42) Pen and brown ink and brown wash over black chalk (loss in standing figure in foreground, folds, splits). 269 x 325 mm. (10 9/16 x 12 13/16 in.) No watermark. Inscribed upper left, pen and brown ink "Bassignano"; verso, pen and brown ink "Anno 1659 [further illegible writing]." PROVENANCE: Professor Henry Johnson. BIBLIOGRAPHY: *Handbook* 1981, p. 165 (as attributed to Balducci).

BALDUCCI STUDIED IN FLORENCE with Giovanni Battista Naldini (ca. 1537–1591), and had accompanied him to Rome by about 1590. They often collaborated on commissions in both cities. Around 1600, Balducci moved to Naples, where he spent the rest of his life, executing numerous important religious commissions.

This sheet carried a traditional attribution to Domenico Cresti, Il Passignano (ca. 1558/60–1638), understandable in the light of his own study with Naldini and his work in Florence during the 1590s.[1] Philip Pouncey was apparently the first scholar to recognize the draughtsmanship as Balducci's.[2] Martin Hopkinson identified the design as a preparatory study for a lunette in the church of San Giovanni Decollato, Rome.[3] It is located above the doorway into the oratory and was painted around 1590.[4]

There is a subsequent study for the same painting in the Fogg Art Museum.[5] The Fogg sheet has been squared for transfer and is quite close to the final composition, even to cuts in the lower corners to allow for protruding moldings in the church.[6] The painting retains such principal figures from the Bowdoin sheet as St. John, the mother and child at lower right, the standing figures at the right, the prominent standing figure at left, and the two reclining figures on the left. Several of the onlookers at the rear are eliminated in the painting; a few of the major figural groups have been differently placed, and two of the figures now look toward the viewer. The Fogg drawing represents an intermediate step in the composition. A drawing quite comparable in graphic style to the Bowdoin and Fogg sheets is a Resurrection in the Louvre, a preparatory study for Balducci's painting in the Oratorio dei Pretori in Florence, also dated 1590.[7]

The Fogg Balducci has at times been attributed to Naldini, which has been the source for some confusion.[8] Coincidentally, another sheet of the same subject in the Fogg collection is indeed a study by Naldini for his painting in the vault of the Altoviti Chapel of SS. Trinità dei Monti in Rome.[9] There are striking parallels between the works by master and student, including the basic composition and several of the prominent figures. The pose of St. John is reversed between the two paintings. Balducci treated the subject of St. John Preaching on at least one other occasion, in a small vertical grisaille oil sketch now in the Walker Art Gallery, Liverpool.[10]

1. He also executed a painting of St. John Preaching (repr. in Freedberg 1979, fig. 282). 2. Note on the mount of the Witt Library photograph. There is an unsigned and undated ascription on the mat of the drawing itself. 3. Letter to the author, 6 November 1974, mentioning that the painting was recorded by Baglione. 4. Cf. Buchowiecki 1967–1974, vol. 2, p. 80. 5. Inv. no. 1969.113: pen and brown ink, brown wash over black chalk, squared in black chalk, 275 x 335 mm. 6. I am grateful to Susan Wegner for a photograph of the painting. 7. Repr. in P. Pouncey, "A 'Modello' at Hampton Court for a Fresco in Rome," *Burlington Magazine*, vol. 93, no. 583 (October 1951), p. 323, fig. 29. 8. Oberhuber and Pillsbury have orally attributed the Fogg drawing to Naldini, connecting it with his Trinità dei Monti ceiling (Fogg files). Röttgen and Kirwin also attributed it to Naldini,

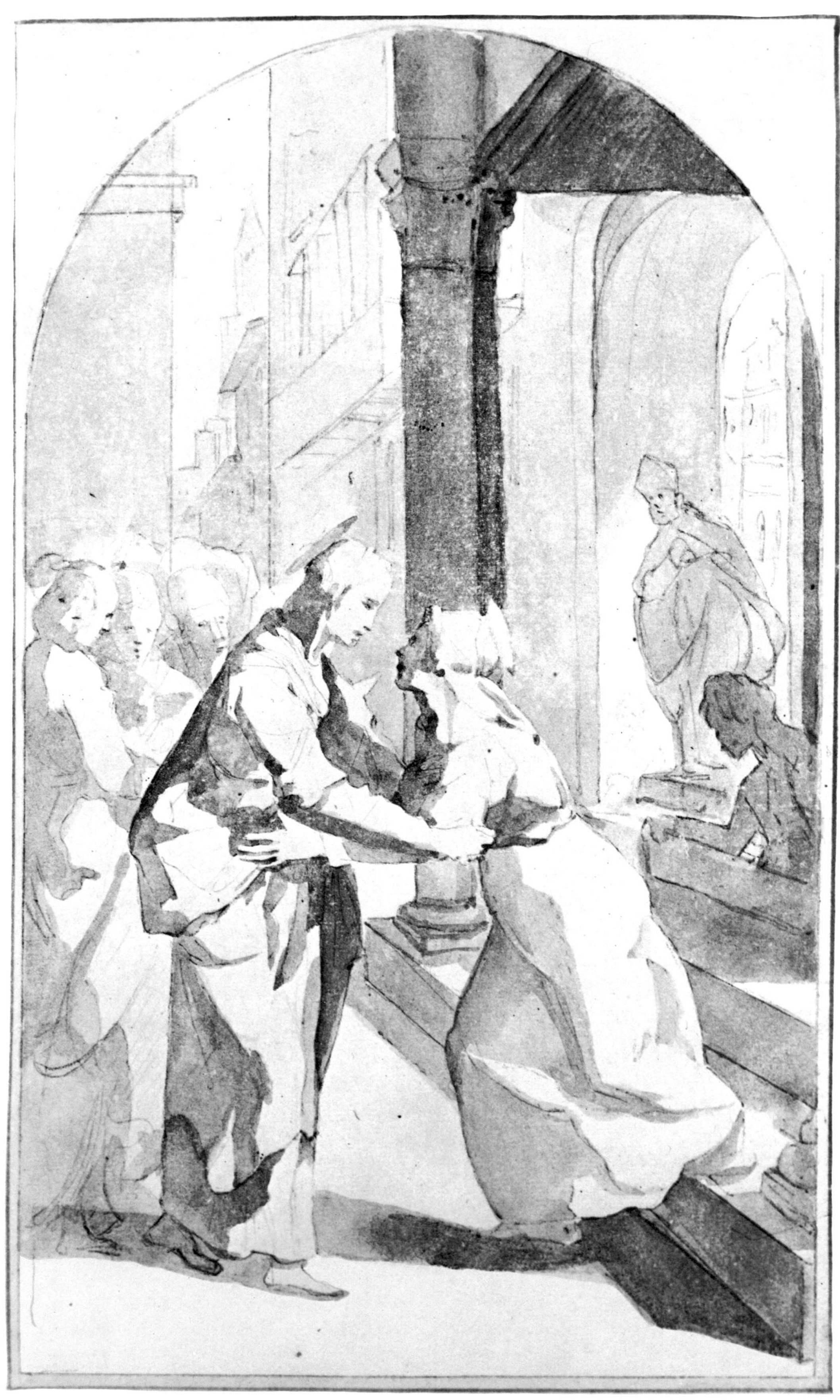

saying that it is preparatory to the S. Giovanni Decollato painting (Fogg files). However, both Turner (letter to Fogg, 11 June 1982) and Pouncey (verbally to author) have recently affirmed the attribution of the sheet to Balducci. 9. Inv. no. 1932.300, formerly attributed as Venetian (Mongan and Sachs 1940, vol. 1, no. 201). The painting is illustrated in P. Barocchi, "Itinerario di Giovambattista Naldini," *Arte antica e moderna*, nos. 31–32 (December 1965), pl. 104b. 10. Sold at Sotheby's London, 9 December 1959, lot no. 2, it measures 11 x 8 3/8 in.; I am grateful to Mr. Hopkinson for a photograph.

ANDREA BOSCOLI

FLORENCE ca. 1560–1607 FLORENCE

47 *The Visitation*

Bequest of James Bowdoin III (1811.7) Brush and grey wash over black chalk and graphite. 232 x 140 mm. (9 1/8 x 51/2 in.) No watermark. Inscribed graphite verso "15"; in graphite on old mount (removed): "Mola." PROVENANCE: James Bowdoin III. BIBLIOGRAPHY: *Catalogue* 1885, no. 20 (as Mola); *Catalogue* 1930, no. 20 (as Mola); *Handbook* 1981, p. 165 (as Boscoli).

AFTER CARRYING an unlikely attribution to a seventeenth-century artist, Pier Francesco Mola, this drawing was recognized as a thoroughly characteristic work by Boscoli.[1] Boscoli pursued a quite individual style within late sixteenth-century Florentine mannerism, after studying with Santi di Tito. He also traveled and worked in Rome, Siena, and Pisa, and between 1600 and 1606 in the province of the Marches. Many drawings of his survive (principally in the Uffizi) and often show the typical facetted surfaces of his figures evident here. He made quite a few copies from other masters. Viatte has remarked on Boscoli's strong stylistic connections with the many northern artists who were working in Italy during the late sixteenth century, forerunners of the later northern mannerists, such as Spranger and Goltzius.[2]

The Bowdoin drawing can be related to an altarpiece in Sant' Ambrogio in Florence, dating from 1596/1597,[3] for which it is a very close study. The major modifications in the painting are the closing of the vista and the enlargement of the ecclesiastical figure in the right background. A related drawing very close in conception and dimensions is in the Museo Cerralbo, Madrid.[4] That sheet is probably earlier than the Bowdoin version, for the figure in the right distance is even less resolved, and the perspective lines of the composition are quite apparent beneath the figures. The Bowdoin sheet appears to be a carefully prepared *modello*, with subtle application of washes. Forlani indicates a probable preliminary study for this commission in a horizontal format in the Uffizi.[5]

1. The source of the correct attribution is unknown; both Bean and Vitzthum affirmed its authorship on visits during the 1960s. 2. Paris 1981–1982, pp. 62, 64. 3. Forlani 1963, p. 129, no. 8, repr. pl. 85. 4. Inv. no. 4938, repr. in its *Catalogo de dibujos* (Madrid, 1976), no. 10. 5. Forlani 1963, p. 146, no. 100, Inv. no. 8218F.

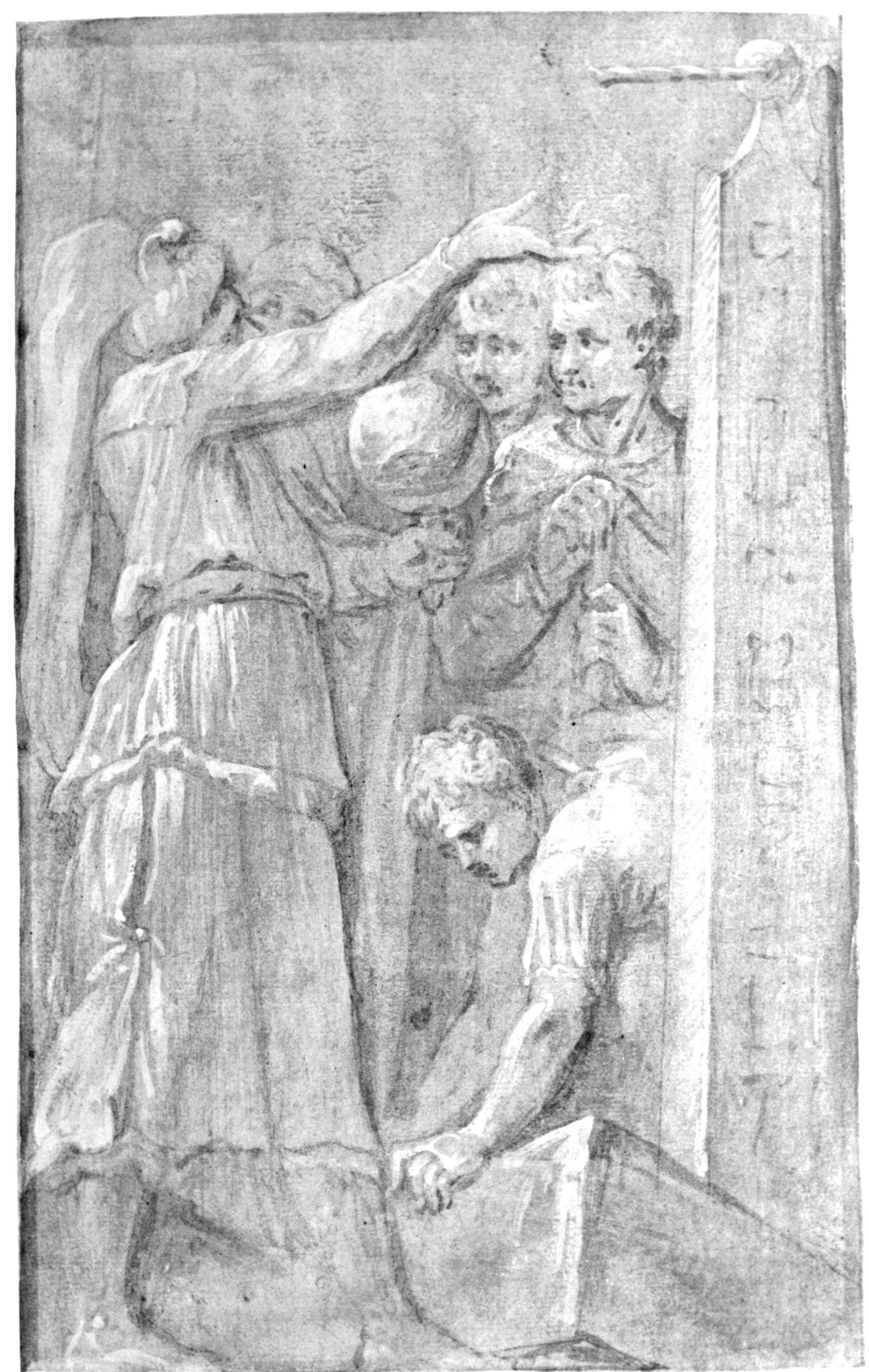

BELISARIO CORENZIO

NAPLES ca. 1560–after 1640 NAPLES

48 *Figures around an Obelisk*

Bequest of James Bowdoin III (1811.58) Brush and grey and blue wash, heightened with white, on brown paper (blue faded from exposure to light). 242 x 152 mm. (9 1/2 x 6 in.) No watermark. PROVENANCE: James Bowdoin III. BIBLIOGRAPHY: *Catalogue* 1885, no. 77 (as Unknown); *Catalogue* 1930, no. 77 (as Unknown); *Handbook* 1981, p. 166 (as Corenzio).

THIS DRAWING was first connected to the school of Polidoro da Caravaggio (1490/1500–ca. 1543) by Filippo di Pietro.[1] The flat, relief-like treatment of the subject and the low viewpoint are characteristic of the style of Polidoro's many grisaille paintings of house facades in Rome. These paintings inspired numerous later artists, who copied them in drawings and engravings. The Bowdoin drawing can be assumed to have been copied from the same source as another drawing in an album taken primarily from Polidoro's designs; that album is now in the Lugt Collection, Institut Néerlandais, Paris.[2] The album is said to have been in the collections of Andrea Sacchi and Carlo Maratti, and the drawings have recently been convincingly attributed to Cherubino Alberti (1553–1615).[3] Sixty-three sheets in the album were engraved in 1791 by Conrad Metz, including the one with the same subject as the Bowdoin work.[4]

Jacob Bean attributed this drawing to Corenzio in 1963, recognizing the characteristic brush style with blue wash. A drawing of Joshua done in the same manner is in the Scholz Collection, New York.[5] Corenzio worked in the Tintoretto shop in Venice during the early 1580s, where, it is thought, he developed his distinctive style.[6] He spent most of his career in Naples and was a prolific decorator of churches there. It is not known specifically when Corenzio copied the presumed Polidoro model for this drawing, which reveals considerably more detail than the Alberti sketch and Metz print after the latter. The specific subject has not been identified;[7] Susan Wegner has tentatively suggested that it might be connected with Polidoro's designs for the Casa Boniauguri in Rome.[8]

1. Note on the verso of an old photograph in museum files. 2. Byam Shaw 1983, vol. 2, pp. 30–31, repr. pl. 47. 3. J. Byam Shaw, review of Gere and Pouncey 1983 in *Burlington Magazine*, vol. 125, no. 966 (September 1983), p. 552. 4. Pl. 34 (reversed) in *Schediasmata selecta*, 1791 (cf. Byam Shaw 1983, vol. 2, pp. 30–31). 5. Stampfle and Bean 1967, cat. no. 16, repr. 6. Ibid., p. 27, under no. 16. 7. Byam Shaw (1983, pp. 30–31) has very tentatively suggested the erection of a sundial. However, the staff of the Department of Egyptian and Near Eastern Art, Museum of Fine Arts, Boston, has informed the author that sundials were not known in ancient Egypt. 8. One subject from those decorations, known from an engraving, is repr. in Marabottini 1969, pl. 129, no. 1.

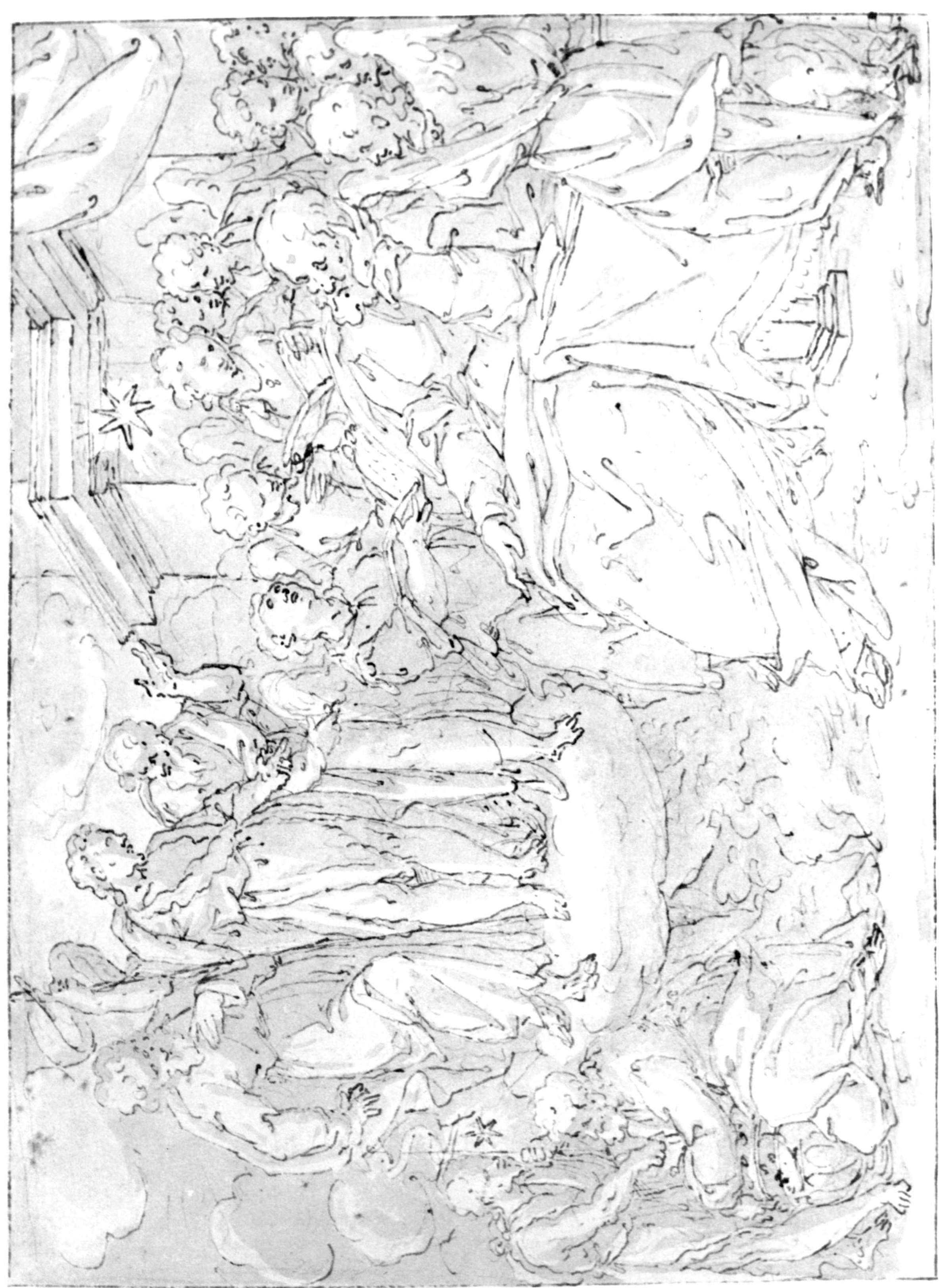

GIOVANNI BATTISTA DELLA ROVERE

MILAN ca. 1561–after 1627 MILAN

49 *The Vision of St. Marcellus*

Bequest of James Bowdoin III (1811.114) Pen and brown ink, brown wash over black chalk (border of pen and black ink). Sheet 207 x 282 mm. (8 1/8 x 11 1/8 in.) Image 173 x 236 mm. (6 13/16 x 9 5/16 in.) Inscribed pen and brown ink verso (crossed out) "2-6." No watermark. PROVENANCE: James Bowdoin III. BIBLIOGRAPHY: *Catalogue* 1885, no. 132 (as Unknown); *Catalogue* 1930, no. 132 (as Unknown).

GIOVANNI BATTISTA DELLA ROVERE and his younger brother, Giovanni Mauro (ca. 1575–1640), both spent their entire careers working primarily for the churches and religious societies in and around Milan. They were sons of a transplanted Flemish glass painter and were both, as a result, known as "Il Fiammenghino."

This drawing was first given by Judson to Marten de Vos, a Flemish artist whose many religious works are compositionally and stylistically similar to those of della Rovere.[1] Yet here the draughtsmanship is more fluid than de Vos's and indicates instead the della Rovere brothers. Jacob Bean gave this sheet to Giovanni Mauro in 1963, and Lawrence Turčić gave it in 1980 to Giovanni Battista. The latter seems closer because of peculiarities of the facial features and pen technique. The Bowdoin sheet is not initialled and dated, as are many of Giovanni Battista's drawings (see Cat. 192 for one at Bowdoin). An apt comparison may be made with a large design in the List Collection of the Death and Transportation of the Body of St. Dionysius, datable about 1599.[2] Another similar sheet is in the Metropolitan Museum, dated 1590.[3]

The subject of the Bowdoin drawing remained obscure until recently, when Susan Wegner identified it as the monk Marcellus's vision of St. John the Baptist. One of the many legends surrounding the relics of St. John after his martyrdom at the order of Herod, this story is told in Jacobus de Voragine, *Legenda Aureum* (*The Golden Legend*), written ca. 1275.[4] Several centuries after his death, the location of St. John's buried head is miraculously revealed to two monks, who move it, only to have it stolen by another, who hides it in a cave near the city of Emissene. St. John reveals himself in a vision to Marcellus, a monk who lives in the cave. The Baptist appears flanked by two figures and preceded by many singers. The next night, the monk sees a star and follows it to a spot where the pot with the head of St. John lies buried, and he recovers it. The author of the *Golden Legend* specifies that this story comes from the *Historia Scholastica*.

Della Rovere's design follows the legend precisely, except that the setting does not resemble a cave. The two episodes of the story are here depicted together. This drawing may be preparatory to a scene from a cycle of frescoes devoted to St. John the Baptist executed around 1580 for the Cathedral at Monza, near Milan.[5]

1. Comments in the museum files on two visits, 1962 and 1968. 2. Repr. in Staatliche Graphische Sammlung, *Stiftung Ratjen—Italienische Zeichnungen des 16.–18. Jahrhunderts* (exh. cat.) (Munich and other places, 1977–1978), cat. no. 17. 3. Bean and Turčić 1982, no. 228, repr. 4. *The Golden Legend, or Lives of the Saints*, trans. W. Caxton, ed. F. S. Ellis (London, 1900), vol. 5, pp. 73–74. 5. Freedberg 1979, p. 709, n. 30.

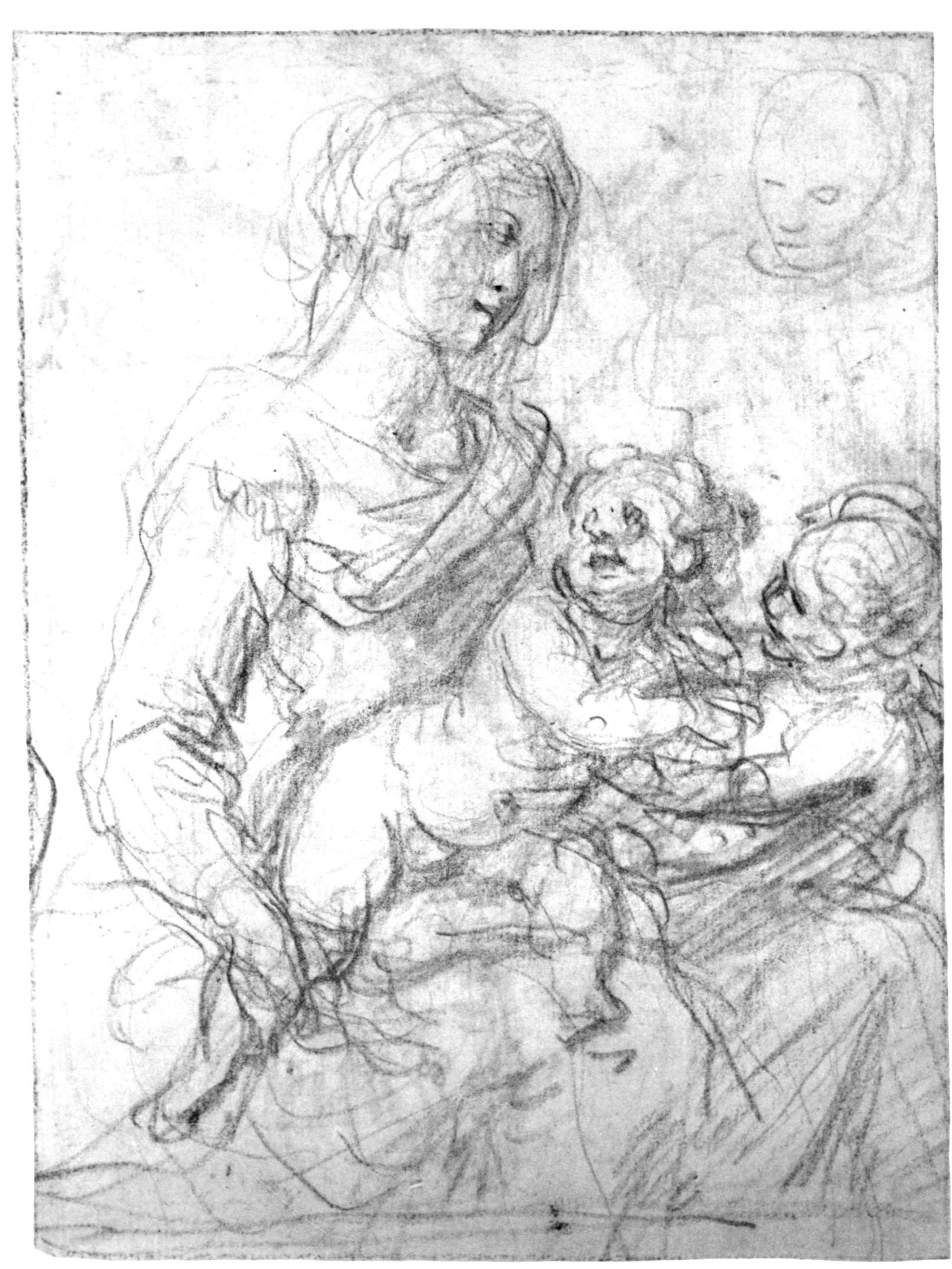

FRANCESCO VANNI
SIENA 1563–1610 SIENA

50 *The Holy Family with St. John* (verso: *Madonna and Child*)

Bequest of James Bowdoin III (1811.9) Red chalk over black chalk. 177 x 134 mm. (7 x 5 1/4 in.) Inscribed pen and ink, verso of former mount (lost) "Vani da Siena." No watermark. PROVENANCE: James Bowdoin III. BIBLIOGRAPHY: *Catalogue* 1885, no. 15; *Catalogue* 1930, no. 15; *Handbook* 1981, p. 166. EXHIBITIONS: Cleveland 1979, cat. no. 72, recto and verso repr.; Miami, Center for the Fine Arts, *In Quest of Excellence—Civic Pride, Patronage, Connoisseurship*, 14 January – 22 April 1984, cat. no. 41, repr.

THE ATTRIBUTION to Vanni of this double-sided sheet is traditional, deriving from the old inscription on the former mount. Vanni first trained in Siena with his stepfather, Arcangelo Salimbeni, and after Salimbeni's death in 1580 he traveled to Rome, where he studied for two years. He worked there with Giovanni de' Vecchi, in addition to studying works of antiquity and Renaissance masterpieces. After journeying to Bologna and Lombardy around 1584, he settled in Siena for the rest of his career. Vanni continued to work for Roman patrons and executed *The Fall of Simon Magus*, a large altarpiece for St. Peter's, in 1603.

Alessandro Bagnoli, Peter Anselm Riedl, and Susan Wegner have accepted Vanni's authorship of the Bowdoin sheet, but recently other scholars have preferred to place it in a Florentine context. Both Pouncey and Turner have tentatively suggested Cigoli, while Chappell has pointed toward Giovanni Bilivert, Baldassare Franceschini (Volterrano), or Pignoni. Chiara d'Afflitto has proposed Ottavio Vannini as a possibility.[1]

However, Wegner has proposed both drawn comparisons with the Bowdoin sheet and convincing relationships with several small devotional paintings executed by Vanni around 1600.[2] The expressive sketchiness of the studies on each side renders precise correspondences difficult, but certain chalk studies in Siena and Florence are comparable. A sheet in Siena contains a close parallel with the two babies on the recto of the Bowdoin drawing.[3] As Wegner has pointed out, the head of the Virgin on both sides of this sheet is shifted between two positions, with the artist developing alternate solutions in each case; another Vanni chalk study in the Uffizi for a painting of St. Thomas Nacci shows a similar treatment of shifting expression.[4]

(Text continued overleaf)

1. Pouncey and Turner in conversation with the author, 1983; Chappell in letters to the author, 8 September and 29 November 1983; d'Afflitto in conversation with Katharine Watson, 1982. 2. A detailed article by Susan Wegner on this sheet is in preparation, from which much of the following information is derived. I am extremely grateful to her for discussing this drawing in great detail and sharing much unpublished information. 3. Biblioteca Comunale, Inv. no. S. III. 9/56 verso; repr. in P. A. Riedl, "Zu Francesco Vannis Tätigkeit für römische Auftraggeber," *Mitteilungen des Kunsthistorischen Institut in Florenz*, vol. 22, no. 3 (1978), p. 345, fig. 42. 4. Inv. no. 1696E, repr. Uffizi, *Disegni dei Barocceschi Senesi—Francesco Vanni e Ventura Salimbeni* (exh. cat. by P. A. Riedl) (Florence, 1976), cat. no. 8, fig. 9.

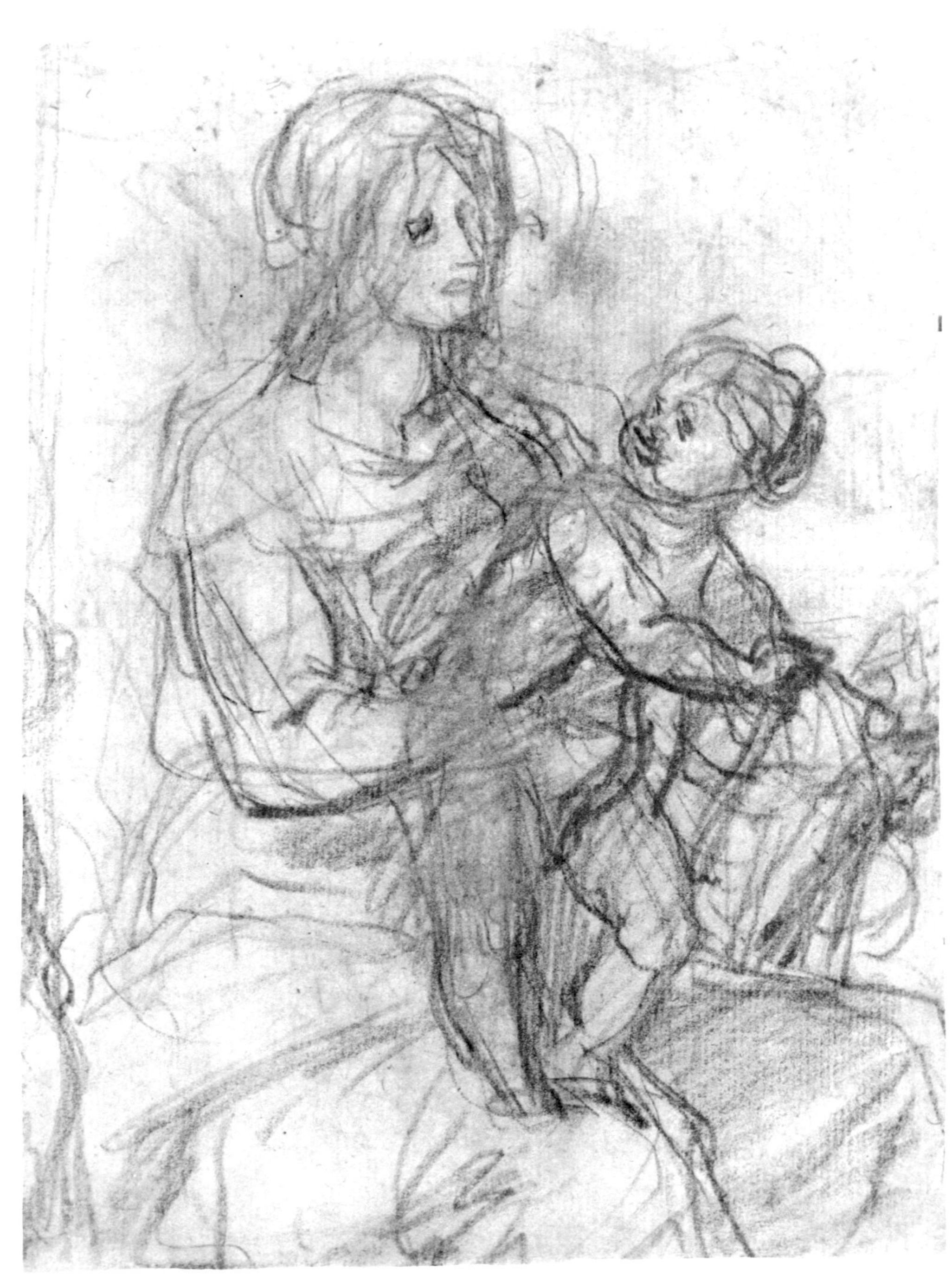

Vanni produced quite a few small-scale paintings of the Virgin and Child, among which Wegner has found similarities to the Bowdoin drawing in *The Madonna and Child with a Book* in the Church Gallery of the Gerolamini, Naples (particularly with the verso), and *Madonna and Child with Saints* in the Borghese Gallery, Rome.[5] All the paintings share with the Bowdoin sheet a carefully refined, almost sweet, relationship of the Christ Child with the Madonna, often involving an upward or backward glance toward his mother as he moves outward in another gesture. The verso of the Bowdoin sketch shows the Christ Child holding a book, as in the Naples painting cited above. None of the paintings cited show the infant St. John as he appears in the recto of the Bowdoin drawing.

This drawing has been cut from a considerably larger sheet of sketches, perhaps including several more variations on the Madonna and Child theme. At the left edge of the verso there is what appears to be a fragment of another sketch of the standing Christ Child.

5. The Borghese painting is Inv. no. 62.

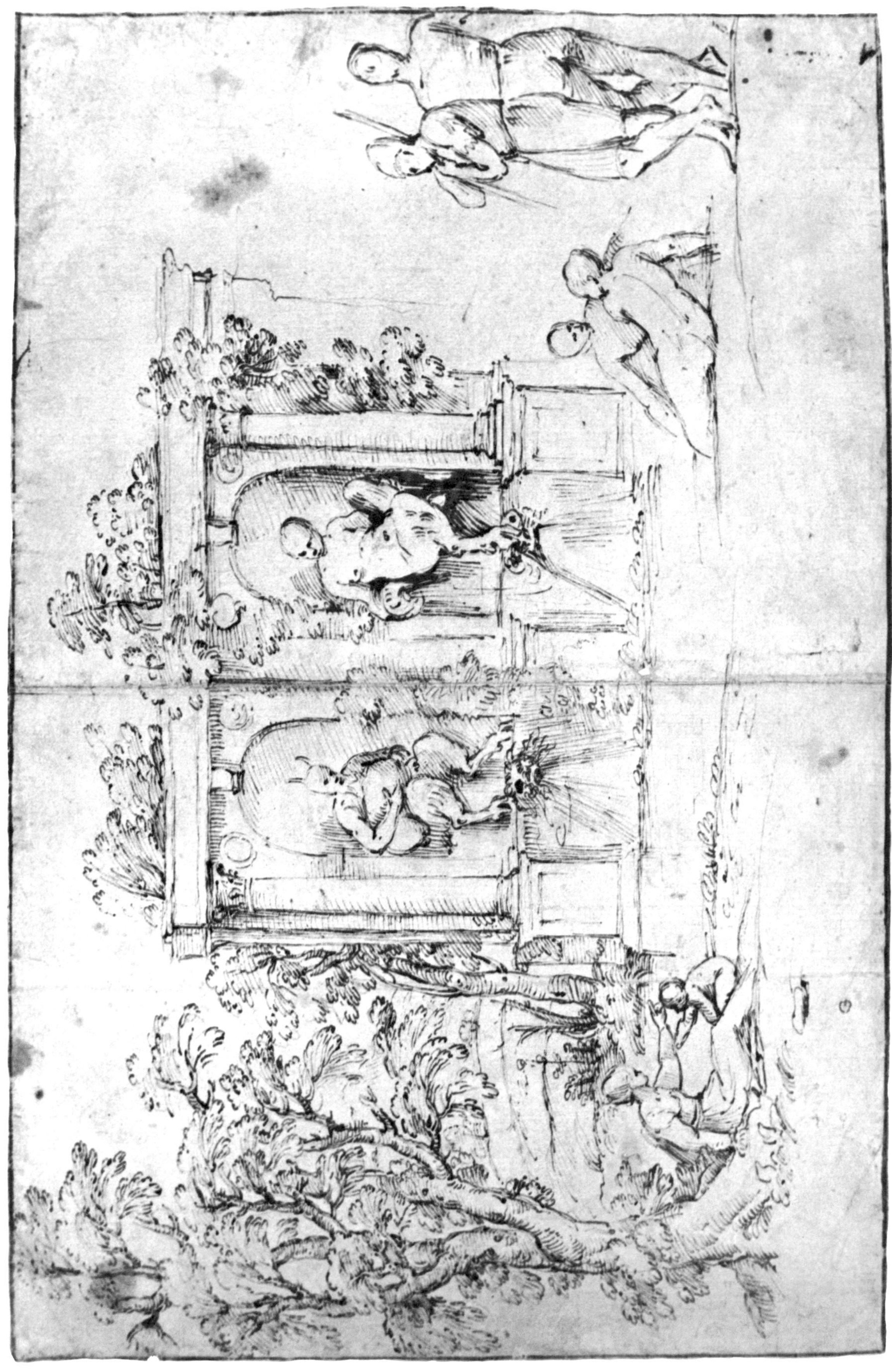

GIOVANNI BATTISTA VIOLA, Attributed to
BOLOGNA 1576–1622 ROME

51 *Landscape with Fountain and Figures*

James Phinney Baxter Fund in Memory of Professor Henry Johnson (1932.11) Pen and brown ink over black chalk. 279 x 426 mm. (11 x 16³/4 in.) Inscribed verso pen and brown ink "Verzano [?] dal Caracci"; on old mount (lost) "Dominichino/Strawberry Hill." Watermark: kneeling saint holding cross within shield. PROVENANCE: Horace Walpole (1717–1797) (according to old note in museum files); Professor Henry Johnson. BIBLIOGRAPHY: *Catalogue* 1930, p. 95, no. 625 (as Domenichino).

THIS SHEET belongs within the Bolognese landscape school founded by the Carracci, but it has as yet eluded a firm attribution. Richard Spear does not accept the traditional attribution to Domenichino. Jacob Bean has suggested looking around Grimaldi; Nicholas Turner does not dismiss an attribution to Annibale Carracci, feeling that the sheet is better than might be expected from Grimaldi.[1] Recently, Laura Giles has suggested the name of Viola as a possibility.

Viola studied with Annibale Carracci in Bologna and later settled in Rome after 1600. He specialized in landscape painting, soon achieving a notable reputation in that field. He collaborated with Domenichino on several projects, including the frescoes in the Villa Aldobrandini at Frascati, which he worked on between 1616 and 1618.[2] Viola's close connections with the Carracci and with Domenichino explain the stylistic resemblance of his work to drawings by those masters. Known sheets by Viola are rare; Marco Chiarini attributes at least two in the Uffizi to him.[3] Though not identical with the Bowdoin sheet, they do offer very close parallels.

1. Conversation with the author, July 1983, and letter to the author, 22 October 1983. 2. The most recent study of Viola's work is R. E. Spear, "A Forgotten Landscape Painter: Giovanni Battista Viola," *Burlington Magazine*, vol. 122, no. 926 (May 1980), pp. 298–315. 3. Inv. nos. 449P (repr. in M. Chiarini, *I disegni italiani di paesaggio dal 1600 al 1750* [Treviso, 1972], no. 13) and 450P (repr. in Uffizi, *Mostra di disegni italiani di paesaggio del seicento e del settecento* [exh. cat.] [Florence, 1973], cat. no. 38).

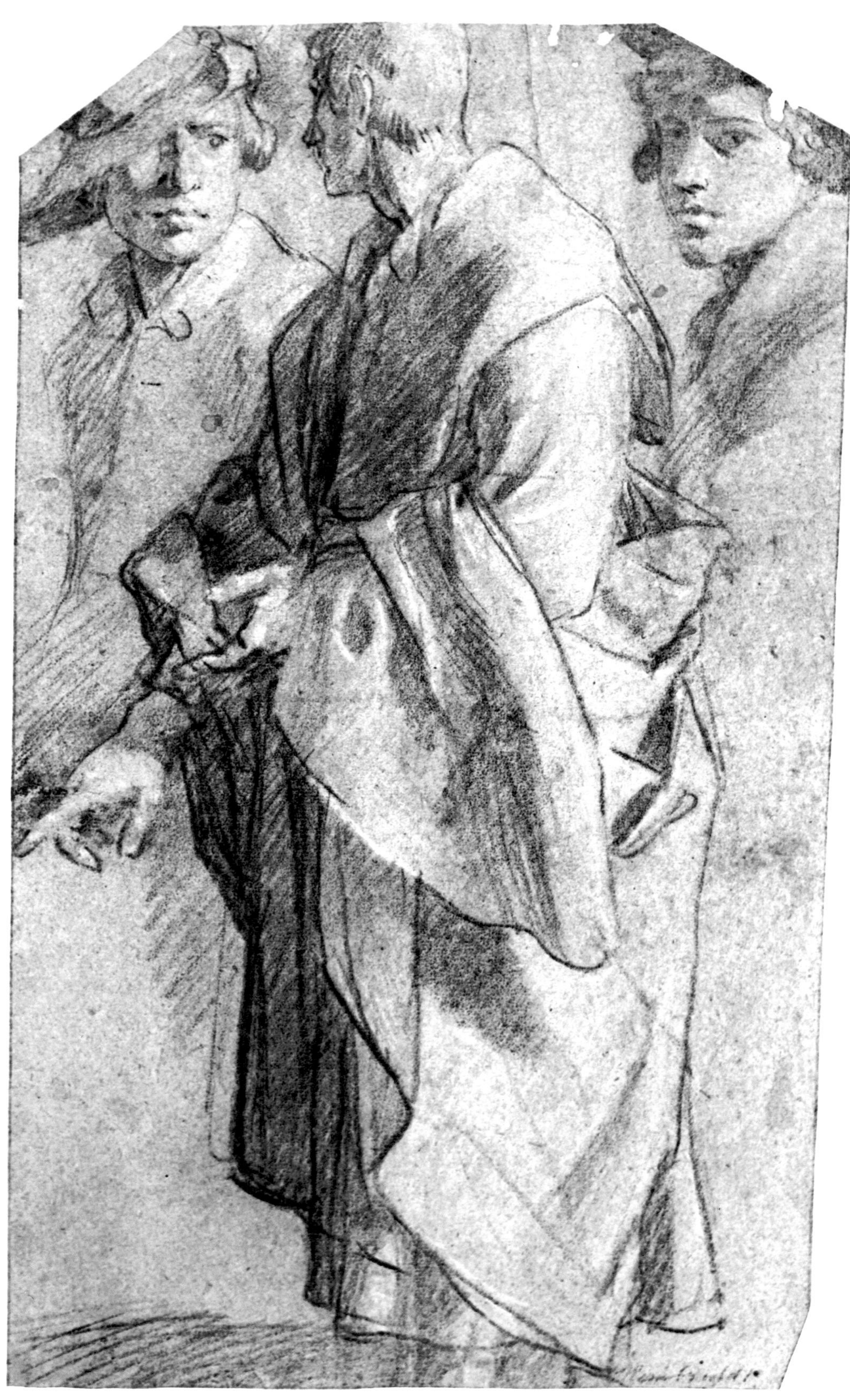

CRISTOFANO ALLORI, Attributed to
FLORENCE 1577–1621 FLORENCE

52 *Study of Three Male Figures*

James Phinney Baxter Fund in Memory of Professor Henry Johnson (1932.41) Black and white chalk on blue laid paper (three corners cut, laid down). 416 x 256 mm. (16³/₈ x 10 in.) Indecipherable inscription in black chalk lower right edge. No watermark visible. PROVENANCE: Professor Henry Johnson. EXHIBITION: Waterville 1978, cat. no. 10, repr. (as Domenichino, attributed).

THIS LARGE DRAWING remains without a firm attribution. Most scholars have agreed with Sir Robert Witt, who was the first to identify the work as seventeenth-century Florentine. However, Michael Jaffé has tentatively proposed an attribution to Domenichino (1581–1641), who worked primarily in Rome. Although this sheet does resemble in feeling Domenichino's large chalk studies at Windsor Castle, Richard Spear rejects a connection with that artist and reaffirms the placement in Florence. Recently, Nicholas Turner and Philip Pouncey have tentatively suggested Allori as the artist. Christel Thiem agrees that the Bowdoin study is Florentine and "could be" by Allori.[1]

Allori entered the Accademia del Disegno in 1613, having studied with his father, Alessandro. He spent his entire career in and around Florence, executing comparatively few works. Several paintings were commissioned by the Medici, including his celebrated *Judith* in the Palazzo Pitti, Florence. Allori was also noted for his psychologically direct portraits, among which is a recently attributed work at Bowdoin, perhaps of the young Lorenzo de' Medici (1599–1648).[2]

Thiem has proposed that, if the Allori ascription is correct for this drawing, it could be placed early in his career, at the time that he painted *Hospitality of Saint Julian*, also in the Pitti, ca. 1604.[3] She relates the technique of the Bowdoin study to that of a similar sheet of a woman in the Uffizi,[4] where there are other comparable drawings. The group of three figures in the Bowdoin sheet could be a study for bystanders in one of the artist's religious paintings, where figures are often seen looking directly out at the viewer.[5] However, no precise correspondence has been found. There seems to be a slight ambiguity of scale between the figures, as though the studies on either side of the full-length figure are variants of the same model, drawn to explore the figure's expression.

1. Comments made in conversation with the author; letter from Thiem to the author, 20 August 1983. 2. Inv. no. 1870.3; the attribution was made by this author and affirmed by Miles Chappell and Claudio Pizzorusso (letters of Chappell to the author, 17 April 1984, and Pizzorusso to the museum, 20 June 1984. 3. Repr. Paris 1981–1982, p. 101. 4. Inv. no. 7900F. Repr. Florence 1974, cat. no. 19. 5. For instance, his *St. Manetti Healing a Cripple* of 1602, SS. Annunziata, Florence (repr. Thiem 1977, p. 329, fig. 269) or his *Christ at Emmaus* in the Uffizi (repr. Florence 1974, cat. no. 2).

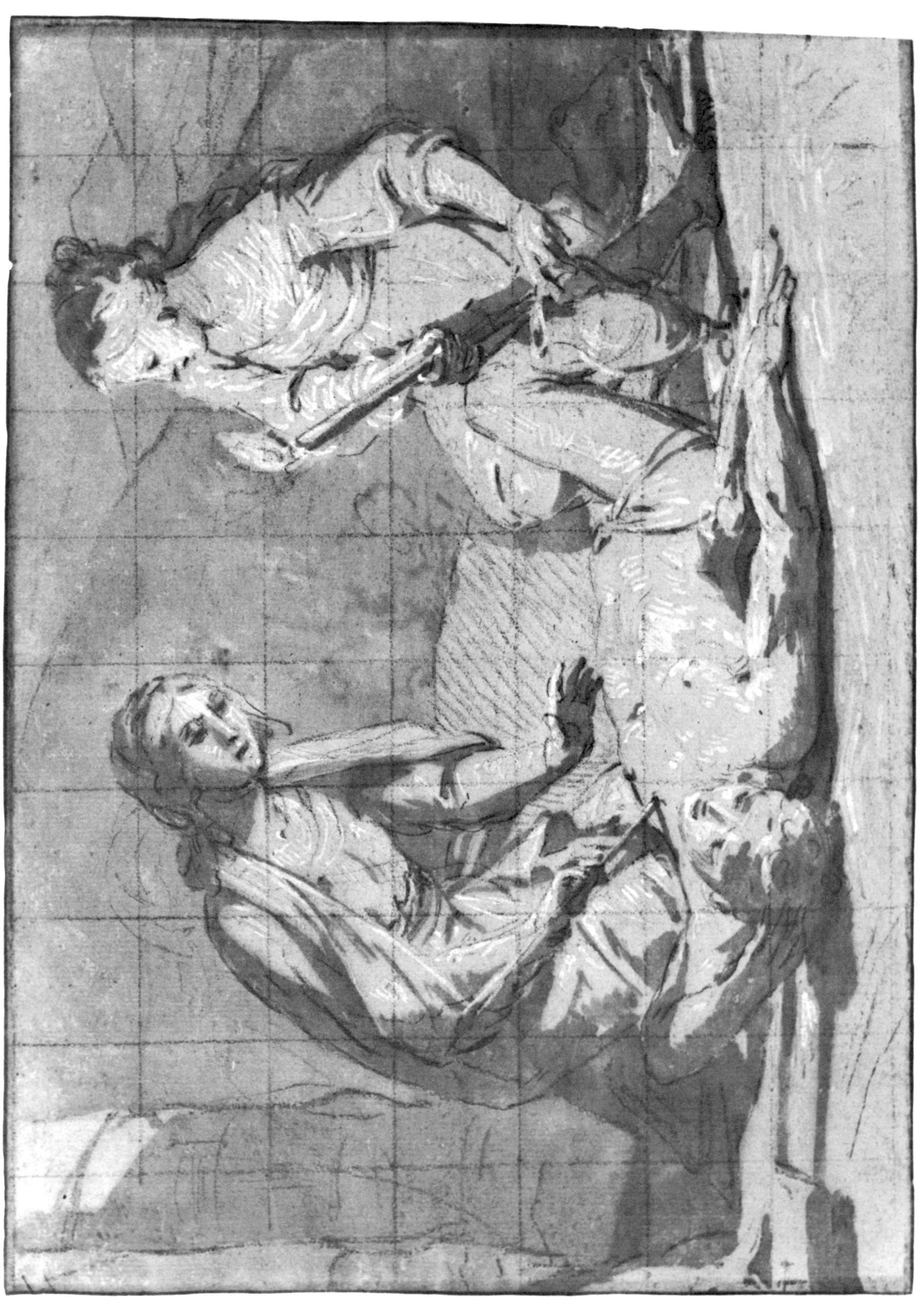

VERONESE, early seventeenth century

53 *St. Sebastian Nursed by St. Irene and Attendant*

Bequest of James Bowdoin III (1811.96) Brush and brown wash over black chalk, heightened with white, squared in black on brown paper. 257 x 355 mm. (10 1/8 x 14 in.) Inscribed pen and ink verso of former mount (lost) "No. 36." Watermark: fleur-de-lis on three mounts within circle, M above (compare with that repr. in Fischer Pace 1979, p. 449, no. 18). PROVENANCE: James Bowdoin III. BIBLIOGRAPHY: *Catalogue* 1885, no. 88 (as Unknown); *Catalogue* 1930, no. 88 (as Unknown); *Handbook* 1981, p. 166 (as Lallemand).

FRITS LUGT was the first to place this sheet as Italian, ca. 1630. In 1977 Konrad Oberhuber thought the drawing could be French, possibly near the style of Georges Lallemand (or Lallemant, ca. 1575/76–1636), a student of Jacques Bellange.[1] Recently, however, Oberhuber has suggested that this drawing is indeed Italian, by a Veronese artist working in the style of Alessandro Turchi (ca. 1582–1650), if not actually by him.

Turchi studied with Felice Brusasorci, worked in Venice, and then settled in Rome by 1614, along with his Veronese compatriot Bassetti (Cat. 54). He was influenced by the Venetian Carlo Saraceni and by the style of Caravaggio, who had died in 1610. Turchi became a member of the Accademia di San Luca in 1619 and participated in the decorations for the Sala Regia of the Palazzo Quirinale, among others.

The Bowdoin drawing resembles certain of Turchi's smaller paintings in its strong chiaroscuro, figural style, and nighttime motif,[2] but comparisons with known Turchi drawings are less certain. Drawings in Munich and Stuttgart datable ca. 1620 and executed in similar technique of wash over black chalk offer the closest parallels,[3] but the forms in the Bowdoin sheet do not seem to have quite the movement of those in Turchi's works.

1. A painting by Lallemand of this subject is repr. in *Burlington Magazine*, vol. 100, no. 660 (March 1958), p. 99, fig. 34 (as Vignon). It is attr. to Lallemand by Rosenberg, in International Exhibitions Foundation, *French Master Drawings from the Rouen Museum* (exh. cat.) (1981–1982), p. 49. 2. Cf. Verona 1974, cat. no. 91, repr. fig. 112, and E. Schleier, "Drawings by Alessandro Turchi," *Master Drawings*, vol. 9, no. 2 (1971), p. 147, fig. 2. 3. Cf. Schleier, op. cit., pp. 147–48, respectively cat. nos. 2, 4, repr. pls. 18, 20.

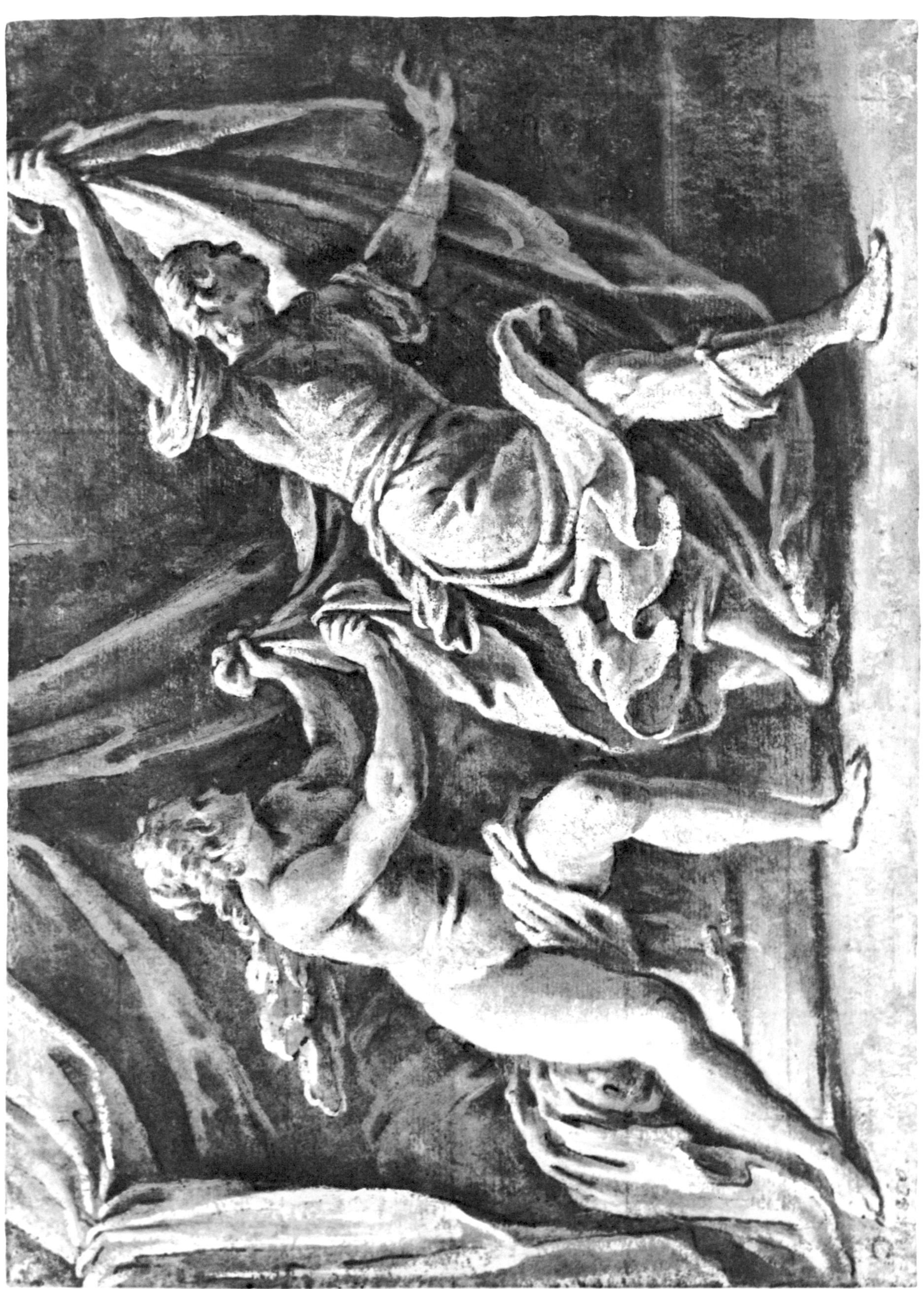

MARCANTONIO BASSETTI
VERONA 1586–1630 VERONA

54 *Joseph and Potiphar's Wife*

Museum Purchase (1930.184) Brown and white oil paint over pen and brown ink, brown wash, over red chalk squaring, on brown prepared paper, laid down. 157 x 215 mm. (6 1/8 x 8 1/2 in.) No watermark. Inscribed lower left in pen and brown ink "Passeto."; verso of old mount pen and brown ink "Bassette"; graphite "Scholar of Felice Ricci (1586–1630)." PROVENANCE: William Bates (1824–1884) (Lugt 2604); Professor Henry Johnson. BIBLIOGRAPHY: *Handbook* 1981, p. 166. EXHIBITION: Regina and Montreal 1970, cat. no. 31, repr.

BASSETTI TRAINED with Felice Brusasorci in Verona and moved to Venice by ca. 1605. There he was influenced by the works of Tintoretto and Bassano and seems to have been an assistant and friend of Palma Giovane. By 1616 he was in Rome, where he worked with Carlo Saraceni. The strong influence of Caravaggio is also seen in Bassetti's work. He returned to Verona by 1620, where he executed commissions for portraits and several church altarpieces. He died during the plague of 1629–1630.

This strongly defined drawing came into the collection with a traditional attribution, supported by the inscriptions recto and verso. Indeed, it is a characteristic work by this artist; the physicality and strong highlights of the fluttering garments are virtual trademarks of both his drawings and paintings. His draughtsmanship has received increasing attention.[1] Other typical drawings quite similar to this one are at the Princeton and Metropolitan Museums.[2] A large group of his drawings is at Windsor Castle.[3]

Bassetti depicted the nude figure relatively rarely, as pointed out by Ottani Cavina, referring to a painting of Danaë in a private collection.[4] In the placement of the figure quite close to the picture plane and the simple setting of a draped bedchamber, that work and the Bowdoin drawing are quite similar. The squaring on the latter indicates that it may have been a study for a painting, but no such work is known. The story of Potiphar's wife falsely accusing Joseph of violating her is told in Genesis 39:7–20. As in most depictions, Joseph is seen running away, while she grabs his cloak to use as evidence against him.

1. An extensive discussion by A. Ottani Cavina and illustrations of Bassetti's painting and drawings is in Verona 1974, pp. 130–62, cat. nos. 111–58. More recent is T. Mullaly, review of Verona 1974 in *Burlington Magazine*, vol. 116, no. 860 (November 1974), pp. 698–99; and V. Ruggeri, "Proposte per il Bassetti disegnatore," *Arte veneta*, vol. 31 (1977), pp. 208–12. 2. Respectively, Gibbons 1977, no. 37, repr.; and Bean 1979, no. 60, repr. 3. Blunt and Croft-Murray 1957, nos. 1–21, pls. 3, 5–8. 4. Verona 1974, p. 151, cat. no. 130, repr. fig. 150.

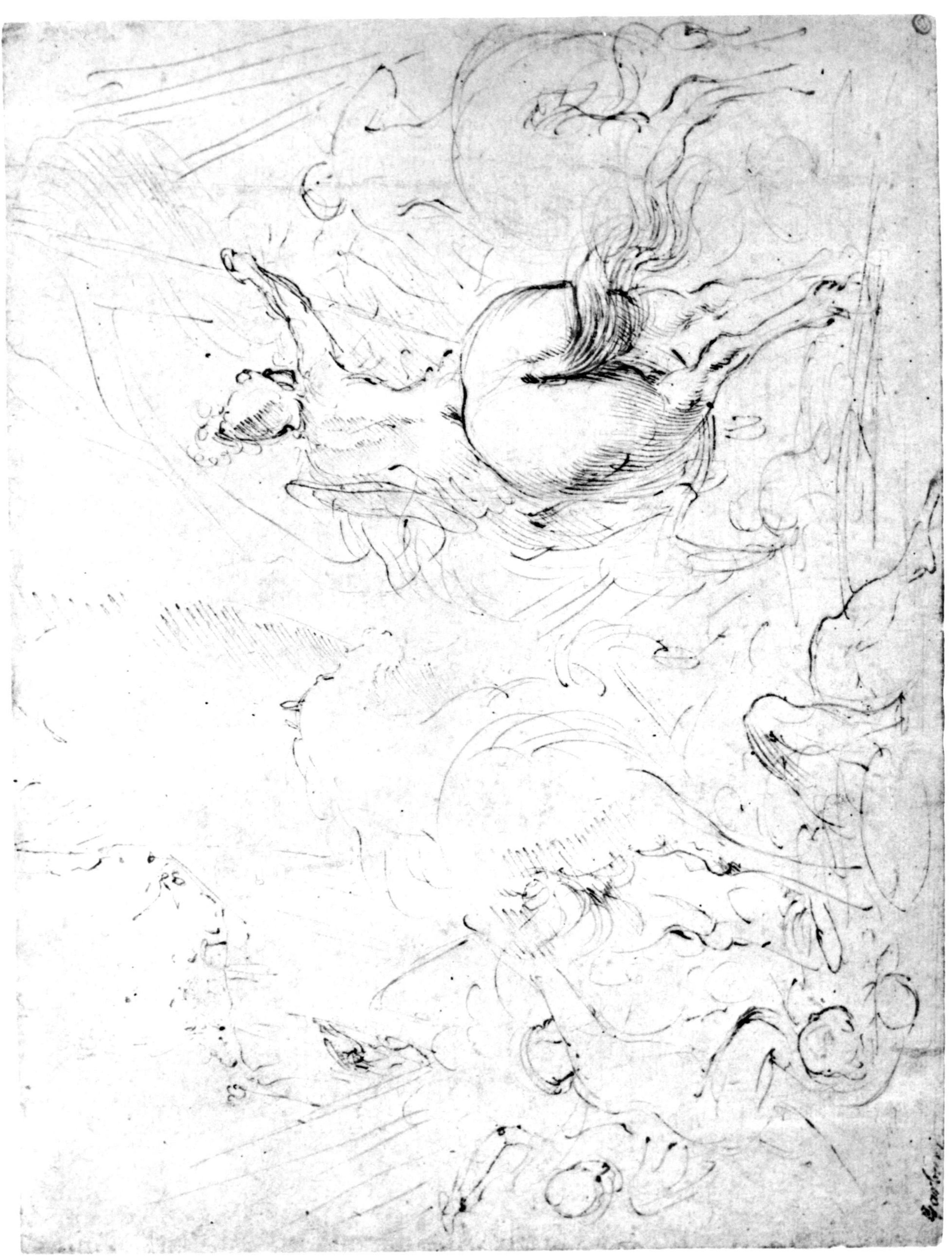

GIOVANNI FRANCESCO BARBIERI, called Guercino
CENTO (near Bologna) 1591–1666 BOLOGNA

55 *Battle Scene*

Museum Purchase (1930.197) Pen and brown ink. 227 x 296 mm. ($8^{15}/_{16}$ x $11^{5}/_{8}$ in.) Inscribed recto lower left pen and brown ink (over earlier inscription) "Garbieri"; verso pen and ink "21g/Lucans sale/Giacomo Cortesi dit il Bourgignon/JB"; verso graphite "H6/Bourguinone." Watermark: winged figure with halo, hands held together in prayer. PROVENANCE: William Bates (1824–1884) (Lugt 2604); Professor Henry Johnson.

NICHOLAS TURNER recently recognized this sheet as an early study by Guercino, convincingly suggesting a connection with Guercino's participation in the execution of the frescoes for the Casa Provenzale, Cento. These are dated by Roli ca. 1614 or later, but before Guercino's removal to Bologna in 1618.[1] The Bowdoin drawing had had traditional attributions to the near-contemporary Bolognese painter Lorenzo Garbieri (1580–1624) and to the noted French-born painter of battle scenes, Jacques Courtois (1621–1676). Like the drawing, several of the Cento frescoes, which were painted by Guercino and collaborators, depict large-scale battle scenes, often dominated by horsemen in the foreground and seen from the rear before a distant view.[2] No painting with a precise correspondence to the Bowdoin sketch is known. The fresco series depicts scenes from the fictional history of the hero Provencus, who had supposedly served in Julius Caesar's army.[3]

The extreme sketchiness of the Bowdoin sheet is not very common in Guercino's work but has a few parallels. One large sheet at Munich, dating from 1617, contains at least six very rapid studies, also done without wash, for a painting of the Prodigal Son.[4] The cursory depiction of heads and limbs, at times with mere curlicue outlines, is quite similar. This feature is present throughout Guercino's career in his rapid figural or compositional sketches. The closely connected parallel strokes to define shading are characteristic. Turner has also noted an intriguing connection with another pen sketch at Windsor Castle of a battle scene, though probably it was executed later.[5] Two studies by Guercino for the figures of Hercules and Neptune in the Cento frescoes are known. They are located in the Duke of Sutherland Collection and the Herzog Anton Ulrich Museum, Brunswick (Germany), respectively.[6]

1. The attribution was made verbally, 1983. The Cento frescoes are discussed in Roli 1968, pp. 43–56. 2. Ibid., pls. 17, 20–21. 3. Ibid., p. 10. 4. Inv. no. 10546, repr. Palazzo dell'Archiginnasio, *Il Guercino—Catalogo critico dei disegni* (exh. cat. by D. Mahon) (Bologna, 1969), cat. no. 23. The Munich sheet also carries the same watermark as the Bowdoin drawing (letter of Richard Harprath to the author, 10 July 1984). 5. Inv. no. 2397, ca. 340 x 228 mm. 6. Repr. in Roli 1968, pls. 10 and 12, respectively.

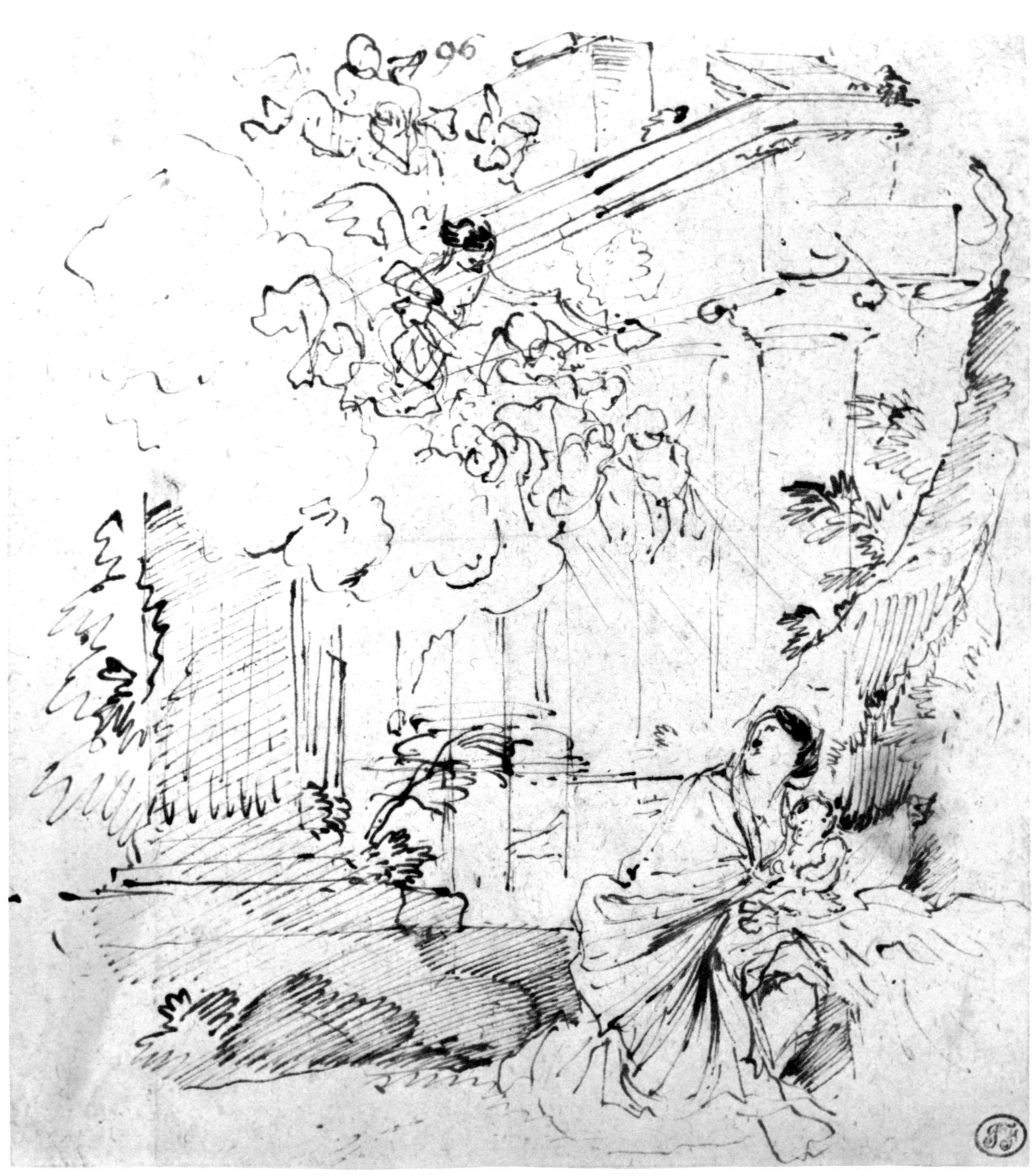

GIOVANNI BENEDETTO CASTIGLIONE
GENOA ca. 1610–1663/65 MANTUA

56 *Madonna and Child with Angels*

Gift of Miss Susan Dwight Bliss (1956.24.196) Pen and brown ink. 214 x 196 mm. ($8^{1}/_{2}$ x $7^{3}/_{4}$ in.) Inscribed pen and brown ink top center "96." Watermark: cross within heart over BR. PROVENANCE: J. Fitchett Marsh (1818–1880) (Lugt 1455); Susan Dwight Bliss. BIBLIOGRAPHY: *Handbook* 1981, p. 167. EXHIBITION: Waterville 1978, cat. no. 18, repr.

CASTIGLIONE is known to have worked in Rome, Naples, Parma, Florence, Venice, Bologna, Modena, and Mantua, as well as in his birthplace, Genoa, where he received his early training. In addition to being a painter and a prolific draughtsman, he was an accomplished etcher and the probable inventor of the monotype medium.

This and the following drawing entered the collection together and were probably once part of the same album of drawings, judging from the numbers inscribed at the top of each sheet.[1] Both are related to a large number of other Castiglione drawings of the same subject. Castiglione executed a major altarpiece of the Nativity in the church of San Luca, Genoa, in 1645.[2] Though that painting includes Joseph and several other figures, it shares many characteristics with these drawings, such as the pose of the Madonna and Child, the classical setting, and the fluttering angels. Percy notes that the San Luca painting stimulated a large series of drawings, etchings, and monotypes produced over the next fifteen years.[3] The pose of the Madonna in his etching *God the Father and Angels Adoring the Christ Child*[4] is quite close to that in both Bowdoin drawings.

Drawings related in technique and subject are at Princeton[5] and Windsor Castle.[6] A date in the late 1640s can be proposed for the Bowdoin works, based on their fluid, energetic pen style.[7] These two compositions are quite similar, despite variations in setting, space, and technique.

1. Cf. A. Percy, "A Castiglione Album," *Master Drawings*, vol. 6, no. 2 (1968), pp. 144–48, for another such album. A sheet in the University of Michigan Museum of Art (Percy 1971, cat. no. 38, repr.), also from the Fitchett Marsh collection, is probably from the same album as the Bowdoin pair. Some Castiglione sheets have been numbered twice. 2. Repr. in Percy 1971, p. 22, fig. 3. 3. Percy 1971, p. 29. 4. Bartsch 7; Percy 1971, cat. no. E 18, repr. The museum owns an impression of this print (Inv. no. 1982.27); a painting, *Christ Cleansing the Temple*, is also in the collections (Inv. no. 1961.100.12). 5. Percy 1971, cat. no. 7, repr. 6. Cf. Blunt 1954, cat. nos. 32–33. 7. Cf. the related Michigan drawing (see note 1).

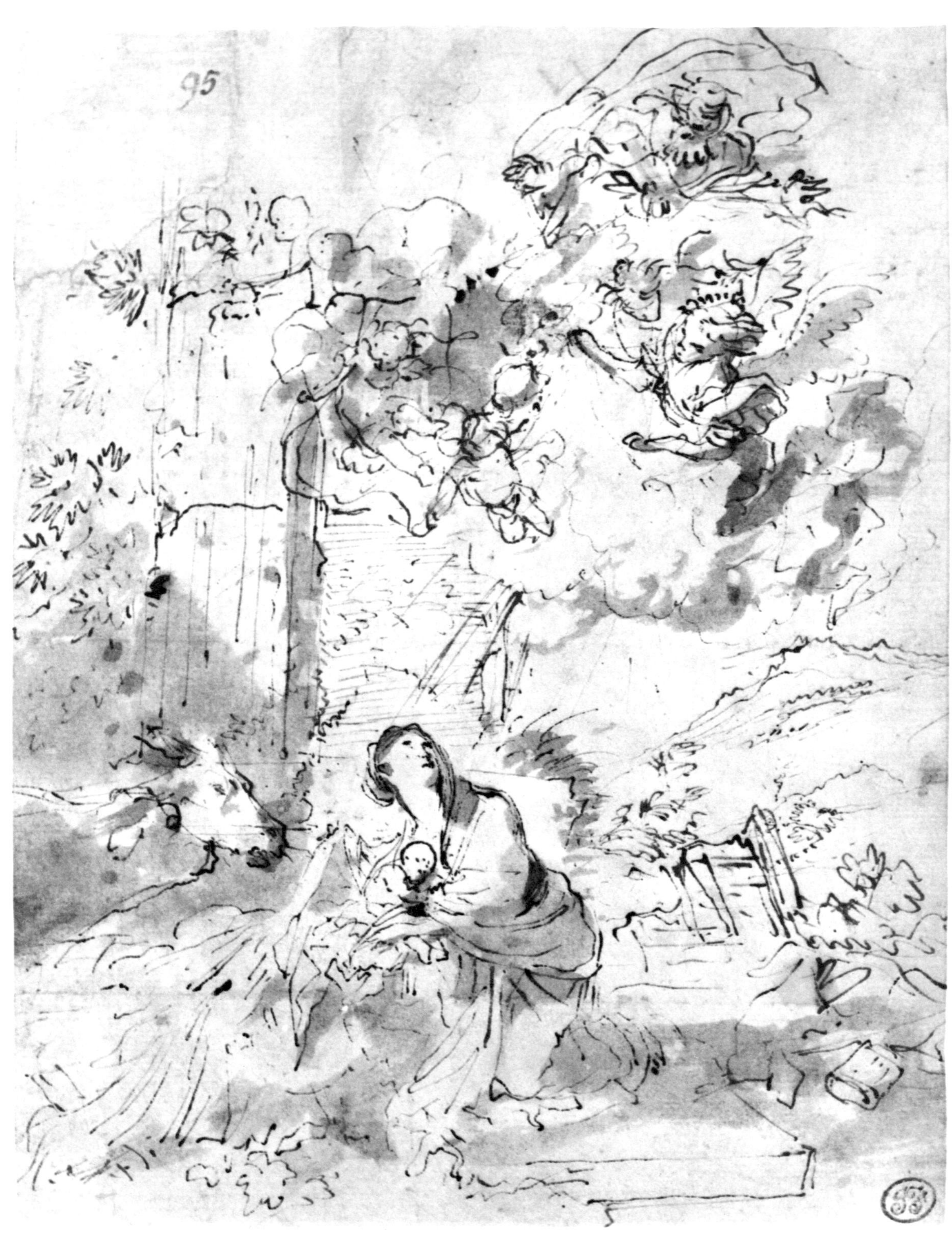

GIOVANNI BENEDETTO CASTIGLIONE

57 *Madonna and Child with God the Father and Adoring Angels*

Gift of Miss Susan Dwight Bliss (1956.24.197) Pen and brown ink and brown wash; large loss upper left. 215 x 170 mm. (8 7/16 x 6 11/16 in.) Inscribed pen and brown ink top center (on an old repair) "95." Watermark: six-pointed star over bird within oval. PROVENANCE: J. Fitchett Marsh (1818–1880) (Lugt 1455); Susan Dwight Bliss. BIBLIOGRAPHY: *Handbook* 1981, p. 167.

See discussion under Cat. 56 above.

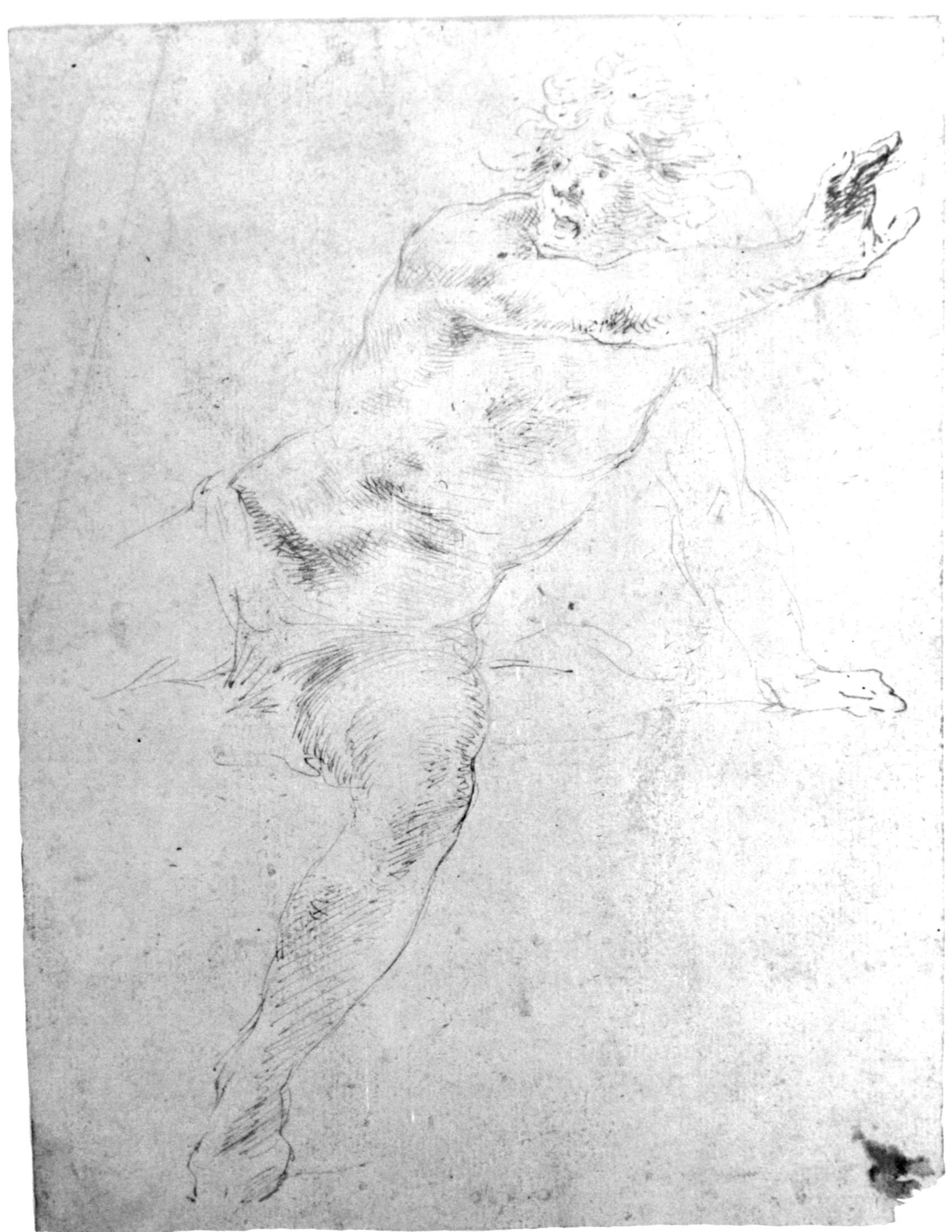

STEFANO DELLA BELLA
FLORENCE 1610–1664 FLORENCE

58 *Gesturing Nude Man*

Museum Purchase (1930.130) Pen and brown ink. 185 x 144 mm. ($7^{1}/_{4}$ x $5^{5}/_{8}$ in.) Fragmentary watermark of bird's feet. PROVENANCE: Professor Henry Johnson. BIBLIOGRAPHY: Cat. Christie's London, 18 March 1975, p. 19 under no. 32. EXHIBITIONS: Regina and Montreal 1970, cat. no. 53, repr.; Waterville 1978, cat. no. 16, repr.

TRAINED IN FLORENCE as a goldsmith, della Bella first began etching in the manner of Jacques Callot (1592–1635), who had worked in that city from ca. 1612 until ca. 1620. In 1633 della Bella was given a stipend by Lorenzo de' Medici and sent to Rome, and by 1639 he was in Paris in the company of the Florentine ambassador. While there, he produced theater and festival designs, topographic works, book illustrations, and ornamental prints for several of the many print publishers then active in Paris. He may have traveled to Holland in 1647; he returned to Florence in 1649. Della Bella enjoyed the patronage of the Medici family throughout his career. He executed over 1,000 prints. Major collections of his drawings are in the Louvre, the Uffizi, the Gabinetto Nazionale in Rome, the Hermitage, Windsor Castle, and the Albertina.

As Phyllis Massar has observed, the Bowdoin study was evidently taken from life.[1] It probably was done in the artist's studio, as the figure appears to be posed on a flat bench or bed. Considering della Bella's sizable drawn oeuvre, such academic studies as this are comparatively rare, numbering perhaps twenty.[2] Most are done in a similar pen and ink technique with delicate cross-hatched modelling, though at least three are in red chalk.[3] Blunt, Massar, and others date the majority of these life studies after della Bella's return to Florence, ca. 1651. They suggest that these may have been intended as study guides for his pupil, Cosimo III de' Medici.[4]

Della Bella also did not execute many prints of academic nudes, the only two exceptions being De Vesme/Massar 411–12. The pose and agitated expression of the Bowdoin study suggest a plausible relationship to a series of prints depicting Death pursuing individuals.[5] Viatte has studied other drawings for this series, of which several relate in feeling and pose to the Bowdoin sheet—in particular, two of a young man with arms outstretched and a horrified expression on his face.[6] In addition, there is a small detail study of a young man's face with his mouth wide in fear at the Gabinetto Nazionale.[7] A study related to the Bowdoin drawing was on the art market in 1975.[8] Viatte dates these studies to the period ca. 1650, just before and after della Bella's return to Florence, when he was exploring allegorical themes of flight, fear, and struggle.[9] It is conceivable that the Bowdoin version could be an academic preparation for one or more of these prints, as it can be dated by comparison with the other nude studies to the same period after 1650.

1. In conversation with the author, 1981. 2. They include drawings in the Ashmolean (Parker 1956, no. 786, repr. p. 173); Windsor Castle (Blunt 1954, nos. 82–83); the Albertina (Stix and Fröhlich-Bum 1932, no. 531, repr.); the Louvre (Viatte 1974, nos. 330–32, repr.); the Blunt Collection (Courtauld Institute, *A. Blunt Collection* [exh. cat.] [London, 1964], no. 16); the Manning Collection (Stampfle and Bean 1967, cat. no. 90, repr.); the Uffizi (Inv. nos. 5890S, 5891S, 5921S); the Gabinetto Nazionale (Rome 1976, nos. 13–14, repr.); formerly in New York, Sotheby Parke-Bernet, 22 October 1970, no. 16, repr.; formerly in London, Christie's, 18 March 1975, nos. 31–33, repr. pls. 19–20; and the Hermitage (Inv. no. 1597, T. Kamenskaya, "L'Art graphique d'Etienne de la Belle," *Annuaire du Musée de l'Ermitage*, vol. 1, fasc. 1 [1936], pp. 33–54, no. 12). 3. Those in the Manning Collection, the Louvre (Viatte 1974, no. 332), and the Gabinetto Nazionale (Rome 1976, no. 13). 4. See Massar, review of Rome 1976 in *Master Drawings*, vol. 15, no. 2 (Summer 1977), pp. 182–83, under nos. 13–14; Blunt 1954, p. 96, no. 83; Viatte 1974, p. 201, no. 330. 5. DeVesme/Massar 87–93 (particularly no. 92, only partially finished); Viatte 1977, pls. 8, 9b. 6. One in the Gabinetto Nazionale, the other in a private collection, repr. in Viatte 1977, pls. 8, 9b. 7. Rome 1976, no. 109, repr. 8. Cat. Christie's London, 18 March 1975, p. 19, no. 32. 9. Viatte 1977, pp. 351–54.

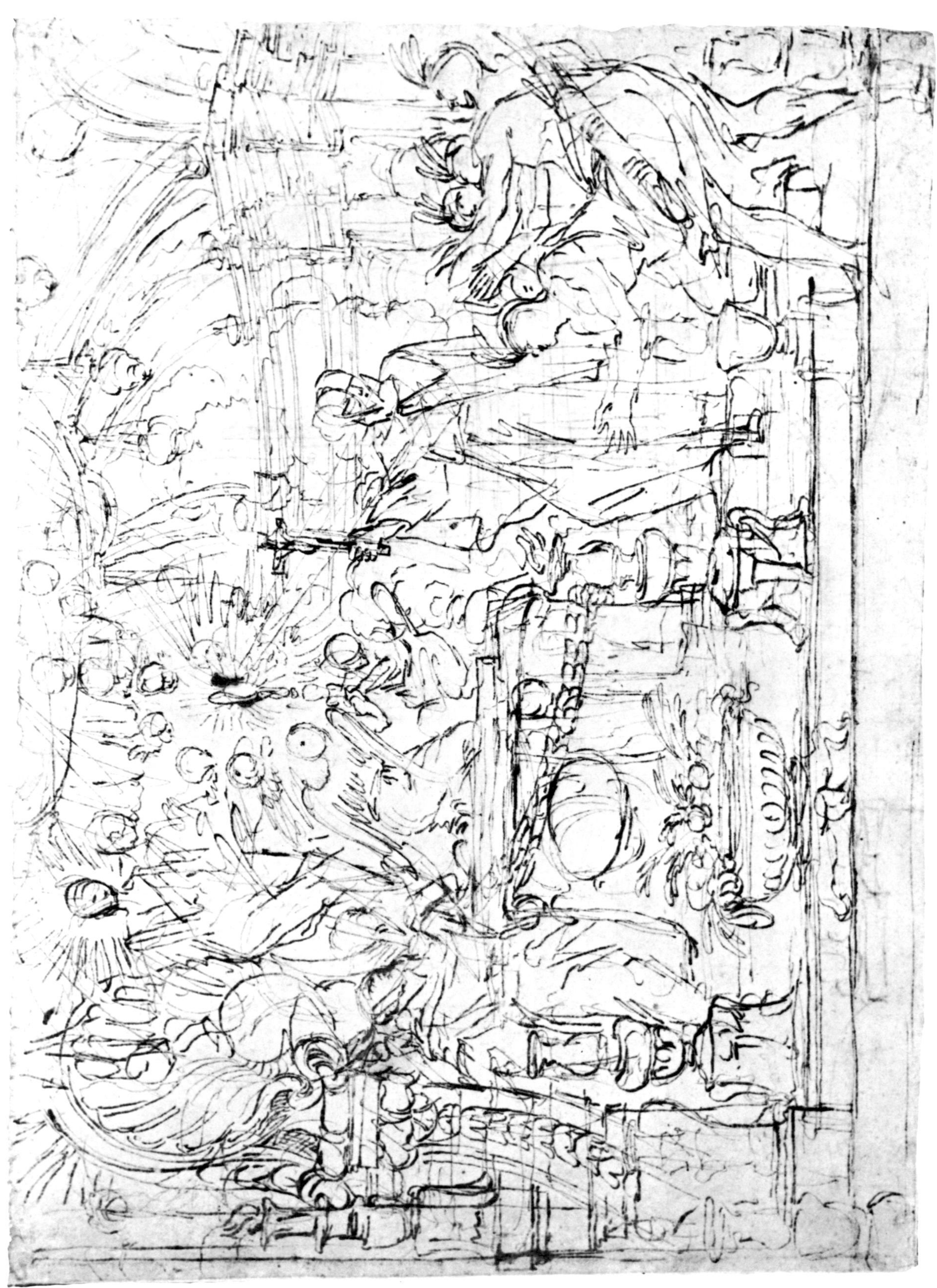

ITALIAN, seventeenth century

59 *Indians Worshipping a Vision of the Madonna*

James Phinney Baxter Fund in Memory of Professor Henry Johnson (1932.39) Pen and brown ink and traces of red chalk, laid down. 262 x 357 mm. (10 5/16 x 14 1/16 in.) PROVENANCE: William Bates (1824–1884) (Lugt 2604); Professor Henry Johnson. BIBLIOGRAPHY: *Catalogue* 1930, p. 95, no. 648 (as Unknown).

THE PURPOSE of this complex and apparently rapidly executed compositional sketch is as yet unknown. The long horizontal format is not usual for an altarpiece, but this could also be a preliminary study for a print.[1] The unusual subject matter is also somewhat unclear, though it is probably related to a Jesuit missionary, most likely St. Francis Xavier (1506–1552), who preached primarily in the Far East. Europeans at the time had little information about the appearance of inhabitants of the Far East; American Indians, who were still thought to come from a land connected to Asia, were sometimes used as exotic types. Behind the altar appears a vision of the Madonna attended by angels, with the heavenly light transmitted through the monstrance to the awed Indians.

The sketchy and confusing pen work makes an attribution difficult; there is another elaborate pen sketch on the verso which shows through and obscures the recto somewhat. The original classification was to the school of Sebastien Leclerc (1637–1714), a French printmaker whose style is normally much more controlled.[2] Sir Robert Witt then tentatively suggested another French artist, Raymond La Fage (1656–1684). Michael Jaffé was the first to suggest an ascription to Pietro Testa (1611–1650), a Roman painter and printmaker, an idea affirmed by Nicholas Turner. Ann Sutherland Harris and Elizabeth Cropper, however, dismiss the Testa attribution.[3] Testa's known drawings, though often as "busy," usually do display slightly more control in the delineation of facial features, for instance.[4] The Bowdoin drawing displays a tantalizing resemblance in technique and subject matter (complete with Indians) to an Adoration of the Magi also attributed to Testa which is in the Louvre,[5] itself related to an etching by Testa of the same subject.[6]

1. As has also been suggested by Ann Sutherland Harris in a letter to the author, 1 January 1984. 2. The attribution is taken from an appraisal in the museum files dated 15 November 1932. 3. Harris, in letter cited above; Cropper, in conversation with the author, October 1984. 4. Recent articles on Testa's drawings include A. S. Harris, "Notes on the Chronology and Death of Pietro Testa," *Paragone*, no. 213 (1967), pp. 35–60; E. Cropper, "*Disegno* as the Foundation of Art: Some Drawings by Pietro Testa," *Burlington Magazine*, vol. 116, no. 856 (July 1974), pp. 376–84; H. Brigstoke, "Some Further Thoughts on Pietro Testa," *Münchner Jahrbuch der bildenden Kunst*, s. 3, vol. 29 (1978), pp. 117–48. 5. Photograph in the Fogg Art Library. 6. Repr. in P. Bellini, *L'Opera incisa di Pietro Testa*, cat. no. 16.

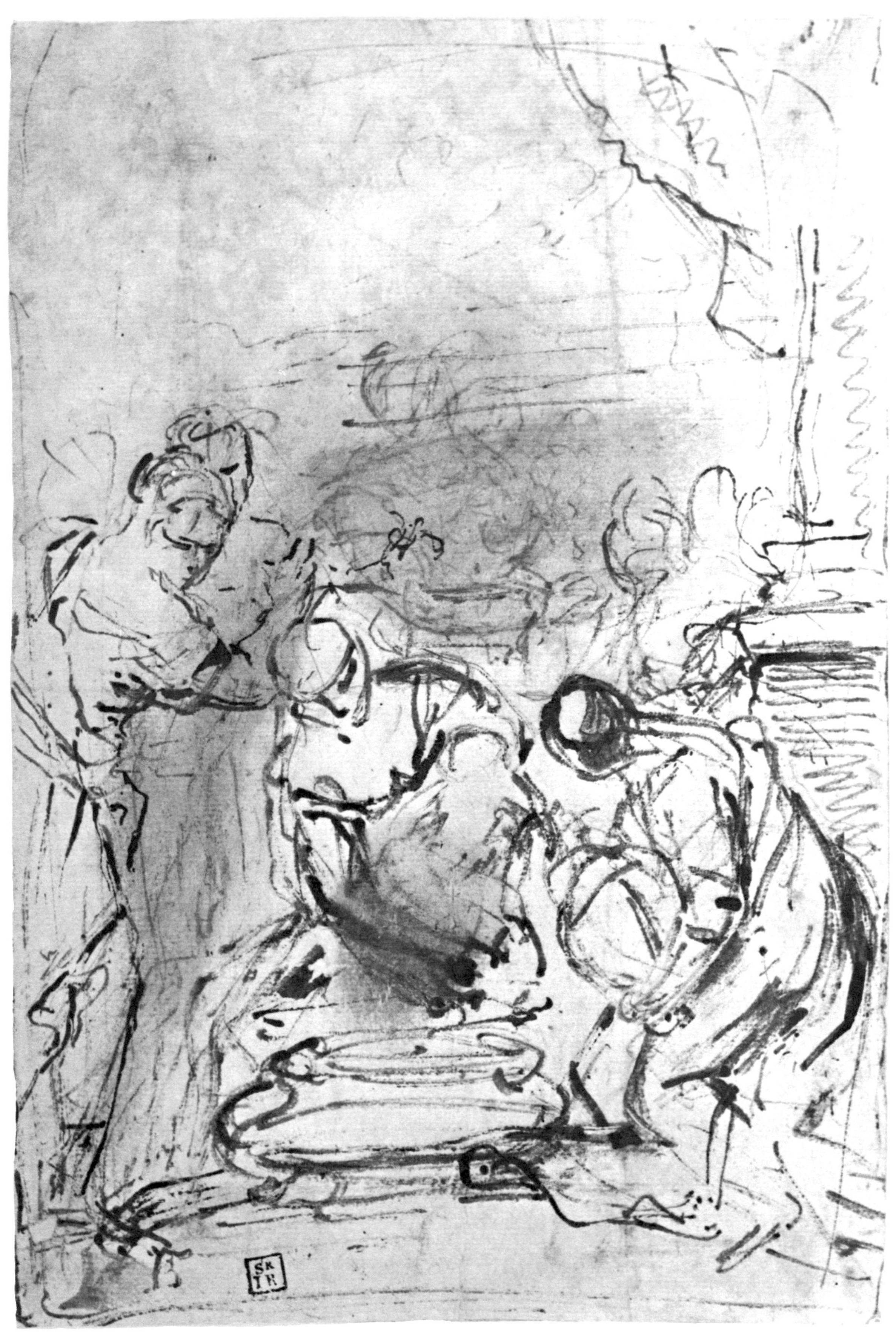

ITALIAN, seventeenth century

60 *The Birth of the Virgin*

James Phinney Baxter Fund in Memory of Professor Henry Johnson (1932.14) Quill pen and brown ink over traces of black chalk with smudging and abrasions, laid down. 324 x 219 mm. (12¾ x 8⅝ in.) PROVENANCE: Sir Joshua Reynolds (1723–1792) (Lugt 2364); William Bates (1824–1884) (Lugt 2604); Professor Henry Johnson. BIBLIOGRAPHY: *Catalogue* 1930, p. 94, no. 628 (as "Calabrese").

THIS SHEET has had a traditional attribution to Mattia Preti, as is indicated by its publication in 1930 under his nickname, Il Calabrese, which was derived from the name of his home region. The comparatively uncharacteristic draughtsmanship and extremely sketchy, rubbed quality of the sheet hamper an accurate attribution, however. In an unpublished catalogue of Preti's drawings, the late Walter Vitzthum did not accept the Preti attribution.[1] The subject traditionally has been thought to be Moses rescued from the Nile, but the presence of the basin in the foreground and indications of architecture at the right would seem to confirm the present title.

1. I am grateful to Catherine Johnston for retrieving this information from Dr. Vitzthum's files.

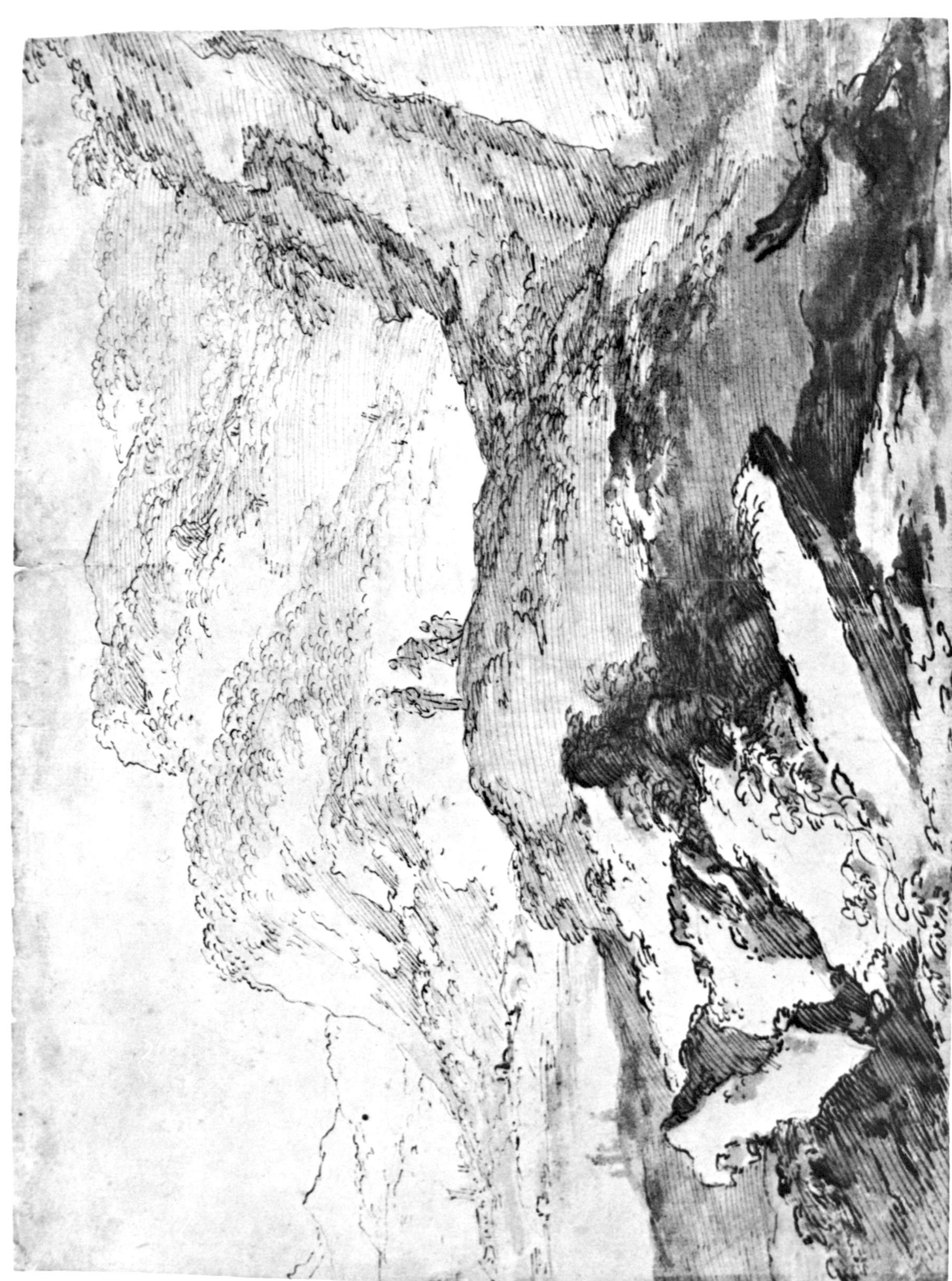

SALVATOR ROSA
ARENELLA (Naples) 1615–1673 ROME

61 *Rocky Landscape*

Bequest of James Bowdoin III (1811.70) Pen and brown ink, brown wash, over traces of black chalk, laid down, tear top center, old vertical folds, small losses at edges. 332 x 446 mm. (13 x 17½ in.) No watermark visible. PROVENANCE: James Bowdoin III. BIBLIOGRAPHY: *Catalogue* 1885, no. 22; *Catalogue* 1930, no. 22; Mahoney 1977, vol. 1, pp. 509–10, no. 55.13; repr. vol. 2; *Handbook* 1981, p. 167.

ROSA TRAINED with the Neapolitan artists Francesco Fracanzona and Aniello Falcone and was also influenced by the style of Jusepe de Ribera. He moved to Rome in 1635, then worked in Florence from 1640 to 1649. There he became a noted poet and satirist. Returning to Rome, Rosa worked independently of normal patronage systems, becoming best known for his often stormy landscapes and battle scenes. He was also an accomplished printmaker. Except for brief journeys, he remained in Rome until his death.

The traditional ascription to Rosa has been accepted by Mahoney and Richard Wallace.[1] Mahoney includes it with a group of twelve other pen landscape studies (although it is considerably larger than the others) and dates them to the late 1650s, indicating that they are composed views, not taken directly from nature.[2] The technique and composition of the Bowdoin sheet are particularly close to the style of a drawing in the Nationalmuseum, Stockholm.[3]

1. Mahoney 1977, p. 509; Wallace affirmed the attribution in conversation with the author, December 1983. 2. Mahoney 1977, pp. 503, 267. 3. Inv. no. 234.1975; Mahoney 1977, p. 505, no. 55.3, repr.

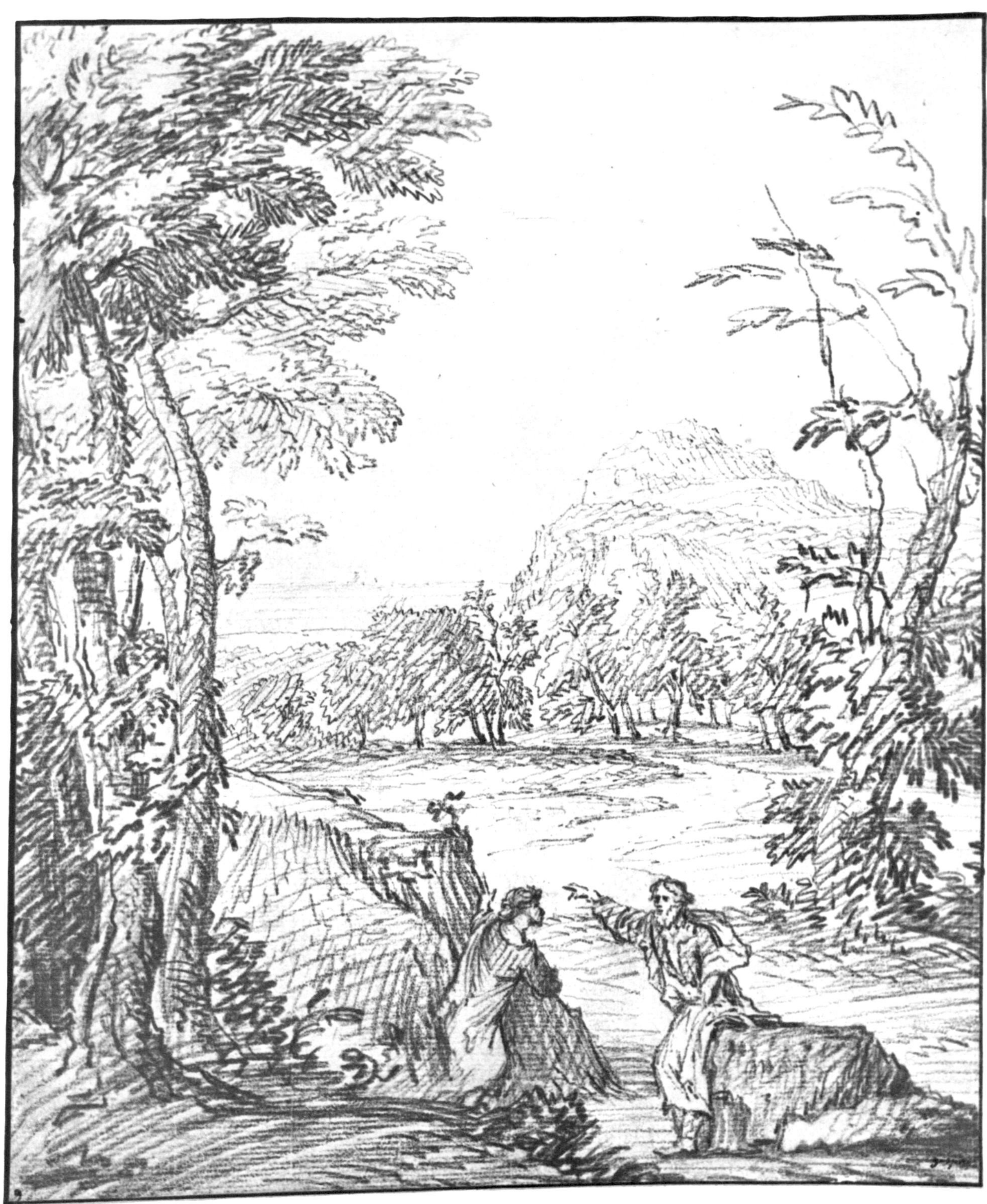

GASPARD DUGHET
ROME 1615–1675 ROME

62 *Landscape with Two Figures*

Gift of Miss Susan Dwight Bliss (1956.24.241) Two kinds of red chalk, laid down. 323 x 270 mm. (12 11/16 x 10 5/8 in.) Inscribed pen and black ink lower right "gaspar[?]"; lower left "9." Watermark: fleur-de-lis within double circle. PROVENANCE: Susan Dwight Bliss. BIBLIOGRAPHY: Toronto 1972, p. 157, under cat. no. 46.[1]

DUGHET WAS THE brother-in-law of Nicholas Poussin and studied with him in the 1630s. He became a well-known and influential landscape painter, working entirely in Rome and its environs, at the same time as Poussin, Claude, and the many northern landscape artists who came to depict the Roman Campagna. Dughet's first important commission was for a series of frescoes in San Martino ai Monti in Rome, executed from 1648 until 1651. He apparently succeeded Giovanni Francesco Grimaldi (1606–ca. 1680) in this task, for the latter artist had finished two frescoes in the church before leaving for Paris in the autumn of 1648.[2] It is one of these which the Bowdoin drawing depicts—Elijah and His Servant See a Cloud Rising from the Sea (I Kings 18:43–44).[3] The Bowdoin sheet clearly duplicates the composition of the Grimaldi painting, with the exception that neither the cloud nor the sea is present.

There is another closely related drawing, presently unlocated, of the same subject without the two figures.[4] Both drawings are clearly in Dughet's style and can be compared to, among others, the large group of chalk drawings in the Kunstmuseum, Düsseldorf.[5] Harris assumed that the existence of the Dughet drawing posited that Grimaldi worked from the former's designs for his fresco (she was unaware of the existence of the Bowdoin drawing).[6] However, Heideman argues that an artist such as Grimaldi would hardly have worked from the designs of the younger, lesser-known Dughet. She therefore assumes that the sketch published by Harris is a "free" drawing after the fresco for the record, as a possible source for later use.[7] The existence of the Bowdoin drawing would reinforce her hypothesis, indicating that Dughet drew that sheet first, reproducing Grimaldi's design closely, then transforming it in the broader treatment of the other sheet. Heideman also points out that, rather than a sea, there are indications of a city in the distance, less clear but still evident in the Bowdoin sketch.

1. According to correspondence in the museum files, Mme Boisclair will be including this drawing in her planned catalogue raisonné. 2. Heideman 1980, p. 544. The article affords a summary of Dughet's work in the church and the relevant literature. 3. The fresco is repr. in A. B. Sutherland, "The Decoration of San Martino ai Monti," *Burlington Magazine*, vol. 106, no. 731 (February 1964), p. 67, fig. 17. 4. Repr. in A. S. Harris, "A Lost Drawing by Gaspard Dughet for a Fresco by Giovanni Francesco Grimaldi," *Burlington Magazine*, vol. 110, no. 780 (March 1968), pp. 143–45, fig. 42. 5. Cf. Düsseldorf, Goethe-Museum, *Gaspard Dughet und die ideale Landschaft—Die Zeichnungen im Kunstmuseum* (exh. cat. by C. Klemm) (Düsseldorf, 1981). 6. Harris, op. cit., p. 142; Dr. Harris retains this view (letter to the author, 1 January 1984). 7. Heideman 1980, p. 544.

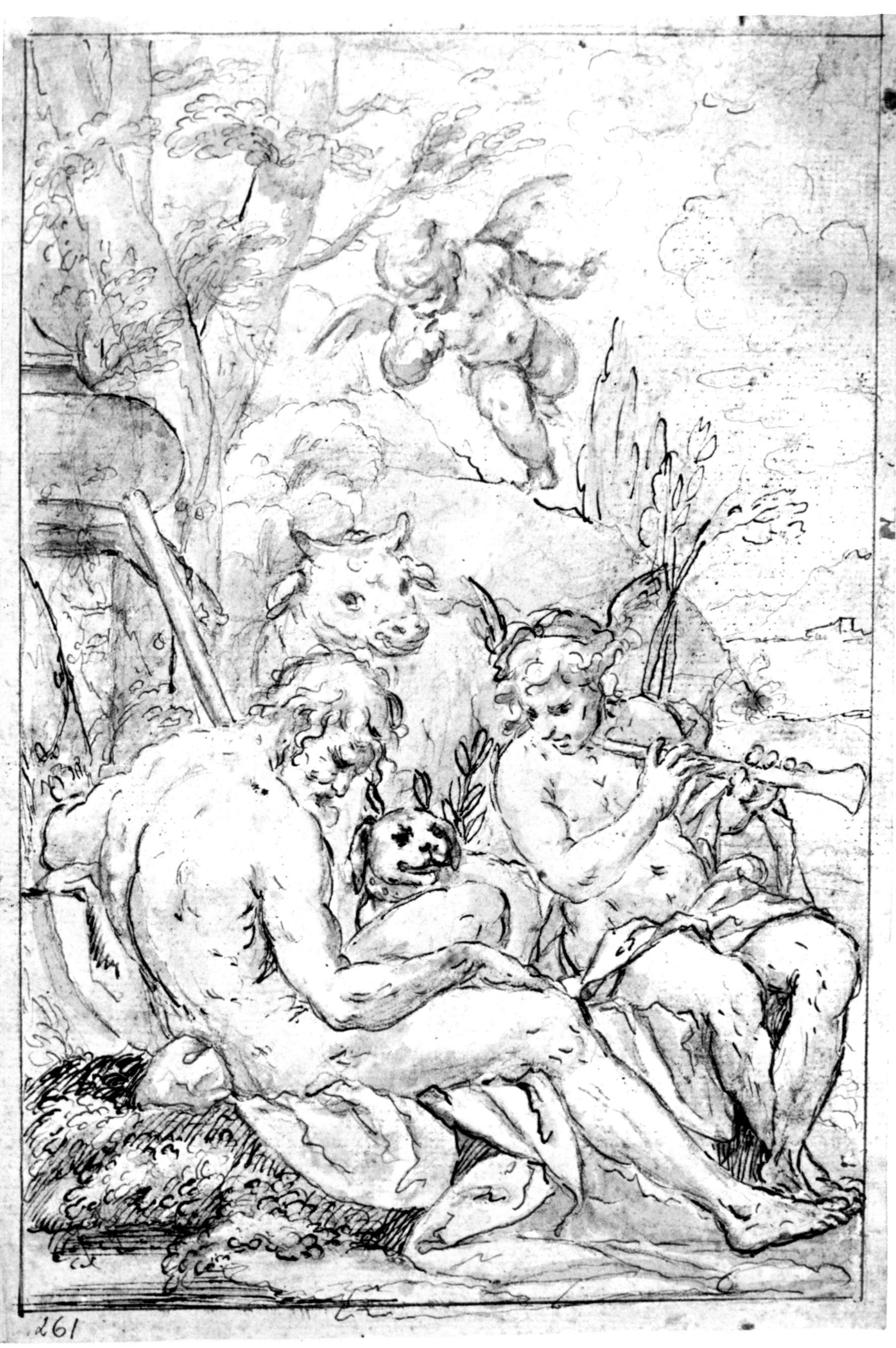
261

GIUSEPPE DIAMANTINI
FOSSOMBRONE (Marches) 1621–1705 FOSSOMBRONE

63 *Mercury and Argus*

Gift of Miss Susan Dwight Bliss (1956.24.270) Pen and brown ink, brown wash over red chalk, pen and brown ink border, traces of red chalk verso. 281 x 193 mm. (11 1/16 x 7 5/8 in.) Inscribed graphite lower left "261"; pen and brown ink verso "Diamantini"; graphite verso "Van der Werft 261f." No watermark. PROVENANCE: Susan Dwight Bliss.

MASKED BY AN OLD ATTRIBUTION to the Dutch artist Adriaen van der Werff, this drawing can certainly be given to Diamantini, an artist trained in Bologna who spent most of his career in Venice.[1] He returned to his native city in 1698. He was a member of the intellectual and artistic circles in Venice, producing works for the nobility and several churches there. He was also an accomplished printmaker. Diamantini's often sketchy style, present in both his prints and drawings, is reminiscent of the light-filled effects of Castiglione's graphic works.[2] The subjects of his prints are primarily allegorical and mythological figures.

The Bowdoin drawing is a study for an etching of the same direction and dimensions.[3] As there are differences between the two works (most apparent in Mercury's legs), the drawing cannot be considered a copy of the print. The artist most often dedicated his prints to members of the Venetian nobility; this one was presented to Ferdinand de Tassis. Diamantini etched another version of Mercury and Argus.[4]

The largest group of drawings by Diamantini (some twenty-four sheets) is in the Staatsgalerie, Stuttgart.[5] Several have the same tentative pen outlines and details worked over the chalk underdrawing as are evident here.[6] The Bowdoin drawing and related etching depict Mercury attempting to lull Argus to sleep with his music, a subject taken from Ovid's *Metamorphoses*, book 1. The hundred-eyed Argus had been appointed by Juno to guard the young maiden Io (transformed into the heifer seen in the background) from the clutches of her husband, Jupiter. Mercury eventually succeeds in his task and slays the dozing guard, thus releasing Io from her captivity.

1. The correct attribution was suggested by the verso inscription and an unsigned notation on the mat. 2. Calabi 1936, p. 27. 3. Calabi 1936, no. 23, repr. fig. 37; Bartsch 21.285.36. 4. Calabi 1936, no. 15, repr. fig. 17. 5. Thiem, Stuttgart, 1977, nos. 281–304, repr., with additional references to drawings in other collections and recent literature. 6. Ibid., esp. nos. 286–87, 289, 295, 300.

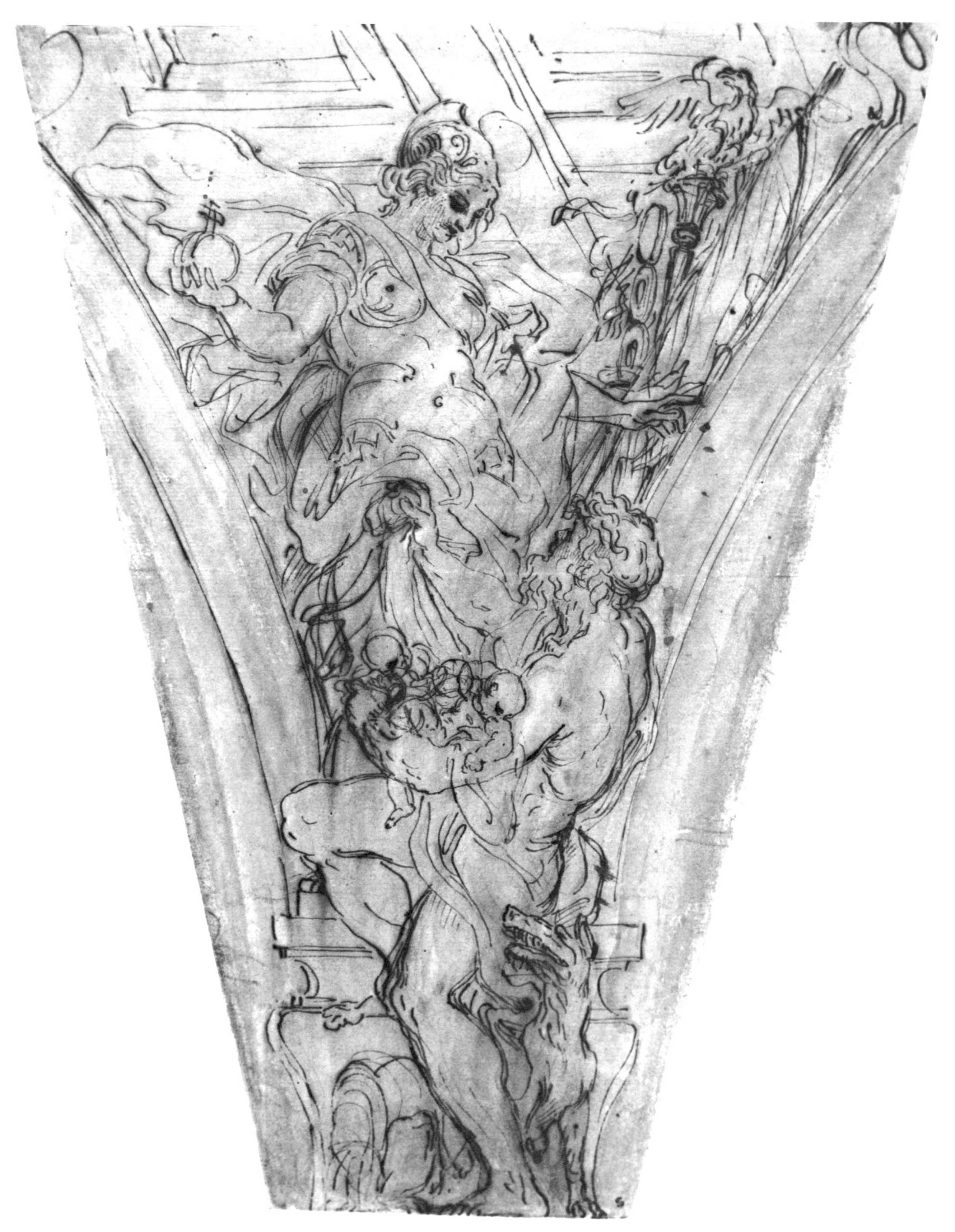

CARLO MARATTI

CAMERANO (Marches) 1625–1713 ROME

64 *Sacred and Christian Rome*

Gift of Miss Susan Dwight Bliss (1956.24.230) Pen and brown ink, brown and grey wash over red chalk, laid down. 475 x 376/144 mm. ($18^{11}/_{16}$ x $14^{13}/_{16}/5^{11}/_{16}$ in.) No watermark visible. Inscribed in pen and brown ink below on mount "Carlo Maratti"; verso of mount, graphite diagram [of a palette?]; ink at top "U/N.º 18." PROVENANCE: Earl Spencer (mid-eighteenth century) (Lugt 1530); Susan Dwight Bliss. BIBLIOGRAPHY: J. Bean, "Carlo Maratta at the Palazzo Altieri," *Burlington Magazine*, vol. 105, no. 728 (November 1963), pp. 511, 519, fig. 49; Stampfle and Bean 1967, p. 74, under no. 112; Montagu 1978, p. 339; Feinblatt 1979, pp. 11, 14, fig. 13; *Handbook* 1981, p. 167. EXHIBITIONS: Regina and Montreal 1970, cat. no. 68, repr.; Storrs 1973, cat. no. 1b, repr. fig. 1; Gainesville, University of Florida, University Gallery, and elsewhere, *Transformations of the Roman Baroque* (exh. cat. by J. K. Westin and R. H. Westin), 1981, cat. no. 16, repr.

MARATTI CAME TO ROME while quite young and was apprenticed to the leading painter Andrea Sacchi (1599–1661). He achieved prominence in his own right by 1650, receiving major religious and secular commissions. He also designed sculpture and etched several prints after his own and others' designs. He remained in Rome for the rest of his long career, becoming head of the Accademia di San Luca in 1664–65 and from 1701 until his death. Maratti's style and teaching methods were quite influential, and he had many pupils and followers. The museum owns a notable group of drawings by Maratti and his school (often called the "Maratteschi"; see Cats. 66, 72, 74–77, 78, 84). Maratti himself was a prolific draughtsman, executing many copies and preparatory studies for his own works; particularly large groups are in Windsor Castle, Düsseldorf, and Madrid.[1]

This impressive sheet came to the collection with an old attribution to Maratti; Jacob Bean first pointed out the connection with the series of designs for the audience chamber of the Altieri Palace, the family seat of Pope Clement X. These were intended to surround Maratti's famous ceiling painting, *The Triumph of Clemency*, executed from 1674 to 1677. The projected ornamentation for the spandrels of the chamber is known from the manuscript iconographic program by Giovanni Pietro Bellori and from some twenty-two drawings by Maratti for the paintings which have been identified so far.[2] Montagu has most fully elucidated Bellori's program, which was intended to complement the ceiling painting and to celebrate the blessings of the Pope's reign.[3] It is not known why this commission was never painted.

The Bowdoin drawing represents Sacred and Christian Rome and is one of five of this subject. The others are in the Academia de San Fernando, Madrid, and the Hessisches Landesmuseum, Darmstadt.[4] In them, the allegorical figure of the Tiber hands the twins Romulus and Remus to the figure of Christian Rome, who is dressed in armor and holding an orb; the she-wolf who had suckled the twins appears at Tiber's feet. Montagu points out that the ancient Roman banners and insignia at the top right probably represent an allegory of Time, incorporated from another projected spandrel.[5] The order of execution of these five designs for this spandrel is difficult to determine, though the Darmstadt drawing is probably the latest, judging from its more finished red chalk technique and more resolved compositional elements. The disposition of the figures in that sheet and in two of those in the Academia de San Fernando[6] indicates a closer relationship to each other. The other Academia sheet[7] seems to be preliminary to the Bowdoin study, which is considerably larger than all the other designs.

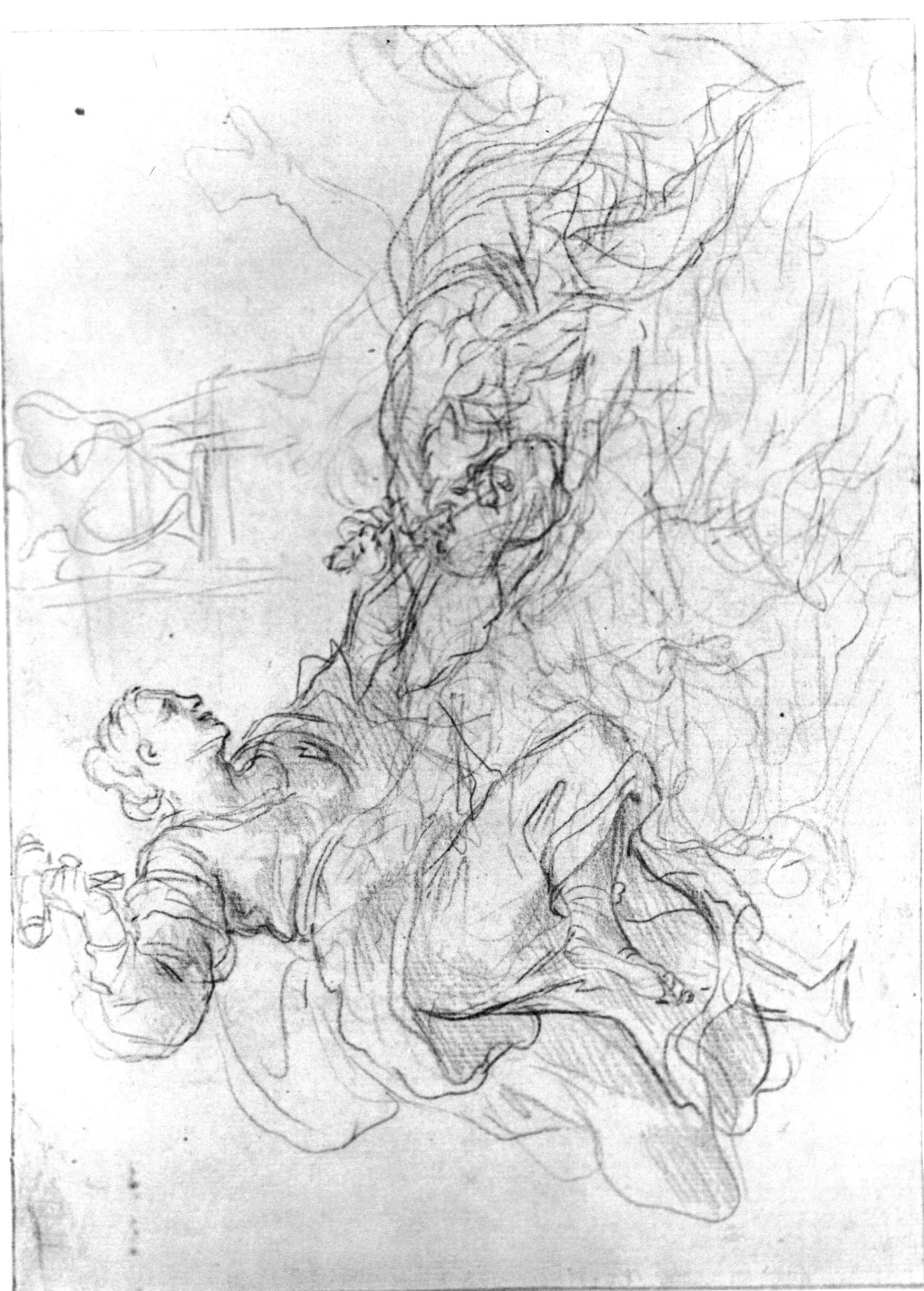

1. Respectively catalogued in Blunt and Cooke 1960, Harris and Schaar 1967, and Nieto Alcaide 1965 (the latter only a selection). 2. Montagu 1978; in an addendum to her article, Montagu noted the acquisition by the Los Angeles County Museum of Art of another study, featured in Feinblatt 1979. All the drawings are reproduced in Feinblatt 1979. 3. Montagu 1978. 4. Ibid., pp. 339–40; repr. in Feinblatt 1979, figs. 10–14. 5. Montagu 1978, p. 336; Bellori had evidently miscounted the available spandrels, so four subjects had to double up. 6. Inv. nos. 605 and 606. 7. Inv. no. 607.

CARLO MARATTI

65 *Jael and Sisera*

Bequest of James Bowdoin III (1811.49) Red chalk. 193 x 264 mm. (7⅝ x 10⅜ in.) No watermark. Inscribed verso of old mount (lost) pen and ink "No. 58 Nicholo Pousin." Verso red chalk sketches for Judith and Holofernes. PROVENANCE: James Bowdoin III. BIBLIOGRAPHY: *Catalogue* 1885, no. 65, repr. in large paper edition (as Poussin); Allen 1886, pt. 2, repr. (as Poussin); Mather 1914, pp. 112, 115, repr. p. 118, figs. 6, 7 (as doubtful Poussin, rather Roman); *Catalogue* 1930, no. 68 (as Poussin); [Siber] 1947, p. 119, fig. 8 (as Roman school). EXHIBITIONS: Cincinnati, Cincinnati Art Museum, *Nicholas Poussin/Peter Paul Rubens*, 1948, cat. no. 24 (as Poussin); American Federation of Arts 1962–1963, no. 50 (as Poussin); Houston, Temple Emmanuel, *Festival of the Bible in the Arts*, 1964, cat. no. 25, repr. (as Poussin).

THE TRADITIONAL ATTRIBUTION of this sheet to Nicholas Poussin was questioned as early as 1914 by Frank Jewett Mather, who ascribed it generally to Rome during the first half of the seventeenth century. Other scholars have most often connected it with Maratti or his school.[1] Recently, Manuela Mena Marqués has affirmed its attribution to Maratti himself.[2] Its subject matter relates to that of Maratti's decorations for the Presentation Chapel dedicated to the Virgin Mary in St. Peter's, Rome. These occupied him for over forty years and remained unfinished at his death. Maratti was responsible for the dome, six half-lunettes, and intervening pendentives. The subjects included both Old Testament prophets and three heroine prefigurations of the Virgin: Miriam, Jael, and Judith. The latter two subjects together formed a lunette above the altar, each flanking a window; they were executed in mosaic after Maratti's painted cartoons. The dome painting of the Virgin Immaculate was finished after Maratti's death by his pupil Giuseppe Chiari.[3]

Maratti developed his design for the half-lunette *Jael and Sisera* through an extensive series of drawings, at least twenty-five of which have been identified.[4] The final design, which was executed, depicts the triumphant Jael standing over the slain Sisera, pointing out his body to her countrymen. However, the earliest sketches known, a group in Würzburg and Madrid, show an earlier moment in the drama, as Jael raises the hammer to drive the nail into the head of the sleeping Sisera.[5]

It is this earlier and more dramatic moment which is shown in the Bowdoin sketch, which does not conform to the eventually established format of the half-lunette. Therefore, it could be among Maratti's preliminary thoughts about his subject, or it could be a later variation on it. He is known to have painted later versions of many of his compositions and was commissioned to do so for these subjects as well.[6] Mena Marqués has indicated a drawing in the Biblioteca Nacional, Madrid, which is related to the Bowdoin depiction of this subject. It also shows the act of murder and likewise does not conform to the St. Peter's composition.[7] The verso of the Bowdoin drawing contains finished sketches of Judith's hands, for the pendant subject of Judith and Holofernes. Jean

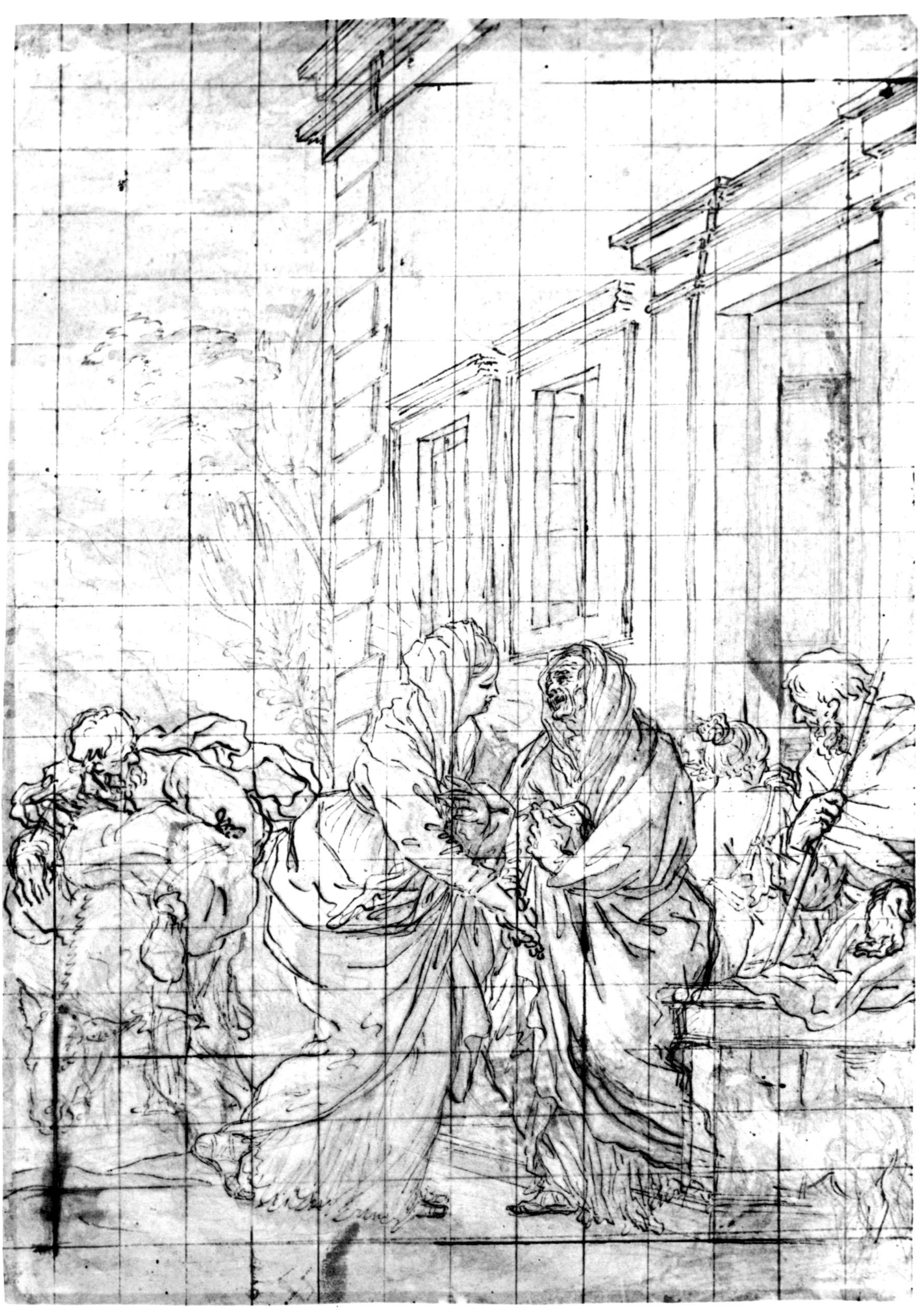

and Robert Westin theorize that Maratti's designs for the Jael and Judith subjects are among the earliest he worked on for the St. Peter's commission, in the early 1670s.[8]

1. Unsigned note on the mount of the Witt Library photograph, "close to Maratti"; Jacob Bean associated it with the Maratti circle, in conversation with the author, 1980; and Oberhuber and Montagu both tentatively suggested an attribution to Maratti himself (comments in museum files). 2. Letter to the author, 29 December 1983. 3. See Macandrew 1980, p. 129, for a concise synopsis of the project. 4. F. H. Dowley, review of Nieto Alcaide 1965 in *Art Bulletin*, vol. 52, no. 4 (December 1970), pp. 458–59. In addition, a sheet in the Clark Bequest at the Philadelphia Museum of Art has been associated with this commission (Philadelphia 1980–1981, cat. no. 1, repr.). 5. The Würzburg sheet is repr. in *Master Drawings*, vol. 3, no. 2 (1965), pl. 37a; the Madrid sheet is repr. in Nieto Alcaide 1965, no. 41, pl. 26. In addition, a detail study in the Metropolitan Museum shows Jael's hand upraised with the hammer (repr. Bean 1979, cat. no. 275). 6. Macandrew 1980, p. 129. 7. Inv. Barcia 8241; the sheet is not by Maratti himself, according to Mena Marqués. 8. Museum of Art, Pennsylvania State University, *Carlo Maratti and His Contemporaries* (exh. cat. by J. K. Westin and R. H. Westin), 1975, p. 65.

ROMAN, late seventeenth century

66 *The Visitation*

Bequest of James Bowdoin III (1811.127) Pen and brown ink, brush and brown wash, red chalk, heightened with white, squared in pen and brown ink (verso: red chalk and pen and brown ink). 384 x 275 mm. (15 1/8 x 10 13/16 in.) Verso sketch of drapery and caricature of man's head. Inscribed pen and brown ink verso "12 Marzo" with various figures and addition table. Watermark: six-pointed star over crossed arrows. PROVENANCE: James Bowdoin III. BIBLIOGRAPHY: *Catalogue* 1885, no. 139 (as Unknown); *Catalogue* 1930, no. 139 (as Unknown).

SEVERAL SUGGESTIONS have been made as to the authorship of this drawing, and all have centered in late seventeenth-century Rome. Filippo di Pietro indicated a relationship to Pietro da Cortona, and others have also seen an influence of Carlo Maratti, the other major figure of the period in Rome.[1] Among more specific names, Jennifer Montagu suggested Lazzaro Baldi (ca. 1624–1703), and Nicholas Turner, the very plausible idea of Daniel Seiter (1649–1705).

Born in Vienna and principally trained in Venice by Carl Loth, Seiter spent virtually his entire career in Italy, eventually settling after 1688 in Turin. Several stays in Rome during the 1680s and 1690s familiarized him with the Roman school, and drawings of his have been connected with both da Cortona and Maratti.[2]

The figures behind Mary and Elizabeth are quite Cortonesque, and the overall composition echoes that of the same subject repeated often by Maratti in paintings, drawings, and an etching.[3] Comparable drawings in technique and figural style by Seiter are in Windsor Castle and Düsseldorf.[4]

1. Both Spear and Oberhuber suggested looking in Maratti's circle. 2. See P. Pouncey, "Two Studies by Daniel Seiter for Ceiling Paintings in Turin," *Master Drawings*, vol. 5, no. 3 (1967), p. 287. 3. See the discussion of Maratti's Visitation grisaille oil sketch at Oxford in Parker 1956, cat. no. 900, and Macandrew 1980, p. 302, no. 900. 4. The Windsor drawings are repr. in Pouncey, op. cit., pls. 28–29; the Düsseldorf sheet is repr. in I. Budde, *Beschreibender Katalog der Handzeichnungen in der Staatlichen Kunstakademie Düsseldorf* (Düsseldorf, 1930), pl. 234, no. 973.

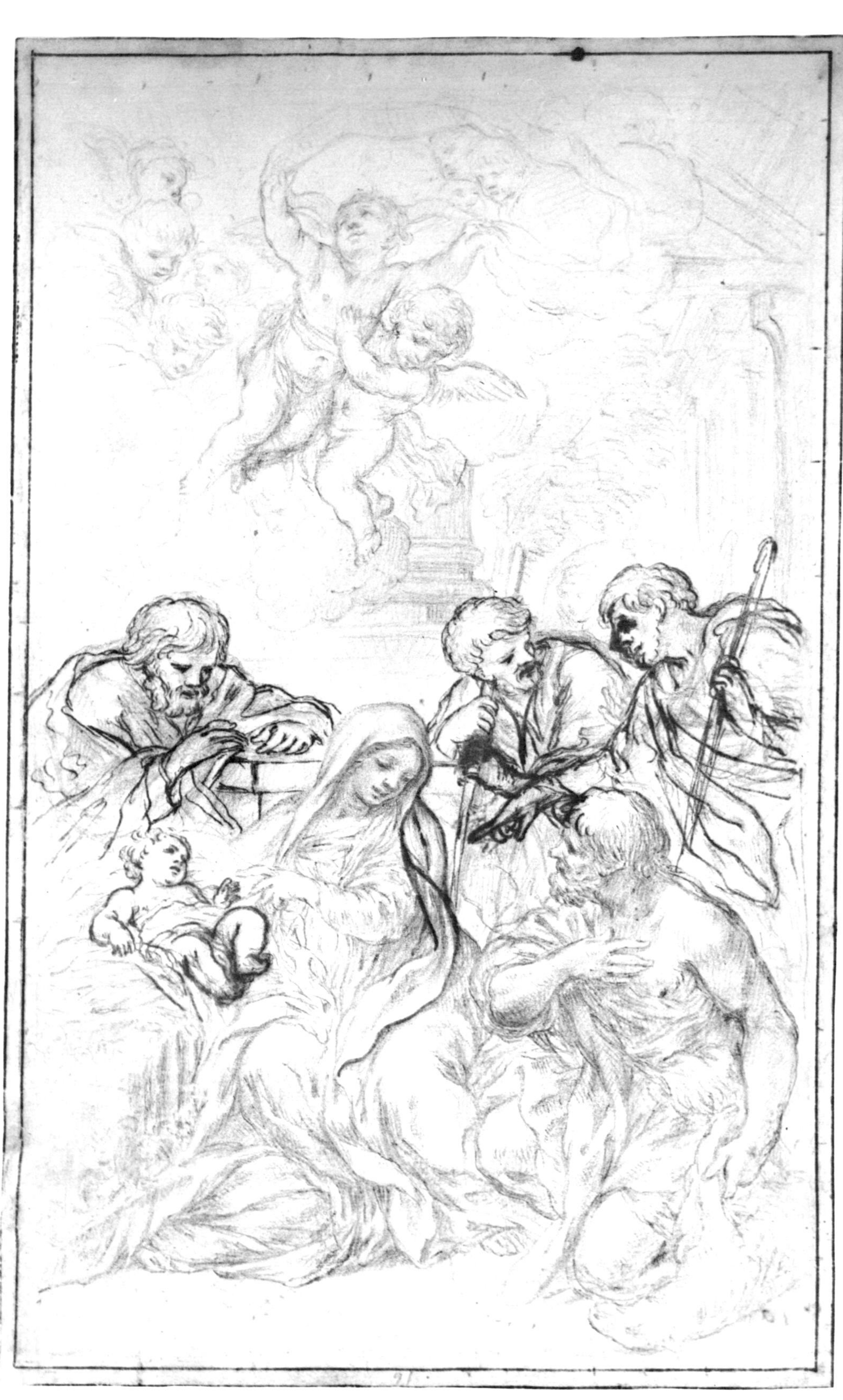

CIRO FERRI
ROME 1634–1689 ROME

67 *Adoration of the Shepherds*

Bequest of James Bowdoin III (1811.65) Black chalk, touches of red chalk, with pen and brown ink (losses in lower left corner below Christ Child). Sheet 396 x 248 mm. (15 5/8 x 9 3/4 in.) Inner pen border 386 x 235 mm. (15 3/16 x 9 1/4 in.) Inscribed black chalk bottom "91"; pen and brown ink verso "S · 10," black chalk "4." No watermark. PROVENANCE: James Bowdoin III. BIBLIOGRAPHY: *Catalogue* 1885, no. 92 (as Unknown); *Catalogue* 1930, no. 92 (as Unknown); Montagu 1973, p. 338, n. 14.

FERRI WAS THE most prominent assistant and imitator of Pietro da Cortona. He became a member of the Accademia di San Luca in 1657 and worked in Florence for Grand Duke Ferdinando de' Medici and others from 1659 until 1665. After working in Bergamo and Venice, Ferri returned to Rome at Pietro da Cortona's death in 1669. He continued to work busily under both Florentine and Roman patronage, participating in the decorations for St. Peter's. Large groups of Ferri's drawings are in Paris and Florence, and numerous engravings, including book illustrations, were executed after his painted and drawn designs.

The basic composition of this Adoration of the Shepherds was an influential and often-repeated design in the da Cortona and Ferri studios.[1] The Bowdoin sheet was first identified with da Cortona's school by Sir Robert Witt, and then with Ferri himself by Vitzthum. It poses several problems of chronology and purpose, however, and it is one of several closely related versions.

The closest is actually a Ferri drawing now lost and known only from an engraved copy by Conrad Metz, published in his *Imitations of Drawings* of 1798.[2] The drawing was then in the collection of Lord St. Helens and was attributed to Ferri. If we trust the accuracy of the Metz copy (which is in reverse to the Bowdoin sheet), the Lord St. Helens sheet corresponds almost exactly to the black chalk portions of the Bowdoin drawing. However, the latter sheet has numerous pen and ink pentimenti in the heads and hands of the shepherds and in the entire figures of Joseph and the Christ Child. Further, there are a few red chalk additions to the shepherd at the right, the Virgin's veil, and the Christ Child. The size of the Bowdoin design and the Metz print are roughly the same.[3] Since the Bowdoin sheet was at the College by 1811 and probably in this country by 1728, it cannot have been the Lord St. Helens model for the Metz print.[4] Nor is it at all likely to be a counterproof of the Metz design.

Two other very close drawn versions of this design exist, one at Berlin attributed to Lazzaro Baldi[5] and a copy in reverse to the Bowdoin sheet at Düsseldorf.[6] The elements of the design are closely related to those in a small oil painting on copper by Ferri in the Denis Mahon Collection (also in reverse).[7] A similar painting in the Prado, formerly given to da Cortona, has been attributed by Bruce Davis to Ferri; he has also identified a preparatory black chalk sketch for it in the Louvre.[8] Nicholas Turner has further attributed a rapid pen sketch at Düsseldorf to Ferri, as a preliminary thought for the Bowdoin–Lord St. Helens composition.[9]

Black chalk is the usual medium for Ferri, even for his engraving studies, but at times his drawings are worked over in pen and ink, as this one is. The red chalk is unusual.

1. Da Cortona treated the subject in altarpieces in San Francesco, Aversa, and San Salvatore in Lauro, Rome (the latter repr. in G. Briganti, *Pietro da Cortona o della pittora barocca* [Florence, 1962], pl. 59). Drawn studies by

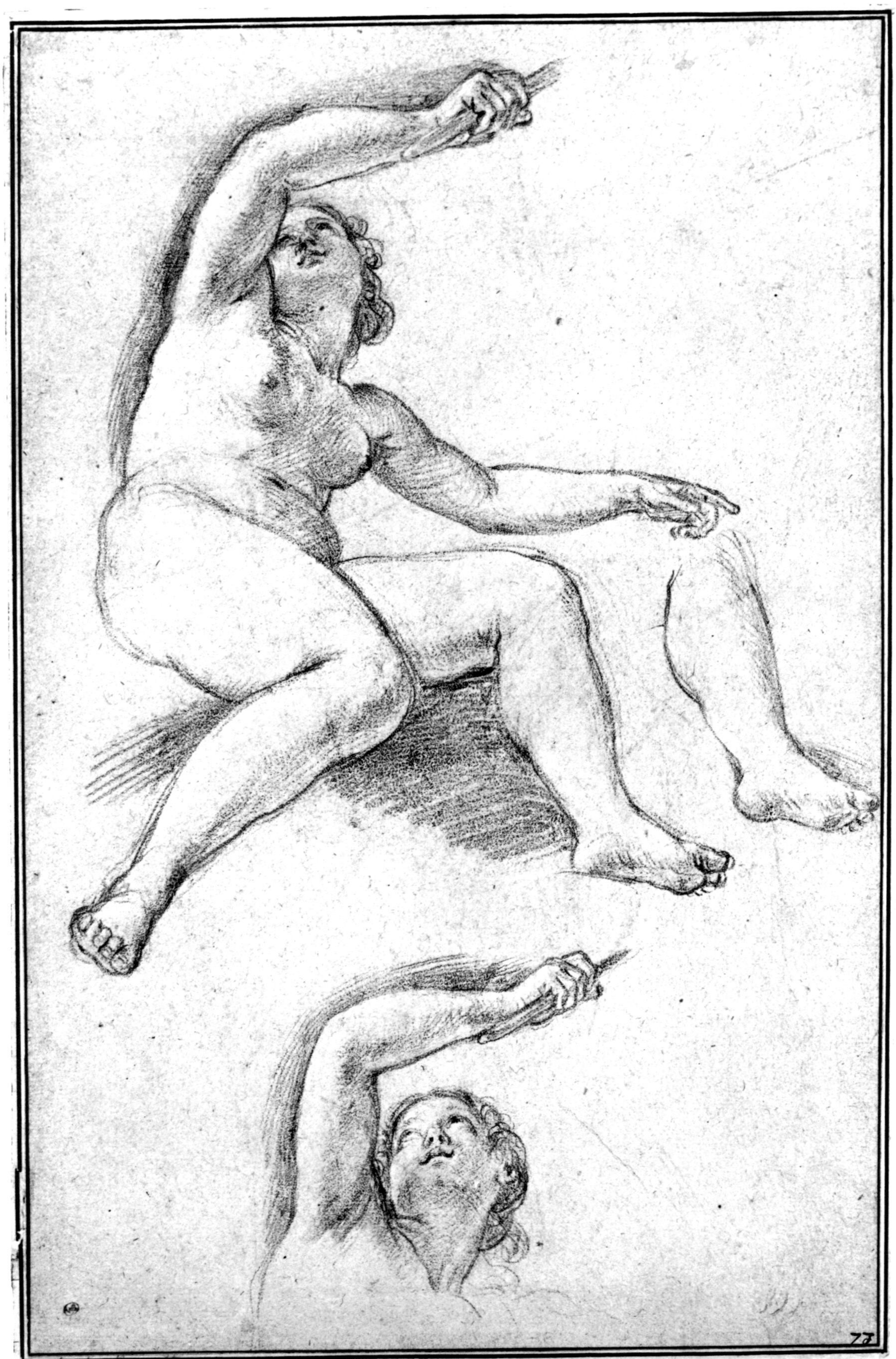

da Cortona of the subject include one formerly with Pietro Scarpa (Paris, Grand Palais, *Dessins anciens* [exh. cat.] [Venice: Pietro Scarpa, 1978], cat. no. 35, repr.) and one in the Gabinetto Nazionale, Rome (Villa della Farnesina alla Lungara, *Disegni di Pietro da Cortona e Ciro Ferri* [exh. cat. by M. Giannatempo] [Rome, 1977] cat. no. 44, repr.). Jennifer Montagu (1973) has pointed out the influence of this composition on the early relief sculpture of Giovanni Battista Foggini. 2. Impression in the Witt Library; also repr. in Montagu 1973, p. 334, fig. 4. 3. The image on the Metz print measures 356 x 223 mm. Among the unknown qualities of the Lord St. Helens original are its direction, size, and medium; this author's tendency is to accept the Metz reproduction as a near-exact facsimile, rather than as a rough translation. 4. The collection would presumably have remained intact until its dispersal at auction in 1840 (F. Lugt, *Répertoire des catalogues de vents publiques*, vol. 2 [1826–1860] [The Hague, 1953], no. 15840 [Christie's London, 26 May 1840]). 5. Inv. no. KdZ 16643, repr. in Dreyer 1969, cat. no. 5, pl. 2. 6. Inv. no. FP 1588; I am grateful to Jörg Merz, through Bruce Davis, for this information. 7. Sold Sotheby's London, 26 April 1950, no. 129; photo in Witt Library. 8. The Davis attribution of the painting is on the Witt Library mount of the photo (under da Cortona); it is repr. in Prado, *Pintura Italiana del Siglo XVII* (exh. cat.) (Madrid, 1970), no. 57. The Louvre drawing photo is in the Ferri file at the Witt Library. 9. Inv. no. FP 11910, pen and brown ink, 89 x 100 mm.; I am grateful to Nicholas Turner for bringing this sheet to my attention and to both him and Bruce Davis for discussing the Bowdoin drawing and its attendant problems in great detail with me.

NICCOLO BERRETTONI

MACERATA DI MONTEFELTRO 1637–1682 ROME

68 *Studies for an Allegory of Love*

James Phinney Baxter Fund in Memory of Professor Henry Johnson (1932.16) Red chalk heightened with white chalk on blue laid paper (faded to grey), laid down. 402 x 264 mm. ($15^{13}/_{16}$ x $10^{3}/_{8}$ in.) Inscribed pen and black ink lower right "77"; graphite verso of mount "Nicolo Berrettoni 3882 No 34." No watermark visible. PROVENANCE: William Bates (1824–1884) (Lugt 2604); Professor Henry Johnson. BIBLIOGRAPHY: *Catalogue* 1930, p. 94, no. 631; Clark 1961, pp. 192–93, repr. fig. 1; Dowley 1966, p. 422; Mena Marqués 1976, p. 53; *Handbook* 1981, p. 167; Byam Shaw 1983, vol. 1, p. 177, n. 7.

AFTER STUDYING with Simone Cantarini in Pesaro, Berrettoni moved to Rome and entered the studio of Carlo Maratti (Cat. 64), where he remained for some twenty years. He was elected to the Accademia di San Luca in 1675 and executed several church and secular commissions. Berrettoni was regarded by his contemporaries as the most gifted of Maratti's followers.

This sheet entered the collections with a traditional attribution to Berrettoni and was recognized by Clark as a study for the central figure in Berrettoni's ceiling painting for the Salone Rosso in the Palazzo Altieri, Rome, executed around 1673–1675.[1] The decorative commissions for the palace (the family home of Pope Clement X) were among the most important in Rome of the time; Maratti himself painted the large ceiling of the audience chamber (see Cat. 64 for another drawing for the commission). The Salone Rosso was the bedchamber of the pope's niece and her husband. The extent of Maratti's influence over the designs for the smaller rooms in the palace, executed in three cases by students of his (the others besides Berrettoni being G. A. Carloni and F. Chiari), has been elucidated by Dowley and Mena Marqués. Dowley assumed that Berrettoni was working after general designs of Maratti's which at that point had not been found.[2] Mena Marqués later discovered two such designs by Maratti in the Academia de San Fernando in Madrid.[3] In addition, she found several figure studies by Berrettoni for his paintings; they are stylistically comparable to the Bowdoin sheet, and some are studies for the same figure.[4]

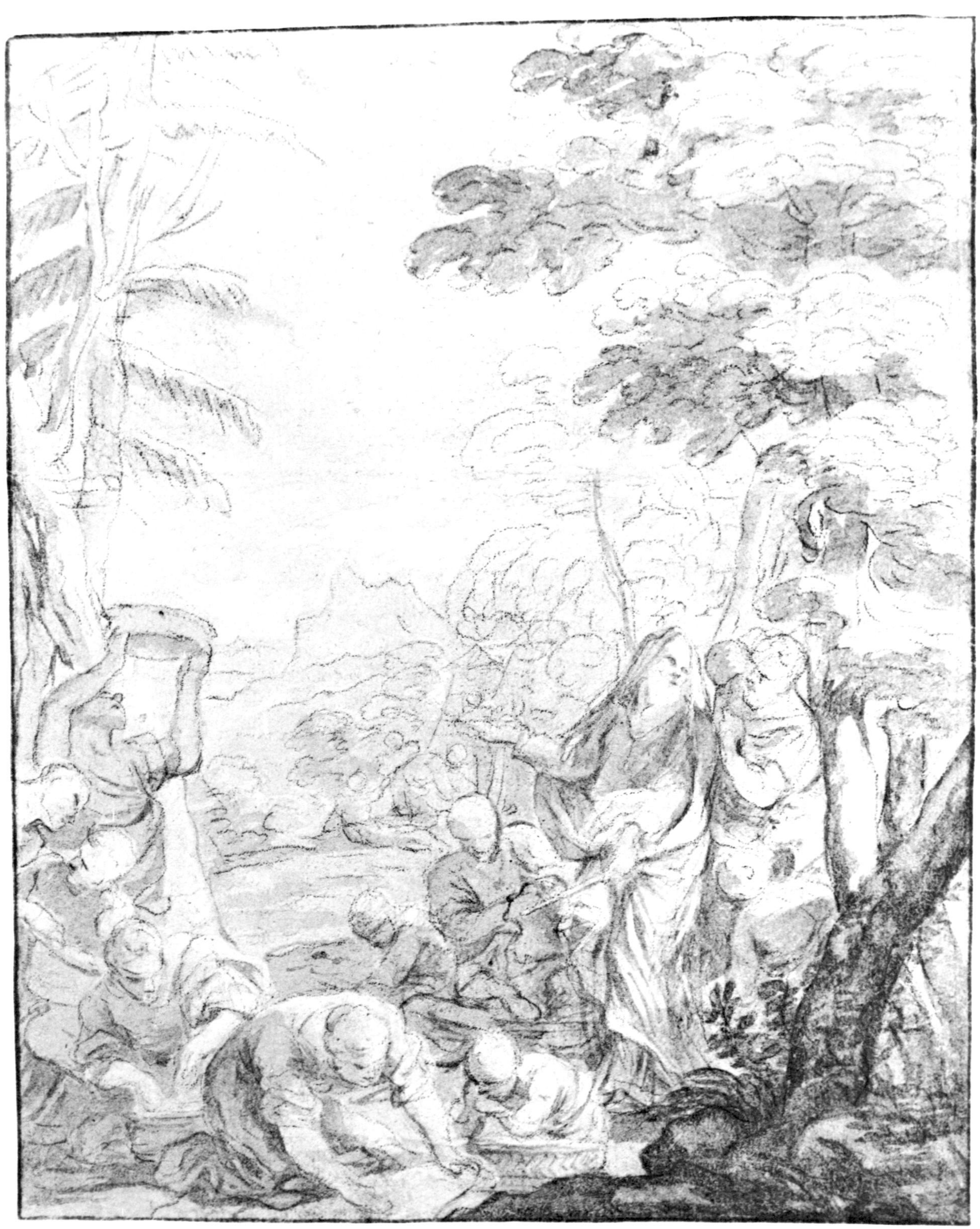

Mena Marqués also proposed that the central figure in Berrettoni's painting *Allegory of Love* is not Venus, as had traditionally been thought, but Aurora, goddess of the dawn, holding a torch being lit by Phosphorus, the morning star. The accompanying figures are Hesperus, the evening light, and the Hesperides. Mena Marqués pointed out that the figure of Aurora would be appropriate for the subject, in consideration of the goddess's "legendary power to renew a lover's passion upon her arrival."[5] Berrettoni's surrounding lunettes represent Venus and Cupid and an allegory of Spring. The Bowdoin study follows a studio practice of the time in depicting figures nude; clothing was usually added in later versions.

1. Clark 1961, p. 192. 2. Dowley 1966, p. 422. 3. Mena Marqués 1976, pp. 52–54. 4. Cf. ibid., p. 53 and pls. 25–32. Another head study is in Düsseldorf (ibid., p. 53). 5. Ibid., p. 52.

LUDOVICO GIMIGNANI

ROME 1643–1697 ZAGAROLA

69 *The Israelites Gathering Manna*

Bequest of James Bowdoin III (1811.16) Black chalk, grey wash, heightened with white, on brown laid paper. 275 x 224 mm. ($10^{13}/_{16}$ x $8^{13}/_{16}$ in.) Inscribed verso of former mount "No. 28 Chero Ferri." Watermark: fragment of initials IHS with cross within circle. PROVENANCE: James Bowdoin III. BIBLIOGRAPHY: *Catalogue* 1885, no. 25 (as Ferri); *Catalogue* 1930, no. 25 (as Ferri); Fischer Pace 1979, pp. 122–23, under cat. no. 402, repr. fig. 119 (as Gimignani, as is following); *Handbook* 1981, p. 167.

TRADITIONALLY ATTRIBUTED to Ciro Ferri, this sheet was recognized by Jacob Bean in 1963 as the work of another Roman, Ludovico Gimignani. He was trained by his father, Giacinto, and studied in Venice for a period under the patronage of his godfather, Giulio Rospigliosi, later Pope Clement IX. Ludovico spent his career entirely in Rome, painting palace decorations and commissions for several churches. He was elected to the Accademia di San Luca in 1672 and became its head in 1688–1689. By far the largest group of Gimignani's drawings—some 722 sheets—is in the Gabinetto Nazionale delle Stampe in Rome.[1] A drawn portrait of him by Giulio Solimena is in the Nationalmuseum, Stockholm.[2]

Ursula Fischer Pace has identified a pendant to the Bowdoin drawing, a depiction of the Finding of Moses, in the Gabinetto Nazionale. It is identical in format, technique, and style but has an attached decorative frame of satyrs, nymphs, and ornament. The frame also includes the device of the Rospigliosi family, leading Fischer Pace to date the sheet to within Clement IX's reign, from 1667 to 1669. Her dating to this point fairly early in Gimignani's career is reinforced by her stylistic comparison of this drawing to two other sheets, in Rome and Düsseldorf, which are studies for paintings datable to 1670.[4] She judges the purpose of the two scenes from the life of Moses to be strictly private and knows of no final work for which the Bowdoin and Rome sheets would have been studies. The story of the miraculous manna which fed the Israelites in their flight from Egypt is told in Exodus 16:4–36.

1. Fully catalogued in Fischer Pace 1979. 2. Repr. ibid., p. 36. 3. Ibid., p. 122, cat. no. 402, repr. The author states that Eric Schleier brought the Bowdoin sheet to her attention. 4. The drawings are repr. ibid., cat. no. 88 (Rome), and fig. 40 (Düsseldorf). The two paintings are repr. ibid., figs. 38 and 41.

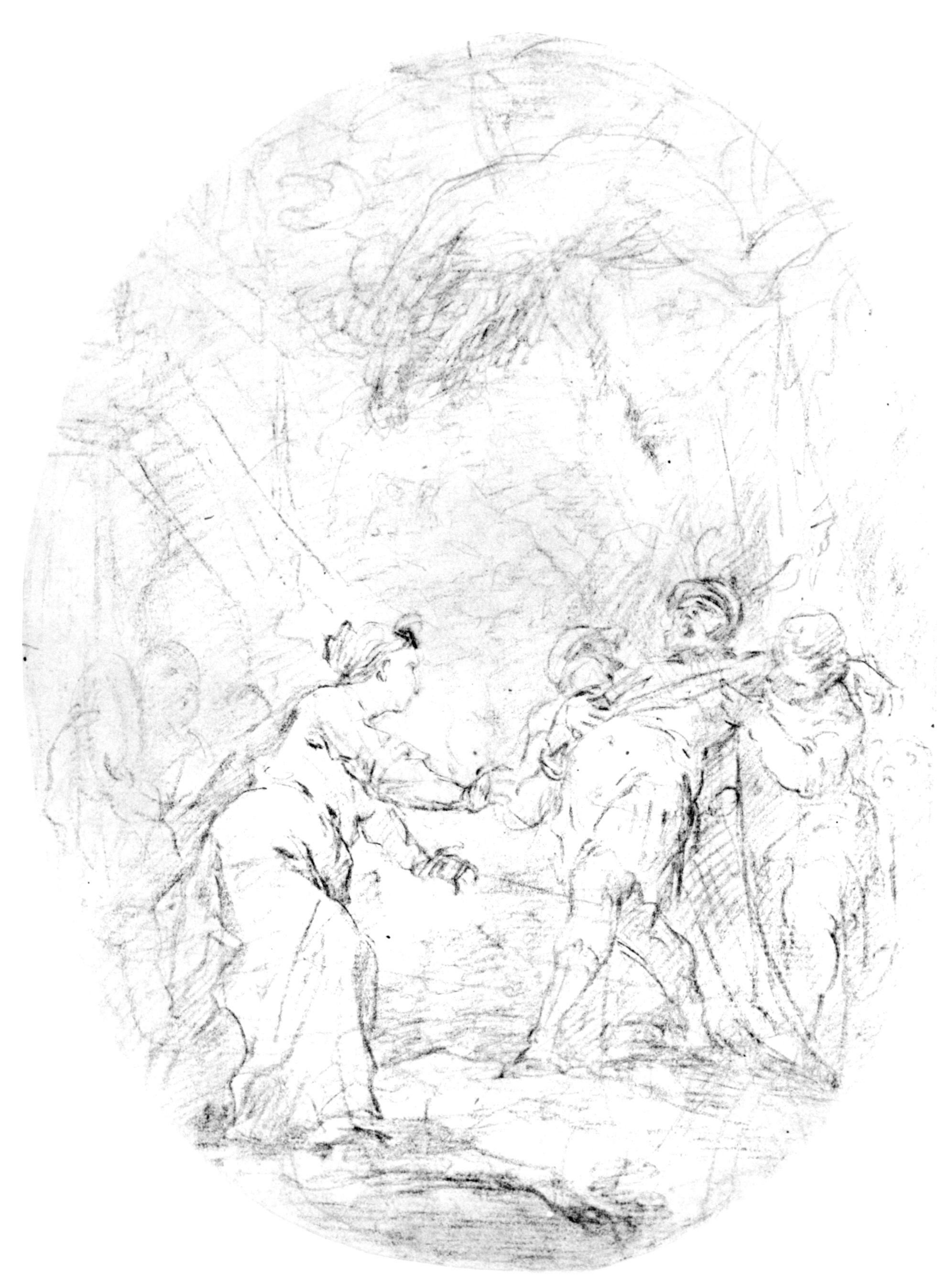

PIETRO DANDINI
FLORENCE 1646–1712 FLORENCE

70 *Jephthah and His Daughter*

James Phinney Baxter Fund in Memory of Professor Henry Johnson (1932.12) Brown and black chalk, partially laid down. Oval 232 x 174 mm. (9 1/8 x 6 7/8 in.) Inscribed on former mount (lost): "Dandini"; "Scuola Toscana." Indecipherable watermark. PROVENANCE: Giovanni Lombardi, Florence (oval stamp in black, verso of mount, not in Lugt); Professor Henry Johnson. BIBLIOGRAPHY: *Catalogue* 1930, p. 95, no. 626.

ACCORDING TO Philip Pouncey and to an unsigned note on the mount of the Witt Library photograph of this drawing (filed under Cesare), Pietro Dandini is more likely to have been the source of this work than is his uncle, Cesare, to whom it was formerly credited.[1] Pietro was a member of a large artistic family in Florence and trained with another uncle, Vincenzo Dandini. After travels to Venice, Lombardy, Emilia, and Rome, Pietro settled in Florence and executed several commissions for members of the Medici family in addition to producing paintings for various churches, palaces, and villas.

The subject of the Bowdoin drawing has traditionally been thought to represent Lucrecia and the Dying Tarquin, but Jennifer Montagu has convincingly suggested that it is instead the tragic story of Jephthah, as recounted in Judges 12:30–40. In return for victory in battle, the warrior leader Jephthah promised the Lord he would sacrifice the first person he saw upon returning to his house. After victory was granted him, the first person who greeted him was his only child and daughter, who emerged with music and celebration. Upon seeing her, Jephthah tore his clothes and lamented his promise, which, however, his daughter insisted he keep. The meeting is depicted here.

As Susan Wegner recently noted, this drawing is apparently carried out over a previous sketch, visible in part when the sheet is turned on its right side. The technique agrees very favorably with a study by Dandini of the Fall of the Damned.[2]

1. In conversation with the author, 1983. 2. Repr. in Palazzo Strozzi and other places, *Disegni antichi di allegoria e mitologia* (Florence, 1975), cat. no. 42.

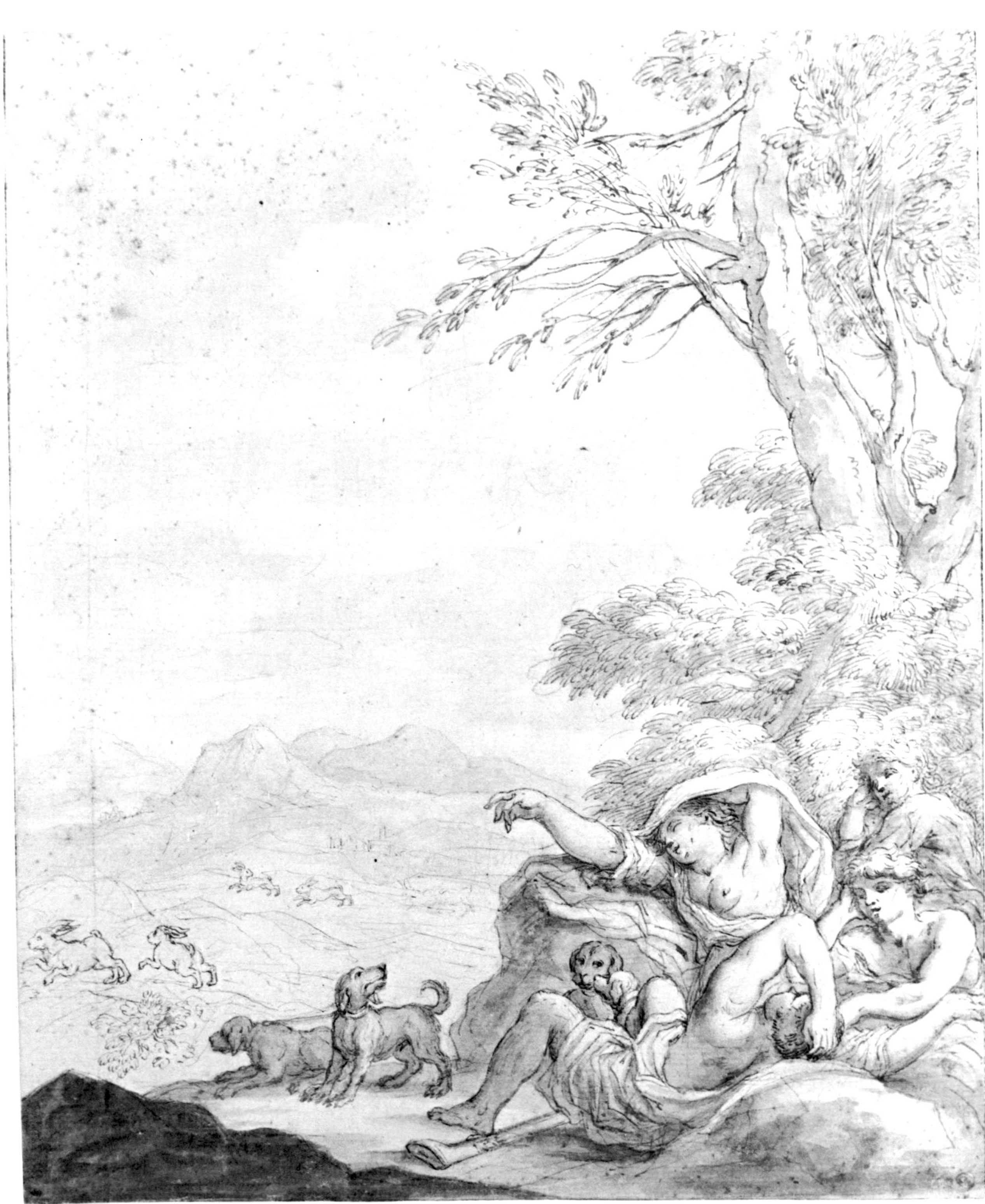

ATANASIO BIMBACCI

FLORENCE ca. 1654–1734 FLORENCE

71 *The Sleeping Hunters*

James Phinney Baxter Fund in Memory of Professor Henry Johnson (1932.18) Pen and brown ink, brown wash, over black chalk (graphite?), traced with a stylus, laid down. Verso sketches of figures (Diana?). 305 x 255 mm. (12 x 10 in.) Inscribed verso of mount pen and brown ink "Atanasio Bimbacci." No watermark visible. PROVENANCE: William Bates (1824–1884) (Lugt 2604); Professor Henry Johnson. BIBLIOGRAPHY: *Catalogue* 1930, p. 94, no. 633.

BIMBACCI TRAINED FIRST in Florence with Livio Mehus, then in Rome with Ciro Ferri (cf. Cat. 67), in both cases under the patronage of the grand dukes of Tuscany. He returned to Florence, where he produced numerous decorations for churches, houses, and theaters. His death date is unknown.[1]

The attribution of this drawing is based on the old inscription on the mount. Works by Bimbacci are so little known that the inscription may be considered reliable. Stylistically the Bowdoin sheet matches a group formerly in the collection of the Instituto Jovellanos in Gijon, Spain, which was destroyed during the Spanish Civil War.[2] This design would likely have been included among the customary hunting scenes used to decorate a summer villa. The sheet has been carefully traced with a stylus for transfer, probably for another drawing, as Bimbacci is not known to have executed any prints. The figures have been identified in the museum files as Venus and Adonis, but specific attributes are lacking; the verso sketches perhaps depict Diana.

1. Bimbacci's manuscript autobiography is in the library at Perugia (Thieme-Becker, vol. 4, p. 35). His work is discussed among others by S. Rudolph in *Arte illustrata*, vol. 7, no. 59 (1974), pp. 279–98. 2. A. Perez Sanchez, *Catalogo de la Coleccion de Dibujos del Instituto Jovellanos de Gijon* (Madrid, 1969), pp. 19–20, cat. nos. 19–26, figs. 29–32.

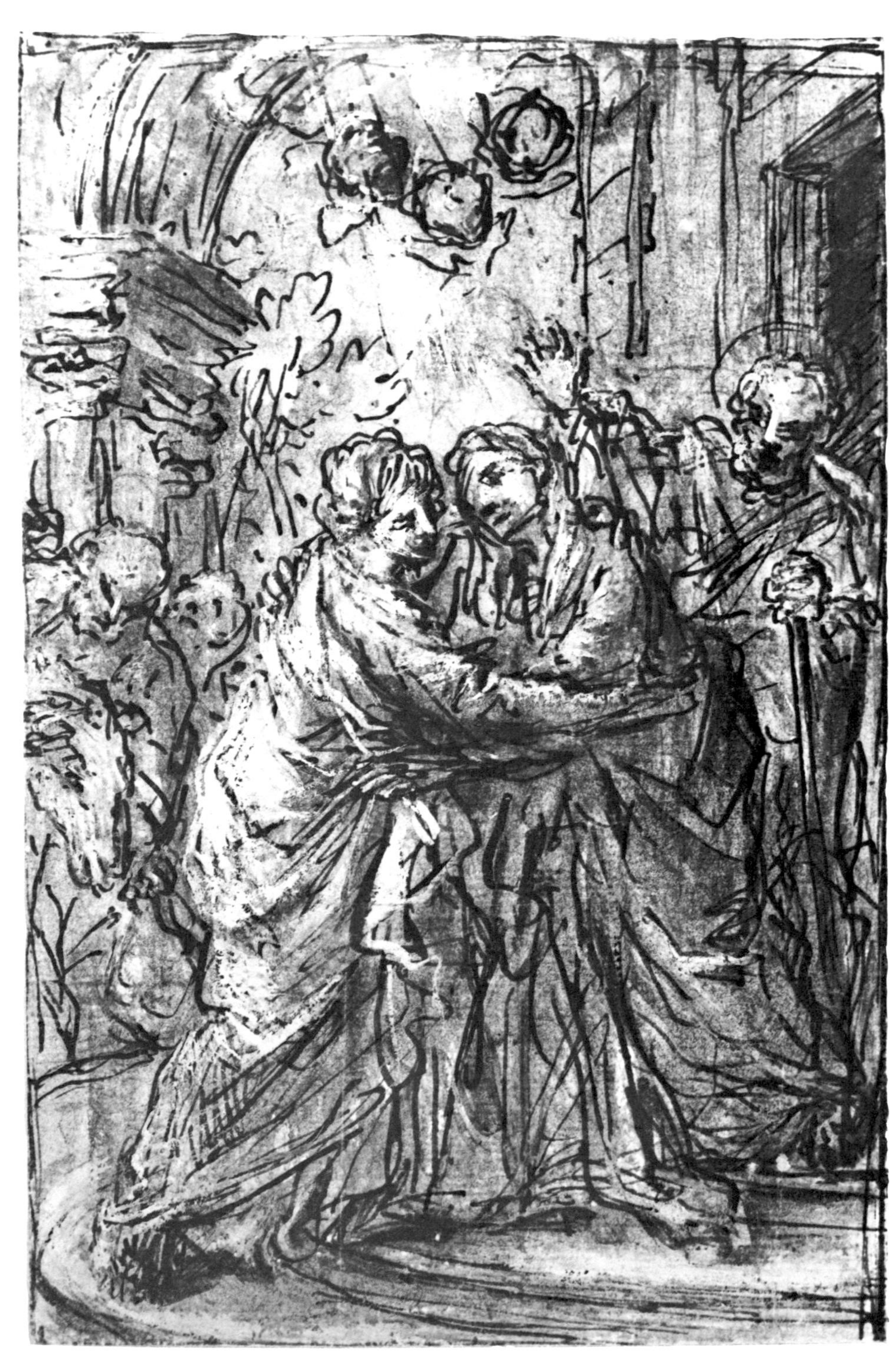

GIUSEPPE PASSERI
ROME 1654–1714 ROME

72 *The Visitation*

Gift of Miss Susan Dwight Bliss (1956.24.234) Pen and black ink, grey wash, red and black chalk, heightened with white (darkened), laid down. 206 x 137 mm. (8 1/8 x 5 3/8 in.) Inscribed verso graphite "G. Passeri sketch for Visitation picture/at Chiesa Nuova Rome 1711/1799." No watermark. PROVENANCE: Susan Dwight Bliss.

PASSERI WAS THE NEPHEW of the biographer Giovanni Battista Passeri and trained briefly with him before entering the studio of Carlo Maratti (Cat. 64). He is said to have been one of Maratti's favorite students, and he collaborated on commissions with his master. Passeri's earliest dated work was in the Palazzo Barberini in 1678. He was elected a member of the Accademia di San Luca in 1693. Besides the usual religious commissions he received, Passeri was known as a portraitist and painter of small easel pictures. Over 1,100 of his drawings are in the Kunstmuseum, Düsseldorf, and other sizable groups are in the Albertina and Windsor Castle.[1]

The attribution to Passeri of this sheet is traditional and entirely consistent with the almost frenetic linear style he used to define his compositions. Many of his chalk drawings, though done on white paper, are composed of a field of dark lines upon which highlights are defined with white, as has been done here. Though the verso inscription indicates that the Bowdoin sheet is a study for a work in the Chiesa Nuova, Rome (S. Maria in Vallicella), neither Buchowiecki nor Waterhouse mention such a Visitation by Passeri in that church.[2] Dieter Graf notes that the Bowdoin drawing is, however, related to an engraving by Jean Charles Allet (active 1690–1732) after Passeri's design in a book by Alessandro Mazzinelli, *Officio della B. Vergine Maria*, first published in Rome in 1706.[3] The engraving is in the same direction as the drawing and agrees with it in composition. Graf indicates that the Bowdoin sketch might also have been used for a painting, but he knows of no such work. Two Passeri drawings for a Deposition, also engraved for Mazzinelli's book, are in Windsor Castle.[4]

1. The Albertina and Windsor drawings are catalogued respectively in Stix and Fröhlich-Bum 1932, cat. nos. 787–98, and Blunt and Cooke 1960, cat. nos. 566–87. 2. Buchowiecki 1967–1974, vol. 3, p. 214, and Waterhouse 1976, p. 102. 3. Letter to the author, 21 September 1984. A copy of the 1744 edition is in the Houghton Library, Harvard University. 4. Blunt and Cooke 1960, cat. nos. 573–74. I am very grateful to Dr. Graf for this information.

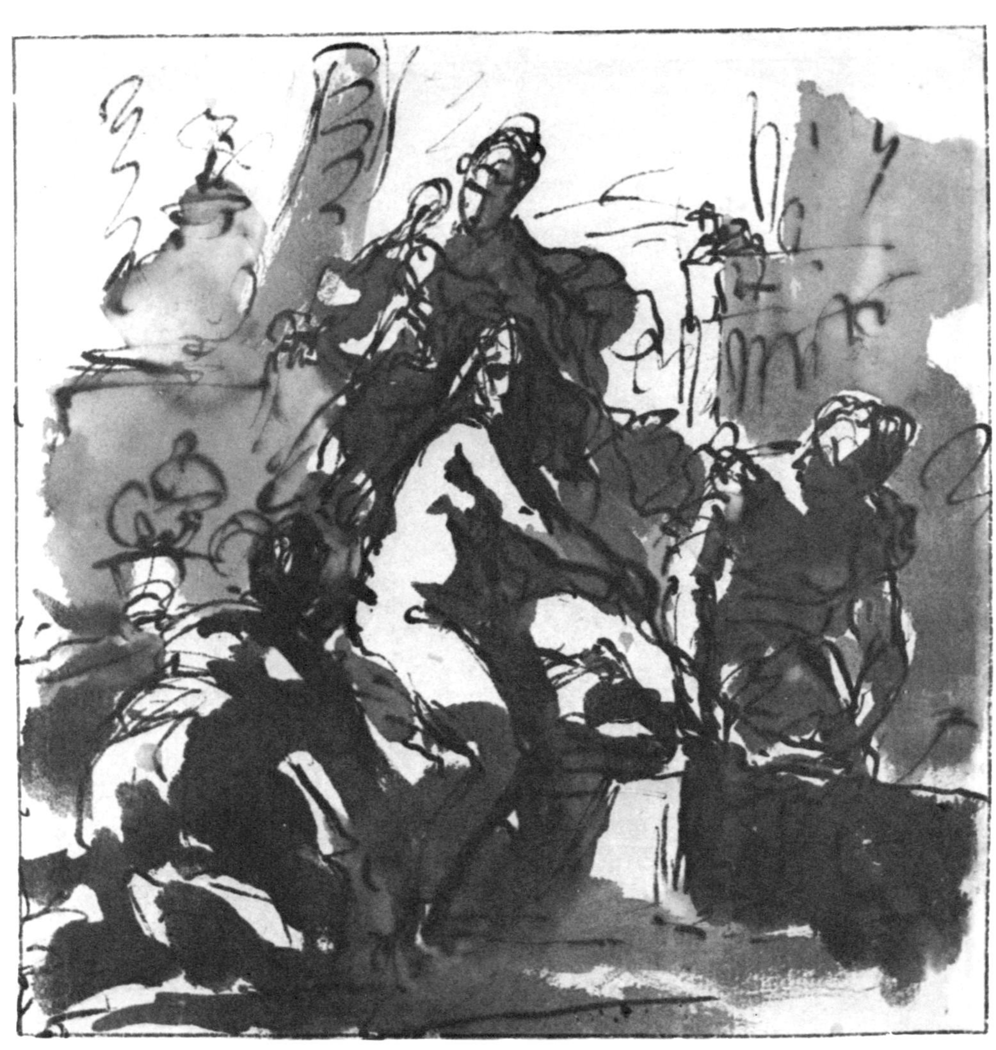

SEBASTIANO RICCI
BELLUNO 1659–1734 VENICE

73 *Bathsheba*

Bequest of James Bowdoin III (1811.41) Pen and brown ink and brown wash (paper darkened from exposure to light). 136 x 131 mm. ($5^3/_8$ x $5^1/_8$ in.) Inscribed verso, graphite "S. Ricci." No watermark. PROVENANCE: James Bowdoin III. BIBLIOGRAPHY: *Catalogue* 1885, no. 75 (as Ricci, as are all following); Mather 1913, p. 248, repr. p. 247, fig. 16; *Catalogue* 1930, no. 48; [Siber] 1947, p. 119, repr. p. 117, fig. IV; Daniels 1976a, p. 14, under no. 41; Daniels 1976b, p. 125, under no. 414; *Handbook* 1981, pp. 167–68. EXHIBITION: Memphis, Brooks Memorial Art Gallery, and Lexington, University of Kentucky Art Gallery, *Sebastiano and Marco Ricci in America* [exh. cat. by M. Milkovich], 1965–1966, cat. no. 20, repr.

RICCI WAS A PUPIL of Federico Cervelli in Venice and worked there between extensive trips within Italy and to England, the Netherlands, and France. During an extended stay in Florence he finished several decorative cycles for the Medici and other patrons. His colorful and energetic painting style was an important forerunner of the eighteenth-century Venetian school, in particular the work of Giovanni Battista Tiepolo. Ricci was the uncle of the landscapist Marco Ricci.

This drawing came to the museum with at least a nineteenth-century ascription to Ricci and was singled out in early publications of the collection. In 1913 Mather published it and stated that it was essentially a "rearrangement" of Tintoretto's *Susannah and the Elders*, which is in the Louvre. At the same time, he entitled the Bowdoin drawing *Susannah*, but the presence of the tiny figure of David on the terrace in the right background establishes this subject as Bathsheba (2 Samuel 11:3–17), as recognized by Richard West.

Jeffery Daniels has connected the Bowdoin study with two painted versions of the subject by Ricci, particularly the one in the Dahlem Museum, which he dates around 1724, in which the pose of Bathsheba is quite similar.[1] The Berlin painting does not include the figure of David, but he does appear in the other version, of which there are two copies, one in Budapest and the other in the Coin Collection, Venice.[2] Daniels dates the Berlin painting around 1724. The rapid flourishes and contrasts of the Bowdoin drawing are seen in several characteristic Ricci sheets in an album in the Accademia, Venice.[3]

1. Daniels 1976a, p. 14, no. 41, repr. fig. 44; cf. also letter from Daniels to Richard West, 18 December 1970, in museum files. 2. Budapest: ibid., p. 21, no. 67, repr. fig. 45; Coin: p. 139, no. 475. A preparatory study for the Budapest drawing is in the Accademia, Venice (Daniels 1976b, fig. 411[1]). 3. Cf. Daniels 1976b, figs. 118, 353, 373[2], and 410[1].

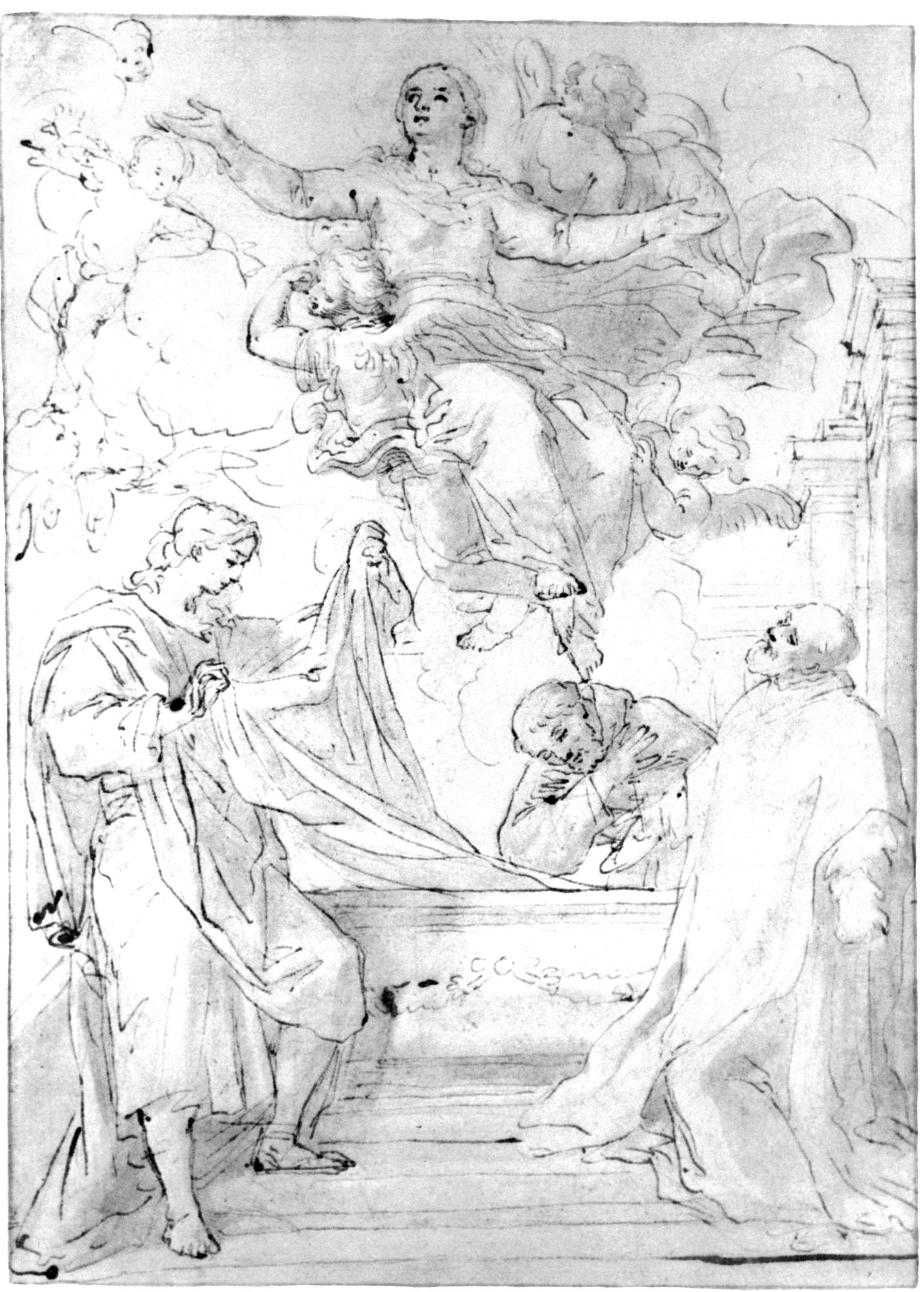

PIETRO ANTONIO DE' PIETRI

PREMIA (Piedmont) 1663/65–1716 ROME

74 *The Assumption, with St. Philip Neri and St. Francis*

Bequest of James Bowdoin III (1811.26) Pen and brown ink, brown wash over black chalk. 266 x 193 mm. (10 7/16 x 7 9/16 in.) Watermark: cardinal's hat over shield. PROVENANCE: James Bowdoin III. BIBLIOGRAPHY: *Catalogue* 1885, no. 35; *Catalogue* 1930, no. 35; *Handbook* 1981, p. 168.

THOUGH VARYING BIRTH DATES are given in early biographies of de' Pietri, Byam Shaw has pointed out that the later date is inscribed on a self-portrait drawing in Stockholm.[1] De' Pietri came to Rome at an early age, studying first with Giuseppe Ghezzi and Angelo Massarotti, then entering Maratti's studio. He executed several commissions for Roman families and churches and was elected to the Accademia di San Luca in 1711. He also executed several prints.[2] Sizable groups of de' Pietri's drawings are in Windsor Castle, Düsseldorf, and Berlin.[3] The group at Bowdoin College is also noteworthy, all coming from the original Bowdoin bequest. If they indeed were acquired by John Smibert in Italy, the presumed breakup of de' Pietri's studio at his death just prior to Smibert's arrival would explain the presence of such a large group at Bowdoin (including other sheets by students of Maratti).

The Bowdoin group includes examples of the two media used most often by de' Pietri—red chalk, and pen and brown ink with wash. Following the system used in Maratti's studio, de' Pietri made many preliminary sketches for his compositions; indeed, he often tried many variations before determining a final disposition of his subjects. A case in point is the subject of this drawing, for which a large number of drawn studies survive. Late in his career, de' Pietri finished both an etching of the Assumption of the Virgin[4] and an oval ceiling of the same scene in the dome of Santa Maria alle Fornaci, Rome.[5] The Bowdoin sheet is closely related to the etching and to several other drawn studies for the same work. Two sheets in the British Museum[6] and the Art Institute of Chicago[7] are particularly close. Also related is a double-sided sheet in the Chrysler Museum, Norfolk.[8] All these drawings include the figures of the two saints at the tomb, with the Virgin being carried upward by angels. Three other studies are at Windsor.[9]

In all these studies, the artist has switched the positions of the figures, reversed the direction of the Virgin, and extensively explored differing attitudes of faces and arms. The multiplicity of changes renders a logical chronology difficult to establish. There is no final painted composition known of this particular scheme. The study in the British Museum clearly establishes the identity of the attendant saints by displaying their attributes of a crucifix and skull (St. Francis) and chasuble and lily (St. Philip Neri). Another, unidentified attendant holds the Virgin's shroud. Here, St. Francis is seen behind the tomb and St. Philip Neri anchors the right side of the composition. De' Pietri drawings are frequently double-sided; the Norfolk study and one of those at Windsor have drawings on both sides of the paper in the same scale.[10]

1. Byam Shaw 1976, vol. 1, p. 177, under no. 656. The Stockholm drawing is repr. in Clark 1967, pl. 4. Another attributed self-portrait drawing was sold at Christie's London, 4 July 1972, lot 110, repr. 2. The Bowdoin museum owns his etching of The Rescue of Souls from Purgatory (Inv. no. 1979.17). 3. An extensive listing of de' Pietri holdings, with references, is included in Philadelphia 1980–1981, p. 17, under cat. no. 7. 4. Bartsch 21.292.1; the Metropolitan Museum of Art owns an impression. 5. A study for this ceiling is in Philadelphia, cf. Philadelphia 1980–1981, checklist no. 149. 6. Inv. no. 1946-2-9-34. 7. Inv. no. 1922.5476. 8. Inv. no. 50.49.62a and b; repr. in E. M. Zafran, *One Hundred Drawings in the Chrysler Museum at Norfolk* (Norfolk, 1979), cat. no. 26. 9. Blunt and Cooke 1960, cat. nos. 686–87a. 10. Ibid., cat. no. 686.

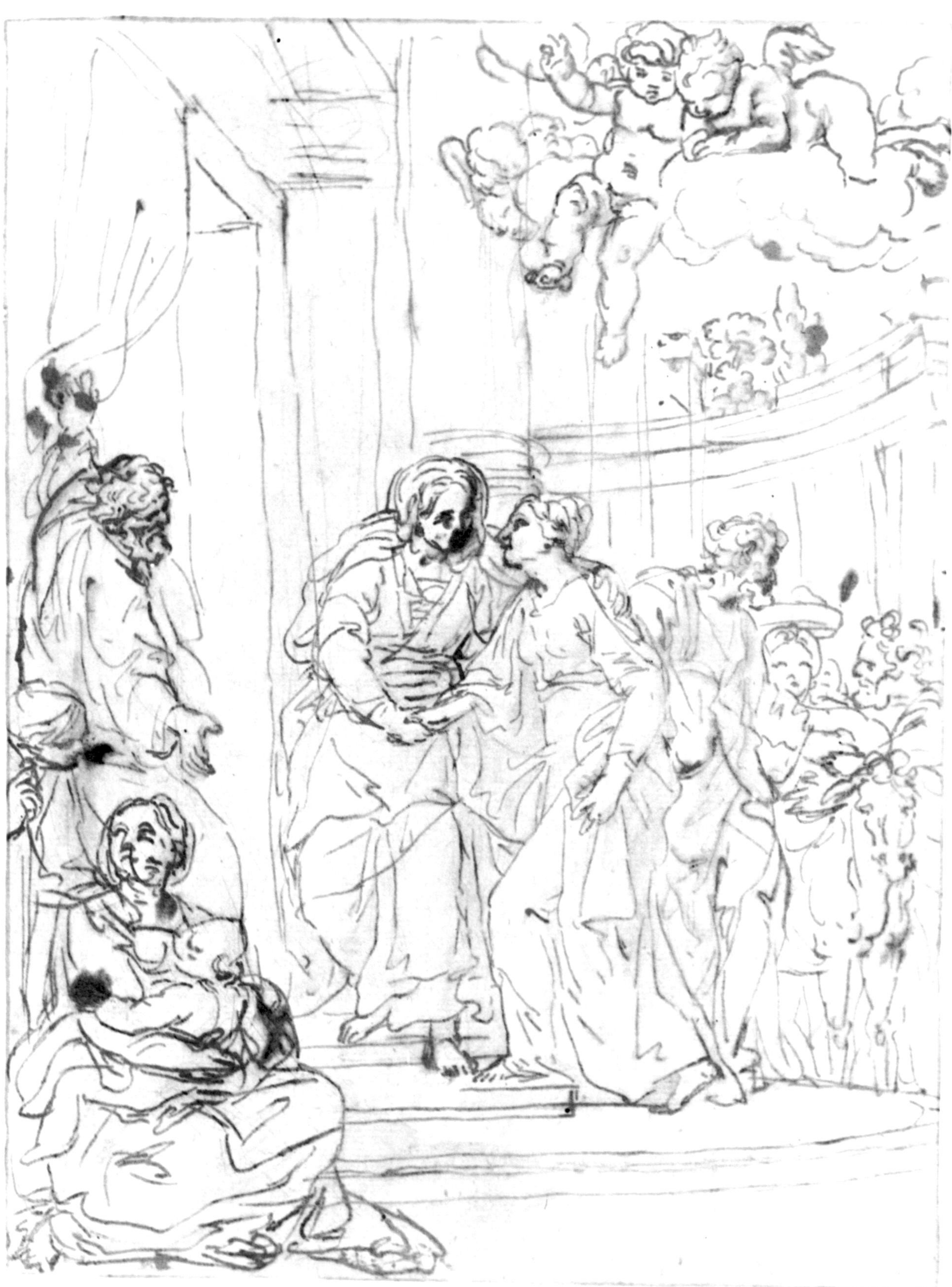

PIETRO DE' PIETRI

75 *The Visitation*

Bequest of James Bowdoin III (1811.24) Pen and brown ink and light brown wash over black chalk. 264 x 198 mm. ($10^{3}/8$ x $7^{15}/16$ in.) No watermark. PROVENANCE: James Bowdoin III. BIBLIOGRAPHY: *Catalogue* 1885, no. 33; *Catalogue* 1930, no. 33; *Handbook* 1981, p. 168.

THE VISITATION is an example of de' Pietri's characteristic pen and wash style, as is *Flight into Egypt* (Cat. 180). These two are more resolved and fluid than studies such as *The Assumption* (Cat. 74), though even here the artist has ventured two alternatives for the head of the mother at lower left. This sheet may be compared with two studies for the *Presentation of the Infant Jesus in the Temple*, one in the Metropolitan[1] and the other in Chicago.[2] Both of the latter sheets are larger and have been further heightened with white gouache. No painted versions by de' Pietri of the Visitation are known.[3] The visit by the Virgin just after the Annunciation to her cousin Elizabeth (who was pregnant with St. John the Baptist) is related in Luke 1:39–56.

1. Inv. no. 1980.122, repr. in Bean and Turčić 1982, p. 316, no. App.15. 2. Inv. no. 1972.323, repr. in Joachim and McCullagh 1979, no. 93, pl. 100. 3. Waterhouse 1976, p. 104.

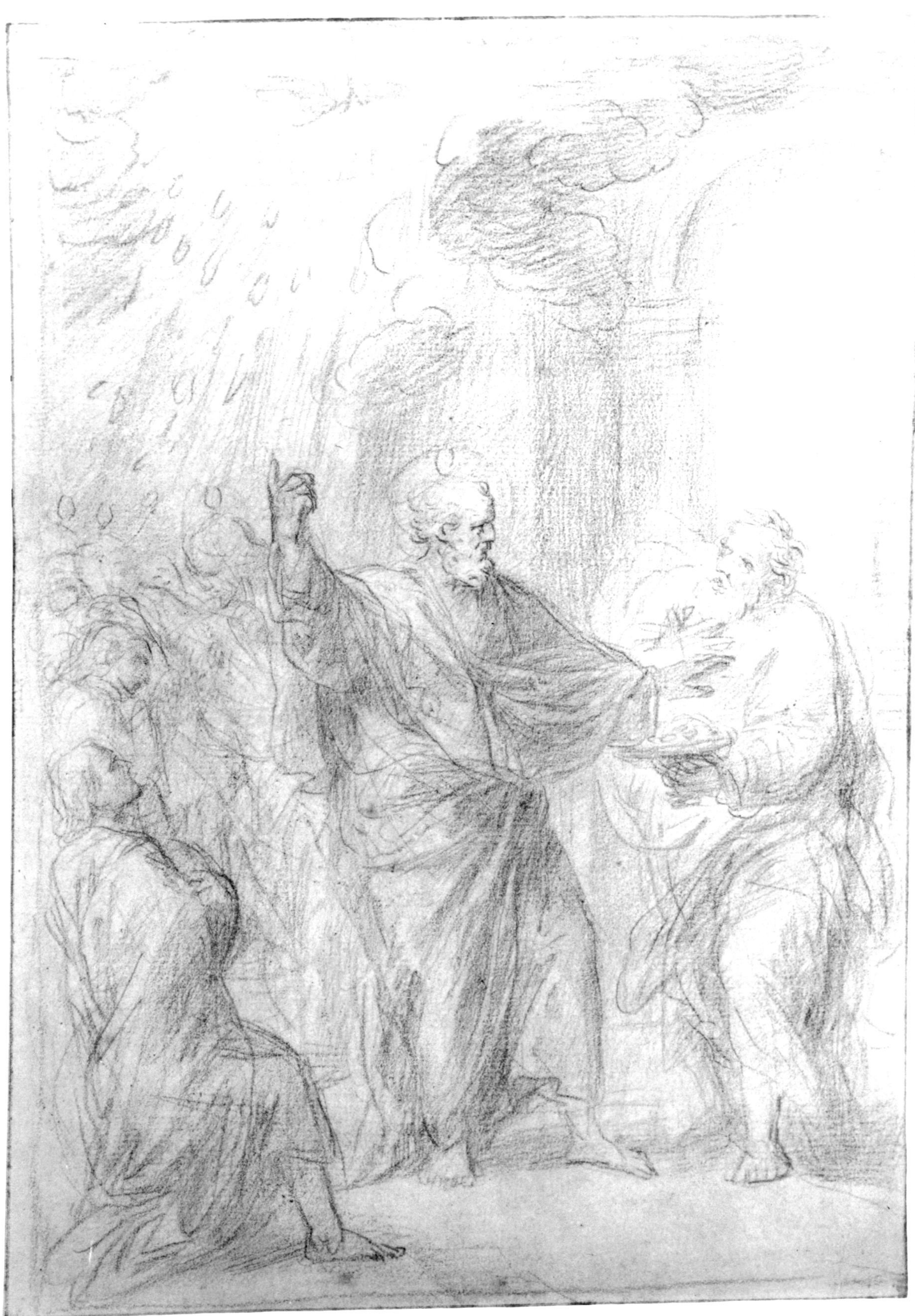

PIETRO DE' PIETRI

76 *Peter Denouncing Simon* (verso: *Christ Delivering the Keys to Peter*)

Bequest of James Bowdoin III (1811.19) Red chalk. 264 x 187 mm. (10 3/8 x 7 3/8 in.) Watermark: six-pointed star above anchor in circle over A. PROVENANCE: James Bowdoin III. BIBLIOGRAPHY: *Catalogue* 1885, no. 28; *Catalogue* 1930, no. 28; Dreyer 1971, p. 189; *Handbook* 1981, p. 168.

AS POINTED OUT by Peter Dreyer, de' Pietri is known to have depicted at least three scenes from the life of the Apostle Peter. A painting of the denouncing of Simon is in the Accademia di San Luca, Rome,[1] for which this sheet and two drawings in Berlin are studies.[2] This episode, in which Simon attempted to offer Peter gold in return for learning the secret of baptism, is described in Acts 8:9–24. The verso of the Bowdoin sheet shows the symbolic delivery of the keys of the Church to St. Peter's care (Matthew 16:8–19). Another double-sided sheet at Bowdoin (Cat. 178) contains two versions of Peter's release from prison in Jerusalem (Acts 12:7–11). No paintings are known of the two latter subjects.

All three studies for the denunciation of Simon are executed in chalk, again with de' Pietri's customary restless experimentation with gestures and disposition of figures. The two Berlin studies are similar to each other. They lack the heavenly shower of the Holy Spirit seen here, but in other respects the three versions are much the same, with the bold figure of Peter dominating the center of the composition. Other red chalk studies like these are found at Bowdoin, Windsor Castle, and Christ Church, Oxford.[3]

1. Dreyer 1971, p. 189. 2. Ibid. 3. Cf. Blunt and Cooke 1960, cat. no. 678; and Byam Shaw 1976, cat. no. 657, repr. pl. 371–72.

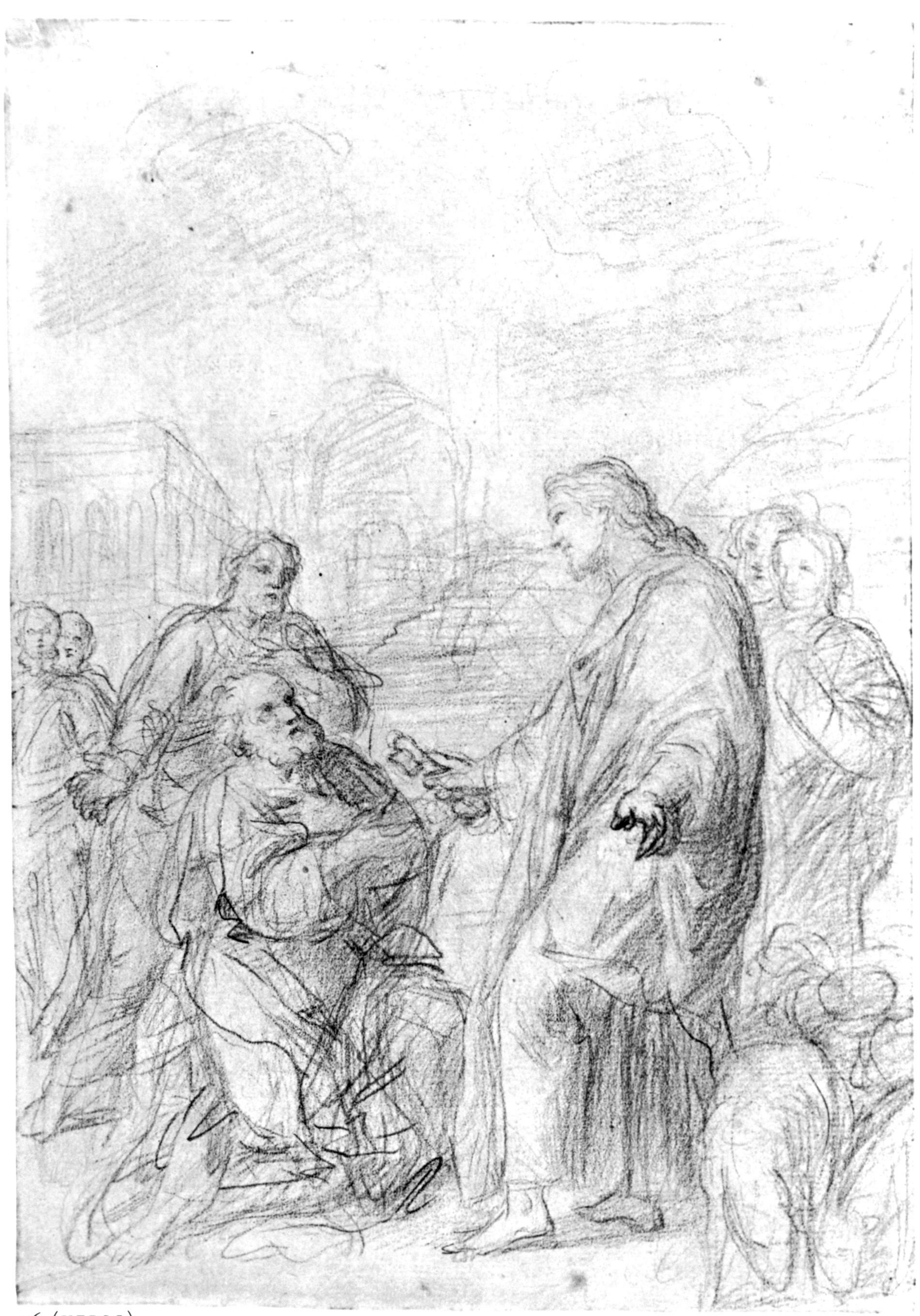

76 (VERSO)

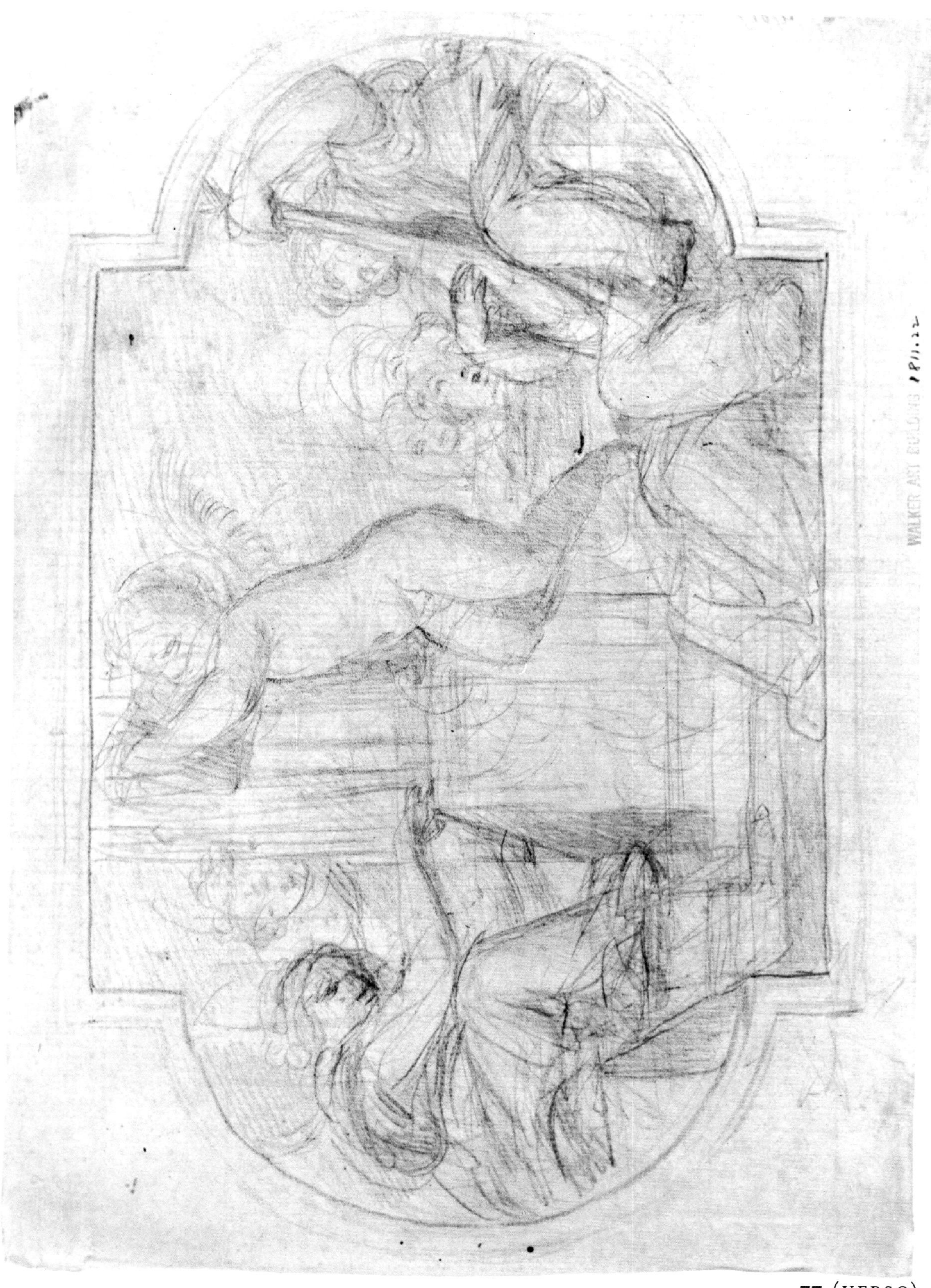

77 (VERSO)

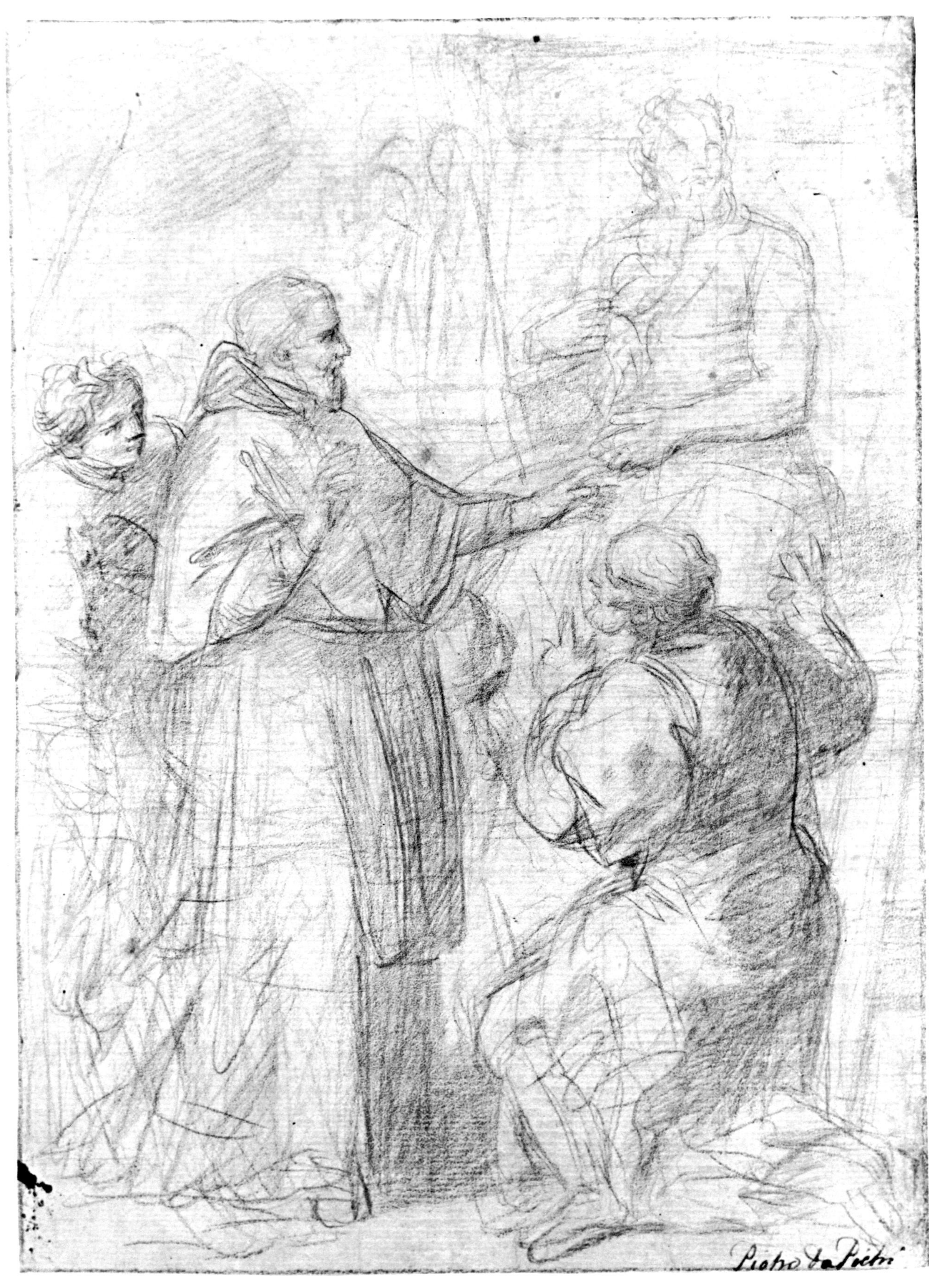
Pietro da Pietri

PIETRO DE' PIETRI

77 *A Pope in Michelangelo's Studio* (verso: *Ceiling Design with Musicians*)

Bequest of James Bowdoin III (1811.22) Red chalk (verso: black chalk). 267 x 195 mm. (10 1/2 x 7 11/16 in.) Inscribed pen and ink lower right "Pietro da Pietri." Watermark: six-pointed star over anchor in circle. PROVENANCE: James Bowdoin III. BIBLIOGRAPHY: *Catalogue* 1885, no. 31; *Catalogue* 1930, no. 31; *Handbook* 1981, p. 168. EXHIBITION: Regina and Montreal 1970, cat. no. 69, repr.

As WALTER VITZTHUM has pointed out, this sheet is particularly interesting for its iconography. He has identified the subject as Pope Julius II looking at Michelangelo's statue of Moses, which was intended for the pope's tomb in St. Peter's. He has further stated that this drawing recalls the decorations of Michelangelo's house in Florence, which were executed in the early seventeenth century by several artists. However, Susan Wegner has suggested that this scene more probably illustrates an anecdote which comes from Vasari's life of Michelangelo and concerns Pope Paul III. Vasari relates that upon the death of Clement VII in 1533, Michelangelo hoped to return to the unfinished project for Julius's tomb, but the newly elected Paul III tried very strongly to secure the artist's services for his own projects. Following Vasari, "the Pope . . . one day called at his house with ten cardinals. He saw and admired all the statues for the tomb of Julius, especially the Moses which the cardinal of Mantua declared sufficient by itself to honour the dead Pope."[1] This explanation receives further support from a closely related de' Pietri drawing of the same subject at Holkham Hall, noted by Vitzthum.[2] The Holkham sheet is considerably more resolved and contains several additional figures, of whom a few are clearly cardinals. It seems to depict the interior of a studio; the pope looks directly at the artist and addresses him. De' Pietri never executed any paintings for Michelangelo's house, the Casa Buonarroti, in Florence, and the final purpose of these two drawings remains obscure.

1. The translation is from G. Vasari, *The Lives of the Painters, Sculptors, and Architects*, trans. A. B. Hinds (London and New York, 1963), vol. 4, pp. 139–40. 2. Red chalk, 264 x 195 mm.; photograph in the Witt Library.

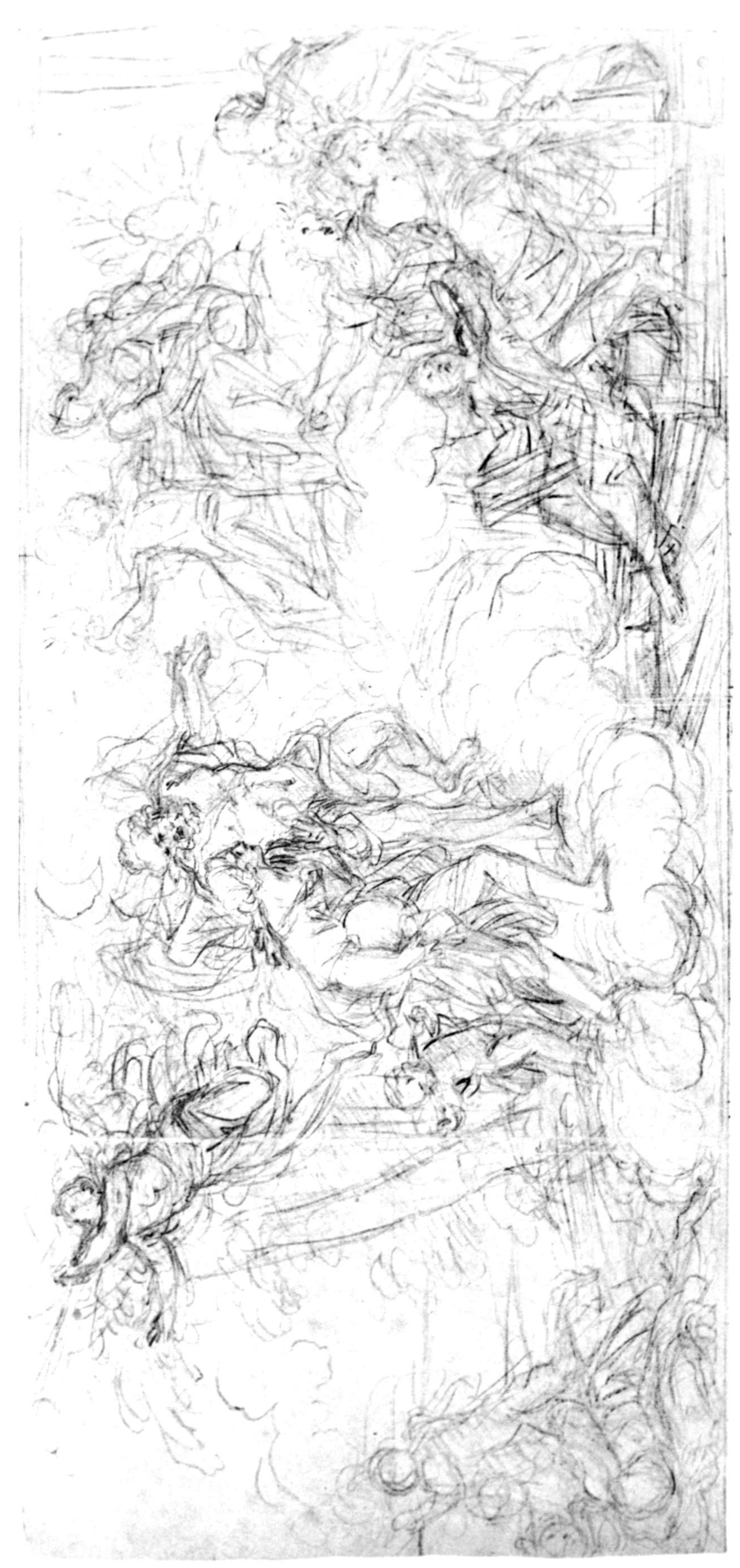

GIOVANNI PAOLO MELCHIORI
ROME 1664–1745 ROME

78 *Cupid Presenting Psyche to the Gods*

Bequest of Helen Johnson Chase (1958.70) Black and red chalk on two sheets of blue laid paper (faded from exposure to light; three old vertical folds). 278 x 595 mm. (11 x 23³/8 in.) Inscribed pen and brown ink verso "W.S." (cf. Provenance). Watermark (countermark): monogram PVL; cf. Churchill 113, 135. Probably the mark of the Dutch papermaking firm Pieter vander Ley, active 1665–1765. PROVENANCE: William Sharp (active mid-nineteenth century) (Lugt 2650); William Bates (1824–1884) (Lugt 2604); Professor Henry Johnson; Helen Johnson (Mrs. Stanley P.) Chase. BIBLIOGRAPHY: *Catalogue* 1930, p. 95, no. 622 (as Figino); *Handbook* 1981, p. 167 (as Maratta).

THIS SHEET was formerly attributed to Ambrogio Figino (ca. 1548–1608) and, more believably, to Maratti. Manuela Mena Marqués doubted the ascription to Maratti upon seeing the drawing several years ago but placed it within his close circle. Recently, she attributed it to Melchiori, a student and follower of Maratti's, and this attribution has been confirmed by Prosperi Valenti Rodinò.[1] After training in Maratti's studio, Melchiori worked in Naples for some time from ca. 1688 but then seems to have spent most of his still obscure career in Rome. His most noted commission was for decorations in San Giovanni in Laterano from ca. 1716 to 1720. He also executed engravings after his and others' (particularly Maratti's) designs. Prosperi Valenti Rodinò has recently defined his accomplished, quite Marattesque draughtsmanship.[2] Sizable collections of his drawings are preserved in Rome at the Gabinetto Nazionale, in Düsseldorf at the Kunstmuseum, and in Berlin.[3] A self-portrait drawing is in the Nationalmuseum, Stockholm.[4]

The loose draughtsmanship and restless working out of gestures in the Bowdoin sheet has parallels in other drawings by Melchiori, particularly several in Düsseldorf.[5] The Bowdoin drawing is a compositional sketch preliminary to the more systematic, careful delineation of individual figures, characteristic of the working method in Maratti's studio (for instance, the Bowdoin Berrettoni study, Cat. 68). The subject of this large-scale, complex work, however, has eluded firm identification. Prosperi Valenti Rodinò knows of no recorded or existing paintings after this design. Presumably it is either an allegory relating to the history of a particular family or an independent iconographic exercise.

The sketchiness of the figures also renders their identities obscure.[6] Prosperi Valenti Rodinò has proposed that the design represents Amor (Cupid) presenting Psyche to the gods, who are seen at the upper right seated upon clouds. (Juno is recognizable by her attribute, a peacock, behind her, and therefore Jupiter is the male figure seated to her left.) Psyche ascends toward them, holding a globe and being led by a bearded, winged figure, presumably Time. Cupid is the small putto behind Psyche's feet. The figures at the lower right may be personifications of the Arts or History. Meanwhile, the flying figure (Fame?) blows a trumpet and banishes the evil forces offstage to the left. The story of the love of Cupid and Psyche is told in Lucius Apuleius's *The Golden Ass, or Metamorphoses*.[7]

This allegory possibly depicts the council of all the gods which was held to grant formal permission for Cupid and Psyche to be married. Psyche was granted immortality by Jupiter at that council; the container she is holding might be the pot of immortality. As Prosperi Valenti Rodinò notes, the same subject was depicted by Raphael in the Loggia di Psiche of the Villa Farnesina. It has also been ventured that this drawing may depict Fame being led to Parnassus. She is often shown standing on a globe but lacks her characteristic trumpet here.[8]

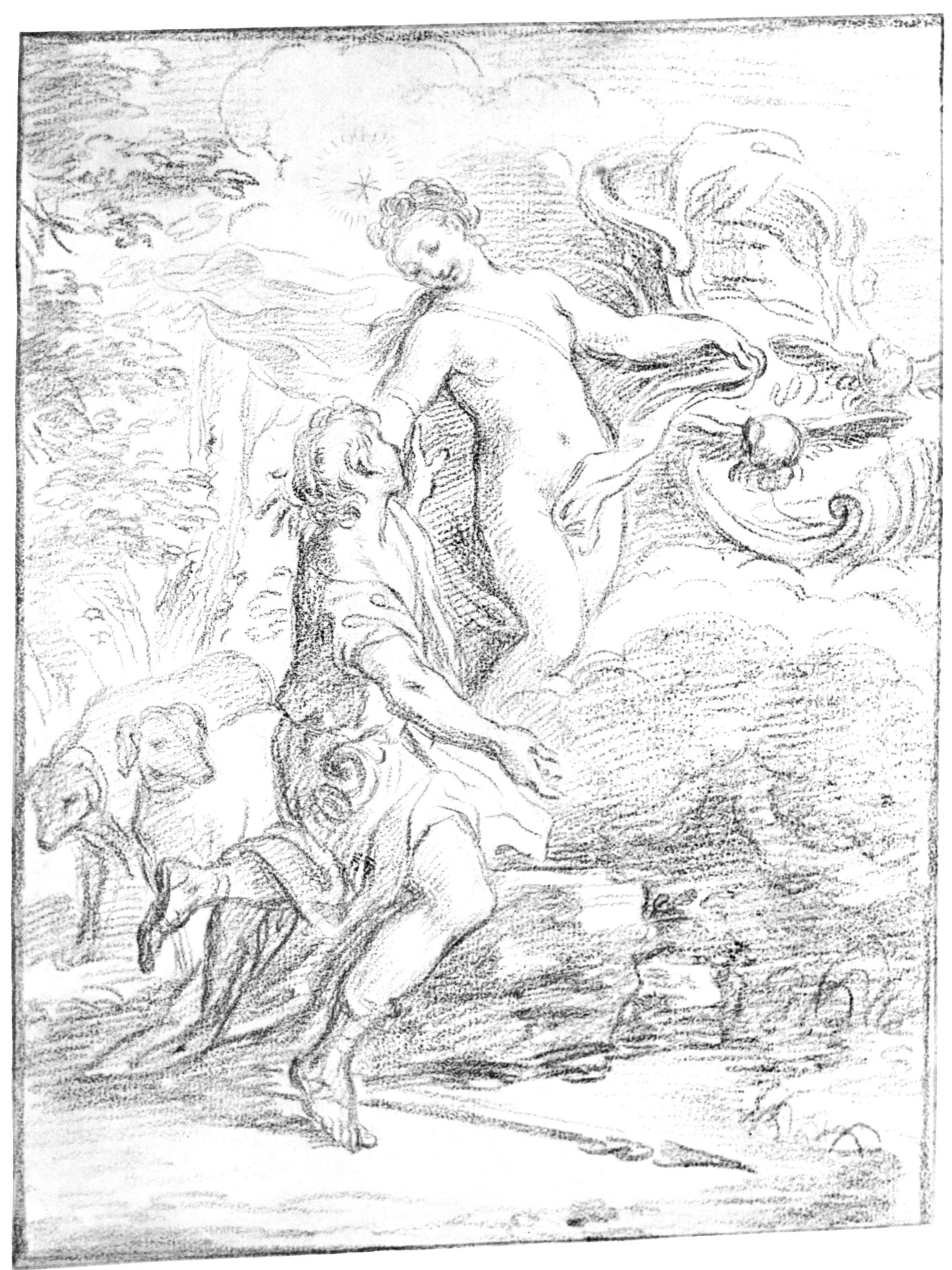

1. Letters from Mena Marqués to author, 29 December 1983, and Prosperi Valenti Rodinò to author, 12 March 1984. 2. S. Prosperi Valenti Rodinò, "Drawings of the Roman Baroque Painter Giovanni Paolo Melchiori," *Master Drawings*, vol. 18, no. 4 (Winter 1980), pp. 351–60. 3. Ibid., p. 352. 4. Repr. ibid., fig. 1. 5. Ibid., pls. 5, 11, and 13. 6. Prosperi Valenti Rodinò (in letter cited above) cites a similarly complex sheet in Düsseldorf, which, however, has each figure labeled (Inv. no. FP 1138). 7. Books 4.28–6.24. 8. The suggestion was made to the author by Oberhuber, 1977.

ROMAN, early eighteenth century

79 *Venus and Adonis*

Bequest of James Bowdoin III (1811.37) Red chalk. 246 x 187 mm. ($9^{11}/_{16}$ x $7^{3}/_{8}$ in.) Inscribed pen and brown ink verso "5" and red chalk monogram with letter P; pen and ink verso of former mount (lost) "No. 61 Il Portoguise." No watermark. PROVENANCE: James Bowdoin III. BIBLIOGRAPHY: *Catalogue* 1885, no. 43, repr. in large paper edition (as "Il Portoguise"); Allen 1886, pt. 3, no. 3, repr. (as "Il Portoguise"); *Catalogue* 1930, no. 43 (as "Il Portoguise"); Benisovich 1955, pp. 113–16, repr. fig. 2 (as Quillard); Eidelberg 1981, p. 29, repr. pl. 29a (as Vieira the Younger).

THIS AND ANOTHER SHEET in the Bowdoin bequest (Cat. 80) came to the collection with identical enigmatic inscriptions to "Il Portoguise," presumably a nickname and reference to the artist's country or city of origin. In 1955, Michel Benisovich interpreted the inscriptions as referring to Pierre Antoine Quillard (ca. 1704–1733), a French follower of Watteau who settled in Portugal. Martin Eidelberg dismissed the Quillard attribution on the basis of comparison with several recently discovered authentic drawings by him.[1] He then proposed ascribing both Bowdoin sheets to Francisco Vieira the Younger (1765–1805), whose nickname was "o Portuense," from his birthplace of Porto. Eidelberg also attributed to Vieira a depiction of Diana and Endymion which is now in a private collection in Paris.[2]

However, the two Bowdoin sheets in question are probably not even by the same hand, despite superficial resemblances. The Paris sheet published by Eidelberg as by Vieira is certainly by yet a third artist. What these three drawings do share, however, is an origin in Rome among the followers and imitators of Carlo Maratti. Benedetto Luti, for one, often depicted scenes of mythological lovers such as Venus and Adonis and Diana and Endymion.[3] The Parmese artist Michele Rocca (ca. 1670/75–after 1751), who worked in Rome during the early eighteenth century, also painted similar themes; an unsigned note on the Witt Library photograph mount of the Bowdoin *Venus and Adonis* ascribes it to Rocca.[4] Nicholas Turner suggested yet another Maratti student, Niccolò Berrettoni, as its author. Although difficult to pin down, the Marattesque technique and figural forms would logically place this sheet in that circle.

1. See Eidelberg 1981, with previous bibliography. 2. Ibid., p. 29, repr. pl. 29b. 3. See discussion in Philadelphia 1980–1981, under cat. no. 9. Two drawings by Luti of Angelica and Medoro are repr. in F. H. Dowley, "Some Drawings by Benedetto Luti," *Art Bulletin*, vol. 44 (September 1962), after p. 224, figs. 13–14. One painting is repr. in G. Sestieri, "Il punto su Benedetto Luti," *Arte illustrata*, vol. 6, no. 54 (August 1973), p. 243, fig. 22. 4. A painting by Rocca of Diana and Endymion is repr. in ibid., p. 243, fig. 23.

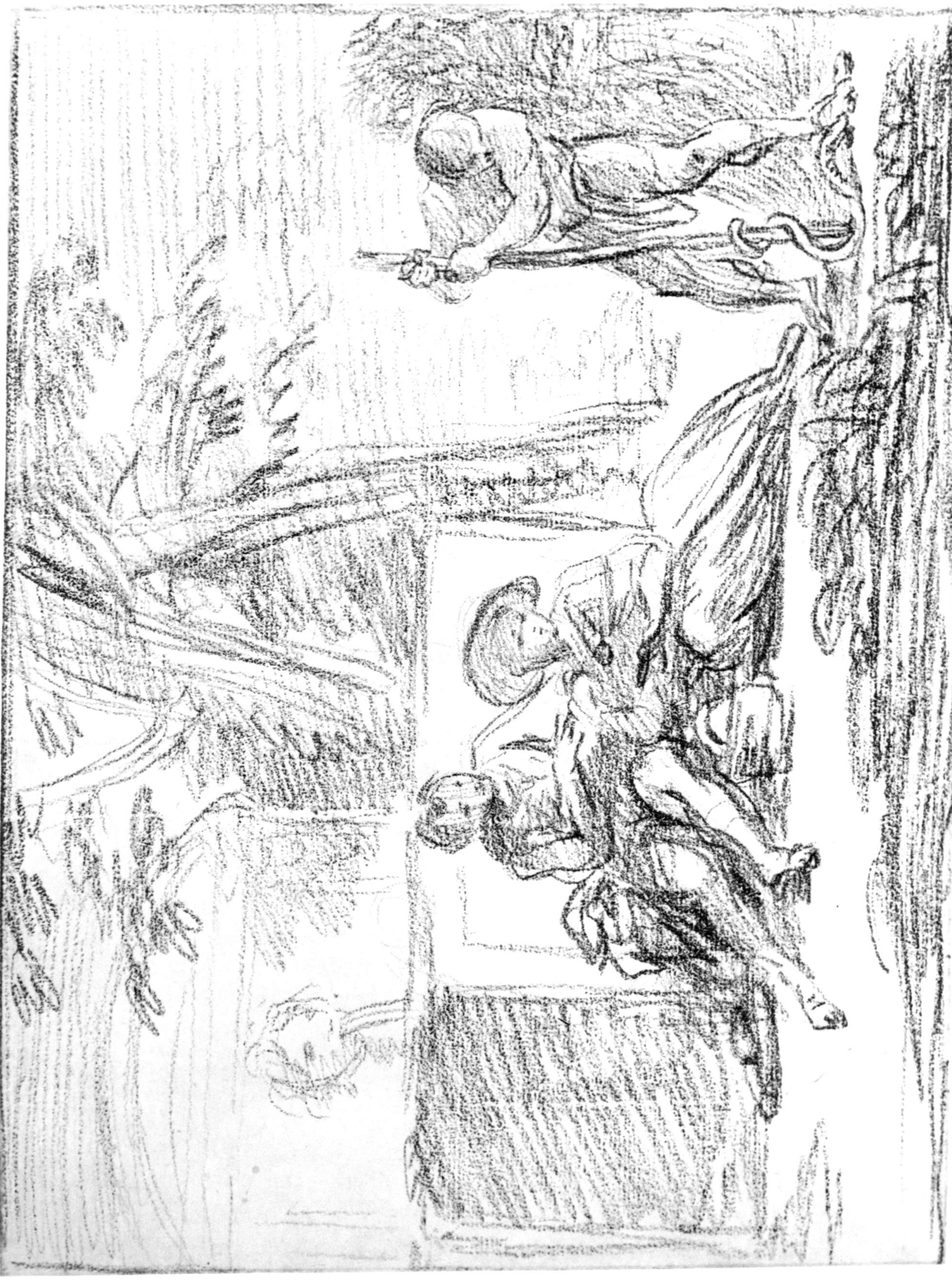

ITALIAN, early eighteenth century

80 *Scene in a Garden*

Bequest of James Bowdoin III (1811.38) Red chalk, laid down. 202 x 265 mm. ($7^{15}/16$ x $10^{3}/8$ in.) Inscribed verso of former mount (lost) "No. 61 Il Portoguise." No watermark. PROVENANCE: James Bowdoin III. BIBLIOGRAPHY: *Catalogue* 1885, no. 44 (as "Il Portoguise"); *Catalogue* 1930, no. 44 (as "Il Portoguise"); Benisovich 1955, pp. 113–16, repr. fig. 1 (as Quillard); *Handbook* 1981, p. 169 (as Quillard); Eidelberg 1981, p. 37 (as Vieira).

WITH CAT. 79, this drawing was attributed in 1955 by Michel Benisovich to the French artist Pierre Antoine Quillard. Both sheets were then given to Francisco Vieira the Younger by Martin Eidelberg in 1981. The two Bowdoin sheets, though bearing similar old inscriptions to "Il Portoguise," are almost certainly by different artists. They both do, however, probably originate in Rome during the early eighteenth century in the large circle of followers and imitators of Carlo Maratti.

The subject of this sheet seems unusual in itself and has not been explained. The purported existence of a painting by Quillard of three figures in a garden with a snake, reported by Benisovich, has been discounted by Eidelberg.[1] The pastoral garden scene has undoubtedly led to the sheet's placement within eighteenth-century French art such as that epitomized by Watteau, but such subjects do turn up in Italy, especially in the work of such later artists as Hubert Robert and even Giovanni Battista Piranesi. The old Italian inscription lends some support to an Italian origin for these two drawings.

1. Eidelberg 1981, p. 37, n. 11.

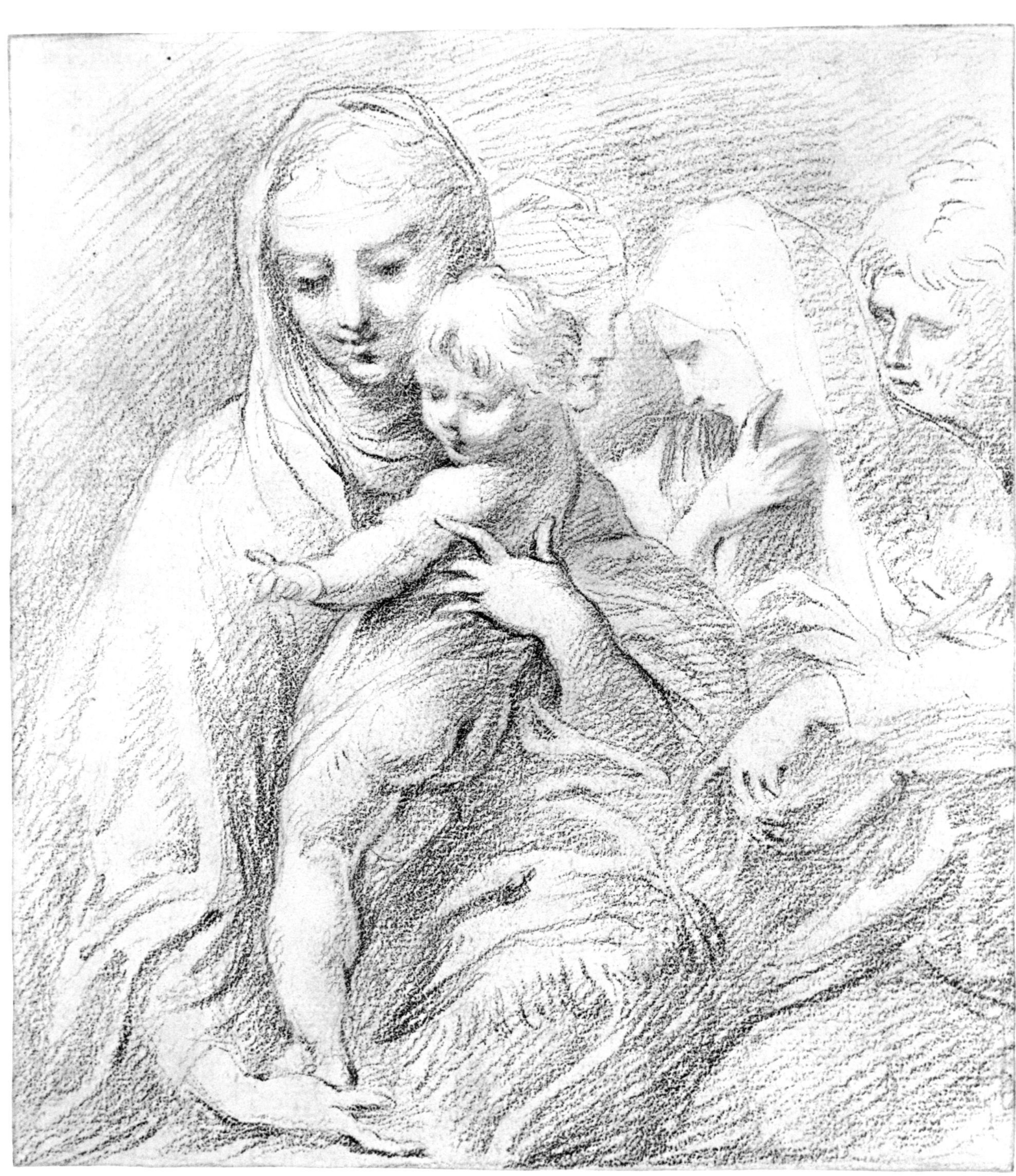

TOMMASO REDI
FLORENCE 1665–1726 FLORENCE

81 *Madonna and Child with Three Holy Women, after Parmigianino*

Bequest of James Bowdoin III (1811.31) Red chalk, rubbed in areas by the artist. 212 x 188 mm. ($8^3/_8$ x $7^3/_8$ in.) Inscribed pen and ink, verso of mount (now removed) "No. 68 Thomas Redi." Watermark: Paschal lamb in double circle. PROVENANCE: John Smibert (?); James Bowdoin III. BIBLIOGRAPHY: *Catalogue* 1885, no. 41; *Catalogue* 1930, no. 41.

REDI STUDIED with Anton Domenico Gabbiani (1652–1726) from the age of eighteen. In 1690 he was sent to Rome on a stipend from Cosimo III to continue his studies with Carlo Maratti (Cat. 64). Ten years later, he returned to Florence, and remained there until his death. Redi executed religious paintings for churches and houses in and near Florence; he was often commissioned by visiting English nobility on the Grand Tour to paint mythological and historical subjects. He also worked for the Danish and Russian courts.

This sheet bears a traditional attribution to Redi. The comparative rarity of drawings by him lends credence to the ascription, particularly since a logical attribution would have been to the originator of the design—Parmigianino. As Pouncey was the first to point out, the Bowdoin drawing is a close copy of a Parmigianino sheet, also in red chalk, in the Uffizi.[1] Chiara d'Afflitto has affirmed the Redi attribution; the style of the Bowdoin sheet agrees with a figure study securely attributed to Redi in the National Gallery of Scotland.[2]

Smibert probably acquired this drawing for his collection directly from the artist. He is known to have visited Redi on 25 May 1720, and purchased a "pictor of his."[3] Perhaps Smibert was particularly interested in buying a reproduction of a design by Parmigianino, as originals may have been difficult to procure. The Uffizi original of this design was engraved by Mulinari, but after Redi's death. Redi himself is known to have copied other old master drawings for reproduction as prints.[4]

1. Pouncey's observation was made in conversation with the author, June 1983. The Parmigianino drawing is catalogued and reproduced in Popham 1971, cat. no. 87, repr. pl. 244. 2. Andrews 1968, p. 103, repr. fig. 707. Another group of Redi drawings in the Louvre is discussed in Paris 1981–1982, pp. 230–35. 3. Cf. Introduction, p. xv: cf. *Smibert Notebook* 1969, p. 100. 4. Thieme-Becker, vol. 28, p. 74; Paris 1981–1982, p. 230.

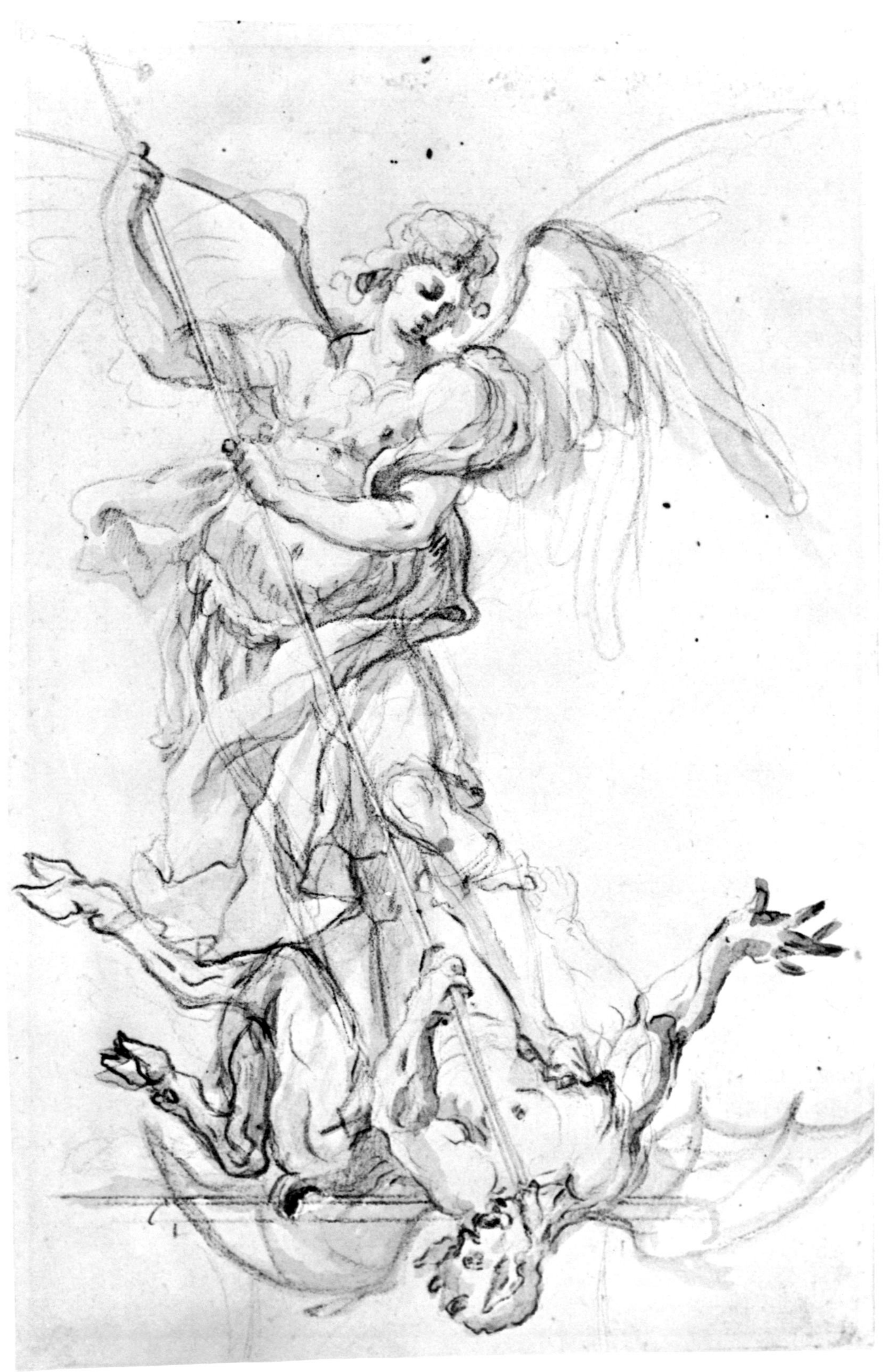

DOMENICO ANTONIO VACCARO, Attributed to
NAPLES 1678–1745 NAPLES

82 *St. Michael and Lucifer*

Museum Purchase (1930.145) Black chalk, touches of red chalk (in Michael's left hand), and grey wash, laid down. 276 x 178 mm. (10⅞ x 7 in.) No watermark visible. PROVENANCE: Professor Henry Johnson.

IAN KENNEDY and Stephen Pepper independently attributed this sheet to Vaccaro, a Neapolitan sculptor and architect. He was the son of the sculptor Lorenzo and the grandson of the painter Andrea. He first trained with his father, who then sent him to learn painting with Francesco Solimena. Domenico received commissions from an early age and became most successful as a sculptural decorator and architect of churches and villas in and around Naples.

Vaccaro's draughtsmanship is not well known. This sheet is related to him primarily through its relationship to several small sculptural groups of this subject recently attributed to Vaccaro and his studio, particularly a silver one now in Berlin.[1] Another drawing of this subject attributed to Vaccaro which was recently on the art market is related stylistically to the Bowdoin sheet, although the Bowdoin version seems more fluid and assured.[2] The Bowdoin drawing is clearly a study for a sculpture, as can be seen in the sketched-in pedestal and the lack of a defined background. Another large sheet of St. Michael battling the rebel angels is in a private collection in Rome,[3] and a drawing in the Fogg Art Museum of the Madonna della Misericordia is attributed to Vaccaro.[4] A famous altarpiece of the same subject by Luca Giordano executed during the 1660s in Naples is now in West Berlin.[5]

1. See F. Bologna, "A Silver Sculpture Ascribed to Domenico Antonio Vaccaro," *Burlington Magazine*, vol. 121, no. 913 (April 1979), pp. 220–25. See also A. González-Palacios, "Un capolavoro della plastica napoletana barocca," *Antologia di belle arti*, n.s., nos. 21–22 (1984), pp. 111–26, esp. fig. 1, also repr. in color on the cover.
2. The other drawing is repr. in ibid., fig. 34. 3. Repr. ibid., fig. 36. 4. Inv. no. 1965.425. 5. See C. Whitfield and J. Martineau, eds., *Painting in Naples 1606–1705 from Caravaggio to Giordano* (exh. cat.) (London, 1982), cat. no. 67, repr. in color p. 96.

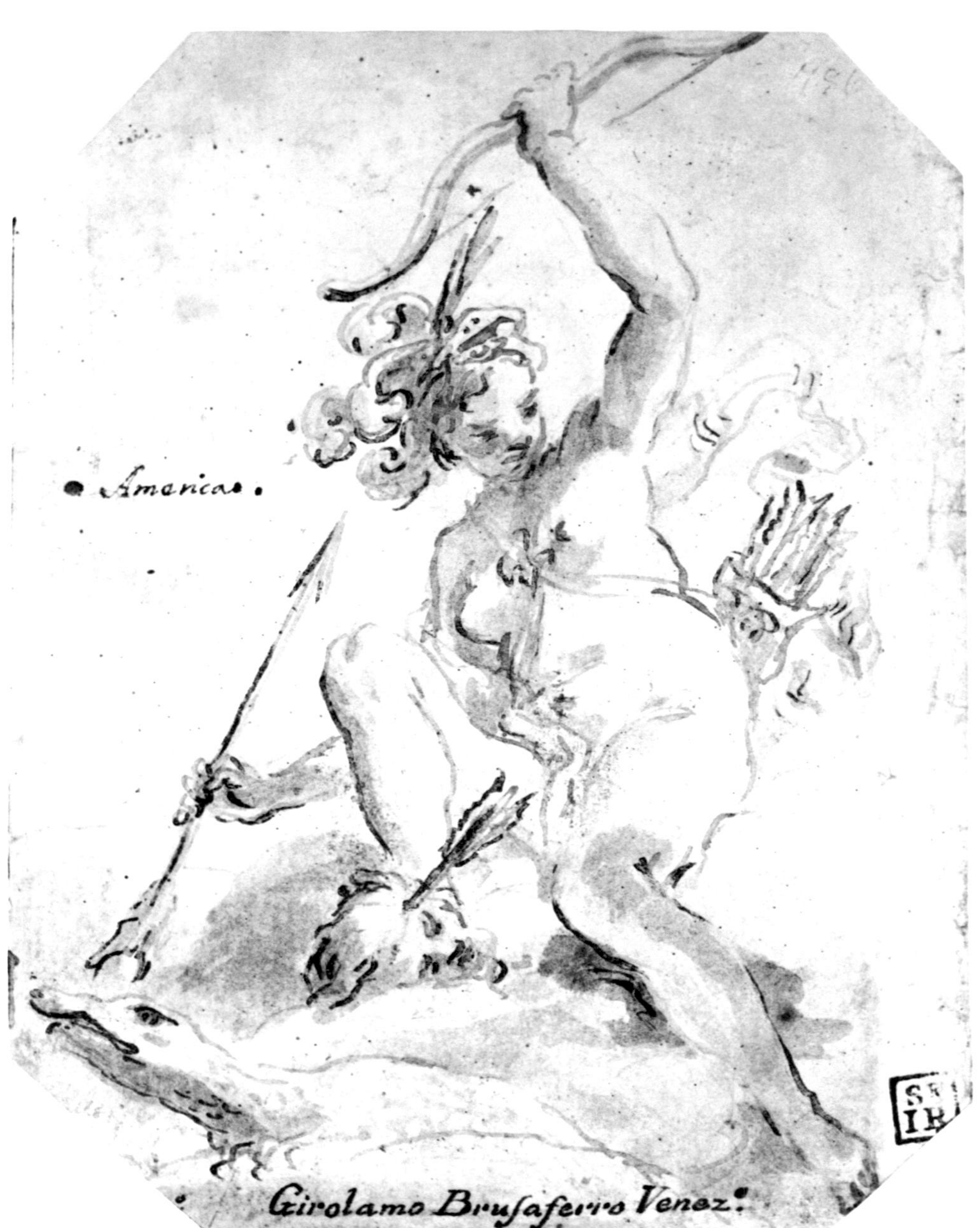
America
Girolamo Brusaferro Venez.

GIROLAMO BRUSAFERRO
VENICE ca. 1680–1760 VENICE

83 *Allegory of America*

Gift of Miss Susan Dwight Bliss (1956.24.193) Pen and brown ink and grey wash, corners trimmed, laid down. 161 x 129 mm. (6¼ x 5⅛ in.) Inscribed pen and brown ink left center "America"; pen and black ink bottom "Girolamo Brusaferro Venez.º" [see Provenance]; graphite upper right "786." No watermark visible. PROVENANCE: "Reliable Venetian Hand" (mid-eighteenth century) (Lugt 3005c–d); Sir Joshua Reynolds (1723–1792) (Lugt 2364); Susan Dwight Bliss. BIBLIOGRAPHY: Venice 1966, p. 115, no. 180, repr.; *Handbook* 1981, p. 169.

BRUSAFERRO studied with Niccolo Bambini (1651–1736) in Venice and spent his career primarily in that city. He furnished numerous paintings for churches and palaces in Venice and is also known to have worked in Mantua. The attribution of this sheet to Brusaferro is based on the old inscription at the bottom, which has been traced to an eighteenth-century collector who similarly labeled a large number of drawings in his collection. The collector's identity remains obscure, and thus he has been dubbed the "Reliable Venetian Hand." An exhibition and catalogue of 183 drawings inscribed by him was compiled in 1966.[1] As the majority of the artists represented are Venetian, the collector is assumed to have been Venetian himself, and the evidence indicates that his attributions for artists who were his contemporaries are more accurate than those he made for artists of earlier centuries.[2]

In addition to the Bowdoin drawing, Alessandro Bettagno reproduced three other Brusaferro sheets with identical inscriptions in his 1966 catalogue. They are from the British Museum, the Albertina, and the Scholz Collection.[3] All are stylistically comparable, so there seems to be no reason to doubt the attribution of the Bowdoin sheet. Other drawings given to Brusaferro are in the Nationalmuseum, Stockholm,[4] the Albertina,[5] and Budapest.[6]

The subject of the Bowdoin study is a personification of America, one of the four parts into which the world was commonly "divided," the others being Europe, Asia, and Africa. Representations of all four were commonly utilized in decorative cycles of paintings, tapestries, and prints, particularly as more distant parts of the world began to be explored. America was classically shown as a near-naked figure, usually a woman, with a feather headdress, holding a bow and arrow, with a severed head at her feet (symbolizing the cannibalism imagined in the new world) and accompanied by a caiman, or alligator. Brusaferro's figure follows the standard iconography and is seated upon clouds, perhaps indicating that this drawing is a study for a ceiling painting meant to adorn one of the four corners of a room. Similar studies by Brusaferro for the other three parts of the world are not known, although there is another very similar study for America which was once in the same collection and was attributed by the anonymous "reliable hand" to Giovanni Antonio Pellegrini.[7]

1. Cf. Venice 1966. 2. Cf. J. Bean, review of Venice 1966, in *Master Drawings*, vol. 4, no. 3 (1966), pp. 309–10. 3. Venice 1966, pp. 87–88, nos. 115–17, repr. 4. Fondation Giorgio Cini, *Disegni veneti del Museo di Stoccolma* (exh. cat.) (Venice, 1974), no. 94, repr. 5. Inv. no. 24338, repr. in A. Stix and L. Fröhlich-Bum, *Die Zeichnungen der venezianischen Schule*, vol. 1 of *Beschreibender Katalog der Handzeichnungen in der Albertina* (Vienna, 1926), no. 342. 6. Inv. no. 58.19K, repr. in Fondation Giorgio Cini, *Disegni veneti del Museo di Budapest* (exh. cat.) (Venice, 1965), cat. no. 86. 7. Venice 1966, p. 63, no. 65, repr.; this sheet was also in the Reynolds Collection.

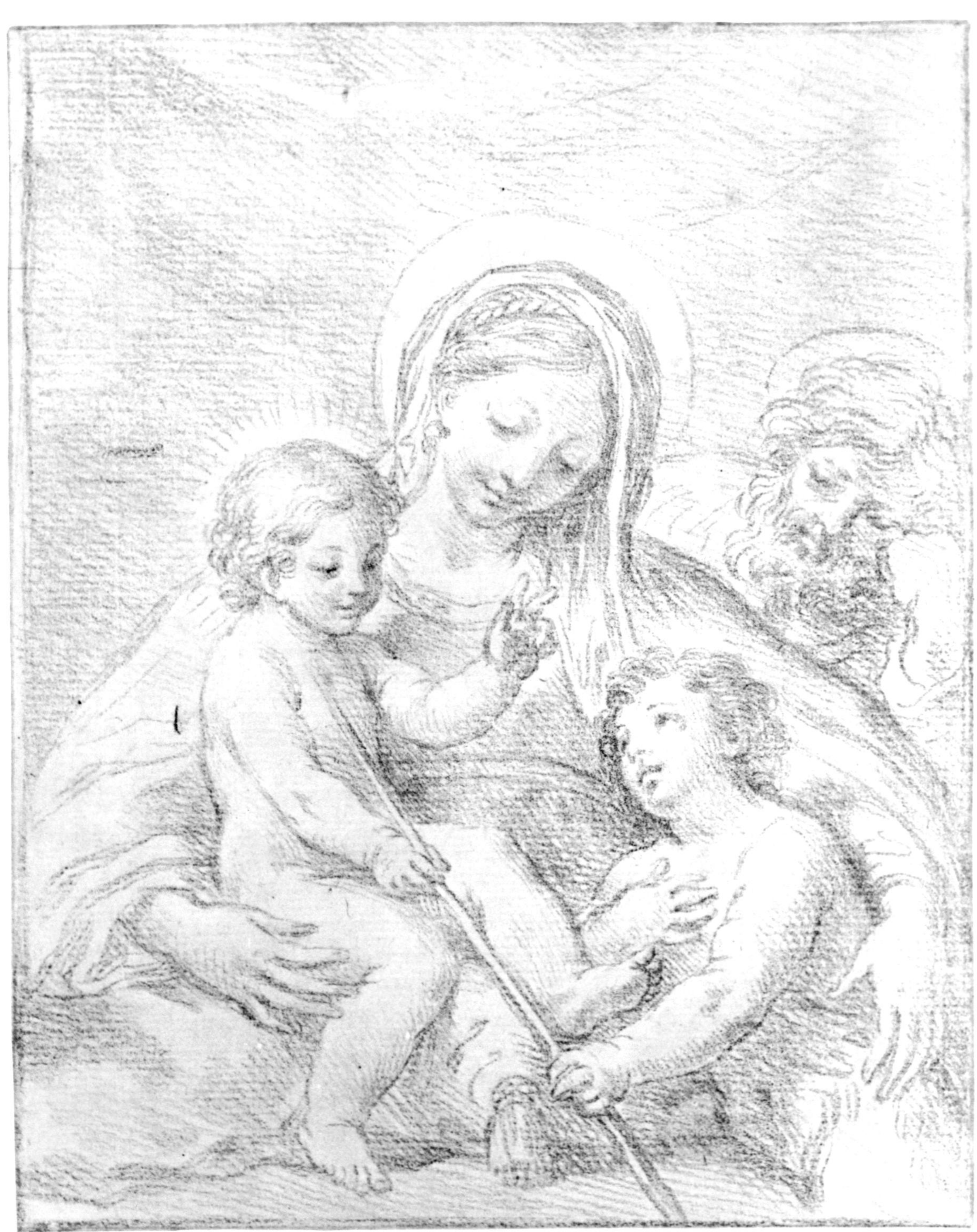

AGOSTINO MASUCCI
ROME 1692–1758 ROME

84 *Holy Family with Infant St. John*

Bequest of James Bowdoin III (1811.61) Red chalk, counterproof. 189 x 152 mm. ($7^{1/2}$ x 6 in.) Watermark: T or F within circle within six-pointed star inscribed within circle surmounted by cross; elaborate F below circle (close to Briquet 6089). PROVENANCE: James Bowdoin III. BIBLIOGRAPHY: *Catalogue* 1885, no. 83, repr. in large paper edition (as Unknown); *Catalogue* 1930, no. 83 (as Unknown).

AMONG THE RELATIVELY LARGE GROUP of Marattesque drawings in the Bowdoin bequest is this carefully finished composition, perhaps intended as an end in itself. Filippo di Pietro first attributed it to the school of Maratti and was followed by Sir Robert Witt.[1] Manuela Mena Marqués has tentatively suggested Masucci as the author.[2]

Masucci studied with Andrea Procaccini and was the youngest of Maratti's pupils. He was elected to the Accademia di San Luca in 1724 and served as its head from 1736 to 1738. He executed altarpieces and was known as a portraitist. Among Masucci's pupils were Pompeo Batoni and Gavin Hamilton.

Other Masucci drawings are in Windsor Castle,[3] Berlin,[4] the Held Collection,[5] and the Nationalmuseum, Stockholm.[6] The latter group are primarily portraits of artists done for Niccolò Pio's biographies. The Bowdoin drawing is probably a counterproof, as indicated by the unusual direction of the shading.[7] A very similar drawing from the Maratti school, now attributed to Giuseppe Chiari, was formerly in the Bick Collection.[8]

1. Comments in the museum files. 2. Letter to the author, 29 December 1983. 3. Blunt and Cooke 1960, cat. nos. 533–35. 4. Dreyer 1971, pp. 202–6, figs. 21–25. 5. Clark Art Institute, *Master Drawings from the Collection of Ingrid and Julius S. Held* (exh. cat. by L. Giles, E. Milroy, and G. Owens) (Williamstown, 1979), cat. no. 25, repr. 6. Cf. Clark 1967, pp. 14–15, several repr. fig. 1, pls. 10–12. 7. For instance, see Dreyer 1971, p. 204, fig. 24, for a finished drawing by Masucci. 8. Dartmouth College, *Italian Drawings: Selections from the Collection of Esther S. and Malcolm W. Bick* (exh. cat.) (Hanover, N.H., 1971), cat. no. 30, repr.; sold Sotheby's London, 2 July 1984, lot no. 90.

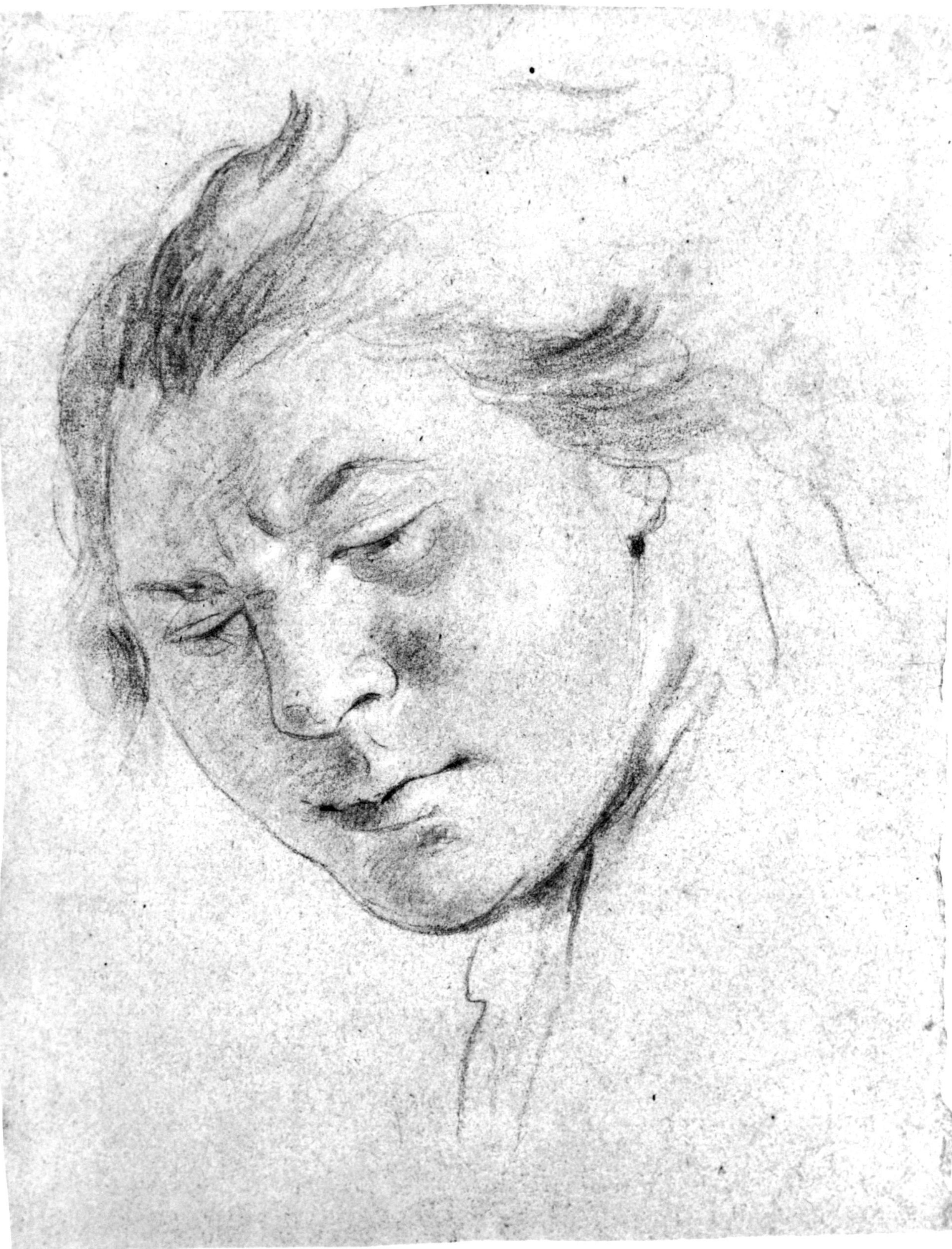

GIOVANNI BATTISTA TIEPOLO
VENICE 1696–1770 MADRID

85 *Head of a Young Man*

Florence C. Quinby Fund in Memory of Henry Cole Quinby H '16 (1972.14) Red chalk on blue laid paper (rubbed in places). 270 x 210 mm. ($10^5/_8$ x $8^1/_4$ in.) Inscribed red pen "44"; blue pen "75"; graphite "$19^1/_2$ x 26." Watermark: triple fleurs-de-lis. PROVENANCE: Count Gregori Stroganoff? (d. 1910) (his mark, Lugt 550, not present); Sotheby's London, 25 November 1971, no. 114, repr.; acquired from Stuart Denenberg '64. BIBLIOGRAPHY: Knox 1980, p. 199, no. L.23; *Handbook* 1981, p. 169 (as Giovanni Domenico Tiepolo). EXHIBITION: Seattle, University of Washington, Henry Gallery, *XVIII Century Venice—Drawings from American Academic Collections*, 1974, cat. no. 21, repr. (as Giovanni Domenico or Lorenzo Tiepolo).

IN ADDITION TO the hundreds of surviving pen and ink drawings by Giovanni Battista Tiepolo and his two sons and collaborators, Giovanni Domenico (1727–1804) and Lorenzo (1736–1776), over fifteen hundred chalk studies by all three exist. They are primarily in red chalk, often heightened with white, on blue paper. The difficult task of separating the hands responsible for individual sheets has been undertaken by George Knox, who made the attribution of the Bowdoin portrait study to Giovanni Battista.[1] He associates it with a group of twenty-four such head studies, most of which are known to have once been together in a single album belonging to Count Stroganoff.[2] Though many of these were formerly attributed to Lorenzo, Knox now believes the majority of these studies to be by Giambattista, reasoning in large part from their quality and from the existence of at least fourteen copies of these drawings known to be by Lorenzo, in a sketchbook now in Würzburg.[3] He dates all these drawings to the period 1752–1753, when the Tiepolos were working in Würzburg, decorating the grand ceremonial rooms of the Kaisersaal and Residenz of the prince-bishop. At that time the young Lorenzo was an apprentice in his father's studio and presumably was copying drawings for his training. Giovanni Battista himself had been trained in Venice and had worked widely in northern Italy before going to Würzburg in 1750. He returned to Venice in 1753 and worked there until he was called to Spain in 1761 by Charles III to decorate the Royal Palace in Madrid.

Several of the studies from the Stroganoff group, including the Bowdoin sheet, depict the same young man, whom Knox theorizes is the model for one of the figures in the Würzburg ceiling frescoes. He tentatively identifies him as Franz Ignaz Neumann, the son of the architect of the Kaisersaal complex, Balthasar Neumann.[4] Two other drawings from the Stroganoff group which depict this model are particularly close to the Bowdoin study—one in the Fogg Art Museum[5] (which owns twelve from the group) and one in the British Museum.[6]

1. Letter to the author, 8 April 1981; see also discussion in Knox 1980, p. 196. 2. Knox 1980, pp. 196–99, cat. nos. L.1–L.24. 3. Ibid.; there is a Lorenzo copy of the Bowdoin drawing at Würzburg (Knox 1980, cat. no. H.53). 4. Ibid., p. 196. 5. Inv. no. 1940.312 (Knox 1980, cat. no. L.10; repr. in Fogg Art Museum, *Tiepolo: A Bicentenary Exhibition 1770–1970* [exh. cat.] [Cambridge, 1970], cat. no. 64). 6. Inv. no. 1949-4-11-89 (Knox 1980, cat. no. L.15; repr. in J. Byam Shaw, review of Fogg 1970 catalogue [cf. note 5 above], in *Master Drawings*, vol. 9, no. 3 [1971], p. 270, fig. 5).

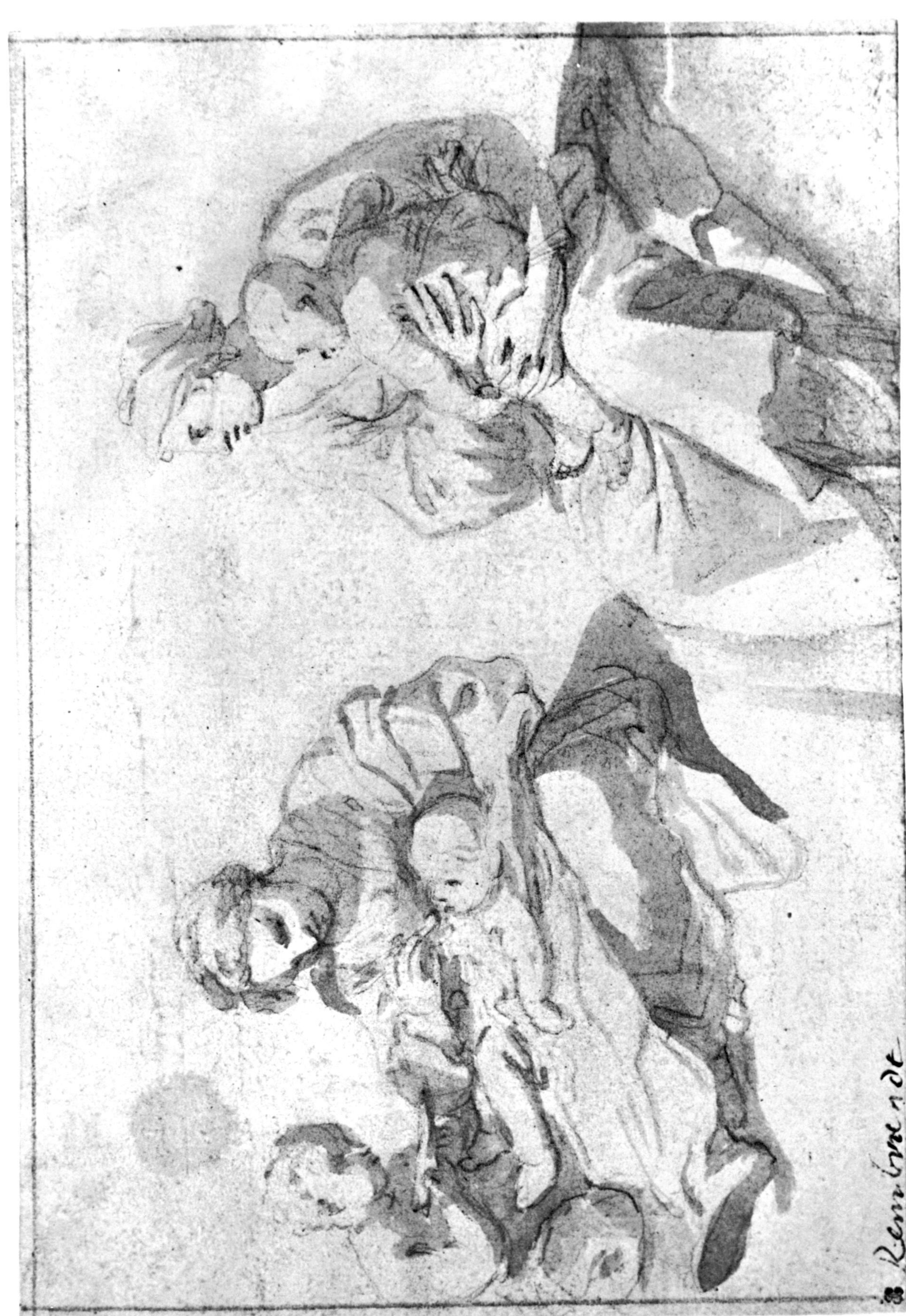

French and British

JACQUES STELLA
LYON 1596–1657 PARIS

86 *Two Mothers with Their Children*

Museum Purchase (1930.187) Brush and brown wash over black chalk; laid down. 165 x 238 mm. (6 1/2 x 9 3/8 in.) Inscribed pen and brown ink lower left "Rembrandt"; graphite verso "A · W · X." Watermark: IHS, the H surmounted by a cross inscribed within an oval; below AR [?] in rectangle (not in Briquet). PROVENANCE: Marquis Philippe de Chennevières (1820–1899) (Lugt 2072/3), his sale, Paris, 4–7 April 1900, probably part of lot 476; Professor Henry Johnson. BIBLIOGRAPHY: P. de Chennevières, "Une collection de dessins d'artistes français," *L'Artiste*, 1894–1897, p. 153; Davidson 1975, pp. 152, 155 (n. 10), 157 (n. 46). EXHIBITION: Toronto 1972, cat. no. 137, repr. pl. 15.

FORMERLY ATTRIBUTED to Rembrandt, presumably only from the inscription on the sheet, this drawing was recognized by Pierre Rosenberg in 1971 as the work of Jacques Stella. Leaving France at the age of twenty, Stella spent almost twenty years in Italy, first in Florence and then in Rome from around 1622. There he studied works of art and produced paintings, drawings, and prints, becoming a close friend of Poussin. He returned to Paris by 1635 and was granted a royal pension and an apartment in the Louvre.

Probably drawn from life, the Bowdoin study can be compared with a group of genre drawings of similar format and technique recognized by Rosenberg and studied in detail by Gail Davidson. Davidson points out quite close relationships in the wash and black chalk technique with drawings in the Louvre[1] and in the Wolf Collection, New York.[2] Other sheets in the Wolf Collection and in the Metropolitan, Fogg, and Ashmolean museums also belong to the larger group depicting similar figures in everyday occupations.[3] All these drawings probably date from the 1650s, as recently affirmed by Davidson.[4] They possibly came from the same sketchbook, which was listed in the inventory of the estate of the artist's niece and pupil, Claudine Bouzonnet Stella.[5] Rosenberg and Davidson have also related the Bowdoin drawing to a painting by Stella, *The Virgin Feeding the Child*, and to an engraving after Jacques by Claudine Bouzonnet Stella.[6]

1. Inv. no. 32896, cf. Davidson 1975, p. 155, no. 10. 2. Repr. ibid., pl. 14. 3. Ibid., pls. 10–13. 4. Fogg Art Museum, *French Drawings from a Private Collection: Louis XIII to Louis XVI* (exh. cat. ed. by K. Oberhuber and B. Schreiber Jacoby) (Cambridge, 1980), p. 48, under cat. no. 5. 5. Davidson 1975, p. 153. 6. Ibid., p. 155, n. 10; the engraving is listed in R. Weigert, *Inventaire du fonds français—graveurs du XVIIe siècle*, vol. 2 (Paris, 1951), p. 80, no. 6.

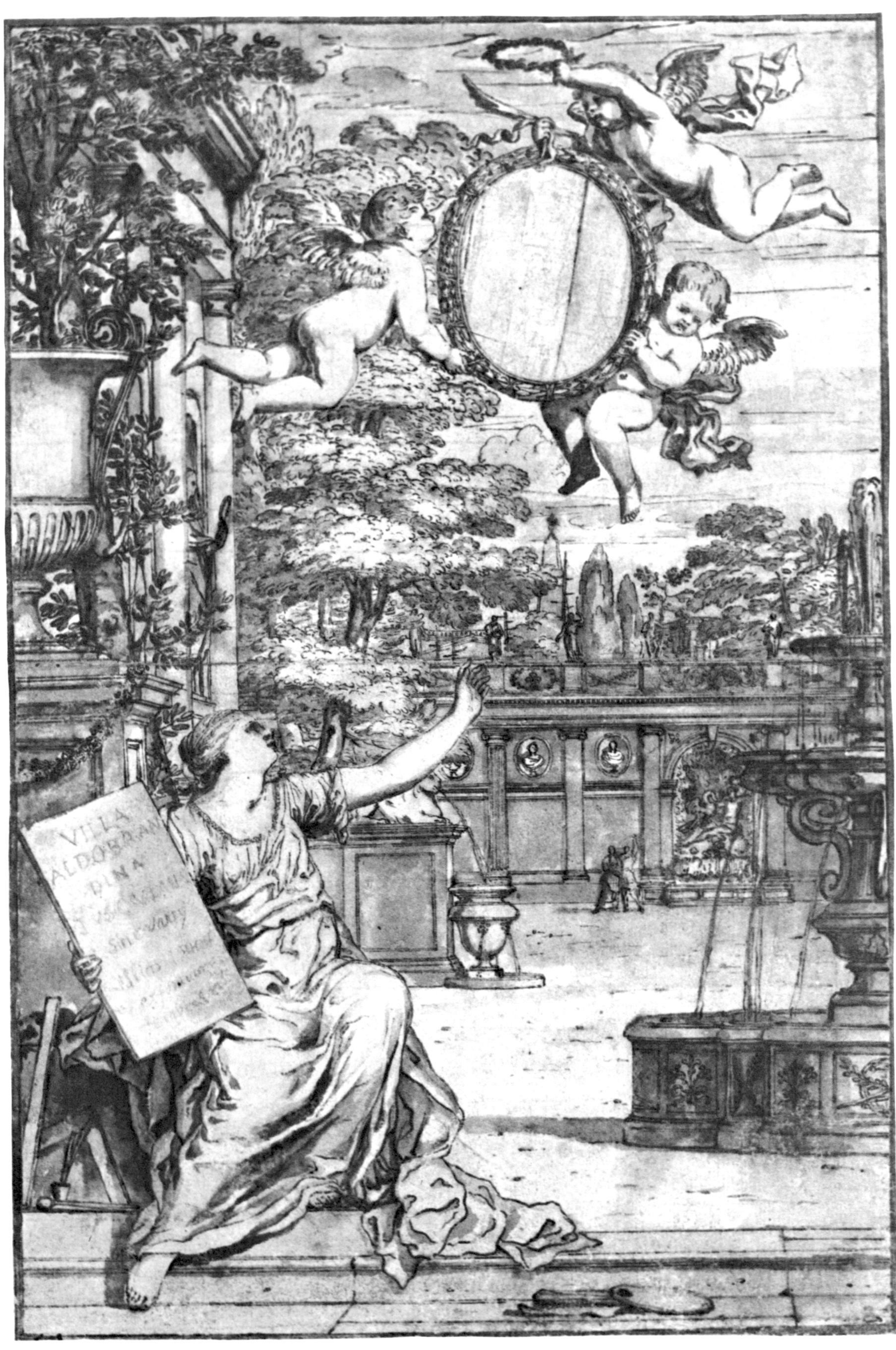
VILLA
ALDOBRAN
DINA

DOMINIQUE BARRIERE

MARSEILLES ca. 1610/20–1678 ROME

87 *Study for a Title Page*

Bequest of James Bowdoin III (1811.136) Pen and brown ink, brown wash, over black chalk, traced with a stylus for transfer, verso prepared with red chalk, laid down. Old horizontal fold, several pin holes, worm damages lower portion, portrait medallion blank. 347 x 234 mm. (13 5/8 x 9 1/4 in.) Inscribed graphite on tablet "VILLA / ALDOBRAN / DINA / TVSCVLANA / sine varij / . . ."; graphite on mount "The Villa Aldobrandina, belonging to the Pamfili family, is near the church of St. Dominico on Monte Quirinale." No watermark visible. PROVENANCE: James Bowdoin III. BIBLIOGRAPHY: *Catalogue* 1885, no. 96 (as Unknown); *Catalogue* 1930, no. 96 (as Unknown).

LITTLE IS KNOWN of Barrière's life or career, save what is left of his fairly numerous prints of topographic and architectural views. These were executed after his own designs and those of other artists, such as Claude Lorrain and Pietro da Cortona. A large two-part study by him for a panoramic view of Rome is in the Nationalmuseum, Stockholm.[1]

This drawing was designed as the title page to one such set of views of the Villa Aldobrandina, the country seat of the Pamphili family at Frascati, in the Roman Campagna southeast of the city.[2] The book is totally etched (with engraved additions), consisting of a title page, a dedication, a preface, eight plates of views of the villa and its gardens, ten plates reproducing the famed Domenichino frescoes in the villa, and a final plan of the villa and its surroundings.[3] The book is dedicated to the young King Louis XIV of France (then nine years old), whose engraved portrait appears on the printed title within a laurel wreath (blank in the drawing). The printed title is reversed from the drawing and is dated 1647. Barrière signed the plate as designer, draughtsman, and etcher.

In this design, an allegorical figure of Painting (with supplies at her feet) sits in a garden of the villa surrounded by classical sculpture and three fountains. The title of the volume is engraved on the tablet she holds. The major changes from drawing to print are the addition of classical figures on the large vase at the left and of a scene of Hercules in combat with an animal in the tablet under Painting's outstretched arm. For the final print Barrière also denied Leda her swan in the sculpture in the far garden wall.

1. Inv. nos. NM 2329/1863 and 2330/1863, repr. in Bjurström 1976, cat. nos. 154–55. The print after the drawing is also repr. 2. The print is catalogued in Robert-Dumesnil, vol. 3.70.144. 3. Ibid., pp. 144–65; the Metropolitan Museum of Art and the Houghton Library have copies of the book.

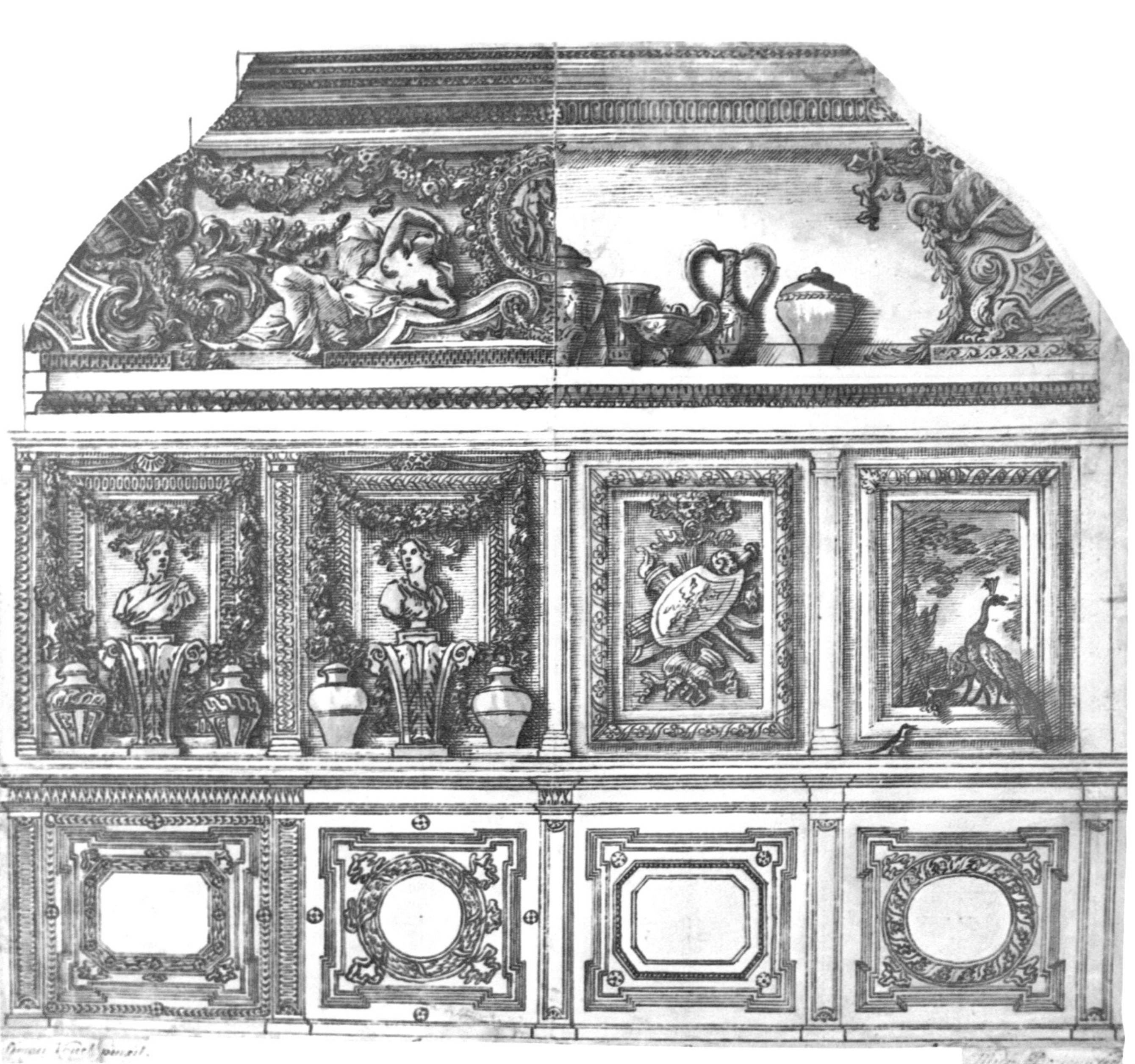
Simon Vouet pinxit.

MICHEL DORIGNY
SAN QUENTIN 1617–1665 PARIS

88 *Design for a Wall Decoration*

Gift of Miss Susan Dwight Bliss (1956.24.273) Pen and brown ink with watercolor, laid down (losses upper right), on two sheets of paper (drapery of reclining woman top left added on four further patches). 376 x 430 mm. (14 13/16 x 16 15/16 in.) Inscribed pen and ink on old mount below "Simon Vouet pinxit."; "Mich! Dorigny feci"; another inscription below design has been cut off. No watermark. PROVENANCE: Susan Dwight Bliss. BIBLIOGRAPHY: *Handbook* 1981, p. 167. EXHIBITION: Toronto 1972, cat. no. 43, repr. pl. 41.

PIERRE ROSENBERG was the first to single out the Bowdoin drawing as an example of Dorigny's relatively little-known draughtsmanship. After an apprenticeship with the painter Georges Lallemand, Dorigny became the son-in-law and collaborator of Simon Vouet (1590–1649). Known primarily as an engraver, Dorigny executed over ninety prints after Vouet's designs alone. He also painted several decorative schemes for private mansions. Dorigny was elected to the Académie royale in 1663 and was appointed professor there the next year.

The specific decoration for which the Bowdoin sketch might have been destined is not known, and there are no specific iconographic or family references in the drawing to aid an identification. It could have been a design meant to be engraved as a model, though no related print is known. Rosenberg has associated this watercolor with a series of twenty-three similar designs at the Château de Vincennes and other sheets in the Louvre and at Chantilly.[1] Like them, this design compresses its various elements into a discontinuous order. Particularly close is a sheet formerly in the Anthony Blunt Collection.[2] The Baltimore and Metropolitan Museums also contain characteristic decorative designs by Dorigny.[3] The strong pen outlines, cross-hatching, and circles forming the eyes are quite typical of Dorigny's drawings. Rosenberg points out that drawings like this are valuable for the documentation they provide for the decorative arts in Paris in the mid-seventeenth century.

1. Toronto 1972, p. 156, under cat. no. 43. 2. Ibid. 3. Ibid.

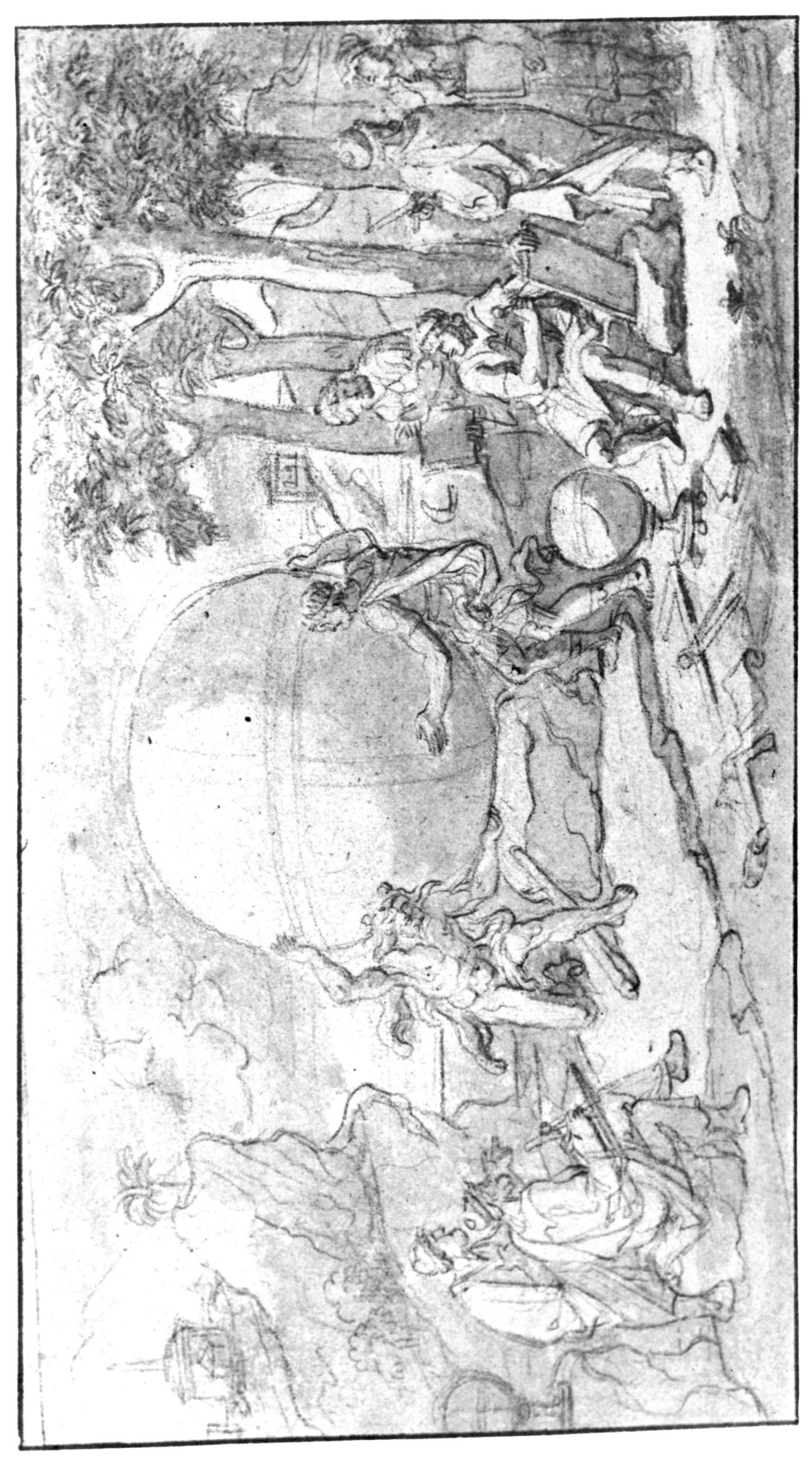

FRANÇOIS VERDIER

PARIS 1651–1730 PARIS

89 *Hercules and Atlas*

Florence C. Quinby Fund in Memory of Henry Cole Quinby H '16 (1969.66) Brush and grey wash over black chalk on brown paper, laid down. 216 x 388 mm. ($8^{1}/_{2}$ x $15^{1}/_{4}$ in.) No watermark visible. PROVENANCE: acquired from H. Schickman Gallery, New York.

VERDIER STUDIED with Charles Lebrun (1619–1690) at the Académie royale and was elected a full member himself in 1678. He left Paris to study at the French Academy in Rome until 1680. Verdier collaborated with Lebrun on several projects at Versailles and in the Louvre and was a close adherent of his master's style. He was a prolific draughtsman, and sheets by him are found in numerous collections; it is said that late in life he executed many drawings independently of Lebrun in order to support himself. There is quite a large group in Stockholm (thirty-three sheets)[1]; the most substantial group in this country is at the Art Institute of Chicago (nine sheets).[2] The vast majority of his subjects are drawn from classical mythology or from history, although he also executed religious works.

Among the themes which Verdier depicted often were the life and labors of Hercules. His reception piece for the Académie was a painting of Hercules battling the monster Geryon.[3] The Graphische Sammlung in Stuttgart owns Verdier drawings of six Hercules subjects, and the Uffizi owns at least two.[4] A sheet in Chicago depicts the attempted rape of Hercules' wife, Deianeira, by Nessus.[5] Several sheets formerly on the art market also show scenes with Herculean themes.[6]

The specific subject and purpose of the Bowdoin drawing are ambiguous. Hercules, with lion skin and club, is shown supporting the world with Atlas, who usually held it. According to legend, Hercules briefly assumed the weight of the world in return for Atlas's agreeing to pick the golden apples of the Hesperides. In the sixteenth century, this motif was used as an allegory of astronomy, for Atlas was said to have also imparted the secrets of that art to Hercules.[7] The presence here of a group of astronomers and geographers measuring and recording data with compasses and armillary spheres supports this explanation. It is not known, therefore, whether this sheet would have been a part of a series of the Liberal Arts or of the Labors of Hercules.

1. Bjurström 1976, cat. nos. 703–35, repr. 2. Joachim 1977, cat. nos. 1F3-1F11, repr. on microfiche. 3. Thieme-Becker, vol. 34, p. 233. 4. See Graphische Sammlung Staatsgalerie, *Zeichnungen des 15. bis 18. Jahrhunderts* (exh. cat.) (Stuttgart, 1984), cat. nos. 182–83, two repr.; and P. Rosenberg, *Disegni francesi da Callot a Ingres* (exh. cat.) (Florence: Uffizi, 1968), cat. nos. 53–54, repr. figs. 39–40. 5. Joachim 1977, cat. no. 1F4, repr. 6. See, for instance, Sotheby's London, 30 October 1980, nos. 186, 264. 7. Hall 1974, p. 150.

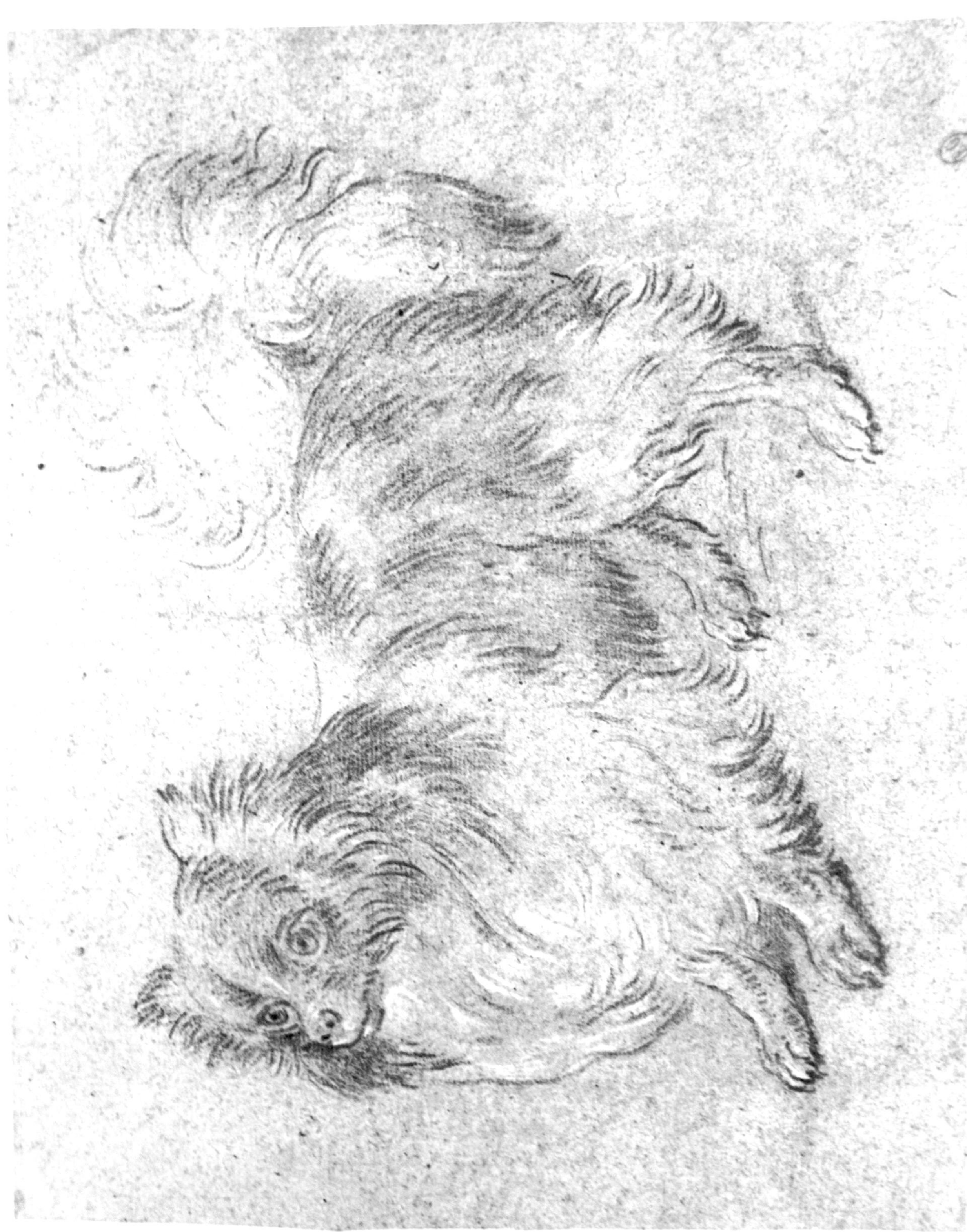

JEAN BAPTISTE OUDRY
PARIS 1686–1755 BEAUVAIS

90 *A Pomeranian*

Museum Purchase (1964.58) Black and white chalk on blue paper. 318 x 396 mm. (12 1/2 x 15 9/16 in.) Watermark: T MOREL / MD [indecipherable letters] / ASSISTE. PROVENANCE: J. B. E. Gallice (1828–1872) (Lugt 855), his sale, Paris, 11 February 1920, no. 150; Galerie Beauvau, Paris, 1961; Sotheby's London, 11 March 1964, no. 213; purchased by the museum from Schaeffer Galleries, New York. BIBLIOGRAPHY: Opperman 1972/77, vol. 2, p. 765, cat. no. D 686; *Handbook* 1981, p. 168.

OUDRY RECEIVED HIS FIRST TRAINING from his father, an artist who owned a small shop selling paintings and other art works. He then apprenticed with Nicholas de Largillière for five years, until ca. 1712. His career improved steadily after he was elected to the Académie de St. Luc and the Académie royale (he became a professor in each), and he received commissions from the royal family and others. In 1734 Oudry was named supervising designer at the Beauvais tapestry works, and in 1748 he was given the same job at the rival Gobelins factory. He had previously designed individual works at both places, the most prestigious being the series of royal hunts commissioned by King Louis XV of France in 1733. Oudry was and is most famous for his portrayals of animals and was "peintre ordinaire" to the king for such subjects.

This characteristic study of a dog is dated by Opperman around 1734–1740; he connects it with a group of individual studies of animals, probably done as ends in themselves.[1] None can be related to known paintings, and this sheet is no exception. All are done in black and white chalk on colored papers; some are highly finished, while others, like this one, are more informal studies. Among Oudry's paintings are single portraits of dogs, including several of the king's favorite hunting dogs.[2]

1. Opperman 1972/77, vol. 1, p. 144; cf. also vol. 2, cat. no. D 678–708. 2. See, for instance, Kimbell Art Museum, *Jean Baptiste Oudry* (exh. cat. by H. N. Opperman) (Fort Worth, 1983), p. 68, fig. 40.

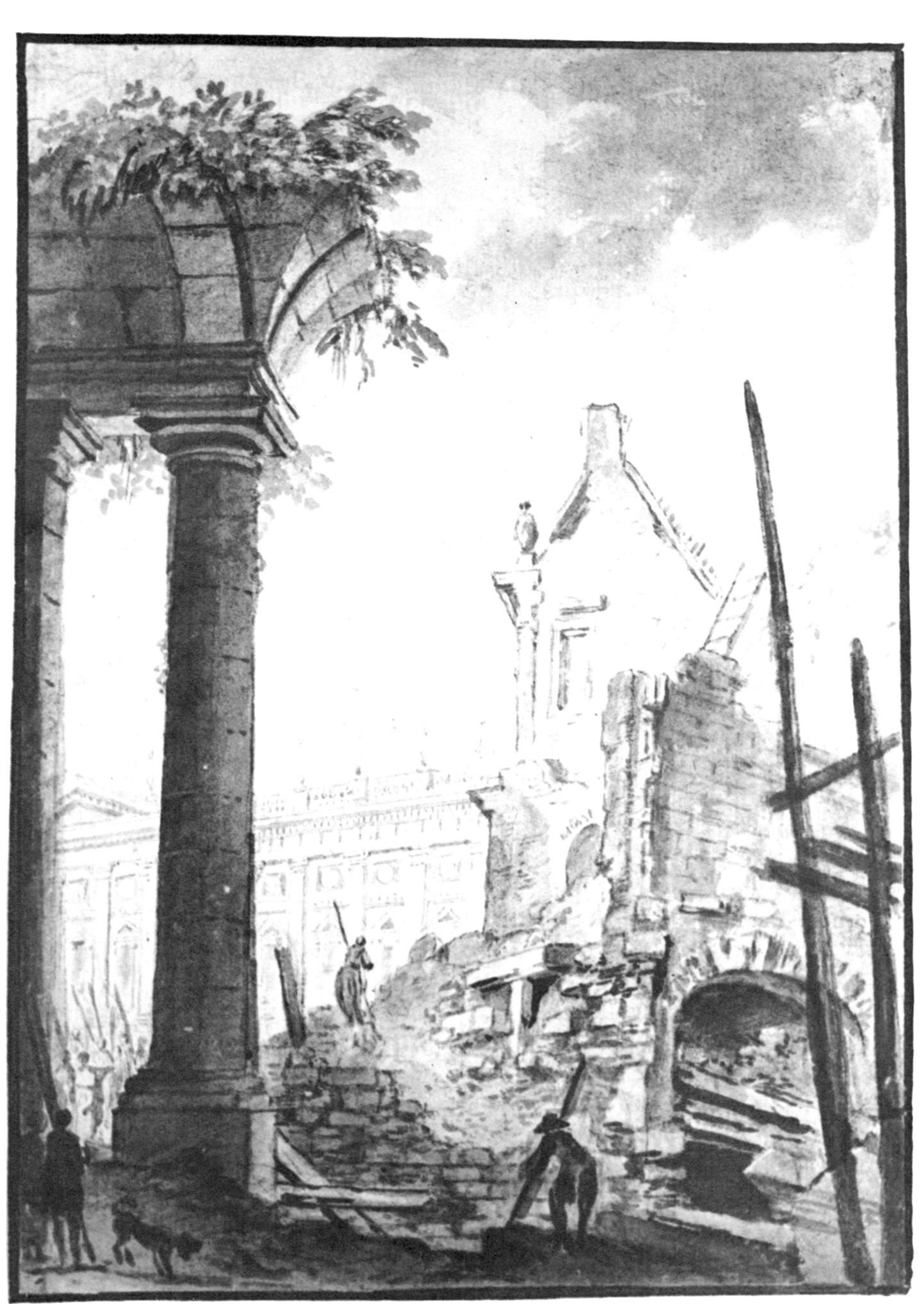

PIERRE ANTOINE DE MACHY
PARIS 1723–1807 PARIS

91 *Demolition of a Building with a View of the Louvre*

Gift of Miss Susan Dwight Bliss (1956.24.253) Pen and black ink and black wash over graphite, laid down. 169 x 121 mm. (6 5/8 x 4 3/4 in.) Inscribed on mount below right "Robert." No watermark. PROVENANCE: Susan Dwight Bliss.

DE MACHY WAS A STUDENT of Giovanni Niccolò Servandoni (1695–1766) and was elected a member of the Académie royale in 1758. He became a professor of perspective there in 1786 and was known as an engraver. He exhibited regularly in the Salon from 1757. De Machy was noted for his skill as an illusionist, and he often depicted views in Paris seen through a foreground of imaginary ruins. Though he apparently never traveled to Italy, he was influenced, as many of his contemporaries were, by Piranesi.[1] A large group of his paintings and several drawings are in the Musée Carnavalet, Paris.

Formerly attributed to Hubert Robert, this sheet was recognized by Pierre Rosenberg in 1971 as typical of De Machy's style. It seems to be a fairly rapid compositional sketch, without elaborate perspective constructions, in contrast to his large, detailed gouache studies.[2]

1. See Académie de France à Rome, *Piranèse et les Français 1740–1790* (exh. cat.) (1976), pp. 114–20.

2. See, for instance, ibid., cat. no. 57, repr.

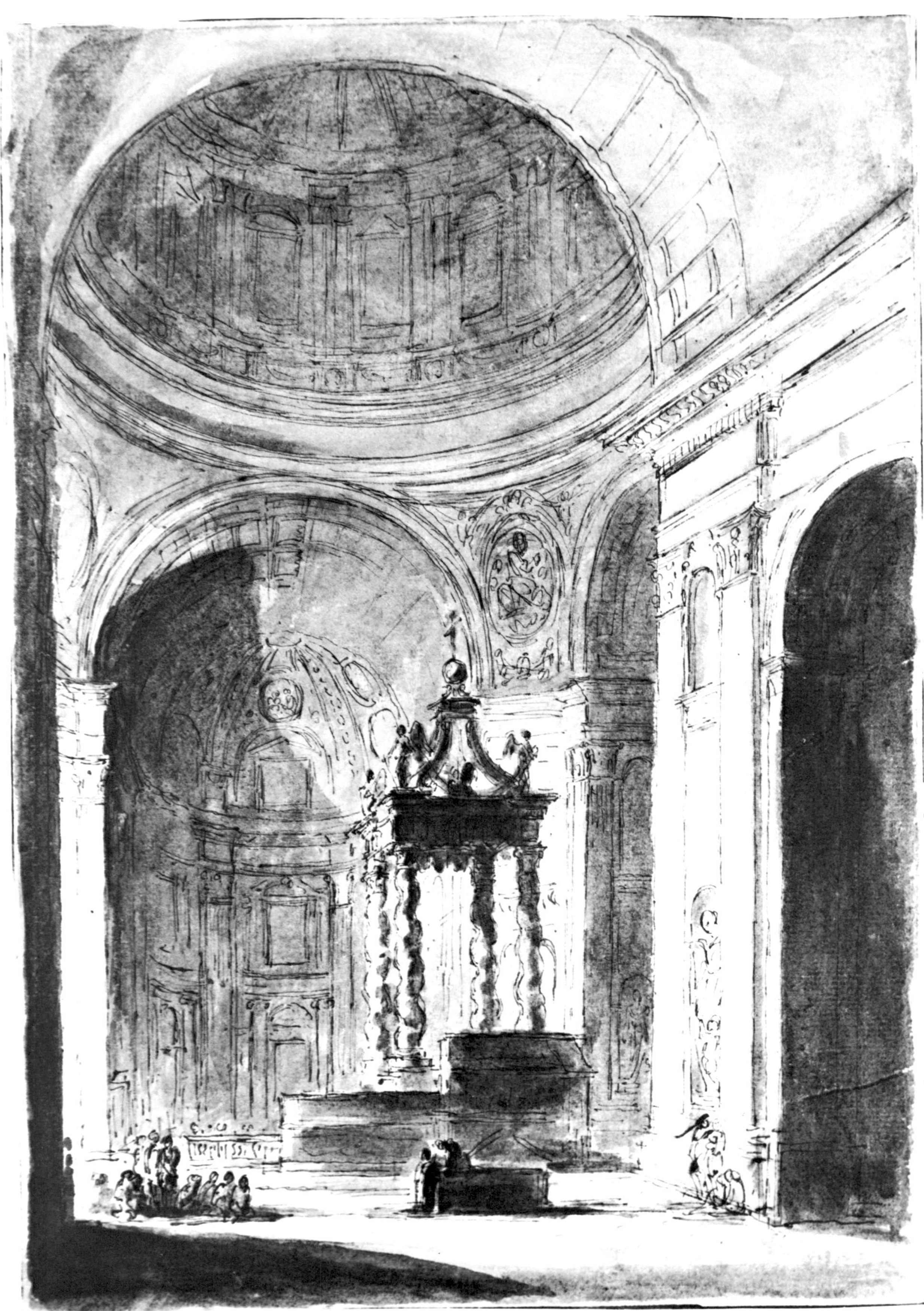

LOUIS JEAN DESPREZ
AUXERRE 1743–1804 STOCKHOLM

92 *Interior of St. Peter's, Rome*

Gift of Miss Susan Dwight Bliss (1956.24.235) Pen and black ink and brown wash over black chalk. 316 x 225 mm. (12 7/16 x 8 7/8 in.) No watermark. PROVENANCE: Susan Dwight Bliss.

THE ATTRIBUTION of this sheet was shifted from Jean le Pautre to Desprez by Pierre Rosenberg in 1971. Originally trained as an architect under Jacques François Blondel (1705–1774), Desprez studied at the Académie royale d'architecture from 1768 to 1776. In that year he won the Grand prix de Rome, which enabled him to go to Italy, where he began to concentrate on painting and drawing. During this time he was commissioned by the Abbé de Saint-Non to travel through southern Italy and Sicily preparing illustrations for the abbé's noted *Le voyage pittoresque, ou description des Royaumes de Naples et de Sicile*, published in Paris from 1781 to 1786. Desprez remained in Italy until 1784, when he was hired by Gustave III of Sweden as an architect and set designer for the royal theater. Desprez spent the rest of his career in Sweden, where a major portion of his work remains.

In 1782, Desprez executed a large pen and wash interior view of St. Peter's, Rome, which was presented to the Académie royale and is now in the Louvre.[1] It depicts the large illuminated cross which was hung in the nave of St. Peter's during Holy Week. The cross contained over six hundred lamps, creating a dramatic spectacle within the darkened cathedral.[2] The Louvre drawing (which was later engraved by Francesco Piranesi) shows both the Bernini altar and the hanging cross, whereas the Bowdoin sketch, drawn from within the opposite transept, shows only the altar reflecting the strong light of the unseen cross.

The Louvre and Bowdoin drawings are comparable in technique, particularly in the pen details of the ceiling and the figural types, but the somewhat tentative perspective of the Bowdoin sketch might betray another draughtsman with a style close to that of Desprez. The illuminated cross in St. Peter's was depicted by many artists of the time.[3]

1. N. G. Wollin, *Desprez en Italie* (Malmö, 1935), pl. 201. 2. Ibid., p. 157. 3. Cf. ibid., pp. 157–59.

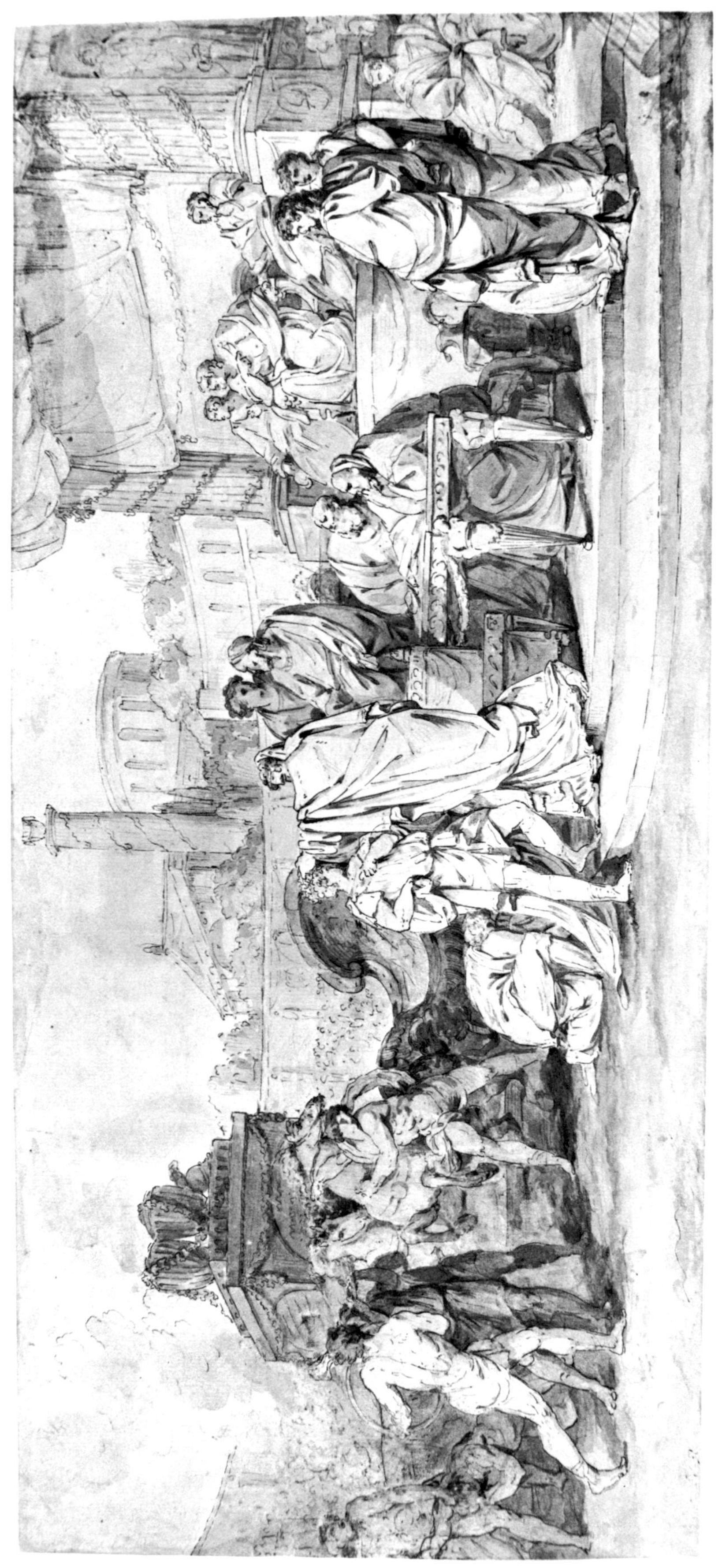

NICOLAS ANDRE MONSIAU, Attributed to
PARIS 1754–1837 PARIS

93 *Classical Award Ceremony*

Gift of Miss Susan Dwight Bliss (1956.24.299) Pen and black ink, red, grey, and brown washes, heightened with white, over graphite. 229 x 505 mm. (9 x 19⁷/₈ in.) Inscription at lower left (signature?) effaced. No watermark. PROVENANCE: Countess von Holstein and Rathbon Collections (according to Bliss Estate inventory); Susan Dwight Bliss.

MONSIAU WAS A STUDENT of Jean François Pierre Peyron (1744–1814) and became a painter of classical and historical subjects and a designer of book illustrations. He was elected to the Académie royale in 1789 and exhibited regularly at the Salon from 1787. The Louvre possesses several chalk portrait studies by him, and a group of forty-one drawings for his illustrations of Ovid are in the Pierpont Morgan Library, New York.[1]

The attribution of this sheet to Monsiau is traditional. He is known to have done pen studies embellished with watercolor, but comparable drawings have not been located. Usually the style of his drawings for book illustrations is more finished than in this fairly sketchy composition, as is to be expected in studies prepared to be engraved. The erasure of what possibly had been a signature at the lower left is troubling. Though the specific subject is unidentified, the grand neoclassical conception certainly is characteristic of Monsiau's works.

1. The Louvre drawings are cat. in Musée du Louvre, Cabinet des Dessins, *Catalogue raisonné—Ecole française*, vol. 11 [cat. by G. Rouchès and R. Huyghe] (Paris, 1938), p. 39, cat. nos. 10831–38, two repr. pl. 38. The Morgan drawings are noted in G. Ray, *The Art of the French Illustrated Book 1700–1914*, vol. 1 (New York and Ithaca, 1982), p. 154, one repr. p. 152. Other drawings by Monsiau are recorded in Baron R. Portalis, *Les Dessinateurs d'illustrations au dix-huitième siècle*, vol. 2 (Paris, 1877), pp. 414, 422–23.

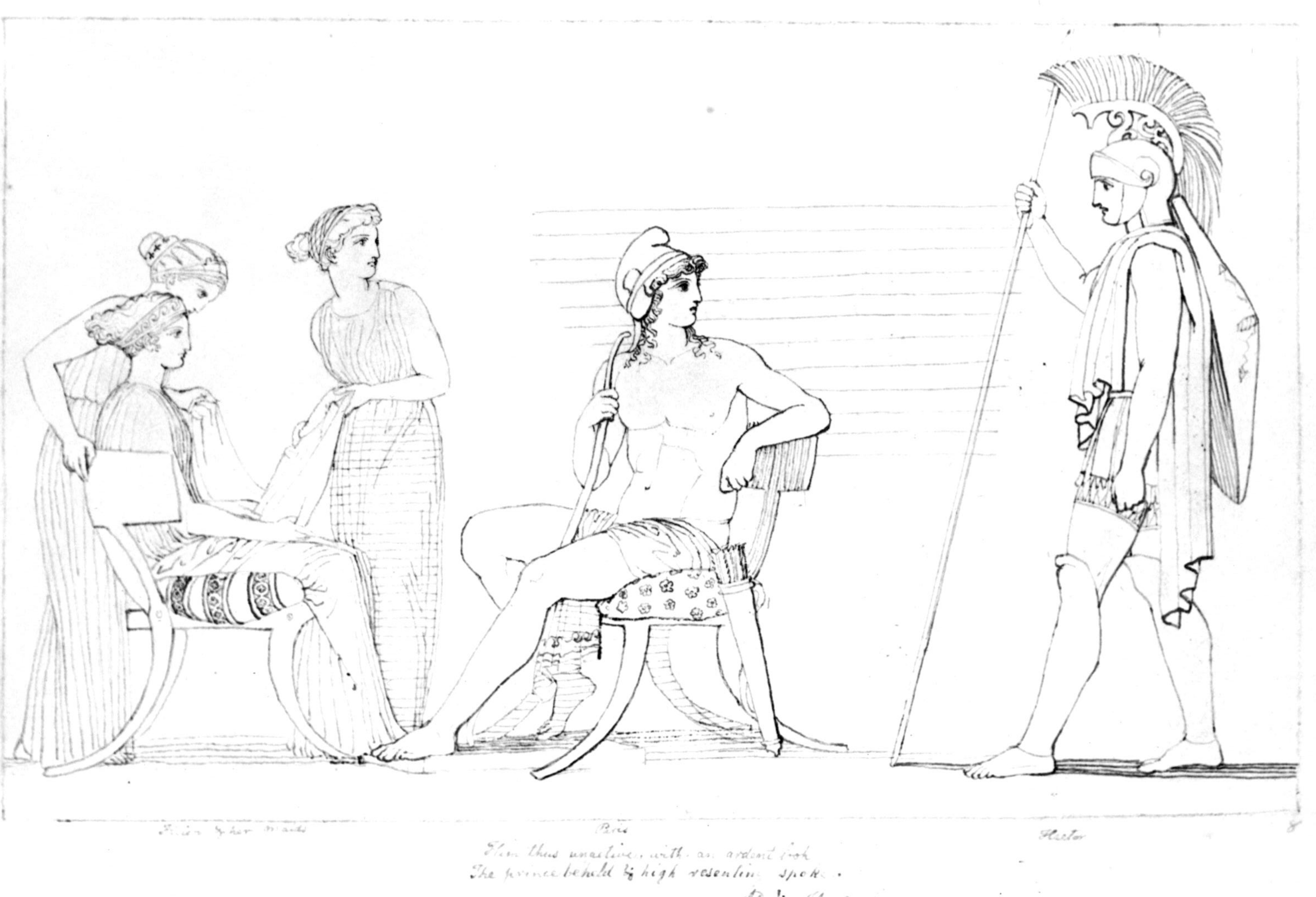

Him thus unactive, with an ardent look
The prince beheld, & high resenting spoke.

Pope's Il: 6: l: 404

JOHN FLAXMAN
YORK 1755–1826 LONDON

94 *Hector Chiding Paris*

Classical Fund (1918.1) Pen and grey ink, brush and black ink over graphite on wove paper. Sheet 212 x 309 mm. (8³/8 x 12¹/8 in.) Image 168 x 270 mm. (6⁵/8 x 10⁵/8 in.) Inscribed by the artist below lower right graphite "8"; below pen and grey ink "Helen & her Maids Paris Hector / Him thus unactive, with an ardent look / The prince beheld & high resenting spoke. / Pope's Il: 6: 1: 404." No watermark. PROVENANCE: Thomas Hope (ca. 1770–1831); acquired from Scott and Fowles, New York (*Catalogue of an Exhibition of Original Drawings by John Flaxman, R. A.*, [New York, 1918], cat. no. 8). BIBLIOGRAPHY: *Catalogue* 1930, p. 104, no. D-1; *Handbook* 1981, p. 169. EXHIBITIONS: Storrs 1973, cat. no. 129a; Wilmington 1976, cat. nos. 1–11, repr.

THE SON OF A MAKER of plaster casts and models, Flaxman began his studies at the Royal Academy School at the age of fourteen and soon exhibited there. In 1775 he began designing reliefs and medallions for the Wedgwood pottery factory, and about ten years later he executed the first of many sculptural commissions for both public and private patrons. Flaxman spent nearly eight years beginning in 1787 on the Continent, primarily in Italy, where he studied antique and Renaissance works of art. Upon his return to London, he was elected to the Royal Academy in 1800 and was appointed its first professor of sculpture in 1810.

Flaxman's taste for the antique and his support for the ideals of neoclassical art are seen clearly in several series of illustrations which he began designing during his Italian sojourn. Primarily classical texts, his sources included Homer, Aeschylus, Hesiod, and Dante. Commissioned by private patrons, he executed drawings which incorporated short captions, usually lines from translations, into the designs. These captions were engraved as parts of the design instead of being superimposed by letterpress, and therefore the works cannot be strictly construed as book illustrations. They are, rather, representations in themselves of the events in a story "on the principles of the ancients."[1]

This drawing is a preliminary study for one of the *Iliad* plates, illustrating line 404 of book 6, in which the Trojan leader Hector upbraids the young Paris for his laziness in the defense of the city. The Homer drawings were executed by Flaxman in Rome in 1792 and 1793 for a Mrs. Hare-Naylor. The first series of engravings was prepared in 1793 by Tommaso Piroli (1750–1824); the prints proved so popular that they were reprinted and copied many times throughout Europe well into the nineteenth century. Flaxman consciously evoked the linear style of Greek vase painting in his spare designs, which are essentially pure outlines drawn with the barest indications of shading, depth, and background setting.

Each of Flaxman's designs evolved through experimental variants and figure studies. The Bowdoin study is considerably different from the final engraving, in which Paris is shown standing somewhat sheepishly facing Hector, and the two handmaidens attending to Helen are eliminated. The figures of Helen and Hector are quite similar to those in the print. A study similar to the Bowdoin sheet is in the Royal Academy, London, and another variant was on the London art market in 1976.[2] A study for Flaxman's *Odyssey* designs is also in the museum collection (Cat. 275). The two drawings are said to have belonged to Thomas Hope, an antiquary and longtime patron of Flaxman. Sizable collections of Flaxman's drawings for his illustrations are in the British Museum; the Royal Academy; University College, London; the Huntington Library and Art Gallery, San Marino; and the Houghton Library, Harvard.

1. D. Irwin, *John Flaxman 1755–1826—Sculptor Illustrator Designer* (London, 1979), p. 68. 2. R. Essick and J. La Belle, intro., *Flaxman's Illustrations to Homer* (New York, 1977), p. xxiii, under no. 13; the latter study is repr. in D. Irwin, *English Neoclassical Art* (London, 1966), pl. 70.

Checklist of Further Drawings

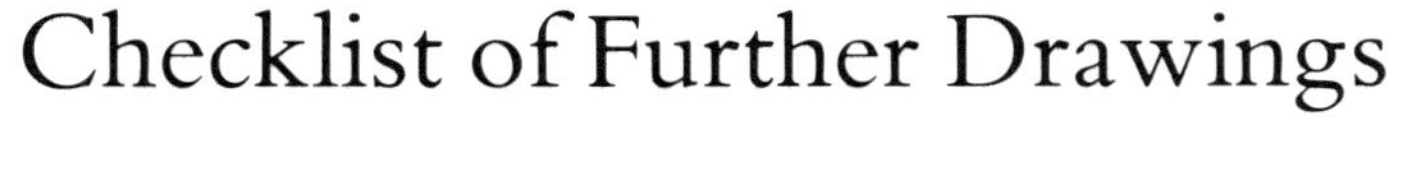

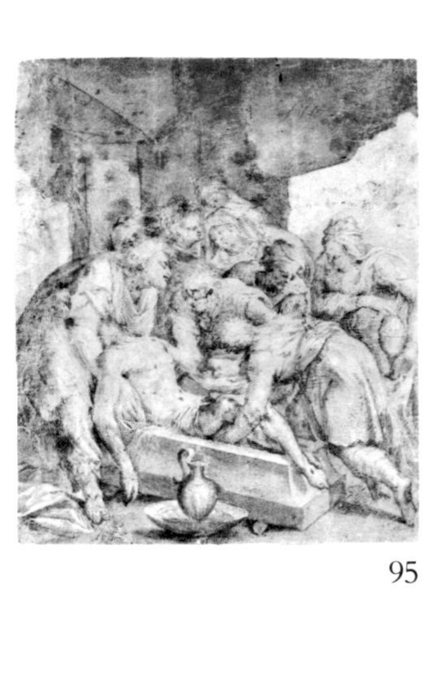
95

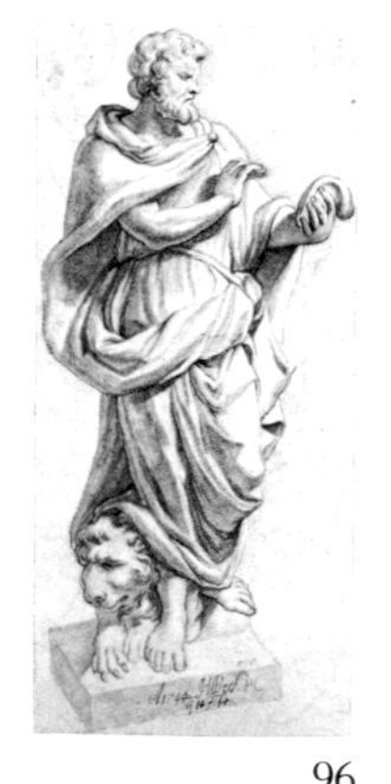
96

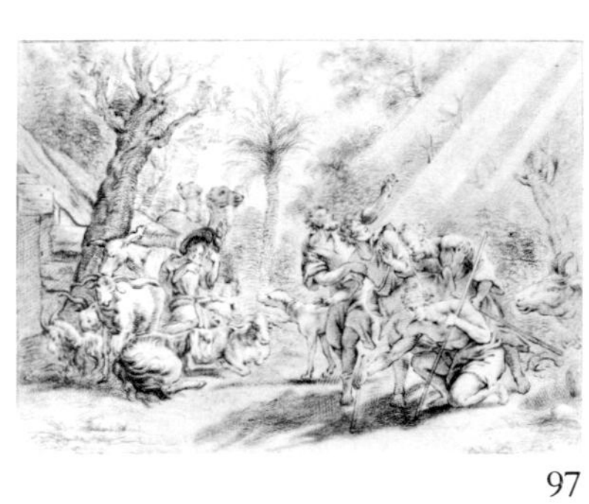
97

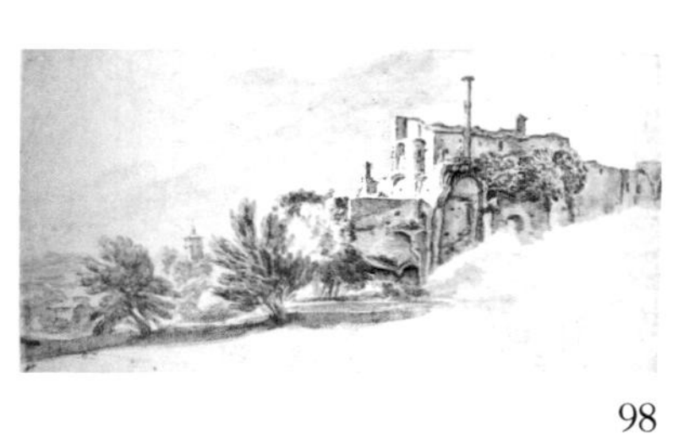
98

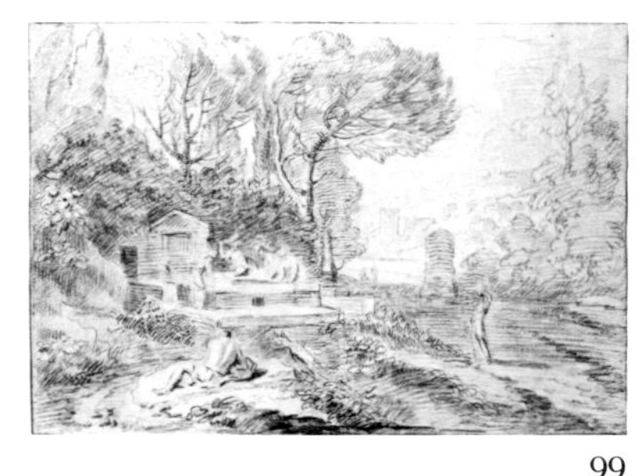
99

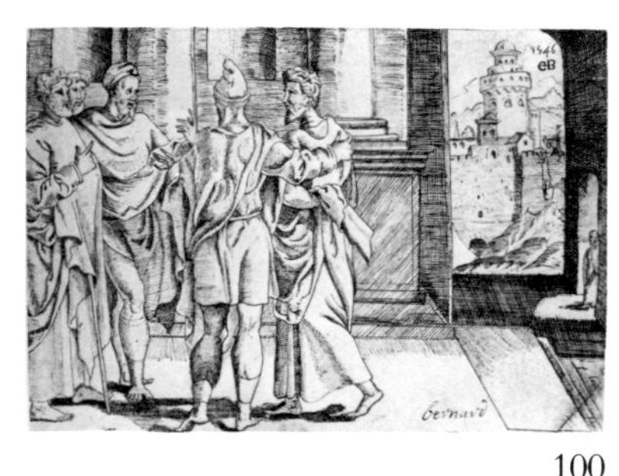
100

101

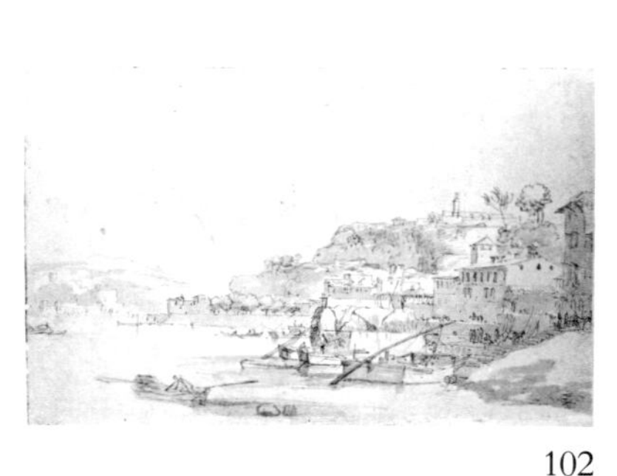
102

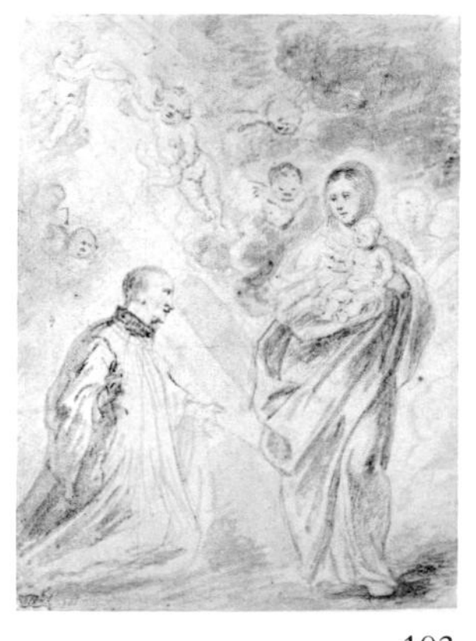
103

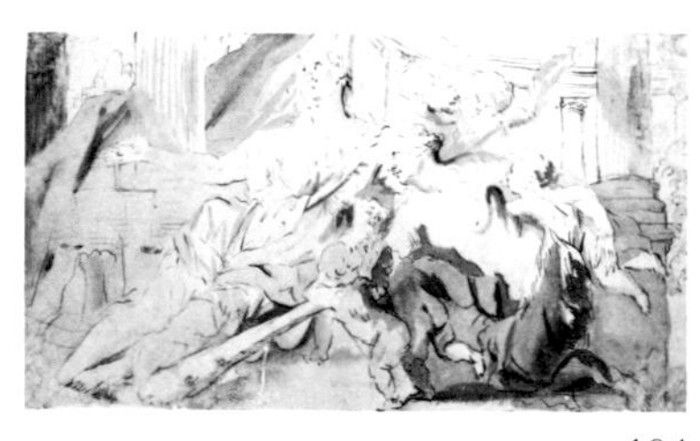
104

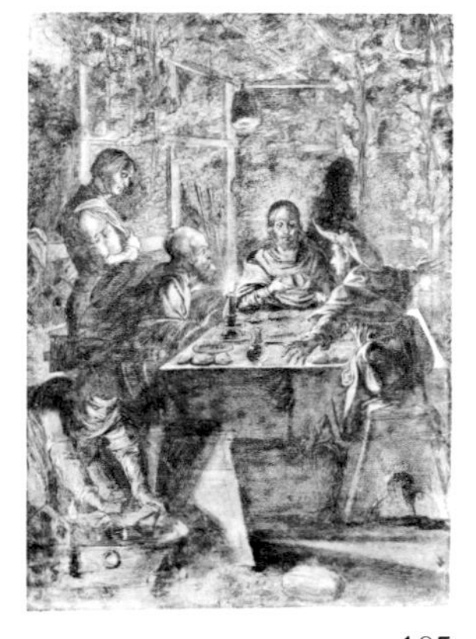
105

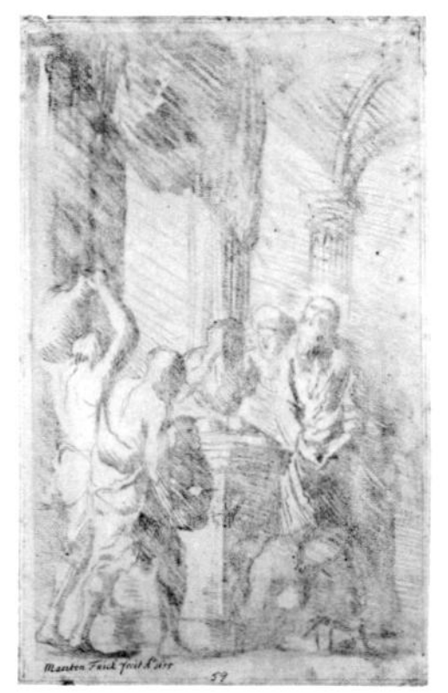
106

THE FOLLOWING CONDENSED ENTRIES are similar in format to the preceding except that watermarks are mentioned only when they are present. The anonymous drawings within each school and century are arranged by their museum accession numbers.

Dutch, Flemish, and German

95

DIRCK BARENDSZ. (1534–1592), copy after, *The Entombment*, brush and brown ink and wash, heightened with white (partly oxidized) on brown laid paper (old wrinkles, stains, fading, losses), 220 x 186 mm. (8 5/8 x 7 5/16 in.). Inscr. verso pen and brown ink "ouden ersamen."

James Phinney Baxter Fund in Memory of Professor Henry Johnson (1932.29). Prov.: Henry Johnson. Bibl.: *Cat.* 1930, p. 94, no. 615 (as Palma Vecchio); Judson 1970, pp. 22, 60–62, 119, no. 58, repr. fig. 26 (as Barendsz., as are all following); W. Wegner, review of Judson 1970, in *Pantheon*, vol. 30, no. 2 (March–April 1972), p. 172; Boon 1978, vol. 1, p. 14; J. Foucart and P. Rosenberg, "Some *Modelli* of Religious Scenes by Dirck Barendsz.," *Burlington Magazine*, vol. 120, no. 901 (April 1978), pp. 198, 201. Exh.: American Federation of Arts 1962–1963, no. 39 (as Palma Giovane).

Attributed by Richard Judson in his monograph to Barendsz. himself, and related to two prints after this subject by Jan Sadeler (Judson 1970, fig. 33) and Dominicus Custos (Hollstein *German*, vol. 6, p. 179, no. 10). A drawing in Amsterdam (Boon 1978, no. 25, repr.; Judson 1970, fig. 26A) in reverse to the Bowdoin sheet and prepared for transfer is the undoubted model for the Sadeler print, which is in the same direction as the Bowdoin sheet. Judson argues that the latter is either a rejected design for the Sadeler print or a later study for the Custos engraved version, stating that the Bowdoin sheet lacks details such as the crown of thorns found in the Sadeler print; however, though almost faded away, the crown is present in the Bowdoin sheet. Therefore, it is likely that it is a copy of very high quality, perhaps contemporary, from the Sadeler engraving.

96

J. H. BECH, *Copy of a Sculpture*, 1744, black chalk and grey wash on blue paper, 391 x 179 mm. (15 3/8 x 7 1/16 in.). Inscr. black chalk on base of sculpture "590/A 1744 J H Bech del/14 Febr."

Museum Purchase (1930.235). Prov.: Prof. Henry Johnson.

The lack of scholarly references to the artist and the stiffness of execution suggest that this is an amateur's copy of an antique sculpture.

97

NICOLAES BERCHEM (1620–1683), copy after (?), *Annunciation to the Shepherds*, red chalk, laid down, 145 x 200 mm. (5 11/16 x 7 7/8 in.).

James Phinney Baxter Fund in Memory of Professor Henry Johnson (1932.36). Prov.: Henry Johnson. Bibl.: *Cat.* 1930, p. 95, no. 641 (as Berchem).

Far from Berchem himself; probably a copy after a painting.

98

JAN FRANS VAN BLOEMEN (1662–1748/49), attr., *Landscape with Classical Ruins*, brush and brown wash over graphite, 223 x 433 mm. (8 3/4 x 17 in.). Wmk.: saint holding cross within shield.

Bequest of James Bowdoin III (1811.124). Prov.: James Bowdoin III. Bibl.: *Cat.* 1885, no. 104 (as Unknown); *Cat.* 1930, no. 104 (as Unknown).

An attribution to Frederic de Moucheron has also been suggested. The composition and technique bear resemblance to those of a sheet attributed to Crescenzio Onofri at Windsor Castle (Inv. no. 6136, repr. Blunt and Cooke 1960, p. 71, fig. 52).

99

JAN FRANS VAN BLOEMEN, copy after, *Landscape with Washerwomen*, black chalk with pen and brown ink, 282 x 411 mm. (11 1/8 x 16 3/16 in.). Inscr. pen and ink verso of old mount (lost) "Horosonti." Wmk.: fleur-de-lis within circle.

Bequest of James Bowdoin III (1811.66). Prov.: James Bowdoin III. Bibl.: *Cat.* 1885, no. 74 (as "Horosonti?"); *Cat.* 1930, no. 64 (as van Bloemen).

The composition is that of a van Bloemen painting in the collection of the Earl of Leicester at Holkham Hall, datable before 1715 (repr. in A. Busiri Vici, *Jan Frans van Bloemen Orizzonte* [Rome, 1974], no. 272). An Zwollo (letter to the author, 13 July 1984) feels it is done after the painting, rather than preliminary to it.

100

CORNELIS BOS (ca. 1506/10–1564), copy after, *Saul Brought by Barnabas to the Apostles*, pen and black ink, touches of red chalk, 165 x 241 mm. (6½ x 9½ in.). Inscr. pen and black ink upper right "1546/CB"; pen and brown ink lower right "bernard."

Museum Purchase (1930.220). Prov.: William Bates (1824–1884) (Lugt 2604); Prof. Henry Johnson.

A copy in the same direction of a Bos engraving dated 1546 (S. Schéle, *Cornelis Bos—A Study of the Origins of the Netherland Grotesque* [Uppsala, 1965], p. 123, cat. no. 41, repr. pl. 15, no. 7). The lower inscription probably refers to Bernard Salomon, a sixteenth-century French designer of book illustrations.

101

LEONARD BRAMER (1596–1674), *Youth Leaping from a Precipice*, pen and brush and black ink (loss in cow), 360 x 288 mm. (14³/16 x 11⁵/16 in.). Inscr. pen and brown ink upper right "62." Wmk.: foolscap.

Bequest of James Bowdoin III (1811.130). Prov.: James Bowdoin III. Bibl.: *Cat.* 1885, no. 107 (as Unknown); *Cat.* 1930, no. 107 (as Unknown).

Although the subject of this sheet is not known, it bears resemblance in technique, dimensions, and composition to a drawing by Bramer in Bremen of Io Plunging into the Sea (Inv. no. 456, Gernsheim 60890).

102

ADRIAEN VAN DER CABEL (1631–1705), *View of a Port* (verso: *Bridge and Tower*), graphite and grey wash, 233 x 368 mm. (9³/16 x 14½ in.). Inscr. pen and brown ink verso "Adriaen van der cabel/Per sopra porte/di [. . .] 2½ rela." Indecipherable watermark.

Bequest of James Bowdoin III (1811.123). Prov.: James Bowdoin III. Bibl.: *Cat.* 1885, no. 64; *Cat.* 1930, no. 61.

103

ABRAHAM VAN DIEPENBEECK (1596–1675), *Madonna and Child Appearing to St. Ignatius* (verso: architectural studies), brush and black ink, grey wash, red chalk (verso: black chalk), 191 x 143 mm. (7½ x 5⁵/8 in.). Inscr. verso graphite "3. guilders/A.V.D."; pen and brown ink "N.º 12"; verso of old mount (removed) "Diepenbeck."

Bequest of James Bowdoin III (1811.42). Prov.: Jan Pietersz. Zomer (1641–1724) (Lugt 1511), James Bowdoin III. Bibl.: *Cat.* 1885, no. 53; *Cat.* 1930, no. 53.

The attribution has been affirmed by Jaffé and by Haverkamp Begemann, who identified the saint.

104

WILLEM DOUDIJNS (1630–1697), attr., *Hercules and Omphale*, pen and brown ink, brown wash (waterstains, wormholes), 202 x 360 mm. (7¹⁵/16 x 14³/16 in.). Wmk.: foolscap with five points.

Museum Purchase (1930.186). Prov.: Johan Conrad Spengler (1767–1839) (Lugt 1434); William Bates (1824–1884) (Lugt 2604); Prof. Henry Johnson.

Haverkamp Begemann doubts the attribution. Hercules' attributes, the lion skin and club, are worn by Omphale; the meaning of the scales of justice is obscure.

105

ADAM ELSHEIMER (1578–1610), follower of, *The Supper at Emmaus*, pen and brown ink, brown wash, heightened with white, on brown prepared paper (losses left edge), 350 x 253 mm. (13¾ x 10 in.).

Bequest of James Bowdoin III (1811.75). Prov.: James Bowdoin III. Bibl.: *Cat.* 1885, no. 89 (as Unknown); *Cat.* 1930, no. 89 (as Unknown).

This drawing was ascribed to the school of Barocci by Sir Robert Witt and to the circle of Elsheimer by Oberhuber. In fact, it is a copy of a painting (in a Swiss private collection) formerly given to Elsheimer himself and then by Andrews to a follower, Thoman von Hagelstein (1588–1653). See Städelsches Kunstinstitut, *Adam Elsheimer* [exh. cat.] (Frankfurt am Main, 1966–1967), cat. no. 19, repr. pl. 17a; also K. Andrews, *Adam Elsheimer* (New York and London, 1977), p. 166, no. A 15. Andrews (letter to the author, 31 March 1982) placed the Bowdoin sheet as a copy, designating the artist as a follower of Elsheimer.

106

MAERTEN FUICK, *Sacrificial Scene*, black chalk (counterproof), 316 x 199 mm. (12⁷/16 x 7¹³/16 in.). Inscr. pen and black ink lower left "Maerten Fuick fecit A°. 1655"; graphite bottom "59."

Bequest of James Bowdoin III (1811.80). Prov.: James Bowdoin III. Bibl.: *Cat.* 1885, no. 60; *Cat.* 1930, no. 60.

The inscription would seem to leave no doubt as to the attribution, but the obscurity of the artist raises the possibility that he was an amateur, or even that he made a counterproof of another artist's drawing.

107

DANIEL KERKHOFF (1766–1831), *Boy Fishing by a Canal*, pen and brown ink, brown wash, black chalk, 308 x 243 mm. (12⅛ x 9⁹/16 in.).

James Phinney Baxter Fund in Memory of Professor Henry Johnson (1932.22). Prov.: Henry Johnson. Bibl.: *Cat.* 1930, p. 95, no. 644.

108

ISAAC MAJOR (1588–after 1642), attr., *Landscape with Stream*, brush and blue ink over black chalk (almost totally faded by light), laid down, 239 x 365 mm. (9³/₈ x 14³/₈ in.). Inscr. pen and brown ink upper right "140." Wmk.: serpent with initials MH.

Bequest of James Bowdoin III (1811.87). Prov.: James Bowdoin III. Bibl.: *Cat.* 1885, no. 115 (as Unknown); *Cat.* 1930, no. 115 (as Unknown); [Siber] 1947, pp. 119–20, repr. fig. 10 (as Flemish, 16th–17th c.).

Closely related to drawings at Yale (Inv. no. 1961.62.62, repr. Princeton-Washington 1982–1983, cat. no. 66) and the Metropolitan Museum (Inv. no. 66.93.5). Attribution is by Spicer (see Princeton-Washington 1982–1983, under cat. nos. 66–67). Previously these drawings had been placed in the Savery school. See following entry for a related sheet.

109

ISAAC MAJOR, attr., *Landscape with River*, brush and blue ink over black chalk (almost totally faded by light), laid down, 241 x 364 mm. (9¹/₂ x 14⁵/₁₆ in.). Inscr. pen and brown ink upper right "144."

Bequest of James Bowdoin III (1811.128). Prov.: James Bowdoin III. Bibl.: *Cat.* 1885, no. 114 (as Unknown); *Cat.* 1930, no. 114 (as Unknown).

See discussion under previous entry.

110

ADAM FRANS VAN DER MEULEN (1632–1690), attr., *Horsemen and Carriages*, brush and grey wash, laid down, 163 x 276 mm. (6³/₈ x 10⁷/₈ in.). Inscr. graphite lower right 'Van der meulen."

James Phinney Baxter Fund in Memory of Professor Henry Johnson (1932.33). Prov.: Henry Johnson. Bibl.: *Cat.* 1930, p. 95, no. 638.

According to notes in the museum files, this sketch is related to depictions of the victories of Louis XIV.

111

CLAES CORNELISZ. MOEYAERT (1590/91–1655), *Tobias Frightened by the Fish*, pen and brown ink, brown wash over black chalk, 212 x 163 mm. (8³/₈ x 6⁷/₁₆ in.).

Bequest of James Bowdoin III (1811.63). Prov.: James Bowdoin III. Bibl.: *Cat.* 1885, no. 131 (as Unknown); *Cat.* 1930, no. 131 (as Unknown); *Handbook* 1981, p. 166 (as Moeyaert). Exh.: Sacramento 1974, cat. no. 18. repr.

Attribution first made by Witt, affirmed by Lugt and other scholars. The story of the subject is related in the Book of Tobit from the Apocrypha, 6:1–6.

112

CLAES CORNELISZ. MOEYAERT, copy after, *Joseph Sold by His Brothers*, pen and brown ink, grey and brown wash over graphite (losses top edge and corners), 210 x 305 mm. (8¹/₄ x 12 in.). Inscr. graphite former mount (lost) "Salvator Rosa." Wmk.: fleur-de-lis in crowned shield, LB below.

Bequest of James Bowdoin III (1811.101). Prov.: James Bowdoin III. Bibl.: *Cat.* 1885, no. 21, repr. in large paper ed. (as Salvator Rosa, as are all following); Allen 1886, pt. 1, no. 3, repr.; *Cat.* 1930, no. 21.

Witt was the first to describe this as Dutch; Lugt recognized it as a copy from Moeyaert. Tümpel has located a painting and three drawings by Moeyaert of this subject (Tümpel 1974, p. 251, cat. no. 41 and figs. 222–24), none precisely like the Bowdoin model. The story is recounted in Genesis 37:25–28.

113

"PSEUDO-AERT ORTKENS" (active ca. 1510–1540), school of, *The Circumcision*, pen and brown ink over traces of black chalk, laid down, 228 mm. diameter (9 in.), cut down at sides to 206 mm. (8¹/₈ in.). Inscr. recto of mount pen and brown ink "Israel van Mentz."

Gift of Miss Susan Dwight Bliss (1956.24.271). Prov.: Thomas Banks (1735–1805) (Lugt 2423); his daughter, Mrs. Lavinia Forster; her son-in-law, Ambrose Poynter (1796–1886) (Lugt 161); his son, Sir Edward J. Poynter (1836–1919), his sale, 24–25 April 1918, no. 255; B. Saklatwalla; Susan Dwight Bliss.

The old inscription probably refers to Israhel van Meckenhem (ca. 1445–1503). Haverkamp Begemann related this sheet to a group of designs for stained glass roundels formerly attributed to Aert Ortkens (active 1513–1538). No drawing has been securely attributed to him (see discussion by Boon in Florence-Paris 1980–1981, pp. 167–69, and Boon 1978, vol. 1, pp. 137–38). The Bowdoin sheet is probably a workshop copy, perhaps several times removed from the original model; another Circumcision by a better hand of the group is in Amsterdam (Boon 1978, cat. no. 384, repr.).

114

JAN (1583/84–1631) or JACOB (ca. 1585–after 1656) PYNAS, attr., *The Visitation*, black chalk (counterproof), touched with white chalk, 214 x 168 mm. (8⁷/₁₆ x 6⁵/₈ in.). Inscr. pen and ink verso of old mount (lost) "Rembrant." Wmk.: fleur-de-lis in shield over W (fragment).

Bequest of James Bowdoin III (1811.78). Prov.: James Bowdoin III. Bibl.: *Cat.* 1885, no. 51 (as Rembrandt);

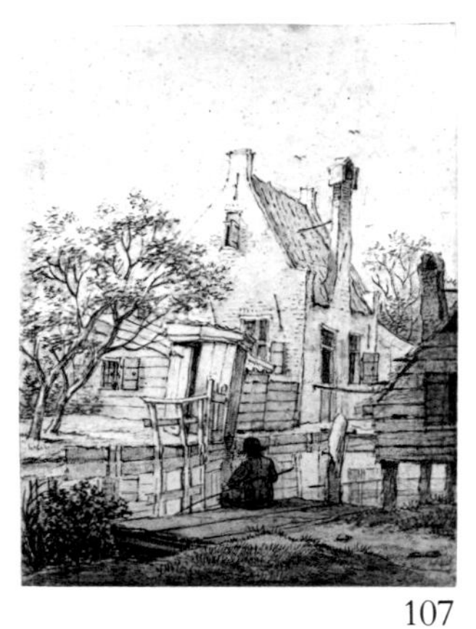
107

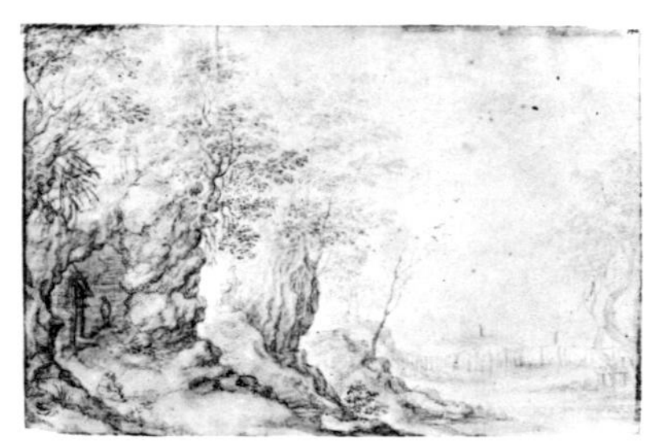
108

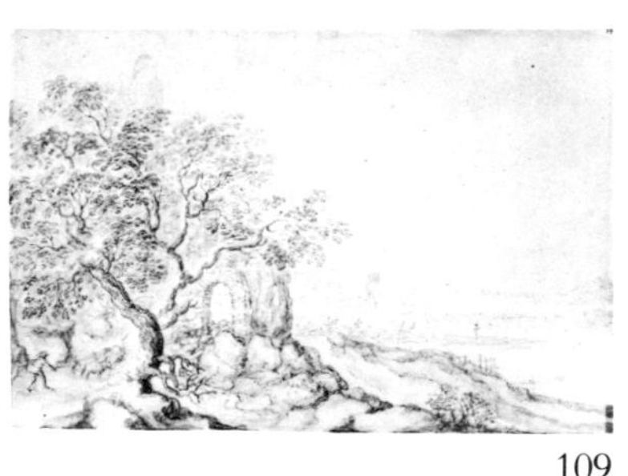
109

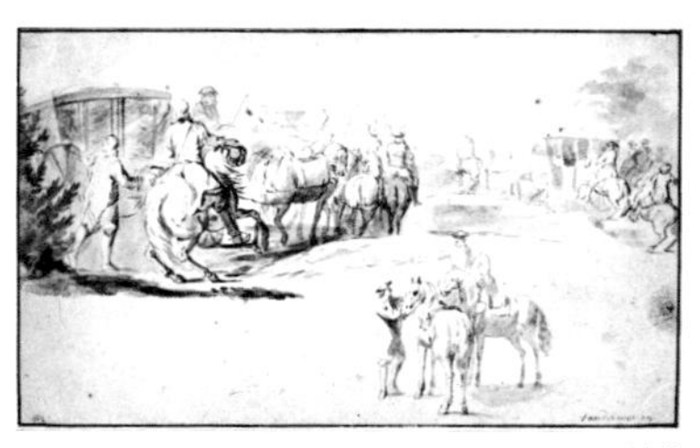
110

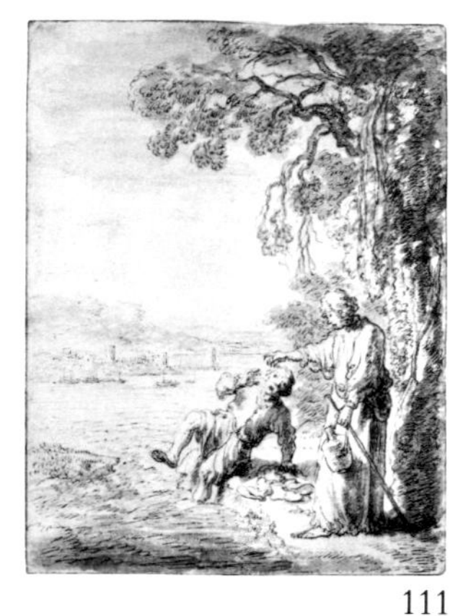
111

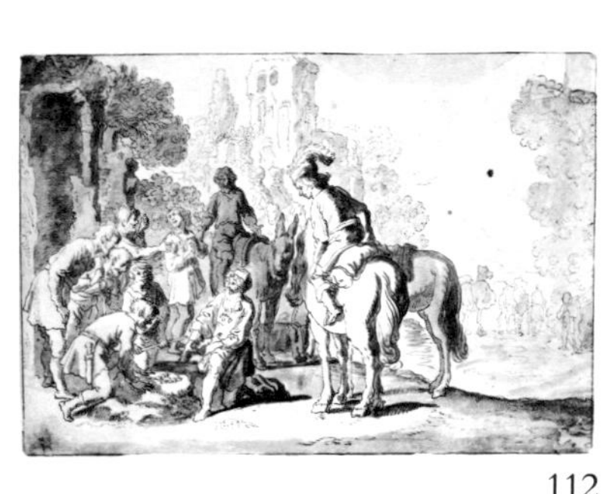
112

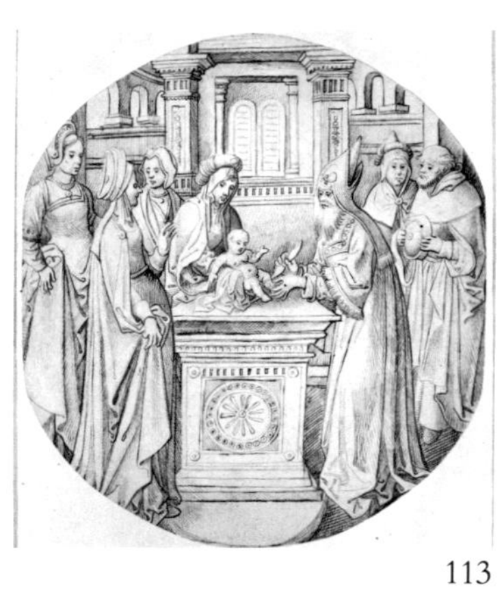
113

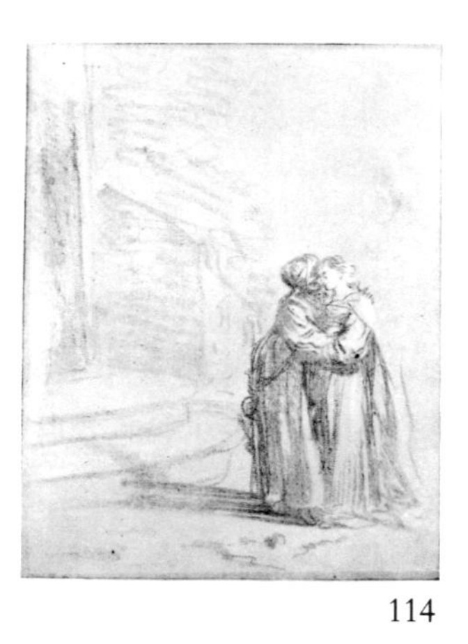
114

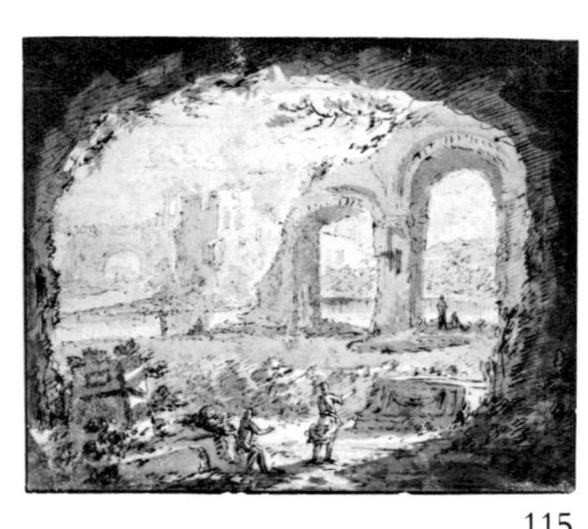
115

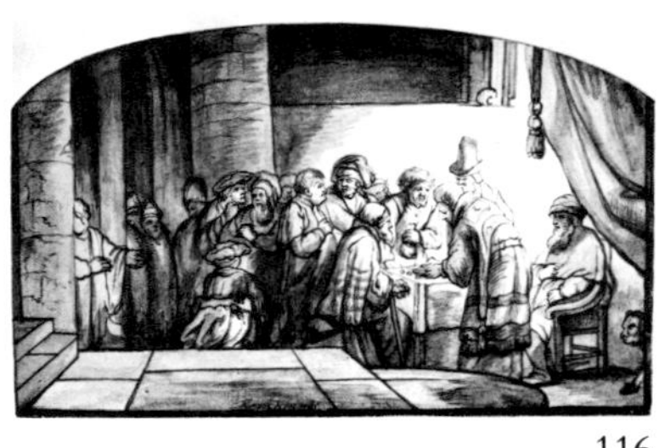
116

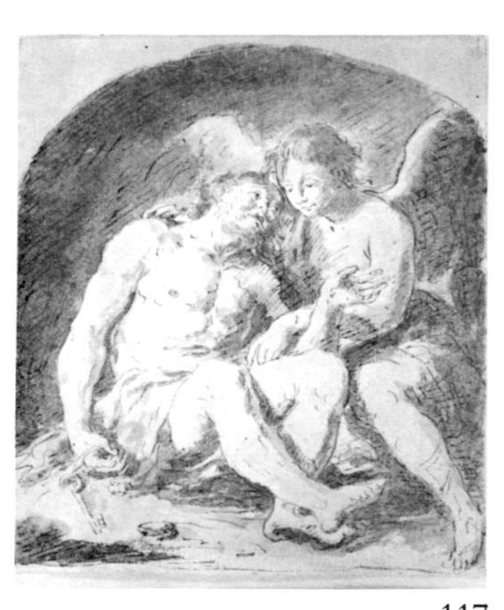
117

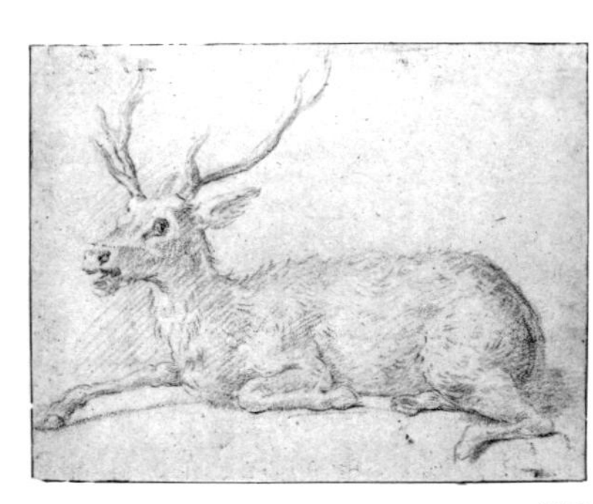
118

Cat. 1930, no. 51 (as Rembrandt); [Siber] 1947, p. 119, repr. fig. 6 (as derived from Rembrandt).

The source of the Pynas attribution is not known; most scholars place this sheet within the school of Rembrandt.

115

ABRAHAM RADEMAKER (1675–1735), attr., *Landscape with Classical Ruins*, pen and brown ink, grey wash over black chalk, 205 x 252 mm. (8 1/16 x 9 15/16 in.). Inscr. graphite on mount "Abr. Rademaker." Wmk.: arms of Amsterdam.

James Phinney Baxter Fund in Memory of Professor Henry Johnson (1932.20). Prov.: William Bates (1824–1884) (Lugt 2604); Henry Johnson.

116

REMBRANDT VAN RIJN (1606–1669) and pupil, copy after, *Judas Receiving the Thirty Pieces of Silver*, brush and brown ink and wash over graphite, laid down, 152 x 253 mm. (6 x 10 in.). Inscr. pen and brown ink bottom "Rembrandt."

Museum Purchase (1930.146). Prov.: Prof. Henry Johnson.

This is a close copy of a drawing in the Devonshire Collection, Chatsworth, by Constantijn van Renesse, corrected by Rembrandt (Benesch, vol. 6, cat. no. 1378, repr. fig. 1613).

117

REMBRANDT VAN RIJN, school of, attr., *St. Peter in Prison* (verso: Nativity scene), pen and brown ink, grey wash, 135 x 120 mm. (5 5/16 x 4 3/4 in.). Inscr. graphite verso "?Rembrandt."

Gift of Miss Susan Dwight Bliss (1956.24.242). Prov.: Susan Dwight Bliss.

118

PHILIPP PETER ROOS (ca. 1655–1706), attr., *Reclining Stag*, red chalk on brown paper, laid down, 260 x 338 mm. (10 1/4 x 13 5/16 in.). Inscr. pen and brown ink verso of mount "di Salvador Rosa."

Bequest of Helen Johnson Chase (1958.66). Prov.: Professor Henry Johnson; Helen Johnson (Mrs. Stanley P.) Chase. Bibl.: *Cat.* 1930, p. 94, no. 630 (as Rosa).

Attributed to a member of the Roos family, possibly Philipp Peter, by Hans Werner Schmidt (letter in museum files, 8 December 1956).

119

JOHANN ROTTENHAMMER (1564–1625), copy after?, *Adoration of the Shepherds*, pen and brown ink, brown wash over black and white chalk on blue laid paper, considerable damage lower right, laid down on Japanese tissue, 316 x 236 mm. (12 7/16 x 9 5/16 in.). Inscr. pen and brown ink bottom "Rottenhammer fe."

Bequest of James Bowdoin III (1811.57). Prov.: James Bowdoin III. Bibl.: *Cat.* 1885, no. 16 (as Rottenhammer); *Cat.* 1930, no. 76 (as Rottenhammer).

The tentative, loose treatment speaks for this being a copy. For other sheets by Rottenhammer in this country, see Princeton-Washington 1982–1983, cat. nos. 30–33, repr.

120

JOHANN ROTTENHAMMER, circle of, *Judgment of Paris*, pen and brown ink, brown wash, heightened with white (oxidized), on rose-colored prepared paper, 286 x 197 mm. (11 1/4 x 7 3/4 in.). Wmk.: five-pointed star over hand with initials CM (somewhat related to Briquet 11351, 11363).

Bequest of James Bowdoin III (1811.105). Prov.: James Bowdoin III. Bibl.: *Cat.* 1885, no. 133 (as Unknown); *Cat.* 1930, no. 133 (as Unknown).

Ascribed to the school of Parmigianino by Filippo di Pietro, this sheet was placed near Rottenhammer by Oberhuber. A drawing by Rottenhammer of the same subject is at Yale (Haverkamp Begemann and Logan 1970, cat. no. 176, repr. pl. 101).

121

SIR PETER PAUL RUBENS (1577–1640), copy after, *Head of Nero*, brush and black ink, 317 x 195 mm. (12 1/2 x 7 11/16 in.). Inscr. graphite lower left "Rubens." Wmk.: posthorn in shield, F below.

Museum Purchase (1930.152). Prov.: Johann Wilhelm Nahl (1803–1880) (Lugt 1954); Prof. Henry Johnson.

As Jaffé recognized, this sheet is a copy of the engraving by Paulus Pontius after a Rubens drawing now in the Fogg Art Museum (Inv. no. 1932.360, repr. Mongan and Sachs 1940, fig. 251).

122

NETHERLANDISH, 16th c. (?), *An Entombment* (?), pen and brown ink, grey wash, 158 x 214 mm. (6 1/4 x 8 7/16 in.). Wmk.: arms of Amsterdam.

James Phinney Baxter Fund in Memory of Professor Henry Johnson (1932.30). Prov.: Horace Walpole (1717–1797) (according to museum files); William Bates (1824–1884) (Lugt 2604); Henry Johnson. Bibl.: *Cat.* 1930, p. 94, no. 624 (as Albani).

Certainly not by Francesco Albani; Oberhuber has suggested a sixteenth-century northern artist, possibly Antonis Blocklandt.

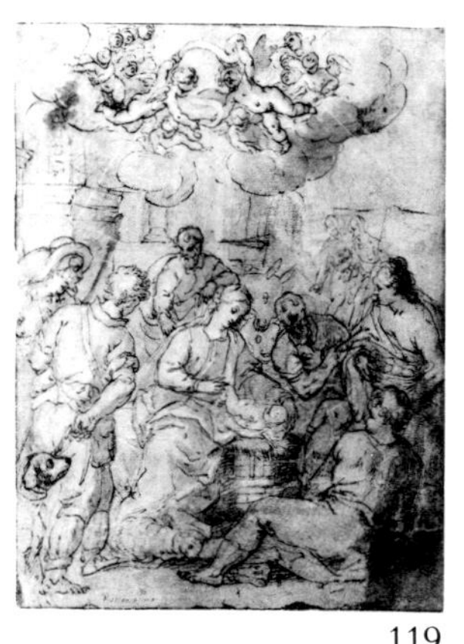

119

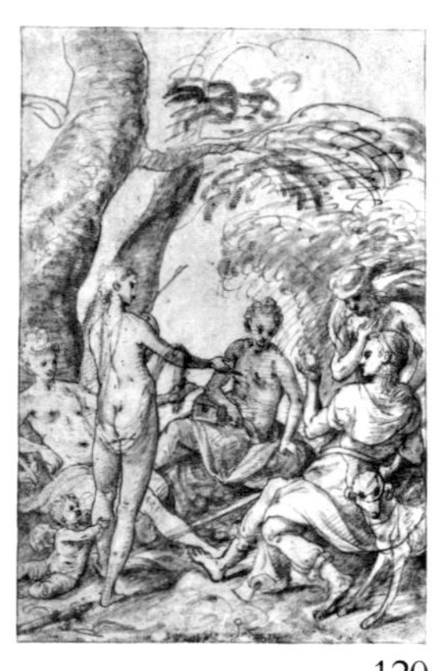

120

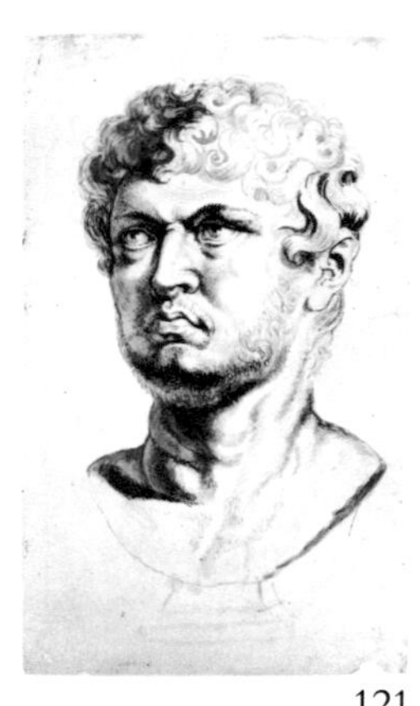

121

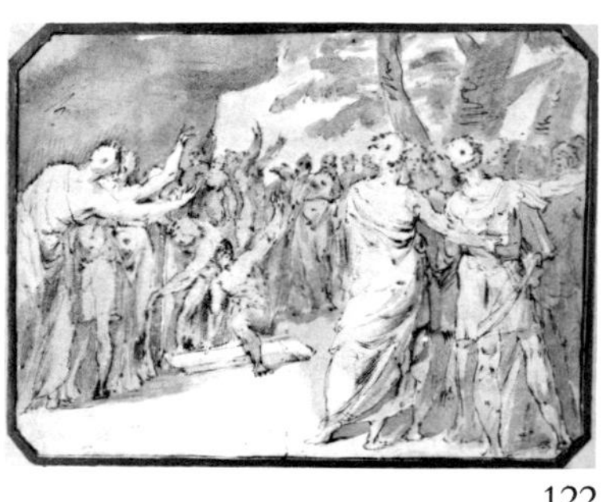

122

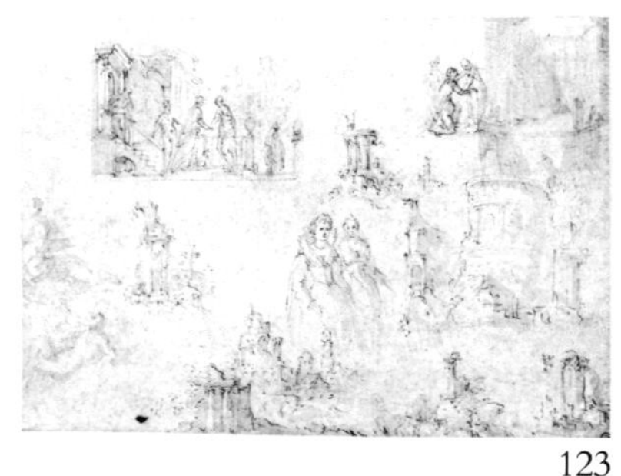

123

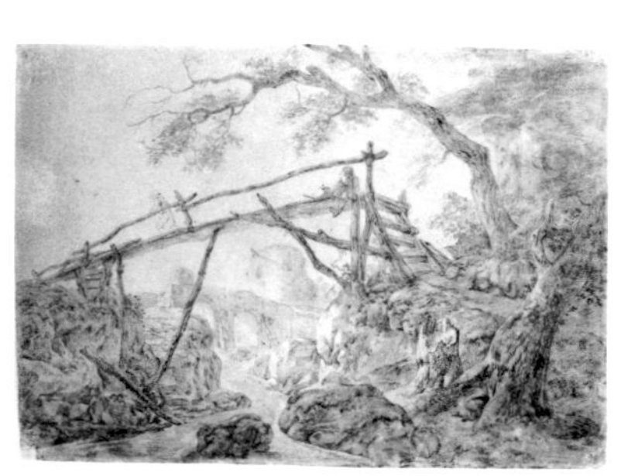

124

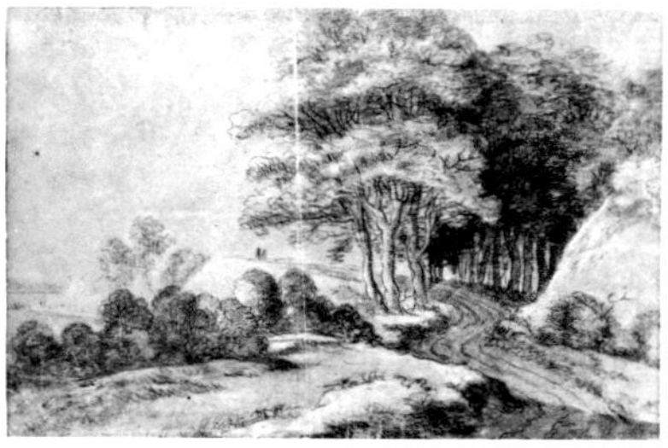

125

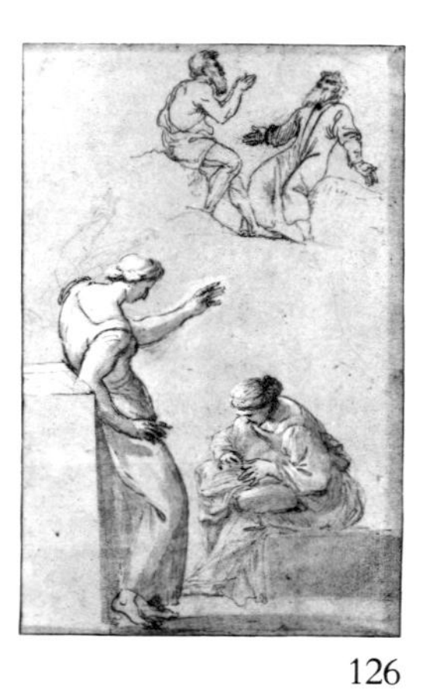

126

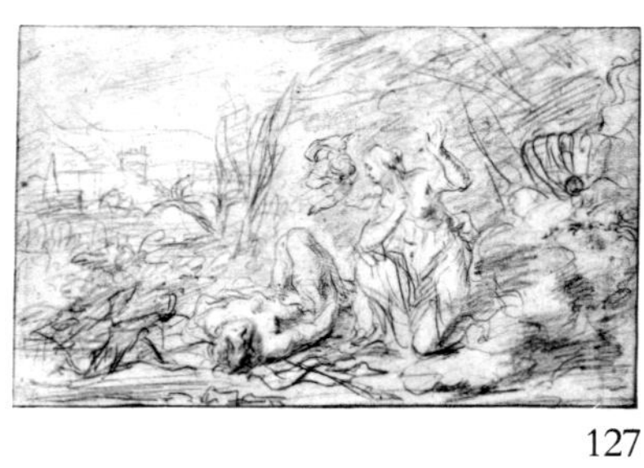

127

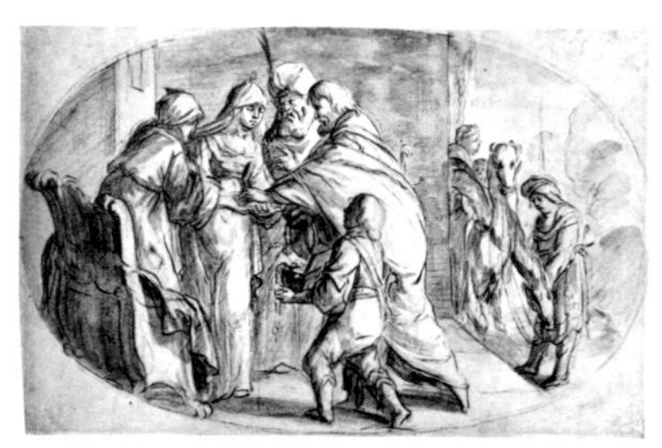

128

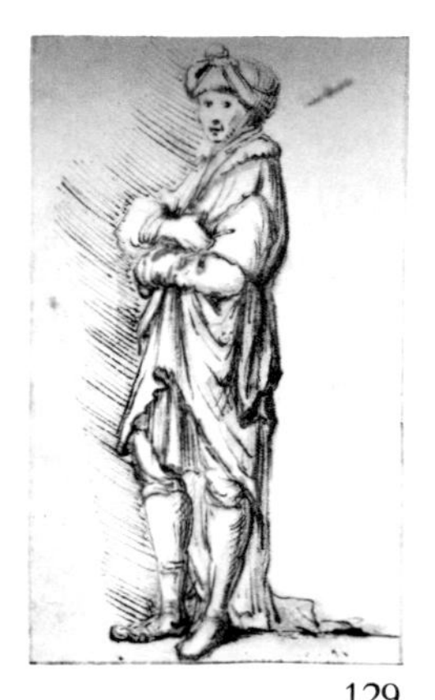

129

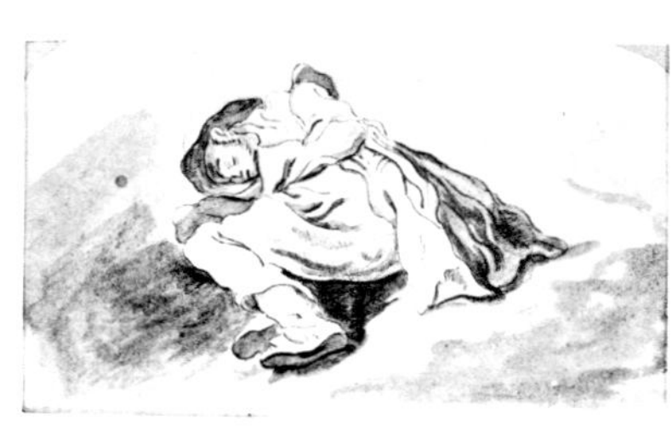

130

123

FLEMISH, late 16th c., *Sketches of Figures and Architecture*, pen and black ink, grey wash, black chalk, laid down, 197 x 282 mm. (7 3/4 x 11 1/8 in.).

James Phinney Baxter Fund in Memory of Professor Henry Johnson (1932.5). Prov.: Nathaniel Hone (1718–1784) (Lugt 2793); William Bates (1824–1884) (Lugt 2604); Henry Johnson. Bibl.: *Cat.* 1930, p. 95, no. 617 (as Polidoro da Caravaggio).

Jaffé attributed this sheet to Perino del Vaga, but Oberhuber places it with a Flemish artist, probably one working in Venice.

124

DUTCH, 17th c., *Landscape with Wooden Bridge*, pen and grey ink, grey wash over black chalk (poor condition, mounted on Japanese tissue), 249 x 350 mm. (9 13/16 x 13 3/4 in.). Inscr. pen and ink verso of former mount (lost) "Wouverman."

Bequest of James Bowdoin III (1811.67). Prov.: James Bowdoin III. Bibl.: *Cat.* 1885, no. 55 (as Wouverman); *Cat.* 1930, no. 55 (as Wouverman).

Traditionally attributed to Philips Wouverman (1619–1668).

125

DUTCH, 17th c., *Landscape*, black chalk on blue paper (faded), 248 x 378 mm. (9 3/4 x 14 7/8 in.). Inscr. pen and ink verso of old mount (lost) "No. 3 Watterlow."

Bequest of James Bowdoin III (1811.68). Prov.: James Bowdoin III. Bibl.: *Cat.* 1885, no 54 (as Waterloo); *Cat.* 1930, no. 54 (as Waterloo).

Traditionally attributed to Anthonie Waterloo (1610–1690).

126

DUTCH, 17th c., *Figure Studies*, pen and brown ink, brown wash, heightened with white over graphite on blue-green paper (faded to brown), 250 x 162 mm. (9 7/8 x 6 3/8 in.).

Bequest of James Bowdoin III (1811.84). Prov.: James Bowdoin III. Bibl.: *Cat.* 1885, no. 118; *Cat.* 1930, no. 118.

Perhaps related to the style of the so-called Pre-Rembrandtists, particularly the Pynas brothers (cf. Sacramento 1974, pp. 27–33, figs. 28, 33, 47).

127

DUTCH, 17th c., *Venus and Adonis*, red and white chalk, 153 x 252 mm. (6 x 9 15/16 in.).

Bequest of James Bowdoin III (1811.86). Prov.: James Bowdoin III. Bibl.: *Cat.* 1885, no. 116; *Cat.* 1930, no. 116.

Though traditionally thought to be Italian, this sheet seems to betray a more northern figure style. Richard Spear suggested a Pre-Rembrandtist origin, such as Lastman, while Oberhuber thought it a work of a Flemish artist.

128

DUTCH, 17th c., *Rebecca and Eleazer*, black chalk, brush and blue wash (faded), traced with a stylus, 229 x 348 mm. (9 x 13 11/16 in.). Wmk.: Strasbourg bend with fleur-de-lis above.

Bequest of James Bowdoin III (1811.88). Prov.: James Bowdoin III. Bibl.: *Cat.* 1885, no. 113; *Cat.* 1930, no. 113.

Oberhuber was the first to recognize the subject, told in Genesis 24:10–60. He tentatively placed the artist in the Pre-Rembrandtist circle, perhaps as a pupil of Pieter Lastman.

129

DUTCH, 17th c., *Standing Man with Turban*, pen and brown ink, grey wash, over red chalk (loss in right edge), 178 x 107 mm. (7 x 4 3/16 in.).

Bequest of James Bowdoin III (1811.91). Prov.: James Bowdoin III. Bibl.: *Cat.* 1885, no. 109; *Cat.* 1930, no. 109.

130

DUTCH, 17th c., *Man Lying Asleep*, red chalk and brown wash, laid down, 68 x 116 mm. (2 11/16 x 4 9/16 in.).

Bequest of James Bowdoin III (1811.92). Prov.: James Bowdoin III. Bibl.: *Cat.* 1885, no. 110; *Cat.* 1930, no. 110.

131

DUTCH, 17th c., *Battle Scene*, pen and brown ink, brown wash over black chalk, 178 x 295 mm. (7 x 11 5/8 in.). Inscr. verso pen and brown ink "Christan Mascall."

Bequest of James Bowdoin III (1811.119). Prov.: James Bowdoin III. Bibl.: *Cat.* 1885, no. 121; *Cat.* 1930, no. 121.

Judson has tentatively suggested Crispin van de Passe; Oberhuber feels the sheet is German. There are resemblances to the style of Nicolas Knupfer (cf. J. I. Kuznetzow, "Nikolaus Knupfer [1603?–1655]," *Oud Holland*, vol. 88, no. 3 [1974], p. 216, fig. 35).

132

DUTCH, 17th c., *Landscape with Buildings* (verso: landscape), pen and brown ink, grey wash, black chalk heightened with white (wash, formerly blue, has faded), 229 x 412 mm. (9 x 16 1/4 in.).

Bequest of James Bowdoin III (1811.131). Prov.: James Bowdoin III. Bibl.: *Cat.* 1885, no. 106; *Cat.* 1930, no. 106.

An Italian subject. Attributed to Frederic de Moucheron by Ian Kennedy.

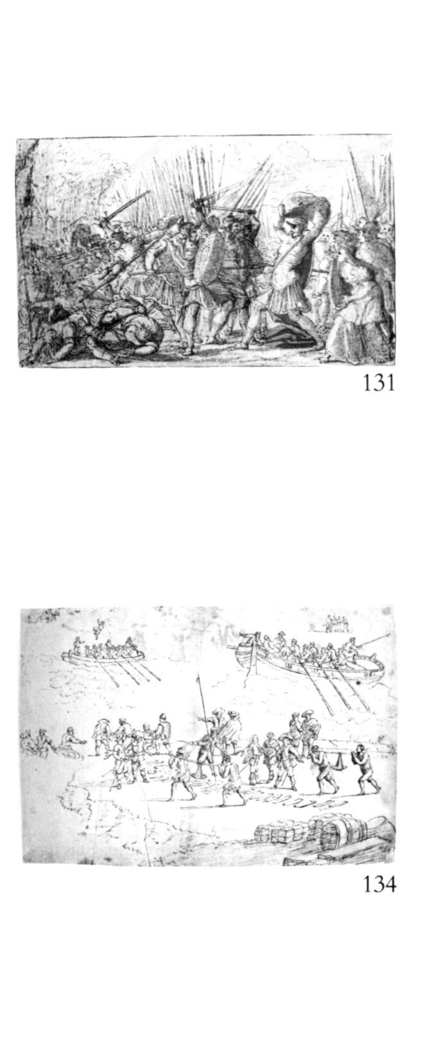

131

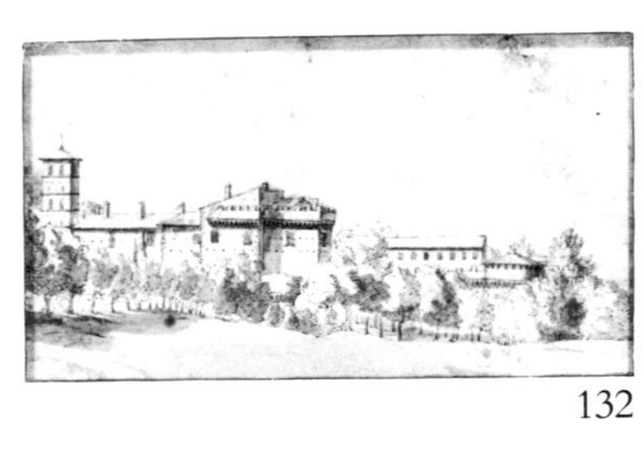

132

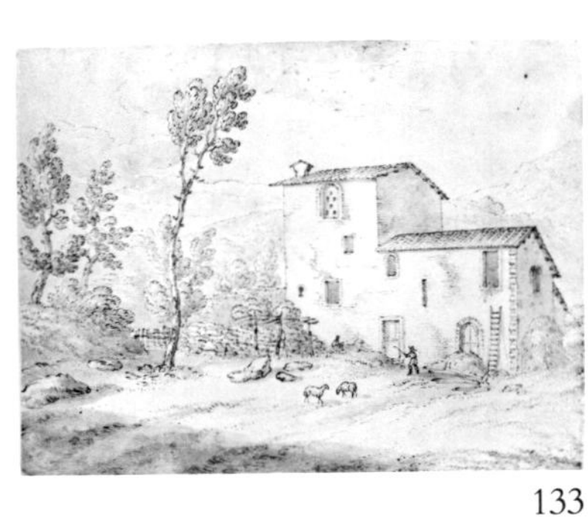

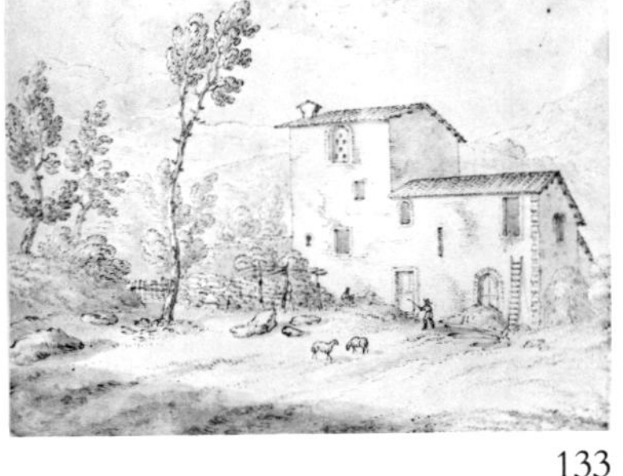

133

134

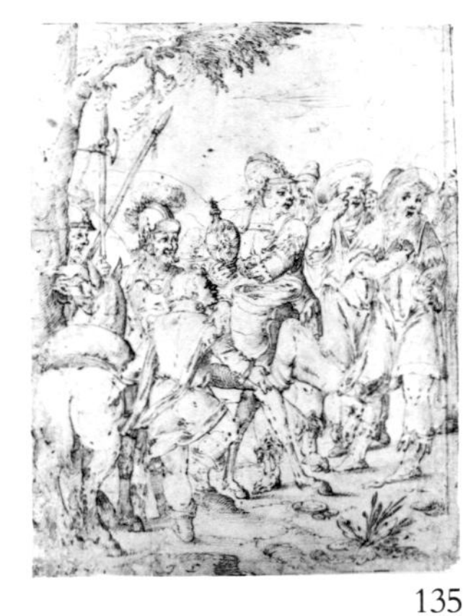

135

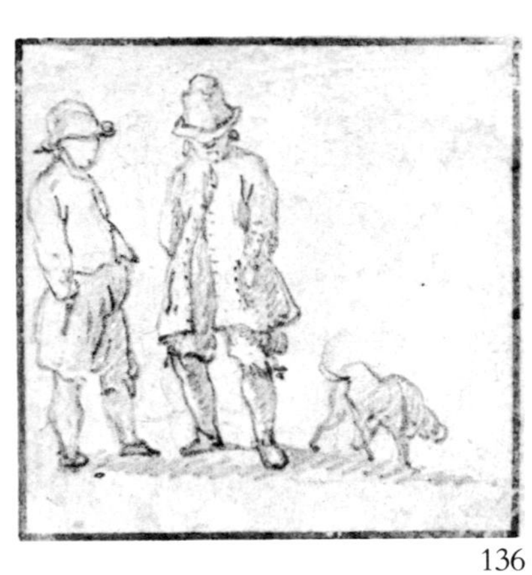

136

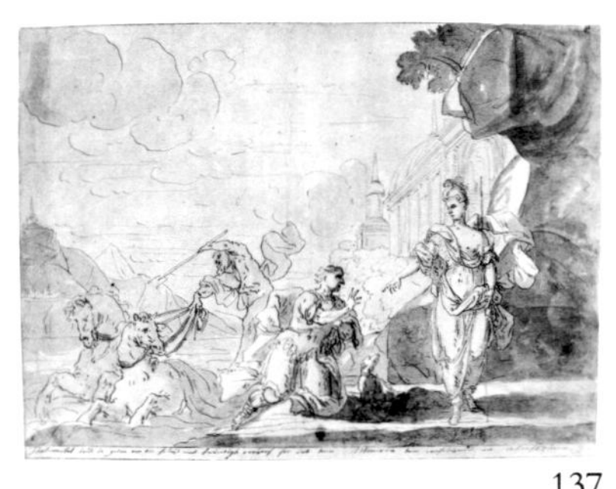

137

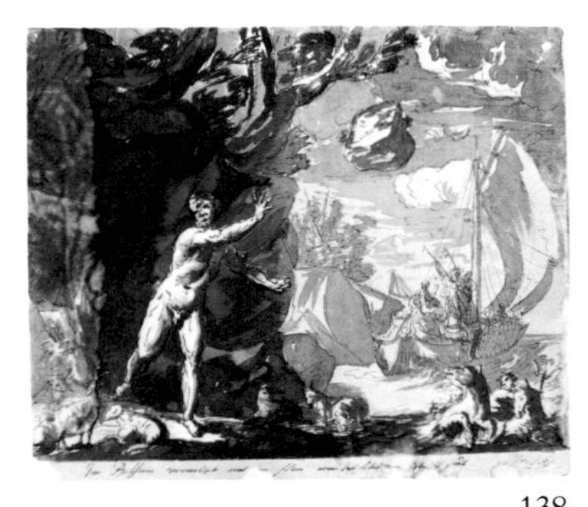

138

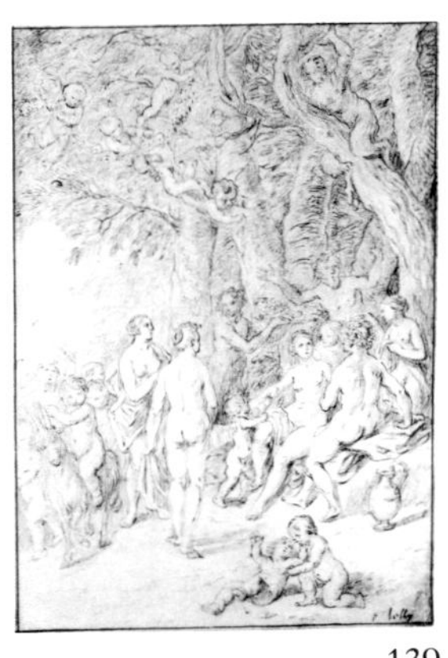

139

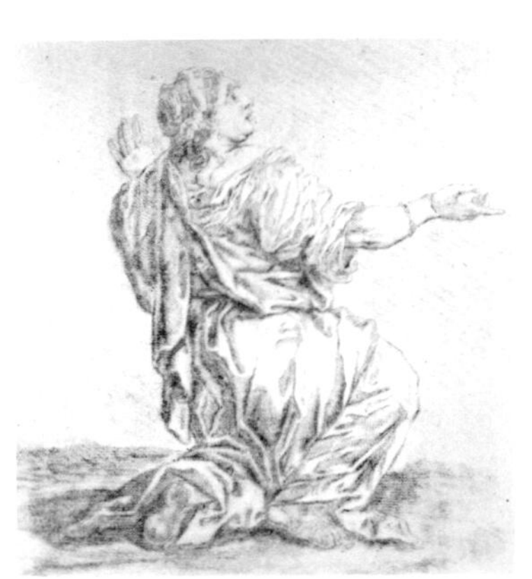

140

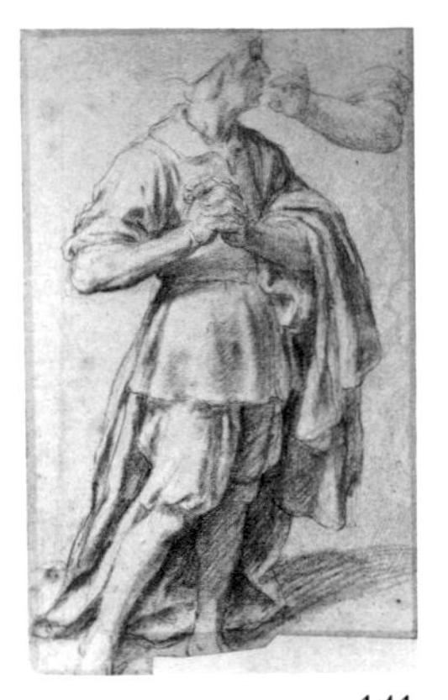

141

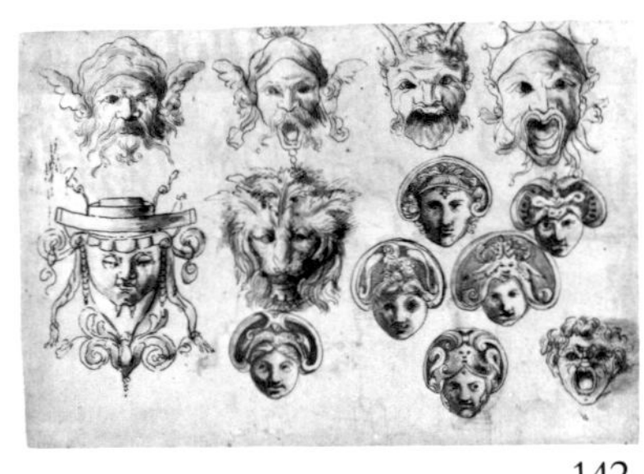

142

133

DUTCH, 17th c., *Landscape with Farm Building*, pen and brown ink, brown wash, over black chalk, 305 x 403 mm. (12 x 15⅞ in.). Inscr. verso pen and brown ink "JW." Wmk.: three crescent moons.

Bequest of James Bowdoin III (1811.138). Prov.: James Bowdoin III. Bibl.: *Cat.* 1885, no. 105; *Cat.* 1930, no. 105.

Probably done by a Dutch artist in Italy.

134

DUTCH, 17th c., *Figures in Boats and on Seashore* (verso: figure studies), pen and brown ink, 297 x 439 mm. (11 11/16 x 17¼ in.). Wmk.: HD (countermark). Inscr. graphite center "by Teniers"; red chalk verso "27/1/28/1/29/1/30/1."

James Phinney Baxter Fund in Memory of Professor Henry Johnson (1932.32). Prov.: Henry Johnson. Bibl.: *Cat.* 1930, p. 95, no. 637 (as David Teniers the Younger).

Lugt suggested the sheet was in the style of Cornelis de Wael, but Haverkamp Begemann feels it is not by him.

135

DUTCH (?), 17th c., *Finding the Cup in Benjamin's Sack*, pen and brown ink (several losses, mounted on Japanese tissue), 223 x 175 mm. (8¾ x 6⅞ in.). Inscr. pen and brown ink lower left "J Ve [. . . .] J D."

Bequest of James Bowdoin III (1811.120). Prov.: James Bowdoin III. Bibl.: *Cat.* 1885, no. 120; *Cat.* 1930, no. 120.

The subject is described in Genesis 44:1–17.

136

DUTCH, 17th or 18th c., *Two Men and a Dog*, graphite, 71 x 72 mm. (2¾ x 2 13/16 in.).

Gift of Miss Susan Dwight Bliss (1956.24.269). Prov.: Susan Dwight Bliss.

This drawing was formerly attributed to Esaias van de Velde. From a photograph, George Keyes (letter to the author, 10 August 1981) does not accept the attribution and feels the drawing is eighteenth-century, particularly from the costumes.

137

DUTCH, 18th c., *Scene from "The Odyssey,"* pen and brown ink, brown and grey wash, heightened with white, over graphite, 333 x 447 mm. (13⅛ x 17⅝ in.). Inscr. pen and brown ink below "Thelmachus bidt de godin om een schip met twintigh roeyerf soo dat hem Minerva hun verschijndt en belooft 't hem 3."

Museum Purchase (1930.221). Prov.: Prof. Henry Johnson.

I am grateful to Professor Held for transcribing the inscription.

138

DUTCH, 18th c., *Scene from "The Odyssey,"* pen and brown ink, brown wash, heightened with white, over graphite (losses and waterstains all sides), 361 x 430 mm. (14 3/16 x 16 15/16 in.). Inscr. pen and brown ink below "Paer Bossum vervuerlijck met [. . .]n Stein nuer het Schip van Ulissis goodt No:j 6." Wmk. (partial): man riding horse with frock coat, hat, and long hair.

Museum Purchase (1930.222). Prov.: Prof. Henry Johnson.

See preceding entry for related sheet.

139

FLEMISH, 17th c., *Bacchus (?), Nymphs, and Satyrs*, black chalk, 311 x 218 mm. (12¼ x 8 9/16 in.). Inscr. pen and brown ink lower right "p Lelly"; pen and ink verso of former mount (lost) "No. 13 Sir Petter Lilly."

Bequest of James Bowdoin III (1811.53). Prov.: James Bowdoin III. Bibl.: *Cat.* 1885, no. 69 (as Lely); *Cat.* 1930, no. 72 (as Lely).

Lugt rejected the Lely attribution, but Jaffé did not. From a photograph, David Brown also rejects the attribution, although he admits it could be by a member of Lely's studio.

140

FLEMISH, 17th c., *Mary Magdalene* (?), red chalk (counterproof), 194 x 186 mm. (7⅝ x 7 5/16 in.).

Museum Purchase (1930.196). Prov.: Prof. Henry Johnson.

Related to the style of Rubens; possibly a study for the figure of Mary Magdalene at the foot of the cross.

141

FLEMISH, 17th c., *Figure Study*, black chalk on blue paper (faded), 430 x 261 mm. (16 15/16 x 10¼ in.). Inscr. black chalk lower right "Rubens." Wmk.: fleur-de-lis within circle, crown above.

Museum Purchase (1930.232). Prov.: Prof. Henry Johnson.

Lugt ascribed this sheet tentatively to a Flemish artist; it could also be Dutch. Perhaps it is a study for a king in the Adoration of the Magi.

142

FLEMISH, 17th c., *Sketches of Grotesque Ornament* (verso: architectural motifs), pen and brown ink, brown and grey washes, 215 x 317 mm. (8 7/16 x 12½ in.). Inscr. graphite verso "Flemish 1650/I.S."

Gift of Miss Susan Dwight Bliss (1956.24.214). Prov.: Susan Dwight Bliss.

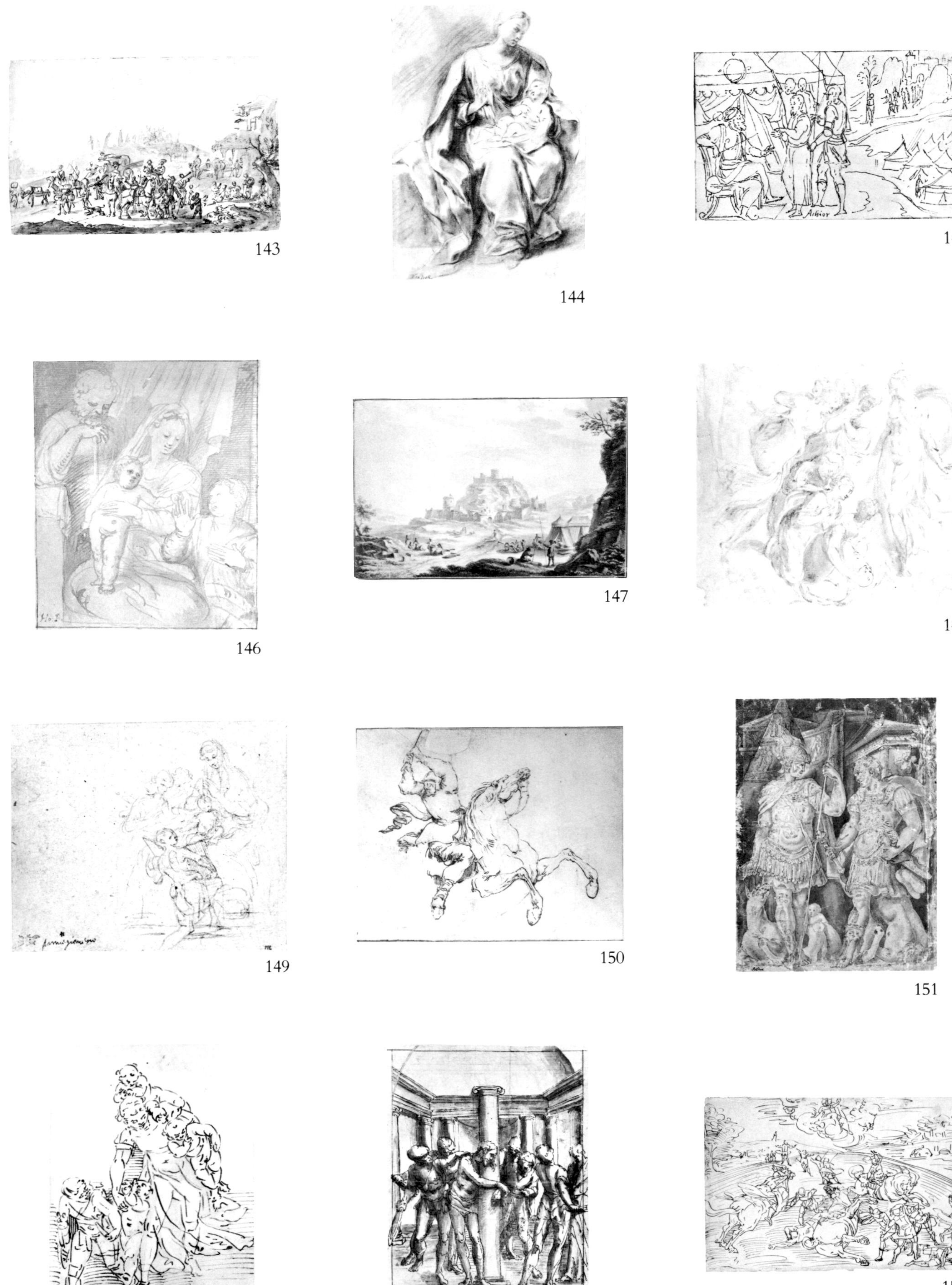

143 144 145 146 147 148 149 150 151 152 153 154

143

FLEMISH (?), 17th c., *Soldiers Stopping to Rest*, pen and brown ink, brown wash, over graphite, 210 x 321 mm. (8 1/4 x 12 5/8 in.). Wmk.: arms of Amsterdam.

Bequest of James Bowdoin III (1811.121). Prov.: James Bowdoin III. Bibl.: *Cat.* 1885, no. 119; *Cat.* 1930, no. 119.

144

FLEMISH (?), 17th c., *Madonna and Child*, black chalk, laid down, 356 x 255 mm. (14 x 10 in.). Inscr. pen and brown ink lower left. "Van Dyck."

James Phinney Baxter Fund in Memory of Professor Henry Johnson (1932.31). Prov.: Henry Johnson (acquired from Karl W. Hiersemann, Leipzig, 27 July 1893, their cat. 112, no. 767, as Van Dyck). Bibl.: *Cat.* 1930, p. 95, no. 636 (as Van Dyck).

Lugt felt that this sheet could be French, in the style of Simon Vouet.

145

GERMAN, 16th c., *Achior before Holofernes*, pen and dark brown ink, old folds through center, traces of black chalk on verso, 82 x 132 mm. (3 1/4 x 5 3/16 in.). Inscr. pen and dark brown ink bottom center "Achior."

Bequest of James Bowdoin III (1811.90). Prov.: James Bowdoin III. Bibl.: *Cat.* 1885, no. 112; *Cat.* 1930, no. 112.

The small format, sketchiness, and narrative nature of this sheet indicate that it was preparatory to a book illustration or other print, but none has yet been found. A different moment in the story was depicted in essentially the same composition by the so-called Master of the Liechtenstein Adoration (repr. *Master Drawings*, vol. 3, no. 1 [1965], pls. 38–39). The story of Achior and Holofernes is related in the apocryphal Book of Judith 5:1–14:10.

146

GERMAN, 16th c., *Holy Family*, pen and brown ink, brown and pink washes, heightened with white (verso: black chalk), 101 x 85 mm. (4 x 3 5/16 in.). Inscr. pen and brown ink lower left "Ho:B"; verso "N° 238."

Bequest of James Bowdoin III (1811.47). Prov.: James Bowdoin III. Bibl.: *Cat.* 1885, no. 63; *Cat.* 1930, no. 93.

Oberhuber very tentatively placed this sheet as German; traditionally thought to be Italian, it could be after an Italian model.

147

GERMAN(?), 18th c., *Landscape with Military Encampment*, pen and black ink with grey wash, 248 x 378 mm. (9 3/4 x 14 7/8 in.). Wmk.: IV.

Museum Purchase (1930.202). Prov.: William Bates (1824–1884) (Lugt 2604); Prof. Henry Johnson.

Traditionally placed as French. Resembles a stage set.

Italian

148

GIOVANNI BATTISTA D'ANGELI, called del Moro (active 1550s), *The Finding of Moses*, brush and purplish ink with touches of pen and brown ink (counterproof?), 187 x 207 mm. (7 3/8 x 8 1/8 in.). Inscr. pen and ink on former mount (lost) "Francisco Permensis." Wmk.: eagle within shield over F (cf. Briquet 142–43).

Bequest of James Bowdoin III (1811.29). Prov.: James Bowdoin III. Bibl.: *Cat.* 1885, no. 39 (as "Permensis"); Mather 1913, p. 250, repr. fig. 18 (as Parmigianino); Mather 1914, p. 125 (as Schiavone); *Cat.* 1930, no. 38 (as Parmigianino); Richardson 1980, pp. 79, 138, cat. no. D221, repr. fig. 228 (as del Moro).

The traditional attribution to Parmigianino was at first affirmed by Mather; then it was changed by him to Andrea Schiavone on the basis of the drawing's resemblance to Schiavone's etching of this subject (Bartsch 2, repr. Richardson 1980, fig. 24). Francis Richardson instead argues that the Bowdoin sheet is del Moro's preparatory drawing (and a copy of Schiavone's print) for his own etching of the subject (Bartsch 1), which is in reverse to both this sheet and the Schiavone print. The unusual texture and flatness of the Bowdoin drawing perhaps indicate that it is a counterproof (or itself was transferred).

149

GIROLAMO BEDOLI, called Mazzola Bedoli (ca. 1500?–ca. 1569), attr., *Madonna and Child with Attendants*, black chalk on blue paper, laid down, 143 x 173 mm. (5 5/8 x 6 13/16 in.). Inscr. pen and brown ink lower left "parmigianino"; pen and brown ink verso of mount "Formerly in the coll of Ld Arundel / P. H. Lanchrinck & / Jon^{n} Richardson / WE N 70."

Gift of Miss Susan Dwight Bliss (1956.24.232). Prov.: Nicholas Lanier (1588–1666) (Lugt 2886); Earl of Arundel (according to inscription verso); Prosper Henry Lankrink (1628–1692) (Lugt 2090); Jonathan Richardson, Sr. (1665–1745) (Lugt 2183); William Esdaile (1758–1837) (Lugt 2617), his inscription verso of mount; unidentified collector with blind stamp of crest with bishop's mitre; Susan Dwight Bliss.

Though Jaffé affirmed the traditional attribution of this sheet to Parmigianino himself, Oberhuber felt it was most likely the work of Parmigianino's follower and cousin by marriage, Bedoli. The closest parallel for this slight sketch is one in the Fitzwilliam Museum, Cambridge (Inv. no. PD 66-1974; repr. in Pierpont Morgan Library, and other places, *European Drawings from the Fitzwilliam* [exh. cat. ed. by M. Jaffé] [New York, 1976–1977], cat. no. 9).

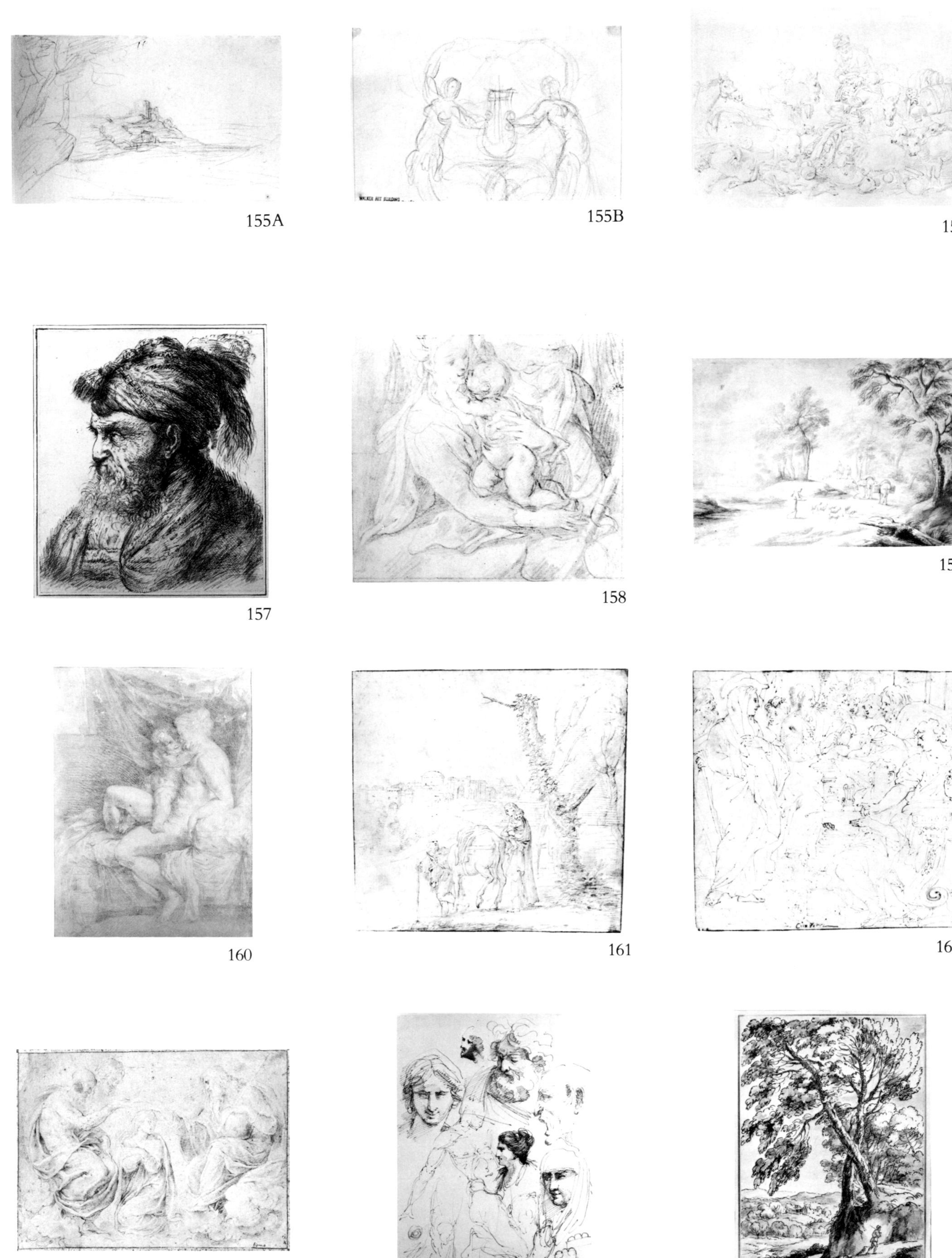

155A

155B

156

157

158

159

160

161

162

163

164

165

150

STEFANO DELLA BELLA (1610–1664), attr., *Soldier on Horseback*, pen and dark brown ink over earlier drawing in pen and brown ink, laid down (loss top left), 124 x 157 mm. (4 7/8 x 6 3/16 in.). Inscr. pen and two brown inks below on mount "Stefano della Bella"; pen and brown ink verso of mount "6·34."

Gift of Miss Susan Dwight Bliss (1956.24.186). Prov.: Earl of Aylesford (1786–1859) (Lugt 58); Paul J. Sachs (1878–1965) (Lugt 2091); Susan Dwight Bliss.

This sheet is actually composed of a crude pen drawing covering most of the lines of a considerably more subtle, earlier one, which appears very faintly and probably was previously damaged. Therefore the attribution of at least the earlier drawing to della Bella is believable. Compare, for instance, other della Bella studies of mounted soldiers in the Louvre (Viatte 1974, cat. nos. 462–63, repr.) and formerly on the art market (Christie's London, 4 July 1972, lot 79, repr.).

151

POLIDORO CALDARA, called da Caravaggio (1490/1500–1543?), copy after, *Two Roman Heroes*, pen and brown ink and brown wash, 375 x 280 mm. (14 3/4 x 11 in.). Inscr. lower left "Polidoro"; lower right of backing "Polidoro."

James Phinney Baxter Fund in Memory of Professor Henry Johnson (1932.6). Prov.: Henry Johnson. Bibl.: *Cat.* 1930, p. 95, no. 618 (as Polidoro).

This is a copy of a section in the second tier of decorations of the Palazzo Milesi in Rome by Polidoro (repr. Marabottini 1969, vol. 2, pl. 147). Oberhuber has tentatively suggested that the draughtsmanship is close to that of Peruzzi. The two figures are identified in the museum files as Caesar and Antony. Another copy of the same two figures is in the Biblioteca Reale, Turin (Bertini 1958, cat. no. 172, repr.).

152

LUCA CAMBIASO (1527–1585), attr., *Charity*, pen and brown ink over black chalk, 123 x 92 mm. (4 7/8 x 3 5/8 in.). Inscr. pen and brown ink verso "N° 74"; pen and ink on former mount (lost) "Di Luca Cangiagio."

Bequest of James Bowdoin III (1811.12). Prov.: James Bowdoin III. Bibl.: *Cat.* 1885, no. 12 (as "Cangiagio di Luca"); *Cat.* 1930, no. 12 (as Cambiaso).

A close version of this subject is in the Witt Collection, Courtauld Institute Galleries (photo, Witt Library). Cambiaso also explored other variants of this composition (see L. Ragghianti Collobi, "Il magistrale Luca Cambiaso," *Critica d'Arte*, vol. 6, no. 33 [1959], p. 171, fig. 101). The Bowdoin sheet could be a studio copy.

153

LUCA CAMBIASO, follower of (?), *The Flagellation*, pen and brown ink, brown wash over black chalk, 187 x 137 mm. (7 3/8 x 5 3/8 in.). Inscr. pen and brown ink bottom "Luca di Genua"; verso "L. Cangiagio 8.1."; pen and ink verso of former mount (lost) "Di Luca Cangiagio." Wmk.: three mounts within circle.

Bequest of James Bowdoin III (1811.11). Prov.: James Bowdoin III. Bibl.: *Cat.* 1885, no. 13 (as "Cangiagio di Luca"); *Cat.* 1930, no. 13 (as Cambiaso); *Handbook* 1981, p. 165 (as Cambiaso, attr.).

Most probably not by Cambiaso himself.

154

LUCA CAMBIASO, copy after, *The Conversion of St. Paul*, pen and brown ink over black chalk, 269 x 417 mm. (10 9/16 x 16 7/16 in.). Inscr. verso pen and brown ink "57.8.34."

James Phinney Baxter Fund in Memory of Professor Henry Johnson (1932.4.1). Prov.: William Bates (1824–1884) (Lugt 2604); Henry Johnson. Bibl.: Mather 1913, p. 248, repr. fig. 17 (as Pordenone); *Cat.* 1930, p. 94, no. 616 (as Pordenone); Finch College Museum of Art, *Drawings of Luca Cambiaso* (exh. cat.) (New York, 1967–1968), under cat. no. 60 (as Cambiaso, as are all following); Manning 1974, p. 31, under cat. no. 41; Crocker Art Gallery, *The Collecting Muse—A Selection from the Nathalie and Hugo Weisgall Collection* (exh. cat.) (Sacramento, 1975), p. 10, under cat. no. 1.

Other versions of this specific composition are in the Manning Collection (repr. in Manning 1974, cat. nos. 41–42), the Uffizi, and the Weisgall Collection (the latter repr. in the Crocker Art Gallery exhibition catalogue cited above). The Bowdoin version is most probably a studio copy.

155

GIOVANNI ANGELO CANINI (1617–1666), attr., *Landscape* (verso: sketch of two angels holding lyre), red chalk (verso: black chalk), 141 x 221 mm. (5 9/16 x 8 11/16 in.).

Museum Purchase (1930.192). Prov.: Prof. Henry Johnson.

Originally catalogued as Dutch, this slight sketch was tentatively given to Canini by Turner. For other Canini sheets, see Blunt and Cooke 1960, cat. nos. 99–105 (no. 99 repr. fig. 11); N. Turner, "Drawings by Giovanni Angelo Canini," *Master Drawings*, vol. 16, no. 4 (Winter 1978), pp. 387–96; and Kate Ganz, Ltd., *Old Master Drawings* (sale cat. no. 4) (London, Summer 1984), cat. nos. 4–5, repr.

156

GIOVANNI BENEDETTO CASTIGLIONE (ca. 1610–1663/65), copy after, *Merchants and Animals*, graphite, laid down (many losses, tears), 200 x 310 mm. (7⅞ x 12³⁄₁₆ in.). Inscr. on former mount (lost) "Berghem." Wmk.: initials DR.

Bequest of James Bowdoin III (1811.43). Prov.: James Bowdoin III. Bibl.: *Cat.* 1885, no. 56 (as Berchem); *Cat.* 1930, no. 56 (as Berchem). Exh.: American Federation of Arts 1962–1963, no. 6 (as Berchem).

Traditionally attributed to Nicolaes Berchem. Jaffé recognized it as a copy after Castiglione; the precise source is not known.

157

GIOVANNI BENEDETTO CASTIGLIONE, copy after, *Oriental Head*, pen and brown ink, grey wash, laid down, 216 x 185 mm. (8½ x 7¼ in.). Inscr. mount below "Castiglione."

Gift of Miss Susan Dwight Bliss (1967.39.4). Prov.: Earl of Shrewsbury (1753–1827) (Lugt 2688); Susan Dwight Bliss.

A copy in the same direction of an etching by Castiglione from the series called Large Oriental Heads (Bartsch 51).

158

GIOVANNI BATTISTA CAVAZZA (active 1620), attr., *Madonna and Child* (recto and verso), red chalk, 153 x 171 mm. (6 x 6¾ in.). Inscr. graphite bottom verso "a Cavatz."

Bequest of James Bowdoin III (1811.32). Prov.: James Bowdoin III. Bibl.: *Cat.* 1885, no. 42 (as "A. Cavatz?"); *Cat.* 1930, no. 42 (as G. B. Cavazza).

159

PIER FRANCESCO CITTADINI (1616–1681), *Landscape with Travelers*, pen and brown ink and brown wash over black chalk (faded), 292 x 417 mm. (11½ x 16⅜ in.). Inscr. pen and brown ink (trimmed) "Sitadini"; verso graphite "Sitadini."

Museum Purchase (1930.203). Prov.: Prof. Henry Johnson. Exh.: Ottawa 1982, cat. no. 66, repr.

Attributed to Cittadini in 1963 by Jacob Bean.

160

PLACIDO COSTANZI (1688–1759), *Woman and Child Seated on Bed*, red chalk, 333 x 243 mm. (13⅛ x 9⁹⁄₁₆ in.). Inscr. verso of former mount (lost) "No. 12 Plaedio Constanei."

Bequest of James Bowdoin III (1811.69). Prov.: James Bowdoin III. Bibl.: *Cat.* 1885, no. 40 (as "Plaedio Constanei (?)"), repr. large paper ed.; Allen 1886, pt. 2, no. 2, repr. (as Constanzi); *Cat.* 1930, no. 40 (as Constanzi).

Possibly a counterproof. Attributed to Tommaso Redi (see Cat. 81) on the mount of the Witt Library photograph. See also three drawings listed in Byam Shaw 1983, vol. 1, p. 189, under no. 189, repr. figs. 41–42 and pl. 203, and one at Christ Church, Oxford (Byam Shaw 1976, cat. no. 672, repr. pl. 365).

161

DOMENICHINO (Domenico Zampieri, 1581–1641), copy after, *The Flight into Egypt*, pen and brown ink over red chalk, 203 x 213 mm. (8 x 8⅜ in.). Fragmentary and undecipherable watermark.

Bequest of James Bowdoin III (1811.102). Prov.: James Bowdoin III. Bibl.: *Cat.* 1885, no. 138 (as Unknown); *Cat.* 1930, no. 138 (as Unknown).

Copy of a Domenichino drawing in the Louvre (Inv. no. R.F. 635. See E. Borea, "Un *Paesaggio con Fuga in Egitto* di Domenichino," *Paragone*, n.s. 19, no. 199 [September 1966], pp. 56–57, repr. pl. 54). The red chalk underneath the pen lines indicates a tracing process.

162

CIRO FERRI (1634–1689), copy after, *The Circumcision*, pen and brown ink over red chalk, 184 x 192 mm. (7¼ x 7⁹⁄₁₆ in.). Inscr. pen and brown ink bottom center "Ciro Ferri"; verso "Romanelli." Wmk.: crossed keys within shield above letter B.

Bequest of James Bowdoin III (1811.17). Prov.: James Bowdoin III. Bibl.: *Cat.* 1885, no. 26 (as Ferri); *Cat.* 1930, no. 26 (as Ferri).

Copy of a design by Ferri for the *Missale Romanum* published in 1662, in the reign of Alexander VII. The Bowdoin copy and the engraving by François Spierre in the missal are both in reverse to the original drawn study by Ferri in a private collection, New York (repr. Stampfle and Bean 1967, no. 126).

163

AMBROGIO FIGINO (1548–1608), attr., *Coronation of the Virgin*, black and white chalk on blue paper, laid down, 182 x 256 mm. (7⅛ x 10¹⁄₁₆ in.). Inscr. pen and brown ink lower right "figino."

James Phinney Baxter Fund in Memory of Professor Henry Johnson (1932.9). Prov.: Henry Johnson. Bibl.: *Cat.* 1930, p. 95, no. 621.

164

MAURO GANDOLFI (1764–1834), attr., *Studies of Heads and Other Figures*, pen and brown ink, 255 x 192 mm. (10 x 7⁹⁄₁₆ in.). Wmk.: BARTOCCI.

Museum Purchase (1930.189). Prov.: Prof. Henry Johnson.

Attributed to Gaetano Gandolfi by Ian Kennedy and to

Gandolfi's son Mauro by Stephen Pepper. A similar pen and ink figure study is in Philadelphia (repr. Ottawa 1982, cat. no. 117).

165

GIOVANNI GHISOLFI (1632–1680), circle of, *Landscape with Walking Figure*, pen and brown ink and brown wash over black chalk, laid down, 297 x 217 mm. (11 11/16 x 8 1/2 in.). Inscr. pen and brown ink verso of mount "1824 WE Ex'd with RF."

Gift of Miss Susan Dwight Bliss (1956.24.224). Prov.: William Esdaile (1758–1837) (Lugt 2617); Victor Winthrop Newman (b. 1860) (Lugt 2540); Susan Dwight Bliss.

Marcel Roethlisberger (letter to museum, 1 June 1964) attributed this sheet to Ghisolfi or his circle; it formerly was attributed to Claude Lorrain.

166

GIULIO ROMANO (Pippi) (ca. 1499–1546), imitator of, *Two Women*, pen and brown ink, brown wash, traces of black chalk (sheet trimmed on right side to silhouette of right figure), 180 x 147 mm. (7 1/16 x 5 3/4 in. irregular). Inscr. pen and brown ink lower left "Perino"; pen and brown ink verso "Perino del Vaga—mori 1547." Wmk. (fragment): three mounts within circle, six-pointed star above.

Bequest of James Bowdoin III (1811.14). Prov.: James Bowdoin III. Bibl.: *Cat.* 1885, no. 9 (as Perino); *Cat.* 1930, no. 9 (as Perino).

Not by Perino; instead, Bernice Davidson, Jaffé, and Oberhuber (comments in museum files) have related this sheet to Giulio Romano as a copy or an imitation.

167

GIOVANNI FRANCESCO GRIMALDI (1606–1680), attr., *St. Jerome in a Landscape*, pen and brown ink (loss lower left corner), 413 x 278 mm. (16 1/4 x 10 11/16 in.). Inscr. pen and ink verso of former mount (lost) "No. 16 Francisco Bollognese"; graphite verso of sheet "anibal carats."

Bequest of James Bowdoin III (1811.73). Prov.: James Bowdoin III. Bibl.: *Cat.* 1885, no. 47 (as Grimaldi); *Cat.* 1930, no. 47 (as Grimaldi); [Siber] 1947, pp. 119–20, repr. fig. 11 (as Italian, 16th c.).

Vitzthum was the first to point out that this sheet is a copy of an Annibale Carracci drawing in Budapest (repr. *Master Drawings*, vol. 5, no. 3 [1967], pl. 9; another, poorer copy is in the Uffizi [ibid., pl. 8]). Grimaldi is known to have made many copies of Annibale's landscape drawings (ibid., p. 259), and the old inscription supports the traditional attribution.

168

GIOVANNI FRANCESCO BARBIERI, called GUERCINO (1591–1666), follower of, *Figure with Cornucopia (Ceres?)*, red chalk, laid down on canvas (numerous losses), 230 x 173 mm. (9 1/16 x 6 13/16 in.). Inscr. verso of mount pen and brown ink "Diseg.º / Del sig Gio. fran^co Barbieri d. to Guercin Cento 1635 / Guercino."

Gift of Miss Susan Dwight Bliss (1956.24.221). Prov.: Susan Dwight Bliss. Exh.: Waterville 1978, cat. no. 11, repr. (as attributed to Guercino), exhibited in Brunswick.

Though not by Guercino himself, this sheet is very close to his style (cf. a red chalk drawing in the Metropolitan Museum [repr. Bean 1979, cat. no. 245]). Nicholas Turner (letter to the author, 15 July 1983) indicates that there are several sheets by the same hand at Windsor Castle and feels that the artist is perhaps a member of the Gennari family. The subject of this sheet is probably Ceres, though her characteristic crown of corn sheaves is not present; the figure of Abundance could also be meant.

169

BENEDETTO LUTI (1666–1724), attr., *Seated Nude Male Figure*, red and white chalk, 418 x 267 mm. (16 7/16 x 10 1/2 in.). Inscr. pen and brown ink lower left "di B:Luti"; pen and brown ink verso "fatto in Roma/nel 1694." Wmk.: Paschal lamb in double circle, V above.

James Phinney Baxter Fund in Memory of Professor Henry Johnson (1932.17). Prov.: William Bates (1824–1884) (Lugt 2604); Henry Johnson. Bibl.: *Cat.* 1930, p. 94, no. 632.

Similar to, but not identical with, other academy studies by Luti in Christ Church, Oxford (Byam Shaw 1976, nos. 662–63, repr.), and the Metropolitan Museum (Bean 1979, no. 269, repr.).

170

RUTILIO MANETTI (1571–1639), attr., *Virgin and Child with St. Bernard of Clairvaux*, pen and brown ink and brown wash over red chalk, laid down, 191 x 153 mm. (7 1/2 x 6 in.). Inscr. graphite below right on mount "V. Salimbeni"; graphite mount verso "Francesco Vanni."

Lloyd O. and Marjorie Strong Coulter Fund (1982.12). Prov.: acquired from James A. Bergquist, Boston.

The three mountains, cross, and olive branch held by the Christ Child are the symbols of the Monastery of Monte Oliveto Maggiore, near Siena, founded by Bernardo dei Tolomei in 1313. His patron saint was St. Bernard of Clairvaux, who is sometimes portrayed with a discarded bishop's mitre, which symbolizes his having declined a bishopric. (I am grateful to Susan Wegner for this information.) Formerly attributed to Vanni and Salimbeni, this sheet is now given to Manetti by Susan Wegner, but Nicholas Turner feels it is later.

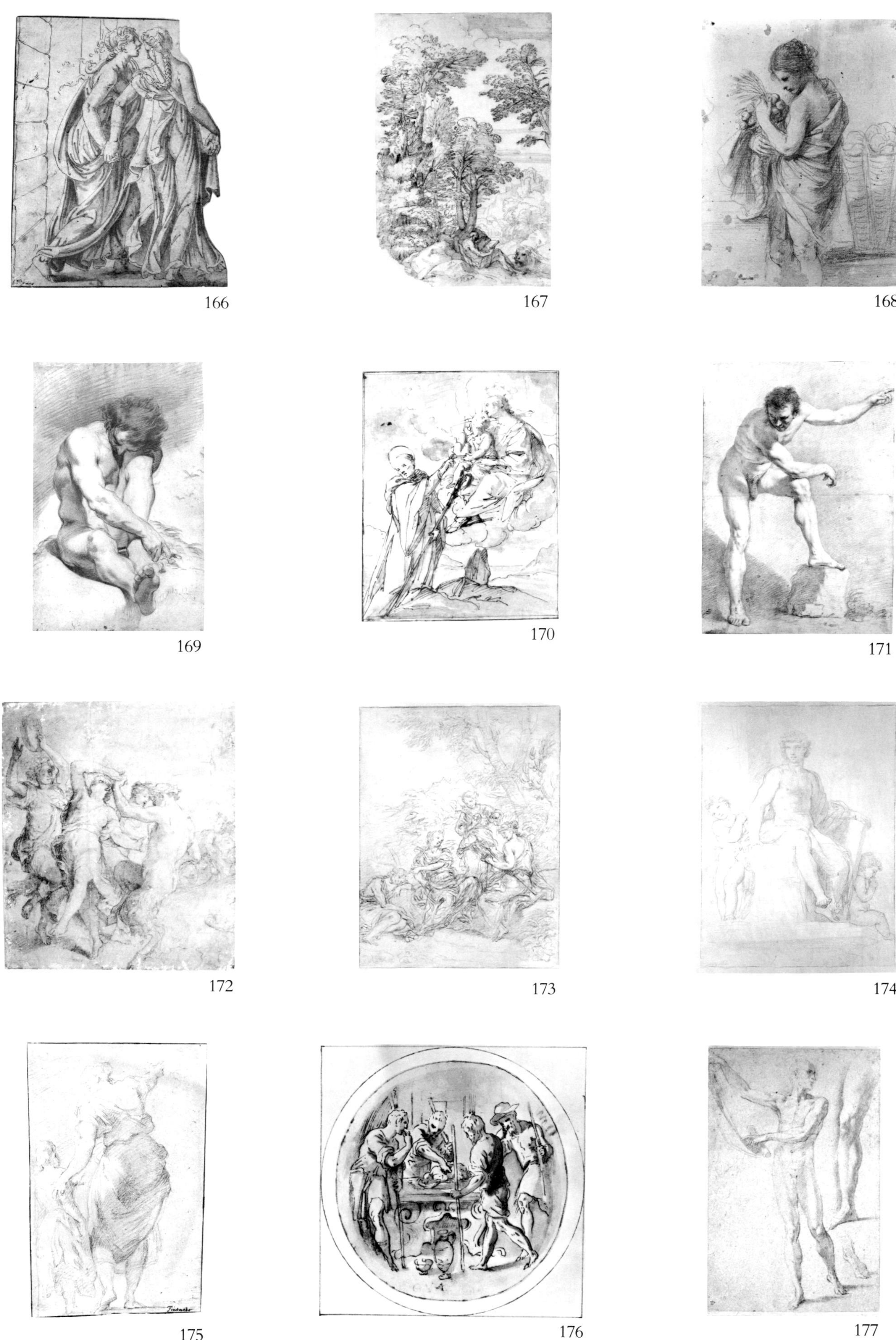

166 167 168

169 170 171

172 173 174

175 176 177

171

GIOVANNI MANNOZZI, called da San Giovanni (1592–1636), attr., *Male Nude*, red chalk, 412 x 293 mm. (16 3/16 x 11 1/2 in.). Inscr. pen and ink verso of original mount (removed) "Giovanni di San Giovanni."

Museum Purchase (1930.217). Prov.: Prof. Henry Johnson.

Chiara d'Afflitto has suggested either Pietro or Vincenzo Dandini as the artist.

172

CARLO MARATTI (1625–1713), circle of, *Bacchanal*, black chalk on joined pieces of grey-green paper, laid down (poor condition—worm holes, repairs, tears, losses), 678 x 591 mm. (26 11/16 x 23 1/4 in.).

James Phinney Baxter Fund in Memory of Professor Henry Johnson (1932.23.4). Prov.: Henry Johnson.

Not by Maratti himself (traditional attribution); perhaps his circle.

173

CARLO MARATTI, school of, *The Three Fates*, black chalk, 236 x 181 mm. (9 1/4 x 7 1/8 in.). Inscr. verso pen and brown ink "N.9/Pp." Wmk.: bird on hill within circle, F above.

Bequest of James Bowdoin III (1811.1). Prov.: James Bowdoin III. Bibl.: *Cat.* 1885, no. 24 (as Maratti); *Cat.* 1930, no. 24 (as Maratti).

Mena Marqués has ventured an attribution to Pietro de' Pietri.

174

CARLO MARATTI, school of, *Statue of Nude Youth with Two Putti* (verso: youth in armor), black chalk, 253 x 189 mm. (10 x 7 7/16 in.). Inscr. black chalk lower left "Maratti"; pen and ink verso of former mount (lost) "Pietro da Petri."

Bequest of James Bowdoin III (1811.2). Prov.: James Bowdoin III. Bibl.: *Cat.* 1885, no. 23 (as Maratti); *Cat.* 1930, no. 23 (as Maratti).

The attribution to de' Pietri written on the lost mount is quite possible. The verso drawing is a copy of a figure in the Sala di Costantino, by Raphael and his studio.

175

CARLO MARATTI, school of, *Woman and Child, after Tintoretto*, black and white chalk on grey-green paper (faded), 280 x 190 mm. (11 x 7 1/2 in.). Inscr. lower right pen and brown ink "Tintoreto."

Bequest of James Bowdoin III (1811.13). Prov.: James Bowdoin III. Bibl.: *Cat.* 1885, no. 10 (as Tintoretto); *Cat.* 1930, no. 10 (as Tintoretto).

Attributed by Jaffé as Roman and by Oberhuber as Maratti school. The style is not inconsistent with de' Pietri, these figures resembling those in a larger compositional study by him in Chicago (Inv. no. 1972.323, repr. Joachim and McCullagh 1979, cat. no. 93, pl. 100).

176

JACOPO PALMA, called Il Giovane (ca. 1548–1628), *The Feast of the Passover*, pen and brown ink and brown wash over black chalk, 107 mm. diam. (4 3/16 in.). Inscr. pen and brown ink bottom "CVM [?]."

Bequest of James Bowdoin III (1811.89). Prov.: James Bowdoin III. Bibl.: *Cat.* 1885, no. 111 (as Unknown); *Cat.* 1930, no. 111 (as Unknown); *Handbook* 1981, p. 165 (as van Mander).

From the fragmentary initials on this sheet, an attribution to the Dutch artist Karel van Mander had been made, but Oberhuber recognized the style of Palma Giovane. Jennifer Montagu was the first to identify the subject tentatively as the feast of the Passover celebrated by the Jews before leaving Egypt (Exodus 12:3–11). Another drawing by Palma Giovane of this subject is in Stockholm (Inv. no. 1479/1863, repr. Bjurström 1979, cat. no. 95).

177

IL PARMIGIANINO (Francesco Mazzola, 1503–1540), copy after?, *Standing Nude Man with Scroll*, black chalk on blue paper, laid down, 289 x 192 mm. (11 3/8 x 7 9/16 in.).

Gift of Miss Susan Dwight Bliss (1956.24.233). Prov.: Jonathan Richardson, Sr. (1665–1745) (Lugt 2184); John Barnard (d. 1784) (Lugt 1420); Sir Edward J. Poynter (1836–1919) (Lugt 874), his sale, Sotheby's London, 24–25 April 1918, lot no. 111, as "School of Parmigianino"; Susan Dwight Bliss.

This drawing is undoubtedly connected with the figure of St. Jerome in the background of Parmigianino's *Madonna dal Collo Lungo* (Florence, Uffizi, repr. Popham 1971, fig. 40), but not specifically related to any of the known studies by Parmigianino for that figure (some repr. Popham 1971, pls. 357–60). There are differences between the Bowdoin sheet and the painting in both of the figure's legs and in its left arm. It is possible that this sheet is a copy of a lost Parmigianino study, or it could be a later study of a figure in the pose of St. Jerome.

178

PIETRO ANTONIO DE' PIETRI (1663/65–1716), *St. Peter Delivered from Prison* (recto and verso), red chalk, 268 x 197 mm. (10 9/16 x 7 3/4 in.).

Bequest of James Bowdoin III (1811.20). Prov.: James Bowdoin III. Bibl.: *Cat.* 1885, no. 29; *Cat.* 1930, no. 29; Dreyer 1971, p. 189; *Handbook* 1981, p. 168.

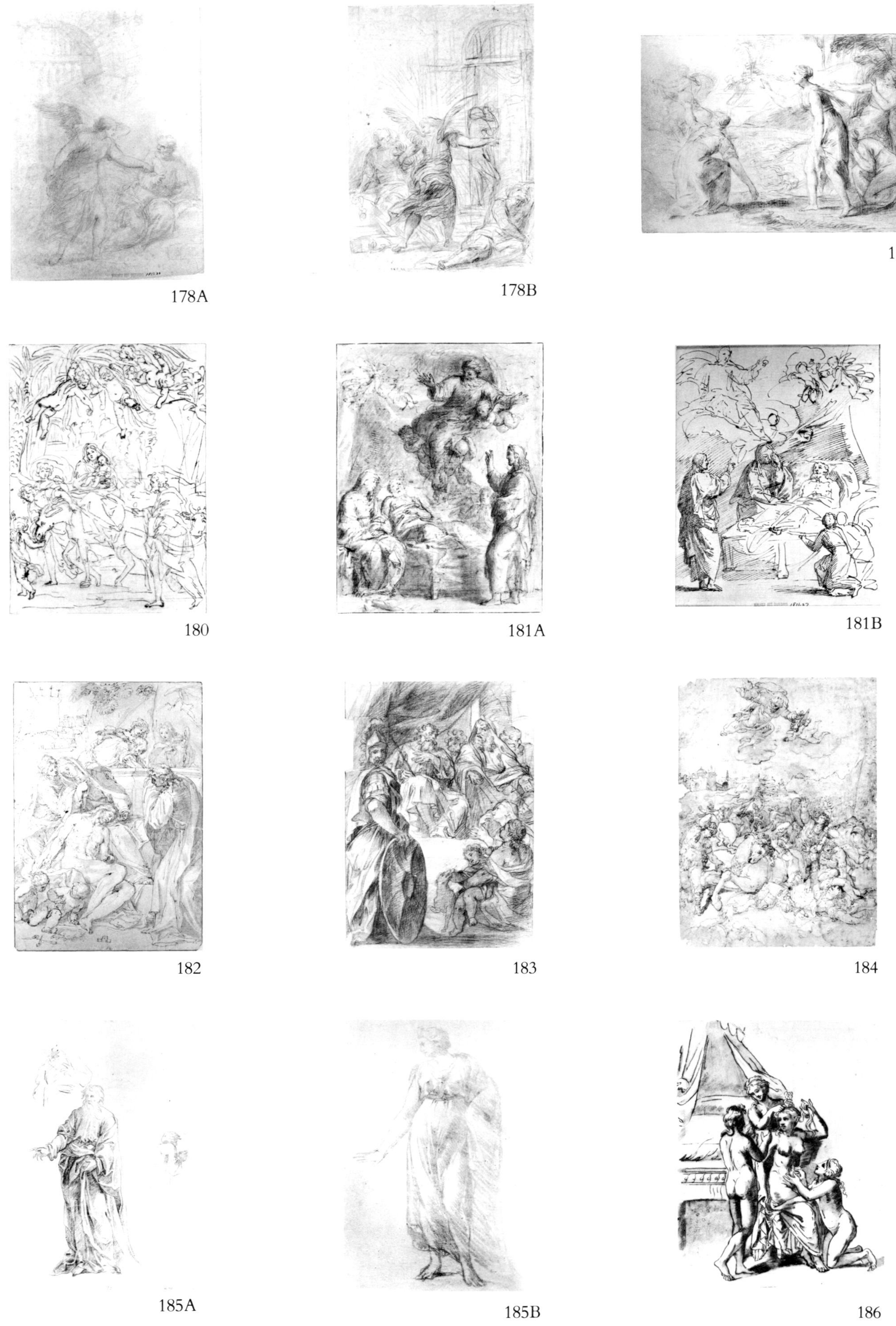

178A 178B 179

180 181A 181B

182 183 184

185A 185B 186

For two other scenes from the life of St. Peter, see Cat. 76. This scene is described in Acts 12:1–11. The artist has apparently traced the outlines of the recto drawing on the verso before changing his composition for the latter.

179

PIETRO ANTONIO DE' PIETRI, *The Rape of Europa*, red chalk, 194 x 267 mm. (7 5/8 x 10 1/2 in.). Inscr. verso of former mount (lost) "Pietro da Petri."

Bequest of James Bowdoin III (1811.23). Prov.: James Bowdoin III. Bibl.: *Cat.* 1885, no. 32; *Cat.* 1930, no. 32; *Handbook* 1981, p. 168.

180

PIETRO ANTONIO DE' PIETRI, *The Flight into Egypt*, pen and brown ink over black chalk, 267 x 197 mm. (10 1/2 x 7 3/4 in.). Inscr. pen and ink verso of former mount (lost) "No. 60 Pietro de Petri."

Bequest of James Bowdoin III (1811.25). Prov.: James Bowdoin III. Bibl.: *Cat.* 1885, no. 34; *Cat.* 1930, no. 34; *Handbook* 1981, p. 168.

181

PIETRO ANTONIO DE' PIETRI, attr., *Death of St. Joseph* (recto and verso), black chalk (verso: pen and brown ink), 259 x 200 mm. (10 3/16 x 7 7/8 in.). Inscr. pen and ink verso of former mount (lost) "Pietro de Petri." Wmk.: anchor in circle, six-pointed star above.

Bequest of James Bowdoin III (1811.27). Prov.: James Bowdoin III. Bibl.: *Cat.* 1885, no. 36; *Cat.* 1930, no. 36; *Handbook* 1981, p. 168.

The attribution is probably correct, though not to the artist's credit. The subject was very popular within the Maratti school.

182

PIETRO ANTONIO DE' PIETRI, attr., *The Entombment* (verso: Holy Women at the Sepulchre?), pen and brown ink and brown wash (verso: pen and black ink), 305 x 215 mm. (12 x 8 7/16 in.). Inscr. pen and ink verso of former mount (lost) "No. 35 Pietro da Petri." Unidentified wmk.

Bequest of James Bowdoin III (1811.28). Prov.: James Bowdoin III. Bibl.: *Cat.* 1885, no. 37; *Cat.* 1930, no. 37; *Handbook* 1981, p. 168. Exh.: Mount Holyoke College Art Museum, *Collegiate Collections*, 1976.

The recto has more claim to be de' Pietri than the verso. The latter probably depicts the morning of the Resurrection, when the three Marys come to Christ's tomb and find it empty, guarded by an angel (sometimes depicted as a young man) who announces the Resurrection.

183

PIETRO ANTONIO DE' PIETRI, copy after (?), *Coriolanus before the Walls of Rome*, red chalk (head of soldier at the left cut out), 268 x 188 mm. (10 1/2 x 7 3/8 in.).

Bequest of James Bowdoin III (1811.21). Prov.: James Bowdoin III. Bibl.: *Cat.* 1885, no. 30 (as de' Pietri); *Cat.* 1930, no. 30 (as de' Pietri); *Handbook* 1981, p. 168 (as de' Pietri, attr.).

For two horizontal versions of this subject by de' Pietri, see Dreyer 1971, figs. 1, 4. By a member of the Maratti school, if not by de' Pietri himself.

184

MARCO PINO (ca. 1520/25–1579/86), copy after (?), *Conversion of St. Paul*, pen and brown ink and brown wash (several worm holes, waterstains), 306 x 227 mm. (12 1/16 x 8 15/16 in.). Inscr. graphite verso "M. da Pino."

Museum Purchase (1930.188). Prov.: Prof. Henry Johnson.

The condition of this sheet impedes an attribution; Oberhuber was the first to recognize the style of Pino (cf. a sheet in Los Angeles, repr. Los Angeles County Museum of Art, *Old Master Drawings from American Collections* [exh. cat. by E. Feinblatt] [1976], cat. no. 28).

185

RAPHAEL (Raffaello Santi, 1483–1520), copy after, *Standing Prophet and Other Studies* (recto/verso), red chalk (verso: counterproof), 320 x 214 mm. (12 5/8 x 8 7/16 in.). Wmk.: armorial shield crowned, initials CMB above.

Bequest of James Bowdoin III (1811.48). Prov.: James Bowdoin III. Bibl.: *Cat.* 1885, no. 93 (as Unknown); *Cat.* 1930, no. 67 (as Poussin).

Oberhuber was the first to recognize these sketches as copies of the Vatican Loggia frescoes designed by Raphael and executed by his studio; specific subjects for two of the figures are Noah Building the Ark and Moses and the Burning Bush.

186

RAPHAEL, copy after, *Lady and Her Attendants*, pen and brown ink and brown wash, 221 x 176 mm. (8 11/16 x 6 15/16 in.).

Museum Purchase (1930.137). Prov.: Prof. Henry Johnson.

Lugt first ascribed this sheet to the school of Raphael, and Oberhuber recognized it as a copy of an engraving by Giulio Bonasone (Bartsch 15.153.167), reproducing a Raphael composition (see British Museum, *Drawings by Raphael* [exh. cat. by J. A. Gere and N. Turner] [London, 1983], p. 202, under no. 161).

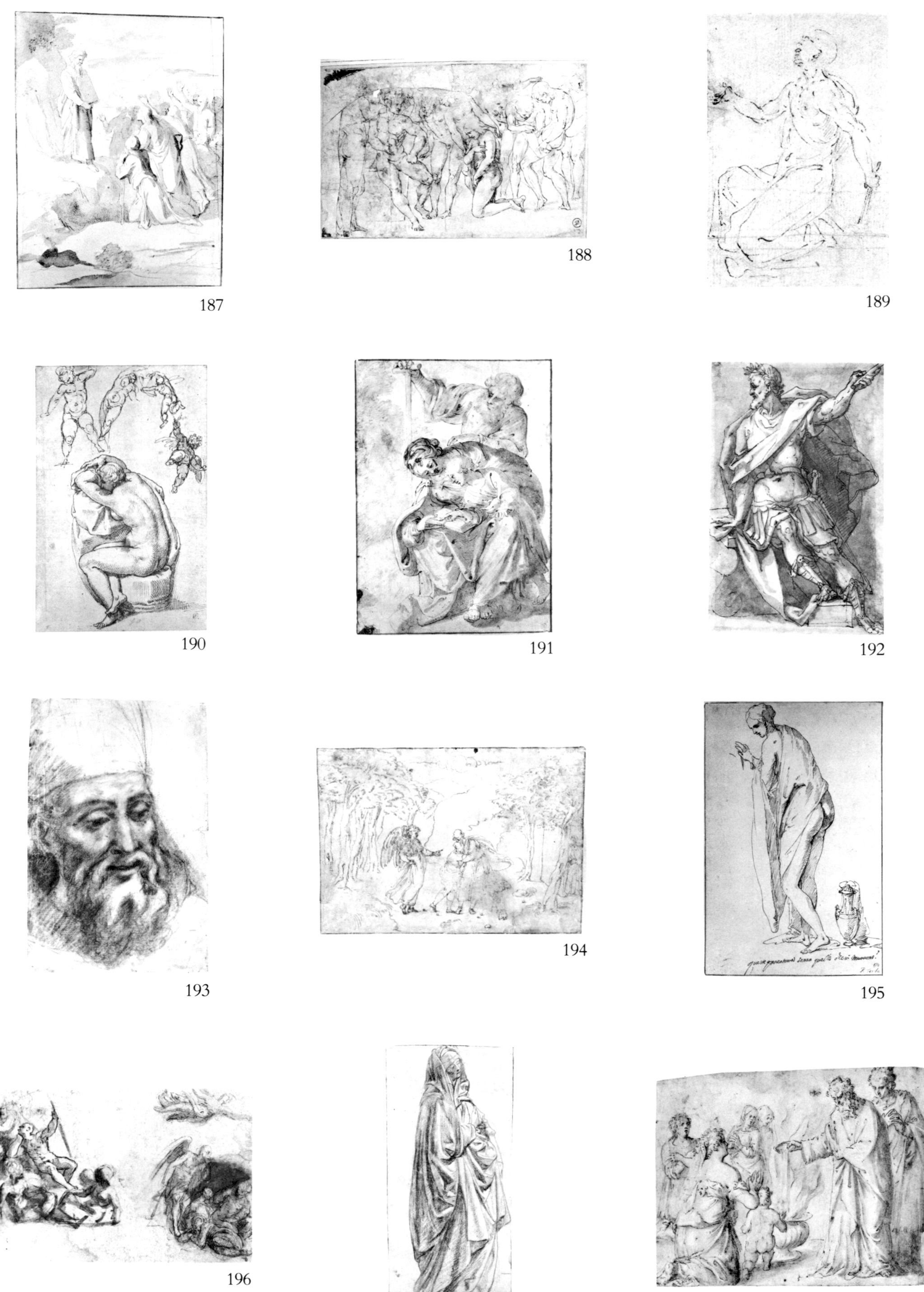

187 188 189

190 191 192

193 194 195

196 197 198

187

RAPHAEL, copy after (perhaps Salomon de Bray, 1597–1664), *Moses and the Tablets*, pen and brown ink, grey wash, touches of red chalk, laid down, 207 x 159 mm. (8 1/8 x 6 1/4 in.).

Museum Purchase (1930.139). Prov.: Prof. Henry Johnson.

Although this sheet was originally classified as Italian, Lugt saw it as Dutch, and Gerson attributed it to Salomon de Bray (letter in museum files, 8 October 1957). The composition is taken directly from the same subject after Raphael's design, which was executed for the Vatican Loggia by his studio (repr. Düssler 1971, pl. 152).

188

RAPHAEL, copy after, *The Continence of Scipio*, pen and brown ink over traces of black chalk, laid down (many losses left and top edges, stains, old folds), 280 x 435 mm. (11 x 17 1/8 in.). Inscr. pen and brown ink verso of mount in hand of Jonathan Richardson, Jr. (see Provenance).

Gift of Miss Susan Dwight Bliss (1956.24.209). Prov.: Jonathan Richardson, Jr. (1694–1771) (Lugt 2170 and 2997), his inscription attributes the sheet to Timoteo Viti and describes the subject as Alexander and Timoclea; Sir Joshua Reynolds (1723–1792) (Lugt 2364); Thomas Banks (1735–1805) (Lugt 2423); his daughter, Mrs. Lavinia Forster; her son-in-law, Ambrose Poynter (1796–1886) (Lugt 161); his son, Sir Edward J. Poynter (1836–1919), his sale, Sotheby's London, 24–25 April 1918, no. 203, as "Timoteo della Vite"; Susan Dwight Bliss (acquired from American Art Association, July 1925). Bibl.: [C. Ruland, comp.] *The Works of Raphael . . . in the Royal Library at Windsor Castle* (London, 1876), p. 162, no. 4.2.

This drawing has been traditionally attributed to Timoteo Viti (1469/70–1523), but it is probably a later copy of a Raphael composition, as Jaffé and Oberhuber recognized. The original model is lost, and the composition is known only from this sheet and from a more complete one in the museum at Lille (repr. Fischel 1913, vol. 5, fig. 192). A photograph of the Bowdoin sheet when it was in the Poynter collection is mounted in the Windsor Castle collection of reproductions of Raphael's works compiled by Carl Ruland for Prince Albert (on loan to the British Museum, Department of Prints and Drawings). The subject has been identified as Alexander and Timoclea but probably is the Continence of Scipio.

189

JUSEPE DE RIBERA (1591–1652), manner of, *Kneeling Man*, pen and brown ink over graphite, 88 x 60 mm. (3 1/2 x 2 3/8 in.).

Gift of Miss Susan Dwight Bliss (1956.24.176). Prov.: Susan Dwight Bliss.

According to Jonathan Brown (letter to the author, 30 June 1981), there are "points of contact" with Ribera's style, but this sheet is not by Ribera's hand.

190

CRISTOFANO RONCALLI (1551/52–1626), attr., *Nude Woman Seated and Four Putti*, pen and brown ink on blue paper (faded), laid down, 218 x 143 mm. (8 9/16 x 5 5/8 in.). Inscr. pen and brown ink bottom "30"; verso "Pomerangio / N.39 / 18/3—Christofano Roncalli bygen il Caval Pomerancio / 55 Florent Sch." Wmk: pilgrim with staff within circle.

Museum Purchase (1930.124). Prov.: William Bates (1824–1884) (Lugt 2604); Prof. Henry Johnson.

The figure of the woman seen from behind is copied from a sheet traditionally attributed to Michelangelo which is in the Albertina (Inv. no. 4868, repr. in Stix and Fröhlich-Bum 1932, cat. no. 133) or from their common model, perhaps an antique sculpture.

191

FRANCESCO MARIA RONDANI (1490–1548), attr., *The Holy Family*, pen and brown ink, reddish brown wash, heightened with white (oxidized), 192 x 139 mm. (7 9/16 x 5 1/2 in.). Inscr. verso of former mount (removed) pen and brown ink "J:B N° 972. / 7 1/2 by 5 1/2. / Francesco Maria Rondani fu Scolaro / del Correggio [see Provenance]."

Museum Purchase (1930.156). Prov.: John Barnard (d. 1784) (Lugt 1420), his inscription verso; William Bates (1824–1884) (Lugt 2604); Prof. Henry Johnson.

The attribution is by John Barnard, a noted English connoisseur (see article under Lugt 1420).

192

GIOVANNI BATTISTA DELLA ROVERE (ca. 1561–1630?), *Seated Emperor in Armor*, pen and brown ink and brown wash, 186 x 121 mm. (7 5/16 x 4 3/4 in.). Inscr. pen and brown ink verso "1588 1/novemb/IBR"; red chalk verso ". . . niji fiamingo."

Museum Purchase (1930.123). Prov.: Prof. Henry Johnson.

This sheet includes the artist's characteristic inscription, including the precise date of execution, as first described by Pouncey (see P. M. Pouncey, review of Bertini 1958, in *Burlington Magazine*, vol. 101 [1959], p. 297, under no. 237). Della Rovere was of Flemish origin, hence his nickname, Il Fiammenghino.

193

SEBASTIANO LUCIANI, called del Piombo (ca. 1485–1547), copy after, *Head of a Bishop* (verso: Seated Bishop), black chalk (verso: black and red chalk), 333 x 225 mm. (13 1/8 x 8 7/8 in.).

Museum Purchase (1930.133). Prov.: Prof. Henry Johnson. Bibl.: *Handbook* 1981, p. 166 (as copy of Sebastiano).

Although Jaffé tentatively suggested that this might be by Sebastiano himself, Oberhuber thought it a copy, perhaps by a 17th-century Florentine draughtsman. It seems to be a copy of a sheet in the de Boer Collection, Amsterdam (see Institut Néerlandais, Museum Boymans–van Beuningen, and Teylers Museum, *Le dessin italien dans les collections hollandaises* [exh. cat.] [Paris, 1962], cat. no. 90, repr.); the de Boer drawing does not include the bishop's mitre.

194

ERCOLE SETTI (1530–1617), *Scene from the Book of Tobit*, pen and brown ink (old stain through central figures), 161 x 229 mm. (6 5/16 x 9 in.).

Bequest of James Bowdoin III (1811.115). Prov.: James Bowdoin III. Bibl.: *Cat.* 1885, no. 130 (as Unknown); *Cat.* 1930, no. 130 (as Unknown); W. Vitzthum, "Drawings by Ercole Setti," *Burlington Magazine*, vol. 97, no. 629 (August 1955), p. 252 (as Setti, as are all following); Parker 1956, p. 376, under no. 699; F. Z. Boccazzi, "An Unpublished Album of Drawings by Ercole Setti," *Master Drawings*, vol. 6, no. 4 (Winter 1968), p. 356.

The attribution of this sheet was apparently first made by Pouncey, as acknowledged by Vitzthum in the article cited above. The scene depicted comes from the apocryphal Book of Tobit and shows either Tobias embracing his blind father, Tobit, or an earlier scene where Tobias meets Raguel.

195

PIETRO TESTA (1612–1650), attr., *Study of a Partially Draped Model*, pen and brown ink over traces of graphite, 234 x 152 mm. (9 3/16 x 6 in.). Inscr. by the artist pen and brown ink bottom "queste per aventura sanar quelle che vi muouona?"; further inscribed lower right "P. Testa"; verso pen and brown ink "Z."

Museum Purchase (1930.199). Prov.: William Bates (1824–1884) (Lugt 2604); Prof. Henry Johnson.

Although marked in the museum files as a copy, this sheet seems related to similar pen figure studies by Testa in Stuttgart (Inv. no. 1383, repr. Thiem, Stuttgart, 1977, cat. no. 400) and the Metropolitan Museum (Inv. nos. 1971.241 and 64.201; repr. Bean 1979, cat. nos. 362, 364). In conversation with the author (1984) Elizabeth Cropper also tentatively attributed this sheet to Testa himself, stating further that the inscription at the bottom is in his hand. The inscription vaguely refers to healing (sanar) by chance those who are dying. (I am grateful to Dr. Cropper for her aid in the attribution and the transcription of the inscription.) She feels it could be a study for a larger composition.

196

DOMENICO TINTORETTO (1560–1635), attr., *Two Groups of Figures with Father Time*, brush and brown ink and brown wash, black chalk on blue paper, laid down, 188 x 300 mm. (7 3/8 x 11 13/16 in.).

James Phinney Baxter Fund in Memory of Professor Henry Johnson (1932.7). Prov.: William Bates (1824–1884) (Lugt 2604); Henry Johnson. Bibl.: *Cat.* 1930, p. 95, no. 619 (as Tintoretto).

Perhaps related to decorations in the Ducal Palace, Venice (note in museum files).

197

MARCELLO VENUSTI (ca. 1512/15–1579), attr., *Standing Draped Woman*, red and black chalk, 278 x 129 mm. (10 15/16 x 5 1/16 in.). Inscr. pen and ink below on former mount (removed) "Andrea del Sarto." Wmk.: double-handled jug with flowers.

Bequest of James Bowdoin III (1811.34). Prov.: James Bowdoin III. Bibl.: *Cat.* 1885, no. 3 (as Andrea del Sarto); Mather 1913, pp. 246–48, repr. fig. 13 (as Pontormo); *Cat.* 1930, no. 3 (as Andrea del Sarto); [Siber] 1947, p. 119, repr. fig. 5 (as Florentine School, 16th c.).

Mather attributed this study to Pontormo, and it is not known who proposed the ascription to Venusti. It would seem to be a study for the figure of the Virgin in a Visitation composition.

198

ITALIAN, 16th c., *Sacrificial Scene*, pen and brown ink and grey wash, heightened with white, 177 x 224 mm. irregular (7 x 8 13/16 in.). Inscr. verso pen and brown ink "2 shilings N° 40"; pen and ink below on former mount (lost) "Del Purdenone."

Bequest of James Bowdoin III (1811.3). Prov.: James Bowdoin III. Bibl.: *Cat.* 1885, no. 2 (as Pordenone); *Cat.* 1930, no. 2 (as Pordenone).

Tietze and Tietze-Conrat were the first to reject the traditional attribution. Oberhuber has suggested investigating such late sixteenth-century mannerist artists as Filippo Bellini (see Cat. 42) or even Friedrich Sustris (see Cat. 11), although he agreed that this sheet is not by either of these artists.

199

ITALIAN, 16th c., *Ecce Homo*, pen and brown ink and brown wash over graphite, squared in red chalk and graphite, 259 x 207 mm. (10 3/16 x 8 1/8 in.). Inscr. graphite verso "Fresco Candidi"; pen and ink below on former mount (lost) "Chev. dal Borgo 25."

Bequest of James Bowdoin III (1811.39). Prov.: James Bowdoin III. Bibl.: *Cat.* 1885, no. 45 (as "Chev. dal Borgo"); *Cat.* 1930, no. 45 (as Raffaello dal Colle); *Handbook* 1981, p. 166 (as Flemish).

The lack of well-known drawings by Raffaello dal Colle (d. 1566) renders the traditional attribution doubtful. The verso inscription refers to Peter Candid (ca. 1548–1628), a Flemish-born painter who worked in Italy and Germany. This sheet is not by him, but it is by a Flemish artist working in Italy, according to Oberhuber. More recently, Lawrence Turčić has tentatively related it to the Genoese artist Paggi (letter to the author, 26 June 1984).

200

ITALIAN, 16th c., *Copy after the Antique*, pen and brown ink (verso: red and black chalk), 100 x 155 mm. (3 15/16 x 6 1/8 in.). Inscr. graphite lower left "319." Unidentified circular watermark.

Bequest of James Bowdoin III (1811.106). Prov.: James Bowdoin III. Bibl.: *Cat.* 1885, no. 129; *Cat.* 1930, no. 129.

Phyllis Pray Bober (letter to the author, 8 March 1984) has not been able to identify the hand or the prototype, although she suspects that the artist has joined two ends of a sarcophagus.

201

ITALIAN, 16th c., *Copy after the Antique*, pen and brown ink and brown wash, 352 x 263 mm. (13 13/16 x 10 3/8 in.).

Bequest of James Bowdoin III (1811. 134). Prov.: James Bowdoin III. Bibl.: *Cat.* 1885, no. 91; *Cat.* 1930, no. 91.

First identified by di Pietro as after an antique model. Though originally catalogued as "nineteen separate sketches," this sheet was recognized by Susan Wegner as a compressed copy of part of an antique sarcophagus in the Villa Medici, Rome. It depicts the Judgment of Paris (repr. in P. P. Bober, *Drawings after the Antique by Amico Aspertini* [London, 1957], fig. 83). Other drawings after this relief are listed in ibid., pp. 68–69. Oberhuber thought the Bowdoin sheet might be by a Flemish artist.

202

ITALIAN, ca. 1600, *The Fall of Icarus*, pen and brown ink and brown wash over black chalk, 267 x 203 mm. (10 1/2 x 8 in.). Inscr. verso pen and brown ink "Fran.co P[. . .]"; pen and ink verso of former mount (lost) "John Smibert / 13."

Bequest of James Bowdoin III (1811.55). Prov.: John Smibert; James Bowdoin III. Bibl.: *Cat.* 1885, no. 71 (as Smibert); *Cat.* 1930, no. 74 (as Smibert); Foote 1950, p. 232 (as "earlier"); Sadik 1966, p. 217 (as not by Smibert); Chappell 1982, p. 137 (as not Smibert).

Placed by Witt as Italian, ca. 1600; by Oberhuber as Florentine, in the Vasari circle; and by Pouncey as possibly Sienese. Somewhat resembles an anonymous sheet in the Ashmolean (Macandrew 1980, cat. no. 61–4, repr. pl. 5). According to Professor Herwarth Röttgen (letter to the author, 14 August 1984), the iconography of Daedalus and Icarus with the prominent fishermen and boat is very unusual. This sheet and Cat. 10 and 209 bear old inscriptions referring to John Smibert's ownership (see Introduction).

203

ITALIAN, 16th–17th c., *St. Mark* (verso: head study), black chalk on blue paper, 390 x 267 mm. (15 3/8 x 10 1/2 in.).

Museum Purchase (1930.229). Prov.: Prof. Henry Johnson.

Oberhuber tentatively placed this as late sixteenth-century Roman; David Scrase has suggested Perugino as a possible prototype for this later drawing. Mark, one of the four Evangelists, is identified by his traditional lion at lower left.

204

UNKNOWN, 17th c., *Female Figure*, red chalk, laid down, 262 x 302 mm. (10 5/16 x 11 7/8 in.).

James Phinney Baxter Fund in Memory of Professor Henry Johnson (1932.38). Prov.: Henry Johnson.

Attributed by Oberhuber to an artist near Giovanni Lanfranco (1582–1647), and by Cazort and Turner to a member of the Gandolfi family.

205

ITALIAN, 17th c., *Moses Pouring Water from the Rock*, pen and brown ink, red wash, over traces of black chalk, 169 x 232 mm. (6 5/8 x 9 1/8 in.). Inscr. on former mount (lost) "Pietro da Cortona"; verso "Ciro Ferri / E. 24." Fragment of unidentifiable wmk.

Bequest of James Bowdoin III (1811.18). Prov.: James Bowdoin III. Bibl.: *Cat.* 1885, no. 27 (as Ferri); *Cat.* 1930, no. 27 (as Ferri).

Possibly derived from a Ferri composition. Oberhuber considered it Genoese; it could also be Dutch. The scene depicts Moses (with characteristic "horns") distributing water to the Israelites after striking the rock of Horeb with his staff (Exodus 17:1–7; Numbers 20:1–13).

206

ITALIAN, 17th c., *Rest on the Flight into Egypt*, pen and brown ink, brown wash, over black chalk (old folds), 280 x 192 mm. (11 x 7 9/16 in.). Inscr. graphite lower right "Domco Zami Fabi [. . .] Cari"; verso pen and brown ink,

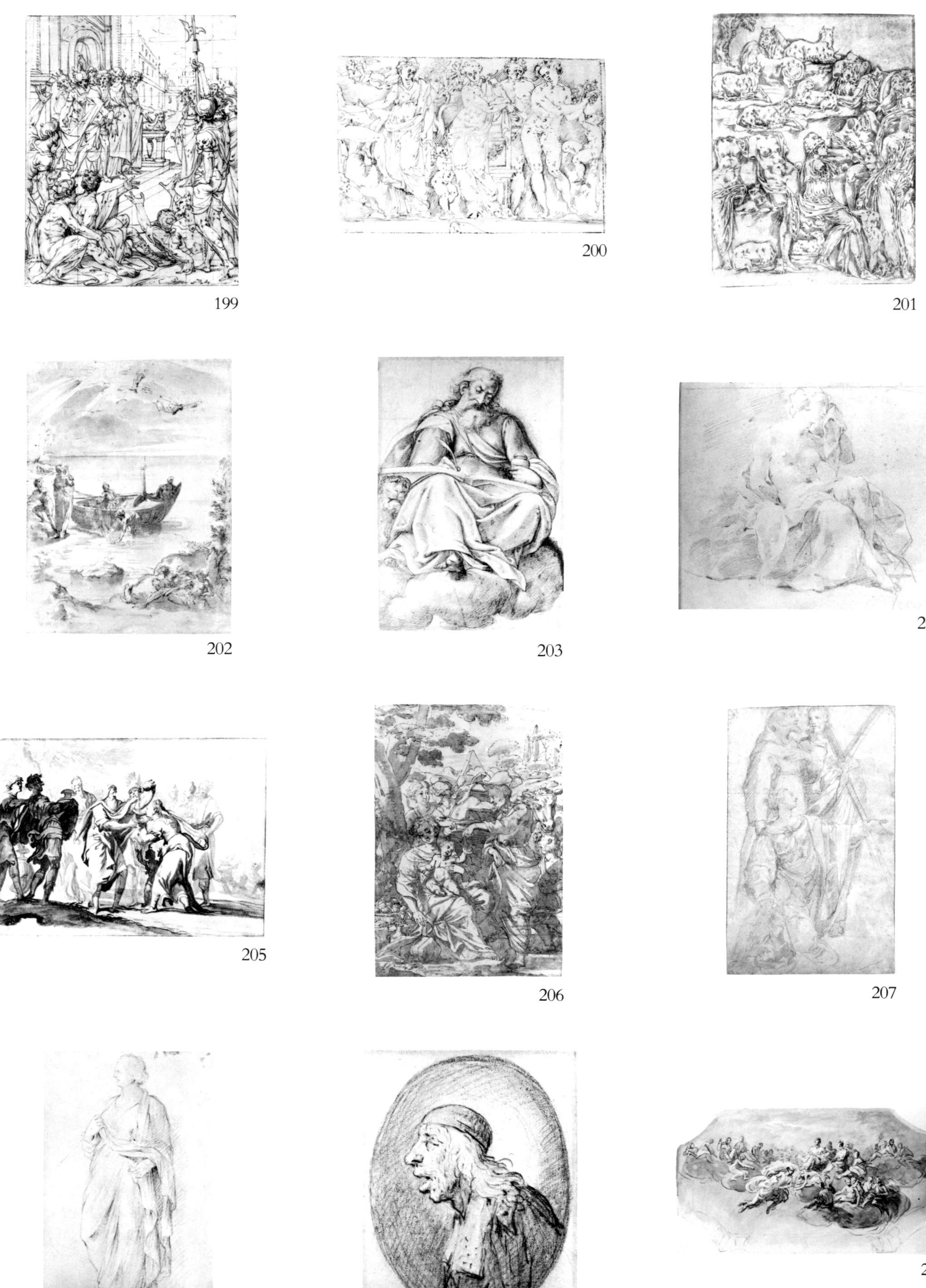

199 200 201

202 203 204

205 206 207

208 209 210

several lines of writing, with "questo disegno e mano di / [. . .] zio Cari." Wmk.: BPR on shield over BERGAMO.

Bequest of James Bowdoin III (1811.30). Prov.: James Bowdoin III. Bibl.: *Cat.* 1885, no. 38 (as "Fabritio Cari"); *Cat.* 1930, no. 39 (as "Fabritio Cari").

The unfortunately obscured inscriptions led to the traditional attribution to "Cari," to whom no reference can be located. Oberhuber tentatively attributed this sheet to a French artist.

207

ITALIAN, 17th c., *Saints Andrew, Catherine, and Francis*, red chalk, 310 x 194 mm. (12 3/16 x 7 5/8 in.). Inscr. pen and brown ink lower left "2"; pen and ink on former mount (lost) "Baptista . . . Anstatile."

Bequest of James Bowdoin III (1811.40). Prov.: James Bowdoin III. Bibl.: *Cat.* 1885, no. 46 (as "Baptista Anstatile"); *Cat.* 1930, no. 46 (as "Baptista Anstatile").

The meaning of the original attribution, taken from the old inscription, is unknown. Oberhuber and Susan Wegner place the drawing as Tuscan. St. Andrew is identifiable by his large cross; Catherine by her spiked wheel; the third saint is probably Francis.

208

ITALIAN, 17th c., *Standing Figure* (verso: figure studies), red chalk, 253 x 167 mm. (10 x 6 9/16 in.). Inscr. pen and brown ink bottom "Nel Palazo del. M [. . .]e"; pen and ink verso of former mount (lost) "No. 58 Nicholo Pousin." Wmk.: bird on three mounts within circle surmounted by six-pointed star.

Bequest of James Bowdoin III (1811.50). Prov.: James Bowdoin III. Bibl.: *Cat.* 1885, no. 66 (as Poussin); *Cat.* 1930, no. 69 (as Poussin).

Oberhuber felt that this sheet could possibly be French or Flemish.

209

ITALIAN, 17th c., *Portrait Caricature of a Man*, black and white chalk on brown paper, 164 x 134 mm. (6 7/16 x 5 1/4 in.). Inscr. pen and brown ink below on old mount "Cosmo the 3d - Grand Duke of Tuscany, from the life, by John Smibert." Wmk. of mount: I VILLEDARY.

Bequest of James Bowdoin III (1811.54). Prov.: John Smibert; James Bowdoin III. Bibl.: *Cat.* 1885, no. 70 (as Smibert); Mather 1914, p. 116, repr. fig. 11 (as Smibert); *Cat.* 1930, no. 73 (as Smibert); O. Hagen, *Birth of the American Tradition in Art*, pp. 50–51, repr. fig. 55 (as copy after Magnasco?); Foote 1950, p. 232 (as not by Smibert, as are following); Sadik 1966, p. 216; Chappell 1982, pp. 134–35, repr. fig. 2. Exh.: Detroit Institute of Arts, *Three Centuries of American Master Drawings* (exh. cat.) (Detroit, 1948), cat. p. 7 (as Smibert).

The traditional inscription on the mount of this sheet has occasioned much comment as to this drawing's subject and artist. Although it was accepted as Smibert's own work for years, scholars such as Sir Robert Witt, Frits Lugt, and Agnes Mongan dismissed the attribution and generally placed the drawing in Italy in the seventeenth century. Hagen suggested that perhaps it is copied from a work by Alessandro Magnasco (ca. 1667–1749). Chappell ventured the tantalizing identification of the subject with Antonio Magliabecchi (1633–1714), the Florentine scholar and librarian to the Medici (the museum owns a 1710 portrait medal of him by Maria Antonio di Gennaro [A. Norris and I. Weber, *The Molinari Collection at Bowdoin College* (Brunswick, 1976), cat. no. 186, repr.]).

210

ITALIAN, 17th c., *Mercury Bearing Psyche to Olympus*, pen and brown ink, brush and black ink, blue-grey wash, heightened with white, over graphite, 257 x 439 mm. (10 1/8 x 17 1/4 in.). Inscr. black chalk lower right "Tolimino"; graphite lower right "(No. 74)." Wmk.: Strasbourg bend, fleur-de-lis above.

Bequest of James Bowdoin III (1811.71). Prov.: James Bowdoin III. Bibl.: *Cat.* 1885, no. 76 (as "Tolomino?"); *Cat.* 1930, no. 16 (as Solimena).

The attribution to Francesco Solimena (1657–1747) is by Charles Eliot Norton, who, in a letter of 23 November 1885 to Henry Johnson (museum files), interpreted the inscription as such. The attribution has not been generally accepted. Montagu identified the subject, which is confirmed by the presence of Cupid rushing to embrace his lover, Psyche, prior to their marriage.

211

ITALIAN, 17th c., *The Finding of Moses* (verso: fragmentary sketch of Pan), pen and brown ink and brown wash over red chalk, on two joined sheets of paper, 140 x 157 mm. (5 1/2 x 6 3/16 in.).

Bequest of James Bowdoin III (1811.76). Prov.: James Bowdoin III. Bibl.: *Cat.* 1885, no. 125; *Cat.* 1930, no. 125.

Filippo di Pietro suggested Passignano as the artist; Witt ascribed this sheet to the school of Poussin. Oberhuber placed it close to Guido Reni; Pepper, however, tentatively suggested Giovanni Baglione.

212

ITALIAN, 17th c., *The Entombment*, black chalk and brown wash heightened with white (severely damaged), 297 x 241 mm. (11 11/16 x 9 1/2 in.). Wmk.: PH.

Bequest of James Bowdoin III (1811.95). Prov.: James Bowdoin III. Bibl.: *Cat.* 1885, no. 90; *Cat.* 1930, no. 90.

Catalogued in the Witt Library as school of Polidoro da

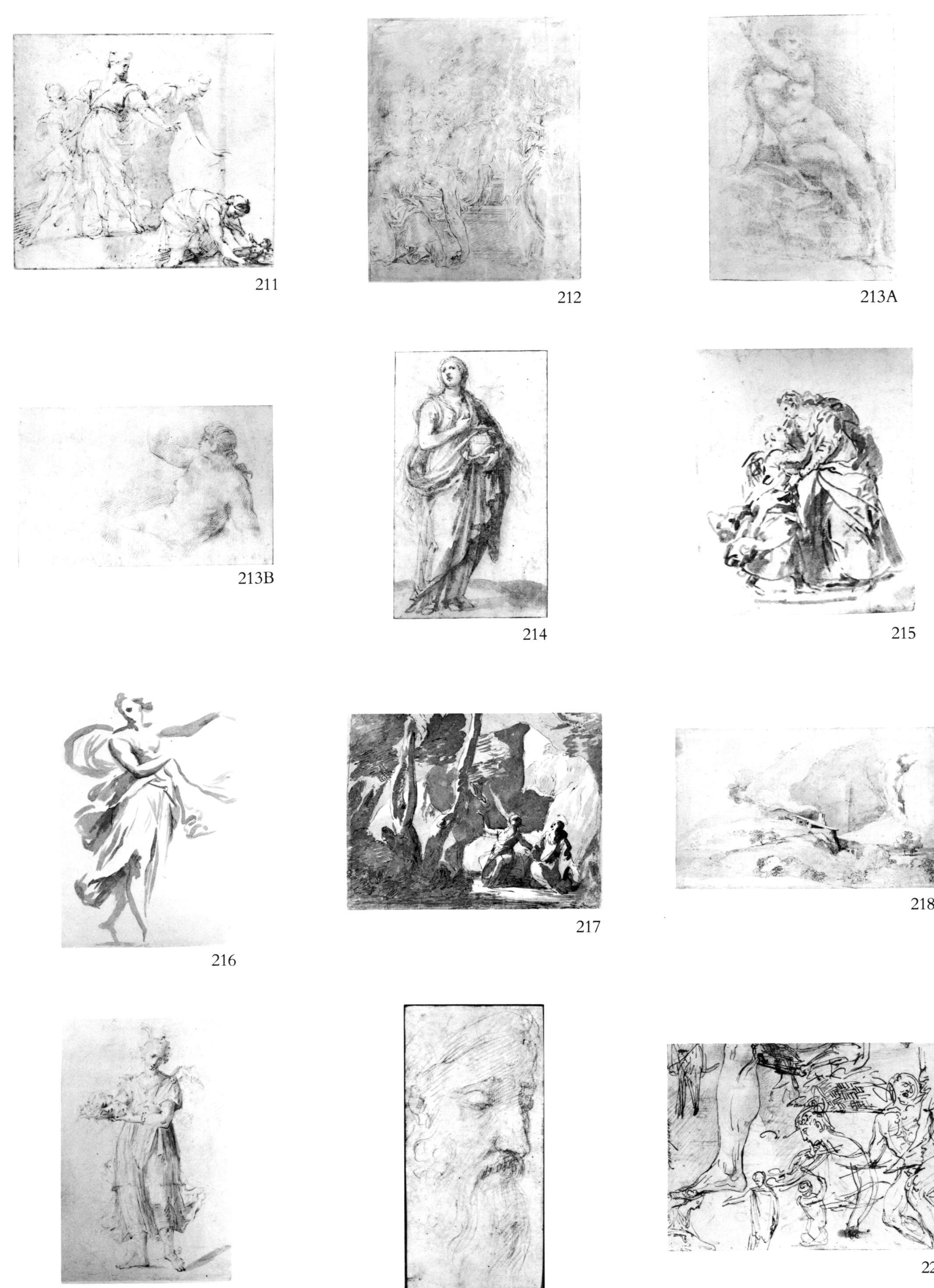

211

212

213A

213B

214

215

216

217

218

219

220

221

Caravaggio; Oberhuber has suggested looking near the work of Theodor van Thulden (1606–1669), a pupil and assistant of Rubens's.

213

ITALIAN, 17th c., *Nude Figure Study* (verso: same), red chalk, counterproof (recto only), 273 x 194 mm. (10¾ x 7⅝ in.). Wmk.: four triangles within circle, GANTON above, BERGAMO below.

Bequest of James Bowdoin III (1811.98). Prov.: James Bowdoin III. Bibl.: *Cat.* 1885, no. 85; *Cat.* 1930, no. 85.

214

ITALIAN, 17th c., *Mary Magdalene*, pen and brown ink and brown wash over red chalk, 256 x 149 mm. (10 1/16 x 5⅞ in.).

Bequest of James Bowdoin III (1811.100). Prov.: James Bowdoin III. Bibl.: *Cat.* 1885, no. 81; *Cat.* 1930, no. 81.

Oberhuber has suggested looking near Guido Reni; Kennedy has ventured Elisabetta Sirani.

215

ITALIAN, 17th c., *The Visitation*, brush and brown ink over graphite (verso: graphite compositional sketch), 149 x 123 mm. (5⅞ x 4⅞ in.). Inscr. black chalk verso "S b."

Bequest of James Bowdoin III (1811.107). Prov.: James Bowdoin III. Bibl.: *Cat.* 1885, no. 124; *Cat.* 1930, no. 124.

This drawing has been placed in the Neapolitan school by di Pietro. Reminiscent of the rapid sketch style of Elisabetta Sirani.

216

ITALIAN, 17th c., *Female Figure*, brush and brown ink over red chalk with touches of black chalk, 195 x 132 mm. (7 11/16 x 5 3/16 in.). Inscr. pen and ink verso of former mount (lost) "Josip Arpinas."

Bequest of James Bowdoin III (1811.110). Prov.: James Bowdoin III. Bibl.: *Cat.* 1885, no. 17 (as Cesari); *Cat.* 1930, no. 17 (as Cesari).

Not Giuseppe Cesari (d'Arpino, 1568–1640). Stephen Pepper has drawn a parallel with Elisabetta Sirani. This sheet also resembles one ascribed to Giovanni Domenico Ferretti in Lille (repr. in E. A. Maser, "Addenda Ferrettiana," in *Kunst des Barock in der Toscana*, vol. 9 of *Italienische Forschungen*, 3rd. ser. [Munich: Kunsthistorisches Institut in Florenz, 1976], p. 389, fig. 9).

217

ITALIAN, 17th c., *Saints Anthony and Paul in the Desert*, pen and brown ink and brown wash, 140 x 180 mm. (5½ x 7⅛ in.).

Bequest of James Bowdoin III (1811.116). Prov.: James Bowdoin III. Bibl.: *Cat.* 1885, no. 128 (as Unknown); Mather 1913, pp. 250–53, repr. fig. 19 (as Spanish, perhaps Velásquez); *Cat.* 1930, no. 128 (as Unknown); [Siber] 1947, pp. 118–19, repr. fig. 3 (as Italian).

Early commentators ascribed great brilliance to this sheet, but it has eluded any firm attribution to artist or school. It displays certain Neapolitan characteristics, but Oberhuber thought it might be by one of the Gandolfis.

218

ITALIAN, 17th c., *Mountainous Landscape*, pen and brown ink and brown wash, 251 x 409 mm. (9⅞ x 16⅛ in.). Wmk.: bunch of grapes.

Bequest of James Bowdoin III (1811.141). Prov.: James Bowdoin III. Bibl.: *Cat.* 1885, no. 101; *Cat.* 1930, no. 101.

Formerly attributed to Guercino, this sheet should rather be called in his manner.

219

ITALIAN, 17th c., *Salome with the Head of John the Baptist*, black chalk and brown wash, 202 x 132 mm. (7 15/16 x 5 3/16 in.). Inscr. graphite verso "61 N 312 / No. 148."

Museum Purchase (1930.125). Prov.: Prof. Henry Johnson.

Panofsky suggested a Florentine origin for the work, although Turner has tentatively associated it with Vittorio Bigari (1692–1776). It resembles a costume design for a festival production.

220

ITALIAN, 17th c., *Head of a Bearded Man* (verso: sketch of drapery), black chalk, 183 x 90 mm. (7 3/16 x 3½ in.). Inscr. graphite on mount "Lodovico Carracci"; pen and brown ink verso of mount "dal Caracci"; black ink "br N 106."

Museum Purchase (1930.126). Prov.: Giovanni Lombardi, Florence (stamp verso, not in Lugt); Prof. Henry Johnson.

Not by Lodovico Carracci.

221

ITALIAN, 17th c., *Figure and Anatomical Studies* (verso: tree study), pen and brown ink and red chalk (verso: pen and brown ink and black chalk), 181 x 249 mm. (7⅛ x 9 13/16 in.). Inscr. pen and brown ink "Straordinaria / biacha."

Museum Purchase (1930.131). Prov.: William Bates (1824–1884) (Lugt 2604); Prof. Henry Johnson.

Oberhuber placed this sheet as Genoese.

222

ITALIAN, 17th c., *Studies for a Deposition*, pen and

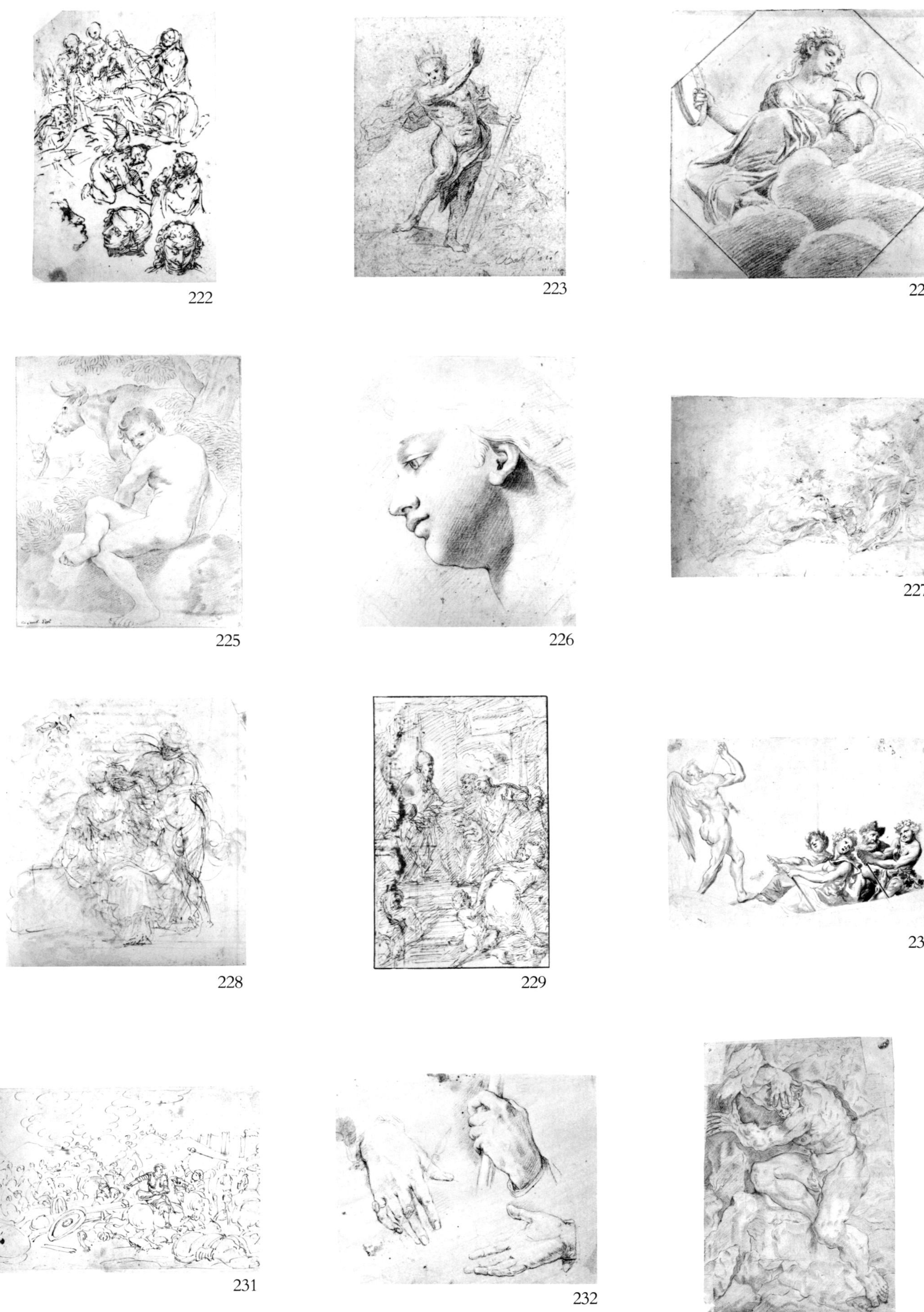

222 223 224

225 226 227

228 229 230

231 232 233

brown ink, left corners trimmed, 302 x 208 mm. (11 7/8 x 8 3/16 in.).

Museum Purchase (1930.132). Prov.: Prof. Henry Johnson.

Oberhuber suggests that this is Genoese, perhaps in the circle of Bernardo Strozzi.

223

ITALIAN, 17th c., *Neptune*, black chalk on "oatmeal" textured paper (darkened within mat opening by light), laid down, 218 x 180 mm. (8 9/16 x 7 1/16 in.). Inscr. black chalk lower right "Bardini."

Museum Purchase (1930.134). Prov.: William Bates (1824–1884) (Lugt 2604); Prof. Henry Johnson.

The subject of this sheet and its ambiguous inscription have led Panofsky and Jaffé to suggest the circle of Bernini for its authorship. The draughtsmanship is not close to Bernini himself.

224

ITALIAN, 17th c., *Seated Figure in the Clouds*, red chalk, corners trimmed to octagonal shape, 206 x 205 mm. (8 1/8 x 8 1/16 in.). Wmk.: dove surmounting COLOMBA.

Museum Purchase (1930.141). Prov.: Prof. Henry Johnson.

Panofsky has identified the figure as Hecate. She is crowned with laurel and holds a tambourine and a jug.

225

ITALIAN, 17th c., *Argus*, black chalk, 287 x 241 mm. (11 5/16 x 9 1/2 in.).

Museum Purchase (1930.143). Prov.: William Bates (1824–1884) (Lugt 2604); Prof. Henry Johnson.

Probably a copy.

226

ITALIAN, 17th c., *Head of a Woman*, red and black chalk, 221 x 186 mm. (8 11/16 x 7 5/16 in.). Wmk.: three mounts.

Museum Purchase (1930.147). Prov.: Prof. Henry Johnson.

227

ITALIAN, 17th–18th c., *Venus and the Slain Adonis*, red and black chalk, 213 x 313 mm. (8 3/8 x 12 5/16 in.). Wmk.: crown above three circles, stacked vertically (AA in center one, S within bottom one).

Museum Purchase (1930.148). Prov.: Prof. Henry Johnson.

This drawing bears an old, unlikely attribution to Francesco Furini (ca. 1600–1646).

228

ITALIAN, 17th c., *Man and Woman* (verso: male nude), pen and brown ink, brown wash, over black chalk (verso: same plus grey wash), 183 x 168 mm. (7 3/16 x 6 5/8 in.). Inscr. pen and brown ink with lines of Italian verse. Wmk.: anchor in circle.

Museum Purchase (1930.154). Prov.: Prof. Henry Johnson.

Probably Bolognese; as suggested by Turner, reminiscent of Giuseppe Rolli (1652–1727).

229

ITALIAN, 17th c., *Presentation of the Virgin* (verso: architectural studies), pen and brown ink over black chalk, 232 x 150 mm. (9 1/8 x 5 7/8 in.). Inscr. graphite verso "1611–1650/B8." Wmk.: FIN DE ANTO [. . .] within cartouche.

Museum Purchase (1930.155.1). Prov.: Prof. Henry Johnson.

Montagu suggested Dorigny as the artist; Kennedy thinks perhaps Luca Giordano.

230

ITALIAN, 17th c., *Time with the Seasons*, brush and grey and black ink over black chalk, laid down, 232 x 325 mm. (9 1/8 x 12 13/16 in.). Inscr. verso of mount pen and brown ink "Lou [. . .]."

Museum Purchase (1930.193). Prov.: Prof. Henry Johnson.

Jennifer Montagu has identified the subject and has indicated that Maratti treated the same theme.

231

ITALIAN, 17th c., *Battle Scenes* (recto/verso), pen and brown ink over graphite, 231 x 343 mm. (9 1/8 x 13 1/2 in.). Wmk.: kneeling saint holding cross within shield.

Museum Purchase (1930.194). Prov.: Prof. Henry Johnson.

Possibly executed as a caricature.

232

ITALIAN, 17th c., *Studies of Hands*, black and white chalk on white paper prepared with brown wash, 191 x 238 mm. (7 1/2 x 9 3/8 in.).

Museum Purchase (1930.195). Prov.: Prof. Henry Johnson.

Agnes Mongan suggested in 1982 that this sheet is Florentine. The hand on the left is shown with an artist's chalk-holder.

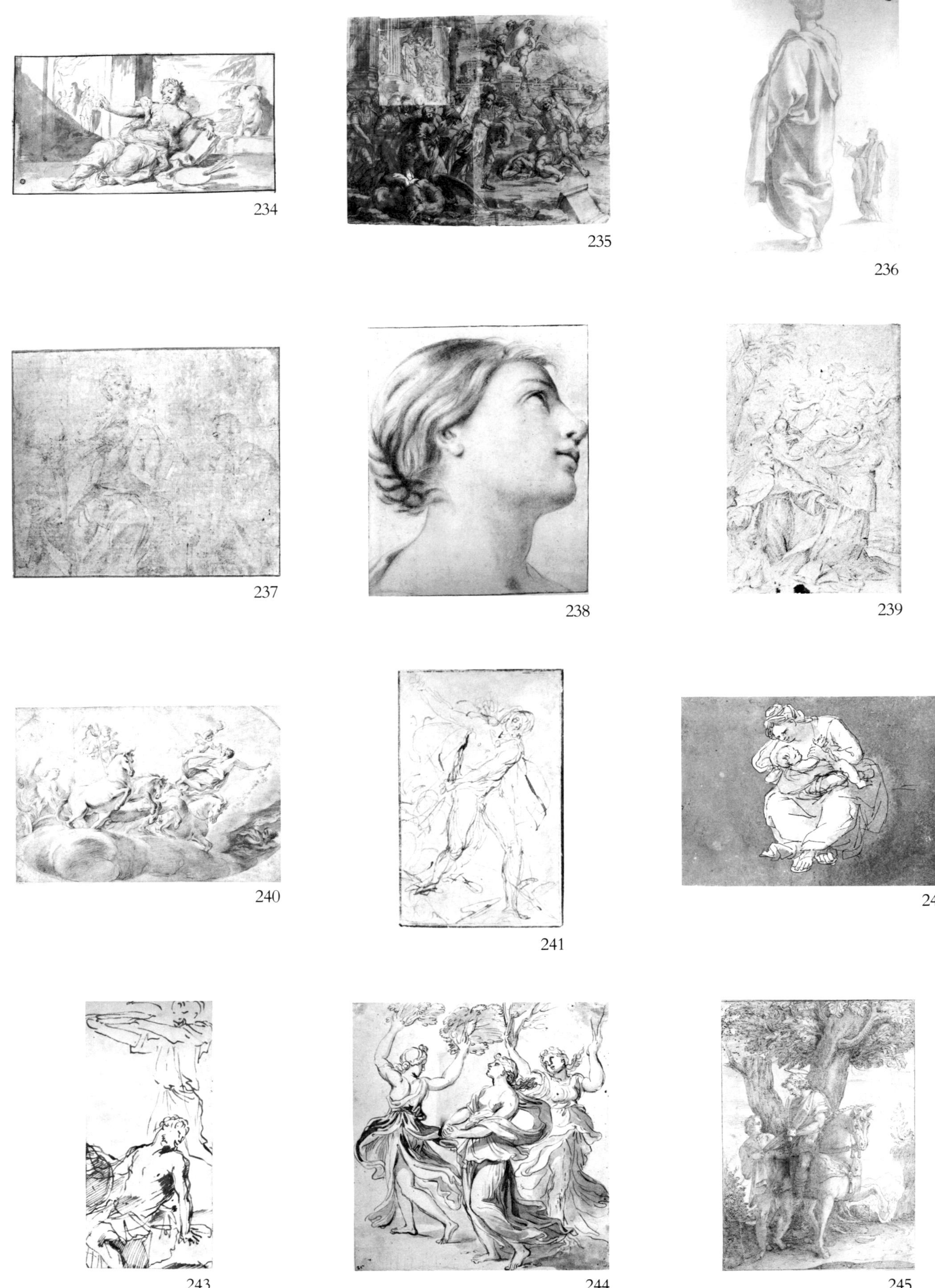

234 235 236

237 238 239

240 241 242

243 244 245

233

ITALIAN, 17th c., *Giant*, red chalk, 386 x 276 mm. (15 3/16 x 10 7/8 in.). Inscr. verso "Questo non e disegnato (da Ferdo Passarotte)." Wmk.: crown above heraldic device with six circles in center.

Museum Purchase (1930.204). Prov.: Prof. Henry Johnson.

234

ITALIAN, 17th c., *Allegorical Figure of the Arts*, brush and brown ink over black chalk, laid down, 230 x 431 mm. (9 1/16 x 17 in.). Inscr. lower right pen and brown ink "D."

Museum Purchase (1930.225). Prov.: William Bates (1824–1884) (Lugt 2604); unidentified collector's mark of Maltese cross (not in Lugt); Prof. Henry Johnson.

Oberhuber thought this drawing Dutch, perhaps by Leonard Bramer (see Cat. 16, 17, and 101), but it seems more likely Italian, perhaps Venetian. There is a resemblance to the style of Andrea Celesti (1637–ca. 1700). Susan Wegner observes that the figure points to the traditional scene of the invention of painting and sculpture, as related by Pliny, in which a woman traces her lover's shadow on a wall so that she can remember him in his absence. This figure has attributes of a palette, a book, and a sculpture.

235

ITALIAN, 17th c., *Jason and the Golden Fleece*, pen and black ink, dark brown wash, laid down (tears, repairs), 420 x 538 mm. (16 1/2 x 21 3/16 in.).

Museum Purchase (1930.228). Prov.: Prof. Henry Johnson.

Probably a copy; according to a note in the museum files, taken from a composition by Ciro Ferri in the Quirinal Palace, Rome. However, Bruce Davis (letter to the author, 26 November 1984) knows of no such composition by him.

236

FLORENTINE, 17th c. (?), *Draped Figure Studies* (verso: Diana at the Bath), red chalk (verso: black chalk), 407 x 266 mm. (16 x 10 1/2 in.).

Museum Purchase (1930.234). Prov.: unidentified armorial collector's stamp upper right; Prof. Henry Johnson.

The attribution is by Oberhuber, who suggested the name of Matteo Rosselli (1578–1651). The drawing can be compared with sheets in the Uffizi (repr. Thiem 1977, pl. 100) and the Louvre (Paris 1981–1982, cat. no. 64, repr.), although the draughtsmanship here (and the paper) appears to be later.

237

ITALIAN, 17th c., *Madonna and Child with Two Saints*, pen and brown ink and brown wash, laid down (faded, losses), 181 x 216 mm. (7 1/8 x 8 1/2 in.). Inscr. pen and ink on mount "Guido."

James Phinney Baxter Fund in Memory of Professor Henry Johnson (1932.10). Prov.: Robert Udny (1722–1802) (Lugt 2248); Henry Johnson. Bibl.: *Cat.* 1930, p. 94, no. 623 (as Guido Reni).

This drawing carries an old unlikely attribution to Guido Reni (1575–1642).

238

ITALIAN, 17th c., *Head of a Woman*, red chalk, 278 x 232 mm. (10 15/16 x 9 1/8 in.).

James Phinney Baxter Fund in Memory of Professor Henry Johnson (1932.13). Prov.: Henry Johnson. Bibl.: *Cat.* 1930, p. 95, no. 627 (as Sacchi).

Formerly attributed to Andrea Sacchi; Oberhuber suggests looking in the circle of Guercino.

239

ITALIAN, 17th c., *Two Dominican Saints Receiving the Christ Child*, black and white chalk on brown paper, laid down, 322 x 215 mm. (12 11/16 x 8 7/16 in.). Inscr. pen and brown ink on mount below "Titian Del."

James Phinney Baxter Fund in Memory of Professor Henry Johnson (1932.28). Prov.: Henry Johnson. Bibl.: *Cat.* 1930, p. 95, no. 614 (as Titian).

Certainly seventeenth-century. Turner very tentatively suggested looking near Luigi Garzi (1638–1721).

240

BOLOGNESE, 17th c., *Apollo and Aurora*, red chalk and brush and red wash, laid down, 238 x 363 mm. (9 3/8 x 14 1/4 in.). Wmk.: fleur-de-lis within crowned shield.

Gift of Miss Susan Dwight Bliss (1956.24.173). Prov.: Susan Dwight Bliss.

Attributed in 1969 by Michael Jaffé to Domenico Maria Canuti and in 1983 by Nicholas Turner as Bolognese, perhaps by Francesco Monti or Giovan Gioseffo dal Sole.

241

ITALIAN, 17th c., *Striding Male Nude*, pen and brown ink, laid down, 87 x 56 mm. (3 7/16 x 2 3/16 in.).

Gift of Miss Susan Dwight Bliss (1956.24.178). Prov.: Susan Dwight Bliss.

242

ITALIAN, 17th c., *Woman and Child*, pen and black ink, brown and grey washes, 92 x 131 mm. (3 5/8 x 5 1/8 in.).

Gift of Miss Susan Dwight Bliss (1956.24.180). Prov.: Susan Dwight Bliss.

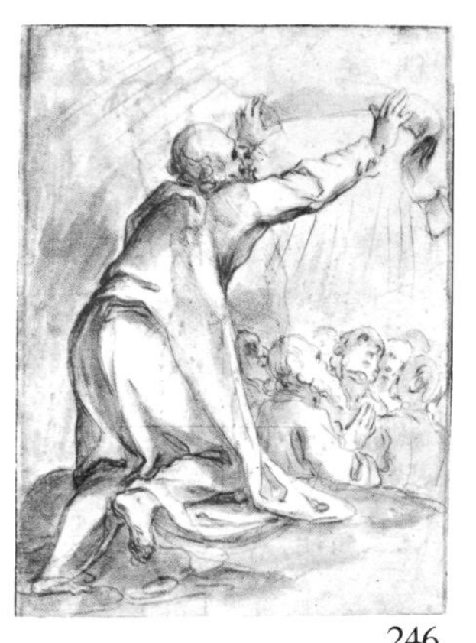
246

247

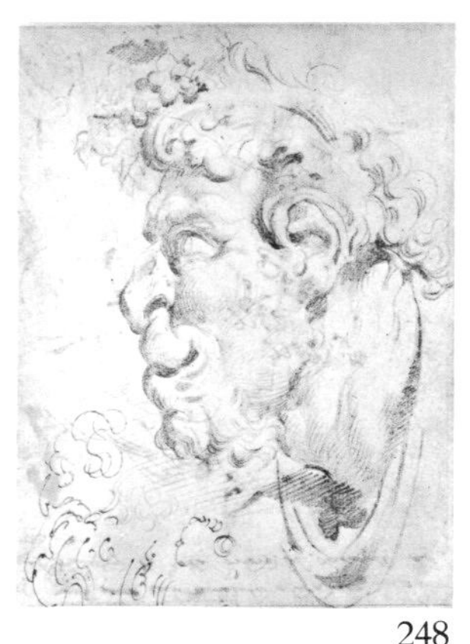
248

249

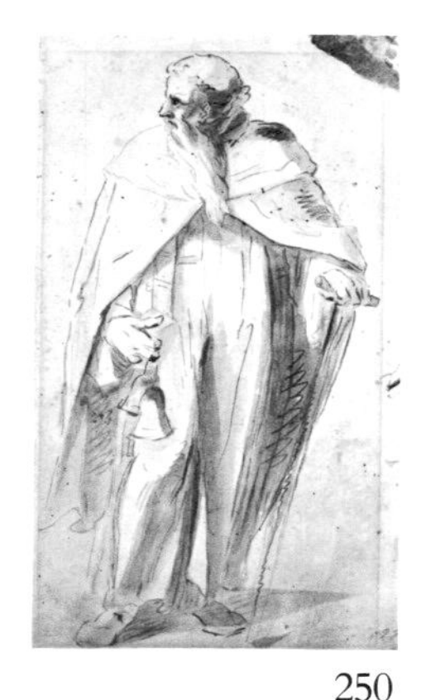
250

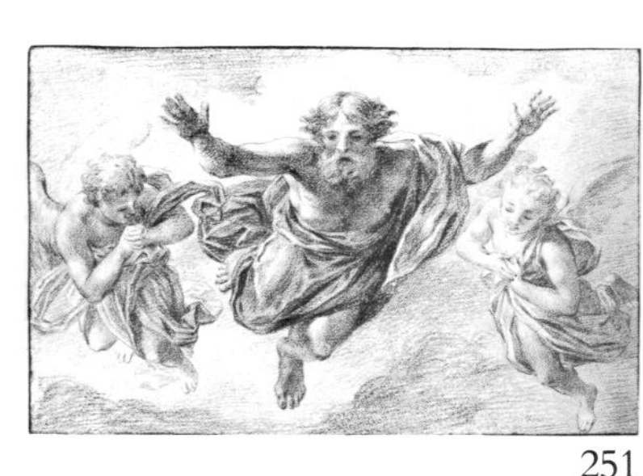
251

252

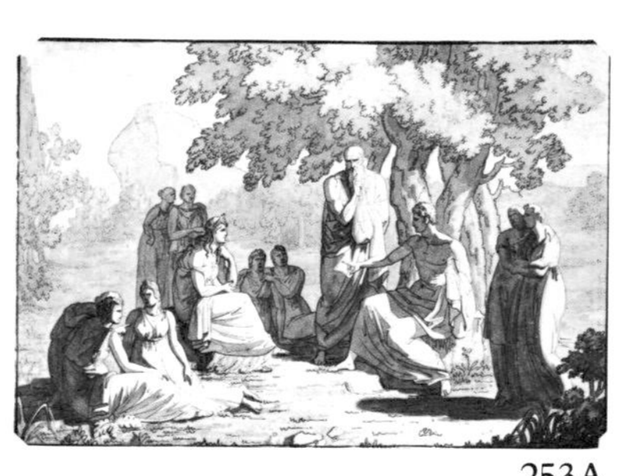
253A

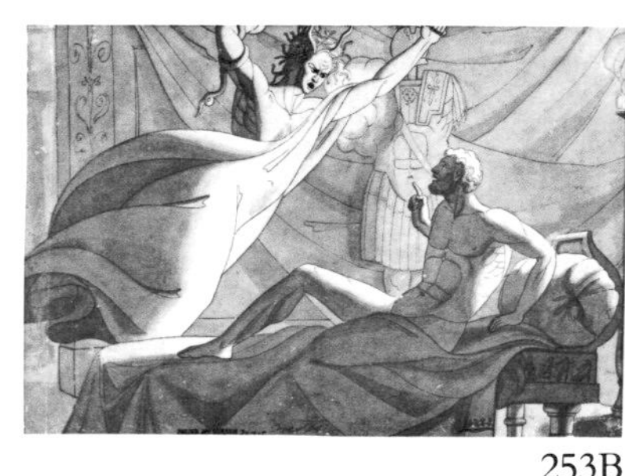
253B

254

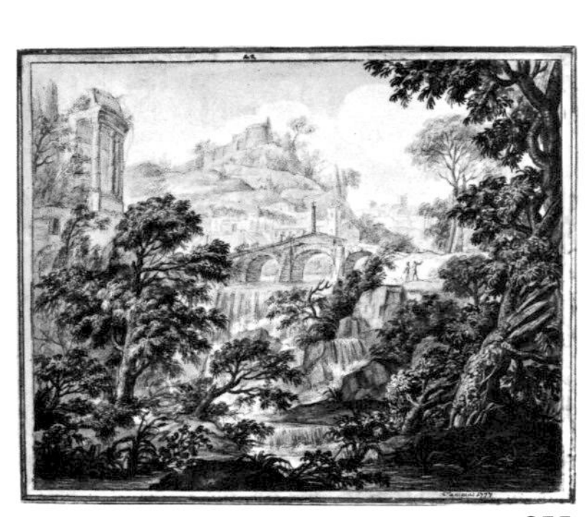
255

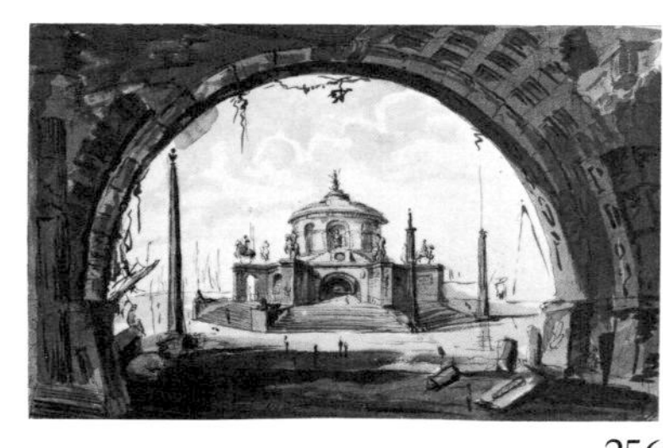
256

243

ITALIAN, 17th c., *Two Figures*, pen and brown ink, laid down, 141 x 69 mm. (5 9/16 x 2 11/16 in.). Inscr. verso graphite "Bertani."

Gift of Miss Susan Dwight Bliss (1956.24.183). Prov.: Susan Dwight Bliss.

In the manner of Castiglione; Jaffé (comment in museum files) associated it with Testa.

244

ITALIAN, 17th c., *The Heliades*, pen and brown ink over black chalk, brush and brown wash, heightened with white (darkened), laid down, 213 x 207 mm. (8 3/8 x 8 1/8 in.). Inscr. pen and brown ink lower left "25"; verso of mount a description of the subject.

Gift of Miss Susan Dwight Bliss (1956.24.210). Prov.: William Bates (1824–1884) (Lugt 2604); Susan Dwight Bliss.

Traditionally attributed to the school of Domenichino; Oberhuber associated it with Michel Corneille (1601/03–1664).

245

ITALIAN, 17th c., *St. Martin Dividing His Cloak*, pen and brown ink, traced with a stylus for transfer, rubbed with red chalk verso, laid down, 278 x 205 mm. (10 15/16 x 8 1/16 in.). Indecipherable watermark.

Gift of Miss Susan Dwight Bliss (1956.24.213). Prov.: unidentified collector's mark; Susan Dwight Bliss.

Prepared for transfer; probably a study for a print.

246

ITALIAN, 17th c., *Figures from the Assumption of the Virgin* (verso: standing male nude from the back), red chalk (verso: pen and brown ink), 302 x 225 mm. (11 7/8 x 8 7/8 in.). Inscr. pen and brown ink verso "Adi:23:di Setembre 1670"; blue pencil lower left "44.Sec. XVII."

Gift of Miss Susan Dwight Bliss (1956.24.254). Prov.: Susan Dwight Bliss.

Formerly attributed to Giovanni Francesco Romanelli (1612–1662); the attribution has been dismissed by Montagu.

247

ITALIAN, 17th c., *Study of a Crown* (verso: sketch of man and woman), brush and brown washes over graphite, compass points and rules at bottom (verso: graphite), 185 x 318 mm. (7 1/4 x 12 1/2 in.).

Museum Purchase (1964.41). Prov.: acquired from Hinckley and Brohel, New York. Bibl.: Bowdoin College Museum of Art, *Recent Acquisitions* (exh. cat.) (Brunswick, 1968). [p. 23], repr. on cover.

Mary Myers suggests that this drawing is Florentine; Held has ventured that it is a sculptural study for a statue of the Virgin.

248

ITALIAN, 18th c., *Head of a Satyr* (verso: sketches of heads), black chalk and pen and brown ink (verso: pen and brown ink), 167 x 127 mm. (6 9/16 x 5 in.). Inscr. verso pen and brown ink with fragment of letter in Italian.

Museum Purchase (1930.128). Prov.: Prof. Henry Johnson.

Tentatively ascribed by Oberhuber to a member of the Gandolfi family.

249

ITALIAN, 18th c., *Charity* (verso: sketch of same subject), brush and brown ink and wash, 156 x 194 mm. (6 1/8 x 7 5/8 in.).

Museum Purchase (1930.140). Prov.: William Bates (1824–1884) (Lugt 2604); Prof. Henry Johnson.

Panofsky recognized the subject of this drawing.

250

ITALIAN, 17th c., *St. Anthony Abbot* (verso: profile portrait), pen and brown ink and brown wash (verso: black chalk), 308 x 184 mm. (12 1/8 x 7 1/4 in.). Inscr. pen and brown ink "25." Wmk.: fleur-de-lis over C & [. . .] Honig.

Museum Purchase (1930.144). Prov.: Prof. Henry Johnson.

The recto seems a copy after Luca Cambiaso (see Cat. 35, 152–54).

251

ITALIAN, 18th c., *God the Father and Two Angels*, red chalk, 144 x 229 mm. (5 11/16 x 9 in.). Inscr. on original mount (lost) "Vittorio Bigari / St. Petronio."

Museum Purchase (1930.198). Prov.: Prof. Henry Johnson.

Has been associated with Vittorio Bigari (1692–1776) and with the circle of Anton Raphael Mengs (1728–1779).

252

ITALIAN, 18th c., *Landscape with View of a City*, pen and brown ink and brown wash over black chalk, 205 x 323 mm. (8 1/16 x 12 3/4 in.). Wmk.: crowned shield with fleur-de-lis over VDL.

James Phinney Baxter Fund in Memory of Professor Henry Johnson (1932.21). Prov.: Henry Johnson. Bibl.: *Cat.* 1930, p. 95, no. 646.

This sheet carries an old attribution to Giovanni Paolo Pannini. Resembles a stage design.

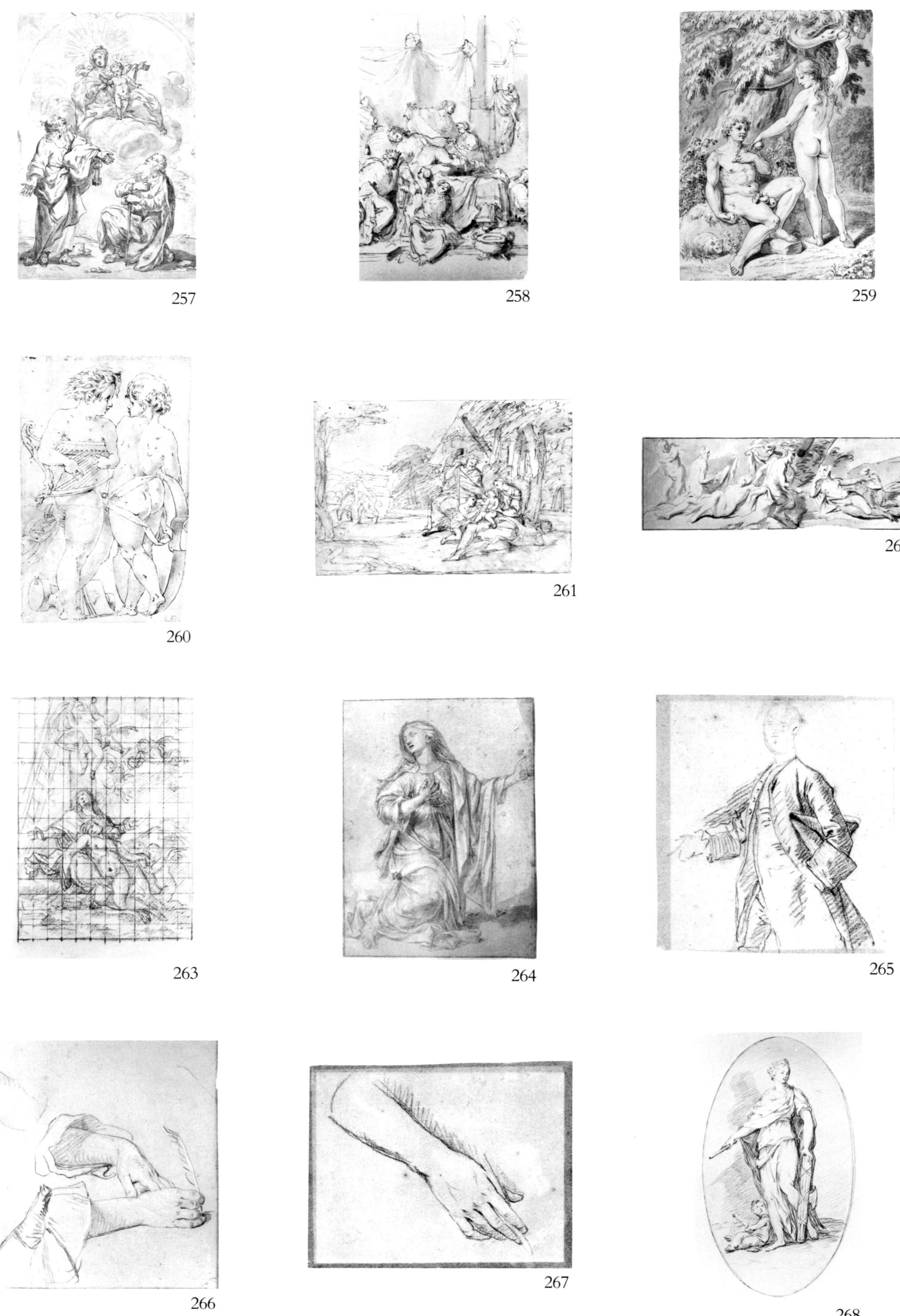
257 258 259 260 261 262 263 264 265 266 267 268

253

ITALIAN, late 18th c., *Aeneas Relating the History of Troy to Dido* (?) (verso: *Orestes*), pen and brown ink, brown wash over black chalk on wove paper, 225 x 332 mm. (8 7/8 x 13 1/16 in.).

Museum Purchase (1930.218). Prov.: William Bates (1824–1884) (Lugt 2604); Prof. Henry Johnson.

According to a note in the museum files, an old inscription on a former mount (lost) contained an attribution to Nicolo Benvenuto, for whom no references can be found in the literature. The tentative identification of the subject is based upon the fact that the chief woman listener wears a crown; the episode is related in the *Aeneid*, beginning in book 2, line 1.

254

ITALIAN, late 18th c., *Scene from Classical History*, pen and black ink and light brown wash, 482 x 649 mm. (19 x 25 9/16 in.).

Museum Purchase (1930.226). Prov.: Prof. Henry Johnson.

The subject is unidentified; one of the figures may be Hercules wearing his customary lionskin.

French

255

LAMBERT FRANÇOIS THÉRÈSE CAMMAS (1743–1804), *The Falls at Tivoli*, 1777, pen and grey ink, grey, brown, and black wash, heightened with white, laid down, 214 x 268 mm. (8 7/16 x 10 9/16 in.). Inscr. by artist pen and black ink on mount below "Cammas 1777"; on mount above "1=2."

Museum Purchase (1930.142). Prov.: William Bates (1824–1884) (Lugt 2604); Prof. Henry Johnson.

The subject is evident from the representation of the Temple of the Sibyl at the left.

256

NOËL COCHIN (1622–1695), attr., *Temple Seen through an Archway*, pen and black ink, brown, grey, and black washes, over graphite, 248 x 405 mm. (9 3/4 x 15 15/16 in.). Inscr. pen and brown ink lower right "Cochin del.t"; graphite verso "Panini." Wmk.: Strasbourg bend with fleur-de-lis.

Gift of Miss Susan Dwight Bliss (1956.24.200). Prov.: Susan Dwight Bliss.

Resembles a stage design.

257

JOSEPH ANTOINE DAVID, called David de Marseilles (1725–1789), attr., *The Virgin and Child Appearing to Saints Peter and Paul*, pen and black and brown ink, grey wash, over black chalk, 322 x 220 mm. (12 11/16 x 8 5/8 in.). Inscr. pen and black ink lower left "David de Marseilles"; graphite bottom "1659"; graphite verso "David de Marseilles 1659/Signed & dated/Woodburn & Devros Collections."

Gift of Miss Susan Dwight Bliss (1956.24.220). Prov.: Samuel Woodburn (1786–1853) and Devros Collections (?—see inscriptions above); Susan Dwight Bliss.

258

JEAN FRANÇOIS PIERRE PEYRON (1744–1814), copy after, *Death of Alcestis*, pen and brown ink, brown and black wash, over graphite, 214 x 138 mm. (8 7/16 x 5 7/16 in.).

James Phinney Baxter Fund in Memory of Professor Henry Johnson (1932.40). Prov.: Henry Johnson. Bibl.: *Cat.* 1930, p. 95, no. 649 (as Unknown); Toronto 1972, p. 194, under cat. no. 109 (as copy of Peyron). P. Rosenberg and V. van de Sandt, *Pierre Peyron 1744–1814* (Neuilly-sur-Seine, 1983), p. 156, no. x8, repr. fig. 99 (as copy of Le Bas print after Peyron painting; print repr. fig. 98).

Recognized in 1971 by Rosenberg as a copy of an engraving by Jacques Philippe Lebas after a Peyron painting of 1785 now in the Louvre.

259

JACQUES STELLA (1596–1657), copy after, *Adam and Eve*, pen and black ink, grey and brown wash, 267 x 195 mm. (10 9/16 x 7 11/16 in.). Inscr. graphite verso "859 Stella/t-27"; pen and black ink "I.A.d.F. Inv." Wmk.: K.

Museum Purchase (1930.185). Prov.: Prof. Henry Johnson.

Most probably after a Stella prototype (cf. a Christ at the Column formerly in the Seligman Collection, repr. Davidson 1975, p. 151, fig. 4).

260

FRENCH, 16th c., *Two Boy Musicians*, pen and brown ink, brown wash, 208 x 134 mm. irregular (8 3/16 x 5 1/4 in.). Inscr. pen and brown ink verso "N. 119 [. . .] Pissa [. . .]."

Bequest of James Bowdoin III (1811.97). Prov.: James Bowdoin III. Bibl.: *Cat.* 1885, no. 87; *Cat.* 1930, no. 87.

Although it has always been considered Italian, this sheet was thought by Oberhuber to be from the school of Fontainebleau, perhaps close to Leonard Thiry (d. ca. 1550).

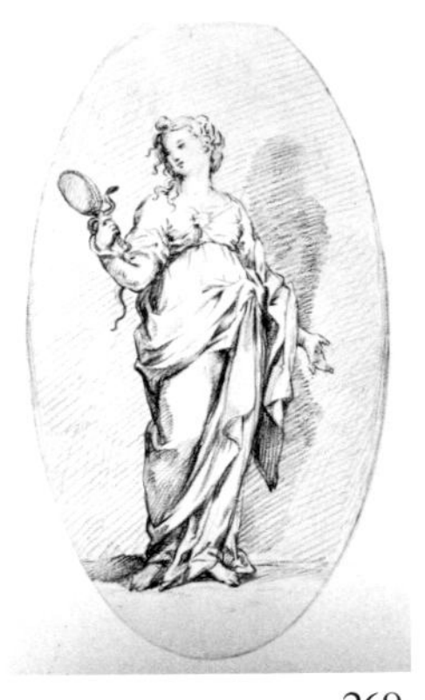
269

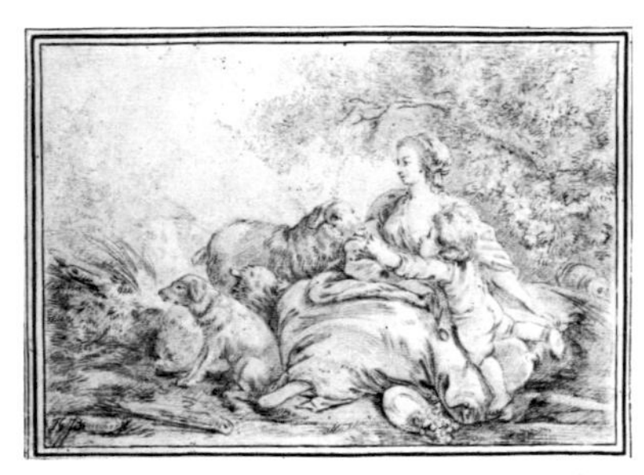
270

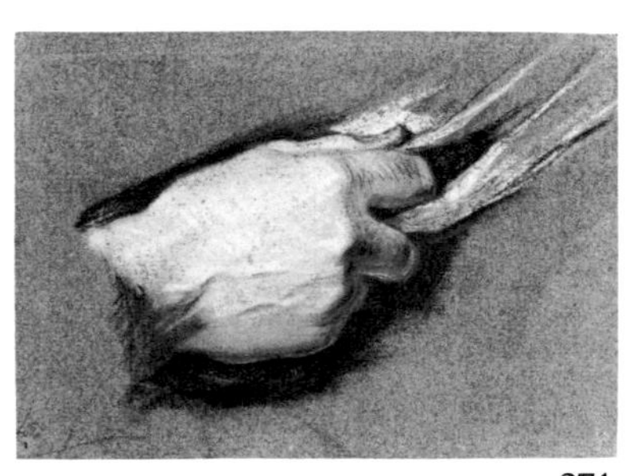
271

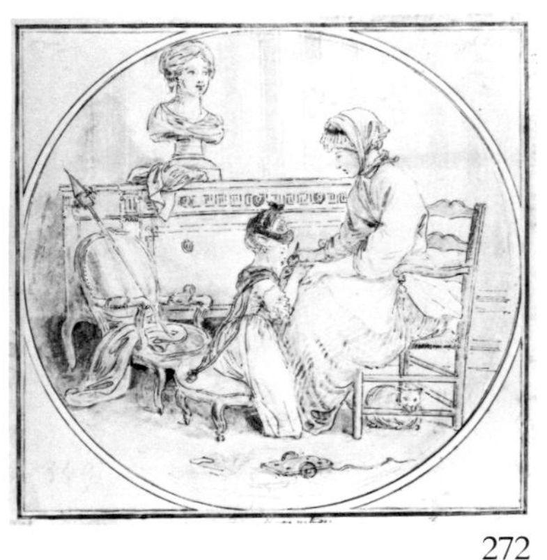
272

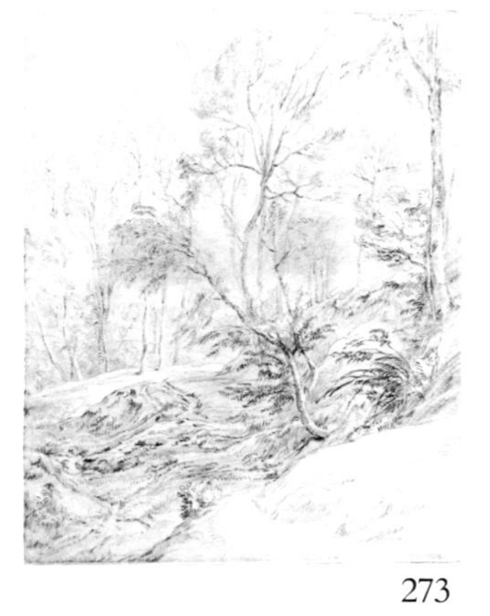
273

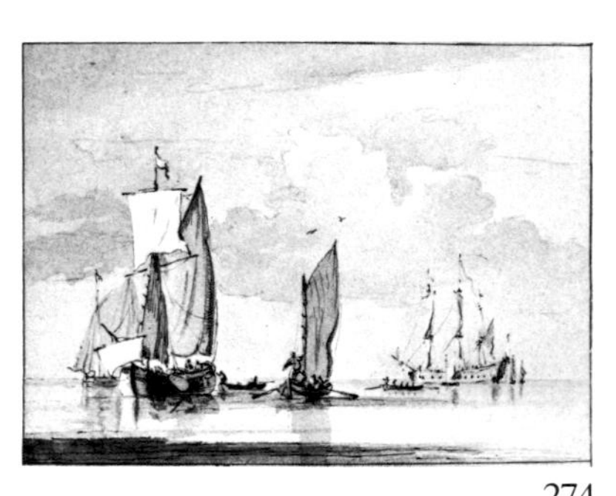
274

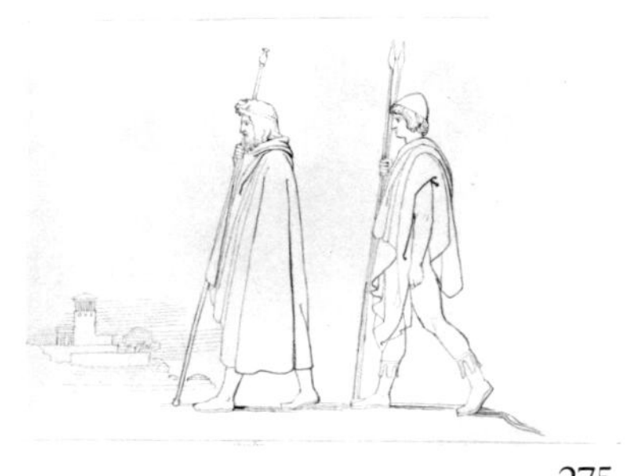
275

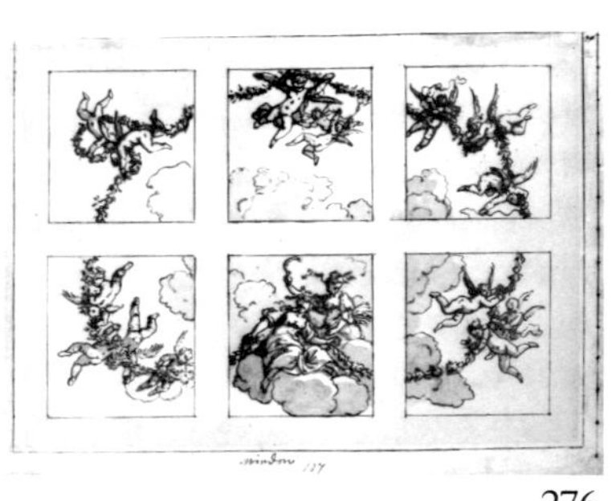
276

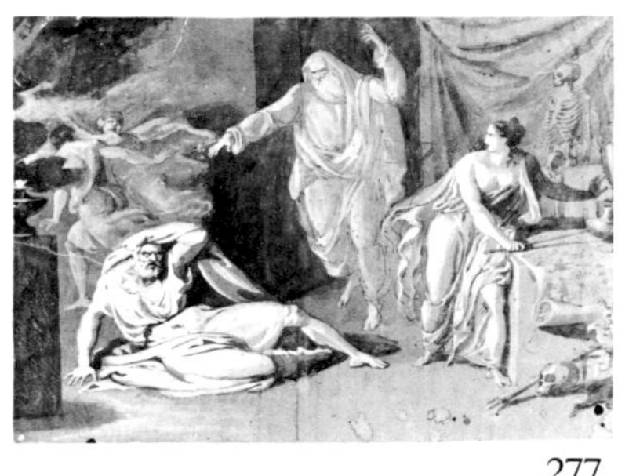
277

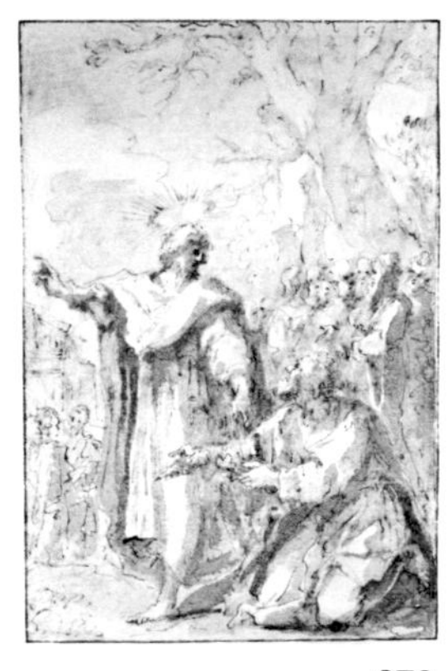
278

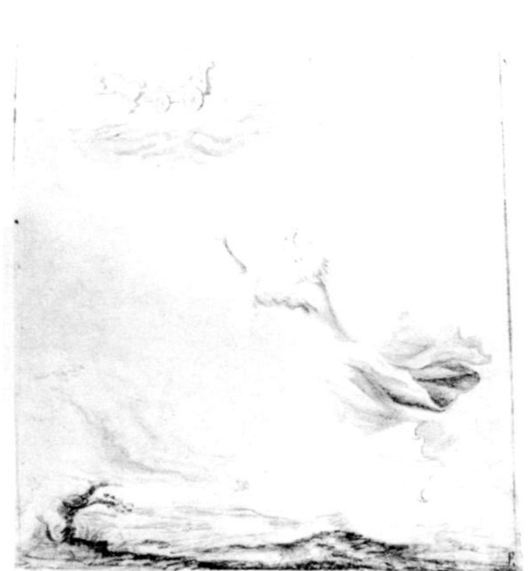
279

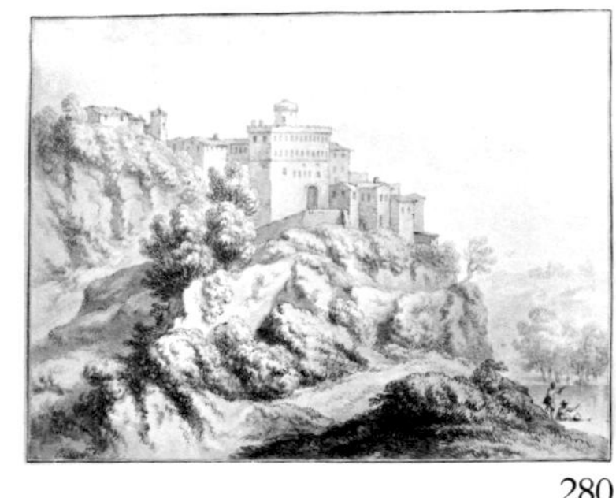
280

261

FRENCH, 17th c., *The Flight into Egypt* (verso: Madonna and Child), pen and brown ink over graphite (verso: red chalk), 170 x 253 mm. (6 11/16 x 10 in.). Inscr. pen and ink verso of former mount (removed) "No. 58 Nicholo Pousin." Wmk.: crowned coat of arms with two fish and two triple fleur-de-lis.

Bequest of James Bowdoin III (1811.51). Prov.: James Bowdoin III. Bibl.: *Cat.* 1885, no. 67 (as Poussin); *Cat.* 1930, no. 70 (as Poussin).

The Poussin attribution has been dismissed by Lugt and subsequently by other scholars; Oberhuber detected the influence of Sebastien Bourdon. Perhaps a copy.

262

FRENCH, 17th c., *Nymphs and Satyrs* (verso: figure sketches), pen and brown ink, grey wash (verso: pen and brown ink), 83 x 244 mm. (3 1/4 x 9 5/8 in.).

Bequest of James Bowdoin III (1811.117). Prov.: James Bowdoin III. Bibl.: *Cat.* 1885, no. 127; *Cat.* 1930, no. 127.

Pierre Rosenberg tentatively suggested a member of the Parrocel family as the artist, while Oberhuber felt the sheet could be earlier, within the influence of Poussin.

263

FRENCH, 17th c., *Pietà*, black chalk, squared in black chalk, 189 x 135 mm. (7 7/16 x 5 5/16 in.).

Bequest of James Bowdoin III (1811.118). Prov.: James Bowdoin III. Bibl.: *Cat.* 1885, no. 126; *Cat.* 1930, no. 126.

This sheet has been traditionally classified as Italian, but both Oberhuber and Eunice Williams feel that it is French. However, considering the large group of drawings by Maratti followers in the Bowdoin bequest, an Italian source is also possible.

264

FRENCH, 17th c., *Study for the Virgin Annunciate*, red chalk, 356 x 260 mm. (14 x 10 in.).

Bequest of James Bowdoin III (1811.133). Prov.: James Bowdoin III. Bibl.: *Cat.* 1885, no. 84; *Cat.* 1930, no. 84.

Felice Stampfle was the first to recognize the subject as a study for the Virgin in an Annunciation. Oberhuber thought this sheet French despite its earlier placement as Italian.

265

FRENCH, early 18th c., *Study of a Man with a Tricorne Hat*, black and white chalk on blue paper, faded, 236 x 224 mm. (9 5/16 x 8 13/16 in.).

Bequest of James Bowdoin III (1811.77). Prov.: James Bowdoin III. Bibl.: *Cat.* 1885, no. 140; Mather 1914, pp. 115–16, repr. fig. 9; *Cat.* 1930, no. 140.

By the same hand as Cat. 266 and 267.

266

FRENCH, early 18th c., *Two Hands of a Woman Writing with a Quill*, black and white chalk on blue paper, faded, 265 x 231 mm. (10 7/16 x 9 1/8 in.).

Bequest of James Bowdoin III (1811.122). Prov.: James Bowdoin III. Bibl.: *Cat.* 1885, no. 142; Mather 1914, p. 116, repr. fig. 10; *Cat.* 1930, no. 142.

Di Pietro placed this sheet in the seventeenth century; Mather placed it later. Pierre Rosenberg tentatively suggested François Lemoyne (1688–1737) as the artist. By the same hand as Cat. 265 and 267. This group may be by an Italian artist.

267

FRENCH, early 18th c., *A Hand Holding a Stylus*, black and white chalk on blue paper, faded, 185 x 239 mm. (7 1/4 x 9 3/8 in.).

Bequest of James Bowdoin III (1811.125). Prov.: James Bowdoin III. Bibl.: *Cat.* 1885, no. 141 (as Unknown); Mather 1914 (as French, 18th c.), p. 116; *Cat.* 1930, no. 141 (as Unknown).

See comments for previous entry, which is by the same hand.

268

FRENCH or ITALIAN, early 18th c., *Allegory of Justice*, red chalk, oval 238 x 142 mm. (9 3/8 x 5 5/8 in.). Inscr. pen and brown ink verso "4.p. / Filippo: B[. . .]."

Bequest of James Bowdoin III (1811.59). Prov.: James Bowdoin III. Bibl.: *Cat.* 1885, no. 79 (as Unknown); *Cat.* 1930, no. 79 (as Unknown); *Handbook* 1981, p. 168 (as Bouchardon).

The attribution of this and the following sheet to Edmé Bouchardon (made by Benisovich) has not been accepted by scholars such as Agnes Mongan, Margaret Morgan Grasselli, and Eunice Williams. The pair is believed to be earlier and conceivably Italian.

269

FRENCH or ITALIAN, early 18th c., *Allegory of Prudence*, red chalk, trimmed at top, oval 228 x 132 mm. (9 x 5 3/16 in.). Inscr. pen and brown ink verso "4.p."

Bequest of James Bowdoin III (1811.74). Prov.: James Bowdoin III. Bibl.: *Cat.* 1885, no. 80 (as Unknown); *Cat.* 1930, no. 80 (as Unknown); *Handbook* 1981, p. 168 (as Bouchardon).

See comments for previous sheet, with which this forms a pair. Traditionally identified as Truth, the subject is confirmed as Prudence by the serpent and mirror together as attributes.

270

FRENCH, 18th c., *Pastoral Subject with a Shepherdess*, black and red chalk and graphite, laid down, 149 x 215 mm. (5 7/8 x 8 1/2 in.). Inscr. initials lower left effaced to read "F. Boucher"; pen and brown ink on mount below "par François Boucher."

Gift of Miss Susan Dwight Bliss (1956.24.191). Prov.: Susan Dwight Bliss.

Not Boucher himself; perhaps a copy.

271

FRENCH, 18th c., *Study of a Hand*, colored chalks on blue paper, 194 x 137 mm. (7 5/8 x 5 3/8 in.). Inscr. graphite "Prud'hon/37."

Gift of Miss Susan Dwight Bliss (1956.24.202). Prov.: Susan Dwight Bliss.

Traditionally attributed to Pierre Paul Prud'hon (1758–1823), this sheet is believed by Agnes Mongan and Eunice Williams to be earlier, in the manner of Maurice Quentin de Latour (1704–1788).

272

FRENCH, 18th c., *Mother and Child*, pen and black ink and watercolor over black chalk, laid down, 225 x 237 mm. (8 7/8 x 9 5/16 in.). Inscr. pen and brown ink on mount below "d'apres nature / Fragonard"; graphite lower left "349."

Gift of Miss Susan Dwight Bliss (1956.24.215). Prov.: Susan Dwight Bliss.

Not near Fragonard; perhaps eighteenth-century.

273

FRENCH, 18th c., *Wooded Landscape*, black and white chalk on blue paper, 519 x 416 mm. (20 7/16 x 16 1/2 in.). Inscr. left (partially obscured) "Ruysdc?"; right corner (partially obscured) "Chilip [. . .]."

Bequest of Helen Johnson Chase (1958.71). Prov.: Prof. Henry Johnson; Helen Johnson (Mrs. Stanley P.) Chase. Bibl.: *Cat.* 1930, p. 95, no. 642 (as Ruisdael).

With a traditional, and unlikely, attribution to Ruisdael, this landscape seems more French in feeling, in the manner of Jean Baptiste Oudry (1686–1755).

British

274

CHARLES BROOKING (1723–1759), *Ships at Anchor, after van de Velde*, pen and brown and black ink, grey wash, heightened with white, on blue paper, laid down, 179 x 242 mm. (7 1/16 x 9 1/2 in.). Inscr. pen and brown ink on label affixed to verso of mount "S [. . .] Dastins Feb-7 / by Brooking after Van dev."

Gift of Miss Susan Dwight Bliss (1956.24.192). Prov.: Victor W. Newman (b. 1860) (Lugt 2540); Susan Dwight Bliss (acquired from American Art Association, February 1921).

The source is probably a painting by Willem van de Velde the Younger (see Cat. 30).

275

JOHN FLAXMAN (1755–1826), *Telemachus in Search of His Father*, pen and black ink over graphite on wove paper; sheet 210 x 276 mm. (8 1/4 x 10 7/8 in.); image 171 x 244 mm. (6 3/4 x 9 5/8 in.). Inscr. by the artist graphite lower right "29"; pen and black ink below "Mentor Telemachus / Telemachus already prest the Shore, / Not first, the power of Wisdom marched before, / Odys: 3–1.15:"

Classical Fund (1918.2). Prov.: Thomas Hope (ca. 1770–1831); acquired from Scott and Fowles, New York (*Catalogue of an Exhibition of Original Drawings by John Flaxman, R.A.* [New York, 1918], cat. no. 29). Bibl.: *Cat.* 1930, p. 104, no. D-2; *Handbook* 1981, p. 169. Exhs.: Storrs 1973, cat. no. 129b; Wilmington 1976, cat. no. 1–12, repr.

A study for Flaxman's series of illustrations for *The Iliad* and *The Odyssey* (see Cat. 94 for another, with further discussion).

276

SIR JAMES THORNHILL (1675–1734), attr., *Stained Glass Window Designs*, pen and brown ink and grey wash, 205 x 286 mm. (8 1/8 x 11 1/4 in.). Inscr. pen and brown ink bottom "Window / 137."

Bequest of James Bowdoin III (1811.103). Prov.: James Bowdoin III. Bibl.: *Cat.* 1885, no. 137 (as Unknown); *Cat.* 1930, no. 137 (as Unknown); J. Harris, *A Catalogue of British Drawings for Architecture, Decoration, Sculpture, and Landscape Gardening 1550–1900 in American Collections* (Upper Saddle River, 1971), p. 260 (as Thornhill).

Attributed tentatively to Thornhill by Lugt. The figure with the sickle in the lower center of the sheet is Ceres.

277

BRITISH, late 18th c., *Samuel Appearing to Saul at the Witch of Endor's*, pen and ink, grey, white, and orange wash, 375 x 533 mm. (14 7/16 x 21 in.).

Museum Purchase (1930.227). Prov.: Prof. Henry Johnson.

Professors Pearl Freiberg and Gert Schiff independently recognized the subject, described in 1 Samuel 28:3–25. Such scenes were favored by the circle of English artists around Henry Fuseli (1741–1825), and Schiff has placed this sheet within that milieu.

Unknown

278

UNKNOWN, 16th c., *Christ Giving the Keys to St. Peter*, pen and brown ink and brown wash, 182 x 124 mm. ($7^{3}/_{16}$ x $4^{7}/_{8}$ in.).

Bequest of James Bowdoin III (1811.113). Prov.: James Bowdoin III. Bibl.: *Cat.* 1885, no. 134; *Cat.* 1930, no. 134.

Judson has placed this sheet as Flemish, within the school of Antwerp, perhaps near Marten de Vos.

279

UNKNOWN, 17th c., *The Translation of Elijah*, brush and red ink and wash, traces of black chalk, 199 x 195 mm. ($7^{13}/_{16}$ x $7^{11}/_{16}$ in.). Inscr. pen and brown ink lower right "P."

Bequest of James Bowdoin III (1811.60). Prov.: James Bowdoin III. Bibl.: *Cat.* 1885, no. 78; *Cat.* 1930, no. 78.

The subject is taken from 2 Kings 2:1–12.

280

UNKNOWN, 17th c., *Landscape with Buildings on a Hill*, pen and black and grey inks, grey wash, 226 x 299 mm. ($8^{7}/_{8}$ x $11^{3}/_{4}$ in.). Inscr. pen and ink verso of former mount (lost) "34."

Bequest of James Bowdoin III (1811.93). Prov.: James Bowdoin III. Bibl.: *Cat.* 1885, no. 100; *Cat.* 1930, no. 100.

281

UNKNOWN, 17th c., *Group of Fisherwomen* (verso: study of a hand), pen and grey ink, grey wash, heightened with white, over red chalk tracing, the central two figures traced with a stylus (verso: red and white chalk), 281 x 460 mm. ($11^{1}/_{16}$ x $18^{1}/_{8}$ in.).

Bequest of James Bowdoin III (1811.126). Prov.: James Bowdoin III. Bibl.: *Cat.* 1885, no. 97; *Cat.* 1930, no. 97.

The composition is in the shape of a lunette and is probably a copy. It is executed over a tracing in red chalk taken from an earlier drawing or print. The central two figures have been traced with a stylus for further transfer.

282

UNKNOWN, 17th c., *Landscape with Buildings*, pen and brown ink and grey wash over black chalk (verso: pen sketches), many losses, mounted on Japanese tissue, 303 x 425 mm. ($11^{15}/_{16}$ x $16^{3}/_{4}$ in.). Wmk.: cross surmounting three circles in vertical line, the center one with an eagle.

Bequest of James Bowdoin III (1811.139). Prov.: James Bowdoin III. Bibl.: *Cat.* 1885, no. 103; *Cat.* 1930, no. 103.

283

UNKNOWN, 17th c., *Standing Soldier*, brush and blue wash, heightened with white (partially oxidized), laid down, 140 x 75 mm. ($5^{1}/_{2}$ x $2^{15}/_{16}$ in.). Inscr. pen and ink verso (showing through on recto) with Greek cross.

Museum Purchase (1930.127). Prov.: Prof. Henry Johnson.

284

UNKNOWN, 17th c., *Sketch Sheet* (recto/verso), pen and brown ink, touched with white, on blue paper, 291 x 200 mm. ($11^{7}/_{16}$ x $7^{7}/_{8}$ in.).

Museum Purchase (1930.138). Prov.: Prof. Henry Johnson.

Traditionally classed as Italian, but could conceivably be northern, near an artist such as Leonard Bramer (cf. Cat. 16, 17).

285

UNKNOWN, 17th c., *Studies of Horses* (verso: copy of a book illustration), black chalk, 225 x 315 mm. ($8^{7}/_{8}$ x $12^{3}/_{8}$ in.). Wmk. (partial): ZOONEN.

Museum Purchase (1930.150). Prov.: William Bates (1824–1884) (Lugt 2604); Prof. Henry Johnson.

Both sides are probably copies.

286

UNKNOWN, 17th c., *Scene at a Well with Figures Fleeing* (verso: anatomical studies), pen and brown ink and brown wash over red chalk (verso: red chalk), 208 x 288 mm. ($8^{3}/_{16}$ x $11^{3}/_{8}$ in.).

Museum Purchase (1930.156.1). Prov.: unidentified armorial collector's stamp lower left; Prof. Henry Johnson.

Though classed as Italian in the museum files, this sheet could be northern.

287

UNKNOWN, 17th c., *Figure and Architectural Studies*, pen and brown ink, brown wash, over graphite, 290 x 424 mm. ($11^{7}/_{16}$ x $16^{11}/_{16}$ in.).

Museum Purchase (1930.224). Prov.: Prof. Henry Johnson.

Oberhuber has suggested that a member of the Holzmair family of German artists may have executed this sheet.

288

UNKNOWN, 17th c., *Kneeling Bishop*, black and white chalk on blue paper (faded, tears upper right, worm holes), 492 x 323 mm. ($19^{3}/_{8}$ x $12^{3}/_{4}$ in.). Inscr. indistinctly pen and black ink lower right "E. hobm[. . .] del."

Museum Purchase (1930.233). Prov.: Prof. Henry Johnson.

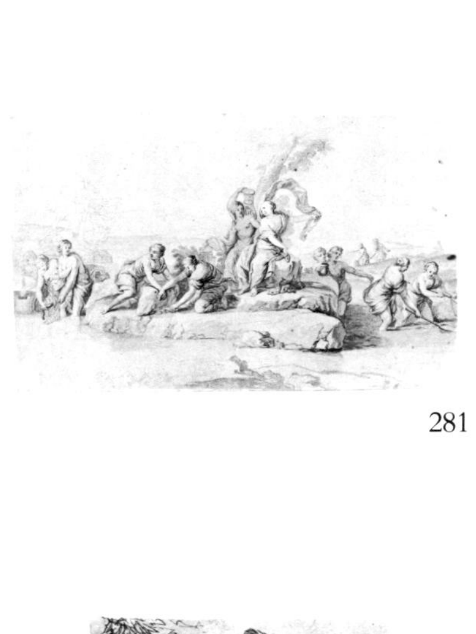

281

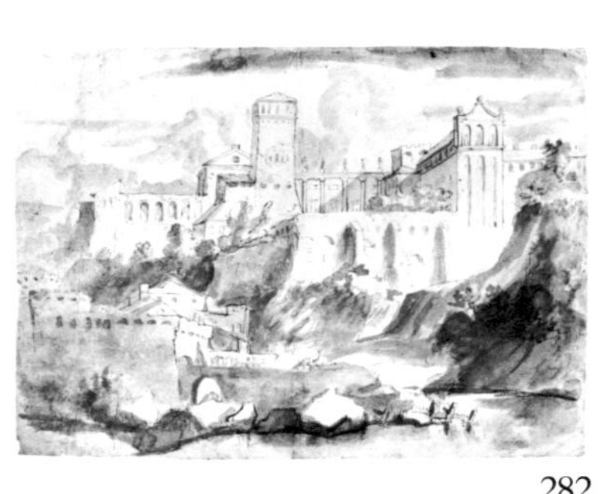

282

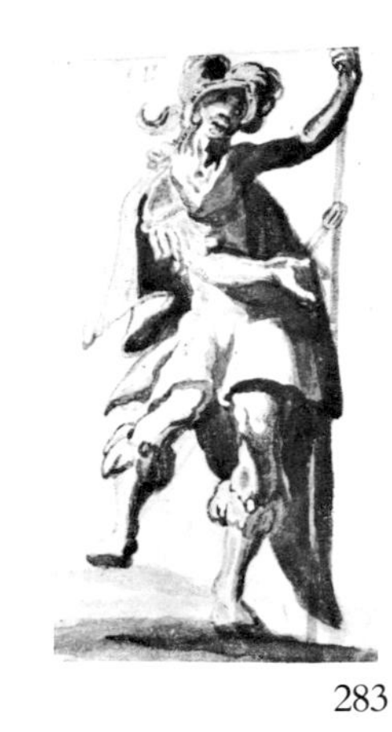

283

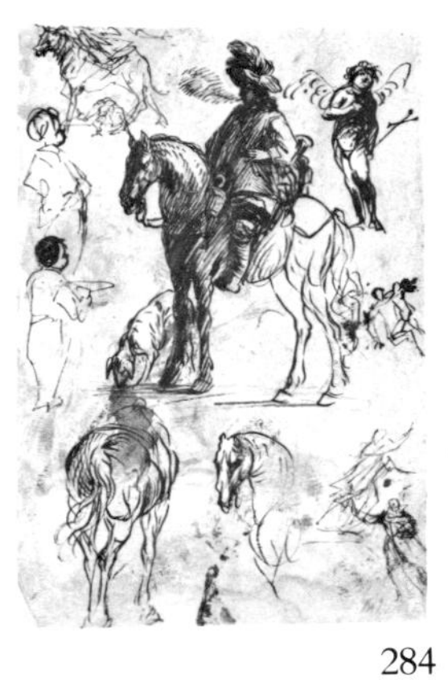

284

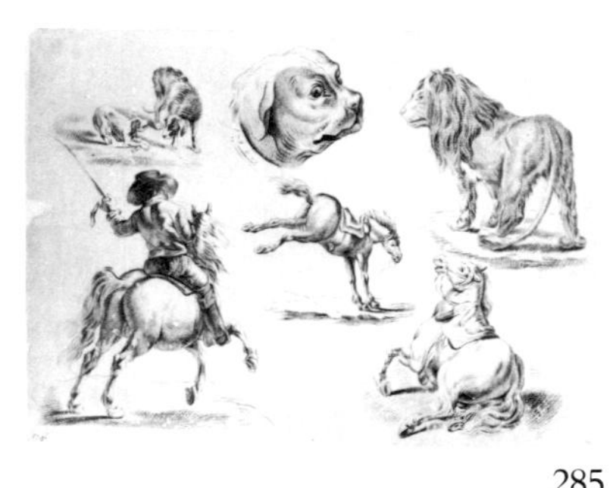

285

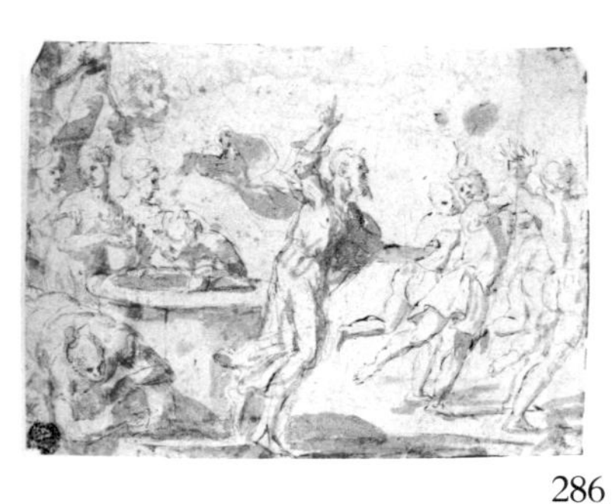

286

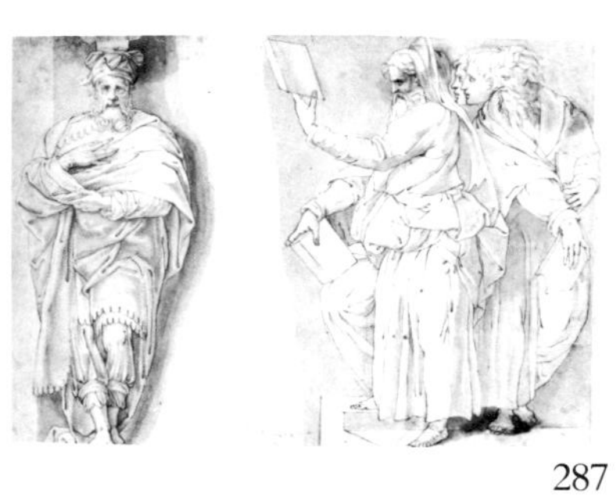

287

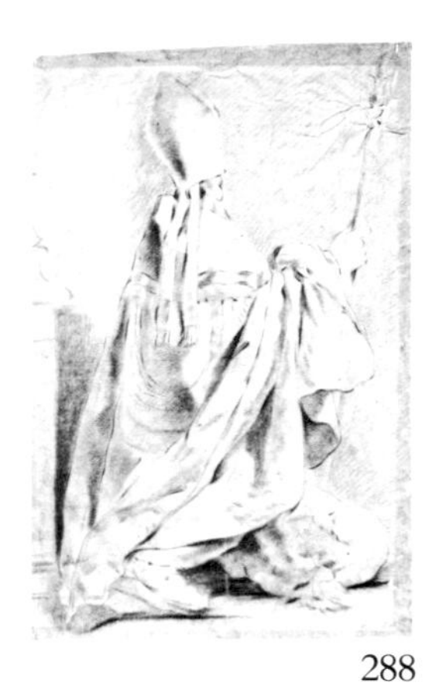

288

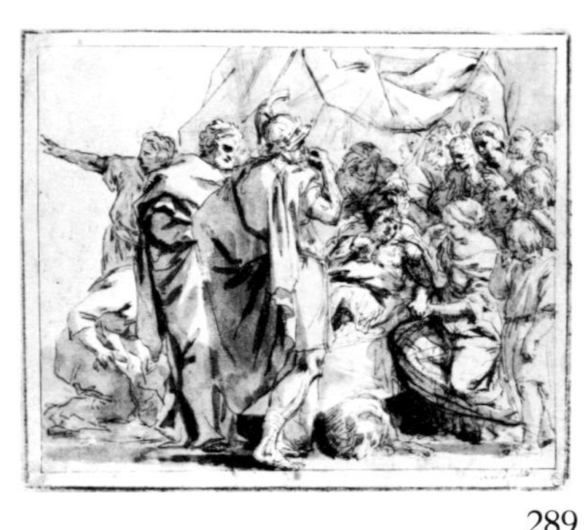

289

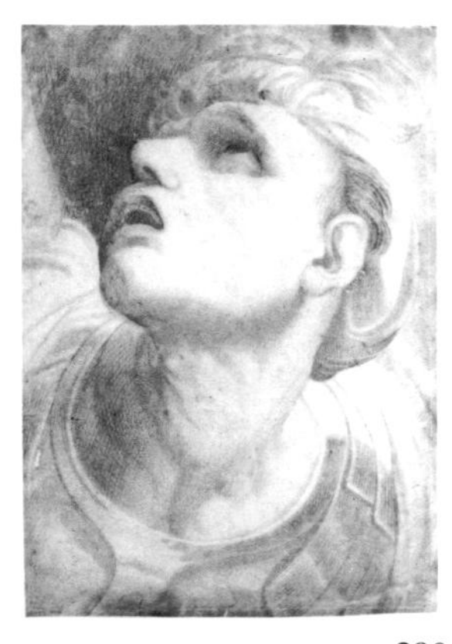

290

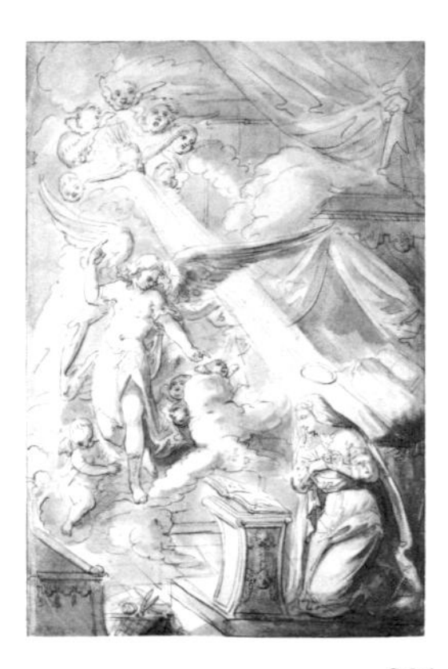

291

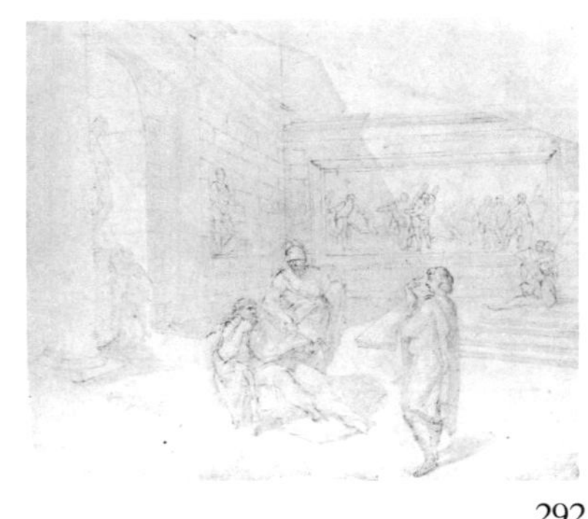

292

Most authorities have thought this sheet Flemish, perhaps by a follower of Rubens, but Oberhuber suggested that it might be French.

289

UNKNOWN, 17th c., *Death of a Hero*, pen and brown ink, brown wash, over red and black chalk, 165 x 199 mm. ($6^{1}/_{2}$ x $7^{13}/_{16}$ in.). Inscr. pen and brown ink lower right "Sandrart."

James Phinney Baxter Fund in Memory of Professor Henry Johnson (1932.19). Prov.: William Bates (1824–1884) (Lugt 2604); Henry Johnson. Bibl.: *Cat.* 1930, p. 95, no. 634 (as "Jacopo di Sandro").

Traditionally attributed to Joachim von Sandrart (1606–1688), but Christian Klemm (letter of 4 April 1975 in museum files) dismisses the ascription. The subject has traditionally been called the Death of Germanicus, but Pierre Rosenberg has suggested that it is the Death of Meleager.

290

UNKNOWN, 17th–18th c., *Head of a Soldier*, red chalk, laid down, 365 x 261 mm. ($14^{3}/_{8}$ x $10^{1}/_{4}$ in.).

Museum Purchase (1930.219). Prov.: Prof. Henry Johnson.

Perhaps copied from Raphael; the drawing carries an unlikely traditional attribution to Guido Reni.

291

UNKNOWN, 17th–18th c., *The Annunciation*, pen and black ink and grey wash, 380 x 260 mm. ($14^{15}/_{16}$ x $10^{1}/_{4}$ in.). Wmk.: fleur-de-lis on crowned shield, initial V below.

Museum Purchase (1930.230). Prov.: Prof. Henry Johnson.

Could be French.

292

UNKNOWN, 18th c., *Classical Scene*, black chalk, grey-brown wash, traces of red chalk (top right and lower left corners trimmed), 222 x 273 mm. ($8^{3}/_{4}$ x $10^{3}/_{4}$ in.).

Bequest of James Bowdoin III (1811.64). Prov.: James Bowdoin III. Bibl.: *Cat.* 1885, no. 136; *Cat.* 1930, no. 136.

The subject and the school remain unidentified.

293

UNKNOWN, 18th c., *Head of a Woman*, black, white, and red chalk, 500 x 348 mm. ($19^{11}/_{16}$ x $13^{11}/_{16}$ in.).

Museum Purchase (1930.200). Prov.: Prof. Henry Johnson.

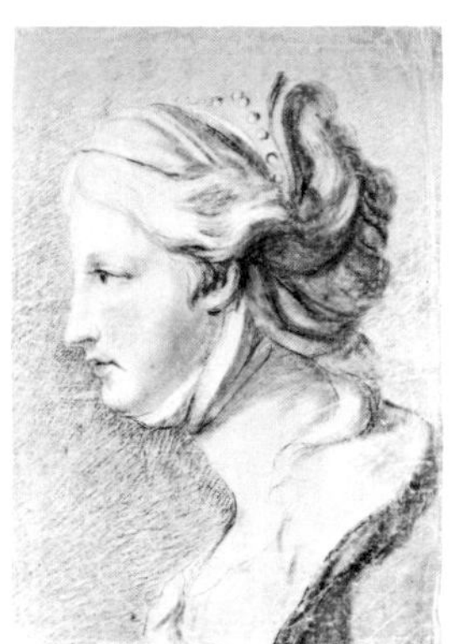

293

Frequently Cited References

ALLEN 1886
Rev. F. H. Allen. *The Bowdoin Collection* [five parts of four illustrations each, with individual texts]. Brunswick, 1886.

AMERICAN FEDERATION OF ARTS 1962–1963
American Federation of Arts [traveling exhibition]. *Old Master Drawings from College and University Collections.* 1962–1963.

ANDREWS 1968
K. Andrews. *National Gallery of Scotland—Catalogue of Italian Drawings.* 2 vols., Cambridge, 1968.

AUNER 1956
M. Auner. "Pieter Bruegel, Umrisse eines Lebenbildes." *Jahrbuch der Kunsthistorischen Sammlungen in Wien*, vol. 52, n.s. 16 (1956), pp. 51–122.

BARTSCH
A. Bartsch. *Le Peintre-graveur.* 21 vols., Vienna, 1803–1821.

BAUER 1981
R. Bauer. *Tapisserien der Renaissance nach Entwürfen von Pieter Coecke van Aelst* (exh. cat.). Eisenstadt, 1981.

BEAN 1979
J. Bean. *17th Century Italian Drawings in the Metropolitan Museum of Art.* New York, 1979.

BEAN and STAMPFLE 1965
J. Bean and F. Stampfle. *The Italian Renaissance* (exh. cat.). Drawings from New York Collections 1. New York, 1965.

BEAN and TURČIĆ 1982
J. Bean and L. Turčić. *15th and 16th Century Italian Drawings in the Metropolitan Museum of Art.* New York, 1982.

BENESCH
O. Benesch. *The Drawings of Rembrandt.* 6 vols., London, 1954–1957.

BENESCH 1928
O. Benesch. *Die Zeichnungen der niederländischen Schulen des XV. und XVI. Jahrhunderts.* Beschreibender Band der Katalog der Handzeichnungen in der graphischen Sammlung Albertina 2. Vienna, 1928.

BENESCH 1953
O. Benesch. Review of De Tolnay, *Die Zeichnungen Pieter Bruegels. Kunstchronik*, vol. 6, no. 3 (1953), pp. 76–82.

BENISOVICH 1955
M. Benisovich. "Quillard aux États-Unis—Une Découverte." *Gazette des Beaux-Arts*, ser. 6, vol. 45 (February 1955), pp. 113–16.

BERLIN 1975
Berlin, Staatliche Museen, Preussischer Kulturbesitz, Kupferstichkabinett. *Pieter Bruegel d. Ä als Zeichner, Herkunft und Nachfolge* (exh. cat.). 1975.

BERNT 1957–1958
W. Bernt. *Die niederländischen Zeichner des 17. Jahrhunderts.* 2 vols., Munich, 1957–1958.

BERTINI 1958
A. Bertini. *I disegni italiani della Biblioteca Reale di Torino.* Rome, 1958.

BJURSTRÖM 1976
P. Bjurström. *French Drawings—Sixteenth and Seventeenth Centuries.* Drawings in Swedish Public Collections 2. Stockholm, 1976.

BJURSTRÖM 1979
P. Bjurström. *Italian Drawings—Venice, Brescia, Parma, Milan, Genoa.* Drawings in Swedish Public Collections 3. Stockholm, 1979.

BLUNT 1954
A. Blunt. *The Drawings of G. B. Castiglione and Stefano della Bella . . . at Windsor Castle.* London, 1954.

BLUNT and COOKE 1960
A. Blunt and H. L. Cooke. *The Roman Drawings of the XVII and XVIII Centuries . . . at Windsor Castle.* London, 1960.

BLUNT and CROFT-MURRAY 1957
A. Blunt and E. Croft-Murray. *Venetian Drawings of the XVII and XVIII Centuries . . . at Windsor Castle.* London, 1957.

BOK-VAN KAMMEN 1980
W. Bok-van Kammen. *Stradanus and the Hunt.* Ph.D. diss., Johns Hopkins University, 1977. Ann Arbor, 1977.

BOON 1964
K. G. Boon. "Two Designs for Windows by Dierick Vellert." *Master Drawings*, vol. 2, no. 2 (1964), pp. 153–56.

BOON 1978
K. G. Boon. *Catalogue of the Dutch and Flemish Drawings in the Rijksmuseum.* Vol. 2, *Netherlandish Drawings of the Fifteenth and Sixteenth Centuries.* The Hague, 1978.

BRIQUET
C. M. Briquet. *Les Filigranes.* 4 vols., Geneva, 1907. Facsimile ed. with addenda. Amsterdam, 1968.

BROOS 1981
B. Broos. *Rembrandt en tekenaars uit zijn omgeving.* Oude tekeningen in het bezit van de Gemeentemusea van Amsterdam waaronder de collectie Fodor. Amsterdam, 1981.

BRUYN 1960
J. Bruyn. "Twee St. Antonius-panelen en andere Werken van Aertgen van Leyden." *Nederlands Kunsthistorisch Jaarboek*, vol. 11 (1960), pp. 36–119.

BUCHOWIECKI 1967–1974
W. Buchowiecki. *Handbuch der Kirchen Roms.* 3 vols. (A–S. Susanna), Vienna, 1967–1974.

BUSIRI VICI 1974
A. Busiri Vici. *Jan Frans van Bloemen Orizzonte*. Rome, 1974.

BYAM SHAW 1976
J. Byam Shaw. *Drawings by Old Masters at Christ Church Oxford*. 2 vols., Oxford, 1976.

BYAM SHAW 1983
J. Byam Shaw. *The Italian Drawings of the Frits Lugt Collection*. 3 vols., Paris, 1983.

CALABI 1936
A. Calabi. "Le acqueforti di Giuseppe Diamantino." *Die graphischen Künste*, n.s., vol. 1, no. 1 (1936), pp. 25–40.

CATALOGUE 1885
H. Johnson. *Catalogue of the Bowdoin College Art Collections*. Pt. 1, *The Bowdoin Drawings*. Brunswick, 1885.

CATALOGUE 1930
Bowdoin Museum of Fine Arts, Walker Art Building—Descriptive Catalogue of the Paintings, Sculpture and Drawings and of the Walker Collection. 4th ed., Brunswick, 1930.

CHAPPELL 1982
M. Chappell. "A Note on John Smibert's Italian Sojourn." *Art Bulletin*, vol. 64, no. 1 (March 1982), pp. 132–38.

CHICAGO 1969–1970
Art Institute of Chicago and elsewhere. *Rembrandt after Three Hundred Years* (exh. cat.; cat. of drawings by E. Haverkamp Begemann and A.-M. Logan). Chicago, 1969–1970.

CHURCHILL
W. A. Churchill. *Watermarks in Paper in Holland, England, France, etc., in the XVII and XVIII Centuries and Their Interconnection*. Amsterdam, 1935.

CLARK 1961
A. M. Clark. "'Lost' Frescoes by Niccolò Berrettoni." *Connoisseur*, vol. 148, no. 597 (November 1961), pp. 190–93.

CLARK 1967
A. M. Clark. "The Portraits of Artists Drawn for Nicola Pio." *Master Drawings*, vol. 5, no. 1 (1967), pp. 3–23.

CLEVELAND 1979
Cleveland, Cleveland Museum of Art. *The Draftsman's Eye—Late Italian Renaissance Schools and Styles* (exh. cat. by E. J. Olszewski and J. Glaubinger). 1979 (published 1981).

COLOGNE 1977
Cologne, Wallraf-Richartz-Museum. *Peter Paul Rubens 1577–1640 Kat. 1 Rubens in Italien* (exh. cat.). 1977.

DANIELS 1976a
J. Daniels. *Sebastiano Ricci*. Hove, 1976.

DANIELS 1976b
J. Daniels. *L'Opera completa di Sebastiano Ricci*. Milan, 1976.

DAVIDSON 1975
G. S. Davidson. "Some Genre Drawings by Jacques Stella: Notes on an Attribution." *Master Drawings*, vol. 13, no. 2 (Summer 1975), pp. 147–57.

DE GRAZIA 1984
D. De Grazia. *Correggio and His Legacy—Sixteenth-Century Emilian Drawings* (exh. cat.). Washington: National Gallery of Art, 1984.

DOWLEY 1966
F. H. Dowley. "A Few Drawings by Carlo Maratti." *Master Drawings*, vol. 4, no. 4 (1966), pp. 422–34.

DREYER 1969
Berlin, Staatliche Museen Preussischer Kulturbesitz, Kupferstichkabinett. *Römische Barockzeichnungen aus dem Berliner Kupferstichkabinett* (exh. cat. by P. Dreyer). 1969.

DREYER 1971
P. Dreyer. "Notizen zum malerischen und zeichnerischen Oeuvre der Maratta-Schule: Giuseppe Chiari—Pietro de' Pietri—Agostino Masucci." *Zeitschrift für Kunstgeschichte*, vol. 34, no. 3 (1971), pp. 184–207.

DÜSSLER 1971
L. Düssler. *Raphael—A Critical Catalogue of His Pictures, Wall Paintings, and Tapestries*. New York and London, 1971.

EIDELBERG 1981
M. Eidelberg. "Quillard as Draughtsman." *Master Drawings*, vol. 19, no. 1 (Spring 1981), pp. 27–38.

FEINBLATT 1979
E. Feinblatt. "A Drawing by Carlo Maratta." *Bulletin of the Los Angeles County Museum*, vol. 25 (1979), pp. 6–23.

FISCHEL 1913
O. Fischel. *Raphaels Zeichnungen*. 8 vols., Berlin, 1913ff.

FISCHER PACE 1979
U. V. Fischer Pace. *Disegni di Giacinto e Ludovico Gimignani nelle collezioni del Gabinetto Nazionale delle Stampe*. Rome, 1979.

FLORENCE 1974
Florence, Palazzo Strozzi. *Disegni e Bozzetti di Cristofano Allori* (exh. cat.). 1974.

FLORENCE 1980
Florence, Gabinetto Disegni e Stampe degli Uffizi. *Disegni di Bernardino Poccetti* (exh. cat. by P. Hamilton). 1980.

FLORENCE-PARIS 1980–1981
Florence, Istituto Universitario Olandese di Storia dell' Arte, and Paris, Institut Néerlandais. *L'Epoque de Lucas de Leyde et Pierre Bruegel—Dessins des Anciens Pays-Bas Collection Frits Lugt Institut Néerlandais Paris* (exh. cat.). 1980–1981.

FOOTE 1950
H. W. Foote. *John Smibert Painter*. Cambridge, 1950.

FORLANI 1963
A. Forlani. "Andrea Boscoli." *Proporzione*, vol. 4 (1963), pp. 85–208.

FREEDBERG 1979
S. J. Freedberg. *Painting in Italy 1500–1600*. Rev. ed., Harmondsworth, 1979.

FRERICHS 1973
Amsterdam, Rijksprentenkabinet. *Italiaanse Tekeningen 1: de 17de Eeuw* (exh. cat. by L. C. J. Frerichs). 1973.

VAN GELDER 1971
J. G. van Gelder. "Jan de Bisschop." *Oud Holland*, vol. 86 (1971), pp. 201–88.

GERE 1969
J. A. Gere. *Taddeo Zuccaro, His Development Studied in His Drawings*. London and Chicago, 1969.

GERE and POUNCEY 1983
J. A. Gere and P. M. R. Pouncey. *Italian Drawings in the Department of Prints and Drawings at the British Museum: Artists Working in Rome ca. 1550 to ca. 1640*. London, 1983.

GERNSHEIM
W. Gernsheim. *Corpus Photographicum* [of drawings in public and private collections]. In progress.

GERSON 1936
H. Gerson. *Philips Koninck*. Berlin, 1936.

GIBBONS 1977
F. Gibbons. *Catalogue of Italian Drawings in the Art Museum, Princeton University*. 2 vols., Princeton, 1977.

GROSSMANN 1954
F. Grossmann. "The Drawings of Pieter Bruegel the Elder in the Museum Boymans and Some Problems of Attribution." *Bulletin Museum Boymans Rotterdam*, vol. 5, nos. 2 and 3 (July and December 1954), pp. 41–63, 76–85.

HALL 1974
J. Hall. *Dictionary of Subjects and Symbols in Art*. New York, 1974.

HANDBOOK 1950
Bowdoin College Museum of Art. An Illustrated Handbook of the Bowdoin College Museum of Fine Arts in the Walker Art Building. Brunswick, 1950.

HANDBOOK 1981
Bowdoin College Museum of Art. *Handbook of the Collections*. Edited by M. R. Burke. Brunswick, 1981.

HARRIS and SCHAAR 1967
A. S. Harris and E. Schaar. *Die Handzeichnungen von Andrea Sacchi und Carlo Maratta*. Düsseldorf, 1967.

HAVERKAMP BEGEMANN and LOGAN 1970
E. Haverkamp Begemann and A.-M. S. Logan. *European Drawings and Watercolors in the Yale University Art Gallery, 1500–1900*. 2 vols., New Haven and London, 1970.

HEAWOOD
E. Heawood. *Watermarks Mainly of the 17th and 18th Centuries*. Monumenta Chartae Papyraceae 1. Hilversum, 1950.

HEIDEMAN 1980
J. Heideman. "The Dating of Gaspard Dughet's Frescoes in San Martino ai Monti in Rome." *Burlington Magazine*, vol. 122, no. 929 (August 1980), pp. 540–46.

HELD 1959
J. S. Held. *Rubens—Selected Drawings*. 2 vols., London and Garden City, 1959.

HIND 1926
A. M. Hind. *Catalogue of Drawings by Dutch and Flemish Artists . . . in the British Museum*. Vol. 3, *Dutch Drawings of the XVII Century (A-M)*. London, 1926.

HOLLSTEIN *DUTCH AND FLEMISH*
F. W. H. Hollstein. *Dutch and Flemish Etchings, Engravings, and Woodcuts c. 1450–1700*. Amsterdam, 1947ff.

HOLLSTEIN *GERMAN*
F. W. H. Hollstein. *German Engravings, Etchings, and Woodcuts 1400–1700*. Amsterdam, 1954ff.

JAFFÉ 1977
M. Jaffé. *Rubens and Italy*. Oxford, 1977.

JOACHIM 1977
H. Joachim. *French Drawings of the Sixteenth and Seventeenth Centuries in the Art Institute of Chicago*. Chicago and London, 1977.

JOACHIM and McCULLAGH 1979
H. Joachim and S. F. McCullagh. *Italian Drawings in the Art Institute of Chicago*. Chicago and London, 1979.

JOANNIDES 1983
P. Joannides. *The Drawings of Raphael with a Complete Catalogue*. Berkeley and Los Angeles, 1983.

JUDSON 1970
J. R. Judson. *Dirck Barendsz., 1534–1592*. Amsterdam, 1970.

KLOEK 1975
W. T. Kloek. *Beknopte catalogus van de Nederlandse tekeningen in het Prentenkabinet van de Uffizi te Florence*. Utrecht, 1975.

KNOX 1980
G. Knox. *Giambattista and Domenico Tiepolo—A Study and Catalogue Raisonné of the Chalk Drawings*. 2 vols., Oxford, 1980.

LUGT and LUGT *SUPPL.*
F. Lugt. *Les Marques de collections de dessins et estampes*. Amsterdam, 1921; *Supplément*. The Hague, 1956.

LUGT 1929
F. Lugt. *Musée du Louvre, Inventaire général des dessins des écoles du nord—école hollandaise*, vol. 1 (A-M). Paris, 1929.

LUGT 1949
F. Lugt. *Musée du Louvre, Inventaire général des dessins des écoles du nord—école flamande*. 2 vols., Paris, 1949.

LUGT 1968
F. Lugt. *Musée du Louvre, Inventaire général des dessins des écoles du nord—maîtres des anciens Pays-Bas nés avant 1550*. Paris, 1968.

MACANDREW 1980
H. Macandrew. *Catalogue of the Collection of Drawings in the Ashmolean Museum*. Vol. 3, *Italian Schools: Supplement*. Oxford, 1980.

MCGRATH 1981–1982
E. McGrath. "Rubens, the Gonzaga, and the 'Adoration of the Trinity.'" In London, Victoria and Albert Museum, *Splendours of the Gonzaga* (exh. cat.). 1981–1982.

MAHONEY 1977
M. Mahoney. *The Drawings of Salvator Rosa*. 2 vols., New York and London, 1977.

MANNING 1974
B. Suida Manning and R. L. Manning. *The Genoese Renaissance, Grace and Geometry: Paintings and Drawings by*

Luca Cambiaso from the Suida-Manning Collection (exh. cat.). Houston, Museum of Fine Arts, 1974.

MARABOTTINI 1969

A. Marabottini. *Polidoro da Caravaggio*. 2 vols., Rome, 1969.

MARLIER 1966

G. Marlier. *La Renaissance flamande—Pierre Coeck d'Alost*. Brussels, 1966.

MATHER 1913

F. J. Mather, Jr. "Drawings by Old Masters at Bowdoin College." *Art in America*, vol. 1, no. 4 (October 1913), pp. 244–53.

MATHER 1914

F. J. Mather, Jr. "Drawings by Old Masters at Bowdoin College Ascribed to Northern Schools: II." *Art in America*, vol. 2, no. 2 (February 1914), pp. 108–25.

MENA MARQUÉS 1976

M. Mena Marqués. "Some Drawings by Carlo Maratta and Niccolò Berrettoni for the Altieri Palace." *Master Drawings*, vol. 14, no. 1 (Spring 1976), pp. 51–55.

MONBEIG GOGUEL 1975

C. Monbeig Goguel. "Filippo Bellini da Urbino della Scuola del Baroccio." *Master Drawings*, vol. 13, no. 4 (Winter 1975), pp. 347–69.

MONGAN and SACHS 1940

A. Mongan and P. J. Sachs. *Drawings in the Fogg Museum of Art*. 3 vols., Cambridge, Massachusetts, 1940.

MONTAGU 1973

J. Montagu. "Il primo rilievo di marmo del Foggini." *Arte illustrata*, vol. 6, no. 55–56 (December 1973), pp. 331–38.

MONTAGU 1978

J. Montagu. "Bellori, Maratti, and the Palazzo Altieri." *Journal of the Warburg and Courtauld Institutes*, vol. 41 (1978), pp. 334–40.

MULLALY 1971

T. Mullaly. *Disegni veronesi del Cinquecento* (exh. cat.). Vicenza, 1971.

MÜLLER HOFSTEDE 1979

J. Müller Hofstede. "Zur Interpretation von Bruegels Landschaft. Ästhetischer Landschaftsbegriff und Stoische Weltbetrachtung." *Pieter Bruegel und seine Welt*. O. von Simson and M. Winner, eds. Berlin, 1979.

MÜNZ 1961

L. Münz. *Bruegel—The Drawings*. London and Greenwich, 1961.

NEILSON 1979

N. W. Neilson. *Camillo Procaccini Paintings and Drawings*. New York and London, 1979.

NEW YORK 1979

New York, Pierpont Morgan Library. *Rubens and Rembrandt in Their Century—Flemish & Dutch Drawings of the 17th Century from the Pierpont Morgan Library* (exh. cat. by F. Stampfle). 1979.

NIETO ALCAIDE 1965

V. M. Nieto Alcaide. *Dibujos de la R. Academia de San Fernando: Carlo Maratti, 43 Dibujos de Tema Religiosa*. Madrid, 1965.

OBERHUBER 1981

K. Oberhuber. "Bruegel's Early Landscape Drawings." *Master Drawings*, vol. 19, no. 2 (Summer 1981), pp. 146–56.

OPPERMAN 1972/77

H. N. Opperman. *Jean Baptiste Oudry*. Ph.D. diss., 1972. New York and London, 1977.

OTTAWA 1982

Ottawa, National Gallery of Canada. *Bolognese Drawings in North American Collections 1500–1800* (exh. cat. by M. Cazort and C. Johnston). 1982.

PARIS 1981–1982

Paris, Louvre, Cabinet des Dessins. *Dessins baroques florentins du musée du Louvre* (exh. cat. by F. Viatte and C. Monbeig Goguel). 1981–1982.

PARKER 1938

K. T. Parker. *Catalogue of the Collection of Drawings in the Ashmolean Museum*. Vol. 1, *Netherlandish, German, French, and Spanish Schools*. Oxford, 1938.

PARKER 1956

K. T. Parker. *Catalogue of the Collection of Drawings in the Ashmolean Museum*. Vol. 2, *Italian Schools*. Oxford, 1956.

PERCY 1971

A. Percy. *Giovanni Benedetto Castiglione—Master Draughtsman of the Italian Baroque* (exh. cat.). Philadelphia, Philadelphia Museum of Art, 1971.

PHILADELPHIA 1980–1981

Philadelphia, Philadelphia Museum of Art. *A Scholar Collects—Selections from the Anthony Morris Clark Bequest* (exh. cat.). 1980–1981.

POPHAM 1932

A. E. Popham. *Catalogue of Drawings by Dutch and Flemish Artists . . . in the British Museum*. Vol. 5, *Dutch and Flemish Drawings of the XV and XVI Centuries*. London, 1932.

POPHAM 1971

A. E. Popham. *Catalogue of the Drawings of Parmigianino*. 3 vols., New Haven and London, 1971.

POPHAM and WILDE 1949

A. E. Popham and J. Wilde. *The Italian Drawings of the XV and XVI Centuries . . . at Windsor Castle*. London, 1949.

PORDENONE 1980

Pordenone, Museo Civico. *Amalteo* (exh. cat.). 1980.

POUGHKEEPSIE 1976

Poughkeepsie, Vassar College Art Gallery. *Seventeenth-Century Dutch Landscape Drawings and Selected Prints from American Collections* (exh. cat.). 1976.

PRINCETON-WASHINGTON 1982–1983

Princeton, University Art Museum, and Washington, National Gallery of Art. *Drawings from the Holy Roman Empire 1540–1680—A Selection from North American Collections* (exh. cat. by T. daC. Kaufmann). 1982–1983.

PROVIDENCE 1973

Providence, Rhode Island School of Design, Museum of Art. *Drawings and Prints of the First Maniera 1515–1535* (exh. cat.). 1973.

RAGGHIANTI COLLOBI 1959
L. Ragghianti Collobi. "Il magistrale Luca Cambiaso." *Critica d'arte*, vol. 6, no. 33 (1959), pp. 166–84.

REGINA and MONTREAL 1970
Regina, Norman Mackenzie Art Gallery, and Montreal, Museum of Fine Arts. *A Selection of Italian Drawings from North American Collections* (exh. cat. by W. Vitzthum). 1970.

VAN REGTEREN ALTENA 1939
I. G. van Regteren Altena. "Aertgen van Leyden." *Oud Holland*, vol. 56 (1939), pp. 17–25, 74–87, 129–38, and 222–35.

RICHARDSON 1980
F. L. Richardson. *Andrea Schiavone*. Oxford, 1980.

ROBERT-DUMESNIL
A. P. F. Robert-Dumesnil. *Le Peintre-graveur français*. 11 vols., Paris, 1835–1871.

ROBINSON 1958–1974
M. S. Robinson. *Van de Velde Drawings—A Catalogue of Drawings in the National Maritime Museum made by the Elder and the Younger Willem van de Velde*. 2 vols., Cambridge, England, 1958–1974.

ROLI 1968
R. Roli. *I fregi centesi del Guercino*. Bologna, 1968.

ROME 1976
Rome, Villa della Farnesina alla Lungara. *Disegni di Stefano della Bella dalle collezioni del Gabinetto Nazionale delle Stampe* (exh. cat. by M. Catelli Isola). 1976.

SACRAMENTO 1974
Sacramento, E. B. Crocker Art Gallery. *The Pre-Rembrandtists* (exh. cat. by A. Tümpel and C. Tümpel). 1974.

SADIK 1966
M. S. Sadik. *Colonial and Federal Portraits at Bowdoin College*. Brunswick, 1966.

SANMINIATELLI 1967
D. Sanminiatelli. *Domenico Beccafumi*. Milan, 1967.

SAUNDERS 1984
R. H. Saunders. "John Smibert's Italian Sojourn—Once Again." *Art Bulletin*, vol. 66, no. 2 (June 1984), pp. 312–18.

SCHATBORN 1981
P. Schatborn. *Dutch Figure Drawings from the Seventeenth Century*. The Hague, 1981.

[SIBER] 1947
[H. C. Siber]. "James Bowdoin and His Collection of Drawings with Notes on Early Art Collecting in America." *Connoisseur*, vol. 120, no. 506 (December 1947), pp. 116–21.

SMIBERT NOTEBOOK 1969
The Notebook of John Smibert. With essays by D. Evans, J. Kerslake, A. Oliver. Boston, 1969.

STAMPFLE and BEAN 1967
F. Stampfle and J. Bean. *The 17th Century in Italy* (exh. cat.). Drawings from New York Collections 2. New York, 1967.

STEADMAN 1973
D. Steadman. *Abraham van Diepenbeeck—17th-Century Flemish Painter*. Ph.D. diss., Princeton University, 1973.

STIX and FRÖHLICH-BUM 1932
A. Stix and L. Fröhlich-Bum. *Die Zeichnungen der toskanischen, umbrischen, und römischen Schulen*. Beschreibender Katalog der Handzeichnungen in der . . . Albertina 3. Vienna, 1932.

STORRS 1973
Storrs, The William Benton Museum of Art. *The Academy of Europe—Rome in the 18th Century* (exh. cat. by F. den Broeder). 1973.

SUIDA MANNING and SUIDA 1958
B. Suida Manning and W. Suida. *Luca Cambiaso, la vita e le opere*. Milan, 1958.

SUMOWSKI 1979ff.
W. Sumowski. *Drawings of the Rembrandt School*. New York, 1979ff.

THIEM 1958
G. Thiem. "Studien zu Jan van der Straet, genannt Stradanus." *Mitteilungen des Kunsthistorischen Institutes in Florenz*, vol. 8 (1958), pp. 88–111.

THIEM 1977
C. Thiem. *Florentiner Zeichner des Frühbarock*. Munich, 1977.

THIEM, STUTTGART, 1977
Stuttgart, Staatsgalerie. *Italienische Zeichnungen 1500–1800* (cat. by C. Thiem). Stuttgart, 1977.

THIEME-BECKER
U. Thieme and F. Becker. *Allgemeines Lexikon der bildenden Künstler von der Antike bis zur Gegenwart*. 37 vols., Leipzig, 1907–1950.

DE TOLNAY 1952
C. de Tolnay. *The Drawings of Pieter Bruegel the Elder*. London, 1952.

TORONTO 1972
Toronto, Art Gallery of Ontario, and elsewhere. *French Master Drawings of the 17th & 18th Centuries in North American Collections* (exh. cat. by P. Rosenberg). 1972.

TÜMPEL 1974
A. Tümpel. "Claes Cornelisz. Moeyaert—Katalog der Gemälde." *Oud Holland*, vol. 88, no. 4 (1974), pp. 245–90.

VAN DE VELDE 1975
C. van de Velde. *Frans Floris (1519/20–1570)—Leven en Werken*. 2 vols., Brussels, 1975.

VENICE 1966
Venice, Fondazione Giorgio Cini. *Disegni di una collezione veneziana del Settecento* (exh. cat. by A. Bettagno). 1966.

VENTURI
A. Venturi. *Storia dell'arte italiana*. 11 vols., Milan, 1901–1939.

VERONA 1974
Verona, Palazzo della Gran Guardia. *Cinquant' anni di pittura veronese 1580–1630* (exh. cat. by L. Magagnato and others). 1974.

DE VESME/MASSAR
A. de Vesme. *Stefano della Bella—Catalogue Raisonné*. With intro. and additions by P. D. Massar. 2 vols., New York, 1971.

VIATTE 1974
F. Viatte. *Dessins de Stefano della Bella 1610–1664*. Musée du Louvre, Cabinet des Dessins, Inventaire général des dessins italiens 2. Paris, 1974.

VIATTE 1977
F. Viatte. "Allegorical and Burlesque Subjects by Stefano della Bella." *Master Drawings*, vol. 15, no. 4 (Winter 1977), pp. 347–65.

VÖGE 1896
W. Vöge. *Raffael und Donatello*. Strassburg, 1896.

WARD-JACKSON 1979
P. Ward-Jackson. *Italian Drawings*. Vol. 1, *14th–16th Century*. Victoria and Albert Museum Catalogues. London, 1979.

WARD-JACKSON 1980
P. Ward-Jackson. *Italian Drawings*. Vol. 2, *17th–18th Century*. Victoria and Albert Museum Catalogues. London, 1980.

WATERHOUSE 1976
E. Waterhouse. *Roman Baroque Painting: A List of the Principal Painters and Their Works in and around Rome*. London, 1976.

WATERVILLE 1978
Waterville, Colby College Museum of Art. *Drawings from Maine Collections* (exh. cat.). 1978.

WAYMENT 1972
H. G. Wayment. *The Windows of King's College Chapel Cambridge*. Supp. vol. 1 of *Corpus Vitrearum Medii Aevi—Great Britain*. London, 1972.

WEGNER 1973
W. Wegner. *Die niederländischen Handzeichnungen des 15.–18. Jahrhunderts*. Kataloge der Staatlichen Graphischen Sammlung München, vol. 1. Berlin, 1973.

WESCHER 1928
P. Wescher. "Holländischer Zeichner zur Zeit des Lucas van Leiden." *Oud Holland*, vol. 45 (1928), pp. 245–54.

WICHMANN 1923
H. Wichmann. *Leonaert Bramer—sein Leben und seine Kunst*. Leipzig, 1923.

WILMINGTON 1976
Wilmington, Delaware Art Museum. *The Pre-Raphaelite Era 1848–1914* (exh. cat. by R. and B. Elzea). 1976.

Index to Former Owners

THE PRESENT INDEX lists all known former owners of the drawings except James Bowdoin III, Henry Johnson, Helen Johnson (Mrs. Stanley P.) Chase, and Miss Susan Dwight Bliss. For those owners, Concordance 2 serves as an index. All of the drawings with accession numbers beginning 1811 were left to the College by James Bowdoin III and presumably had been acquired by him from John Smibert's studio. The three inscribed "John Smibert" are listed in this index. Drawings with accession numbers beginning 1930 were probably bought for the museum by Professor Henry Johnson. Those with accession numbers beginning 1932 were bought from the Johnson family as a memorial to Professor Johnson after his death. Professor Johnson's daughter, Helen Johnson (Mrs. Stanley P.) Chase, gave the College the drawings with 1958 accession numbers; they had previously belonged to her father. The drawings with 1956 accession numbers came to the collection from the bequest of Miss Susan Dwight Bliss. Please see the Introduction for a full discussion of these donations. Drawings are listed in this index by catalogue number, not by page number.

Concordance 1

Cat. 1885 no.	*Cat.* 1930 no.	*Cat.* 1985 no.	*Cat.* 1885 no.	*Cat.* 1930 no.	*Cat.* 1985 no.	*Cat.* 1885 no.	*Cat.* 1930 no.	*Cat.* 1985 no.	*Cat.* 1885 no.	*Cat.* 1930 no.	*Cat.* 1985 no.
1	1	34	37	37	182	65	—	65	90	90	212
2	2	198	—	38	148	66	—	208	91	91	201
3	3	197	38	—	206	—	66	37	92	92	67
4	4	42	39	—	148	—	67	185	—	93	146
5	5	36	—	39	206	67	—	261	93	—	185
7	7	31	40	40	160	68	—	15	94	94	14
8	8	11	41	41	81	—	68	65	95	95	20
9	9	166	42	42	158	—	69	208	96	96	87
10	10	175	43	43	79	69	—	139	97	97	281
11	11	38	44	44	80	—	70	261	98	98	8
12	12	152	45	45	199	70	—	209	99	99	28
13	13	153	46	46	207	—	71	15	100	100	280
14	14	41	47	47	167	71	—	202	101	101	218
15	15	50	48	—	12	72	—	10	102	102	27
—	16	210	—	48	73	—	72	139	103	103	282
16	—	119	49	49	24	73	—	16	104	104	98
17	17	216	50	50	25	—	73	209	105	105	133
18	18	39	51	51	114	—	74	202	106	106	132
19	19	45	52	52	19	74	—	99	107	107	101
20	20	47	53	53	103	—	75	10	108	108	5
21	21	112	54	54	125	75	—	73	109	109	129
22	22	61	55	55	124	—	76	119	110	110	130
23	23	174	56	56	156	76	—	210	111	111	176
24	24	173	57	57	21	77	77	48	112	112	145
25	25	69	58	58	29	78	78	279	113	113	128
26	26	162	59	59	29	79	79	268	114	114	109
27	27	205	60	60	106	80	80	269	115	115	108
28	28	76	—	61	102	81	81	214	116	116	127
29	29	178	61	—	37	82	82	44	117	117	32
30	30	183	—	62	12	83	83	84	118	118	126
31	31	77	62	—	18	84	84	264	119	119	143
32	32	179	—	63	16	85	85	213	120	120	135
33	33	75	63	—	146	86	86	40	121	121	131
34	34	180	—	64	99	87	87	260	122	122	2
35	35	74	64	—	102	88	88	53	123	123	4
36	36	181	—	65	18	89	89	105	124	124	215

(Continued from previous page)

Cat. 1885 no.	Cat. 1930 no.	Cat. 1985 no.	Cat. 1885 no.	Cat. 1930 no.	Cat. 1985 no.	Cat. 1885 no.	Cat. 1930 no.	Cat. 1985 no.	Cat. 1885 no.	Cat. 1930 no.	Cat. 1985 no.
125	125	211	140	140	265	—	626	70	—	642	273
126	126	263	141	141	267	—	627	238	—	644	107
127	127	262	142	142	266	—	628	60	—	645	3
128	128	217	—	614	239	—	630	118	—	646	252
129	129	200	—	615	95	—	631	68	—	648	59
130	130	194	—	616	154	—	632	169	—	649	258
131	131	111	—	617	123	—	633	71	—	p. 104, no. D-1	94
132	132	49	—	618	151	—	634	289			
133	133	120	—	619	196	—	635	13	—	p. 104, no. D-2	275
134	134	278	—	620	35	—	636	144			
135	135	43	—	621	163	—	637	134			
136	136	292	—	622	78	—	638	110			
137	137	276	—	623	237	—	639	17			
138	138	161	—	624	122	—	640	23			
139	139	66	—	625	51	—	641	97			

Concordance 2

Accession no.	Cat. 1985 no.	Accession no.	Cat. 1985 no.	Accession no.	Cat. 1985 no.	Accession no.	Cat. 1985 no.
1811.1	173	1811.37	79	1811.74	269	1811.110	216
1811.2	174	1811.38	80	1811.75	105	1811.111 & .112	29
1811.3	198	1811.39	199	1811.76	211	1811.113	278
1811.4	42	1811.40	207	1811.77	265	1811.114	49
1811.5	36	1811.41	73	1811.78	114	1811.115	194
1811.6	31	1811.42	103	1811.79	25	1811.116	217
1811.7	47	1811.43	156	1811.80	106	1811.117	262
1811.8	45	1811.44	16	1811.81	12	1811.118	263
1811.9	50	1811.45	18	1811.82	24	1811.119	131
1811.10	41	1811.46	37	1811.83	19	1811.120	135
1811.11	153	1811.47	146	1811.84	126	1811.121	143
1811.12	152	1811.48	185	1811.85	32	1811.122	266
1811.13	175	1811.49	65	1811.86	127	1811.123	102
1811.14	166	1811.50	208	1811.87	108	1811.124	98
1811.15	11	1811.51	261	1811.88	128	1811.125	267
1811.16	69	1811.52	15	1811.89	176	1811.126	281
1811.17	162	1811.53	139	1811.90	145	1811.127	66
1811.18	205	1811.54	209	1811.91	129	1811.128	109
1811.19	76	1811.55	202	1811.92	130	1811.129	5
1811.20	178	1811.56	10	1811.93	280	1811.130	101
1811.21	183	1811.57	119	1811.94	14	1811.131	132
1811.22	77	1811.58	48	1811.95	212	1811.132	21
1811.23	179	1811.59	268	1811.96	53	1811.133	264
1811.24	75	1811.60	279	1811.97	260	1811.134	201
1811.25	180	1811.61	84	1811.98	213	1811.135	20
1811.26	74	1811.62	40	1811.99	44	1811.136	87
1811.27	181	1811.63	111	1811.100	214	1811.137	28
1811.28	182	1811.64	292	1811.101	112	1811.138	133
1811.29	148	1811.65	67	1811.102	161	1811.139	282
1811.30	206	1811.66	99	1811.103	276	1811.140	27
1811.31	81	1811.67	124	1811.104	43	1811.141	218
1811.32	158	1811.68	125	1811.105	120	1811.142	8
1811.33	34	1811.69	160	1811.106	200	1918.1	94
1811.34	197	1811.70	61	1811.107	215	1918.2	275
1811.35	38	1811.71	210	1811.108	4	1930.123	192
1811.36	39	1811.73	167	1811.109	2	1930.124	190

(Continued from previous page)

Accession no.	Cat. 1985 no.	Accession no.	Cat. 1985 no.	Accession no.	Cat. 1985 no.	Accession no.	Cat. 1985 no.
1930.125	219	1930.194	231	1932.13	238	1956.24.202	271
1930.126	220	1930.195	232	1932.14	60	1956.24.209	188
1930.127	283	1930.196	140	1932.16	68	1956.24.210	244
1930.128.	248	1930.197	55	1932.17	169	1956.24.213	245
1930.130	58	1930.198	251	1932.18	71	1956.24.214	142
1930.131	221	1930.199	195	1932.19	289	1956.24.215	272
1930.132	222	1930.200	293	1932.20	115	1956.24.220	257
1930.133	193	1930.202	147	1932.21	252	1956.24.221	168
1930.134	223	1930.203	159	1932.22	107	1956.24.224	165
1930.135	9	1930.204	233	1032.23.4	172	1956.24.229	93
1930.137	186	1930.209	229	1932.28	239	1956.24.230	64
1930.138	284	1930.217	171	1932.29	95	1956.24.232	149
1930.139	187	1930.218	253	1932.30	122	1956.24.233	177
1930.140	249	1930.219	290	1932.31	144	1956.24.234	72
1930.141	224	1930.220	100	1932.32	134	1956.24.235	92
1930.142	255	1930.221	137	1932.33	110	1956.24.241	62
1930.143	225	1930.222	138	1932.34	17	1956.24.242	117
1930.144	250	1930.223	7	1932.35	23	1956.24.253	91
1930.145	82	1930.224	287	1932.36	97	1956.24.254	246
1930.146	116	1930.225	234	1932.37	3	1956.24.266	6
1930.147	226	1930.226	254	1932.38	204	1956.24.268	30
1930.148	227	1930.227	277	1932.39	59	1956.24.269	136
1930.150	285	1930.228	235	1932.40	258	1956.24.270	63
1930.152	121	1930.230	291	1932.41	52	1956.24.271	113
1930.153	33	1930.231	22	1932.42	46	1956.24.273	88
1930.154	228	1930.232	141	1956.24.173	240	1958.66	118
1930.155	1	1930.233	288	1956.24.176	189	1958.67	13
1930.155.1	229	1930.234	236	1956.24.178	241	1958.70	78
1930.156	191	1930.235	96	1956.24.180	242	1958.71	273
1930.156.1	286	1932.4.1	154	1956.24.183	243	1964.41	247
1930.184	54	1932.5	123	1956.24.186	150	1964.58	90
1930.185	259	1932.6	151	1956.24.187	26	1967.39.4	157
1930.186	104	1932.7	196	1956.24.191	270	1969.66	89
1930.187	86	1932.8	35	1956.24.192	274	1972.14	85
1930.188	184	1932.9	163	1956.24.193	83	1982.12	170
1930.189	164	1932.10	237	1956.24.196	56		
1930.192	155	1932.11	51	1956.24.197	57		
1930.193	230	1932.12	70	1956.24.200	256		

1811.72 is a woodcut. See p. xxi, note 19.

Index to Artists and Subjects